Freedom's Racial Frontier

Race and Culture in the American West
Quintard Taylor, Series Editor

Freedom's Racial Frontier

African Americans in the Twentieth-Century West

Edited by Herbert G. Ruffin II and Dwayne A. Mack

Foreword by Quintard Taylor

UNIVERSITY OF OKLAHOMA PRESS : NORMAN

Library of Congress Cataloging-in-Publication Data

Names: Ruffin, Herbert G., 1969– editor. | Mack, Dwayne, 1968– editor.
Title: Freedom's racial frontier : African Americans in the twentieth-century west / edited by
  Herbert G. Ruffin II and Dwayne A. Mack ; foreword by Quintard Taylor.
Description: Norman : University of Oklahoma Press, 2018. | Series: Race and culture in the
  American West series ; volume 13 | Includes bibliographical references and index.
Identifiers: LCCN 2017036436| ISBN 978-0-8061-5977-5 (hardcover : alk. paper) | ISBN
  978-0-8061-5976-8 (pbk. : alk. paper)
Subjects: LCSH: African Americans—West (U.S.)—History—20th century. | West (U.S.)—
  Race relations—History—20th century.
Classification: LCC E185.925 .F74 2018 | DDC 305.800978—dc23
LC record available at https://lccn.loc.gov/2017036436

Freedom's Racial Frontier: African Americans in the Twentieth-Century West is Volume 13 in
the Race and Culture in the American West series.

The paper in this book meets the guidelines for permanence and durability of the Committee
on Production Guidelines for Book Longevity of the Council on Library Resources, Inc. ∞

Copyright © 2018 by Herbert G. Ruffin II and Dwayne A. Mack. Published by the University of
Oklahoma Press, Norman, Publishing Division of the University. Manufactured in the U.S.A.

1 2 3 4 5 6 7 8 9 10

Contents

List of Illustrations. ix

List of Tables xi

Foreword xiii
 Quintard Taylor

Acknowledgments. xvii

Introduction: The African American West in
Twentieth- and Twenty-First-Century History. 3
 Herbert G. Ruffin II and Dwayne A. Mack

Part 1. Place
 1. "Beautiful People": Community Formation
  in Houston, 1900–1941 45
   Bernadette Pruitt

 2. The Las Vegas Press and the Westside:
  The Moulin Rouge Agreement 87
   Shared History Program, University of Nevada, Reno

 3. The More Things Change, the More They Stay the Same:
  Structural Racism and African American Community
  Formation in the North Bay Area 99
   April L. Harris

 As Seattle Gets Richer, the City's Black Households Get Poorer 108

 Aurora's Growth Reflects That African-Americans Are Finding Base
 in Denver 'Burbs. 110

Part 2. Racial Frontier

4. "Turn Our Faces to the West": Refugees, Pioneers,
   and the Roots of "All-Black" Oklahoma 115
   Kendra T. Field

5. Poetic Justice: Bay Area Afro-Asian Women's Activism
   through Verse. 128
   Jeanelle Hope

6. Apartheid in Arizona? HB 2281 and Arizona's Denial
   of Human Rights to Peoples of Color 146
   Julian Kunnie

   Black Population of Fargo-Moorhead Has Nearly Tripled in Past Decade 157

Part 3. Political Expression

7. Multiracial Garveyism in the Far West 163
   Holly Roose

8. Brothers Taking Action: African American Soldier Activism
   at Fort Hood, Texas, 1948–1972 181
   Herbert G. Ruffin II

9. Black Women in Spokane: Emerging from the
   Shadows of Jim and Jane Crow 202
   Dwayne A. Mack

   Albina Residents Picket the Portland Development Commission, 1973 229

Part 4. Entertainment and Representation

10. The New Negro Frontier: Jean Toomer, Wallace Thurman,
    and African American Modernism in the West 233
    Emily Lutenski

11. Containing "Perversion": African Americans and
    Same-Sex Desire in Cold War Los Angeles. 252
    Kevin Allen Leonard

12. "Something 2 Dance 2": Electro-hop in 1980s Los Angeles
    and Its Afrofuturist Link 278
    Gabriela Jiménez

Ku Klux Klan's 1925 Attack on Malcolm X's Family Home in
Omaha Heralded the Fight to Come 293

The Black 14: Race, Politics, Religion, and Wyoming Football 296

Part 5. Reconsiderations

13. African Americans in Albuquerque, 1880–1930:
    A Demographic Analysis 303
    Randolph Stakeman

14. Obscured Collaboration: African American Presence
    in the Myth of the White West .320
    Tracey Owens Patton

15. *Kama'āina*s and African Americans in Hawaii:
    Making Sense of the Black Hawaiian Experience
    with Dr. Kathryn Waddell Takara 337
    Herbert G. Ruffin II and Kathryn Takara

Blanche Louise Preston McSmith: An Alaska Civil Rights Icon 359

African American History Month Enacted in Alaska, 2015 361

Bibliographic Essay: The Twentieth- and
Twenty-First-Century West 363
    Herbert G. Ruffin II
Contributors 387
Index 393

Illustrations

Figures

Joshua Houston family, October 1898 49

Lubertha Johnson, 1987 88

Sisters on the Reading Edge book club and
Napa Valley Wine Train, 2015 .100

Main Street, looking north, in Boley, Oklahoma,
circa 1905 116

Sonia Sanchez during her years at San Francisco
State College, 1969 129

Asian American protesters in front of
Oakland courthouse, 1969 131

Mexican American studies supporters shut down
Tucson school board meeting, 2012 153

United Negro Improvement Association Meeting in
Oakland, 1924. 166

GIs outside of the Oleo Strut in Killeen, Texas, circa 1970 189

Rosa Malone Greeting the Women's Army Corps,
Spokane, 1945. 208

James and Lydia Sims 221

Jean Toomer in Taos, New Mexico, 1935. 235

Langston Hughes and Wallace Thurman in California, 1934. . . .244

Drag ball at legendary Central Avenue jazz club,
Club Alabam, 1945 259

Uncle Jamm's Army, circa 1982. 281

Bryant Messenger Service, circa 1912 314

Myrtis Dightman at 1970 National Finals Rodeo,
Oklahoma City. 329

College of Hawaii, class of 1915, including Alice Augusta Ball . . . 354

Maps

Black communities in the western United States 5

Oklahoma's African American towns and settlements 123

African American home ownership and
rentals in Albuquerque, 1900 310

Tables

I.1. U.S. West populations, 1890–1940 6

I.2. U.S. West populations, 1960–2010 10

I.3. Population growth in the fastest-growing
      suburban cities, 1950–2010 22–23

13.1. African American home ownership in
       Albuquerque, 1900–1920 309

13.2 African American occupations in Albuquerque, 1900 311

Foreword

Quintard Taylor

In 1928, W. Sherman Savage, a young professor of history at Lincoln University in Missouri, published "The Negro in the History of the Pacific Northwest" in the *Journal of Negro History*. Although the article got scant attention at the time, this was the first attempt to write a history of African Americans beyond the Ninety-Eighth Meridian (west of Austin, Texas) that did not focus on slavery. Over the decades since then, numerous other historians, including Kenneth W. Porter, Lawrence B. de Graaf, Albert Broussard, Douglas Flamming, Shirley Moore, and me, to name a few, have added to that history and have usually posed similar questions. Was the black experience in the West different from the black experience in the rest of the nation? Was there a racial frontier beyond which black people could find freedom and justice? Black western history is no longer just an interesting footnote to African American and western history.

With *Freedom's Racial Frontier: African Americans in the Twentieth-Century West,* Herbert Ruffin and Dwayne Mack extend historical scholarship into the contemporary era. They and their contributors grapple with the questions raised by Savage and his successors even as they raise new questions about black life in the region. Their focus is exclusively on the black West since 1900, expressly addressing the African American population in cities from Omaha and Houston to Anchorage and Honolulu. They argue that the modern urban black West should be at the heart of the examination of the western African American historical experience. Yet they make a second argument equally significant and often overlooked: that the black urban experience in the West often differs sharply from the historical narrative of black folks in the East, the Midwest, and the South.

The book begins with an extended introduction that is a tour-de-force exploration of black western history. While the introduction reminds us of the eighteenth-
and nineteenth-century roots of contemporary black western communities, it
also explores the region's twentieth- and now twenty-first-century history. It
calls us to reexamine the Great Migration as an exclusively South-to-North
narrative by reminding us of the early-twentieth-century migration to Dallas,
Houston, and Tulsa. The latter suffered one of the worst race riots of the twentieth
century precisely because of the success of the black migrants. World War II
western migration is covered as well, not simply to explore the extraordinary
growth of black communities in cities like San Francisco, Oakland, Las Vegas,
Los Angeles, San Diego, Portland, and Seattle, but as a prelude and catalyst
for the western freedom struggles of 1950–1975. Ruffin and Mack are careful to
include smaller cities heretofore overlooked in such discussions, such as Salt Lake
City, Albuquerque, Wichita, and Spokane. To their credit the authors extend
the discussion to the rapidly grown suburbs of western cities such as Arlington
(Dallas–Fort Worth), Aurora (Denver), Federal Way (Seattle), Moreno Valley
(Los Angeles), North Las Vegas (Las Vegas), Santa Rosa (San Francisco), and
Scottsdale (Phoenix). As Ruffin and Mack and their contributors show, African
American suburbanites are writing a new narrative about race and class, and
they comprise the next cultural and social frontier in the region's history.

The larger significance of this anthology lies in its original articles. *Freedom's
Racial Frontier* speaks to how western black history parallels and differs from
that of the rest of African America and the rest of the West. I advanced this
argument nearly two decades ago with *In Search of the Racial Frontier*, but Ruffin
and Mack have gone far beyond what was comprehensible to me at that time. To
accomplish this, they have brought together a cadre of younger historians who
view the region through a variety of historical lenses, ranging from traditional
community biographies to the "infrapolitics" of political dissidence. The impact
of black western suburbanization is one example, as reflected in "The More Things
Change, the More They Stay the Same," by April Harris. Questions of racial,
ethnic, and gender identity are explored in Jeanelle Hope's "Poetic Justice," Ruffin
and Kathryn Takara's "Kama'ainas and African Americans in Hawaii," and Kevin
Leonard's "Containing 'Perversion.'" The rich and heretofore mostly ignored
cultural heritage of the black West is explored in various ways, as reflected in
Emily Lutenski's essay on Jean Toomer as well as Gabriela Jimenez's provocative
"Something 2 Dance 2" on hip-hop and Afrofuturism.

Even as it examines these rich new themes, *Freedom's Racial Frontier* also keeps politics and the long, ongoing freedom struggle as a central focus, as Holly Roose in "Multiracial Garveyism in the Far West" explores the relationship of the United Negro Improvement Association to Asian nationalism. Coeditor Mack analyzes the long and mostly hidden history of black women activists in Spokane, while Julian Kunnie's "Apartheid in Arizona" looks at the state's banning of ethnic studies in 2010 and links it with larger concerns about the growing numbers of Latinos, blacks, and other people of color in Arizona. Coeditor Ruffin's "Brothers Taking Action" links nineteenth- and early-twentieth-century Buffalo Soldier protests with black military activism at the nation's largest military base during the Vietnam War.

These explorations represent exciting new directions in African American western history. The answers to the questions advanced in *Freedom's Racial Frontier* represent the most important contribution to the history of the more than seven million African Americans who now call the West their home.

Seattle, Washington
July 2016

Acknowledgments

This book derives from the experiences that contributors to this anthology have had with the African American West. For editors Ruffin and Mack, this experience formally traces back to the mid-1990s when both started researching the topic for their respective academic programs and began networking with scholars in the field of African American West history and studies. For Ruffin, a San Francisco Bay Area native, this work resulted in the coproduction of the Smithsonian Institution symposium "A Quest for Freedom: The Black Experience in the American West" (2001), the Web page "Africans on the North American Frontier, 1528–1864" (2000–2004), and the conversion of his dissertation into the book *Uninvited Neighbors: African Americans in the Silicon Valley, 1769–1990* (University of Oklahoma Press, 2014). For Mack this work took him from his native Brooklyn, New York, to Washington State University in Pullman, where he researched blacks in the Northwest, published many peer-reviewed book chapters on the African American West, and converted his dissertation, "Triumphing through Adversity," into the book *Black Spokane: The Civil Rights Struggle in the Inland Northwest* (University of Oklahoma Press, 2014). Ruffin and Mack began conceptualizing their joint book in 2012, shortly after they met at the Western Historical Association meeting in Oakland.

Freedom's Racial Frontier is a five-year project that features some of the best African American West scholars. We would like to humbly thank everyone who has contributed to this important volume, in the order in which their chapters appear: Bernadette Pruitt, April L. Harris, Kendra T. Field, Jeanelle Hope, Julian Kunnie, Holly Roose, Emily Lutenski, Kevin Allen Leonard, Gabriela Jiménez, Randolph Stakeman, Tracey Owens Patton, and Kathryn Takara.

We especially thank our editor, Kathleen A. Kelly, and managing editor Steven Baker at the University of Oklahoma Press and freelance copy editor Chris Dodge for improving our volume's prose. They made the publication of the book a pleasant process. We also thank freelance copy editor Genevieve Beenen for her work on an early version of the manuscript.

We must also thank Dr. Quintard Taylor, who will always be the dean of blacks in the West. His guidance and scholarly conceptualization of the African American West put us on the path to better examine such a complex and dynamic region. He helped us broaden the scope of our research to articulate a more complete interpretation of the black West.

This book could not exist in its current form without its illustrations. We thank all those who gave us permission to use these graphics on very generous terms: Syracuse University cartographer Joe Stoll; African American Museum of Oakland; Center for Southwest Research at the University of New Mexico; Dickinson Research Center at the National Cowboy and Western Heritage Museum; Egyptian Lover (Greg Broussard); estate of Langston Hughes; Beinecke Rare Book and Manuscript Library, Yale University; estate of Marjorie Content, estate of Will Seberger; the *Forum* (Fargo, N.D.); #LaughingWhileBlack's Lisa Renee Johnson; Northwest Museum of Arts and Culture; Oklahoma History Center; Roz Payne; Michael C. "Mikey" Sproat and staff at Sam Houston Memorial Museum; Sonia Sanchez; *Spokesman-Review* (Spokane, Wash.); University of Hawai'i at Mānoa Library, Phil White and Tom Rea at the Wyoming Historical Society; David Zeiger; *Blackpast.org*; *Denver Post*; *Omaha World-Herald*; Amy E. Platt and the Oregon Historical Society; State of Alaska, Office of the Governor; Anita J. Watson and the Shared History Program at the University of Nevada, Reno; Dr. Linda Strong-Leek and her Office of the Academic Vice President at Berea College; and the University of Texas Press.

Finally, we would be remiss not to give thanks to family and friends Dr. Carol Alleyne; Herbert, Sadie, Talya, and Michael Ruffin; Mrs. Jerrelene Williamson; Ms. Susan Giffin; Dr. Felicia Mack; and Charity, Liberte, Jelani, and Kosey Mack.

Herbert G. Ruffin II and Dwayne A. Mack

Freedom's Racial Frontier

Introduction

The African American West in
Twentieth- and Twenty-First-Century History

Herbert G. Ruffin II and Dwayne A. Mack

In 1971 a young professor, Quintard Taylor, launched his career as a specialist in the study of the African American West following what might have been no more than a classroom discussion. In a course on African American history at Washington State University, undergraduate Billy Ray Flowers asked Taylor about black history in the West. As Taylor later recalled, he confidently replied that none existed, but, "undaunted, Billy Ray challenged me to document what he knew to be true from his practical experience and community experiences."[1] Soon Taylor was interviewing African Americans throughout the western United States and studying the pioneering scholarship of Lawrence De Graaf, Kevin Mulroy, Kenneth Hamilton, Gretchen Lemke-Santangelo, Shirley Ann Wilson-Moore, Albert Broussard, Kenneth Mason, and Lonnie Bunch, to name a few. The result was the 1998 publication of *In Search of a Racial Frontier*, and Taylor was en route to becoming a preeminent scholar on the subject.[2]

Flowers's challenge to Taylor, which initiated a profound inquiry into what was until that time no more than a footnote to African American and U.S. history, was one of many similar unrecorded exchanges between experts on African American history and life and the people who actually experienced and represented the black West. This included westerners, such as most of the pioneer scholars noted above (and most of this volume's contributors), who became motivated to examine the African American West as histories of the communities within which they lived. Since 1970, these "coming to consciousness" moments have resulted in a growing number of scholars of African American western history producing an exciting new branch of scholarship. In 2017 the largest and most dynamic area of this study focuses on the black urban experience in the twentieth and twenty-first centuries. This focus has taken the field beyond the classical Frederick Jackson Turner and Walter Prescott Webb frameworks. The former author was centered on the presence and contributions of white males on the early western frontier, and the latter, Webb, extended that focus to the West in the years just before World War II.[3]

The first regional synthesis to conceptualize how the African American western frontier was connected to twentieth-century industrial-urban America was Taylor's *In Search of a Racial Frontier*. Taylor's book was conceived and written in a manner mindful of the regional syntheses that had preceded it—"new western history" and studies of the West as a place (see the bibliographic essay concluding this book). What resulted was the opening up of a previously marginalized area of human history, the African American West. Fresh stories were discovered and published that fluidly interconnected consideration of race, class, gender, multiculturalism, and black community formation and political expression west of the Ninety-Eighth Meridian (west of Austin, Texas) and in states that rest on that meridian, including North Dakota, South Dakota, Nebraska, Kansas, Oklahoma, and Texas. The history ranged from the story of enslaved Spanish explorer Esteban to that of the Los Angeles rebellion of 1992.[4] Since *In Search of a Racial Frontier*, several regional surveys have been published that have used the racial frontier framework. The result has been an invaluable expansion of how the story of the U.S. West has been told in the twentieth and twenty-first centuries. These surveys include *African American Women Confront the West, 1600–2000*, edited by Quintard Taylor and Shirley Ann Wilson Moore (University of Oklahoma Press, 2003); *African Americans in the West*, by Douglas Flamming (ABC-CLIO, 2009); and *Expectations of Equality: A History of Black Westerners*, by Albert S. Broussard (Harlan Davidson, 2012). In this current volume, *Freedom's Racial Frontier*, we seek to add to this rich, ever-growing tradition by focusing on black western experience from 1900 to 2015, a period of great population growth. According to the 2010 census, the region's black population grew from 1,343,931 persons in 1940 to almost seven million.[5]

From Western Frontier to Great Migration

At the beginning of the twentieth century most black westerners lived and worked in rural-agrarian communities in Central Texas, East Texas, Oklahoma, and Kansas. This was a pattern established in the 1820s in Texas, the 1830s in Oklahoma, and the 1860s in Kansas. In the aftermath of slavery, by means of migration, self-determined African Americans actively searched for promised lands that bordered former slave states and ideally offered the greatest potential for

Black communities in the western United States. *Cartography by Joe Stoll.*

TABLE I.1 U.S. West populations, 1890–1940

	1890	1900	1910	1920	1930	1940	% 1890 & 1940	% Change
Total Population	8,292,721	10,615,163	16,679,890	20,254,448	25,177,247	27,532,135		
Black	574,901	710,400	942,380	1,042,507	1,229,191	1,343,931	6.9 / 4.9	−0.2
White	7,549,046	9,562,791	15,222,426	18,601,587	23,033,508	25,263,156	91.0 / 91.8	0.8
Other Races	164,476	1,052,372	515,084	375,407	487,497	468,364	2.0 / 1.7	−0.3

Source: Social Explorer Datasets (SE), Census 1890–1940.

their dreams of freedom to be actualized.[6] Prior to 1915, when African American migration patterns fundamentally shifted toward settlement in the industrial-urban West—which resulted in the western U.S. black population growing from 574,901 people in 1890 to 1,343,931 in 1940—most blacks worked in the region as farmers, community makers, cowboys, and soldiers.[7]

Most African American communities west of Austin, Texas, were minute and were tolerated by whites (at least prior to the influx of war industry workers in the 1940s). In contrast, where the South transitioned into the West, black communities experienced Jim Crow and did not see racial desegregation until after landmark U.S. Supreme Court rulings that led to the passage of civil rights legislation for fair voting and educational practices—for example, *Smith v. Alright* (1944), *Sipuel v. Board of Regents of the University of Oklahoma* (1948), *Sweatt v. Painter* (University of Texas) (1950), and *McLaurin v. Oklahoma State Regents* (1950).[8] According to historian Alwyn Barr, in Texas, segregation and disenfranchisement laws traced back to when "black social life in the late nineteenth century became. . . . more self-contained than during Reconstruction, because of continued economic limitations and anti-black violence coupled with growing segregation and discrimination by law and custom."[9] By 1900, most African American Texans struggled to make a living as sharecroppers and independent farmers. They worked on extremely small plots and lacked sufficient financial resources (including credit) and up-to-date technology (such as tractors) to make a quality living on par with their white counterparts.[10] Nevertheless, blacks such as the Amos and Doris Ball family were determined to counter segregation as land-owning farmers. In South Central Texas, the Ball family formed the core of two of the first five African American families in Greater San Antonio. In 2015 they owned more than one thousand acres of arable land in Seguin's Zion Hill area, much of which they had purchased in the 1940s.[11] Ball family member Joseph Ruffin purchased a two-hundred-acre cotton farm in nearby New Berlin through a determined, charismatic appeal to the local power structure of German Americans, hard work, and the Ball-Ruffin-Hysaw family network. Ruffin obtained a prime loan from a banker—a Ball who publicly passed as a white German American.[12]

Other early-twentieth-century black westerners countered racial subordination by establishing all-black towns. This development was rooted in Seminole-Maroon settlements in places such as Fort Mose, Augustine, Florida (1738), and after the Civil War in the all-black town of Davis Bend, Mississippi. These self-segregated, self-governed utopias presented hope to African Americans, shielding community members from hostile race relations, and sometimes provided them a reprieve from poverty as entrepreneurs and farmers on fertile soil.[13] The formation of black towns as the ultimate expression of African American self-determination and economic self-sufficiency had its greatest development in Nicodemus, Kansas (founded in 1879); Langston City, Oklahoma (founded in 1890); Boley, Oklahoma (founded in 1903); Allensworth, California (founded in 1908); and Dearfield, Colorado (founded in 1921). Most black towns went into decline in the 1910s and 1920s following the death of their patriarchs (such as Colonel Allen Allensworth), due to the postwar agriculture depression, and as residents moved to western cities like Boise, Idaho, to pursue waged employment.[14] Following World War I (1914–18), the African American West experienced a profound shift from the frontier to the city through the movement known as the Great Migration.

Since the 1980s, historians have been challenging the traditional South–North narrative of the Great Migration, from Rudolph Lapp, who traced the voluntary mass movement of African Americans to California during the gold rush in the 1850s to Bernadette Pruitt and her work on the early twentieth-century mass black migration to Houston, which she referred to as "the other Great Migration."[15] Similar to Dallas and Omaha, Houston became a booming industrial city as whites, blacks, Mexicans, and others moved there from nearby places in the region, including Walker County, Texas. Black pioneers like Luther and Louis McBride resettled in Houston, taking on the risk that they could find quality housing and employment that would pay a living wage.[16] Unlike the First and Second

Great Migrations (ca. 1915–1970) this movement was not sparked by industrial recruiters. Instead, African Americans chain-migrated to cities like Houston and Kansas City on the premise that there they might safely live quality lives free from poverty, debt bondage, lynching, criminalization, prison labor, and substandard education and housing. From 1917 to 1923, this mass search for living conditions and rights equal to those of whites came into direct conflict with segregationists in places like Houston, Omaha, and Tulsa, and widespread racial violence and property destruction sometimes ensued.[17] The Houston Riot of 1917, sometimes known as the Camp Logan Mutiny, was preceded by a wave of police abuse of African American soldiers and sparked by the police assault and arrest of Corporal Charles Baltimore. The retaliatory response of nearly 150 members of the all-Black 104th Infantry led to the courts-martial of 118 soldiers, 28 death sentences, 63 life sentences, and only 7 acquittals, and black units were removed from combat. These events in Houston—mutiny, riot, and unjust punishment of black soldiers—were a watershed. No longer did urban African American political expression predominantly accommodate Jim Crow. Now there was agitation against it. An urgent new brand of black politics rose in the West, one joined the fights for black suffrage, fair labor practices, equal education and fair media representation, and self-help and economic empowerment. By 1924, these "New Negro" politics had expanded to small black communities such as that in El Paso, whose NAACP branch launched the nationwide fight to end the white Democratic primary after black physician Lawrence A. Nixon was denied the vote in that city.[18]

Unlike border cities such as Houston and Kansas City, most cities and towns west of Austin did not undergo a great black migration process until after 1915. Inconsistent and short-lived economic booms (linked to the transcontinental railroad), the Depression of 1893–98, and environmental disasters (earthquakes, fires, droughts and tornados) kept the West and its cities from being attractive. This changed somewhat during the postwar era, stimulated by rumors that in cities like Los Angeles blacks could escape Jim Crow and experience better living, better schools, and dignified jobs that paid decent wages.[19]

In this book the phrase "the black community" refers to people of African descent who share a similar sociohistorical heritage that encompasses African ancestors, involuntary migration, chattel slavery, colonialism, and de facto and de jure racial discrimination that intimately informs their continued search for equality and social justice. Lawyer McCants Stewart and Portland civil rights advocate Beatrice Morrow Cannady came to the West with their families hoping to fulfill the promise of equal opportunity outlined in the Fourteenth

Amendment of the U.S. Constitution. What they and most black westerners encountered instead was another U.S. region that defaulted on the promissory note of "unalienable rights of life, liberty, and the pursuit of happiness."[20] Conscious of a late-developing "color line" that increasingly feminized poverty in western black communities and restricted most African Americans to low-paying manual labor and domestic work, people like Stewart and Cannady developed a collective sense of community and political urgency to make the U.S. West live up to their expectations of equality.[21] For example, in Los Angeles this modern quest for freedom was sparked in 1915 by local NAACP efforts to censor the white supremacist motion picture *The Birth of a Nation*.[22] In 1920s Portland, a new era of protest combined the concepts of "self-help, hard work, thrift, and racial solidarity" with civil rights and women's rights activism for first-class citizenship, which arose in direct opposition to the rise of Oregon's Ku Klux Klan.[23] From these efforts emerged the modern freedom rights movement in the U.S. West, which included the working-class struggle for fair employment practices, safe, decent housing, and racial regeneration and advancement. For instance, in 1910s Los Angeles, rapid black population growth and the formation of the first involuntary ghetto west of the Ninety-Eighth Meridian resulted in the first election of an African American to public office since 1901, California State Assembly member Frederick M. Roberts (R)—the first black politician in high office on the West Coast. By the 1930s, New Negro politics and the ghettoization of most black Los Angelenos resulted in what historian Douglas Flamming refers to as "one the most significant political realignments in American history" through the election of liberal Democrats, Franklin Delano Roosevelt (as president) and African American Augustus F. Hawkins (to the California State Assembly).[24]

World War II and the Postwar Era West

African American life and culture made its greatest impact on the western United States during World War II and the postwar period. From 1940 to 1970 the black western population nearly tripled, going from 1,343,931 to 3,409,006.[25] Academics call this period the Second Great Migration. It was launched on June 25, 1941, the date that the March on Washington Movement pressured President Roosevelt into issuing Executive Order 8802, which outlawed segregation in defense industries with federal government contracts. The order was enforced by the Fair Employment Practices Commission and War Manpower Commission, which set a precedent for the federal government to combat legal segregation more broadly.[26] Its immediate impact was arguably felt the greatest on the West

Table I.2   U.S. West populations, 1960–2010

	1960	1970	1980	1990	2000	2010	% 1960 & 2010	% Change
Total Population	47,902,122	53,575,692	65,703,960	77,612,936	92,394,936	107,008,695		
African American	2,548,495	3,409,006	4,355,790	5,290,705	5,973,758	6,948,958	5.7 / 6.5	0.8
European American	43,858,892	48,340,508	53,610,249	59,691,970	64,924,335	73,465,379	91.6 / 68.7	−22.9
Native American	390,008	—	1,019,967	1,312,045	1,613,849	1,984,634	0.8 / 1.9	1.1
Asian American	712,292	—	2,244,254	4,448,626	5,961,911	7,815,196	1.5 / 7.3	5.8
Other race and Latino	176,484	—	4,473,700	6,872,848	10,348,627	11,911,153	0.4 / 11.1	10.7

Source: Social Explorer Datasets (SE), Census 1960–2010.

Coast, where for the first time African Americans in cities like Tacoma became the largest minority population, dwarfing until the 1980s Asian Americans and Asian immigrants and, in the Southwest, Mexican Americans and Mexican immigrants. Most of these black westerners, such as San Jose civil rights activist Inez Jackson and family, migrated from the South, Midwest, and Great Plains. In 1944 the Jacksons moved to the San Francisco Bay Area from Oklahoma City, spurred by the commonly heard rumor that racial discrimination did not exist in California. It was only after being excluded from teaching in San Jose's Unified School District that fully credentialed Inez Jackson realized in many ways California was no better than Oklahoma. Determined to thrive in Northside San Jose, black migrants like the Jacksons overcame the region's racial intolerance and underemployment by working multiple jobs, pooling their resources, and staying grounded in black southern culture—soul food, social clubs, music, and worship—cultural heritage that has had an immeasurable impact on the U.S. West. The black West meant enjoying family recipes at Denver's CoraFaye's Cafe, hearing cutting-edge jazz and R&B from Seattle's Quincy Jones and Ray Charles "RC" Robinson at the Central District's YMCA, and participating in churches whose leaders—like San Francisco reverends Howard Thurman and Cecil Williams—extended salvation beyond the sanctuary to the civil rights arena and the streets.[27]

In western areas that bordered the South, the immigration that began during the 1900s continued after 1940. This intraregional urban movement paralleled the rapid development of southwestern cities with defense industries and military bases. One such city was Beaumont, Texas, which saw an increase in the black population sparked by employment opportunities at Pennsylvania Shipyards—with concomitant racial tensions. On June 15–16, 1943, an alleged rape of a white woman by a black man sparked a race riot.[28] Things were different in sundown towns, like Killeen, Texas, that became military boomtowns after 1940.[29] In Killeen the adjacency of Fort Hood, a massive federal economic presence, and the army's demand for black GIs, led to desegregation. Change came not only due to government pressure but also from activists like members of the 761st "Black *Panthers*" *Tank* Battalion, which included Jackie Robinson, who would go on to become a baseball legend. This pattern was replicated in cities such as Honolulu (home of Pearl Harbor), Monterey, California (near Fort Ord), and Spokane (home of Fort George Wright).[30]

The most dramatic black growth occurred in West Coast cities as 443,000 blacks were pulled to Washington, Oregon, and California in the 1940s to work in defense industries at shipyards, food plants, and airplane factories. More than 338,000 of these migrants settled in California, with most black laborers working in shipbuilding in Los Angeles and in the San Francisco Bay Area.[31] Here segregated black communities formed, sometimes spilling into adjacent abandoned Japantowns. These overcrowded neighborhoods were centered at Fillmore and Western Addition in San Francisco, Logan Heights in San Diego, and in North Richmond, South Central Los Angeles, and West Oakland.[32] Meanwhile, in places like Inner Northeast Portland, Southwest Anaheim, and West Las Vegas, blacks represented less than 3 percent of the general population and continued living lives impacted by de facto race discrimination that represented both socioeconomic freedom and the constant struggle for freedoms deferred.[33]

Segregated housing was the first signal to most African American westerners that structural racism was getting worse after the U.S. Supreme Court decision in *Shelley v. Kraemer* (1948), which made restrictive covenants unenforceable.[34] The ghettoes in which most black westerners were segregated were brought about through redlining, the antithesis of the development of the promising postwar suburb. This was the practice of systematically denying home loans to persons of color and working poor people in certain areas (such as suburbs). Central to this suburban policy bias was the Federal Housing Authority mortgage program. Its participation in the postwar housing market profoundly restructured race relations, restricting people of color to central cities and allowing only whites access into new suburbs.[35] Thus, in the U.S. West from 1945 to 1980, suburbs from Alamo Heights (outside San Antonio) to Orange County, California, were enclaves where Euro-Americans enjoyed white privilege.[36]

Following the passage of the 1949 National Housing Act, which provided for slum clearance, urban renewal, and warehousing of black and poor people in public housing, statewide fair housing campaigns were launched throughout the West. From 1950 until passage of the Fair Housing Act of 1968, this struggle was waged in conjunction with grassroots organizations and local NAACP chapters that also pursued broader civil rights agendas. These included the Phoenix and Topeka NAACP chapters, the latter best known for desegregating public education.[37] In California, black assemblymen Gus Hawkins and William Byron Rumford made the postwar struggle for open housing a statewide issue. In 1954 their efforts were supported by a new multiracial civil rights coalition called the California Committee for Fair Employment Practices, and a new generation of civil-rights-oriented politicians, led by Governor Edmund G. "Pat" Brown eventually enacted change. In 1959 the California Fair Employment Practices Act was passed, and within four years a fair higher education bill and three fair housing bills were passed. The latter—the Hawkins Act, Unruh Act, and California Fair Housing Act (aka Rumford Act)—covered public-assisted housing, fair business transactions in housing, and single-family housing.[38] The passage of these bills made California central to the success of the national movements for fair housing, equal opportunity in education, and civil rights.

A western color line also existed in employment. Despite having advanced in industrial labor during the war, from 1950 to 1970 most African American westerners continued to work as domestics, manual laborers, and in service-related industries. This was a huge blow for black westerners such as former Kaiser Shipyard worker Margaret Starks, who had come from Pine Bluff, Arkansas, to Richmond, California, on the gamble that she and her family would gain industrial employment and recover from the Great Depression. They had hoped not only for personal success but also to participate in compressing the "wage differentials between African American and white workers."[39] The civil rights struggle extended to the workplace during the summer of 1943. California and Portland shipbuilders fired more than 950 African American workers who had protested being segregated in auxiliary unions and restricted from full membership in the International Brotherhood of Boilermakers and affiliated unions. One of the fired workers, San Francisco NAACP president Joseph James, then led a collective assault against auxiliary unions, participating in federal hearings and in a class action lawsuit against the Marinship Corporation in 1944, a case heard in the Supreme Court of California. This effort resulted in the court ordering the Boilermakers to immediately dismantle the auxiliary unions and integrate the fired black workers within their membership.[40]

A year later, however, World War II ended, and black workers like James were the first people fired when defense industries downsized and military bases closed, despite the fact that many had acquired a high level of skill and advanced education. What followed was chronic unemployment and underemployment, a reversal of the wartime black middle-class growth in metropolitan areas from Beaumont to Oahu, especially among Americans in their twenties and thirties. In cities such as Omaha, Albuquerque, and Seattle, African American economic decline was anchored by deunionization, suburbanization, redlining, red-baiting, white flight, and the capital flight and exclusive hiring practices of corporations like Seattle's Boeing Airplane Company.[41] Concomitant to this decline was the postwar rise of street gangs and a youth culture informed by infrapolitics— masked political dissidence. It was in this milieu, in West Oakland, that future Black Panther Party founder and leader Huey P. Newton began to come of age.[42] Many black westerners tried to overcome the losses by combining their resources with like-minded members of color and becoming community activists. After the war, this is what veteran fighter pilot Lincoln J. Ragsdale, his wife Eleanor, and his brother Hartwell did in South Phoenix to survive and even thrive in an increasingly white supremacist Arizona. Having moved from their native Oklahoma to Arizona, the Ragsdales sustained their mortuary business in the face of structural racial discrimination. The family's strong sense of dignity was their mainstay, and this dignity was connected to involvement in the black church and civil rights organizations like the Greater Phoenix Council for Civic Unity, which they helped found.[43]

The postwar civil rights politics that informed black westerners like the Ragdales was rooted in freedom struggles of the early twentieth century and lived experience. For example, in 1940s Texas, African Americans were still fighting for the right to vote in Democratic primary elections, a struggle that had begun in 1924. Black Houstonian Lonnie E. Smith set the precedent for fair voting with a 1944 Supreme Court decision, *Smith v. Allwright*. In his suit against Harris County election official S. S. Allwright, Smith was represented by NAACP's Legal Defense and Education Fund director Thurgood Marshall. In Texas the decision immediately led to the massive increase in registered African American voters (from 30,000 in 1940, the number rose to 100,000 in 1947).[44] The *Smith v. Allwright* decision paralleled a moderate increase in the region's number of black politicians. The likes of California's Byron Rumford and Texas state senator Barbara Jordan were pioneers in uniting the black vote and cultivating broad interracial support for the election of black politicians despite minority black populations (ranging from 1 to 35 percent in western states.[45] In the post–civil rights movement era, multiracial coalitions and nationalized local elections abnormally impacted by national political party agendas (often at the expense of local concerns) have resulted in numerous African American politicians being elected to high office in the West. Among these are U.S. congresswomen Maxine Waters (D-CA) and Mia Love (R-UT) and mayors Tom Bradley (Los Angeles), James Chase (Spokane), Willie Brown (San Francisco), Norm Rice (Seattle), and Ivy Taylor (San Antonio), to name a few.[46]

More commonly told in civil rights historiography is how the movement exposed the illegal separate and unequal structure of local schools and school districts that violated the Equal Protection Clause in the Fourteenth Amendment of the U.S. Constitution. Since the 1910s, this was the claim that western civil rights organizations had made, such as the Albuquerque NAACP had done in fighting to integrate New Mexico school districts in 1915 and the University of New Mexico from 1915 to 1921. In southeastern New Mexico, school segregation was constant until after the passage of *Brown v. Board of Education*. Similar to other parts of the Southwest, Jim Crow in New Mexico targeted students who lived in public school districts with a majority of Mexican Americans. Most blacks were clustered within these communities, and by the late 1940s this got the NAACP involved in what essentially was a multiracial struggle for freedom.[47] Forty years later, African Americans in cities such as Phoenix and Topeka were engaged in a similar fight, the main difference being that in most parts of the West these new battles were not sparked in multiracial communities with small black populations but in ones with larger, concentrated black communities. Similar to what was done in the struggle for black suffrage, blacks turned the potential ills of the ghetto into a base of political and economic empowerment. Organizations such as the Greater Phoenix Council for Civic Unity and the Topeka NAACP fought segregation in employment, housing, and public accommodations such as restaurants and theaters, but education was their greatest target. Breakthroughs for this struggle began in 1935, during the NAACP's courtroom assault on public universities that denied qualified African Americans admission to graduate programs that had no corresponding "separate and equal" graduate programs for blacks. In the Southwest, this led to desegregation decisions in *Sipuel v. Board of Regents of the University of Oklahoma* (1948), *Sweatt v. Painter* (University of Texas) (1950), and *McLaurin v. Oklahoma State Regents* (1950). These set precedents for national school desegregation verdicts.[48]

Arguably having more impact was the movement that followed: the movement to desegregate public primary and secondary education. During the fall of 1951 in Arizona, this struggle led to the voluntary desegregation of Tucson's School District 1. Two years later, in 1953, it resulted in the voluntary desegregation of Phoenix's Encanto School District and the court-ordered desegregation of Phoenix Union High School.[49] These desegregation efforts and the *Mendez et al. v. Westminster School District* decision (1947) set the precedent for the national defeat of segregation in public education a year later in *Brown v. Board of Education at Topeka* (1954–55). That said, it is important to note the complex and uncommon nature of the western civil rights movement. For example, the *Mendez* decision desegregated public education for Mexican Americans (and implicitly African Americans) in Orange County, California, using social scientific evidence to support the argument that segregated education conditioned Mexican children to feel inferior and harmed their capacity to be productive citizens, because "separate but equal" will always be unequal. Assisting Mendez family attorney David Marcus was the NAACP's Thurgood Marshall who, along with California governor Earl Warren, took close note of this case. Both would be justices in U.S. Supreme Court that would consider the *Brown v. Board of Education*. Less frequently noted in most histories is that several months after the 1947 *Mendez* decision, Warren "signed [a] bill ending school segregation in California, making it the first state to officially desegregate its public schools." As chief justice, he would later write the 1954 opinion in *Brown*.[50] From *Brown* to the present, community members, courts, and policy makers have been grappling with racially imbalanced public education and the re-segregation of public education.[51] In the meantime the Civil Rights Act of 1964 was passed; the NAACP and the American Civil Liberties Union effectively linked residential housing patterns to separate and unequal education, when municipal busing plans were established; and black lawyers such as Denver's Morris Cole and civil rights activists like Santa Clara County's Maurice Hardeman became municipal judges.[52]

African American postwar demand for legal justice came not only from Kansas, the Southwest, and the West Coast. Albert Fritz pushed for social justice in Salt Lake City, and his work for civil rights in Utah and integration of the Church of Latter Day Saints (LDS) stemmed from the belief that he was just as good as any white person. As Salt Lake City's NAACP president (1955–64), Fritz led successful efforts to end segregation in employment and public accommodations for African Americans and Mexican Americans, then the largest minority in Utah.[53] Similar those of other black western communities such as nearby Cheyenne, Wyoming, which passed a public accommodation bill in 1957, Salt Lake City's movement was bolstered by the unprecedented increase in its black population.[54] According to anatomy professor and black Utahn Charles "Chuck" Nabors, the LDS had instigated much of the discrimination by excluding blacks "from its priesthood as proof of their inferiority [in life and in death]" while taking an indifferent stance on civil rights and insisting that "we only get into politics on moral issues."[55] By 1964, Utah's civil rights movement had snowballed into an international struggle, attracting the participation of civil rights leaders such as Dr. Martin Luther King Jr., entertainers like Ella Fitzgerald, college athletes who refused to play against Brigham Young University, prospective converts around the world, and, at least rhetorically, Mormon politicians seeking national office. In 1964, this activity pressured the passage of the state's first civil rights bill, the Public Accommodations Act, which allowed blacks access to city motels in compliance with Title II of the Civil Rights Act of 1964. Nine years later, in 1973, the movement forced Utah legislators to further desegregate public accommodations. This was followed by the 1978 LDS "Revelation on Priesthood," which granted qualified black men (and later black women) the priesthood. This decision has arguably had the most far-reaching impact on social relations in the state, and it provided the model that gay LDS members are currently using to fight for their own access to the priesthood.[56]

In other parts of the West, African Americans and their allies used tactics popularized by the southern civil rights movement. Sit-ins were organized in 1958 in Wichita, Kansas, and Oklahoma City—two years before the more famous sit-ins in Greensboro, North Carolina, sparked the national tactical shift to nonviolent direct action. The Wichita sit-in was led by cousins Carol Parks, nineteen, and Ron Walters, twenty, leaders of the city's NAACP youth council. The two organized the sit-in to end segregation at Dockum Drugs. Parks (now Parks-Haun) remembers that requesting a meal at Dockum's popular lunch counter was always humiliating for blacks. "You'd come in and go to the end of this counter and when you were served anything, it was in disposable containers." For Walters, Wichita was "Mississippi up north. So we tried to break it down and we deliberately chose Dockum because Dockum was part of a chain . . . and we felt if we could do something there in the heart of town, it might have a consequence." For a month the NAACP youth quietly sat at Dockum's lunch counter for dinner on Tuesday, Thursday, and Saturday until the owner broke down and told his manager, "Serve them—I'm losing too much money."[57] Eight days later, in Oklahoma City NAACP, youth adviser Clara Luper and "fourteen well-groomed children ranging in age from six to fifteen walked into Katz Drugstore, sat down, and ordered soft drinks. The waitress refused to serve them."[58] In Oklahoma this triggered a new phase in the civil rights movement, direct action rooted in local empowerment in black towns and the *Sipuel, McLaurin,* and *Brown* court cases. The most important aspect of this phase was that blacks broke local color lines and demanded immediate change by placing their bodies in the crosshairs of potential white terror.[59] One action led to another as westerners waged sympathy strikes, participated in voter registration drives, and demanded their freedom from racial discrimination in housing, education, and public accommodations, and at department stores, grocery stores, and other retailers.[60]

By 1965, the slow-to-moderate pace of racial and economic reform led to calls for "Freedom Now" and "Black Power" in the West as throughout the country. Despite passage of civil rights legislation for public accommodations, equal employment opportunity, and fair voting, the white majority not only safeguarded its privilege but in some cases rolled back changes, as in California's Proposition 14 in 1964—which nullified the Rumford Fair Housing Act. Eventually President Lyndon Johnson would need to establish the National Advisory Commission on Civil Disorders (the Kerner Commission) to deal with the rash of urban disturbances and near disturbances that followed.[61]

On August 11, 1965, in the Los Angeles ghetto of Watts, a six-day rebellion began against poverty, police abuse, residential isolation, a growing racial wealth gap, and inadequate education. As with the Los Angeles uprising that would take place twenty-seven years later, the Watts "riots" were sparked by police brutality. In this instance it was Marquette Frye and his mother and brother who were arrested and badly abused by California Highway Patrol officers. What ensued was arguably the most unforeseen urban rebellion in U.S. history. It took place in an area larger than Manhattan and resulted in thirty-four deaths, one thousand reported injuries (most of them suffered by African Americans), and property damage estimated at $200 million.[62] From Watts's ashes emerged nothing more than failed promises to invest in the South Central Los Angeles black community, and from this failure arose the West's Black Power movement. This movement, Quintard Tayor writes, "began with the ideal that African Americans should define and control the major institutions in their community, whose economic and political resources should be mobilized for its development and eventual parity alongside other communities."[63] Prior to 1965, elements of this movement were developed by black nationalists like the Nation of Islam (NOI) and black student activists inspired by the NOI's message, such as the Afro-American Association (AAA) at University of California, Berkeley, in 1962—"California's first indigenous Black nationalist organization."[64] In the aftermath of Watts (and the February 1965 assassination of Malcolm X) black activists formed organizations that transcended the initial quest of the AAA to fight injustice through the creation of a black middle class. In Watts, former AAA member Maulana Karenga founded the US Organization, based on a philosophy that Karenga referred to as Kawaida, which wedded communitarian culture, black nationalism, pan-Africanism, and socialism. The US Organization, whose name meant "us African people," was intended to put Kawaida principles into practice.[65]

In Oakland, former AAA member Bobby Seale used the Oakland Neighborhood Anti-Poverty Center to empower community members with federal Community Action Program resources and to encourage young adults to be critical and to voice their opinions. Former AAA member Huey P. Newton frequented the Anti-Poverty Center to talk politics and read the center's law books. On October 15, 1966, the two founded the Black Panther Party for Self-Defense. This revolutionary nationalist organization demanded full socioeconomic equality and creatively used media, self-defense, survival programs, and police-control tactics. The Panthers rapidly evolved from being one of many Bay Area freedom rights organizations to the vanguard of the international struggle within little more than a year.[66] Blacks in the U.S. West contributed to this struggle in a variety of powerful ways. San Francisco State University saw the formation of a black student union and ethnic studies departments. A black arts movement took hold whose goal was to "end discrimination in the motion-picture industry, recording studios, and musicians' unions" through groups like L.A.'s Underground Musicians Association. Black amateur athletes stood up for black empowerment, human rights, and democratization of U.S. education and sport. San Jose State University track and field athletes Tommie Smith and John Carlos are remembered today in association with the 1968 Summer Olympics, where made their famous black fist salute after being award medals. Activism also emerged among other communities, partly modeled on the black freedom movement: not only the American Indian Movement, Asian American movement, and Chicana/o movement but also the environmental justice, LGBTQ, feminist, and antiwar movements.[67]

After Watts, offshoot freedom movements typically began with counterculture youth forging interracial alliances reminiscent of black-brown coalitions formed in Albuquerque, Los Angeles, Phoenix, and Westminster, California (in Orange County) during World War II to promote human rights and to combat discrimination. These coalitions used the courts as well as nonviolent protest and mass demonstrations.[68] In Seattle in the 1960s, black youth and third-generation Japanese youth (Sansei) forged a campaign centered on human rights and using nonviolent protest, which contradicted the sensibilities of their parents. For decades African Americans and Japanese Americans had been seemingly indifferent to each other's culture and ambitions. African Americans wanted to end structural racism, especially in housing. Second-generation Japanese Americans (Nisei)—who had survived internment and Washington State's Anti-Alien Land Act (1921–52) were focused more conservatively on intermarriage with Chinese and Filipinos.[69] By 1967, the consolidation of freedom movement centered on the campaign for civil rights and black empowerment forced entrenched white supremacists to acknowledge that black lives mattered. For black communities and their allies the result was increased harassment from the FBI's Counterintelligence Program (COINTELPRO) and a white backlash from "kitchen table activists" in suburbs such as Scottsdale, Arizona, and Garden Grove, California. Whites, like politicians Barry Goldwater and Ronald Reagan in those two states, equated freedom with anticommunism, capitalism, low taxes, limited regulation, private property, Protestant family values, small government, and being tough on law and order.[70] By the mid-1970s the West's freedom rights movement slowed to a crawl because of growing conservatism, agent provocateurs and internal conflicts, stagflation, hetero-patriarchal chauvinism, and the arrests, assassinations and resignation of key black leaders.

The Contemporary West

For black professionals and their children, the democratization of the U.S. West was closely connected to affirmative action and the Fair Housing Act of 1968. These gains, however, would be challenged in high courts and partially undone, as in the 1978 *Regents of the University of California v. Bakke* case, which ruled the use of racial "quotas" unconstitutional in university admissions but maintained that the use of affirmative action programs can be constitutional in other instances. Ronald Reagan's presidential administration (1981–89) saw a conservative realignment of the U.S. political economy, reversing the growth of civil rights legislation and rerouting federal grants from central cities, public education, and social welfare to corporations, the Pentagon, plutocrats, and the prison-industrial complex. Most African American westerners who thrived during this time were college-educated, worked in predominantly white professional environments, and lived in communities where the black poor were absent.[71] Following the Fair Housing Act of 1968, African Americans contributed to a demographic revolution as their migration saw the black population in suburbs nationwide grow from 13 percent in 1960 to 34 percent in 2000. The nation's African American population increased from 2.5 million people in 1960 to 11.9 million people in 2000.[72] A significant percentage of this growth occurred in the Southwest and on the West Coast.[73] To blacks such as San Antonio's Rae Lowry, now a retired AT&T customer service manager, this movement of African Americans into the middle class and the suburbs symbolized the transformation of the United States into a democratic nation. "I have my own home," Lowry says. "[I] have money in the bank. I live comfortably. . . . I am not poverty-stricken. I have a car. I'm okay, [because] my dream could be what I want it to be."[74] She is not alone. Many black westerners in the late twentieth century were able to move into suburban communities like Converse, Live Oak and Windcrest (outside San Antonio) and socialize with people with whom they felt comfortable. Lowry's neighborhood was adjacent to inner city East San Antonio where she had earlier lived.[75]

In booming metropolises such as San Antonio, African Americans like Rae Lowry came from working families that had modest, middle-class aspirations and consciously looked to supplant race with class to determine their life chances. This resulted in black residents dispersing throughout western communities such as Tarrant County (Texas) and Orange County (California) as part of an intraregional urban–suburban migration. In these two cases, blacks moved from communities of South Dallas and Northwest Santa Ana to nearby Fort Worth and Fullerton, respectively.[76] As with earlier migrations, African Americans migrants had an immeasurable impact on regional culture, including education (protesting on the frontlines of landmark anti-affirmative legislation at the University of Texas at Austin) entertainment, foodways, music, political expression, and worship. However, this impact has been achieved without blacks forming a single black community (giving the illusion of integration), except for the black church, black chamber of commerce, and black clubs and restaurants. African Americans commonly moved away from ghettos undergoing the gentrification, such as Northwest Santa Ana, which had a black student population peaking in the mid-1970s at almost 10 percent, only to drop to 1.5 percent in 1994.[77] Most black migrants to western suburbs moved for better education and employment opportunities in strong economies (opportunities that matched their job train-ing), lower living costs, and for what they saw as crime-free and environmentally places where black individuals and interculturalism were accepted by the majority population.[78]

The communities that black suburbanites entered were the fastest growing places in the postwar United States.[79] Some rapidly became accidental metropo-lises that survived the post-1970s deindustrialization in cities like San Jose, Dallas–Fort Worth, and Portland. Their postindustrial economies entailed entertainment, finance, high technology, medicine, the military, petroleum, and even retirement (as many senior communities and nursing homes would be built in these suburbs).[80] Throughout the West, black suburban population growth has outpaced the general growth patterns. For example, the black population of the city of Moreno Valley, California, outside Riverside, grew 113 percent in 1990–2010 while the general population grew 20 percent from 1990 to 2010. Prior to the 1970s, the small number of blacks given the opportunity to live in the suburbs, such as first black police officer in Inglewood, California, Harold P. Moret, were often steered into "ring suburbs" or transitional housing in older, declining suburbs within a particular region that extended a ghetto by artificially creating one in an adjacent suburb.[81] After the 1970s, black migration into western suburbs such as Federal Way (outside Seattle) was influenced by both structural racism and the high cost of urban living—an increasingly expensive housing market (and lack of low-cost urban housing), high inflation, and gentrification.[82]

One of the most unfortunate and misunderstood western developments involved the physical and cultural bifurcation of formerly centralized black com-munities. Since the 1980s, black flight—the exodus of potential African American leaders and role models from central cities to the suburbs—has widened the gulf between the black middle class and the black working poor. This has been a major factor in keeping poor populations perpetually poor. Many black business owners took jobs with them. So did many blacks whose educational and professional successes might have led others to aspire to the same.[83] This outmigration of so many high achievers, like San Jose's T. J. Owens and his family, often took with them the heart of their inner city communities, and in places like suburban South San Jose went from being part of a black community to simply representing a black community everywhere they went. The people left behind dealt with the loss as best they could, and migrants did not necessarily cut ties: Owens and family continued their race work in central city San Jose.[84] But the street culture that developed after the deindustrialization of the inner city in the 1950s

TABLE I.3 **Population growth in the fastest-growing suburban cities, 1950–2010**

Community	State	Metro Area	Year Started	Start Pop.	Black Pop.	2000 Pop.	Black Pop.	Change (Gen. %)	Change (Bl. %)
Chandler	AZ	Phoenix	1950	3,799	13	176,581	11,276	4,548	86,638
Gilbert	AZ	Phoenix	1980	5,717	42	109,697	6,987	1,819	16,536
Glendale	AZ	Phoenix	1950	8,179	361	218,812	13,686	2,575	3,691
Mesa	AZ	Phoenix	1950	16,790	271	396,375	15,289	2,261	5,542
Peoria	AZ	Phoenix	1960	2,593	0	108,364	5,182	4,079	518,200
Scottsdale	AZ	Phoenix	1960	10,026	0	202,705	3,652	1,922	365,200
Tempe	AZ	Phoenix	1950	7,684	18	158,625	9,551	1,964	52,961
Anaheim	CA	Los Angeles	1950	14,556	52	328,014	9,347	2,153	17,875
Corona City	CA	Los Angeles	1950	10,223	22	124,966	8,934	1,122	40,509
Costa Mesa	CA	Los Angeles	1960	37,550	38	108,724	1,640	190	4,216
Fontana	CA	Los Angeles	1960	14,659	1	128,929	19,574	780	1,957,300
Fullerton City	CA	Los Angeles	1950	13,958	33	126,003	3,138	803	9,409
Irvine	CA	Los Angeles	1980	62,134	916	143,072	3,718	130	306
Lancaster	CA	Los Angeles	1950	3,594	2	118,718	32,083	3,203	160,050
Moreno Valley	CA	Los Angeles	1990	118,779	16,402	142,381	34,889	20	113
Ontario	CA	Los Angeles	1950	22,872	112	158,007	10,561	591	9,329
Orange	CA	Los Angeles	1950	10,027	2	128,821	2,227	1,185	111,250
Oxnard	CA	Los Angeles	1950	21,567	496	170,358	5,771	690	1,064
Rancho Cucamonga	CA	Los Angeles	1980	55,250	1,221	127,743	15,246	131	1,149
Riverside	CA	Los Angeles	1950	46,764	888	255,166	21,421	446	2,312
San Bernardino	CA	Los Angeles	1950	63,058	915	185,401	31,582	194	3,352
Santa Ana	CA	Los Angeles	1950	45,533	214	337,977	4,856	642	2,169
Santa Clarita	CA	Los Angeles	1990	110,642	1,695	151,088	5,623	37	232
Simi Valley	CA	Los Angeles	1970	56,676	183	111,351	1,739	96	850

Community	State	Metro Area	Year Started	Start Pop.	Black Pop.	2000 Pop.	Black Pop.	Change (Gen. %)	Change (Bl. %)
Thousand Oaks	CA	Los Angeles	1960	2,934	4	117,005	1,674	3,888	41,750
Chula Vista	CA	San Diego	1950	15,927	39	173,556	11,219	990	28,667
Escondido	CA	San Diego	1950	6,544	2	133,559	3,585	1,941	179,150
Oceanside	CA	San Diego	1950	12,881	87	161,029	7,873	1,150	8,949
Daly City	CA	San Francisco	1950	15,191	5	103,621	3,600	582	71,900
Fremont	CA	San Francisco	1960	43,790	8	203,413	7,103	365	88,676
Santa Rosa	CA	San Francisco	1950	17,902	23	147,595	4,079	724	17,635
Sunnyvale	CA	San Francisco	1950	9,829	12	131,760	2,735	1,241	10,242
Aurora	CO	Denver	1950	11,421	6	276,393	51,196	2,320	853,167
Lakewood	CO	Denver	1960	19,338	45	144,126	2,231	645	1,333
Westminster	CO	Denver	1960	13,850	NA	100,940	1,505	629	62,900
Henderson	NV	Las Vegas	1950	3,643	1	175,381	13,142	4,714	1,314,100
North Las Vegas	NV	Las Vegas	1950	3,875	0	115,488	43,153	2,880	4,315,300
Salem	OR	Portland	1950	43,140	63	136,924	2,283	217	3,524
Arlington	TX	Dallas	1950	7,692	171	332,969	68,792	4,229	40,129
Carrolton	TX	Dallas	1960	4,242	137	109,576	10,001	2,483	7,200
Garland	TX	Dallas	1950	10,571	217	215,768	32,980	1,941	15,098
Grand Prairie	TX	Dallas	1950	14,594	311	127,427	35,390	773	11,279
Irving	TX	Dallas	1950	2,621	0	191,615	26,522	7,211	2,652,200
Mesquite	TX	Dallas	1960	27,526	101	124,523	30,534	352	30,132
Plano	TX	Dallas	1960	3,695	880	222,030	19,697	5,909	2,138
West Valley City	UT	Salt Lake City	1980	72,378	497	108,896	2,533	50	410
Bellevue	WA	Seattle	1960	12,809	14	109,569	2,815	755	20,007

Sources: See note 79.

often dissolved into destructive survival strategies in the 1980s, in response to entrenched poverty, the lack of organizing for black empowerment, and the rise of conservatism, neoliberalism, and the War on Drugs. In communities such as Houston's Third Ward, the ghetto was not a thing of the past—it was becoming more concentrated with poor people of color, as addressed by Houston's Geto Boys in songs like "City under Siege" (e.g., "Police brutality is not a formality, they're kickin' our ass, and we're payin' their salary").[85] As individual pursuits of the American Dream continued to be thwarted, some African American westerners worked diligently to make the region live up to their expectations of equality.[86] In 1972, West Las Vegas's Ruby Duncan and like-minded people formed the antipoverty program Operation Life to help revitalize Las Vegas's poorer communities. Lobbying under the banner "We can do it and do it better," they raised millions of dollars, leading to the community's first daycare center, job training center, library, medical center, and senior housing. Operation Life functioned until the 1980s when Great Society community organizations declined due to the Reagan administration's drastic funding cuts.[87]

Throughout the West the black presence was evident in annual events such as Black History Month ceremonies and forums, Juneteenth, and Dr. Martin Luther King Jr. commemorations.[88] Blacks empowered themselves as business professionals, entrepreneurs, students, and active members in civil, political, and social organizations. As mentioned above, the middle-class African Americans and multiracial liberalism blacks being elected to high office, such as Tom Bradley. During his twenty years as mayor of Los Angeles (1973–1993) liberal coalition politics dominated, with the promise that black, brown, and working poor people in South Central and East Los Angeles would not be left behind during the city's booming redevelopment—the likes of which were occurring in western cities from Honolulu to San Antonio.[89] Western municipal governments, including that of Los Angeles, were rebuilding downtowns and claiming that the money going into this redevelopment would spark socioeconomic growth for those on the bottom—which it usually did not.[90] Similar to President Reagan's touting of "trickle-down economics," neoliberal economic policies such as Bradley's produced a false sense of economic prosperity for most westerners. In culturally diverse Los Angeles, structural discrimination remained, and a highly diversified labor market was maintained that led to "sharply uneven outcomes for different segments of the population."[91] For African American westerners those uneven outcomes included being the main target of War on Drugs policy, unfair prison sentencing, and police repression.[92]

Persistent police repression in particular has played a role in black youth addressing politics through hip-hop (taking a cue from the 1960s Black Arts Movement). In the West and Southwest, artists such as L.A.'s Ice-T, NWA, and Yo-Yo, Oakland's Too Short and Digital Underground, Port Arthur's UGK (aka Underground Kingz), and Seattle's Sir Mix-a-Lot were in the forefront of developing a business centered on hypermasculine authenticity and being true to "the streets."[93] Their pioneering music featured lyrics centered on drug culture, gangs, hustling, police abuse, and prison—an infrapolitics that managed to both entertain and connect with young, disempowered listeners. These soundscapes broke from the James Brown beat-breaks that dominated the New York hip-hop scene and instead was influenced by artists like Curtis Mayfield and Parliament-Funkadelic that dominated western radio. This movement produced the sharpest social commentaries on the state of African America in albums such as Ice Cube's *Death Certificate* (1991), which presaged the Los Angeles uprising of 1992.[94]

Today, as we approach the third decade of the twenty-first century, we seem stuck in time, as events echo the 1992 Los Angeles uprising, triggered by the acquittal of four Los Angeles Police Department officers despite video evidence of their beating of motorist Rodney King.[95] Some things have changed, and some have not. Today's urban and suburban communities in the West are heavily impacted by ethnocentrism, Asian and Latina/o population growth, globalization, racialized policing, reality television, borderline stagflation, and politics of fear. In spite of this, however, through social media and grassroots activism black westerners continue to create models for empowerment and dignity. Intersectional organizations and movements such as Black Lives Matter simultaneously fight structural racism, classism, sexism, and heterosexism. Aided by Twitter and the hashtag #LaughingWhileBlack, eleven women successfully settled an $11 million lawsuit after being ejected from a wine train in Napa Valley. Silicon Valley De-Bug, a multiracial organization led by legal workers, activists, and their families and friends (such as San Francisco 49er Colin Kaepernick), fights social injustice in the courts. Finally, as during the New Negro, Black Arts, and hip-hop movements of the 1920s, 1960s, and 1980s, individual black westerners speak out through arts and entertainment. This includes Kaepernick's national anthem protests and Beyoncé's Black Panther–themed performance of the pro-black feminist trap song "Formation" at Super Bowl 50. Throughout the West, blacks and their allies fight to make reality match their idea of freedom and equality. The West is still a frontier for most African Americans.[96]

Organization of the Book

Freedom's Racial Frontier is divided into five parts that explore community formation, multiculturalism, civil rights and black empowerment, artistic empowerment and identity, and U.S. West scholarship in a twenty-first century context. Part 1, "Place," examines community formation and cultural landscape formation in Houston, Las Vegas, the North San Francisco Bay Area, Seattle, and Denver-Aurora. Chapter 1, Bernadette Pruitt's "'Beautiful People': Community Formation in Houston, 1900–1941," examines black migration and settlement from Huntsville to Houston, Texas, with special consideration given to the importance of black institutions and Pruitt's concept of "the other Great Migration." In chapter 2, "The Las Vegas Press and the Westside: The Moulin Rouge Agreement," the Shared History Program at the University of Nevada, Reno, presents a 1987 interview with Lubertha Johnson on black life in West Las Vegas, the mainstream press on local race relations, and how African Americans desegregated the Las Vegas Strip. In chapter 3, "The More Things Change, the More They Stay the Same: Structural Racism and African American Community Formation in the North Bay Area," April Harris examines regional sustainability through the construction of the postwar ghetto in the North Bay Area's Marin City and Vallejo. The part concludes with two documents that detail the latest great African American migration. The first, "As Seattle Gets Richer, the City's Black Households Get Poorer," reminds us that although western cities such as Seattle have been booming since the 1970s, most blacks have been left behind in areas undergoing urban renewal and gentrification. The second, "Aurora's Growth Reflects That African-Americans Are Finding Base in Denver 'Burbs," reveals why black middle-class westerners have been leaving central districts for unprecedented access into postsuburban communities.

Part 2, "Racial Frontier," expands the discussion of African American West community formation to cover how these communities intermingled with other communities of color. In chapter 4, "'Turn Our Faces to the West': Refugees, Pioneers, and the Roots of 'All-Black' Oklahoma," Kendra T. Field examines African American and Native American relations after 1907 (Oklahoma statehood) and explores the complexity of African American migrants negotiating over land and space with Native Americans and white settlers and oil speculators. In Chapter 5, "'Poetic Justice': Bay Area Afro-Asian Women's Activism through Verse," Jeanelle Hope focuses on the agency of African American and Asian American women, many affiliated with the Black Panther Party and Asian

American Political Alliance, and argues for the use of poetry as an authentic source of knowledge. The discussion of what constitutes a legitimate source of knowledge continues with chapter 6, Julian Kunnie's "Apartheid in Arizona? HB 2281 and Arizona's Denial of Human Rights to Peoples of Color." In this essay the author connects the formation of black studies departments to Arizona's Mexican American–led ethnic studies movement and makes a strong case for why the Arizona law outlawing ethnic studies represents a human rights violation. The part ends with an excerpt on how the black population of Fargo-Moorhead (North Dakota and Minnesota) has grown greatly in recent years.

Part 3, "Political Expression," examines the black response to Jim Crow and de facto racial discrimination in the West. In Chapter 7, "Multiracial Garveyism in the Far West," Holly Roose draws out the complexity of the multicultural and multiracial Garvey movement on the West Coast in the 1920s. In chapter 8, "Brothers Taking Action: African American Soldier Activism at Fort Hood, Texas, 1948–1971," Herbert G. Ruffin II extends the chronology of African American military history from the Buffalo Soldiers on the early frontier to the Black Power era, through a close examination of the black GI movement in Vietnam War–era Texas. In chapter 9, "Black Women in Spokane: Emerging from the Shadows of Jim and Jane Crow," Dwayne A. Mack focuses on agency of African American women in the Inland Northwest's largest city and explores the intersections of racism and sexism there. The part concludes with "Albina Residents Picket the Portland Development Commission, 1973," which reveals intense grassroots black agency in 1970s Portland.

Part 4, "Entertainment and Representation," explores identity and hidden transcripts in the arts, entertainment, sports, and public history. In chapter 10, "The New Negro Frontier: Jean Toomer, Wallace Thurman, and African American Modernism in the West," Emily Lutenski examines New Negro Renaissance writers, editors, and provocateurs Toomer and Thurman in regard to their differing associations with New Mexico and Utah and excavates their western writings that reveal a view of race intersected with gender and sexuality, complicating the dominant critical narratives of these writers. In chapter 11, "Containing 'Perversion': African Americans and Same-Sex Desire in Cold War Los Angeles," Kevin Allen Leonard focuses on African American newspapers' negative coverage of homosexual relationships in Los Angeles and considers how middle-class black beliefs about morality and normality and class shaped the these views. Chapter 12, Gabriela Jiménez's "'Something 2 Dance 2': Electro-hop in 1980s Los Angeles and Its Afrofuturist Link," examines the formation of L.A. hip-hop, tracing it to the Watts uprising of 1965, and exposes the political underpinnings to break dancing and Afrofuturistic funk, disco, electro-hop among black and brown youth in South Central L.A. Part 4 concludes with a document on public memory and one on sports. The first, "Ku Klux Klan's 1925 Attack on Malcolm X's Family Home," looks at Malcolm X's legacy in his birthplace of Omaha, Nebraska, and considers how that legacy could help transform the community. "The Black 14: Race, Politics, Religion, and Wyoming Football" profiles black athletes sanctioned in 1969 for their protest of LDS policy barring black men from the priesthood.

Part 5, "Reconsiderations," focuses on African American westerners in understudied sites and uses transdisciplinary scholarship whose aim is to produce new sites of knowledge. Chapter 13, Randolph Stakeman's "African Americans in Albuquerque 1880–1930," uses quantitative and qualitative methods to examine African American community and shows how Albuquerque blacks avoided social isolation by creating their own institutions, laying the groundwork for civil rights activism in the city after the 1940s. In chapter 14, Tracey Patton's "Obscured Collaboration: African American Presence in the Myth of the White West" reconsiders the western frontier by addressing white supremacy in the popular media and the history of absence, invisibility, and erasure of the African American West. Chapter 15, "Kamaʻāinas and African Americans in Hawaiʻi: Making Sense of the Black Hawaiian Experience with Dr. Kathryn Waddell Takara," by Herbert G. Ruffin II and Kathryn Takara, is an oral history of a black Hawaiian scholar whose story arcs from Jim Crow Alabama to the Northeast and then to the Black Panther Party in Oakland before it moves to Hawaii. The part concludes with two documents on the black Alaska experience: a profile ("Blanche Louise Preston McSmith: An Alaska Civil Rights Icon") and a government proclamation ("African American History Month Enacted in Alaska, 2015").

The book closes with a bibliographic essay by Herbert G. Ruffin II that examines contemporary trends in African American West scholarship, most of which include interdisciplinary and transdisciplinary work on the black urban experience.

Notes

1. Quintard Taylor, "In Search of African American History in the West," in *A Quest for Freedom: The Black Experience in the American West* (Washington, D.C.: Smithsonian National Museum of American History, 2001), 6.

2. Ibid., 8. See also Lawrence B. de Graaf, "Negro Migration to Los Angeles, 1930–1950" (PhD diss., University of California at Los Angeles, 1962); Kevin Mulroy, *Freedom on the Border: The Seminole Maroons in Florida, the Indian Territory, Coahuila, and Texas*

(Lubbock: Texas Tech University Press, 1993); Kenneth Hamilton, *Black Towns and Profit* (Champaign: University of Illinois Press, 1991); Gretchen Lemke-Santangelo, *Abiding Courage: African American Migrant Women and the East Bay Community* (Chapel Hill: University of North Carolina Press, 1996); Shirley Ann Wilson Moore, *To Place Our Deeds: The African American Community in Richmond, California, 1910–1963* (Berkeley: University of California, 2000); Albert S. Broussard, *Black San Francisco: The Struggle for Racial Equality in the West, 1900–1954* (Lawrence: University Press of Kansas, 1993); Kenneth Mason, *Paternal Community: African Americans and Race Relations in San Antonio, Texas, 1867–1937* (Milton Park, UK: Taylor & Francis, 1998); Lonnie G. Bunch, *Black Angelenos: The Afro-American in Los Angeles, 1850–1950* (Los Angeles: California Afro-American Museum, 1988).

3. See Quintard Taylor, *In Search of the Racial Frontier: African Americans in the West, 1528–1990* (New York: W. W. Norton, 1998), 19, 21; Patricia Nelson Limerick, *The Legacy of Conquest: The Unbroken Past of the American West* (New York: W. W. Norton, 1987), 17–34, 322–50; Walter Prescott Webb, "The American West: Perpetual Mirage," *Harper's Magazine*, May 1957, 25–31.

4. Mark Baldassare, ed., *The Los Angeles Riots: Lessons for the Urban Future* (Boulder, Colo.: Westview Press, 1994), 1–18; Gerald Horne, "Black Fire: 'Riot' and "Revolt' in Los Angeles, 1965 and 1992," in *Seeking El Dorado: African Americans in California*, ed. Lawrence B. de Graaf, Kevin Mulroy, and Quintard Taylor (Seattle: University of Washington Press, 2001), 377–404; Taylor, *In Search of the Racial Frontier*, 17–26, 311–16.

5. Social Explorer Datasets (SE), Census 1890–2010, digitally transcribed by Interuniversity Consortium for Political and Social Research, edited, verified by Michael Haines, compiled, edited and verified by Social Explorer.

6. Alwyn Barr, *Black Texans: A History of Negroes in Texas, 1528–1971* (Norman: University of Oklahoma Press, 1973), 3–8; Randolph B. Campbell, *An Empire for Slavery: The Peculiar Institution in Texas, 1821–1865* (Baton Rouge: Louisiana State University Press, 1991); Paul D. Lack, *The Texas Revolutionary Experience: A Political and Social History, 1835–1836* (College Station: Texas A&M University Press, 1995), 238–52; Mulroy, *Freedom on the Border*, 35–60; Kevin Mulroy, *The Seminole Freedmen: A History* (Norman: University of Oklahoma Press, 2007), 22–83; Kenneth W. Porter, *The Black Seminoles: History of a Freedom-Seeking People* (Gainesville: University Press of Florida, 1996), 111–34; Richard B. Sheridan, "From Slavery in Missouri to Freedom in Kansas: The Influx of Black Fugitives and Contrabands into Kansas, 1854–1864," *Kansas History* 12, no. 1 (Spring 1989), 28–47; Richard B. Sheridan, *Freedom's Crucible: The Underground Railroad in Lawrence and Douglas County, Kansas, 1854–1865: A Reader* (Lawrence: University of Kansas, 2000); Harriet C. Frazier, *Runaway and Freed Missouri Slaves and Those Who Helped Them, 1763–1865* (Jefferson, N.C.: McFarland, 2010); James Patrick Morgans, *The Underground Railroad on the Western Frontier: Escapes from Missouri, Arkansas, Iowa and the Territories of Kansas, Nebraska and the Indian Nations, 1840–1865* (Jefferson, N.C.: McFarland, 2010).

7. For census data, see Social Explorer Datasets (SE), Census 1890–1940; Social Explorer Tables (SE), Census 1960 (US, County & State); Social Explorer Tables/Datasets

(SE), Census 1970–2010. Also see Shirley Boteler Mock, *Dreaming the Ancestors: Black Seminole Women in Texas and Mexico* (Norman: University of Oklahoma Press, 2010), 144–56; Bailey C. Hanes, *Bill Pickett: Bulldogger* (Norman: University of Oklahoma Press, 1989); Joe Holley, "Sgt. Mark Matthews Dies; at 111, Was Oldest Buffalo Soldier," *Washington Post*, September 13.

8. See Darlene Clarke Hine, "The Elusive Ballot: The Black Struggle against the Texas Democratic White Primary, 1932–1945," in *The African American Experience in Texas: An Anthology*, ed. Bruce A. Glasrud and James M. Smallwood (Lubbock: Texas Tech University Press, 2007), 280–82; Bernadette Pruitt, *The Other Great Migration: The Movement of Rural African Americans to Houston, 1900–1941* (College Station: Texas A&M University Press, 2013), 166–70; Charles L. Zelden, *The Battle for the Black Ballot: Smith v. Allwright and the Defeat of the Texas All-White Primary* (Lawrence: University Press of Kansas, 2004); Dwonna Goldstone, *Integrating the 40 Acres: The Fifty-Year Struggle for Racial Equality at the University of Texas* (Athens: University of Georgia Press, 2012), 14–30; Cheryl Brown Henderson, "Lucinda Todd and the Invisible Petitioners of *Brown v. Board of Education of Topeka, Kansas*," in *African American Women Confront the West, 1600–2000*, ed. Quintard Taylor and Shirley Ann Wilson Moore (Norman: University of Oklahoma Press, 2003), 312–27; Linda Williams Reese, "Clara Luper and the Civil Rights Movement in Oklahoma City, 1958–1964," in Taylor and Moore, *African American Women Confront the West*, 331–33; Cheryl Elizabeth Brown Wattley, *A Step toward* Brown v. Board of Education: *Ada Lois Sipuel Fisher and Her Fight to End Segregation* (Norman: Oklahoma University Press, 2014); Matthew C. Whitaker, *Race Work: The Rise of Civil Rights in the Urban West* (Lincoln: University of Nebraska Press, 2007), 133–72. Also see Brent M. S. Campney, "'Hold the Line': The Defense of Jim Crow in Lawrence, Kansas, 1945–1961," *Kansas History* 33 (Spring 2010), 22–41, http://www.kshs.org/publicat/history/2010spring_campney.pdf.

9. Quoted in Barr, *Black Texans*, 110. Also see ibid., 70–111; Glasrud and Smallwood, *African American Experience in Texas*, 173–79.

10. Glasrud and Smallwood, *African American Experience in Texas*, 153, 156.

11. See Herbert G. Ruffin, "I Try To Do the Best Job I Can: Herbert Ruffin I and Life in Central Texas and the San Francisco Bay Area, 1946–2002," *Lone Star Legacy: African American History in Texas* 2, no. 2 (Fall 2013), 7–34; Herbert G. Ruffin, "The Forging of an African American Community on the Outskirts of Alamo City: African American Suburbanization in San Antonio, 1980–2000," in *Lone Star Suburbs: The Suburban Process in a Super-State*, ed. M. Scott Sosebee and Paul Sandul (Norman: University of Oklahoma Press, forthcoming). Members of the Ball family interviewed by Ruffin at San Antonio and Seguin from July 2009 to November 2015 include A. J. Ball, Alfred Smith, Bernice Ball, Doris Ball, James Ball, Wade Leroy Ball, Renee Harris, Lilian Kyle, Earl Reddix, Wanda Louis Revels, Delores Ruffin, Honey Ruffin, Jozette Ruffin, and Ruby Ruffin.

12. Based on Ruffin interviews with Wade Leroy Ball, Honey Ruffin, and Wanda Louis Revels in San Antonio, Live Oak, and Seguin, Texas, November 2015. Joseph Ruffin was married to Robert Ball's eldest daughter, Alvernia.

13. Mulroy, *The Seminole Freedmen*, 8–9; Kathleen Deagan and Darcie MacMahon, *Fort Mose: Colonial America's Black Fortress of Freedom* (Gainesville: University Press of Florida, 1995); Jane Landers, *Black Society in Spanish Florida* (Champaign: University of Illinois Press, 1999), 29–106; Janet Sharp Herman, "Isaiah Montgomery's Balancing Act," in *Black Leaders of the Nineteenth Century*, ed. Leon Litwack and August Meier (Urbana: University of Illinois Press, 1991), 291–98.

14. See Hamilton, *Black Towns and Profit*, 5–42, 99–148; Delores Nason McBroome, "Harvests of Gold: African American Boosterism, Agriculture, and Investment in Allensworth and Little Liberia" in De Graaf, Mulroy, and Taylor, *Seeking El Dorado*, 149–80; Taylor, *In Search of the Racial Frontier*, 136–54; Trevor Hughes, "For a Time, All-Black Town Was Dear Field of Dreams," *USA Today*, February 25, 2015.

15. Rudolph M. Lapp, *Blacks in Gold Rush California* (New Haven: Yale University Press, 1977), 12–48, 94–117; Pruitt, *The Other Great Migration*, 1–15.

16. Pruitt, *The Other Great Migration*, 76

17. For early-twentieth race riots, see Taylor, *In Search of the Racial Frontier*, 17981; Barr, *Black Texans*, 115; Robert V. Haynes, *A Night of Violence: The Houston Riot of 1917* (Baton Rouge: Louisiana State University Press, 1976); Pruitt, *The Other Great Migration*, 141–47; Calvin C. Smith, "The Houston Riot of 1917, Revisited," *Houston Review: History and Culture of the Gulf Coast* 13 (Fall 1991): 85–102; Alonzo Smith, "The Omaha Courthouse Lynching of 1919," *Blackpast.org*, http://www.blackpast.org/aaw/omaha-courthouse-lynching-1919; Alfred L. Brophy, *Reconstructing the Dreamland: The Tulsa Riot of 1921* (New York: Oxford University Press, 2002); Scott Ellsworth, *Death in a Promised Land: The Tulsa Race Riot of 1921* (Baton Rouge: Louisiana State University Press, 1982); Hannibal B. Johnson, *Black Wall Street: From Riot to Renaissance in Tulsa's Historic Greenwood District* (Fort Worth, Tex.: Eakin Press, 1998); James S. Hirsch, *Riot and Remembrance: The Tulsa Race War and Its Legacy* (Boston: Houghton Mifflin, 2002); Tim Madigan, *The Burning: Massacre, Destruction, and the Tulsa Race Riot of 1921* (New York: Thomas Dunne Books / St. Martin's Press, 2001).

18. Hine, "The Elusive Ballot," 280–82; Pruitt, *The Other Great Migration*, 166–70; Charles L. Zelden, *The Battle for the Black Ballot*.

19. See Lonnie G. Bunch III, "'The Greatest State for the Negro': Jefferson L. Edmonds, Black Propagandist of the California Dream," in De Graaf, Mulroy, and Taylor, *Seeking El Dorado*, 129–48; Douglas Flamming, *Bound for Freedom: Black Los Angeles in Jim Crow America* (Berkeley: University of California Press, 2005), 92–125; Darnell Hunt and Ana-Christina Ramon, eds., *Black Los Angeles: American Dreams and Racial Realities* (New York: New York University Press, 2010), 34–38. In cities dominated by overt white supremacist activity, such as Portland, Oregon, black population growth stagnated until the 1940s. For more on this history and the general First Great Migration narrative, see Kimberley Mangun, *A Force for Change: Beatrice Morrow Cannady and the Struggle for Civil Rights in Oregon* (Corvallis: Oregon State University Press, 2010), 5–39, 76–93; Elizabeth McLagan, *A Peculiar Paradise: A History of Blacks in Oregon, 1788–1940* (Portland: Georgian Press, 1980), 108–46; Albert

S. Broussard, *Expectations of Equality: A History of Black Westerners* (Wheeling, Ill.: Harlan Davidson, 2012), 60–95; Taylor, *In Search of the Racial Frontier*, 222–50.

20. Charles P. Henry, *Long Overdue: The Politics of Racial Reparations* (New York: New York University Press, 2007), 1. Also see Mangun, *Force for Change*; Albert S. Broussard, *African-American Odyssey: The Stewarts, 1853–1963* (Lawrence: University of Kansas, 1998).

21. "Expectations of equality" borrowed from Broussard, *Expectations of Equality*, xi–xvi. For more on African American economic opportunities prior to the enactment of affirmative action and Title VII of the Civil Rights Act of 1964, see Broussard, *Expectations of Equality*, 62–72; Bruce Nelson, "The 'Lords of the Docks' Reconsidered: Race Relations among West Coast Longshoremen, 1933–61," in *Waterfront Workers: New Perspectives on Race and Class*, ed. Calvin Winslow (Chicago: University of Illinois, 1998), 155–92; Josh Sides, *L.A. City Limits: African American Los Angeles from the Great Depression to the Present* (Berkeley: University of California, 2006), 57–94; Terry H. Anderson, *The Pursuit of Fairness: A History of Affirmative Action* (New York: Oxford University Press, 2005); Title VII of the Civil Rights Act of 1964, U.S. Equal Employment Opportunity Commission, https://www.eeoc.gov/laws/statutes/titlevii.cfm; Shirley Ann Wilson Moore, "Your Life Is Really Not Just Your Own: African American Women in Twentieth-Century California," in De Graaf, Mulroy, and Taylor, *Seeking El Dorado*, 211–12.

22. Broussard, *Black San Francisco*, 77–81; Flamming, *Bound for Freedom*, 88–90, 146–47, 198, 200–201; Moore, "Your Life Is Really Not Just Your Own," 213, 217.

23. Mangun, *Force for Change*, 7.

24. Douglass Flamming, "Becoming Democrats: Liberal Politics and the African American Community in Los Angeles, 1930–1965," in De Graaf, Mulroy, and Taylor, *Seeking El Dorado*, 279, 281–86. The last black politician to be elected to office before 1918 was North Carolina Republican George Henry White (1901), which is covered in Benjamin R. Justesen, *George Henry White: An Even Chance in the Race of Life* (Baton Rouge: Louisiana State University Press, 2001), 276–311. Also see Michelle M. Mears, *And Grace Will Lead Me Home: African American Freedmen Communities of Austin, Texas, 1865 to 1928* (Lubbock: Texas Tech University Press, 2009), 25–56, 137–53.

25. Social Explorer Datasets (SE), Census 1940; Social Explorer Tables (SE), Census 1960 (US, County & State); Social Explorer Tables/Datasets (SE), Census 1970–2010.

26. For more on the Fair Employment Practices Commission and the Great Migration in the West, see Broussard, *Black San Francisco*, 145–46; Dwayne Mack, *Black Spokane: The Civil Rights Struggle in the Inland Northwest* (Norman: Oklahoma University Press, 2014), 19–31; Herbert G. Ruffin, *Uninvited Neighbors: African Americans in the Silicon Valley, 1769–1990* (Norman: Oklahoma University Press, 2014), 82–83; Sides, *L.A. City Limits*, 36–56; Quintard Taylor, "Urban Black Labor in the West, 1849–1949: Reconceptualizing the Image of a Region," in *The African American Urban Experience: Perspectives from the Colonial Period to the Present*, ed. Joe W. Trotter, Earl Lewis, and Tera W. Hunter (New York: Palgrave MacMillan, 2004), 107–114; Moore, *To Place Our Deeds*, 40–70.

27. Jessica B. Harris, *High on the Hog: A Culinary Journey from Africa to America* (New York: Bloomsbury, 2011), 139–66; "Hello and Welcome," CoraFaye's Cafe, http://cora-fayes.com/about-us; Peter Blecha, "Jones, Quincy (b. 1933)," HistoryLink.org/; Quincy Jones, Q: *The Autobiography of Quincy Jones* (New York: Three Rivers Press, 2002); "Howard Thurman," in *This Far By Faith*, PBS, http://www.pbs.org/thisfarbyfaith/ people/howard_thurman.html; "Guide My Feet," transcript, *This Far By Faith*, PBS, http://www-tc.pbs.org/thisfarbyfaith/transcript/episode_3.pdf; Johnetta Richards, "Thurman, Howard (1900–1981)," *Blackpast.org*, http://www.blackpast.org/aaw/ thurman-howard-1900-1981; Sudarshan Kapur, *Raising up a Prophet: The African American Encounter with Gandhi* (Boston: Beacon Press, 1992), 83–96.

28. James S. Olson, "Beaumont Riot of 1943," in *Handbook of Texas Online*, Texas State Historical Association, http://www.tshaonline.org/handbook/online/articles/jcb01; Robert Robertson, "Beaumont Race Riots of 1943," C-Span, http://www.c-span.org/ video/?304139-1/beaumont-race-riots-1943.

29. See James Loewen, *Sundown Towns: A Hidden Dimension of American Racism* (New York: Touchstone, 2006).

30. See "Killeen Pioneer Interviews," Spring 1977, Killeen City Library Archives ("Win-ifred Bell," 17–18; "Ted Connell," 4; "John Cough," 14; "Marion Denton," 6; "Levy," 4; "Hellen Little," 9); Gra'Delle Duncan, *Killeen: Tale of Two Cities, 1882–1982* (Killeen, Tex: G. Duncan, 1984), 17–32; "History of the Great Place," Fort Hood, http://www. hood.army.mil/history.aspx; John R. M. Wilson, *Jackie Robinson and the American Dilemma* (Upper Saddle River, N.J.: Pearson, 2009), 25–39; Beth Bailey and David Farber, *The First Strange Place: Race and Sex in World War II Hawaii* (Baltimore: Johns Hopkins University Press, 1992), 133–66; Carol Lynn McKibben, *Racial Beachhead: Diversity and Democracy in a Military Town* (Stanford: Stanford University Press, 2012), 1–14; Mack, *Black Spokane*, 19–31, 32–148.

31. Taylor, *In Search of a Racial Frontier*, 251; *Historical Census Browser: County-Level Results for 1850–1960*, https://mapserver.lib.virginia.edu.

32. Demographic data can be found at "City of Richmond, 1940–1970," Bay Area Census, http://www.bayareacensus.ca.gov/cities/Richmond.htm; Campbell Gibson and Kay Jung, "Historical Census Statistics on Population Totals by Race, 1790 to 1990, and by Hispanic Origin, 1970 to 1990, for Large Cities and Other Urban Places in the United States: California—Race and Hispanic Origin for Selected Cities and Other Places: Earliest Census to 1990," U.S. Census Bureau, Population Bureau, Working Paper 76, February 2005, Table 5, https://www.census.gov/population/www/documentation/ twps0076/CAtab.pdf.

33. Darrell Millner, "Blacks in Oregon" in *The Oregon Encyclopedia*, http://www.orego-nencyclopedia.org/articles/blacks_in_oregon/#.V1NmYof2ajs; Lawrence De Graaf, "African American Suburbanization in California, 1960 through 1990," in De Graaf, Mulroy, and Taylor, 405–49; Emory J. Tolbert and Lawrence B. de Graaf, "'The Unseen Minority': Blacks in Orange County," *Journal of Orange County Studies* (Fall 1989/ Spring 1990): 54–61; Jamie Coughty and R. T. King, eds., *Lubertha Johnson: Civil*

Rights Efforts in Las Vegas, 1940s–1960s (Reno: Oral History Program, University of Nevada–Reno, 1988), 31–44, 47–54, 59–66.

34. *Shelley v Kraemer,* 334 U.S. 1 (1948).

35. Ruffin, *Uninvited Neighbors,* 160–68; David M. P. Freund, *Colored Property: State Policy and White Racial Politics in Suburban America* (Chicago: University of Chicago Press, 2007), 99–139; Kenneth T. Jackson, *Crabgrass Frontier: The Suburbanization of the United States* (New York: Oxford University Press, 1985), 195–230; George Lipsitz, *The Possessive Investment in Whiteness: How White People Profit from Identity Politics* (Philadelphia: Temple University Press, 2006), 1–23; Robert A. Beauregard, *When America Became Suburban* (Minneapolis: University of Minnesota Press, 2006), 83.

36. Carl Abbott, *The New Urban America: Growth and Politics in Sunbelt Cities* (Chapel Hill: University of North Carolina Press, 1987), 83, 88, 91, 155–56, 232–41, 250; De Graaf, "African American Suburbanization in California," 3–20, 262–74; Tolbert and de Graaf, "The Unseen Minority," 54–61; Rodolfo Rosales, *The Illusion of Inclusion: The Political Story of San Antonio, Texas* (Austin: University of Texas Press, 2000), 14, 92–95, 100.

37. Bureau of Labor Statistics, U.S. Department of Labor, "Provisions of the Housing Act of 1949," *Monthly Labor Review* 69, no. 2 (August 1949), 155–59; De Graaf, "African American Suburbanization in California," 415; Henderson, "Lucinda Todd and the Invisible Petitioners," 312–27; Whitaker, *Race Work,* 1–21.

38. Ruffin, *Uninvited Neighbors,* 107–15; Martin Schiesl, ed., *Responsible Liberalism: Edmond G. "Pat" Brown and Reform Government in California, 1958–1967* (Los Angeles: Edmond G. "Pat" Brown Institute of Public Affairs, 2003), 101–24.

39. Gretchen Lemke-Santangelo, "Deindustrialization, Urban Poverty, and African American Community Mobilization in Oakland, 1945 through the 1990s," in De Graaf, Mulroy, and Taylor, *Seeking El Dorado,* 347. Also see Moore, *To Place Our Deeds,* 47.

40. See Broussard, *Black San Francisco,* 158–65; Delores Nason McBroome, *Parallel Communities: African Americans in California's East Bay 1850–1963* (New York: Garland, 1993), 106–12; Sides, *L.A. City Limits,* 66–69.

41. Kevin Boyle, *The UAW and the Heyday of American Liberalism, 1945–1968* (Ithaca: Cornell University Press, 1995), 61–131; Lemke-Santangelo, "Deindustrialization, Urban Poverty, and African American Community Mobilization"; Quintard Taylor, *The Forging of a Black Community: Seattle's Central District from 1870 through the Civil Rights Era* (Seattle: University of Washington Press, 1994), 159–84, 192–93. Before the 1960s, the small percentage of black westerners who were members of itrade unions either were members of all-black unions like the Brotherhood of Sleeping Car Porters or racially egalitarian unions like the International Longshoremen's and Warehousemen's Union and Congress of Industrial Organizations affiliated unions like the United Rubber Workers and United Auto Workers. This is further discussed in Broussard, *Expectations of Equality,* 141–47; Nelson, "'Lords of the Docks' Reconsidered," 173–92; Ruffin, *Uninvited Neighbors,* 119–120, 215; Taylor, *In Search of the Racial Frontier,* 289–91; Whitaker, *Race Work,* 146–47.

42. Horne, "Black Fire," 377, 381, 385–87, 393; Robin D. G. Kelley, *Race Rebels: Culture, Politics, and the Black Working Class* (New York: Free Press, 1996), 7–9; Donna Jean Murch, *Living for the City: Migration, Education, and the Rise of the Black Panther Party in Oakland, California* (Berkeley: University of California Press, 2010), 45–49; Sides, *L.A. City Limits*, 169–98; Taylor, *Forging of a Black Community*, 233.

43. Whitaker, *Race Work*, 1–21.

44. Hine, "The Elusive Ballot," 279–301; Sanford N. Greenberg, "White Primary," in *Handbook of Texas Online*, Texas State Historical Association, https://tshaonline.org/handbook/online/articles/wdw01.

45. Barr, *Black Texans*, 179, 231; Lawrence P. Crouchett, *William Byron Rumford, the Life and Public Services of a California Legislator: A Biography* (El Cerrito, Calif.: Downey Place Publishing House, 1984). For demography, see Taylor, *In Search of the Racial Frontier*, 286–87.

46. "U.S. Congresswoman Maxine Waters," http://waters.house.gov/; Stephanie Mencimer, "Mia Love: Representative from Nowhere: Utah's New Congresswoman Is a Symptom of What Happens When Local Elections Are Nationalized," *Mother Jones*, http://www.motherjones.com/politics/2014/11/mia-love-congress-utah-representative-nowhere; Darron T. Smith, "She Looks Black, but Her Politics Are Red: What Mia Love's Victory Means for the Face of the GOP," *Huffington Post*, http://www.huffingtonpost.com/darron-t-smith-phd/mia-love_b_6116466.html; Raphael J. Sonenshein, "Coalition Building in Los Angeles: The Bradley Years and Beyond," in De Graaf, Mulroy, and Taylor, *Seeking El Dorado*, 450–44; Mack, *Black Spokane*, 124–48; James Richardson, *Willie Brown: A Biography* (Berkeley: University of California Press, 1997); Taylor, *Forging of a Black Community*, 3; Josh Baugh, "The Evolving Mayor Taylor," *San Antonio Express-News*, March 26, 2016.

47. "The Civil Rights Era in Albuquerque," City of Albuquerque, https://www.cabq.gov/humanrights/public-information-and-education/diversity-booklets/black-heritage-in-new-mexico/the-civil-rights-era-in-albuquerque.

48. See Goldstone, *Integrating the 40 Acres*, 14–30; Henderson, "Lucinda Todd and the Invisible Petitioners"; Reese, "Clara Luper and the Civil Rights Movement in Oklahoma City," 331–33; Brown Wattley, *A Step toward Brown v. Board of Education*; Whitaker, *Race Work*, 133–72. Also see Campney, "Hold the Line."

49. "Bridging Three Centuries: 'One of the Most Progressive and Advanced Systems in the United States,' 1940–1959," in *District History*, Tucson Unified School District, http://www.tusd.k12.az.us/contents/distinfo/history/history9305.asp; Whitaker, *Race Work*, 113–24.

50. "Background–Mendez v. Westminster Re-enactment," United States Courts, http://www.uscourts.gov/educational-resources/get-involved/federal-court-activities/mendez-westminster-re-enactment/mendez-westminster-background.aspx. Also see Henderson, "Lucinda Todd and the Invisible Petitioners," 312–27.

51. Nikole Hannah-Jones, "Segregation Now: Investigating America's Racial Divide," April 16, 2014, *ProPublica*, https://www.propublica.org/article/segregation-now-full-text; Jonathan Kozol, *The Shame of the Nation: The Restoration of Apartheid*

Schooling in America (New York: Broadway, 2006); W .J. Rorabaugh, *Berkeley at War: The 1960s* (New York: Oxford University Press, 1990); *San Jose Mercury News,* "Why Court Ruled against San Jose," May 18, 1984; "Jackson v. Pasadena City School Dist.," Supreme Court of California Resources, Stanford Law School, Robert Crown Law Library, http://scocal.stanford.edu/opinion/jackson-v-pasadena-city-school-dist-27149.

52. Natalie Munio, "Morris Cole, Ground-Breaking Denver Judge, Dies at 83," *Denver Post,* May 21, 2016); "Keyes v. School District No. 1, Denver, Colorado," Legal Information Institute, Cornell University Law School, https://www.law.cornell.edu/supremecourt/text/413/189); Ruffin, *Uninvited Neighbors,* 82–83.

53. Leslie G. Kelen and Eileen Hallett Stone, *Missing Stories: An Oral History of Ethnic and Minority Groups in Utah* (Logan: Utah State University Press, 1996), 101–6.

54. Ronald G. Coleman, "Blacks in Utah History: An Unknown Legacy," in *Utah History to Go* http://historytogo.utah.gov/people/ethnic_cultures/the_peoples_of_utah/blacksinutahhistory.html; preface to "African-American Community Oral History Section," in Kelen and Stone, *Missing Stories,* 66–69; Kim Ibach, and William Howard Moore, "The Emerging Civil Rights Movement: The 1957 Wyoming Public Accommodations Statute as a Case Study," *Annals of Wyoming* 73 (Winter 2001): 2–13, http://www.uwyo.edu/robertshistory/civil_rights_movement.htm.

55. Quoted in Kelen and Stone, *Missing Stories,* 115.

56. Thomas G. Alexander, "The Civil Rights Movement in Utah" in *Utah History to Go,* http://historytogo.utah.gov/utah_chapters/utah_today/thecivilrightsmovementinutah.html; Newell Bringhurst, *Saints, Slaves, and Blacks: The Changing Place of Black People within Mormonism* (Westport, Conn.: Greenwood, 1981), 166–74, 178, 180–96; Newell G. Bringhurst, and Darron T. Smith, eds., *Black and Mormon* (Champaign: University of Illinois Press, 2006), 1–12, 82–115, 148–66; Kelen and Stone, *Missing Stories,* 72, 77–78, 114–15; "Title II of the Civil Rights Act (Public Accommodations)," United States Department of Justice, https://www.justice.gov/crt/title-ii-civil-rights-act-public-accommodations; Tad Walch, "Elder Christofferson Explains Updated LDS Church Policies on Same-Sex Marriage and Children," *Deseret News.*

57. Carla Eckels, "Kansas Sit-In Gets Its Due at Last," *NPR,* October 21, 2006, http://www.npr.org/). For more on this subject, see Gretchen Cassel Eick, *Dissent in Wichita: The Civil Rights Movement in the Midwest, 1954–72* (Champaign: University of Illinois Press, 2001), 1–11.

58. Reese, "Clara Luper and the Civil Rights Movement in Oklahoma City," 328.

59. Ibid., 331–33; Wattley, *A Step toward Brown v. Board of Education.*

60. Broussard, *Expectations of Equality,* 141–47; Coughty and King, "Lubertha Johnson," 47–54, 59–66; Eick, *Dissent in Wichita,* 45–52; Mack, *Black Spokane,* 100–120; Robert A. Goldberg, "Racial Change on the Southern Periphery: The Case of San Antonio, Texas, 1960–1965," in *African Americans in South Texas History,* ed. Bruce A. Glasrud (College Station: Texas A&M University Press, 2011), 280–312; Ruffin, *Uninvited Neighbors,* 119–120, 215; Taylor, *In Search of the Racial Frontier,* 289–91; Whitaker, *Race Work,* 46–147; Moore, "Your Life Is Really Not Just Your Own," 218–223.

61. Mark Brilliant, *The Color of America Has Changed: How Racial Diversity Shaped Civil Rights Reform in California, 1941–1978* (New York: Oxford University Press, 2010), 190–227; De Graaf, "African American Suburbanization in California," 415; National Advisory *Commission* on *Civil Disorders, The Kerner Report* (Princeton: Princeton University Press, 2016), xiii–xxxvi; Ruffin, *Uninvited Neighbors*, 93; Taylor, *Forging of a Black Community*, 201–9.

62. Robert Bauman, *Race and the War on Poverty: From Watts to East L.A.* (Norman: University of Oklahoma Press, 2008), 31–52; Horne, "Black Fire," 377–81; Gerald Horne, *The Fire This Time: The Watts Uprising and the 1960s* (Charlottesville: University of Virginia Press, 1995), 69–73; Hunt and Ramon, *Black Los Angeles*, 243–65; Laura Pulido, *Black, Brown, Yellow, and Left: Radical Activism in Los Angeles* (Berkeley: University of California Press, 2006); Sides, *L.A. City Limits*, 169–93; Errol Wayne Stevens, *Radical L.A.: From Coxey's Army to the Watts Riots, 1894–1965* (Norman: University of Oklahoma Press, 2014), 306–17. Also see Baldassare, *Los Angeles Riots*, 1–18.

63. Taylor, *Forging of a Black Community*, 217. Also see Scot Brown, *Fighting for US: Maulana Karenga, the US Organization and Black Cultural Nationalism* (New York: New York University Press, 2003); Hasan Kwame Jeffries, *Bloody Lowndes: Civil Rights and Black Power in Alabama's Black Belt* (New York: New York University Press, 2009), 1–5, 117–207; Peniel Joseph, ed., *The Black Power Movement: Rethinking the Civil Rights-Black Power Era* (New York: Routledge, 2006); Peniel Joseph, *Waiting 'Til the Midnight Hour: A Narrative History of Black Power in America* (New York: Henry Holt, 2007); Murch, *Living for the City*, 3–14; Jeffrey O. G. Ogbar, *Black Power: Radical Politics and African American Identity* (Baltimore: Johns Hopkins University Press, 2005), 1–10; Robert O. Self, *America Babylon: Race and the Struggle for Postwar Oakland* (Princeton: Princeton University Press, 2003), 217–55.

64. Murch, *Living for the City*, 71. Rich discussions on the black student movement also include David Hilliard, ed., *The Huey P. Newton Reader* (New York: Seven Stories Press, 2002), 45–46; Peniel E. Joseph, "Black Studies, Black Student Activism, and the Black Power Movement" in *Black Power Movement*, 259–62; Bobby Seale, *Seize the Time: The Story of the Black Panther Party and Huey P. Newton* (New York, Random House, 1970), 12–25, 30, 46.

65. Molefi Kete Asante, *Maulana Karenga: An Intellectual Portrait* (Malden, Mass.: Polity Press, 2009), 107–13, 119–24; Brown, *Fighting for US*, 33–36, 74–106, 159–62; Maulana Karenga, *Kawaida and Questions of Life and Struggle* (Los Angeles: University of Sankore Press, 2008); Keith A. Mayes, *Kwanzaa: Black Power and The Making of the African-American Holiday Tradition* (New York: Routledge, 2009), 47–134.

66. Joshua Bloom and Waldo E. Martin, Jr., *Black against Empire: The History and Politics of the Black Panther Party* (Berkeley: University of California Press, 2013) 1–16; Seale, *Seize the Time*, 35–73, 113–25; Hilliard, *Huey P. Newton Reader*, 9–19.

67. Quote is from Daniel Widener, *Black Arts West: Culture and Struggle in Postwar Los Angeles* (Durham, N.C.: Duke University Press, 2010), back cover, 1–15, 52–89. Other sources include Brian D. Behnken, ed., *The Struggle in Black and Brown: African*

American and Mexican American Relations during the Civil Rights Era (Lincoln: University of Nebraska, 2011); Martha Biondi, *The Black Revolution on Campus* (Berkeley: University of California Press), 43–78; Douglas Hartmann, *Race, Culture, and the Revolt of the Black Athlete: The 1968 Olympic Protests and Their Aftermath* (Chicago: University Of Chicago Press, 2004); Jeanelle Hope, "Black, Yellow, and Shades of Purple: Radical Afro-Asian Collective Activism in the San Francisco Bay Area from the Perspectives of Women in the Struggle, 1966–1972" (master's thesis, Syracuse University, 2014); Joseph, "Black Studies, Black Student Activism, and the Black Power Movement," 264–77; Jeffrey O. G. Ogbar, "Rainbow Radicalism: The Rise of the Radical Ethnic Nationalism," in Joseph, *Black Power Movement*, 193–228; Pulido, *Black, Brown, Yellow, and Left*, 1–8, 89–122, 153–79; Ibram H. Rogers, *The Black Campus Movement: Black Students and the Racial Reconstitution of Higher Education, 1965–1972* (New York: Palgrave Macmillan, 2012), 89–126; Fabio Rojas, *From Black Power to Black Studies: How a Radical Social Movement Became an Academic Discipline* (Baltimore: Johns Hopkins University Press, 2010), 45–92; Ruffin, *Uninvited Neighbors*, 163–200; Herbert G. Ruffin II, "'Doing the Right Thing for the Sake of Doing the Right Thing': The Revolt of the Black Athlete and the Modern Student-Athletic Movement, 1956–2014," *Western Journal of Black Studies* 30, no. 4 (2014): 260–78.

68. See Kevin Leonard, *The Battle for Los Angeles: Racial Ideology and World War II* (Albuquerque: University of New Mexico Press, 2006), 147–98; Lisa Y. Ramos, "Not Similar Enough: Mexican American and African American Civil Rights and the Causes of Black-Brown Disunity," in Behnken, *Struggle in Black and Brown*, 19–48.

69. Taylor, *Forging of a Black Community*, 223–33; David Mura, *Turning Japanese: Memoir of a Sansei* (New York: Grove Press, 2007); Ronald Takaki, *Strangers from a Different Shore: A History of Asian Americans* (Little, Brown, 1989), 212–29"; and Nicole Grant, "White Supremacy and the Alien Land Laws of Washington State," in Seattle Civil Rights & Labor History Project, University of Washington, http://depts.washington. edu/civilr/alien_land_laws.htm. Washington State's Alien Land Law was an act of government-sponsored white supremacy passed in 1921. It was the first such act passed in Washington since 1864, when it was a territory. The 1864 act led to white settlers conquering indigenous Americans through the dispossession of their land and denial of citizenship. This was followed by the systematic exclusion of Chinese immigrants from the state and on the West Coast from 1875 to 1943. White nativism and intense racism reemerged in Washington during World War I and lasted until the Great Depression (1915–ca. 1930s). The 1921 law displaced most Japanese Americans from their land—mostly agricultural—and relegated the Issei (first-generation Japanese Americans) to alien status. Many Issei countered by purchasing leased land in the names of the their second-generation (Nisei) children's. In 1923, lawmakers closed this loophole, forcing Japanese Americans who wanted to keep their land to place their trusts in the possession of white lawyers.

70. For more on the "kitchen table activists" concept, see Lisa McGirr, *Suburban Warriors: The Origins of the New American Right* (Princeton: Princeton University Press, 2001), 3–19, 111–46. Also see Murch, *Living for the City*, 168–70.

71. Michelle Alexander, *The New Jim Crow* (New York: New Press, 2012), 1–19, 59–96; "University of California Regents v. Bakke, 1978," Blackpast.org, http://www.blackpast. org/primarywest/university-california-regents-v-bakke-1978; Broussard, *Expectations of Equality*, 167–94; Douglas Flamming, *African Americans in the West* (Santa Barbara: ABC-CLIO, 2009), 273–83; Chrystia Freeland, *Plutocrats: The Rise of the New Global Super-Rich and the Fall of Everyone Else* (New York: Penguin Press, 2012), 38–87; Darlene Clark Hine, William C. Hine, and Stanley Harrold, *African Americans: A Concise History*, vol. 2 (New York: Pearson, 2014), 537–46, 571–86; Ray Kiely, *Empire in the Age of Globalisation: US Hegemony and Neo-Liberal Disorder* (London: Pluto Press), 88–119; Mack, *Black Spokane*, 141; Carl Husemoller Nightingale, "The Global Inner City," in Michael B. Katz and Thomas J. Sugrue, eds., *W. E. B. DuBois, Race, and the City: "The Philadelphia Negro" and Its Legacy* (Philadelphia: University of Pennsylvania Press), 217–58; Ruffin, *Uninvited Neighbors*, 201–28; Robert O. Self, *All in the Family: The Realignment of American Democracy since the 1960s* (New York: Hill and Wang, 2012), 3–16; Whitaker, *Race Work*, 225–62.

72. Andrew Weise, *Places of Their Own: African American Suburbanization in the Twentieth Century* (Chicago: University of Chicago Press, 2004), 255.

73. Robert E. Lang and Patrick A. Simmons, "'Boomburbs': The Emergence of Large, Fast-Growing Suburban Cities in the United States," *Fannie Mae Foundation Census Notes*, no. 6 (June 2001); 1; Robert E. Lang and Patrick A. Simmons, "'Boomburbs': Fast-Growing Suburban Cities," in Bruce Katz and Robert E. Lang, eds., *Redefining Urban and Suburban America: Evidence from Census 2000* (Washington D.C.: Brookings Institution Press, 2003), 106; Social Explorer, *Census Tracts, 1970–2010*; Lawrence B. De Graaf, "African American Suburbanization in California," 405–49; Ruffin, *Uninvited Neighbors*, 201–28.

74. Rae Lowry interviewed by Herbert G. Ruffin II, July 2012, San Antonio.

75. See Ruffin, "Forging of an African American Community."

76. Doreen Carvajal, "Bittersweet Nostalgia: Housing Gains Disbanded Much of Santa Ana's Black Community," *Los Angeles Times*, January 30, 1994; Selwyn Crawford and Michael E. Young, "Census Shows Black Population Expanding in Dallas-Fort Worth Suburbs," *Dallas Morning News*, February 27, 2011.

77. Carvajal, "Bittersweet Nostalgia"; Robert Johnson and Charlene Riggins, "Introduction—Black Orange County, 1930–1980," in *Santa Ana History*, Santa Ana Preservation Society, http://www.santaanahistory.com/articles/Intro-BlackOrangeCounty.html); Flamming, *African Americans in the West*, 299–301.

78. Ruffin, *Uninvited Neighbors*, 207–8, 222–23.

79. In 2000, Forty-six of the fifty quickest growing postsuburban cities were in the U.S. West (see Table I.3). Excluded from this chart are Coral Springs, Hialeah, and Pembroke Pines, Florida, and Naperville, Illinois. Lang and Simmons, "Boomburbs" (2003), 106; U.S. Census, 1950–80, http://www.census.gov/prod/www/decennial.html; Social Explorer.

80. Robert D. Bullard, *Invisible Houston: The Black Experience in Boom and Bust* (College Station: Texas A&M University Press, 1987), 3–14; Sig Christenson, "S.A., Texas

Could Gain in Wake of Troop Cuts, BRAC," *San Antonio Express News*, March 3, 2014; John M. Findlay, *Magic Lands: Western Cityscapes and American Culture after 1940* (Berkeley: University of California Press, 1992), 1–13; Mike Gallagher, "S.A. Must Preserve 'Military City, USA,'" *My San Antonio*, July 9, 2015, http://www.mysanantonio.com/; Katz and Lang, *Redefining Urban and Suburban America*, 106; Ruffin, *Uninvited Neighbors*, 141–99, 202–5, 212–26; John Virtue, *The Black Soldiers Who Built the Alaska Highway: A History of Four U.S. Army Regiments in the North, 1942–1943* (Jefferson, N.C.: McFarland, 2012), 6–17, 185–94.

81. Rings suburbs are discussed in De Graaf, "African American Suburbanization in California," 407; Bruce D. Haynes, *Red Lines, Black Spaces: The Politics of Race and Space in a Black Middle-Class Suburb* (New Haven: Yale University Press, 2001), 60; Mark Gottdiener and Ray Hutchison, *The New Urban Sociology* (New York: Westview Press, 2006), 205; Sheryll Cashin, *The Failures of Integration: How Race and Class Are Undermining the American Dream* (New York: PublicAffairs, 2005), 43. Harold P. Moret is mentioned in "Inglewood, CA," World Library, http://www.worldlibrary.org/articles/inglewood,_ca.

82. Tyrone Beason, "Seattle's Vanishing Black Community," *Seattle Times*, May 28, 2016; "Quickfacts: Federal Way City, Washington," U.S. Census Bureau, http://www.census.gov/quickfacts/table/RHI125215/5323515; "Federal Way, Washington Population: Census 2010 and 2000 Interactive Map, Demographics, Statistics, Quick Facts," Census Viewer, http://censusviewer.com/city/WA/Federal%20Way; Taylor, *Forging of a Black Community*, 208–9.

83. For more information on bifurcation of the Black community, see Karyn R. Lacy, *Blue-Chip Black: Race, Class, and Status in the New Black Middle Class* (Berkeley: University of California Press, 2007), 43–71; *San Francisco Chronicle*, "Prosperity Still Out of Reach for Many Blacks," March 28, 1998; *San Jose Mercury News*, "Urban Racial Isolation Persists," April 9, 1991; William Julius Wilson, *The Ghetto Underclass: Social Science Perspectives* (London: Sage Publications, 1993); Nightingale, "The Global Inner City," 217–58; "Economic and Social Statistics on Black America," *Frontline*, PBS, http://www.pbs.org/wgbh/pages/frontline/shows/race/economics; "Interview: William Julius Wilson," *Frontline*, PBS, http://www.pbs.org/wgbh/pages/frontline/shows/race/interviews/wilson.html.

84. Ruffin, *Uninvited Neighbors*, 107, 194; Whitaker, *Race Work*, 267–83.

85. Baldassare, *Los Angeles Riots*, 1–13; Lawrence Bobo, Melvin L. Oliver, James H. Johnson Jr., and Abel Valenzuela Jr., eds., *Prismatic Metropolis: Inequality in Los Angeles* (New York: Russell Sage Foundation, 2000); Broussard, *Expectations of Equality*, 185–94; Bullard, *Invisible Houston*, 3–14; Carvajal, "Bittersweet Nostalgia"; Maco L. Faniel, *Hip Hop in Houston: Origin and Legacy* (Charleston, S.C.: History Press, 2013), 97–130; Hunt and Ramon, *Black Los Angeles*; Geto Boys, "City under Siege," in *The Geto Boys* (Def American/Warner Bros., 1990); Robin D. G. Kelly, *Race Rebels: Culture, Politics, and the Black Working Class* (New York: Simon and Schuster, 1996), 183–228; Brad "Scarface" Jordan and Benjamin Meadows Ingram, *Diary of a Madman: The Geto Boys, Life, Death, and the Roots of Southern Rap* (New York: Dey Street Books,

2015); Nightingale, "The Global Inner City," 217–58; Jeffrey O. G. Ogbar, *Hip-Hop Revolution: The Culture and Politics of Rap* (Lawrence: University Press of Kansas, 2007), 1–8, 105–38; Sides, *L.A. City Limits*, 199–205.

86. See Broussard, *Expectations of Equality*, xi–xvi.

87. Annelise Orleck, *Storming Caesars Palace: How Black Mothers Fought Their Own War on Poverty* (Boston: Beacon, 2005), 1–6, 208–44.

88. France Davis, *Light in the Midst of Zion: A History of Black Baptists in Utah, 1892–1996* (Las Vegas, Nev: Empire Publishing, 1997); Jasmine Johnson and Shaun Ossei-Owusu, "'From Fillmore to No More': Black-Owned Business in a Transforming San Francisco," in Ingrid Banks, Gaye Johnson, George Lipsitz, Ula Taylor, Daniel Widener, and Clyde Woods, eds., *Black California Dreamin': The Crises of California's African-American Communities* (Santa Barbara: UC Santa Barbara Center for Black Studies Research, 2012), 75–92; Rojas, *From Black Power to Black Studies*; Ruffin, *Uninvited Neighbors*, 1–3, 201–28; Ruffin, "Forging of an African American"; Whittaker, *Race Work*, 256–60, 278, 282.

89. Raphael J. Sonenshein, "Coalition Building in Los Angeles: The Bradley Years and Beyond," in De Graaf, Mulroy, and Taylor, *Seeking El Dorado*, 450–74; Baldassare, *Los Angeles Riots*, 1–13; Bobo, Oliver, Johnson, and Valenzuela, *Prismatic Metropolis*, 3–50. Also see Dennis Branch, "The Lack of Economic Development on the Eastside of San Antonio" (master's thesis, Trinity University, 1983); Tommy Calvert Jr., "Look to the Eastside for San Antonio's Revitalization," *Rivard Report*, August 23rd, 2012, http://therivardreport.com/look-to-the-eastside-for-san-antonios-revitalization; Beverly Creamer, "Kakaako's Building Boom," *Hawaii Business Magazine*, September 2012, http://www.hawaiibusiness.com/kakaakos-building-boom; Bob Wise, "Building San Antonio; It Takes a Village to Revitalize a Community," *San Antonio Express-News*, November 28, 2010.

90. Sonenshein, "Coalition Building in Los Angeles," 456.

91. Bobo, Oliver, Johnson, and Valenzuela, *Prismatic Metropolis*, 3, 3–50; Sonenshein, "Coalition Building in Los Angeles," 450–74; Baldassare, *Los Angeles Riots*, 1–13.

92. Alexander, *New Jim Crow*, 53–139; Baldassare, *Los Angeles Riots*, 1–13; Herbert G. Ruffin II, "Black Lives Matter: The Growth of a New Social Justice Movement," *Blackpast.org*, http://www.blackpast.org/perspectives/black-lives-matter-growth-new-social-justice-movement; Herbert G. Ruffin II, "Welcome Back to Claremont: The Professor Who Was Almost Another Dead Black Person Because He 'Fit the Profile,'" *Conscious*, March 5, 2016, http://theclaremontconscious.altervista.org/; Jon Swaine, Oliver Laughland, Jamiles Lartey, and Ciara McCarthy, "Young Black Men Killed by US Police at Highest Rate in Year of 1,134 Deaths," *Guardian*, December 31, 2015; Sonenshein, "Coalition Building in Los Angeles," 450–74.

93. Faniel, *Hip Hop in Houston*, 20–26, 97–98, 115, 137–39; Nelson George, *Hip Hop America* (New York: Penguin), 129–41; Ice-T, *Rhyme Pays* (Hollywood, Calif.: Sire/Warner Bros., 1987); Ice-T and Douglas Century, *Ice: A Memoir of Gangster Life and Redemption-from South Central to Hollywood* (New York: One World/Ballantine, 2012); NWA, *Straight Outta Compton* (Los Angeles: Ruthless Records/Priority

Records, 1988); Ogbar, *Hip-Hop Revolution*; Tricia Rose, *The Hip Hop Wars* (New York: Basic Books, 2008); Too Short, *Born to Mack* (New York: Jive/RCA Records, 1987); Digital Underground, *Sex Packets* (New York: Tommy Boy/Eurobond Records, 1990); UGK, *Too Hard to Swallow* (New York: Jive Records, 1992); Sir Mix-a-Lot, *Swass* (Los Angeles: Def American Recordings, 1988); Harris Rosen, *N.W.A—The Aftermath: Exclusive Interviews with Dr. Dre, Ice Cube, Jerry Heller, Yella and Westside Connection* (Toronto: Peace! Carving, 2015).

94. Ice Cube, *Death Certificate* (Los Angeles: Priority/EMI Records, 1991).

95. Horne, "Black Fire," 380–81.

96. Ruffin, "Black Lives Matter"; Katie Rogers, "#LaughingWhileBlack Wine Train Lawsuit Is Settled," *New York Times*, April 20, 2016; "About Silicon Valley De-Bug," Silicon Valley De-Bug, http://www.siliconvalleydebug.org/about; "Respect to Colin Kaepernick for Investing His Time, Resources, and Spirit to Communities Fighting for Justice," Silicon Valley De-Bug, November 22, 2016, http://www.siliconvalleydebug.org/; Alicia Garza, "Black Lives Matter Co-Founder to Beyonce: 'Welcome to the Movement,'" *Rolling Stone*, February 11, 2016, http://www.rollingstone.com/; Steve Wyche, "Colin Kaepernick Explains Why He Sat During National Anthem," NFL.com, August 27, 2016, http://www.nfl.com/.

⊠ PART 1

Place

1 "Beautiful People"

Community Formation in Houston, 1900–1941

Bernadette Pruitt

Scholars trace African American community formation to the social construct accommodation. A compromise of practicality that originated in slavery, racial appeasement—the willingness of a subservient caste (slaves and freed blacks) to acquiesce to the philosophies and actions of a dominant group (slaveholding and nonslaveholding whites)—incongruously aided and hindered African-origin peoples. For example, public appeasement never translated into complete subjugation. Enslaved African-descent people learned that their ability to create two distinct identities—one exclusively for their own community and another in the presence of whites—provided them a crucial emotional, spiritual, and political outlet for contesting and surviving their ordeal. In addition, partly as a result of West African and West Central African syncretism and the formation of a single African American identity, the sustainable bonds that comprised the slave community and defined free blacks before slavery's demise inspired what historians refer to as community formation, the racialized self-help and autonomy that continues to this day.[1]

On the other hand, appeasement among black people contributed to feelings of inadequacy, inferiority, and self-hatred since enslaved Americans often embraced the negative concepts that defined them as a debased people. And along with community agency, making a double-edged sword, these negative effects of appeasement became one of the most lasting legacies of slavery, passed down from generation to generation. In the years that followed slavery, freedmen and freedwomen continued the practice of racial accommodation in an effort to withstand structural racism. When not acquiescing to whites directly, they relied on racial autonomy in their endeavor to create homes, institutions, and organizations, and to sustain hope, and so did their children and grandchildren, as the first generations of freeborn African Americans.[2]

Community formation derives from self-help. Organizing institutions, formulating agendas, building coalitions, and cultivating shared cultural and political ideas—also known as community building—entails community agency, hope, self-respect, and self-reliance. Within the black community of Houston, Texas, this almost always translated also into a desired fight for social justice or human and civil rights, despite the notion of self-destruction that remained intact. This viewpoint derives from the scholarship of Robin D. G. Kelley, Jacqueline Rouse, Merline Pitre, Darlene Clark Hine, Amilcar Shabazz, Michael Botson, Tera Hunter, Allison Dorsey, Stephanie Shaw, Brian Behnken, and others who place the actions of black southerners within the context of racial independence, interdependence, and a Long Civil Rights Movement.[3] The term "Long Civil Rights Movement," coined by historian Jacqueline Dowd Hall, is based on four theories: (1) the Modern Civil Rights Movement derived from individualized local modes of activism; (2) the nation, not simply the South, attempted to re-create racial slavery through exclusion and marginality; (3) the Modern Civil Rights Movement formed the traditional movement and the Black Power transformation that followed; and (4) the movement took place during a longer period than is typically thought, not simply in 1954–68 or 1954–75.[4]

This chapter examines the tools black Houstonians used to accomplish the goal of community formation between the start of the twentieth century and the end of World War II, a period during which the African American population of the city grew eightfold, from 15,000 to 125,000, mainly due to the internal migrations of African American southerners mostly from eastern Texas and Louisiana, although several hundred blacks would immigrate to the city from the Caribbean. It takes a holistic look at the communities, organizations, institutions, and philosophies that emerged in the city for the purpose of securing racial autonomy and social justice. It also examines community formation through the lens of the Great Migrations. Houston served as an important destination for 50,000 African-descent people in the first half of the twentieth century. Investigating where people settled, the jobs they secured, the groups they joined, and the goals they initiated reveals something about community, compromise, conflict, blackness, and justice in the first half of the twentieth century. This essay focuses on the southwestern and southern city of Houston to explain why community formation remains the backbone of blackness in the United States.[5]

If Americans regard St. Louis as the nation's gateway to the West, Houston is the southernmost urban center that bridges the historic Spanish and Mexican Southwest and West with the United States South. According to University of Houston architecture professors Rafael Longoria and Susan Rogers, Houston sits on the edges of two important United States regions: the once-Antebellum South, which went to war with its national government to maintain African American slavery and led the nation in isolating its African-descent citizenry through legal racial exclusion and social control through violence; and the Southwest and West, whose cultural designs, economy, people, and historical geography forever link the region with New Spain and a young, multicolored republic called Mexico. Houston, perhaps more than any other Texas city, straddles these two worlds with its historical legacy of subsistence agriculture, ranching, the legendary vaqueros, and spacious rural-like neighborhoods while engaging in innovative transportation, industrialization, commercial expansion, and urban-suburban development. Black Houstonians, with the help of community formation, without question, embraced both definitions of Houston.[6]

First, I examine the roots of community formation in black Houston, the post–Civil War African American communities that gave the city its first institutions, and the rise of agency in the surrounding countryside and towns that provided the city its workforce, community activists, educators, and businesspeople. One of those adopted Houstonians, Joshua Houston Jr., along with his immediate family, represents the generational transformation from that of appeasement to the New Negro activists of the twentieth century. A direct link to the slavery past, Joshua Houston's generation ensured that the community would never lose sight of that slave past and the construct of prudent accommodation.

Roots of Twentieth-Century Community Formation in Black Houston

Joshua Houston Sr., the literate ex-slave of famed Texas politician and military leader Sam Houston, raised his seven children to thrive in the post–Civil War South and Southwest. Leading by example in slavery and freedom, the blacksmith, wheelwright, coachman, landholder, lay church leader, Reconstruction politician, and former overseer taught his offspring to be industrious, to value education, and to aid others in need. Houston himself sought the best for his entire community but especially its children. He served two terms as a Huntsville alderman and Walker County commissioner and used his influence in prominent white circles to raise funds for enterprises including Huntsville's Union Church and

Freedmen's Bureau school, built in 1867, for which he served as a trustee, as well
as established the short-lived Bishop Ward College, founded in 1883 for blacks.
Community builder Joshua Houston Sr. and his spouses over the years—slave
Anneliza Halyard of Alabama and Crockett, Texas, whom as a teenager and
young adult in his twenties, conceived three children between 1836 and 1848;
the enslaved Mary Green of Walker County, Texas, who gave him two children
before her death in the early 1860s; and freedwoman Sylvester Baker Houston,
a younger wife who also preceded him in death in the 1870s after the births of
the couple's two children—adored their progeny and hoped that one day they
would be free. As chattel and the offspring of chattel, the Houston children
particularly understood appeasement. Before and after Emancipation, Joshua
Houston and his wives instilled in their children the importance of respecting
and fearing whites, believing that the ability to cultivate such nonthreatening,
lasting relationships could benefit their family and community for years to come.[7]

The children of Joshua Houston took all this to heart. They did well for several
reasons but mainly because their financially shrewd father aptly invested in
their pursuits, whether trade school, farming, light manufacturing, or liberal
arts education. The Houston offspring triumphed as parents, professionals, and
community builders, thriving under racial conciliation and segregation.[8]

One of Joshua Houston's middle children, born into slavery at the start of
the Civil War, Joshua Houston Jr., knew the "peculiar institution" and slave
community firsthand. He therefore learned early in life the importance of using
racial appeasement, particularly for self-interest. Following slavery, in 1867 he
entered the Huntsville Freedmen's Bureau school—the Union School, excelling
in reading and mathematics. Ultimately, he studied one of his father's trades,
blacksmithing, at Prairie View State and Industrial College (today Prairie View
A&M University) and in his father's blacksmith shop.[9]

Perhaps because his training and career took precedence over a social life,
Joshua Houston Jr. did not marry until thirty-seven. On October 11, 1898, he wed-
ded Georgia Orviss, a Mary Allen Seminary education major and the daughter
of a prominent biracial Baptist pastor and local postmaster, George Orviss. The
couple raised two daughters, Constance Houston (Thompson), born in 1899,
and Hortense Houston (Young), born in 1902. The Joshua Houston Jr. family
lived on Huntsville's Thirteenth Street and Avenue N near what became "The
Drag," the African American commercial center, and on the edge of the Avenues
district, an exclusive middle-class and upper-middle-class white subdivision.
Initially Joshua and Georgia Houston felt good about raising their daughters in

Joshua Houston family at the wedding of Joshua Houston Jr. and Georgia Carlina Orviss in October 1898. *Back row, left–right*: Lawrence Wilson, John Wilson, Israel Wilson, Wesley (C. W.) Wilson. *Second row*: Clarence Wilson, Joshua Houston Jr., Georgia Carolina Orviss, George Wilson, unidentified woman, Samuel Walker Houston. *Third row (seated)*: Cornelia Orviss, Cadolie Wilson, Reverend Brooks, Joshua Houston Sr., Ellen Houston, Ida Wilson. Front *row*: Viola Wilson, Minnie Houston. *Courtesy Sam Houston Memorial Museum, Sam Houston State University.*

Huntsville. The two earned good livings: Joshua as the owner of a blacksmith shop and Georgia as a schoolteacher and beauty consultant for white women.[10]

Family and the community doted on the Houston girls. According to Constance Houston Thompson in an interview with historian Naomi Ledé, "Our parents protected us as much as possible. My family life was one of contentment, free of most restraint and worries."[11] One of the most enduring forces in their lives was their uncle Sam, educator Samuel Walker Houston, whose vocational high school they attended. Samuel, the youngest son of Joshua Houston Sr., had been a classmate of James Weldon Johnson while attending Atlanta University (now Clark-Atlanta University) in the late 1880s and early 1890s and had founded Huntsville and Walker County's first high school for African Americans, the

Houstonian Normal Institute (later the Samuel Houston Industrial and Training School) in the Galilee community of western Walker County in 1906, five miles west of Huntsville. The first high school for African Americans in Walker County, it would also serve coeds in surrounding counties for thirty years. Then the Huntsville Independent School District named Houston the first principal of its African American high school, established in 1930. The esteemed Samuel Walker Houston also served on the Texas Commission on Interracial Cooperation (TCIRC), the post–World War I civil rights organization headed by black and white civic leaders from across the state, including woman's rights and human rights activist Jessie H. Daniel Ames, Houston clubwoman Jennie Covington, Wiley College president Matthew W. Dogan, Prairie View College principal W. R. Banks, and Sam Houston State Teacher's College (now Sam Houston State University) History Department chair Joseph L. Clark. A lifelong defender of racial conciliation, Samuel Houston taught his nieces that a quality education and respectability could upstage racial animosity.[12]

For other reasons racism seems never to have hampered the Houston girls. Elite whites are said to have often stepped in to protect the teens from insults or threats of violence: "That's Joshua's girl. Leave her [alone]."[13] Constance and Hortense also learned to ignore insults and epithets when around whites, particularly students at Sam Houston State Normal Institute (later Sam Houston State Teacher's College) but also when downtown attending affairs and while running errands for their parents.[14] According to Hortense Houston Young, "My parents would always explain racial etiquette to us before we attended [the Henry Opera House, for example]. They would tell us that we should look beyond the discrimination to the long-range benefits."[15] Furthermore, they learned from their parents the many subtle ways to challenge institutional racism. For example, family and friends taught them to legitimize racial appeasement over demands for immediate integration, as the latter only antagonized whites. Public conciliation, on the other hand, could lead to real benefits—such as recommendations, internships, scholarships or fellowships, jobs, and financial perks—according to loved ones. The long-term benefits, according to the girls' parents, overshadowed short-term racial subjugation.[16]

Their mother had other ideas in mind. Women's rights advocate Georgia Houston never used her full name when doing business and while working in the homes of white clients, who referred to her as G. A. Houston. This way neither she nor the girls had to hear whites call her Georgia—they called her Mrs. Houston. Self-respect and a quality education would win out over racial bigotry, according to mother Georgia Houston. Houston thus exposed her daughters to the best in American and world literature, classical music, operas, and off-Broadway musicals and plays. Truly the Houston daughters lived in a world apart from most of their peers—European American, Latin American, and African American. With the help of their community's protection, the parents worked hard to shield the girls from structural inequality.[17]

The middle-class Houstons nonetheless felt stifled by Jim Crow segregation and structural injustice in the new century. Their elite status perhaps obscured the strain placed on the black middle class to both succeed and remain in their socially mandated place beneath whites. The family therefore could never completely safeguard the teens from racial bigotry, particularly during World War I, when interracial animosity intensified in the United States. Occasionally, even in Huntsville, racial violence surfaced and reminded all African Americans of whites' pejorative perception of them as inferior.[18]

In June 1918, whites in the unincorporated community of Dodge in Walker County, ten miles east of Huntsville, massacred an entire black family, in an alleged shootout at the family home. This unfortunate event followed the arrest and beating of farmer George Cabiness, a member of the family, for protesting allegations that he had evaded the draft. A frightened Georgia Houston persuaded Joshua that the family needed to leave their hometown.[19] According to Constance Houston Thompson years later, "We moved to Houston because our mother became concerned—very concerned—after they took a man from the prison in Huntsville and lynched him."[20] Racial accommodation alone no longer served the family's needs. The family left for Houston not long afterward that year.[21]

The family settled in Fifth Ward, primarily a working-class area north of downtown and near the city's industrial district and Port of Houston, living in a quaint one-story structure on 1303 Bayou Street. Joshua Houston Jr. had bought the property earlier in the decade, perhaps in preparation for an inevitable trek into the city and away from his hometown's lingering racial injustice. One hundred miles south of Huntsville, the city of Houston pleased the family, and unsurprisingly they prospered in their adopted hometown. Joshua opened a blacksmith shop on Lyons Avenue along Fifth Ward's African American business district. Georgia Houston, who held memberships in several fraternal orders, would teach at several Fifth Ward elementary schools for the next forty years.[22]

Financially secure, the Houstons lived well. They employed a maid. They continued to invest in their adolescent daughters, providing them with ballet and music lessons along with charm school. More importantly, the Houston area afforded the family the means to give Constance and Hortense a strong liberal arts education. Constance graduated from Prairie View Normal and Industrial School with her high school diploma and teaching certificate in home economics in 1918 and 1924, respectively, while younger sister Hortense graduated from Colored High School in 1920 and Fisk University in Nashville, Tennessee, with a bachelor's degree in English in 1924. Both went on to have distinguished careers in education and serve their communities as their grandfather had done a half-century earlier. The grand-daughters of Joshua Houston Sr. made the best of their opportunities, ultimately using their multiple skills to improve the lives of others, even advancing the cause of the New Negro Long Civil Rights Movement over accommodationism.[23]

The opportunities of the black middle class and to a smaller extent the working class unquestionably came as a result of the city's booming economy and rising black population. In the blossoming city, emerging civil-rights activists such as the Houston daughters were often allowed to obscure their advocacy agendas and create practical strategies aimed at nonviolent persuasion and continuous resistance to structural racism. Indeed, the perspective of the third-generation Houstons would differ considerably from those of their accommodationist grandparents and parents when it came to improving race relations and condi-tions for African Americans. The new generations of the twentieth century, often known as New Negroes, expanded the self-help, racially autonomous strategy of community formation to include social justice. Like their predecessors they joined institutions such as churches and sororities and built women's clubs, but they also formed civil rights groups and were determined to slowly and pragmatically engage the larger society in showdowns to dismantle racial discrimination.[24]

There were some tensions in Houston's black community since some of the newcomers and established residents who had come of age earlier prioritized self-preservation through modest accommodation and even white hegemony. Some enjoyed their privileges as middle-class and upper-middle-class blacks, while members of the black working class at times felt politically and financially vulnerable and thus uneasy about engaging in protests that would publicly expose them to white backlash. At times the black elites hoped to wield enough power to influence whites but on their own terms. They wished to enter integrated neighborhoods and elite universities while distinguishing themselves from the masses of African Americans living in inner-city ghettos and semirural slums. Many New Negroes combined limited militancy with accommodation. On the whole, though, the overwhelming majority of African-descent Houstonians sought permanent social equality.[25]

Agency differed, based largely on class. Black elites often sought ways to retain their power in society and felt strongly that they alone should speak on behalf of the race when in the presence of nonblacks. Often, however, they wanted to retain for themselves the possibilities that might come out of interracial community building—for example, integrated communities, monetary benefits, superior educational opportunities, and white friends and acquaintances. Social acceptance from whites often meant more to these activists than true coalition building.[26]

Middle-class African Americans also felt strongly that they had the personal experiences, education, finances, and moral strength to challenge the racial status quo. Sometimes, due to overlapping circumstances, they worked alongside poorer African-descent peoples, forming agendas that benefited the entire race. The working-class masses, of course, believed in the notion of self-preservation, usually for all. They generally used their institutions toward progress for themselves and others, whether these institutions were fraternal orders and benevolent societies, churches, unions, or places of entertainment such as nightclubs and bars.[27]

Not everyone advocated community agency or self-help agency for all. Many, perhaps because of self-hatred and fear, opposed advancing change. To these individuals and groups, represented in all socioeconomic classes, self-preservation by way of going along with white hegemony was more legitimate than social justice for all. This notion of inadequacy and paranoia had its roots in African American slavery, when many African cultural mandates disappeared and white American cultural and social constructs were embraced, even at the emotional and spiritual expense of blackness. Nevertheless, as argued by historian Grace Elizabeth Hale, any form of racial autonomy—progressive or conservative, intraracial or interracial—appeared threatening and problematic to many whites.[28]

As for the origins of community formation or agency in black Houston, historians point to the nineteenth century when free blacks and slaves interacted occasionally in religious settings, in taverns, at work, and in passing. Agency expanded in the city's African American community during Reconstruction, when the first longstanding black institutions came into existence. Largely thanks to internal migrations from the surrounding environs in East Texas and places in nearby Louisiana, the black community grew more than threefold between 1860 and 1870, from one thousand to thirty-four hundred, as emancipated slaves made their way into the city hoping for jobs and land.[29] The actions of former slaves turned politicians, voters, tenant farmers, educators, paid domestics, civil servants, and property owners set the stage for twentieth-century community building. Rev. Elias Dibble established the first African American church in 1865—Trinity Methodist Episcopal Church (today Trinity United Methodist Church). Rev. John Henry "Jack" Yates, the first permanent pastor of Antioch Baptist Church (currently Antioch Missionary Baptist Church) in 1866, established Emancipation Park in 1872, the first black-owned park in the South and West. In 1885 he opened Houston College, later known as Houston Baptist Academy, the forerunner for Houston Colored Junior College (now Texas Southern University). Mariah Sharkie formed the first women's auxiliary of the Black Baptist Convention in 1886, and she also established the first kindergartens for African Americans in the city. Others, such as grocer John Bell Brown and politician and contractor Richard Allen, invested in numerous institutions and organizations that catered to the needs of blacks.[30]

As former slaves, these first black community agents for change in Houston did not publicly push for racial equality. Nor did they confront whites in an effort to change life for their people. As accommodationists, they realized their limits. Even if they hoped for better days, they did not dare demand immediate social justice. They did, however, work cleverly to improve conditions for blacks through the institutions they created. Working within the black community almost exclusively, they set the path for the next generation of activists.[31]

The Philosophy of Community Formation in the New Century

The children of former slaves, women and men who came of age in the 1870s, 1880s, 1890s, and 1900s borrowed from the playbooks of their predecessors. With very few exceptions, they rarely spoke out against structural racism. Nor did they evoke public protests from their community. Like their parents and grandparents they quietly worked within the community to improve the lives of their people. As mentioned, however, they did modify their acquiescence, and they formulated a new strategy that borrowed from the Booker T. Washington model of calculated accommodation. According to scholar Maceo Crenshaw Dailey Jr., young professionals such as James D. Ryan, E. O. Smith, Mabel Wesley, and Emmett Jay Scott developed a paradigm that he calls "constructionalism." According to Dailey, this refers to the careful formulating of an agenda that benefited both blacks and whites.[32] While on the surface this equated to sheer accommodation, underneath the veneer of passivity and silence these women and men privately found ways to bolster their own agendas for themselves and their communities. The community-formation strategy remained dominant in black society until the rise of the New Negro Movement during and after World War I.[33]

In commemoration of the fiftieth anniversary of Emancipation, the city's black elite compiled *The Red Book of Houston: A Compendium of Social, Professional, Religious, Educational, and Industrial Interests of Houston's Colored Population* in 1915. The book recognized the contributions of local African Americans, from ministers and businessmen to educators and clubwomen, and it highlighted the progress blacks had made in the half century since the Civil War. Native Houstonian Emmett Jay Scott, confidant, personal assistant, publicist, and ghostwriter to Booker T. Washington, wrote the introduction. His viewpoint, not surprisingly, mirrored the constructionalism of the time, again, as defined by Maceo C. Dailey. Black Houstonians, according to Scott, had much to feel good about in 1915. The city had a significant concentration of African American middle-class professionals, and growing industry employed thousands of African-descent southerners. Like Washington, he believed that "the Afro-American knows and has always known that the prosperity of the white race has always meant his prosperity and the common-sense element of the white race is learning fast that the progress and prosperity of the Afro-American race is good for both races."[34]

The Red Book of *Houston* promoted the interests of the city's African American elite. Mostly the products of slavery as former slaves or their children, the black elite emerged in the aftermath of Emancipation as they sought to provide goods and services to African Americans. As prominent pastors, educators, politicians and civic leaders, insurers, grocers, restaurant owners, physicians, newspaper publishers, attorneys, contractors, licensed artisans, funeral home operators, blacksmiths, tailors, boutique owners, et cetera, they put a public face on African American success. They gave the black poor hope and challenged notions of white superiority. As well, their notoriety and prosperity assured them respectability in black circles. As the Great Migration of the early twentieth century brought more people into the city, black enterprises expanded. The owners and spokespersons for these institutions, businesses, and programs—the black elite—also made money and grew in stature.

The interests of this burgeoning black middle-class and upper-middle-class elite expanded as well. The chief representatives of their communities, these businesspersons, professionals, and civic leaders also cultivated ties with whites. Their connections to the white establishment reflected the groups' shared pasts. While some members of the African American elite used their influence to push for social justice, most did not. As former slaves or their direct offspring, the black elite adhered to the philosophy of racial conciliation over immediate civil

rights. Perhaps out of fear, often due to self-interest, but possibly also as supporters of the ideology of constructionalism, Houston's black bourgeoisie shrewdly
stayed clear of controversial issues that would upset whites. The publication *The
Red Book of Houston* confirms this observation. *The Red Book of Houston* as a
nonthreatening compendium praised blacks and whites for the successes of
African American Houston a half century after Emancipation.

The book, on the other hand, did not discuss racism at all. According to the
publishers and contributors, Houston harbored less racial tension than many
places in the South. The publishers, said Scott, produced the book not to stir up
racial animosity "but merely to give credit where credit is due and to set down
in permanent form the record of some of the members of the African race who
stand for the uplift." The work focused extensively on community formation,
highlighting the ways in which black Houstonians created institutions. Black
leaders believed in their people, and the black community in return celebrated
them. When Scott discussed whites or the social construct of the day, racial
segregation, he argued that it benefited African Americans, assisting in the
expansion of black business ventures. In addition, God had formed racial segregation for a reason. According to Scott, it forced blacks to have a more meaningful
relationship with God, who saw in segregation racial autonomy and interracial
cooperation. Scott asserted that "every individual owes it to his race to remain
true to the racial lines and . . . to work up, through the mediums offered, to the
best life possible under these conditions."[35]

Perhaps motivated by his mentor Washington, Scott himself held fast to
constructionalism, which allowed blacks autonomy and independence. From
black elites, black schools received needed funds for building projects and scholarships, while business owners could depend on inexpensive advertising in black
newspapers. Pastors received both anonymous and publicized gifts for their
congregations. As Dailey argues, constructionalism proved useful to the black
elite, even if the masses did not always enjoy the fruits of their labor. Most kept
their mouths closed when it came to the subject of racial segregation, often in
fear of violent retaliation, while their community leaders reaped benefits at their
expense. Scott believed that black excellence, as exhibited in his life and that of
other elites described in *The Red Book of Houston*, did much to improve race
relations in the country. In his opinion it would compel whites to implement
real racial reform. Scott served as a special advisor on black affairs to Secretary
of War Newton Baker during World War I, secretary of the National Negro
Business League, and American diplomat in Liberia, and he went on to write

five books, including *Negro Migration during the War* (1918). Scott never shifted his political views regarding racial segregation. As the Modern Civil Rights Movement took off following the *Brown v. Board of Education of Topeka* decision in 1954, Scott expressed dismay at the rapidly changing South. As early as World War I, a budding new phase of the Long Civil Rights Movement, the New Negro Movement had threatened the tenet constructionalism. But before it took hold of the masses, the Great Migrations of the twentieth century would permanently reconfigure the nation, Texas, and Houston's African American population.[36]

The Great Migrations to Houston

Migration was a long-standing self-help method used by African Americans seeking agency. Fifty thousand African Americans moved to Houston in the first half of the twentieth century. They were part of the nationwide Great Migrations, in which an estimated seven million migrants left the South for cities and manufacturing, especially in the North, Midwest, and West. Houston immigrants came mostly from rural communities and small towns in four East Texas regions: the surrounding cotton belt west and south of the city, smaller industrial centers along the Upper Texas Gulf Coast manufacturing area, mixed-economy centers immediately north of the city, and the far northeast timber belt along the San Jacinto, Trinity, and Red River bottoms. These counties represent the eastern two-fifths of the state west of the Brazos and Colorado Rivers. Nearly 90 percent of the state's African American population for nearly two hundred years has resided in this section of the state.[37]

One quarter of migrants left Louisiana parishes, primarily those in the Sugar Bowl region near New Orleans and Baton Rouge, the rice belt communities of Cajun Country in the southwest, and the cotton region in central Louisiana. These diverse peoples relocated to the city for a number of reasons. Like most in the Great Migrations, they were influenced by poverty and racial discrimination. Most black farmers—sharecroppers primarily—rarely earned enough to pay off their recurring debts. Educationally, they had less formal schooling than whites. Disenfranchisement by means of poll taxes and Texas's white primary prevented them from contributing to the political process individually and as a voting bloc. Jim Crow southern segregation meant separate, subpar public facilities, legally mandated to ensure African American debasement. When descendants of slaves challenged the system, they were liable to suffer violence at the hands of whites, violence means of social control, often through mob actions such as lynching.[38]

Not that the city was much better. Houston too had inadequate public facilities, disfranchisement, wage inequality, restrictive housing covenants, bias in schooling, and police brutality and other racialized violence. But blacks who had trekked to the city as temporary migrant workers or to visit family and friends felt comfortable with Houston, and they saw that its burgeoning economy could provide a means for socioeconomic and sociocultural independence. The city's proximity to migrants' home communities also made migration practical, and some favored moves that would allow them to remain near family and friends left behind. This became more important as parents and grandparents aged. Houston's spaciousness, its trees, high grasses, coastal flatlands, and pace of living reminded newcomers of what they loved about the South. Unlike blacks in the North and West (west of Austin), most established black residents of the city came from the same places newcomers had left behind, and they all could point to parents and grandparents who had experienced slavery. This meant for greater solidarity between newcomers and established residents, who themselves had once been migrants. Three-quarters of Houston's black immigrants had fled surrounding southeastern Texas cotton communities and places in the East Texas timber belt.[39]

Nearly a quarter of the city's black immigrants came from Louisiana. Two hundred thousand African Americans fled Louisiana, Mississippi, Arkansas, and Tennessee in the wake of the Great Mississippi Flood of 1927. Nearly sixty thousand lived in Texas in 1930, with many having relocated becasue of the flood. Of this number, nearly twelve thousand reached Houston. These newcomers mainly relocated to Fifth Ward, with a good number of Louisiana Creoles settling Frenchtown, a small neighborhood there, in 1922. As with other black immigrants, community formation by this group had its roots in slavery and Reconstruction, and it soon became an intricate part of the city's larger black community.[40]

Chain migration networks made settlement easier. Sociologists John and Leatrice MacDonald and historian Earl Lewis define chain migration as the process by which residents—namely relatives or friends, themselves former migrants—use their social contacts to introduce newcomers and potential immigrants to employment options, transportation choices, schools, and churches, and provide them with initial, temporary housing. Black Houstonians often urged loved ones to uproot and come to the city. In the 1990s former labor organizer Luther Stullivan reminisced about his 1920s childhood and recalled the times when his rural New Caney, Texas, family visited loved ones in Houston. For a time, Stullivan and his siblings attended school in Fifth Ward after their father secured work at a local construction firm. Although the family only stayed in the city for a year, Stullivan would later occasionally return to Houston for job opportunities until finding permanent employment with Southern Pacific Railroad in the early 1930s.[41]

Other factors helped spur migration to the city. Newspaper stories, editorials, and advertisements all played a role, and they also aided newcomers to Houston. Black railroad employees, including potential migrants, not only provided information about destination cities such as Houston, they also distributed newspapers from those cities. Church engagements, which were often announced in black community papers, reassured rural blacks that the city was not entirely a place of sin. A hugely popular weekly, the *Houston Informer*, fostered interest in the city among rural readers through its "News and Views from Texas Towns," which cemented bonds between rural and urban people. Covering church and other community events (e.g., banquets, high school graduations, and college socials) and reporting not only on marriages but also divorces, the paper made Houston seem attractive. These stories lured people to Houston who would might otherwise left the region for northern or more western cities, as did job advertisements, sometimes from white prospective employers.[42]

In addition to encouraging migration, the *Houston Informer* fostered pride among its readers. Like northern black newspapers such as the *Chicago Defender*, *New York Age*, and *Pittsburgh Courier*, the *Informer* ("the South's Greatest Race Newspaper," it called itself) advocated the New Negro ideology of the period. As editor and publisher of the newspaper (and later of its rival, the *Houston Defender*), Clifton Frederick Richardson Sr. advanced the New Negro creed of racial pride, intelligent accommodation, economic empowerment, solidarity, and equality. Born in 1892 in Marshall, Texas, to sharecroppers, Richardson excelled academically and graduated from Marshall's Bishop College with a degree in journalism and printing in 1909. The same year he married Ruby Leola Rice, a childhood friend. By the time of his death in 1939, the Texan had left a lasting impression on his adopted city. He had founded two successful newspapers, one of which serves the community to this day. Along with George Webster, Richardson owned the Webster-Richardson Publishing Company, which printed the *Houston Informer*. Richardson deplored racial exclusion, especially disfranchisement, and was not circumspect about sharing his opinions with readers.[43] He also publicly denounced anti-black violence. *Informer* articles immediately following World War I labeled anti-black violence as "hellish and hunnish." Richardson often mentioned this in connection with migration. He wrote, for example, "The colored citizens of Huntsville are all excited and many are anxious to sell out their little belongings and holdings and migrate to more civilized [places]" like Houston.[44]

Settling and Building Communities

Clifton and Ruby Richardson moved into their single-family home on Robin Street in Fourth Ward. Unlike most African Americans in the Great Migrations to the North, who tended to land large-scale, densely populated ghettoes, Houston's black newcomers moved into multiple communities and neighborhoods surrounding downtown Houston, sometimes outside the city limits. Third Ward, Fourth Ward, Fifth Ward, Sunnyside, Independence Heights, Acres Homes, Trinity Gardens, Clinton Park, and Pleasantville were some of the neighborhoods that attracted African Americans in the early twentieth century. Often blacks moved to the same communities their friends and family members had settled years earlier. Many lived near their jobs. Other settled in the first black communities they found after arriving in the city. Migrants from cotton farms south and southwest of the city typically moved to Third and Fourth Wards. Those from farms and towns east and northeast of Houston usually moved into Fifth Ward, Independence Heights, Acres Homes, Clinton Park, places just north of downtown. Inside these communities, newcomers and established residents built upon and reinvented the institutions that former slaves and their children had formed in the late nineteenth century: churches, schools, lodges, political groups, and businesses.[45]

Aside from remaining dependent on the city for utilities, first responders, street improvements, and public schools, blacks lived their daily lives separately from whites. As discussed above, racial segregation discriminated against African Americans in a myriad of ways. The segregation of African-descent Houstonians, however, allowed for enormous creativity. They relied heavily on themselves and their own institutions and organizations for self-esteem, spiritual sustenance and intellectual development, entertainment, political consciousness, and ultimately hope.[46]

All migrants needed a place to live. Although most black Houstonians rented homes inside the city limits or owned land and dwellings in unincorporated areas on the outskirts of the city, occasionally property owners successfully formed alternative communities. In 1908 Alfred Alexander Wright, an up-and-coming white developer from Ohio, provided low-interest loans to blacks desiring land in the Houston area. The Wright Land Company sold property in what became Highland Heights, Acres Homes, and Sunnyside. In 1915 residents incorporated Independence Heights, making it probably Texas's first African American municipality. The city's population burgeoned, from several hundred in 1915 to one thousand in the late 1920s.[47]

For a brief period through 1929, the founders of Independence Heights formed permanent institutions, created jobs, elected their own public officials, and provided residents with modest city services: water and sewage, street lighting and maintenance, plank sidewalks, telephone, and limited public transportation. The town comprised eight groceries, four restaurants, a taxi service, a blacksmith shop, a grain mill, a watch repair shop, a shoe repair shop, a millinery shop, a drug store, and an ice cream parlor.[48] Trades represented included an electrician, builders, and plumbers. Historian and educator Vivian Hubbard Seals, whose father, Oliphant Hubbard, served as the town's second mayor, would fondly remember her childhood home: "I can remember when I used to ride [D]addy's back to Lindsay's Ice Cream Parlor to buy a 'Say-So,' an ice cream cone."[49]

Oliphant Hubbard, a teacher, served two terms as mayor from 1919 to 1923, and city services improved modestly during his tenure.[50] Hubbard encouraged residents to take pride in their city: So let us all try and build up a city that every person who lives here or may come will feel proud of it."[51] Houston annexed Independence Heights in 1929. At a time when the overwhelming majority of blacks rented and had limited work skills, Independence Heights symbolized real progress. A half-century after Emancipation, the town sustained its residents and their political dreams just as its residents created a culture of racial interdependence and independence.[52]

Other Houston neighborhoods with substantial numbers of African-Americans functioned similarly. Residents of Fifth Ward, located northeast of downtown Houston, usually worked in the city's chief industrial district and the Houston Ship Channel. Black railroad workers, cotton-compress workers, refinery laborers, steelworkers, mill workers, meatpacking employees, and teamsters usually lived in Fifth Ward, but many other occupations were represented among the black population there, including domestics, chamber maids, porters, chauffeurs, sextons, waiters and waitresses, cooks, laundresses and seamstresses, blacksmiths, carpenters, teachers, physicians, nurses, attorneys, and social workers.[53]

Music represented an important component of the Fifth Ward and helped usher in a cultural revolution known as the Houston Renaissance, a term first used by historian Neil Sapper in "Black Urban Texas Culture: A Lone Star Renaissance" in 1981. Houston's spectacular cultural beauty, seen, felt, and heard in her music, art, photography, literature, and political commentary, provided African-descent people with a new weapon in the long civil rights struggle for social justice. The whole city, including whites, would come to embrace its black cultural influences: blues, zydeco, gospel, jazz, and African American art, photography, political satire, and comedy. Perhaps unclear to whites, blacks used their culture to comment on, if not draw attention to, their debased experiences as second-class citizens. Under the leadership of brothers Russell and Percy McDavid, the jazz program at Fifth Ward's Phillis Wheatley High School gained national notoriety in 1934 when Duke Ellington visited and praised the program. Wheatley former students include musicians Milt Larkin, Illinois and Russell Jacquet, Tom Archia, Cedric Haywood, Arnett Cobb, and Eddie Vinson, whose sounds provided commentary about black life in the Jim Crow South. And, needless to say, they did more than play music. Percy McDavid, for example, helped integrate musicians' labor unions in the 1950s.[54]

Fifth Ward, because of its neighborhood Frenchtown and its proximity to U.S. Highway 90, which extended east into Louisiana, attracted Louisianans. After the Great Flood of 1927, the city's Louisiana-born population increased from a few thousand to nearly twelve thousand, and Louisiana emigrants started schools, churches, fraternal orders and benevolent associations, and even the likes of zydeco nightclubs and Creole restaurants. One of the community's enduring institutions, Our Mother of Mercy Catholic Church, opened in June 1929 and became the congregation of half of the city's African American Catholics. Its parish school educated Catholics and non-Catholics alike.[55]

Third Ward also had a significant number of African Americans, ranging from the working poor to the city's black elite. Third Ward by the 1930s replaced Fourth Ward as Houston's premier community for influential African American migrant families such as those of Lulu B. and Julius White, Carter and Doris Wesley, Jennie and Benjamin J. Covington, and Thelma and Ira Bryant. In 1934, Crockett, Texas, native Ira Bryant and his wife built their two-bedroom, pink-trimmed cottage on Holman Street and Tierwester Avenue. Bryant, a teacher, had just obtained his master's degree from the University of Kansas. His wife, Thelma, a graduate of Howard University and niece of Emmett Jay Scott, helped Bryant research his many projects. Both graduates of Houston's Colored High School (later renamed Booker T. Washington High School), they would travel to and from California as Bryant completed his doctorate in education at the University of Southern California. He would eventually become principal of Booker T. Washington High.[56]

Home to the working poor as well as the African American elite, Third Ward, which remained predominately white through the first half of the twentieth century, contained existing shotgun homes and modest frame houses in the areas of the ward bordering downtown. New homes were built south along

Holman Avenue, Dowling Avenue, Truxillo Street, Nagle Street, Rosalie Street, Alabama Street, Wheeler Avenue, and Cleburne Street. Third Ward institutions included Houston Negro Hospital, the *Houston Informer* and *Houston Defender* newspapers, Houston Junior College, an NAACP office, Blue Triangle YWCA, and black-owned business such as Franklin Beauty School and Teal Portrait Studios. Whether living in Independence Heights, Fourth Ward, Fifth Ward, or Third Ward, blacks shaped their neighborhoods through their institutions and organizations.[57]

Formation of Institutions and Organizations

The organizations and institutions created by the Houston's black population early in the twentieth century would not only serve as the backbone of black community but also aid future community activists who would abandon the community's long-held accommodationism and work for civil rights.[58] Black social clubs, lodges, and voluntary associations often formed to meet a particular task—for example, to provide life insurance. In 1907 seven African American educators, including post-Reconstruction migrants and recent newcomers to the city, led by Alabama native and Fisk College graduate E. O. Smith, formed the Pilgrim Congregational Church and Library Association to raise public awareness about the need for an African American library. In 1909 a temporary library with three hundred volumes opened inside the city's African American high school. With the support of community leaders Emmett Jay Scott, his mentor Booker T. Washington, and Julia Ideson, director of the Houston Lyceum and Carnegie Library (the city's white public library), the association procured $15,000 from philanthropist and industrialist Andrew Carnegie to build the Colored Carnegie Library (CCL). The CCL, completed in 1914, brought together an ensemble of black Houston's best and brightest—including teachers, ministers, fraternal leaders, and business owners—for the common good of the community. Recent migrants to the city played a pivotal role in the project. They chaired boards, reached out to the community for funds and other resources, persuaded people to give, and themselves donated and loaned thousands of dollars for this and numerous other charitable causes.[59]

Jamaican-born educator Henry Cohen Hardy formed the first Ancient Order of Pilgrims in Houston in 1882. With thirty-one chapters by 1915, the fraternal order wielded significant influence in the community. In the 1920s, the order built the Pilgrim Building on San Filipe (later West Dallas) and Bagby Streets, a four-story structure that housed black-owned businesses. Black Houstonians also formed chapters of white-dominated organizations such as the Prince Hall Masons and Grand United Order of the Odd Fellows. Perhaps the first black business entity in the community after Emancipation, these lodges in many ways shaped the ideals of the city's first African American business owners.[60]

Black women too operated lodges and mutual aid societies. Black women found lodges appealing, mostly because they provided an important outlet for political creativity and helped foster socioeconomic independence and business development. In some instances, women successfully created thriving institutions that functioned independently of male orders. In Texas and specifically in Houston, women headed some of the most successful fraternal societies. Like male lodges, they provided needed services to community members. They offered loans, life insurance policies, and health-care benefits to members, and they provided employment opportunities to women of color. The organizations endorsed the concept of group economy among women of color and increasingly opened doors for African American women with clerical skills, accounting experience, college degrees, and exceptional leadership ability.[61]

One of the most successful such enterprises, the Grand Court Order of Calanthe (GCOC), was founded in Houston in 1898. The organization did more than establish insurance policies and benefits for its female members. It also invested in real estate, government bonds, and the stock market. With an annual income of $600,000 and assets totaling $250,000 in the 1930s during the Great Depression, a time when many African American fraternal orders went into bankruptcy, it provided an important service to eligible members. It also brought together migrant women from differing socioeconomic backgrounds, professions, and education levels. Domestic workers and laundresses attended meetings, socials, teas, and church services with civil rights leader Lulu White, social work advocate Jennie Covington, physician Thelma Patten Law, educators Georgia Houston and Mary L. Jones Johnson, and other members of the African American elite. Unlike similar African American organizations of the twentieth century, it did not limit its members to the well-to-do. Members included chambermaids, homemakers, and entertainers along with the likes of teachers and physicians, and high-school dropouts along with the highly educated.[62]

Women did much, much more. In 1920, reformers Jennie Covington, Mary L. Jones, Martha Sneed, and others, with the assistance of the local and national boards of the Young Women's Christian Association (YWCA), opened the Blue Triangle Branch of the YWCA. Through the years, the branch would provide Houston African Americans, especially women and girls, with an employment office, cafeteria meals, a travelers' aid program for recent migrants in need of assistance, public aid to families in need, recreation facilities for children, and a camp retreat as well as educational and Christian conferences. Because of the generosity of Covington and other newcomers to the city, the Blue Triangle YWCA, during its existence from 1920 to 1998, served many thousands of people.[63]

Covington, the wife of prominent physician Benjamin Jesse Covington, worked closely with blacks and whites in an effort to improve lives. She worked as a volunteer caseworker with the Bethlehem Center, Darcus Home for Delinquent Girls, and Boy Scouts of America. In the Married Ladies Social, Art & Charity Club, founded in 1902, prominent African American women held fund-raisers for poor people and schoolchildren.[64]

Service sororities also used the power of community agency to aid others in need. Lullelia Harrison, a Zeta Phi Beta Sorority national president, teacher, guidance counselor, wife, and mother whose parents settled in Fourth Ward in the 1900s or 1910s from southern Louisiana and Dayton, Texas, pulled double duty to complete her roster of regular activities that mostly benefited others. Harrison also worked with her church, Mount Vernon Methodist Episcopal Church (now Mount Vernon United Methodist Church), as well as the NAACP, serving on the local committee that testified before the Texas legislature in 1946 to lobby for the establishment of a black public school in Houston. At the same time, Harrison, like other active women, had children to raise, a husband to tend to, and other family responsibilities waiting at home every evening. Institution building never waned for these women, and it usually began in the church.[65]

The need for spiritual sustenance in daily living led to the growth and dispersal of African American congregations around the country in the late nineteenth and early twentieth centuries, particularly as the first Great Migrations began at that time. Black church building began immediately following Emancipation and these institutions remained the bedrock of black communities well before the population shift that came later. Church growth symbolized African Americans' need for solace and autonomy. Churches especially expanded as migrants flocked to African American communities throughout Houston. In 1915 almost fourteen thousand people had memberships at thirty-two Baptist and Methodist African American congregations in the city. In 1929, ninety-five churches held worship services in African American neighborhoods in the Houston area. These ninety-five churches represented well over thirty thousand people, although, of these, only seventeen thousand attended church regularly. Black Christians, whether Protestant or Catholic, used the church as a platform to do good deeds in their community.[66]

Often unsung, black Christian women were amazing institution builders in Houston. Kathleen Evans Stewart was one such individual. Born in the Piney Woods town of Teague, Texas, in the early twentieth century, Kathleen Stewart and husband W. H. Stewart moved to Houston in 1938 and joined St. John's Baptist Church on Dowling Street in Third Ward, where for the next forty years she worked as an ardent supporter of disability rights. Because of her ardent generosity toward hearing-impaired people, St. John's soon developed a reputation as an oasis for them. Growing up with a hearing-impaired sibling had given Kathleen Stewart a compassionate temperament and understanding. She had learned sign language at a young age and would become a dedicated signer for the hearing impaired, even establishing a "Silent Department" at St. John's that prioritized the needs of hearing-impaired people. Without a formal college education, Stewart became one of the most visible people in Houston's religious community, always until her death in 1981 promoting the welfare of hearing-disabled people. For Stewart and other dutiful newcomers to the city in the early twentieth century, faith did not begin and end in the sanctuary.[67]

Like Kathleen Stewart, African American educators in Houston understood the meaning of community building. They did not allow inequality of pay to discourage them from working to ensure that the next generation of black Houstonians would receive the best education possible. As the black school-age population grew substantially in the first half of the twentieth century, these committed educators worked to counter a racist system that deemed African American children inferior and undeserving of the public school system's resources.[68]

Beneath the pretense of accommodation, James Ryan, like so many other black migrants to Houston, cultivated a form of cautious self-help. Born in Navasota, Texas, in Grimes County on October 25, 1872, James Delbridge Ryan completed his initial education at Prairie View College in 1890. That same year, at the age of seventeen, the recent migrant began teaching mathematics for the Houston school system. A decade later he began a long career at Colored High School, first as a math instructor. In 1912, he became the school's principal. He later earned a Master of Science degree from Wiley College (in Marshall, Texas) and became principal of the new Jack Yates High School in Third Ward in 1926. Racial inequities were obvious to Ryan, and he discussed them at great length at a Colored Teachers' Association of Texas convention. However, he never challenged white peers, administrators, or city officials to reform African American schools, pay equal salaries, or eradicate other racial disparities.[69]

Instead "Professor Jimmie," as many students called him, used his own resources to fund programs, purchase school supplies, and finance the careers of skillful teachers and help pay them. Ryan persuaded mail clerk Will J. Jones in 1912 to form choral clubs at African American schools, paying Jones a modest fee for this himself. Jones, a former student of music at the New England Conservatory of Music in Boston, loved teaching music. Regrettably, the school system did not pay the salaries of African American music teachers in the early decades of the century. Jones would serve African American children in the Houston Independent School District (HISD) for twenty-two years before the district officially recognized him as a music teacher. By the 1930s, African American schools, largely because of generous benefactor Ryan, enjoyed choirs, music departments, bands, and music textbooks.[70]

Ryan, with others, started additional programs. He was instrumental in the development of athletics in Houston's African American high schools. Before 1925, Ryan purchased uniforms and equipment for the Colored High School football team, and R. G. Lockett and YMCA secretary H. P. Carter volunteered as head coaches. Community builders definitely addressed the needs of schoolchildren, and Ryan used his personal resources to implement and sustain programs and help initiate policy. The actions of Ryan, Smith, and other accommodationists paid off. With the help of extracurricular activities, many of their students at Booker T. Washington, Jack Yates, and Phillis Wheatley went on to have fruitful and lucrative careers in medicine, dentistry, nursing, accounting, library science, mortuary science, music, journalism, and education.[71]

Thanks to Ryan's generosity as well as the successful transition of kinesiology into the HISD curriculum, high school sports grew enormously in the early twentieth century for blacks in Houston. This in turn aided African Americans in numerous ways. Sports afforded African Americans an important gateway to college, and with this a professional career was possible. Athletics also bolstered the New Negro mantra of racial pride. Migrants and their children not only enjoyed participating in sports in Houston, particularly on the high-school level. It also mean that more went on to college and became leaders in their community, contributing greatly to their city's cultural and racial rebirth.[72]

John E. Codwell Sr., while athletic director of the new Wheatley High School, organized the Turkey Day Classic, a football game that would be held annually on Thanksgiving Day between Wheatley (Fifth Ward) and Jack Yates (Third Ward). Houston native Codwell had graduated from Colored High School in

1922 or 1923 and then entered Howard University, earning a degree in physical education in 1927, the same year the Wheatley principal hired the young man as his school's athletic director. That same year, Terre Haute, Indiana, native William S. Holland began teaching and serving as athletic director at Yates High School, headed by principal James D. Ryan. Codwell and Holland, who respected each other as coaching peers and educators, helped organize the first football games between Yates, Wheatley, and Booker T. Washington (formerly Colored High School) in 1927. It would be another twenty years before principals Holland and Codwell successfully lobbied for the Turkey Day Classic, supervised by the Texas Interscholastic League for Colored Schools. Also known as the Prairie View Interscholastic League, the school district soon realized the financial rewards that came with marketing the game. For the black community, however, the game represented the beauty of black Houston, and the entire African American community supported the game.[73]

Black medical professionals, like educators, believed in community formation. Excluded from white hospitals, refused entry into the state's health-science training programs or dismissed as inept, stupid, and lazy, these professionals relied on themselves and the benevolence of their communities' limited resources. They opened practices throughout the Houston area to provide medical assistance to the members of their community, wanting to practice medicine as their white peers did daily. In the wake of Houston's spectacular growth in the twentieth century, these health professionals slowly saw their practices bloom. Their chief concern, however, centered on quality care for the critically ill, especially individuals in need of surgery. Their dream of offering African Americans quality medical care soon turned into a reality.[74]

A charity hospital for whites—Hermann Hospital—opened in 1925 and eventually became the gateway to the Texas Medical Center. Predating this and inspired by racism in the medical profession, black doctors and civic leaders founded medical facilities for Houston's African Americans. They established the People's Sanitarium in 1911 on Andrews Street; tiny Union Hospital—a six-bed and single surgical area facility—in 1918 on Howard and Nash; the New Union Hospital, also on Andrews, between 1919 and 1923; and Union-Jeremiah Hospital, an eleven-bed facility on Andrews and Genesee in 1923, all in Fourth Ward. African American doctors in the mid-1920s petitioned the city to provide adequate medical care for blacks. They particularly felt flustered by the steady growth of private and public hospitals in the city—including Hermann, Methodist Hospital (1924), and Jefferson Davis (1924)—that refused the services of African American physicians.

Even those hospitals that treated African American patients refused African American doctors and nurses. An unlikely benefactor donated the funds for the construction of a new facility for African Americans. In 1925, Houston oil tycoon and philanthropist Joseph S. Cullinan, the founder of Texaco Oil, donated $80,000 for the construction of the Houston Negro Hospital on Ennis Street and Elgin in Third Ward, in memory of his son, Lieutenant John H. Cullinan, who had died in battle in 1918 in World War I. The city gave the hospital three acres of land on which to build the facility. The hospital, completed in 1926, opened in May 1927. For the city's twenty-five African American physicians, the facility represented a new chapter in medical history, as one of eleven southern and southwestern hospitals open to African American medical professionals, allowing new doctors the opportunity to work closely with experienced practitioners.[75]

The coalition that successfully petitioned civic leaders to open a hospital for blacks in the 1920s also helped spearhead the rise of the city's New Negro Movement. Influenced by national and local events, including the death of Booker T. Washington, the rise of Marcus Garvey and the Universal Negro Improvement Association and African Communities' League, the beginning of the first Great Migration, World War I, the growth of the NAACP, and, most importantly, the Houston mutiny and riot August 1917, the period unleashed perhaps the greatest period of protest by black Houstonians up to that point.[76] The Houston riot commenced at dusk on August 23, 1917, when over one hundred soldiers from the all-black Twenty-Fourth Infantry ignored direct orders and marched onto the streets of Fourth Ward, Houston, in protest of examples of racial discrimination against the soldiers. It ended two hours later with four black soldiers, one white National Guardsman, and fifteen white and Hispanic civilians dead, including one who died sometime later. Local blacks, who had nothing to do with the skirmish, publicly condemned the actions of the military men but privately sympathized with the fallen soldiers, who were blamed for the affair. After three courts-martial, the War Department would execute twenty-nine men, and sixty-three would serve life sentences. Black Americans, especially Houstonians, felt this unfair. The melee helped precipitate the rise of a new phase in black political mobilization—the New Negro Movement.[77]

Not since Reconstruction had African Americans been so actively engaged in politics in Houston, as in the period following the Houston Riot of 1917. The riot motivated blacks to become more proactive about ending discrimination; if the Twenty-Fourth Infantry could risk their lives to come to the defense of black Houstonians, certainly Houstonians can take up the mantle themselves.

The emerging African American leaders mostly comprised migrants from the surrounding region. Organizations evidencing this political activity include the Texas Federation of Colored Women's Clubs, NAACP, Lincoln League, Negro Voters Civic, Independent Colored Voters Leagues, Progressive Voters League, Civic Betterment League, Harris County Negro Democratic Club, Third Ward Civic Club, National Negro Business League, Negro Chamber of Commerce, and the Interdenominational Ministerial Alliance. African American churches, fraternal orders, women's clubs, and newspapers also propelled political and civic engagement in the community. Although sometimes affluent African Americans, usually political conservatives such as Jennie Covington, worked alongside white allies (such as members of the TCIRC), most did not. Blacks did support the NAACP and other groups that sought the immediate dismantling of racial discrimination in all areas of society. These efforts would ultimately pave the way for numerous victories, including *Smith v. Allwright* (1944), which overturned Texas's white Democratic primary.[78]

Conclusion

For decades blacks saw insular racial autonomy and quiet resistance to racism as measures of racial progress. As had their forebears who had relocated to the city immediately following slavery or decades later in the nineteenth century, they emphasized self-help strategies and community building from the inside out, and they established successful institutions and organizations. Early migrants and established residents gave back to their communities in numerous ways, and they offered African Americans alternative solutions to pressing problems and challenges facing their families, neighborhoods, and the larger society. The institutions and self-help programs created by early-twentieth-century black Houstonians did something else. They created the impetus for achieving civil rights.[79]

Constance Houston Thompson and Hortense Houston Young, accommodationists who became New Negroes, speak to this transformation. The adolescents who did well for themselves in the 1910s and 1920s represented the "New Negro" of the new century. Joshua and Georgia Houston's youngest daughter, Hortense, entered Booker T. Washington High School in the fall of 1918.[8] Founded in 1893, the school offered its students classes in industrial training and domestic science, applied mathematics and science, and the liberal arts, including Greek and Latin. After high school, Hortense enrolled in Fisk University in Nashville, Tennessee, and she graduated in the mid-1920s with an English degree. After briefly teaching at the newly built Jack Yates High School, Hortense married C. Milton Young Jr., a medical doctor from Nashville, Tennessee.[80]

The couple moved to Louisville, Kentucky, where Young established a practice. Both eventually did graduate work at the University of Illinois and had two children—C. Milton Young III (who would become a physician) and Yvonne Young Clark (who would become a mechanical engineer). In the 1950s Hortense Young was the first African American woman to attend the Louis Brandeis Law School at the University of Louisville. Like her older sister would in Houston, she supported public housing, election rights, desegregation efforts, and financial security for people of color, living in Louisville from the 1930s until her death in 1977.[81]

Eldest daughter Constance Houston entered Prairie View College in 1918 and earned her bachelor's degree in home economics in the early 1920s. For the next twenty years, she taught at Booker T. Washington High School in Houston, her sister's alma mater. She obtained a master's degree and later chaired the Department of Home Economics at Texas State University for Negroes (now Texas Southern). The schoolteacher married tall, dark, and handsome hotel waiter Tracy Thompson in October 1926. The clubwoman also found time for social causes. As a member of the National Council of Negro Women, an organization founded in 1935 by Mary McLeod Bethune, Constance worked with other clubwomen to bring attention to African American slums. Eventually her efforts propelled the construction of some of the city's—and country's—first federal housing projects for poor people. Undoubtedly her family's underpinnings in Huntsville and Houston contributed to later success. The Houstons' move to Fifth Ward not only benefited their immediate family but also ultimately helped numerous people, from descendants and extended family to friends, acquaintances, students, and clients. Constance Houston Thompson, died in Houston on June 10, 1992.[82]

Borrowing from their parents and grandparents, Constance Houston Thompson and Hortense Houston Young broadened the agenda of accommodationists from community formation. In bridging generations, they helped set the stage for the Modern Civil Rights Movement in Houston and the nation.[83]

Notes

1. For more on the evolution of the historiography of African American slavery, see Frances G. Couvares, Martha Saxton, Gerald Grob, and George Athan Billias, ed., "Slave Culture: African or American?" in *Interpretations of American History: Patterns and Perspectives*, vol. 1, 8th ed. (New York: Bedford/St. Martin's Press, 2009), 274–308); John W. Blasingame, *The Slave Community*, new rev. ed. (New York: Oxford University Press, 1979); Lawrence W. Levine, *Black Culture, Black Consciousness:*

Afro-American Folk Thought from Slavery to Freedom (New York: Oxford University Press, 1977); Ira Berlin, *Generations of Captivity: A History of African American* Slaves (Cambridge: Belknap Press, 2004); and John Hope Franklin and Elizabeth Brooks Higginbotham, *From Slavery to Freedom: A History of African Americans* (New York: McGraw-Hill, 2010).

2. Raymond Gavins, "Diasporic Africans and Slavery," in *Africana Studies: A Survey of Africa and the African Diaspora*, ed. Mario Azevedo (Durham: Carolina Academic Press, 1998), 89–106; Daudi Ajani ya Azibo, "Articulating the Distinction between Black Studies and the Study of Blacks: The Fundamental Role of Culture and the African-Centered Worldview," in *The African American Studies Reader*, ed. Nathaniel Norment Jr. (Durham: Carolina Academic Press, 2001), 420–41; Francis Cress Welsing, *The Isis Papers: Keys to the Colors* (Chicago: Third World Press, 1991); Chandler Williams, *The Destruction of Black Civilization: Great Issues of a Race from 4500 BC to 2000 AD*, 3rd ed. (Chicago: Third World Press, 1987); Na'im Akbar, *Breaking the Chains of Psychological Slavery* (Tallahassee: Mind Productions and Associates, 1996), 1–26; and Alvin Morrow, *Breaking the Curse of Willie Lynch: The Science of Slavery Psychology* (St. Louis: Rising Sun Publishers, 2004), 1–30.

3. This work draws on the scholarship of several scholars who have attempted to redefine the parameters of the Modern Civil Rights Movement, including Stephanie J. Shaw, "Black Club Women and the Creation of the National Association of Colored Women," in *"We Specialize in the Wholly Impossible": A Reader in Black Women's History*, ed. Darlene Clark Hine, Wilma King, and Linda Reed (New York: Carlson Publishing, 1995); Merline Pitre, *In Struggle against Jim Crow: Lula B. White and the NAACP, 1900–1957* (College Station: Texas A&M University Press, 1999); Jacqueline Ann Rouse, "Out of the Shadow of Tuskegee: Margaret Murray Washington, Social Activism, and Race Vindication," *Journal of Negro History* 81 (1996): 31–46; Obadele-Starks, *Black Unionism in the Industrial South* (College Station: Texas A&M University Press, 1999), 3–26; Darlene Clark Hine, *Black Victory: The Rise and Fall of the White Primary in Texas*, new ed. (Columbia: University of Missouri Press, 2003); Michael R. Botson, *Labor, Civil Rights, and the Hughes Tool Company* (College Station: Texas A&M University Press, 2005); Dwight Watson, *Race and the Houston Police Department, 1930–1990: A Change Did Come* (College Station: Texas A&M University Press, 2005; Amilcar Shabazz, *Advancing Democracy: African Americans and the Struggle for Access and Equity in Higher Education in Texas* (Chapel Hill: University of North Carolina Press, 2004); Brian D. Behnken, *Fighting Their Own Battles: Mexican Americans, African Americans, and the Struggle for Civil Rights in Texas* (Chapel Hill: University of North Carolina Press, 2011); Eric Arnesen, *Brotherhoods of Color: Black Railroad Workers and the Struggle for Equality* (Cambridge: Harvard University Press, 2002), 1–13; Steven A. Reich, "Soldiers of Democracy: Black Texans and the Fight for Citizenship, 1917–1921," *Journal of American History* 82, no. 4 (1996): 1478–1504; and Robin D. G. Kelley, *Race Rebels: Politics, Culture and the Black Working Class* (New York: Free Press, 1996).

4. This chapter draws attention to theory four, what scholars Sundiata Keita Cha-Jua and Clarence Lang call the "reperiodization" of the Civil Rights Movement. For some, the movement for Afro-American equality began on the shores of West Africa and slave

ships when kidnapped humans sought to disentangle themselves from the Middle Passage. For others, the fight for racial inclusion originated with colonial or antebellum slavery when African people ran away from their slave homes, sought their loved ones sold away, and resisted their unfortunate lot by breaking tools, slowing down their work, poisoning their masters and mistresses, and mocking whites they encountered on a daily basis. Some see the genesis of modern social equality in the eras of the Emancipation and Reconstruction, when African Americans secured citizenship. Many others, however, associate the civil rights fight with the founding of the National Association for the Advancement of Colored People (NAACP). Many others pinpoint the New Negro Movement, the New Deal, and World War II, whether jointly or separately, as the time of unprecedented African American demands for social justice. For works that examine the concept of long civil rights, first conceptualized by historian Jacqueline Dowd Hall, see Kevin Boyle, "Labor, the Left, and the Long Civil Rights Movement," Social *History* 30, no. 3 (August 2005): 366–72; Judith Stein, "Why American Historians Embrace the Long Civil Rights Movement," *American Communist History* 11, no. 1 (April 2012): 55–58; Sundiata Keita Cha-Jua and Clarence Lang, "The 'Long Movement' as Vampire: Temporal and Spatial Fallacies in Recent Black Freedom Studies, "*The Journal of African American History* 92, no. 2 (Spring 2007): 265–88; Jacqueline Dowd Hall, "Long Civil Rights Movement and the Political Uses of the Past," *Journal of American History* 91, no. 4 (March 2005): 1233–63; Danielle L. McGuire and John Dittmer, ed., *Freedom Rights: New Perspectives on the Civil Rights Movement* (Lexington: University Press of Kentucky, 2011); Eric Arneson, "Reconsidering the 'Long Civil Rights Movement,'" *Historically Speaking* 10, no. 2 (2009): 31–34; and Glenda E. Gilmore, *Defying Dixie: The Racial Roots of Civil Rights, 1919–1950* (New York: W. W. Norton, 2008).

5. U.S. Bureau of the Census, *Twelfth Census of the United States Taken in the Year 1900*, vol. 1, *Population; Population of States and Territories* (Washington, D.C.: Government Printing Office, 1901), 132; U.S. Bureau of the Census, *Negro Population in the United States, 1790–1915* (1918; repr., New York: Arno Press, 1969), 92, 205; U.S. Bureau of the Census, *Fourteenth Census of the United States, 1920*, vol. 2, *Population: General Reports and Analytical Tables* (Washington, D.C.: Government Printing Office, 1923), 354; U.S. Bureau of the Census, *Sixteenth Census of the United States, 1940: Population and Housing*, vol. 2, *Characteristics of the Population* (Washington, D.C.: Government Printing Office, 1943), 1044; *A Report of the Seventeenth Decennial Census, 1950*, vol. 2, pt. 43, 509–10; "A Life Sketch of Dr. M. L. Price," Rev. Moses L. Price Papers, 277: 1, folder 1, Houston Metropolitan Research Center, Houston Public Library, Houston, Texas; Thelma Scott Bryant, interview by author, July 24, 1996, Houston; Lullelia Harrison, oral history interview, March 8, 2000, Houston, Texas, in possession of author; Lullelia Harrison, oral history interview, September 23, 1999, Houston, Texas, in possession of author (hereafter cited as Harrison interviews). Bernadette Pruitt, "The Hayes Family of Third Ward: African American Agency in Houston during the Great Migration, 1900–1941," *Houston History Magazine* 13, no. 2 (2015): 8–12, 46, https://houstonhistorymagazine.org/; Bernadette Pruitt, *The Other Great Migration: The Movement of Rural African Americans to Houston, 1900–1941* (College Station: Texas A&M University Press, 2013), 141–282.

6. Rafael Longoria and Susan Rogers, "The Rurban Horseshoe: Historic Black Neighbor-hoods on the Periphery," *Cite* 73 (Winter 2008), Rice Design Alliance, http://offcite.org/wp-content/uploads/2009/10/Cite_73_Rurban_Horseshoe_LongoriaRogers.pdf; Rafael Longoria and Susan Rogers, *Collaborative Community Design Initiative* (Houston: Gerald D. Hines College of Architecture, University of Houston, 2010). The most significant evidence of this geographic duality—Houston as both a southern city and a southwestern and western city that attracted African American newcomers, according to architects Longoria and Rogers, is best seen in six black communities that surround downtown Houston, working-class vicinities that have been in existence since the early twentieth century. The "horseshoe ring" created by Independence Heights, Acres Homes, Sunnyside, Settegast, Clinton Park, and Houston Gardens, they say, speaks of this urban-rural or "rurban" nexus and points to the durability of racial exclusion, even in the twenty-first century. The original settlers of these communities and other African-descent neighborhoods have nevertheless remained vigilant about their ability to survive structural prejudice through community building.

7. Margaret Houston to Sam Houston, 24 May 1848, letter, Franklin Williams Collection, Sam Houston Memorial Museum, Sam Houston State University, Huntsville, Texas; Manuscript Census, Walker County, 1870, roll M593_1607, Bureau of Census, Record group T1232, from Ancestry.com; Manuscript Census, Walker County, 1880, roll 1607, microfilm pub T1134, record group 29, Bureau of Census, record group M593, from Ancestry.com; U.S. Bureau of the Census, *Nonpopulation Census Schedules for Texas, 1850–1880*, rolls 2–49, microfilm pub T1134, Records of the Bureau of the Census, record group 29, from Ancestry.com, http://search.ancestry.com/; Joe Houston, death certificate, 33206, Texas Department of Health, Bureau of Vital Statistics, Standard Certificate of Death, Crockett, Houston County, Texas, August 15, 1938, from Ancestry.com; Naomi Ledé, *Precious Memories of a Black Socialite: A Narrative of the Life and Times of Constance Houston Thompson* (Houston: D. Armstrong, 1991), 40–106; Kirsten R. Willis, "Reconstruction and the Reorientation of African American Energy in Walker County, Texas" (master's thesis, Syracuse University, 2013), 44–86; Patricia Smith Prather and Jane Clements Monday, *From Slave to Statesman: The Legacy of Joshua Houston, Servant to Sam Houston* (Denton: University of North Texas Press, 1993), 29–175; Thomas H. Kreneck, "Houston, Samuel," in *Handbook of Texas Online*, https://tshaonline.org/handbook/online/articles/fho73; Jane Monday, "Houston, Joshua," in *Handbook of Texas Online*, https://tshaonline.org/handbook/online/articles/fhohq; "Houston, Joshua," in *African American National Biography*, ed. Henry Louis Gates Jr. and Evelyn Brooks Higginbotham (New York: Oxford University Press, 2005), 336–37.

8. David Williams, "A Brief History of St. James Methodist Church," 1934, in possession of author; Barry Crouch, *The Freedmen's Bureau in Texas* (Austin: University of Texas Press, 1995), 20–75; Naomi Ledé, *Samuel W. Houston and His Contemporaries: A Comprehensive History of the Origin, Growth, and Development of the Black Educational Movement in Huntsville and Walker County* (Houston: Pha Green Printing, 1981), 12–77; Naomi W. Ledé, ed., *Pathfinders: A History of the Pioneering Efforts of African Americans—Huntsville, Walker, County, Texas* (Virginia Beach, Va.: Donning

Company, 2004), 37; Ledé, *Precious Memories of a Black Socialite*, 40–106; Prather and Monday, *From Slave to Statesman*, 29–175; "Houston, Joshua"; Paul M. Lucko, "Houston, Samuel Walker," in *Handbook of Texas Online*, https://tshaonline.org/handbook/online/articles/fhobs.

9. Manuscript Census, Walker County, 1870; Freedmen's Bureau Records, Series M1912, reels 23–24, Texas Room, Houston Metropolitan Research Center, Julia Ideson Building, Houston Public Library, Houston, Texas; U.S. Bureau of the Census, *Nonpopulation Census Schedules for Texas, 1850–1880*; Joshua Houston Jr., student transcript, "Prairie View Industrial College, 1882–83," Registrar's Office, Prairie View A&M University, Prairie View, Texas.

10. George B. Orviss, Postmaster, Macedonia, Walker County, 1895, 12.71, *Official Register of the United States, Containing a List of the Officers and Employees in the Civil, Military, and Naval Service Together with a List of Vessels Belonging to the United States, 1863–1959*, from Ancestry.com; "The Rev. George B. Orviss" and "Mrs. George B. (Mary) Orviss," photographs, in Ledé, *Precious Memories of a Black Socialite*, 40; David Williams, "A Brief History of St. James Methodist Church"; Houston Family, 1898, Joshua Houston Family Collection, 437–6, Houston Metropolitan Research Center, Julia Ideson Building, Houston Public Library (hereafter cited as Joshua Houston Family MSS); Cornelia Orviss Houston and Georgia C. Orviss Houston, Houston Family MSS, 437–3.

11. Quoted in Ledé, *Precious Memories of a Black Socialite*, 73.

12. Minutes of the Annual Meeting of the Texas Commission on Interracial Cooperation, November 6, 1926, Texas Commission on Interracial Cooperation Records, RG E-12, box 1, folder 1, Houston Metropolitan Research Center, Houston Public Library, Houston, Texas (hereafter cited as TCIRC, RG E-12); M. W. Dogan to Texas Commission on Interracial Cooperation, November 5. 1926, TCIRC, RG E-12, box 1, folder 1; M. W. Dogan to Texas Commission on Interracial Cooperation, November 5, 1926, TCIRC, RG E-12, box 1, folder 1; Minutes of the Annual Meeting of the Texas Commission on Interracial Cooperation, November 1 and 2, 1929, TCIRC, RG E 12, box 1, folder 1; Minutes of the Annual Meeting of the Texas Commission on Interracial Cooperation, November 3 and 4, 1933, TCIRC, RG E 12, box 1, folder 1; Minutes of the Annual Meeting of the Texas Commission on Interracial Cooperation, December 7 and 8, 1934, TCIRC, RG E 12, box 1, folder 2; Minutes of the Annual Meeting of the Texas Commission on Interracial Cooperation, December 6 and 7, 1940, TCIRC, RG E 12, box 1, folder 2. 49.

13. Quoted in Ledé, *Precious Memories of a Black Socialite*, 73.

14. Ibid., 56–74.

15. Quoted in ibid., 81.

16. Ibid., 46–84.

17. Ibid.

18. Ibid.

19. For more on the events referred to by Constance Houston Thompson, see "Six Negroes Slain for Alleged Plot to Wipe Out Family," *San Antonio Express*, June 1, 1918; "Six

Negroes Die after Battle with Citizens Posse," *San Antonio Express*, June 2, 1918; Christine's Genealogy Website, "Six Negroes Die after Battle with Citizen's Posse," http://ccharity.com/; Ralph Ginzburg, *100 Years of Lynchings* (Baltimore: Black Classic Press, 1988), 269.

20. Quoted in Ledé, *Precious Memories of a Black Socialite*, 71.

21. Ibid.

22. Ibid., 40–106; Prather and Monday, *From Slave to Statesman*, 200–38; Ledé, "Constance Houston Thompson," in *Pathfinders*, 70–72; Ledé, "Hortense Houston Young," in *Pathfinders*, 84–86.

23. Ledé, *Precious Memories of a Black Socialite*, 40–106; Prather and Monday, *From Slave to Statesman*, 200–38; Ledé, "Constance Houston Thompson," in *Pathfinders*, 70–72; Ledé, "Hortense Houston Young," in *Pathfinders*, 84–86.

24. *The Red Book of Houston: A Compendium of Social, Professional, Religious, Educational, and Industrial Interests of Houston's Colored Population* (Houston: Sotex Publishing, 1915); Pruitt, *Other Great Migration*, 141–212; Merline Pitre, *In Struggle against Jim Crow: Lulu B. White and the NAACP, 1900–1957* (College Station: Texas A&M University Press, 1999); Darlene Clark Hine, *Black Victory: The Rise and Fall of the White Primary in Texas* (1979; repr., Columbia: University of Missouri Press, 2003).

25. Pruitt, *The Other Great Migration*, 141–212; Pitre, *In Struggle against Jim Crow*, 24–139; Hine, *Black Victory*, 84–220.

26. Thelma Scott Bryant, *Pioneer Families of Houston (Early 1900s) as Remembered by Thelma Scott Bryant* (Houston, 1991); *Red Book of Houston*; National Urban League, *A Review of the Economic and Cultural Problems of Houston, Texas as They Relate to Conditions of the Negro Population* (New York, 1945), 17; Bryant interview; Harrison interviews; *Who's Who in American Education*, vol. 21, 1963–64, Olee Yates McCullough Papers, 370: 1, Houston Metropolitan Research Center, Julia Ideson Building, Houston Public Library (hereafter cited as Olee Yates McCullough MSS); obituary of Olee Yates McCullough, Olee Yates McCullough MSS, 370: 9; "Precious Memories," autobiographical portrait, Olee Yates McCullough MSS, 370: 9; Historical Context Sheet, Sneed Family Collection, 293–1: 1, Houston Metropolitan Research Center, Houston Public Library (hereafter cited as Sneed Family MSS); Pruitt, *Other Great Migration*.

27. May Childs Nerny to Henry Mims, February 6, 1915, reel 19 of 20, Papers of the National Association for the Advancement of Colored People, part 12: Selected Branch Files, 1913–939, States A: The South, ed. John H. Bracey Jr. and August Meier, Bethesda, Maryland, University Publications of America, M. D. Anderson Library, University of Houston, Houston, Texas (hereafter cited as part 12, reel 19 of 20, Papers of the NAACP); Martha Gruening, "National Association for the Advancement of Colored People—Houston: An NAACP Investigation," *The Crisis: A Record of the Darker Races*, November 15, 1917, 14–19; Luther Stullivan, interview by author, July 23, 1996, Houston.

28. Grace Elizabeth Hale, *Making Whiteness: The Culture of Segregation in the South, 1890–1940* (New York: Vintage Books, 1999), 1–88; Pruitt, *Other Great Migration*,

141–82; Botson, *Labor, Civil Rights, and the Hughes Tool Company*, 33–108; Hine, *Black Victory*, 135–94.

29. Houston at this time sat inside a largely rural county—Harris County—that consisted of farms. Blacks, especially in the early twentieth century, bought plots of land on the outskirts of the city and built homes a few miles from downtown Houston or the city proper.

30. Rutherford B. H. Yates Sr. and Paul L. Yates, *The Life and Efforts of Jack Yates* (Houston: Texas Southern University Press, 1985), 4–13; Olee Yates McCullough, "Yates, John Henry," in *Handbook of Texas Online*, https://tshaonline.org/handbook/online/articles/fya07; Louise Passey Maxwell, "Freedmantown: The Origins of a Black Neighborhood in Houston, 1865–1880," in *Bricks without Straw: A Comprehensive History of African Americans in Texas*," ed. David A. Williams (Austin: Eakin Press, 1997), 139–52; Scott L. Stabler, "Free Men Come to Houston: Blacks During Reconstruction," *Houston Review of History and Culture* 3 (Fall 2005): 40–43, 73–76; "Allen, Richard," in *Handbook of Texas Online*, http://tshaonline.org/handbook/online/articles/fal24; Andrew Webster Jackson, *A Sure Foundation and a Sketch of Negro Life in Texas* (Houston: Webster-Richardson, 1940); "Biography of J. B. Bell, Capitalist," in *Red Book of Houston*, 80–84; Audrey Crawford, "'To Protect, to Feed, and to Give Momentum to Every Effort': African American Club-women in Houston, 1880–1910," *Houston Review of History and Culture* 1 (Fall 2003): 15–23; and Pruitt, *Other Great Migration*.

31. Pruitt, *Other Great Migration*.

32. Maceo Crenshaw Dailey Jr., *When the Saints Go Hobbling In: Emmett Jay Scott and the Booker T. Washington Movement* (El Paso: Sweet Earth Flying Press, 2015); Maceo C. Dailey, "Neither 'Uncle Tom' nor 'Accommodationist': Booker T. Washington, Emmett Jay Scott, and Constructionalism," *Atlanta History: A History of Georgia and the South* 38, no. 4 (January 1995): 20–33. Dailey coined the term "constructionalism" for the strategic political ideology deemed necessary for African-descent Americans who, in the years of violent social control, disfranchisement, and racial segregation, needed a socioeconomic and sociopolitical tool—public deference—that would reverberate into real benefits for the masses of people. This scheme would work best at the time of what Rayford Logan calls the nadir of African American life. Logan, *The Betrayal of the Negro: From Rutherford B. Hayes to Woodrow Wilson* (Cambridge, Mass.: Da Capo Press, 1965), xiv, 79–96.

33. Jackson, *A Sure Foundation*; Pruitt, *Other Great Migration*.

34. Emmett J. Scott, introduction to *Red Book of Houston*, 2.

35. Ibid., 1.

36. Ibid.; Jackson, *A Sure Foundation*, 219–20; Ira Bryant, *Houston's Negro Schools* (Houston: Informer, 1935), 169–70; Nancy Ruth Eckols Bessent, "The Publisher: A Biography of Carter W. Wesley" (master's thesis, University of Texas, 1981), 3–5 ; Crawford, "To Protect, to Feed, and to Give Momentum."

37. Pruitt, introduction to *Other Great Migration*, 3–5.

38. Pruitt, *Other Great Migration*.

39. Ibid., 24–50.

40. Bureau of the Census, *Negro Population in the United States, 1790–1915* (1918, repr., New York: Arno Press, 1969), 78; Bureau of the Census, *Fourteenth Census of the United States, Taken in the Year 1920: Population*, vol. 2. *Population: General Reports and Analytical Tables* (Washington, D.C.: Government Printing Office, 1923), 639; John M. Barry, "After the Deluge: In the Wake of Hurricane Katrina, A Writer Looks Back at the Repercussions of Another Great Disaster—the Mississippi Flood of 1927," *Smithsonian*, November 2005, http://www.smithsonianmagazine.com/issues/2005/november/pom.php; and *Fatal Flood: A Story of Greed, Power, and Race*, directed and produced by Chana Gazit, *American Experience*, 2001.

41. John S. MacDonald and Leatrice D. MacDonald, "Chain Migration, Ethnic Neighborhood Formation and Social Networks," *Millbank Memorial Fund* 42 (1964): 82–97; Earl Lewis, "Expectations, Economic Opportunities, and Life in the Industrial Age: Black Migration to Norfolk, Virginia, 1910–1945," in *The Great Migration in Historical Perspective: New Dimensions of Race, Class, and Gender*, ed. Joe William Trotter (Bloomington: Indiana University Press, 1991), 24; *Encyclopedia of the Great Black Migration*, s.v., "Chain Migration" (by Bernadette Pruitt), vol. 1, edited by Steven A. Reich (Westport, Connecticut: Greenwood Press, 2005), 168-70; Luther Stullivan, *Roots of the Stullivan Family* (Houston, 1981), 1–10; Luther Stullivan, interview by author, July 23, 1996, Houston.

42. Ellis Elizabeth Newell, "The Life and Works of C. F. Richardson" (senior thesis, Houston College for Negroes, 1941), 5; "Colored Americans in Walker County Victims of Wholesale Depredations," *Houston Informer*, June 7, 1919; "Dyer Mob-Violence Killed," *Houston Informer*, June 11, 1919; Howard Jones, *The Red Diary: A Chronological History of Black Americans in Houston and Some Neighboring Harris County Communities* (Austin, Tex.: Nortex Press, 1991), 54–55, 61; "News and Views from Texas Towns," *Houston Informer*, June 10, 1933; "The Catholic Circle," *Houston Informer*, November 24, 1934; Pruitt, *Other Great Migration*.

43. Biographical note, C. F. Richardson Papers, 1457, Houston Metropolitan Research Center, Julia Ideson Building, Houston Public Library (hereafter cited as C. F. Richardson Sr. MSS).

44. Clifton Richardson, "Colored Americans in Walker County Victims of Wholesale Depredations," *Houston Informer*, June 7, 1919.

45. Biographical note, C. F. Richardson Sr. MSS; "C. F. Richardson Sr. Family Home on Robin Street," photograph identification sheet, C. F. Richardson MSS, 1457:0007, http://digital.houstonlibrary.org/cdm/singleitem/collection/archival/id/296; Clifton Richardson Jr., interview by Louis Marchiafava, transcript, Houston Oral History Project, http://digital.houstonlibrary.net/oral-history/cliff-richardson.php.

46. "The Rev. George B. Orviss" and "Mrs. George B. (Mary) Orviss"; "National Council of Negro Women," circa 1940s, Joshua Houston Family MSS, 0437:0001; "The Wedding Party Takes a Group Photo at The Houston Place," Fifth Ward, Houston, October 1928, Joshua Houston Family MSS 0437:0022; "Young, Hortense Houston," Notable Kentucky African Americans, University of Kentucky Libraries, http://nkaa.uky.edu/; "Young, Coleman Milton III," ibid.; K. Dawn Rutledge-Jones, "Minority Engineer

Watched Evolution of Industry," *Nashville Business Journal*, February 20, 1998; "Oral-History: Yvonne Clark and Irene Sharpe," *Engineering and Technology History Wiki*, http://ethw.org/Oral-History:Yvonne_Clark_and_Irene_Sharpe; "Constance Houston Thompson," in Ledé, *Pathfinders*, 70–72; Ledé, *Precious Memories*; Kreneck, "Houston, Samuel."

47. "B. G. Gaffney to Mrs. Leona Walls, July 22, 1988," in *Independence Heights, Texas: The First Black City in Texas, 1915–1928*, ed. Vivian Hubbard Seals (V. H. Seals, 1986), unpaged; "The Wright Company," in ibid.; J. Spencer, "Our Neighbor," in ibid.

48. J. Spencer, "Our Neighbor.

49. Ibid.; author interview with Kimberly McCullough, June 25, 2017, Houston. McCullough is the great-great-great niece of Independence Heights mayor Arthur McCullough Sr. Using a tractor, the municipality shelled 31st 1/2 Street (nicknamed Short Shell) and 32nd Street over the basic mud roads and maintained these shelled thoroughfares by grading the roads each month or every other month. Some Fourth Ward roads also went through this process, which goes back to antiquity throughout the world. In Texas, Indigenous peoples used oyster shells and clamshells for a variety of purposes including construction of dwellings. In the early twentieth century, Texas shelling grew, and dredging firms used the seashells to produce lime. Businesses invested in shell-based lime to manufacture paper, soda ash, magnesium hydroxide, and concrete for roads. Because of its close location to the Gulf of Mexico and an almost unlimited abundance of shell reefs along the coast, Independence Heights could easily access the important resource. For road construction, limestone aggregate, for which a major component was oyster shells, served as an important component of concrete. Independence Heights could not afford to pave most of its streets with oyster shells even with a sizable abundance of oyster reefs. White-owned manufacturing firms dominated the market, and the state taxed this as a way of generating revenue. For more on the history of oyster shelling and uses of shells in Texas, see Edwin Doran Jr., "Shell Roads in Texas," *Geographical Review* 55, no. 2 (April 1965): 223–40.

50. Seals, *Independence Heights, Texas*.

51. Quoted in ibid.

52. Vivian Hubbard Seals, "Oliphant Lockwood Hubbard Sr., 1880–1968," in *Independence Heights, Texas*, 1–10; Vivian Hubbard Seals, interview by author, May 17, 1999, Houston; Seals, *Independence Heights, Texas*.

53. Hazel Young, interview by author, Houston, Texas, August 7, 1996; Bryant interview; Harrison interviews; Bryant, *Pioneer Families of Houston*, 437–54; Stullivan, *Roots of the Stullivan Family*, 1–10; Stullivan interview; Diana J. Kleiner, "Fifth Ward, Houston," in *Handbook of Texas Online*, https://tshaonline.org/handbook/online/articles/hpfhk; Jones, *Red Diary*, 67; Clyde McQueen, *Black Churches in Texas: A Guide to Historic Congregations* (College Station: Texas A&M University Press, 2000), 156; Howard O. Beeth and Cary D. Wintz, "Economic and Social Development in Black Houston during the Era of Segregation," in *Black Dixie: Afro-Texan History and Culture in Houston* (College Station: Texas A&M University Press, 1992), 87–88.

54. Neil Sapper, "Black Urban Texas Culture: A Lone Star Renaissance," *Red River Valley Historical Review* 6, no 1 (1981): 69–73; Milton Larkin, interview by Louis Marchiafava, tape recording, January 5, 1988, Milton Larkin Collection, 252: 1, Houston Metropolitan Research Center, Julia Ideson Building, Houston Public Library; Lorenzo Thomas, "Milt Larkin: Houston Jazz Bandleader," paper presented at the Texas State Historical Association Annual Meeting, Austin, March 5, 1998; Lorenzo Thomas, *Don't Deny My Name: Words and Music and the Black Intellectual Tradition*, edited by Aldon Lynn Nielsen (Ann Arbor: University of Michigan Press, 2008), 64–73; Rick Mitchell, "Houston Jazz Legend Larkin Dies at 85," *Houston Chronicle*, August 31, 1996; Roger Wood, *Down in Houston: Bayou City Blues* (Austin: University of Texas Press, 2012), 82, 85; Dave Oliphant, "Jazz," in *Handbook of Texas Online*, https://tshaonline.org/handbook/online/articles/xbjyb; Alan Govenar, "Blues," in *Handbook of Texas Online*, https://tshaonline.org/handbook/online/articles/xbb01; Glen Alyn, "Fight, Flight, or Blues: Mance Lipscomb, Musician, Farmer, Storyteller, Philosopher, Legend, Gatekeeper of the Centuries," 1995, Lipscomb-Alyn Collection, 2.325: A112, Dolph Briscoe Center for American History, University of Texas, Austin; Illinois Jacquet, interview by Louis Marchiafava and Charles Stephenson, tape recording, Houston, Texas, June 1, 1990, Illinois Jacquet Collection, 403: 1, Houston Metropolitan Research Center, Julia Ideson Building, Houston Public Library.

55. Marie Lee Phelps, "Frenchtown," *Houston Post*, May 22, 1955; David Kaplan, "Houston's Creole Quarter," *Houston Post*, March 19, 1989; Patricia Smith Prather, "A Unique Houston Neighborhood Called Frenchtown," *Houston Chronicle*, September 15, 1986; Cyprian Davis, *The History of Black Catholics in the United States* (Crossroad Publishing, 1995), 238–39, 245; Robert C. Giles, "Our Mother of Mercy Church, Houston," in *125th Anniversary: Diocese of Galveston-Houston, 1847–1972* (Houston: Diocese of Galveston-Houston, 1972), 141–42; Robert C. Giles, "St. Nicholas Church, Houston," in *125th Anniversary: Diocese of Galveston-Houston, 1847–1972*, 104–6; Kaplan, "Houston's Creole Quarter"; Raymond Lewis, interview by author, February 14, 1998, Houston; "St. Joseph's Society of the Sacred Heart, Inc., Parish Annual Report by Year, St. Nicholas," Archives, Diocese of Galveston-Houston, Houston; Frances Jerome Woods, *Marginality and Identity: A Colored Creole Family through Ten Generations* (Baton Rouge: Louisiana State University Press, 1972), 20–22; Carl A. Brasseaux, Keith P. Fontenot, and Claude F. Oubre, *Creoles of Color in the Bayou County* (Jackson: University Press of Mississippi, 1994), xi; Kathy Russell-Cole, Midge Wilson, and Ronald E. Hall, *The Color Complex: Politics of Skin Color in a New Millennium*, 2nd ed. (New York: Anchore, 2013), 2–7, 16–18.

56. Bryant interview; Bryant, *Pioneer Families of Houston*; Thelma Scott Bryant, *Our Journey through Houston and US History*, 2nd ed. (Houston, 1997); "Funeral Service: Mrs. Jennie B. Covington," Dr. Benjamin Covington MSS, 170: 1, folder 1, Houston Metropolitan Research Center, Houston Public Library, Houston, Texas (hereafter cited as Covington MSS); John S. Gray III, "Covington, Benjamin Jessie," in *Handbook of Texas Online*, https://tshaonline.org/handbook/online/articles/fcocp; Jean Walsh, "Dr. Covington, at 90, Is Still Practicing," *Houston Post*, March 12, 1961; Henry

Coleman, interview by author, February 13, 1998. Ira Bryant's publications include *Andrew Jackson Young, Mr. Ambassador: United States Ambassador to the United Nations* (Houston: Armstrong, 1979).

57. Betty T. Chapman, "Old City Wards Developed Unique Economic and Political Identities," *Houston Business Journal*, March 15–21, 1988; Betty T. Chapman, "Fifth Ward: Ethnic Melting Pot and Industrial Business District," *Houston Business Journal*, n.d., in Houston—Subdivisions—Wards, Vertical Files, Texas Room, Julia Ideson Building, Houston Public Library; Kleiner, "Fifth Ward, Houston"; Arnoldo De León, *Ethnicity in the Sunbelt: Mexican Americans in Houston* (Houston: Center for Mexican Americans Studies, University of Houston, 1989), 22–31; James L. Kessler, "Jews," in *Handbook of Texas Online*, https://tshaonline.org/handbook/online/articles/pxj01; Jan L. Perkowski and Jan Maria Wozniak, "Poles," in *Handbook of Texas Online*, https://tshaonline.org/handbook/online/articles/plp01; A. Alexander, *Houston Street Guide* (Houston: J. M. Kelsen, 1913); *Houston Northeast*, 1922 map, Historical Maps of Texas Cities, Map Collection, Perry-Castañeda Library, University of Texas Libraries, University of Texas at Austin; *Polk's Houston City Directory* (Houston: R. L. Polk, 1917); McQueen, *Black Churches in Texas*, 151–57.

58. Pruitt, *Other Great Migration*, 95–212, 223–50.

59. Jones, *Red Diary*, 72, 81–98; Thomas, Jessie O., *A Study of the Social Welfare Status of Negroes in Houston, Texas* (Houston: Webster-Richardson, 1929), 68–69; Theda Skoepol and Jennifer Lynn Oser, "Organization Despite Adversity: The Organization and Development of African American Fraternal Associations," *Social Science History* 28, no. 3 (2004): 367–477; Malone, Cheryl Knott. "Autonomy and Accommodation: Houston's Colored Carnegie Library, 1907–1922," *Libraries & Culture* 34, no. 2 (1999): 95–112; Merah Steven Stuart, *An Economic Detour: A History of Insurance in the Lives of American Negroes* (1940; repr., College Park, Md.: McGrath, 1969), 11–34, 190–94; James M. SoRelle, "The Emergence of Black Business in Houston, Texas: A Study of Race and Ideology," in *Black Dixie: Afro-Texan History and Culture in Houston*, ed. Howard Beeth and Cary D. Wintz (College Station: Texas A&M University Press, 1992), 108; Crawford, "To Protect, to Feed, and to Give Momentum," 15–17.

60. *Red Book of Houston*, 96–98; Alwyn Barr, *Black Texans: A History of African-Americans in Texas, 1528–1995*, 2nd ed. (Norman: University of Oklahoma Press, 1996), 106–7; Crawford, "To Protect, to Feed, and to Give Momentum," 15–17; Thomas, *Study of the Social Welfare Status of Negroes*, 68–69; Jones, *Red Diary*, 48–99; Bryant, *Pioneer Families of Houston*, 7; Skocpol and Oser, "Organization Despite Adversity," 377; "'Ancient Order of Pilgrims,' 300 W. Dallas," in "Early Architecture of Houston," http://www.sloanegallery.com/newpage44.htm.

61. Crawford, "To Protect, to Feed, and to Give Momentum," 15–17; Lorenzo Greene, *Selling Black History for Carter G. Woodson: A Diary, 1930–1933*, edited and with an introduction by Arvarh E. Strickland (Columbia: University of Missouri Press, 1996), 124–28; Ruthe Winegarten, *Black Texas Women: 150 Years of Trial and Triumph* (Austin: University of Texas Press, 1995), 186–87; Pitre, *In Struggle against Jim Crow*, 134.

62. "Minutes, Knights of Phythias, Court of Calanthe, Omega Tent #26, 1952," Helen G. Perry Family Collection, 276, box 1, folder 3, Houston Metropolitan Research Center, Julia Ideson Building, Houston Public Library (hereafter cited as Perry Family MSS); "Club Matinee, Lyons Avenue, 5th Ward, Houston, Members of the Princes of Omar, Court of Calanthe," Perry Family MSS, 276, box 2, folder 1–R54; Greene, *Selling Black History for Carter G. Woodson*, 124–28; Winegarten, *Black Texas Women*, 186–88; Pitre, *In Struggle against Jim Crow*, 134.

63. Mary M. Standifer, "Covington, Jennie Belle Murphy," in *Handbook of Texas Online*, https://tshaonline.org/handbook/online/articles/fcoyp; "Funeral Service: Mrs. Jennie B. Covington" and "Seventeen Years with the YWCA in Houston," newspaper clippings, Covington MSS, 170; Bryant, *Houston's Negro Schools*, 58–63; Shaw, "Black Club Women and the Creation of the National Association of Colored Women," 10–25; Rufus E. Clement, "Educational Programs for the Improvement of Race Relations: Interracial Committees," *Journal of Negro Education* 13, no. 3 (1944), 316–20; Pamela Faith Wille, "More Than Classes in Swimming and Making Hats: The YWCA and Social Reform in Houston, Texas, 1907–1977" (PhD diss., Texas Tech University, 2004), 54–91; Alice Dunbar-Nelson, "Negro Women in War Work," in *Scott's Official History of the American Negro in the World War*, ed. Emmett J. Scott (Washington: Emmett J. Scott, 1919), http://net.lib.byu.edu/estu/wwi/comment/scott/ScottTC.htm; Historical Context Sheet, Sneed Family MSS ; Harrison interview; "History of the Blue Triangle Branch," Houston Young Women's Christian Association Collection, RG F 017, box 1, folder 5, Houston Metropolitan Research Center, Julia Ideson Building, Houston Public Library; "YWCA Chronological Highlights and Leaders" [Houston], ibid., box 1, folder 3; Bryant interview; Bryant, *Pioneer Families of Houston*, 7.

64. "Jennie Belle Murphy Covington"; "Funeral Service: Mrs. Jennie B. Covington"; "Seventeen Years with the YWCA in Houston, Covington MSS; Agency History, Finding Aid, Harris County Social Services, CR08, Harris County Archives, Houston, Texas, http://www.cclerk.hctx.net/harriscountyarchives/doc/Records/FA-Social%20Services1CR08.pdf (accessed October 7, 2017); Charles W. Leavens, "Historical Development of the Harris County Welfare Department in Houston, Texas" (master's thesis, Sam Houston State University, 1971), 19–25.

65. Photo identification sheet, "Youth Council Competition Sponsor by the Houston Chapter of the National Association for the Advancement of Colored People, 1946," Perry Family MSS, 276–2: R63; "Funeral Service: Mrs. Jennie B. Covington"; Winegarten, *Black Texas Women*, 97; "Who's Who in American Education," Olee Yates McCullough MSS, 370: 1, folder 9; Crawford, "To Protect, to Feed, and to Give Momentum to Every Effort,'" 15–23; "A Musical Panorama, 42nd Anniversary of the Married Ladies Social, Art and Charity Club," Mary and General Jones Johnson Collection, MSS 119, box 4—Programs, Houston Metropolitan Research Center, Julia Ideson Building, Houston Public Library; Seals interview; photo identification sheet, Alpha Kappa Alpha Sorority, Inc., Alpha Kappa Omega Alumnae Chapter, circa 1942, Sneed Family MSS 293–26; photo identification sheet, Members of the Houston Chapter of The Links, Inc., Sneed Family MSS, 293–33; Ledé, *Precious Memories of a Black Socialite*, 124–66; Ledé, "Constance Houston Thompson," in *Pathfinders*,

70–72; Ledé, "Hortense Houston Young," in Pathfinders, 82–84; Bryant, *Pioneer Families of Houston*; Pitre, *In Struggle against Jim Crow*, 88; Teresa Tomkins-Walsh, "Thelma Scott Bryant: Memories of a Century in Houston's Third Ward," *Houston Review of History and Culture* 1, no. 1 (2003): 53–54; "Biographical Directory of Zeta Women, Zeta Women Bicentennial, 1976," Zeta Amicae Collection, RG E 50, box 2, Houston Metropolitan Research Center, Julia Ideson Building Houston Public Library; "Zeta Phi Betas Stage Their 1st Public Affair," *Houston Informer*, May 12, 1934; Harrison interviews; "Hundreds Honor Lifelong Civil-Rights Fight," Christia Adair Collection, MSS, 109, box 4, folder 1, Houston Metropolitan Research Center, Julia Ideson Building, Houston Public Library.

66. Thomas, *Study of the Social Welfare Status of Negroes*, 72–77; National Urban League, *Review of the Economic and Cultural Problems of Houston*, 160–65; Barr, *Black Texans*, 165–66; W. H. Logan, "Progress of Negro Churches in Houston since Emancipation or the Civil War," in *Red Book of Houston*, 21–23; Rev. Lights, "Brief Sketch of Houston Baptists," in Red *Book of Houston*, 24–25; Karen Kossie-Chernyshev, "A 'Grand Old Church' Rose in the East: The Church of God in Christ (COGIC) in East Texas," *East Texas Historical Journal* 31 (Winter 2003), 26–33; Gary B. McGee, "William Seymour and the Azusa Street Revival," *Enrichment Journal: A Journal for Pentecostal Ministry, Assemblies of God* (Fall 1999), http://web.archive.org/web/20160304190631/http://enrichmentjournal.ag.org/199904/026_azusa.cfm; Cecil M. Robeck Jr., "Azusa Street Revival," in *Dictionary of Pentecostal and Charismatic Movements*, ed. Stanley M. Burgess and Gary B. McGee (Grand Rapids, Mich.: Zondervan, 1988), 31–36; Karen Lynell Kossie, "The Move Is On: African American Pentecostals/ Charismatics in the Southwest" (PhD diss., Rice University, 1998), 50–57, 60–61, 71–82. The term "shotgun houses" usually describes small row houses built for working-class and poor families at the turn of the century. The wood-frame houses, very common in Houston's older neighborhoods like Third Ward, were one room wide and comprised just two or three rooms, including the kitchen. They rarely provided indoor plumbing. People compared them to a shotgun barrel because they were so narrow. See Dorothy Knox Houghton, *Houston's Forgotten Heritage: Landscape, Houses, Interiors, 1824–1914* (Houston: Rice University Press, 1991), 145; Robert C. Giles, "St. Nicholas Church, Houston," in *125th Anniversary: Diocese of Galveston-Houston, 1847–1972* (Houston: Diocese of Galveston-Houston, 1972), 104–6; Peter E. Hogan, "The Catholic Church and African Americans in Texas" (paper presented at the Texas Catholic Historical Society, Austin, 1993), 1–2, in possession of author; Davis, *The History of Black Catholics*, 238–39; Robert C. Giles, Curtis, M. Dowell, and Vivian J. Zermeno, "Josephites Close Centennial Year," in *125th Anniversary: Diocese of Galveston-Houston, 1847–1972*; Giles et al., "Josephites Have Logged 90 Years in the Diocese," supplement to the *Texas Catholic Herald*, September 10, 1993 ; Prather, "A Unique Houston Neighborhood Called Frenchtown"; Brasseaux, Fontenot, and Oubre, *Creoles of Color in the Bayou Country*, 115, 117–20; Woods, *Marginality and Identity*, 44; Giles, "Our Mother of Mercy Church," 141–42; Kaplan, "Houston's Creole Quarter"; Raymond Lewis interview. Although Thomas's study puts the number of black churches at 95, Barr gives a higher number for the year 1930: 160. It is not likely

that sixty-five churches sprang up in the city between 1929 and 1930. In his work, Thomas probably omitted church services held in homes. It is also possible that, given Thomas's bias against smaller congregations, he simply ignored numbers of storefront churches and ad hoc gatherings. On the other hand, Barr does not reveal his sources, making it difficult to corroborate his higher number.

67. "A Service of Christian Worship in Memory of Sister Kathleen Stewart, Saturday, October 10, 1981," obituary, in possession of author.

68. Pruitt, *Other Great Migration*, 116–17.

69. Jackson, *A Sure Foundation*, 116–17; Bryant, *Pioneer Families of Houston*, 9–56; Bryant, *Houston's Negro Schools*, 115–20.

70. Jackson, *A Sure Foundation*, 116–17; Bryant, *Pioneer Families of Houston*, 9–56; Bryant, *Houston's Negro Schools*, 64–93, 115–20.

71. Jackson, *A Sure Foundation*, 116–17; Bryant, *Pioneer Families of Houston*, 9–56; Bryant, *Houston's Negro Schools*, 64–93; 115–20.

72. Jackson, *A Sure Foundation*, 116–17; Bryant, *Pioneer Families of Houston*, 9–56; and Bryant, *Houston's Negro Schools*, 115–20; Bernadette Pruitt, "Codwell, John Elihue Sr.," in *Handbook of Texas Online*, https://tshaonline.org/handbook/online/articles/fcoen; Debbie Z. Harwell, "William S. Holland: A Mighty Lion for Yates High School," *Houston History Magazine* 8, no. 1 (2008), https://houstonhistorymagazine.org/wp-content/uploads/2010/12/vol-8-no-1-Holland.pdf, 1–5, 50; Thurman W. Robins, *Requiem for a Classic: Thanksgiving Turkey Day Classic* (Bloomington, Ind.: Author House, 2011), 1–65; *Wheatley High School Anniversary Commemorative Book* (Houston, 2006).

73. Pruitt, "Codwell, John Ellue Sr."; Harwell, "William S. Holland," 1–5, 50; Robins, *Requiem for a Classic*, 1–38.

74. Thomas, *A Study of the Social Welfare Status of Negroes*, 30–51; "The Emergence of a Black Neighborhood: Houston's Fourth Ward, 1865–1915," in *Urban Texas: Politics and Development*, ed. Char Miller and Heywood Sanders (College Station: Texas A&M University Press, 1990), 106; Bryant, *Pioneer Families of Houston*, 10–13; Bryant interview; *Red Book of Houston*, 170; Mary Jane Schier, "Golden Anniversary of Black Hospital's Founding Tonight," *Houston Post*, October 30, 1975"; Standifer, "Covington, Jennie Belle Murphy"; Gray, "Covington, Benjamin Jesse"; "Funeral Service: Mrs. Jennie B. Covington"; Walsh, "Dr. Covington, at 90, Is Still Practicing"; "Seventeen Years with the YWCA in Houston"; "Marian Anderson to Be Guest of Dr. and Mrs. B. J. Covington," Covington MSS, 170: 1, folder 1; Mr. Read to Dr. and Mrs. B. J. Covington, "John Hope Memorial Fund Committee," Covington MSS, 170: 1, folder 4; Alwyn Barr, "Lone Star State Medical, Dental, and Pharmaceutical Association," in *Handbook of Texas Online*, https://tshaonline.org/handbook/online/articles/sa101; John S. Gray III, "Majors, Monroe Alpheus," in *Handbook of Texas Online*, https://tshaonline.org/handbook/online/articles/fmacq.

75. A. Fletcher, M.D., to Whom It May Concern, October 30, 1923, Houston Negro Hospital, 1923–25, Houston Negro Hospital, Joseph Stephen Cullinan Family Papers, 69, box 22, folder 1, Houston Metropolitan Research Center, Julia Ideson Building,

Houston Public Library (hereafter cited as Houston Negro Hospital, Joseph S. Cullinan Family MSS); O. M. Terrell to Mr. J. S. Cullinan, 30 October 1923, Houston Negro Hospital, 1923–25, Joseph S. Cullinan Family MSS 69, box 22, folder 1; "Houston Negro Hospital Offered to the City: Unknown Philanthropist Donates $75,000 through Dr. Slaughter," *Houston Post-Dispatch*, January 1, 1925; Oscar F. Holcombe to Mr. J. S. Cullinan, 24 January 1925, Houston Negro Hospital, Joseph S. Cullinan MSS 69, box 22, folder 1; "Houston's Union Hospital (1900–1926, Section 8)," in *To Bear Fruit for Our Race: A History of African-American Physicians in Houston*, Center for Public History, University of Houston, http://classweb.uh.edu/cph/tobearfruit/story_1900-1926_section08.html; Betty L. Martin, "Fourth Ward Freedmen's Town Minister's Home Gets Historical Marker," *Houston Chronicle*, April 2, 2009; Bryant, Pioneer Families of Houston, 10–13, 55; *Red Book of Houston*, 171; Wintz, "The Emergence of a Black Neighborhood," 106; Schier, "Golden Anniversary of Black Hospital's Founding Tonight"; Walsh, "Dr. Covington, at 90, Is Still Practicing"; Dan Gerig, "Joseph Stephen Cullinan and the Houston Negro Hospital, 1925–1937" (paper presented at the East Texas Historical Association Fall Meeting, September 25, 2008, Nacogdoches, Texas).

76. "16 Dead—22 Injured from Riot," *Houston Press*, August 24, 1917; "Martial Law Declared—Result of Riot Started by Negro Regulars Who Mutinied, Fired Upon Their Officers and Left Camp, Slaying 13, Wounding 19: One Officer of Illinois Regiment Slain and 9 Policemen Are Dead or Wounded," *Houston Post*, August 24, 1917; "17 Killed; 21 Are Injured in Wild Night," *Houston Chronicle*, August 24, 1917; "Murderous Riot Replaces Negro Watermelon Party," *Houston Chronicle*, August 24, 1917; "The Effects of Martial Law: Mad Riot Clouds Disappear before Shining Guns of Regulars," *Houston Chronicle*, August 25, 1917; "Peace Restored throughout the Riot Zone," Houston Chronicle, August 26, 1917; Robert V. Haynes, *A Night of Violence: The Houston Riot of 1917* (Baton Rouge: Louisiana State University Press, 1977), 143–75, 208–96; Garna Christian, *Black Soldiers in Jim Crow Texas, 1899–1917* (College Station: Texas A&M University Press, 1996), 152–72; C. Calvin Smith, "The Houston Riot of 1917, Revisited," *Houston Review* 13: 96–102.

77. Courts-martial: Quintard Taylor, *In Search of the Racial Frontier: African Americans in the West, 1528–1990* (New York: W. W. Norton, 1998), 181.The data for executions and life sentences vary. Most book sources say that nineteen, twenty-eight, or twenty-nine men were executed and sixty-three were sentenced to life terms. New Negro Movement: Jeffrey B. Perry, "Harrison, Hubert Henry," in *Africana*, vol. 3, 2nd ed., ed. Henry Louis Gates (New York: Oxford University Press, 2005), 171–73; Alain Locke, *The New Negro: An Interpretation* (1925; repr., New York: Simon & Schuster, 1992), 3–18. For a comprehensive list of works about the New Negro Movement, including the evolution of the term, see Franklin and Higginbotham, *From Slavery to Freedom*, 660–62; *Encyclopedia of the Harlem Renaissance*, 2 vols., ed. Cary D. Wintz and Paul Finkelman (New York: Routledge, 2004); "New Negro," *Encyclopedia of the Great Black Migration*, vol. 2, 614. Alain Locke (first black Rhodes Scholar to study at Oxford University, Howard University professor of philosophy, and

noted scholar and artist of the Harlem Renaissance) popularized the use of the term "New Negro" in 1925 to describe a cultural and social movement among blacks after World War I. The "New Negro" combined Booker T. Washington's self-help and accommodation philosophy, Marcus Garvey's Pan-Africanism, W. E. B. Du Bois's push for social equality, educational equity, and political mobilization with sound economic independence and interdependence. See Cary D. Wintz, *Black Culture and the Harlem Renaissance* (Houston: Rice University Press, 1988), 1, 30–31; Cary D. Wintz, *The Harlem Renaissance: A History and an Anthology* (Upper Saddle River, N.J., 2003), 1–18; William M. Tuttle, *Race Riot: Chicago in the Red Summer of 1919* (1970; repr., Urbana: University of Illinois Press, 1996), 2–41; *Red Book of Houston*; Jackson, *A Sure Foundation*; Jon Ralph Wilson, "Origins: The Houston NAACP, 1915–1918" (master's thesis, University of Houston, 2005); Jones, *Red Diary*; Beeth and Wintz, *Black Dixie*.

78. For specific examples of African American political mobilization in Houston in the early twentieth century, see "Constitution and By-Laws, Civic Betterment League of Houston and Harris County, 1918," reel 19 of 20, Papers of the NAACP; "Miscellaneous," Rev. Lee Haywood Simpson & Pleasant Hill Baptist Church Collection, 239: 6, folder 6, Houston Metropolitan Research Center, Julia Ideson Building, Houston Public Library; "Membership Cards, Third Ward Civic Club, 1946–1948," Harrison Family Collection, 182: 1, file 10, Houston Metropolitan Research Center, Julia Ideson Building, Houston Public Library, (hereafter cited as Harrison Family MSS, 182); Director of Branches to E. O. Smith, June 19, 1923, part 12, reel 19 of 20, Papers of the NAACP; Wilson, "Origins: The Houston NAACP, 1915–1918"; "Membership Cards, NAACP, 1945, 1967," Harrison Family MSS, 182: 1, file 9; Stullivan, *Roots of the Stullivan Family*; Stullivan interview; "Constance Houston Thompson and National Council of Negro Women Photograph, circa 1940s," Joshua Houston Family MSS, 437: 1; William L. Sherrill, "We the Negro," Opinions, *Houston Informer*, January 17, 1942; "Biography of J. B. Bell, Capitalist," in *Red Book of Houston*, 81–85; Jackson, *A Sure Foundation*; Pitre, *In Struggle against Jim Crow*, 13–24; Hine, *Black Victory*, 95–103.

79. Pruitt, *Other Great Migration*, 142–87.

80. Ledé, *Precious Memories of a Black Socialite*, 40; "National Council of Negro Women," circa 1940s, Joshua Houston Family MSS, 0437:0001; "The Wedding Party Takes a Group Photo at the Houston Place"; "Constance Houston Thompson," in *Pathfinders*, 70–72; Kreneck, "Houston, Samuel."

81. "Young, Hortense Houston"; "Young, Coleman Milton III"; K. Dawn Rutledge-Jones, "Minority Engineer Watched Evolution of Industry," *Nashville Business Journal*, February 20, 1998; "Oral-History: Yvonne Clark and Irene Sharpe."

82. Ledé, *Precious Memories of a Black Socialite*, 40; "National Council of Negro Women," circa 1940s, Joshua Houston Family MSS, 0437:0001; "The Wedding Party Takes a Group Photo at the Houston Place"; "Constance Houston Thompson," in *Pathfinders*, 70–72.

83. Pruitt, *Other Great Migration*.

2 The Las Vegas Press and the Westside

The Moulin Rouge Agreement

Shared History Program, University of Nevada, Reno

This oral history with Lubertha Johnson documents one black professional woman's service in the cause of civil rights. The interview, conducted by Jamie B. Coughtry, took place in 1987 when the Shared History Program was not yet incorporated with the University of Nevada Oral History Program (UNOHP). A year later UNOHP cataloged the oral history as *Lubertha Johnson: Civil Rights Efforts in Las Vegas, 1940s–1960s*. In this history Johnson explains how the Las Vegas NAACP pressured the city's mayor and business owners into ending public accommodation restrictions on the Strip and desegregating Las Vegas. The agreement that led to improved race relations in Las Vegas was called the Moulin Rouge Agreement.

About Lubertha Johnson

Born in 1906 in rural Mississippi, Lubertha Johnson (née Miller) left the Deep South in response to declining economic opportunities and increasing racial hostility. In 1923 she and her parents made the difficult decision to follow other family members to Chicago.

Already educated beyond the dreams of most southern women of her background, the young Lubertha augmented a boarding school degree with college classes in education and social work in Chicago and Nashville. During the 1930s, Franklin Roosevelt's New Deal provided her with a job in a local WPA recreation program. Equally important was her introduction to the sophisticated worlds of northern black culture and politics. In Chicago not only could one read about black life across the country in papers such as the *Chicago Defender*, but one could also work through the Urban League and the NAACP to improve life for oneself and one's people.

Lubertha Johnson, 1987. *Courtesy Shared History Program, University of Nevada, Reno.*

By the early 1940s, her father's declining health necessitated another move, this time to the West. After a brief interlude in Pasadena, California, Lubertha Johnson settled in Las Vegas in November 1943. After a six-month stay, she returned to Pasadena, continuing her work in the field of public housing, this time for the Urban League. Within a year, she was back in Las Vegas, where she would reside until her death in February 1989.

Despite the vast differences between the dusty desert gambling oasis and her previous homes, there was one constant. Jim Crow preceded her to the southern part of the Silver State and was everywhere in evidence by the time of her arrival. Indeed, blacks who had thronged to the area from the South to get their first crack at high-wage, wartime industrial employment had already dubbed Las Vegas "the Mississippi of the West." City officials took the lead in the racial transformation of the city by rezoning the small prewar black residential area known as Westside for commercial and residential development. Restrictive licensing and housing covenants then kept blacks there, creating a modern ghetto. This was part of a concerted effort to discourage black defense plant workers from staying in the county and to segregate thoroughly those who did remain.

Lubertha Johnson's first job in Clark County was with the federally funded Carver Park housing project across the highway from the Basic Magnesium,

Incorporated (BMI) plant in Henderson. As recreation director, she found herself responsible for maintaining morale among black families residing in this so-called "Model Negro Community." Only a month before her arrival, black workers coming off a shift were ordered to change and shower in facilities separate from those used by their white coworkers before joining their families across the road in segregated apartments. Ultimately, however, most blacks preferred the rude, crowded conditions of the segregated Las Vegas Westside.

Lubertha Johnson balked too. "I had plenty of courage in those days," she recalls in this memoir, which details a life of principle lived primarily in the civil rights trenches. After the war, she and her allies, following the lead of blacks in the South, drove Jim Crow from one haunt after another: hospitals, casinos, theaters, schools, and housing. When federal antipoverty funds became available in the mid-1960s, she was instrumental in launching and guiding Operation Independence, a comprehensive antipoverty program in Las Vegas.

Lubertha Johnson Interview on the Las Vegas Press, the Westside, and the Moulin Rouge Agreement

You didn't need to guess what the *Review-Journal* [Las Vegas's daily paper] thought about black people in general. Because of the way they presented their news, you would think Westside people were from another planet. In those years, the *Review-Journal* would always refer to us as "colored people." Everything was more or less presented in a comical manner. If they quoted some black person, they always did their best to do it in the way that black people are *supposed* to speak, not necessarily the way they *did*. Any time they quoted you, they would say "y'all" and that sort of thing. They were very, very . . . unkind is about the best way I can say it. In their way, they made it a lot worse than it really was, as far as the ignorance was concerned. You were supposed to be so ignorant that you hardly knew up from down. We didn't respond in a way that was pleasant, because we all certainly were aware of it and detested their manner and attitude and the way they treated the black people.

I had a personal experience with the *Review-Journal*. There was a family that had lived in Carver Park—I don't think they lived in Carver Park at the time. There was this young lady who was protecting her mother. She did something to the stepfather; she probably stuck him with an ice pick or something like that. She was placed in some kind of a detention home. We had a law even then that juveniles were supposed to be treated entirely differently, but the police went in and woke her up in the middle of the night with her gown on, took pictures of her and put them on the front page. I got her mother to sue the *Review-Journal*, and we won our case. At that time I was chairman of the grievance committee of NAACP, but we didn't sue them as NAACP. We had her sue them as a citizen. I don't think we went to court. We did get a pretty nice settlement for the family.

Anything that the *Review-Journal* had to do reporting the news involving blacks was always ugly. John Cahlan and Al Cahlan were editing the *Review-Journal* in the 1940s and 1950s. We tried to speak to them, but they didn't want to accept or discuss it. It was a very bad situation. They would more or less make a joke out of events on the Westside. They would treat a situation as if it was an incident dealing with somebody in a comic situation, like in a show. It was never reported in any intelligent or straightforward manner, as it would have been if the person was not Negro.

Florence Lee Jones, the wife of John Cahlan, covered the Westside. She and I had some discussions. In the mid-1950s there was some type of organization of social workers that was planning to have a convention in Las Vegas. The NAACP complained to them so that they wouldn't come to Las Vegas for their convention because of the prejudiced situation here. Why would a social service organization want to come here when the black social workers couldn't stay in the hotels or get any decent kind of accommodations? Florence Lee was very unhappy about that. The social workers just didn't come. There were a lot of discussions about it. I think Florence must have written an article about it. I called her and talked to her about it and told her what I thought. She was very unhappy, and that's why she wrote an article criticizing our not wanting these people to come. It was just a part of the battle as far as we were concerned.

I don't know if Florence visited places on the Westside and tried to write up news; I don't remember that. I think she made her comments from the items that came into the paper more than going over there and speaking to people. I got the feeling that she didn't appear to have any real animosity toward Negroes or the Westside. She was part of a system, and I don't think she would have been allowed to do anything else. You can't afford to go too far out if you *are* sympathetic. I think the family would have objected, even if she had been interested or sympathetic or wanted to do anything in favor of the Negro people.

There was another paper called the *Age*. It was very small and had no power. There was no black paper here in 1945. We started a paper later with the NAACP, called the *Missile*. Then Dr. Charles West took it over in 1963, renamed it the *Las*

Vegas Voice, and published it for a number of years. It was purchased two or three times over, and it's still being run by some gentleman here as the *Sentinel Voice*.

Mr. Hank Greenspun, who is Jewish, was *very, very* friendly as far as we could tell. When he came and started his paper, the *Las Vegas Sun* in 1950, we were so happy. Hank Greenspun's paper was entirely different in the way it approached news. It was quite acceptable to the average Negro person. We considered him very friendly, and we really thought about him as in our corner. I do remember wanting to meet him because of his attitude and the way he published the paper—the way he treated the news as it came from West Las Vegas. We noticed a change right away. He didn't use these words that were changed to make black people sound like old-fashioned people from years and years back. He treated the news like any other paper in any other city. It wasn't quite perfect, and it still isn't. But it was so much better. He used to come to NAACP meetings. I have a picture showing the time that he took out a life membership. I suppose Mr. Greenspun was sincere. At least if he won the people of West Las Vegas, I guess it brought some sort of strength to the paper. He was having problems getting the *Sun* really established.

I don't consider that Mr. Greenspun is as friendly now as he was earlier. For instance, he doesn't affiliate with the NAACP anymore, for one thing. He had a young black man working for him who wrote the news about black folk only, which many of us resented. It sort of opened the door for people to use him against other black people. You know how that can happen. Sometimes things were printed that were not really true. We resented that and told him so. Mr. Greenspun always acted as if he felt that it was the thing to do; it was all right. But then it finally got so bad that he did eliminate this young man. I felt that he should have replaced him. He should have found someone who was capable and have them represent black people *only* as any other reporter, and let him write about everybody. I didn't see the need of having somebody *just* to write about the Negro people. Mr. Greenspun seemed to think that was a very fine idea; we should be proud of that.

We gave Mr. Greenspun an award; we just thought he was really grand in the old days. He did act as a mediator at the Moulin Rouge meeting in 1960 when we worked out a general agreement to discontinue discrimination in the places of public accommodation. It was an important event to those of us who were really in the fight. This kind of discrimination was being practiced all over the country for the most part. Even in the South they were breaking down these discriminatory patterns in the restaurants. The NAACP decided that we were going to discontinue having to put up a fight.

We decided that what we were going to do was march down on the Strip. We had our meetings, and we organized our people into groups. We had committees. About seven or eight of us had a group that they were supposed to supervise, so that everyone who went would do the same thing. The action would be just exactly the way we planned it. We had meetings where we set up certain rules and regulations that we were going to follow. We didn't want to have any violence. When we started our meetings, we were holding them in an office and actually called them "secret meetings." Somebody tipped off the newspapers that we were planning to march on the Strip on a Saturday night. The word went out with the newspaper headlines saying, "Negroes to March on Strip." Somehow it got to Mr. Greenspun. We knew that it had been reported, that we were planning to march.

Mr. Greenspun was not in on the secret that I know of. We preferred to surprise. We were going to march, but we wanted it to be a shock—a surprise. We wouldn't have leaked it, otherwise we wouldn't have been meeting secretly at night. I believe Mr. Alan Jarlson, the person who reported for the *Sun*, told somebody else about our plans. I don't know how he found out, but he did. I felt that he was sympathetic to blacks. I didn't know him that well, but I met him. Generally, in his conversation and all, I had the feeling that he was at least sympathetic. At least he had a kind of show of concern for the problems. NAACP meetings were covered.

Mr. Jarlson probably saw a letter that Dr. McMillan [dentist and Civil Rights activist] had written, and then he went to Hank Greenspun. Dr. McMillan was always writing letters and always making speeches on television and saying the same thing. It wasn't anything different. I don't think that particular letter would have frightened . . . not any more than all of the other things that we did—all the letters that were written. Everybody tried to talk to the governor and had meetings with him and several leading people. Mr. Greenspun was one who attended some of the meetings, so he heard all the talk about something was going to happen, something has to be done and that sort of thing. So it wasn't anything unusual. People had heard this kind of talk before.

Prior to the planning we had made efforts to talk to some of the hotel owners, to the governor and to some of the city officials, but we didn't make any headway. We were told that they were out of town or they were not able to receive us or they were too busy. Mostly they were supposed to be out of town. Interestingly enough, when this headline came out, "Negroes to March on Strip," everybody got back to town: the governor, the hotel owners, everybody. Naturally, they were very upset. They contacted us. They made some effort to see if they could talk us into some kind of compromise. By that time there was a lot of talk. Everywhere there was quite a lot of interest on the part of most citizens.

I don't know how Mr. Greenspun happened to become the person who would actually act as the mediator, but that's what happened. Evidently they had this meeting among themselves. Mr. Greenspun came up with the plan as to what we would do: we would have a meeting with some of the hotel owners, the governor, the city mayor, the commissioners and so forth. That's when we met in the Moulin Rouge on a Sunday morning.

It felt as if something important was going to happen. We *really* felt this way because at least some of us were surprised that these people would even come to this meeting. I know I was. Some of them had expressed themselves in such a way that we expected them to continue to hold out for these practices forever. Just a few days before this incident I had talked to a person in one of the hotels, and he said to me, "I wouldn't even let my mother into this hotel if I thought she would lose business for me. That's what would happen if we allowed Negroes to come in." With that kind of sentiment, it really was something very special to have these people actually come to this meeting, including the governor, the power structure representing the hotels and the city and the county, and the representatives from the police department.

I didn't have any inkling of what the agreement would be before we went in. I don't know if anybody did. I think there certainly was a feeling on everybody's part that this was something that was going to mean a great deal in the city of Las Vegas. I thought the establishment would come in with some phony offer. When Negroes did participate in political activities they'd always give you $1,000 or $500. I didn't think too much of money, but I thought it would be some kind of a compromise offer.

We knew that we couldn't accept a compromise, because we had all these people behind us who had put their money in and had made these meetings. They were sincere, and they had decided that we just were not going to put up with this practice any longer, whatever the cost. Prior to this time, we had several meetings in churches. We had a large church; about the largest one—and people put in all the money they could afford to support some activities. We didn't talk too much about what we were going to do. Everybody knew that we were going to make a supreme effort to have this discrimination discontinued.

The march was just one of the things that we planned to do. Many things were happening in other places. People were boycotting, and they were doing many different things. We decided that in this city, particularly, the march was the thing that we would use. You have all these people coming in here over the weekend. This would not only show Las Vegas how we felt and how determined we were, but it would also show thousands of people who were coming from other cities, other parts of the United States. This would affect their business in some way. We knew it was bound to.

The decision to march was a group decision. You can't have everybody making decisions. You have to have some people who have been in the forefront for the most part trying to make policy. But you talk to everybody; you listen. When we had a big meeting everybody would have a chance to get up and make a suggestion. We didn't just do this overnight. We planned it, and we had meeting after meeting; we raised funds. You have to inspire people. To get them concerned, you have to have people make speeches and give their opinion. For instance, we could cite examples in the South, and we would say, "Now, if people can do this in Mississippi, Alabama, Georgia, Florida, we certainly can do it here." I'm *sure* that we had the approval of the majority of the people. We talked about how we would do it, how we would go about it, how we would conduct ourselves.

We asked everybody to cooperate with our plan, and I'm sure we would have had enough support. I still believe that we would have had enough people to win, because at that time people in this part of the country were very sensitive to marching or picketing. Depending on tourists for the money that they needed to make, they certainly did not want to lose that money. They had never experienced anything of this sort. They were concerned, very much concerned as to what would happen. In those days I was gung ho. I had complete confidence in what I was doing. I didn't think anything about violence, but I had experienced violence, and it wasn't anything new. It wouldn't have surprised me if it had happened.

We had some white people who were very active in NAACP, but I don't think any whites would have marched with us on the Strip. We never approached any whites about marching that I remember. The white citizens of Las Vegas may have become so concerned about this incident because this was the first time we had really taken any action. You can talk about things for years, but nobody pays too much attention. But this time they *knew* that we *really planned to do it!* We weren't just talking about something having to be done. We were in the process of doing it for the first time.

[Until the newspaper headlines] there was nothing that the public saw or heard in advance. As I mentioned before, we were having night meetings that we thought were secret meetings, which they were. Most people didn't know that we had gone that far with our plans, that we were setting up our strategy at the time, the few days before we planned to actually take this action. When the announcement was made, it wasn't made saying that Negroes plan to do this or that plan . . . it said, "Negroes will march." We *were* going to march on the Strip *that very week*.

There was tension at the Moulin Rouge meeting. Some people were completely silent, and others spoke up. Some of them did not particularly like having to face the situation and change it, but they felt that they really had no choice. Most of the people at the meeting I didn't even know. I didn't know what their attitudes had been before. There were some of them who appeared to me to be slightly unhappy with the situation, but I think they had *made* their decision before we actually got a chance to observe their attitudes.

Mr. Greenspun was the person who actually carried the discussion, and they met all our demands fully. We were surprised by that, but it happened. It was unbelievable! We did accept the plan that Mr. Greenspun offered, that this practice of discrimination should be discontinued, period. It was pretty clear and pretty plain. Everybody seemed to have been resigned to the fact that it would be a decision in our favor. It probably was recorded, but we didn't really get the final decision of all of the people until after the meeting.

When I left, I didn't have the sense of victory. I wondered if this was going to be another one of those things where you get a promise and it isn't followed through on, whether this was going to be one of those things where you are sold a bill of goods. I think we all felt more or less the same way. Maybe somebody had a little more confidence than I, and then maybe someone else didn't have as much. The meeting was the talk for months.

After the decision was made, it was immediately evident that blacks were going to be served. We just went in and tried to gamble. I didn't go, but several people did. I was surprised at the ease with which the system fell apart. I expected that a certain portion of them would comply, and some wouldn't, and then we'd have to have the fight all over again.

We had one person (he wasn't at the meeting) who said he would *never* accept Negro people into his place of business. This was Abe Miller, who owned the Sal Sagev [Hotel] on the corner of Main and Fremont. We were told by people who went into his place after this agreement that he refused to serve black people. He was the only one, and he held out for quite some time.

At this time we established a human relations commission that was supported by the city, the county, and North Las Vegas. At our meetings we talked about it.[1] A couple of times we went down to talk to Mr. Miller, and he said he wasn't going to change. About the third time that we went to talk to him, before we could get in the door to sit down, he said, "Here's my letter. Here's my letter." He said, "I've written to my constituents, and I have told them that I am turning over the hotel . . . turning over the stock," or whatever it was, "because I just don't think I can stand the pressure." So that was that. There may have been other little places here and there, but I know all of the main hotels except this one followed the agreement.

Eventually it became easier for blacks to find work in hotels. We did get more jobs along with service. That was another one of our fights—to get more people employed, and we finally did. It took something like two or three years. We even established a committee. Once each month we held meetings with the hotel representatives. Hotel owners themselves seldom came, but they sent representatives from their personnel departments. We'd talk about whether they had followed through on their agreement regarding employment. We finally got help from the federal government. We even got the hotels to promise to make a pledge to hire a certain number of black people.

For instance, James (Jimmy) Gay used to work in the hotels. They gave him some jobs that were supposed to be prestigious. I think they were trying to use Mr. Gay. For instance, an uptown hotel had him as assistant manager or some such thing. That's a name, of course. Then in a couple of other hotels, he had a very prestigious-sounding job. Of course, he's a wonderful person. Mr. Gay is a very fine person. He's about lost his health, however. He lives right around the corner from me.[2]

As a result of these meetings and these activities, we certainly became a people who had more of a sense of change and more respect and a better life. We got a state law prohibiting race discrimination in employment. We got a law prohibiting discrimination in housing. We were more or less fighting all these battles at the same time.[3]

A little side thought: sometimes I wish that we *had* marched on the Strip. But maybe we wouldn't have had as many people as we had hoped, if we had actually had to go through with the march. We came up with several different numbers that we expected. It's possible that most of the people would have watched too.

We all discussed all angles of this situation—what might happen and what we hoped would happen. But we were so enthusiastic until we just knew that we were going to win. You *have* to feel that way or else you can't go on and do what you are trying to do. You have to have confidence that you are going to win. And we had it. I think we expressed this thought (after we were successful) saying that *maybe* it was a good thing that we didn't have to march.

There were people who were not in favor of the march. There were several black people employed as janitors and maids, and some people felt that we would lose the fight and that these people then would actually be eliminated. That was their thinking. Some of the ministers did express this same idea—that the people who had jobs would lose them. It wasn't anything about whether marching was the wrong thing. The jobs were the major concern.

After blacks were able to patronize Strip establishments, businesses on the Westside lost some business. That's one of the negative situations. That happened all over the country. (In Chicago, I know that personally.) You see, it's very difficult for people to establish clubs or hotels that could compete in any way with the Strip hotels. You would think that maybe out of loyalty most people would go to the black-owned hotel, but it doesn't work that way. I suppose it's a normal thing. If I owned a hotel here—let's say even in this spot—and I couldn't provide the kind of entertainment and accommodations that Caesar's Palace could provide, I guess I'd go to Caesar's Palace *if* I didn't feel the way I do, because I never go. The only time I *really* went to the hotels very much was when I was just going to see what would happen during the days of segregation. It bothers me; it still bothers me a great deal, because I feel that with all the problems and with all of the years of denial, I can't see blacks supporting a group of people who for so long were so partial. I'm sure that a lot of people might not think too much about it.

There are a *lot* of black people who come into this town never knowing that there is a Westside. They read the casino ads and everything, and then people talk about Las Vegas. When they come, there's nothing interesting enough compared to what they can see in the other part of the city. The white hotels really made an effort to get black people in, because money looks good—anybody's money looks good. After people started going in and the walls didn't fall down, then they thought they might as well take advantage of it. And they still do. Some of them actually went after black patronage. For instance, if a black person runs a newspaper, the hotels will put in ads; they'll advertise their activities.

Notes

This oral history originally appeared in University of Nevada Oral History Program Catalog No. 148 as "Lubertha Johnson: Civil Rights Efforts in Las Vegas, 1940s–1960s" (1988), pp. 59–66. Copyright by Shared History Program, University of Nevada, Reno. Reprinted with permission.

1. The Southern Nevada Human Relations Commission was formed as part of the agreement.
2. Gay was assistant personnel director for the Sands Hotel and Casino from 1952 to 1970.
3. A bill passed by the state legislature in March 1956 outlawed discrimination in public accommodations and employment. Legislation outlawing residential segregation did not pass the state legislature until 1971.

3 The More Things Change, the More They Stay the Same

Structural Racism and African American Community Formation in the North Bay Area

April L. Harris

The summer of 2015 was reminiscent of past "long, hot" summers that saw significant social change. It included Black Lives Matter activists' calls for reforms in policing and, in the North Bay region of the San Francisco Bay Area, the appearance of the Twitter hashtag #LaughingWhileBlack. The famed Napa Valley Wine Train was called out on social media for having removed members of a predominately African American female book club for "being too loud." Within hours of the hashtag's first posting, the perception that the women in the party were not welcome in the Wine Country became salient. In the aftermath of this event, multiple television interviews occurred, followed by public apologies on behalf of the train company, mandatory cultural competency training for its employees, and ultimately a lawsuit and a multimillion-dollar award. During an interview announcing the filing of the lawsuit, Dr. Amos Brown, president of the San Francisco chapter of the NAACP, concluded: "California never wanted us here from the beginning." He then asked his audience to refer to the history of the state.[1]

The region just north of San Francisco and the Golden Gate Bridge, known as the North Bay, encompasses six counties that are primarily rural and agricultural (Marin, Sonoma, Lake, Mendocino, Napa, and Solano). To tourists this area is famous for bucolic rolling hills, rows of grapevines, NASCAR racing, and the spectacle of the Pacific Ocean. Although there is an abundance of literature on the North Bay's wine industry, tourism, agribusinesses, and environment, little has been written about this area's African American experience, with the exception of references to the lack of that group's presence.[2] This chapter rectifies some of this by examining regional sustainability through the construction of the postwar ghetto in Marin City and in Vallejo. Unlike nearby Oakland and San

Members of Sisters on the Reading Edge book club in 2015 before they were kicked off the Napa Valley Wine Train for allegedly laughing and talking too loudly. *Courtesy Lisa Renee Johnson.*

Francisco, whose black communities immediately underwent the concentrated and unequal residential processes of the 1950s, in the North Bay the first wave of that development did not occur until after the 1970s.[3]

African American Entrance into the North Bay

Thousands of African Americans were first drawn to the North Bay from the South at the onset of World War II. On June 25, 1941, President Franklin Delano Roosevelt issued Executive Order 8802, which mandated that there would be no racial discrimination in national defense industries. To enforce the order Roosevelt established the Fair Employment Practices Committee (FEPC), which gave people of color and women opportunities to obtain stable employment with relatively fair wages.[4] Before this period, of the 1,574 black people who resided in the region in 1940 (1 percent of the total population there), most, by far, were black men housed at San Quentin Prison in Marin County.[5] During the war, that demographic fundamentally changed as thousands of black southerners migrated into the region in search of jobs at shipbuilding companies protected by the FEPC, namely Marinship in Sausalito and at Mare Island Naval Shipyard in Vallejo.[6]

In 1940 Marin City did not yet exist. During World War II, however, the W.A. Bechtel Company of San Francisco was given the contract to construct transport vessels for the U.S. Navy. It created Marinship, which during World War II built nearly one hundred "Liberty ships" and tankers. The Bechtel Company was also given permission to develop a community to house some of its workers. Marin City's first buildings were constructed in 1942 to house workers at the Marinship facility in neighboring Sausalito. One year after its founding, it had a population of 5,500, with African Americans comprising 10 percent of that total.[7] In an era when segregation was widely practiced in California as well as across the South, Marin City was a peculiarly diverse and racially integrated community. It was peculiar because government housing programs placed black and white residents in the same migrant ghetto, making it one of the first "integrated" housing developments in California—nearly two decades before fair housing laws were enacted in state in 1959.[8] North Bay public policy makers, along with Bechtel and the wartime National Housing Agency, had arranged for public housing to be established in what became Marin City and in the Canal District of San Rafael.[9]

After the war, in late 1945, base closures and deindustrialization pushed most cities with defense-driven economies into decline. Marin City, with Marin County's largest housing project, survived the close of its shipyards with blue-collar employment. Meanwhile the North Bay's wine industry was growing, as was agribusiness in the region and gradual suburbanization anchored by structural development of predominantly white communities in the cities of Santa Rosa, Fairfield, and Napa.[10] Unlike Oakland and San Francisco, the postwar economic decline did not lead to poverty until after 1970. Most North Bay African Americans, such as civil rights and labor leader Joseph James (see introduction), simply moved to more vibrant cities in California, such as nearby San Francisco, in search of fair economic opportunities. There strong community and familial structures allowed them to survive and temporarily prevent formation of a postwar ghetto.[11] The characteristics of the black ghetto, described by historian Gretchen Lemke-Santangelo in writing about Oakland: "overcrowded, substandard housing, declining employment opportunities, and a sharp rise in poverty."[12] Black flight from the North Bay gradually reversed after 1965, during a first period of urban revitalization of Marin City and Vallejo and after the passage of civil rights legislation and court cases in education, labor (affirmative action), and housing.[13] Concerning the latter, fair housing was implicit in Title VI of the Civil Rights Act of 1964. But not until passage of the Fair Housing Act, Title VII of the Civil Rights Act of 1968, was there a prohibition against "discrimination in the sale, rental and financing of dwellings based on race, color, religion, sex or national origin."[14]

The North Bay in the Contemporary Period

Similar to in north Richmond, California, on the other side of the bay, discriminatory housing practices before the Fair Housing Act of 1968 widened the gap in wealth and opportunities between black and white people in cities like Marin City and Vallejo.[15] Since 1970 most North Bay whites have fully capitalized on the wealth accumulated thanks in part to postwar home loans and GI Bill grants to attend college. Many of these suburbanites were able to purchase homes, fund their children's college educations, and invest in retirement accounts. This process prompted sociologist Lingxin Hao to ask, "Why does the lack of inheritance severely damage African American prospects of wealth, and hence life chances, but not seem to affect those of immigrant racial-ethnic minority groups?" She was referring here to Asian American immigrants and Mexican Americans immigrants.[16] The short answer given by the director of planning and development for Santa Clara County, Ignacio "Nash" Gonzalez, was that most people hold their wealth in the form of home equity and that "if you are a renter, you do not gain equity, and therefore you have no wealth to transfer to the next generation."[17] For a growing population of middle-class blacks, who have been able to access living wage employment and own single-family housing in middle-class communities, Gonzalez's analysis does not apply. However, most black migrants who settled in the North Bay after 1970 were manual laborers employed in manufacturing, not in the region's agricultural or growing high-tech and telecommunications industries. In addition, unfair land use policies led to the systematic loss of the region's affordable housing for the African American working poor.[18]

Demographically, since 1970 the North Bay African American population has risen from 24,445 (3 percent of the total) to 79,869 (6 percent) in 2010. In this period the counties with the lowest number of black residents have been Lake, Mendocino, Napa, and Sonoma. In 1970, their populations ranged between 0 and 1 percent, and this gradually grew to populations that ranged between 1 percent and 2 percent in 2010. The counties with the largest black populations have been Marin and Solano. For Marin, proportionality has always been a problem, with most blacks living in Marin City and most whites living in the county's suburbs. For example, in 2010 approximately 3 percent of Marin County's population was African American, yet in Marin City it was 38 percent.[19] During the 1970s, part of the draw for African Americans was that Marin City was one of the few locations in the county where public support for subsidized housing remained relatively strong.

The other North Bay region that has been a magnet for African American migration and settlement has been Solano County. In 1970, it had an African American population of 10 percent, which represented 68 percent of the African American population in the North Bay region. In 2010, that share of the population increased to 15 percent, which represented 76 percent of the African American population in the North Bay. Similar to population distribution in Marin County, most Solano County blacks lived in the region's most vibrant city, in this instance Vallejo, which in 2010 represented 32 percent of the African American population in the county. This was followed by notable growth in North Bay cities that boomed after 1980, such as Fairfield, whose population is primarily composed of people who fled the lower half of the San Francisco Bay Area because of congestion and the high cost of living.[20]

In Marin City and Vallejo, which were formed before 1980, housing dated from the significant blue-collar and defense industry buildup of World War II. Within these jurisdictions local government agencies had assumed responsibility for public housing in the 1960s and 1970s, but public policy makers refocused and began whittling away at public housing in the early 1980s. As traditional industrial employment opportunities declined, high technology, casino gaming, and the service economy began to explode throughout the North Bay, with concomitant single-family housing development.[21] This process was exacerbated by the Base Realignment and Closures Commission, which in 1988 started scaling back and closing defense and military installations at Mare Island (Vallejo) and Hamilton Army Airfield in Novato.[22] During this transition period, African Americans were in the same boat as most North Bay residents: they were not prepared for how abruptly the region's socioeconomic change occurred. Their experiences differed, however, in their ability to attain living-wage, unionized employment in the building trades.

By the 1990s, large numbers of African immigrants from Eritrea began competing for North Bay jobs historically held by American-born blacks, particularly in manual labor.[23] Simultaneously, as deindustrialization and displacement of workers occurred in blue-collar employment, the booming computing and telecommunications industry throughout the North Bay ushered in greater affluence for some. Santa Rosa's Hewlett-Packard divided two of its divisions and created Agilent Technologies, for example. But employment in these fields was predicated largely on one's education in science, technology, engineering, and mathematics

(STEM), fields whose black presence was limited in part by student-of-color preparatory deficiencies in Marin City and Vallejo public schools.[24] In the twenty-first century the continuing growth of STEM-related industries and North Bay's increased integration into the Silicon Valley's economy has dramatically increased its socioeconomic value but raises questions for African Americans. Will African Americans be forced out because they are poorly represented in STEM fields?

The viability of the North Bay's black and working poor population depends on the will of regional policy makers and taxpayers to develop affordable housing, including housing for the elderly and people with disabilities.[25] Will Marin City and Vallejo revitalize their housing market for all its residents, or will they allow conversion of residential rental properties into condominiums as has been happening throughout the Bay Area? Advocates for fair housing and against slum gentrification in Marin City and Vallejo can only hope that the more things change, the more they *don't* stay the same. Only time will tell.

Notes

1. Author interview with Amos Brown, October 2015, Napa, California. Also see Janet O, "Women File $11 Million Lawsuit Against Napa Valley Wine Train," ABC7.com, http://abc7.com/news/women-file-$11m-lawsuit-against-napa-valley-wine-train/1013804; "#laughingwhileblack," https://twitter.com/.

2. "Here Is the Whitest State University in California," *Journal of Blacks in Higher Education*, no. 64 (2009): 55. I conducted searches in academic databases using terms such as "black" and "negro" in lieu of "African American."

3. For more on the formation of the postwar ghetto, see Albert S. Broussard, *Black San Francisco: The Struggle for Racial Equality in the West, 1900–1954* (Lawrence: University Press of Kansas, 1993), 205–38; Gretchen Lemke-Santangelo, "Deindustrialization, Urban Poverty, and African American Community Mobilization in Oakland, 1945 through the 1990s," in *Seeking El Dorado: African Americans in California*, ed. Lawrence De Graaf, Kevin Mulroy, and Quintard Taylor (Seattle: University of Washington Press, 2001), 343–76; Gretchen Lemke-Santangelo, *Abiding Courage: African American Migrant Women and the East Bay Community* (Chapel Hill: University of North Carolina Press, 1996); Shirley Ann Wilson Moore, *To Place Our Deeds: The African American Community in Richmond, California, 1910–1963* (Berkeley: University of California Press, 2000), 94–126; Donna Jean Murch, *Living for the City: Migration, Education, and the Rise of the Black Panther Party in Oakland, California* (Chapel Hill: University of North Carolina Press, 2010), 15–70; Delores Nason McBroome, *Parallel Communities: African Americans in California's East Bay 1850–1963* (New York: Garland, 1993); Marilynn S. Johnson, *The Second Gold Rush: Oakland and the East Bay in World War II* (Berkeley: University of California Press, 1993), 209–34; Quintard Taylor, *In Search of the Racial Frontier: African Americans in the West, 1528–1990* (New York: W. W. Norton, 1998), 273–75.

4. For more on the FEPC and Great Migration in the West, see Broussard, *Black San Francisco*, 145–46; Dwayne Mack, *Black Spokane: The Civil Rights Struggle in the Inland Northwest* (Norman: University of Oklahoma Press, 2014), 19–31; Herbert G. Ruffin, *Uninvited Neighbors: African Americans in the Silicon Valley, 1769–1990* (Norman: Oklahoma University Press, 2014), 82–83; Josh Sides, *L.A. City Limits: African American Los Angeles from the Great Depression to the Present* (Berkeley: University of California, 2003), 36–56; Quintard Taylor, "Urban Black Labor in the West, 1849–1949: Reconceptualizing the Image of a Region," in *The African American Urban Experience: Perspectives from the Colonial Period to the Present*, ed. Joe W. Trotter, Earl Lewis, and Tera W. Hunter (New York: Palgrave MacMillan, 2004), 107–14; Moore, *To Place Our Deeds*, 40–70.

5. "Marin County, and San Rafael Township," in *1940 Census*, http://1940census.archives .gov/.

6. Roger Lotchin, "Mobilization for the Duration: The Bay Area in the Good War," in *National Parks and Services, World War II in the San Francisco Bay Area*, https:// www.nps.gov/nr/travel/wwiibayarea/mobilization.html.

7. April L. Harris, "Marin City, California (1942–)," *Blackpast.org*, http://www.blackpast. org/aaw/marin-city-california-1942.

8. Ruffin, *Uninvited Neighbors*, 107–15; Martin Schiesl, ed., *Responsible Liberalism: Edmond G. "Pat" Brown and Reform Government in California, 1958–1967* (Los Angeles: Edmond G. "Pat" Brown Institute of Public Affairs, 2003), 101–24.

9. Charles Wollenberg, *Marinship at War: Shipbuilding and Social Change in Wartime Sausalito* (San Francisco: Heritage House, 1990); April L. Harris, and National Parks and Services, "Ships of Marinship 1942–1945," pictorial exhibit, Rosie the Riveter National Park, Home Front Festival at the Ford Assembly Building, Richmond, California, October 2009; April L. Harris, and National Parks and Services, "Pictorial History of Marin City: Marinship, Ahoy! An Integrated Community 1942–1945," pictorial exhibit, Rosie the Riveter National Park, October 2008.

10. Social Explorer Datasets (SE), Census 1960–2010, Social Explorer and U.S. Census Bureau.

11. For more information on the postwar Bay Area, see Lemke-Santangelo, *Abiding Courage*, 87, 91–94, 167–68; Moore, *To Place Our Deeds*, 71–73; "James v. Marinship Corporation, 25 Ca1.2d 721," SCOCAL, Supreme Court of California Resources, http://scocal.stanford.edu/opinion/james-v-marinship-corp-29267; Ruffin, *Uninvited Neighbors*, 122, 137, 73–91. Also see Quintard Taylor, *In Search of the Racial Frontier: African Americans in the American West 1286–1990* (New York: W. W. Norton, 1990); Robert O. Self, *American Babylon: Race and the Struggle for Postwar Oakland* (Princeton: Princeton University Press, 2003); Ingrid Banks, et al., *Black California Dreamin': The Crises of California's African-American Communities* (Santa Barbara: UCSB, Center for Black Studies Research, 2012).

12. Lemke-Santangelo, "Deindustrialization, Urban Poverty, and African American Community Mobilization," 345.

13. Myra Wysinger, "An African American Trail Blazer of California: Edmond Edward Wysinger (1816–1891)," https://web.archive.org/web/20060228050615/http://wysinger .homestead.com/courtcase.html; "Wysinger v. Crookshank (1890)," opinion by Judge Foote, *Blackpast.org*, http://www.blackpast.org/?q=primarywest/wysinger-v-crookshank-1890; "Background–Mendez v. Westminster Re-enactment," United States Courts, http://www.uscourts.gov/educational-resources/get-involved/federal-court-activities/mendez-westminster-re-enactment/mendez-westminster-background.aspx.

14. "The Fair Housing Act," in "Programs Administered by FHEO, U.S. Department of Housing and Urban Development, http://portal.hud.gov/hudportal/HUD?src=/program_offices/fair_housing_equal_opp/progdesc/title8).

15. Dalton Conley, "Economic Calculations," in *Reparations for Slavery: A Reader*, ed. Ronald P. Salzberger and Mary C. Turck (New York: Rowman & Littlefield, 2004), 289–300.

16. Lingxin Hao, *Color Lines, Country Lines: Race, Immigration and Wealth Stratification in America* (New York: Russell Sage Foundation, 2007), 31–32.

17. Ignacio "Nash" Gonzalez interview with author, April 2015, Mendocino Community College, Ukiah, California.

18. There is a plethora of state and local legislation aimed at land use regulations. A few were precedent-setting, such California's 1965 Land Conservation Act (1965) and 1988 Native Plant Protection Act." See also Laurence M. May, "The California Open-Space Easement Act: The Efficacy of Indirect Incentives," *Santa Clara Law Review* 16, no. 2 (January 1976), 359–77; "California Conservation Easement Act," California Conservation Connection, http://www.stateconservation.org/california/local-resources/California-Conservation-Easement-Act/28222; Michael L. Weber and Burr Heneman, "Guide to California's Marine Life Management Act," December 2000, http://www.bu.edu/ecologyonline/projects/california/mlma.pdf.

19. Social Explorer Tables (SE), Census 2010, "Marin City," Social Explorer and U.S. Census Bureau; County of Marin Community Development Agency, "Marin County Housing Element, 2015–2023," http://www.marincounty.org/.

20. Social Explorer Tables (SE), Census 1970–2010, Social Explorer and U.S. Census Bureau.

21. 500 Nations, "Northern California Casinos," http://500nations.com/Northern_California_Casinos.asp.

22. "Base Realignment and Closures (BRAC) Sites by States," U.S. Environmental Protection Agency, https://www.epa.gov/fedfac/base-realignment-and-closure-brac-sites-state.

23. Christopher Coen, "Eritrean Refugee Discouraged; Wants to Return to Africa," Friends of Refugees, https://forefugees.com/.

24. "Report: Sausalito School District Funneling Funds from Marin City School to Charter School," KPIXTV, n.d., http://sanfrancisco.cbslocal.com/video/category/spoken-word-kpixtv/3463670-report-sausalito-school-district-funneling-funds-from -marin-city-school-to-charter-school/; Mark Prado, "State: Sausalito–Marin City

Board Hurts Minorities with Focus on Charter School," *Marin Independent Journal*, August 11, 2016, http://www.marinij.com/article/NO/20160811/NEWS/160819961. R. Deborah Davis and April Harris, "Putting on the Armour Everyday: Influences of Student Socialization Based on Culture and Ethnicity," in National Association of African American Studies, *Harnessing the Future by Studying the Past*, vol. 1, Monograph Series (Biddleford, Me.: National Association of African American Studies, National Association of Hispanic and Latino Studies, National Association of Native American Studies, International Association, 2004), 344–61.

25. *Marin Countywide Plan* (Marin County Community Development Agency, 2007), http://www.marincounty.org/~/media/files/departments/cd/he/cwp_cd2.pdf; *Sonoma County General Plan 2020*, Sonoma County Permit and Resource Management Department, http://www.sonoma-county.org/PRMD/gp2020/index.htm; *Mendocino County General Plan*, County of Mendocino, http://www.co.mendocino.ca.us/planning/plans/planGeneralTOC.htm; *Lake County General Plan (2008)*, County of Lake, http://www.co.lake.ca.us/Page3939.aspx; *Napa County General Plan*, Napa County, http://www.countyofnapa.org/generalplan; *Solano County General Plan*, Solano County, http://www.co.solano.ca.us/depts/rm/planning/general_plan.asp.

⌘ As Seattle Gets Richer, the City's Black Households Get Poorer

Seattle-based megacorporations Microsoft, Starbucks, and Boeing serve as the premier employers of the area's middle and upper middle class. Such is not the case for black wage earners in the area. This piece serves as a sobering reminder of the increasing wage disparity between whites and blacks during the Obama presidency. The steady decline in black wages and household income is also responsible for the gentrification of Seattle's Central District, a once culturally and economically vibrant African American community. Another contributor to the outmigration of Africans Americans from the Central District is the decade-long influx of immigrants from Ethiopia and Eritrea.

It may feel like boom times in Seattle, but at least one group is being left out: the city's black residents.

While Seattle's median household income soared to an all-time high of $70,200 [in 2013], wages for blacks nose-dived to $25,700—a 13.5 percent drop from 2012. Among the 50 largest U.S. cities, Seattle now has the ninth lowest income for black households.

Seattle, which has the largest black community in the Pacific Northwest, also lags behind the country as a whole. Nationally, black households have median earnings of $34,800—35 percent higher than Seattle.

While last year's decline is particularly dramatic, black household wealth in Seattle has in fact been spiraling downward for years. Remarkably, the earnings were higher in 2000 than they are today, *before* adjusting for inflation: The 2000 household median was $32,000, equal to $44,800 in 2013 dollars.

Also, the rate of homeownership has dropped by nearly half since 2000. Today, just one out of five black households in Seattle own its home. (The census defines a black household as one in which the person identified on census forms as "householder" is black.)

Source: Gene Balk, "As Seattle Gets Richer, the City's Black Households Get Poorer," *Seattle Times*, November 12, 2014.

However, the reasons behind the decline are complex, and the area's shifting demographics play a key role.

For decades, the Central District was the heart of Seattle's African-American community—a stable, working-class neighborhood where many residents owned their homes. But with gentrification beginning in the late 1980s, blacks began leaving the neighborhood—and the city. By 2010, the Central District [CD]—which was nearly 80 percent black in 1970—had become majority white.

Despite changes in the CD, Seattle's overall black population has held steady in number, at around 47,000. But the composition of that population changed dramatically with the arrival of a new wave of émigrés from Africa—particularly Ethiopia and Eritrea—who settled mostly in Rainier Valley. In 2000, just 13 percent of blacks in Seattle were born outside the United States. Today, it's 30 percent.

Many of those immigrants are low-wage workers, which has contributed to the overall decline in income for black households here.

In an interesting demographic twist, as more whites are moving into the city, more blacks are relocating to the suburbs. If you're wondering where Seattle's African-American middle class went, check out parts of King County south of Seattle. In Renton, for example, where the black population has doubled since 2000, the median household income is $42,400—65 percent higher than Seattle.

But do demographic shifts alone adequately explain why the black community in affluent Seattle is among the poorest of any big city—and why Seattle's recent good economic fortune has coincided with less, rather than more, equality?

▓ Aurora's Growth Reflects That African-Americans Are Finding Base in Denver 'Burbs

In a selection from a larger article, Kurtis Lee and Jeremy P. Meyer reveal that black Denver has a phenomenon occurring that is similar to the outmigration of blacks in Seattle: the flight of black middle-class people from central districts like Five Points in Denver to the postsuburban community of Aurora, Colorado. Along with the Seattle story this piece complements the book's chapters on black community formation and illuminates social and economic challenges to the survival of black urban America.

When Ryan Ross began looking for a home to start a family with his new bride, he knew he was already priced out of the historic black neighborhood in Denver where he grew up. Instead, Ross moved to the Saddle Rock Ridge subdivision in southeast Aurora, finding a two-story, three-bedroom home with a large backyard in the Cherry Creek School District. "I love where I live," said Ross, 31, who is dean of students at the Community College of Denver. "Our neighborhood is great. Every time a friend of mine calls to say they are moving to Denver, I tell them about Aurora."

Ross is part of a migration occurring across the country and in the Denver metro area over the past decade. Young black people are abandoning the inner city and its historic black enclaves for the suburbs.

In the city and county of Denver, blacks were the only major racial and ethnic group that declined in numbers between 2000 and 2010, with about 200 fewer black residents. Denver's population is listed at 600,158. Aurora, however, added nearly 14,000 black residents over the same span—the largest increase in Colorado. Now, almost 16 percent of Aurora's 335,105 residents are black, up from 13 percent in 2000.

Source: Kurtis Lee and Jeremy P. Meyer, "Aurora's Growth Reflects That African-Americans Are Finding Base in Denver 'Burbs," *Denver Post,* March 24, 2012.

The change has had a rippling effect, causing historic black districts in Denver to wrestle with how to define themselves, forcing new black transplants to the suburbs to seek a community, and highlighting an increasing disparity of political representation.

"The world is changing," said Ronald Springer, owner of Akente Express, an African novelty and hair/skin-care emporium that has been a hub on the outskirts of Five Points for 21 years. Springer on a recent weekday stood on the steps of his Park Avenue West shop and pointed to the new buildings that surround it. "That is a condominium; those are town houses," he said, adding that homes nearby not long ago selling for less than $100,000 now fetch more than $300,000. "You'd think with all these people coming with their Audis, Porsches and Infinitis, that this place would be happening," he said. "It's not. I've seen my business go down 35 percent over the last six years. They aren't shopping in the neighborhood."

Springer points to the demise of traditional black storefronts in Denver like M&Ds Cafe, Capri Lounge & Fried Chicken and the Hue-Man Book Store. Not far from his shop is Coffee at the Point—a trendy gathering place in Five Points that offers gelato, lattes and free Wi-Fi. The cafe sits across from the historic Rossonian Hotel that in the 1930s and '40s hosted famous jazz greats like Duke Ellington and Charlie Parker.

Coffee at the Point co-owner Donovan Cobbins says the neighborhood has changed, and businesses must adapt to survive. His cafe has been successful by catering to the wide-ranging clientele. "It's tough. I have strong opinions about respecting the history of the Points, but you need to look toward the future," he said. "It's about finding that balance."

Suburban shift

Demographer William Frey of the Brookings Institution has studied national migration trends and found nearly every big city in the country shows a flight of blacks to the suburbs or to Southern states. "We have had such a long history of segregated inner-city neighborhoods," he said. "People grew up in them; their parents and grandparents grew up in them. Now we are several generations away from the civil-rights movement. There has been a great upgrading of standing for African-Americans in the country—better education, better jobs, higher incomes. Like most middle-class Americans, the suburbs have tended to be a symbol of prosperity, and it's especially true for African-Americans because for many years they have been shut out of the suburbs."

In 1994, Tim Dudley moved from Roanoke, Va., to Denver, buying a house in the Park Hill neighborhood near East 29th Avenue and Fairfax Street—where at the time, he says, 70 percent to 80 percent of his neighbors were black. Years later, Dudley and his wife sold the home they had lived in to a white couple, choosing to eventually move to southeast Aurora and into the Cherry Creek School District. "We liked Denver, but for us it was a matter of the education our kids were receiving. We wanted better," Dudley said.

From 2000 to 2010, Denver Public Schools lost 2,669 black students from its overall student population. In the same time span, Cherry Creek School District added 2,600 black students. State Rep. Rhonda Fields, who is one of two black legislators and the only one from Aurora, said schools and housing prices are two prominent factors pushing the trend. "The city (Aurora) is a great place to live and educate our children," Fields said. "I never lived in Denver; I've always lived in Aurora, and for me, personally, it was because of the school system." Fields' children attended schools in the Cherry Creek School District.

In many instances, blacks also are choosing to follow the culture. Omar Montgomery relocated from California to the Denver metro area in 2002, settling in Aurora after asking his black friends already here where he should live. "Aurora just has that feel," Montgomery said. "It's culturally diverse; there's large groups of people from all over the world that call this city home. It's a great place because it's still trying to define itself, and it's still growing."

Former Denver Mayor Wellington Webb said he saw the trend of blacks leaving Denver begin in the mid-1990s, understanding that people want bigger homes. But he said often those moving away soon discover there are extra charges for trash, and they are suddenly dealing with a longer commute. Politically, Webb said, the changing demographics are putting pressure on officeholders to develop crossover appeal. . . .

The next Five Points?

Ed Wingfield is perhaps the perfect example of what is happening with black migration from Denver to Aurora. The real estate broker moved to Aurora years ago, lured by cheaper housing and a sense that now the black community seems to be congregating in the metro region's second-largest city. Wingfield wanted to live in Denver where he had grown up, watching his father sing the blues in Five Points nightclubs. But homes in the Whittier and Five Points neighborhoods now sell for $125 a square foot, while Aurora homes are around $84 a square foot. Wingfield said he is pleased about his choice and is seeing traditional black businesses moving to Aurora, where he can now find soul food restaurants, barber shops and nightclubs. "I don't know if it is the right thing to say, but I love it here," Wingfield said. "I am always promoting Aurora as the next Five Points, the next black hot spot. I like the fact that my neighbors look like me and talk like me. It gives us a sense of culture that we shouldn't lose." He said he is happier that the region celebrates all cultures and races. "We are no longer a melting pot," he said. "We are more like a salad, where a tomato looks like a tomato, the lettuce look like lettuce. But mixed up together, it still tastes good."

PART 2

Racial Frontier

4 "Turn Our Faces to the West"

Refugees, Pioneers, and the
Roots of "All-Black" Oklahoma

Kendra T. Field

When ten-year-old Lomie Davis and her family left the Mississippi Delta and struck out for the new state of Oklahoma, they did so under the cover of night. "I remember they made a pallet on the floor. And we all went to bed," Lomie recalled seventy years later. A few hours into the night, Alexander and his wife, Della, awakened their children. "We left way in the middle of the night. To keep anyone from seeing us," Lomie Davis remembered. "It must have been midnight. . . . And we went to Oklahoma." Like many freedpeople at the turn of the century fleeing debt peonage and rising racial violence in the deep South, Lomie Davis's family "had to slip away" at night, leaving behind "whatever they couldn't carry." Davis recalled how another Mississippian left town: "One man, they put him in a box like he was a dead man. Made holes. And they shipped him away." Leaving the Delta was no easy feat. Nevertheless, in the fall of 1907, ten members of the Davis family arrived in the town of Wetumka, just as the surrounding territory became the new state of Oklahoma. In Oklahoma, they had heard, "everything was different."[1]

The same year that the Davises migrated to Oklahoma, Booker T. Washington recorded his observations of Indian Territory and early Oklahoma, describing his earlier visit in 1905 as having been "an opportunity for the first time to see the three races—the negro, the Indian, and the white man—living side by side, each in sufficient numbers to make their influence felt." Washington was especially thrilled by the influence of African American settlers: "One sees them everywhere, working side by side with white men." He described "their banks, business enterprises, schools, and churches," and especially their towns. He called particular attention to the town of Boley, which, "like the other negro towns that have sprung up in other parts of the country, represents a dawning race

Main Street looking north in Boley, Oklahoma, circa 1905. *Courtesy Research Center, Oklahoma Historical Society, Oklahoma City.*

consciousness, a wholesome desire to do something to make the race respected; something which shall demonstrate the right of the negro, not merely as an individual, but as a race, to have a worthy and permanent place in the civilization that the American people are creating."[2]

In their efforts to establish black towns and settlements in Indian Territory and Oklahoma, black journalists and professional town boosters—including, by this time, Washington—trumpeted a promising racial future in the West. They focused on the black towns as proud experiments in racial self-determination and domestic black enterprise. Unlike the Kansas "Exodusters" who had migrated in the 1870s, by the close of the century Oklahoma's migrants and boosters (some of whom had participated in the Kansas movement) had the advantages of newly "opened" lands and a burgeoning black press with which to publicize their visions and actions. Decades later, Oklahoma towns like Boley and Clearview would be nearly emptied by the Great Depression, the Dust Bowl, the world wars, and urban migration, but African-American citizens would continue to use the story of the black towns as evidence of the potential of "the race" for "civilization" and greatness, as indeed the towns were, in part, created to prove.[3]

This destinarian message of uplift and entrepreneurship papered over the pervasive national rhetoric of racial inferiority and obscured the reality of racial violence that was central to the origins of the black towns. The Davis family's migration to Indian Territory and early Oklahoma was part of a strategic political response to the violent conditions of the post-Reconstruction era, conditions that prompted tens of thousands of black southerners to take the leap. These women, men, and children set in motion the Great Migration. At the same time, their lives and choices illuminate the painstaking construction of race and nation in the United States at the turn of the twentieth century, and the centrality of violence therein.

At first, Lomie's eldest brother, Thad, stayed behind in the Mississippi Delta. A few years later, however, in spite of his desire to stay put, Thad was forced to leave. By this time, white landowners had threatened Thad and his young family with violence. Soon, "they went and set the house afire," Lomie relayed the story, "to burn him up." Her brother recalled "guns shooting," and afterward, she noted, these white men were "so sure that my brother had been killed." When they went to Thad Davis's house the next morning, however, they "saw he wasn't dead. He wasn't even there. He left and come to Oklahoma."[4] African American family histories resound with such stories of women, men, and children heading west in the middle of the night, fleeing violence.

This was not the first time that southern violence and western migration coincided. Two decades prior, in Carroll County, Mississippi, an armed force of one hundred white men on horseback had "moved on the court house, surrounded it, and opened . . . fire" on a group of "peaceable, unarmed" African Americans who "had shown their respect for the law by going to the court house" to attend a trial. Like thousands of former slaves during this time, more than twenty were killed for attempting to participate in the democratic process—that is, for appearing to be citizens, for appearing to be free. The next night, in Memphis, Ida Wells wrote in her journal, "O God, when will these massacres stop?" A few weeks later, Frederick Douglass spoke out. "In any other country such a frightful crime as the Carrolton massacre—in any other country than this," Douglass wrote, "a scream would have gone up from all quarters of the land for the arrest and punishment of these cold-blooded murderers . . . The heart of this nation is torpid, if not dead, to the natural claims of justice and humanity where the victims are of the colored race."[5]

In the violent aftermath of Reconstruction, murderous responses to black political and economic participation compelled African Americans to strategize a collective way out. "The disfranchised citizens of Mississippi and other states where the minority rules by force and fraud," the *National Republican* reported after the Carrollton Massacre, "should be helped to emigrate with their families to states where they will not be liable to massacre, where they will not be robbed of their political rights, nor defrauded of their wages." The paper added that it was the "duty of patriotic citizens" of the North to organize for the purpose of "transferring the oppressed from bondage to freedom, from darkness to light, from danger to safety." Later that summer, the *Chicago Observer* noted that the "most important act" of the Colored Press Association's August 1886 convention was an adopted resolution "urging migration of colored people from the South to the West."6

A few years following the Carrollton Massacre, one August night in 1892, Tom Moss, Calvin McDowell, and Will Stewart were murdered in Memphis. Although the local *Appeal-Avalanche* claimed that the murders had committed by a mob of "unknown" individuals, they nonetheless reported that Moss had "begged for his life, for the sake of his wife, his little daughter and his unborn infant." These infamous Memphis lynchings "opened my eyes," wrote Ida B. Wells, "to what lynching really was." In 1889, Tom Moss, Wells's friend and a respected Memphis postman, had founded the Peoples' Grocery, a cooperative grocery store that he co-owned with nine other prominent black Memphians. Three years later, William Barrett, a white nearby storeowner, perceived his business threatened by the competition from this black business. Barrett enlisted off-duty deputy sheriffs to destroy the People's Grocery. When Moss, McDowell, and clerk Stewart resisted, a gun battle broke out, and afterward they and one hundred African American supporters were arrested. While imprisoned, vigilantes removed Moss, McDowell, and Stewart from their cells, took them to a railroad yard, and shot them to death. Wells spoke out against the Memphis police and their refusal to arrest the men who committed these murders, and she launched her unprecedented investigation into "what lynching really was," that is, "an excuse to get rid of Negroes who were acquiring wealth and property." Months later, Wells recalled this moment as "our first object lesson in the doctrine of white supremacy."7

A lesser-known consequence of the Memphis lynchings, however, was western emigration. After begging for his life for the sake of his family, according to the *Appeal-Avalanche*, Moss's last words were: "If you will kill us, turn our faces to the West." Wells wrote from her office at the *Free Speech*, "There is therefore only one thing left that we can do; save our money and leave a town which will neither protect our lives and property, nor give us a fair trial in the courts, but takes us out and murders us in cold blood when accused by white persons." Alongside the *Free Speech*, black ministers and business owners urged black Memphians to "leave a community whose laws did not protect them." Wells later recalled that "a great determination seized upon the people to follow the advice of the martyred Moss and 'turn our faces to the West,' whose laws protect all alike." Within weeks, hundreds of black Memphians "left on foot to walk four hundred miles between Memphis and Oklahoma." One Baptist minister "went to the territory, built a church and took his entire congregation in less than a month." Just like that, historian Paula Giddings notes, "the nation's first antilynching movement had begun."[8]

Oklahoma was the place. As early as 1881, black Missouri promoter James Milton Turner said that thousands of freedpeople were prepared to enter Oklahoma Territory. In 1882 forty-five delegates said to represent sixty thousand African Americans convened in Parsons, Kansas to lobby Congress for the establishment of an all-black state. In the aftermath of the Oklahoma land runs of 1889, white newspaper editor Murat Halstead entertained the possibility of an all-black state within Oklahoma: "It would afford the colored people a rallying point, a land of actual liberty and equality, a place where they could develop according to their capacity, where there would be none to molest and make them afraid, and there is no question of the importance of the popularity of the movement. . . . It is not only possible, but probable, that this is the beginning of a solution of the question of the races, the most important and dangerous question for the people of the U.S. . . . a black state, populous, prosperous, enlightened, and honored." African American newspaper editor William Eagleson organized a company in Topeka, Kansas, that actively recruited African Americans, including Exodusters who had migrated to Kansas, to migrate to Oklahoma.[9]

Envisioning black freedom and economic opportunity in the Oklahoma Territory, former Kansas state auditor Edward McCabe traveled to Washington in the spring of 1890, where he conferred with President Harrison about the possibility of a "Black state" under his leadership. "We are here, first, as American citizens," McCabe said. "We are here because, as such, we have the right to be here." When Harrison questioned why Oklahoma, McCabe replied, "We wish to remove from the disgraceful surroundings that so degraded my people, and in the new territory in Oklahoma show the people of the U.S. and of the world that we are not only loyal citizens, but that we are capable of advancement, and that we can be an honor to those who broke down barriers of our slavery." By 1890, those "disgraceful surroundings" included the disfranchisement of black voters across the South through poll taxes, literacy tests, and other deliberate measures, as well as racial violence in response to economic success. Responding to this last straw in their political and economic disfranchisement, as well as the promise of a more free place, freedpeople "voted with their feet," heading to Oklahoma at the turn of the century by the thousands, on wagons, by foot, and railways.[10]

By the turn of the century, an expansive black press carried the torch for migration to Oklahoma. "Once to Every Man and Nation comes the moment to decide," Oklahoma's *Lincoln Tribune* declared in 1904. "Follow the Procession WESTWARD to the land of NOW. . . . The better class of colored people are invited to come and dwell in a land of freedom."[11] Notwithstanding such appeals to black capital, the movement straddled the diversity of class backgrounds, employment, and origins that comprised African American communities at the time. Moreover, racial violence and ritualized murder shaped all black lives at the close of the nineteenth century; this migration was, in part, refugee movement. "Like most black Oklahomans," biographer Lawrence Jackson writes, African American migrant Lewis Ellison (Ralph Ellison's father) was "something of a pioneer, something of a refugee."[12]

Facilitated by the press and stories of "free land," the scale of westward migration was unprecedented, and soon white and black settlers turned their eyes to the adjacent Indian Territory, home of the Creek, Cherokee, Choctaw, Chickasaw, and Seminole nations for the half-century since removal from their earlier, ancestral homelands in the present-day states of Georgia, Tennessee, Alabama, and Mississippi in the 1830s. In this way, African American settlers participated in the appropriation of Indian land. As one settler forecast in 1894, "The next move will then be upon the five civilized tribes, who own their lands in common. Then the whole of Indian Territory will have been swallowed by the white man. Many lots of black men help in the swallowing."[13] African American migration to Indian Territory was driven both by broad-based rumors of free land and the specific historical circumstances of the territory, especially the history and legacies of Native American slaveholding within the Creek, Cherokee, Chickasaw, Choctaw, and Seminole nations.

Before and after emancipation, many African-descended members of these Indian nations, free as well as enslaved, served as cultural brokers, ministers, negotiators, and interpreters, as Native Americans contended with tribal divisions, Indian removal, and the Civil War. After the war, the U.S. government made treaties with the Indian nations, requiring these nations to make certain provisions, including land, for freedpeople formerly enslaved within the Indian nations. Bolstered by the promise of citizenship and an equal share of tribal funds following emancipation, African-descended Creeks, for instance, had established themselves as subsistence farmers, as well as traders, merchants, and cattle ranchers in Creek country.[14]

Building upon such knowledge of slavery and freedom in Indian Country, rumors of redistributed Indian lands for freedpeople—especially among those who claimed Native ancestry—spread far beyond the territory, mingling with the post-emancipation promise of "forty acres and a mule." In 1881, Secretary of the Interior Samuel Kirkwood asked the commissioner of the General Land Office, Curtis W. Holcomb, to review whether freedpeople had rights to settle in the Oklahoma Territory in accordance with the postwar treaties with the so-called Five Civilized Tribes. Holcomb replied, "The treaty stipulations, as uniformly understood and construed, have no application to any other freedmen" except in the case of "freedom from Indian bondage." A decade later, however, such rulings mattered little in the face of the federal Dawes Commission, which converted collectively held Indian lands into individual allotments.[15]

Responding to land-hungry settlers within and beyond Indian Territory, as well as to rhetoric about private property as the cornerstone of "progress" and Indian assimilation, Congress passed the Dawes General Allotment Act in 1887. By the early 1900s, all collectively held Indian lands had been individually allotted by the Dawes Commission. In turn, many of these Native American (and black Indian) allotments were quickly sold or ceded to white and some newer black settlers. Moreover, the government offered the remaining "surplus" lands to new settlers. The Dawes Act depleted the indigenous land base and forced Native Americans into capitalist land markets. While the Creek, Cherokee, Choctaw, Chickasaw, and Seminole nations were initially exempted from this act, a decade later the federal government coerced their compliance with the passage of the Curtis Act of 1898. What underwrote this decision was the presence of so many non-Native settlers in Indian Territory. By 1900, there were more than three times as many non-Indians as Indians in Indian Territory, including tens of thousands of African American settlers. Five years later, on the eve of Oklahoma statehood, Booker T. Washington visited the territory and later commented on the rapid change: "One cannot escape the impression, in traveling through Indian Territory, that the Indians, who own practically all the lands, and until recently had the local government largely in their own hands, are to a very large extent regarded by the white settlers, who are rapidly filling up the country, as almost a negligible quantity. . . . The Indians have either receded—'gone back,' as the saying in that region is on the advance of the white race, or they have intermarried with and become absorbed with it."[16]

In spite of the history of shared resources among some African Americans, Native Americans, and black Indians, the advent of Oklahoma statehood gradually fractured such alliances. Facing the specter of statehood and segregation, some African American settlers who had previously invested in the promise of a "black state" turned toward the establishment of black towns and settlements, especially within the Creek and Seminole nations, where freedpeople had a long history of political participation and economic success. Government officials and humanitarian reformers pushed policies that would ensure the assimilation of Native peoples and land into Anglo-American society while at the same time seeking to define and segregate African Americans within a rigid racial dichotomy. Many Native Americans resisted allotment and Oklahoma statehood to the bitter end, momentarily advocating a separate State of Sequoyah in 1905, in order to retain control of their lands. Meanwhile, African-descended residents were excluded from both the Oklahoma statehood convention in 1905 and the Sequoyah Convention the same year. Subsequently, when Native American representatives to the Oklahoma constitutional convention objected to sharing schools and other facilities with African Americans as a result of constitutional segregation, Democratic delegate Robert Lee Williams offered an amendment; regarding the constitution, "the words 'colored' or 'colored race,' 'negro' or 'negro race' . . . shall be construed to apply to all persons of African descent. The term 'white race' shall include all other persons." In effect, "the provision defined Indians as legally white," one historian notes, and this became part of the 1907 constitution.[17]

In response to such developments, African Americans organized a separate convention of their own. Launching the Negro Protective League of Oklahoma and Indian Territories in August 1905 "for the purpose of arousing our people in the two territories to the importance of safeguarding our political and civic rights," hundreds of African Americans and black Indians ultimately condemned the segregationist state constitution. They nevertheless attempted to negotiate the best deal they could within the new system of allotment and the racial hierarchy codified therein. African American settlers of some means purchased allotments from Creek and Cherokee freedpeople, an increasingly common practice following federal allotment of Indian lands. In fact, the vast majority of the celebrated

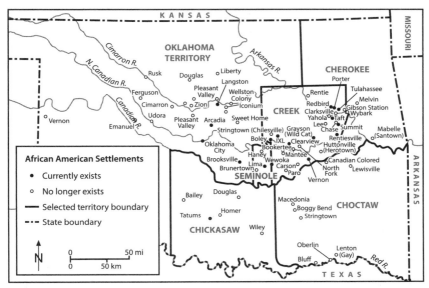

Oklahoma's African American towns and settlements. *Cartography by Joe Stoll.*

"all-black" towns of Oklahoma that emerged in the early twentieth century were built upon Indian allotments. These towns were often publicized by motivated white railroad investors, who hired black town promoters. On the eve of statehood in 1907, Oklahoma claimed more than sixty black towns and settlements.[18]

This complex moment of African American participation in the expropriation of Indian Territory was remarkably short-lived. Between 1890 and 1910, one hundred thousand African Americans migrated to the territory and early Oklahoma. Yet in the years following Oklahoma statehood in 1907, African American access to Indian land ended abruptly, with the advent of political exclusion, Jim Crow segregation, and oil speculation. Many African American migrants lost their land and the associated mineral rights to white settlers and oil speculators through a combination of legal and extralegal exploitation. Within months of statehood, the legislature effectively segregated all facilities within the state. As the *New York Times* reported, "The Democrats carried Oklahoma on the race issue. They planned Jim Crow [railroad] cars and all the other means of segregating the races which are in vogue in the Southern States." In turn, they "were expected by the people to lose no time in making good the issue on which they were elected." One after another, Jim Crow laws were passed to restrict African Americans from assembling and to impose segregation in housing, schools, railroad cars, and beyond. Moreover, African Americans were effectively prohibited, through policy and racial violence, from participating in state and local politics. On Christmas Eve following statehood, African American James Garden became the victim of Oklahoma's first lynching. Over the next eight years, nearly forty people were lynched in the new state, and the victims were almost exclusively black.[19]

When Lomie Davis's family arrived in Oklahoma in 1907, they settled on the outskirts of an "all-white" town, before moving on to a black settlement in Okfuskee County. With little property to their name, the family rented a one-room house, with a kitchen in an attached tent. By this time, white Oklahomans had begun officially prohibiting African American access to land. In 1911, white farmers throughout Davis's county signed oaths pledging to "never rent, lease, or sell land in Okfuskee County to any person of Negro blood, or agent of theirs; unless the land be located more than one mile from a white or Indian resident." This was a far cry from the dream of Oklahoma as an "all-black state" for freedpeople that had circulated—and received momentary consideration by President Harrison—just two decades prior.[20]

Two years later, Lomie Davis's father joined thousands of black Oklahomans as "African Pioneers" in the Chief Sam (Charles Alfred Sam) back-to-Africa movement, while thousands of others migrated instead to Canada and Mexico. By 1926, driven by a transnational vision of a "potential black space," black Oklahomans had launched twenty-eight chapters of Marcus Garvey's Universal Negro Improvement Association, renowned for its commitment to African repatriation. Challenging the notion of a static and withdrawn African American political life at the turn of the twentieth century, African-descended people led bold political lives in Indian Territory, and, when faced with the emergence of statehood and Jim Crow segregation, many refused to acquiesce and chose instead to emigrate. African American experiences in Indian Territory thus prefigure the emergence of Garveyism, the "New Negro" movement, and the Great Migration.[21]

Notes

1. Lomie (Davis) Reed, conversation with Cecil Cade and Mark A. Phillips, March 22, 1988, Houston, Texas, transcript in possession of author.
2. Booker T. Washington, "Boley: A Negro Town in the American West," *Outlook*, January 4, 1908, 28–31.

3. On exodus to Kansas, see Nell Irvin Painter, *Exodusters: Black Migration Kansas after Reconstruction* (1977; repr., New York: W. W. Norton, 1992). On emigration "fever" in Arkansas, see Kenneth C. Barnes, *Journey of Hope: The Back-to-Africa Movement in Arkansas in the Late 1800's* (Chapel Hill: University of North Carolina Press, 2004). On the press and nationalism, see Benedict Anderson, *Imagined Communities: Reflections on the Origin and Spread of Nationalism* (New York: Verso, 1983), chap. 3. For early historical treatment of Oklahoma's black towns, see, for instance, Arthur Tolson, *The Black Oklahomans: A History, 1541–1972* (New Orleans: Edwards Print, 1974); Norman L. Crockett, *The Black Towns* (Lawrence: Regents Press of Kansas, 1979).

4. Lomie (Davis) Reed conversation.

5. "The Latest Mississippi Massacre," *National Republican*, March 22, 1886; Frederick Douglass, "Southern Barbarism," speech on the occasion of the twenty-fourth anniversary of Emancipation in the District of Columbia, Washington, D.C., April 16, 1886, in *Frederick Douglass: Selected Speeches and Writings*, ed. Philip S. Foner, abridged and adapted by Yuval Taylor (Chicago: Lawrence Hill, 1999), 696–705; Ida Wells, diary entry, March 18, 1886, quoted in Paula J. Giddings, *Ida, a Sword among Lions: Ida B. Wells and the Campaign against Lynching* (New York: Amistad, 2008), 91.

6. *National Republican*, March 22, 1886; *Chicago Observer*, quoted in *Washington Bee*, August 28, 1886.

7. Ida B. Wells, *Crusade for Justice: The Autobiography of Ida B. Wells* (Chicago: University of Chicago Press, 1991), chap. 6; Giddings, *Sword among Lions*, chap. 6; Mia Bay, *To Tell the Truth Freely: The Life of Ida B. Wells* (New York: Hill and Wang, 2010), chap. 3; "what lynching really was" and "I then began": Wells, *Crusade for Justice*, 64.

8. *Appeal-Avalanche* quoted by Ida B. Wells at speech at Boston's Tremont Temple, "Lynch Law in All Its Phases," February 13, 1893, published in *Our Day* (Boston: Our Day, 1893), 333–47, reprinted in Ida B. Wells, *The Light of Truth: Writings of an Anti-Lynching Crusader*, ed. Mia Bay (New York: Penguin, 2008); Wells, *Free Speech*, quoted in Giddings, *Sword among Lions*, 189; "leave a community . . . a great determination . . . less than a month": *Appeal-Avalanche* quoted by Wells, "Lynch Law in All Its Phases," reprinted in Wells, *The Light of Truth*, 100–102; Giddings, *Sword among Lions*, 189.

9. Hannibal Johnson, *Acres of Aspiration: The All-Black Towns in Oklahoma* (Woodway, Tex.: Eakin, 2002), 29; Tolson, *Black Oklahomans*, 43; Murat Halstead, *Junction City (Kans.) Weekly Union*, March 15, 1890, 2. On Eagleson et al., see Jimmie Lewis Franklin, *Journey toward Hope: A History of Blacks in Oklahoma* (Norman: University of Oklahoma Press, 1982), 12, 30–31.

10. "Black state": Tolson, *Black Oklahomans*, 81; "To Make a Negro State; Western Black Men Organizing in Oklahoma. They Propose to Control that Territory—Equality Demanded—A Race War Threatened," *New York Times*, Feb. 28, 1890; "We are here": *Langston City Herald*, April 9, 1890; "We wish to remove": Tolson, *Black Oklahomans*, 79; "voted with their feet": Leon Litwack, *Trouble in Mind: Black Southerners in the Age of Jim Crow* (New York: Vintage, 1998), 484. See also Franklin, *Journey toward Hope*, 40.

11. *Lincoln Tribune* (Clearview, Indian Territory), September 17, 1904.

12. Lawrence Jackson, *Ralph Ellison: Emergence of a Genius* (University of Georgia Press, 2007), 2.

13. "The Next Move," *Memphis Scimitar*, reprinted in *Indianapolis Journal*, September 10, 1894. See also Daniel F. Littlefield Jr. and Lonnie Underhill, "Black Dreams and 'Free' Homes: The Oklahoma Territory, 1891–1893," *Phylon* 34, no. 4 (December 1973), 42.

14. On African-Creek communities during the immediate post-emancipation period, see Gary Zellar, *African Creeks: Estelvste and the Creek Nation* (Norman: University of Oklahoma Press, 2007), 34; Miles, *Ties that Bind: An Afro-Cherokee Family in Slavery and Freedom* (Berkeley: University of California Press, 2005); Celia Naylor, *African Cherokees in Indian Territory: From Chattel to Citizens* (Chapel Hill: University of North Carolina Press, 2008); Barbara Krauthamer, *Black Slaves, Indian Masters: Slavery, Emancipation, and Citizenship in the Native American South* (Chapel Hill: University of North Carolina Press, 2013); Kevin Mulroy, *The Seminole Freedmen: A History* (Norman: University of Oklahoma Press, 2007); Fay A. Yarbrough, *Race and the Cherokee Nation: Sovereignty in the Nineteenth Century* (Philadelphia: University of Pennsylvania Press, 2007); Circe Sturm, *Blood Politics: Race, Culture, and Identity in the Cherokee Nation of Oklahoma* (Los Angeles: University of California Press, 2002); Daniel Littlefield, *Africans and Creeks: From the Colonial Period to the Civil War* (Westport, Conn.: Greenwood, 1979); Claudio Saunt, *Black, White, and Indian: Race and the Unmaking of an American Family* (New York: Oxford University Press, 2005); Perdue, *Mixed Blood Indians: Racial Construction in the Early South* (Athens: University of Georgia Press, 2003).

15. Curtis W. Holcomb to S. J. Kirkwood, April 25, 1881, quoted in Arthur Lincoln Tolson, "The Negro in Oklahoma Territory, 1889–1907: A Study in Racial Discrimination" (PhD diss., Univ. of Oklahoma, 1966), 4.

16. Records relating to Intruders, Records of the Five Civilized Tribes Agency, National Archives, Fort Worth, Texas; Zellar, *African Creeks*, 161–62; Carter, *Dawes Commission*, 33–68. On parallel developments in New Mexico Territory, see Pablo Mitchell, *Coyote Nation: Sexuality, Race, and Conquest in Modernizing New Mexico, 1880–1920* (Chicago: University of Chicago Press, 2005). The Curtis Act of 1898 was an amendment to the Dawes Act of 1887. See Carter, *Dawes Commission*, 34–38; Washington, "Boley," 28–31.

17. Constitution of the State of Oklahoma, 1907, sec. 2, art. 23, and sec. 35, art. 6; untitled manuscript, n.d., folder 4, box 1, Robert Lee Williams Collection, Oklahoma Historical Society; "State of Sequoyah": *New York Times*, October 5, 1905; "the provision defined": David A. Chang, *The Color of the Land Race, Nation, and the Politics and Landownership in Oklahoma, 1832–1929* (Chapel Hill: University of North Carolina Press, 2010), 160–61.

18. On the Negro Protective League of Oklahoma, see Tolson, "Negro in Oklahoma Territory," 110–144; "for the purpose of": *Oklahoma Guide*, August 31, 1905, quoted in ibid., 110. On the role of railroads in settlement patterns, see Hamilton, *Black Towns and Profit: Promotion and Development in the Trans-Appalachian West, 1877–1915*

(Urbana: University of Illinois Press, 1991). On allotment sales and leasing, see Chang, *Color of the Land*, 161–62.

19. On the U.S. federal government and the dissolution of Indian Territory, see Chang, *Color of the Land*. See also "Lynching in New State," *New York Times*, December 25, 1907; "Democrats carried Oklahoma": "Give Roosevelt No Chance," *New York Times*, January 2, 1907; "Oklahoma Negro Issue Put up to Roosevelt," *New York Times*, February 2, 1907; "Grandfather's Clause," *New York Times*, October 27, 1910.

20. "Never rent, lease, or sell": *Okemah Ledger*, August 31, 1911, quoted in Crockett, *Black Towns*, 167.

21. Lomie Davis conversation; see "Chief Alfred Sam," in *The Marcus Garvey and UNIA Papers*, vol. 1, *1826–August 1919*, ed. Robert A. Hill and Carol A. Rudisell (Berkeley: University of California Press, 1983), 536–57, 483–84; Robert Hill, "Before Garvey: Chief Alfred Sam and the African Movement, 1912–1916," in *Pan-African Biography*, ed. Robert Hill (Los Angeles: University of California Press, 1987), 57; Kendra T. Field, "'No Such Thing as Stand Still': Migration and Geopolitics in African American History," *Journal of American History*, December 2015, 693–719; Kendra Field and Ebony Coletu, "The Chief Sam Movement, a Century Later: Public Histories, Private Stories, and the African Diaspora," *Transition* 114 (July 2014); William E. Bittle and Gilbert L. Geis, *The Longest Way Home: Chief Alfred Sam's Back-to-Africa Movement* (Detroit: Wayne State University Press, 1964); "potential black space": Tiya Miles and Sharon Holland, *Crossing Waters, Crossing Worlds: The African Diaspora in Indian Country* (Durham, NC: Duke University Press, 2006), 4.

On the UNIA in Okmulgee, see Robert A. Hill, Emory J. Tolbert, and Deborah Forczek, eds., *The Marcus Garvey and United Negro Improvement Association Papers*, vol. 3, *1920–1921* (Berkeley: University of California Press, 1984), 470; "Okmulgee U.N.I.A. Holds Monster Meeting," *Negro World*, March 19, 1921. On Weleetka and the UNIA, see Robert A. Hill, Tevvy Ball, and Erika A. Blum, et al., eds., *The Marcus Garvey and United Negro Improvement Association Papers*, vol. 9, *Africa for the Africans, 1921–1922* (Berkeley: University of California Press, 1995), 316n1. On continuing civil rights activism at home, see Melissa Stuckey, "All Men Up: Race, Rights, and Power in the All-Black Town of Boley, Oklahoma, 1903–1939," PhD diss., Yale University, 2009. On Garveyism in the rural South, see Hahn, *A Nation under Our Feet: Black Political Struggles in the Rural South, from Slavery to the Great Migration* (Cambridge, MA: Belknap Press of Harvard University Press, 2005), epilogue; Mary G. Rolinson, *Grassroots Garveyism: The University Negro Improvement Association in the Rural South, 1929–1927* (Chapel Hill: University of North Carolina Press, 2007).

5 Poetic Justice

Bay Area Afro-Asian Women's
Activism through Verse

Jeanelle Hope

who's gonna make all
that beautiful blk/rhetoric
mean something.
Like
I mean
Who's gonna take
The words
Blk/is/beautiful
And make more of it
  —Sonia Sanchez, 1970

In 1967, poet Sonia Sanchez, then in her early thirties, was approached by the Black Student Union (BSU) at San Francisco State University's Experimental College and asked to teach black literature and help found the first black studies department in the nation. Two years later, the institution became home to the very first college of ethnic studies, inspiring student activism across the nation. Because of her efforts during the Black Power movement and ability to brilliantly capture the black experience through verse, Sanchez is revered as one of the great black women poets. Her work goes beyond artistic expression; it tells a story, evokes images of lived experience, and serves as a call and form of activism, a poetic disruption to the status quo that verbally challenges systems of oppression. Sanchez's call, "Who's gonna make all that beautiful [black] rhetoric mean something?" stands as a critique of Black Power and the Black Arts Movement (BAM), which she was immersed in, pushing artists and activists to "make

Sonia Sanchez during her years at San Francisco State
College, 1969. *Courtesy Sonya Sanchez.*

more of" the black aesthetic, moving beyond idealism and theory and into a
sustainable movement and praxis, broadening the way in which we discuss the
paradoxical struggle and beauty of being black. This call was certainly manifest
physically during the years immediately following its publication. The brief but
pioneering period of 1970–72 brought forth the height of the Black Panther Party
(BPP) and its "intercommunal" survival programs, as well as solidarity and
collective activism among organizations of color throughout the San Francisco
Bay Area: the Red Guard Party, Black Panther Party, Asian American Political
Alliance (AAPA), American Indian Movement (AIM), Brown Berets, and others.

Beyond the physical manifestations of Sanchez's call, it also emerged meta-
phorically and within the space of art and poetry—a space where writers and
activists of color vividly expressed their experiences, struggles, and tactics for
organizing and displayed solidarity by articulating elements of shared struggle.
James Smethurst calls the articulation of early Black Power politics through
poetry "literary nationalism."[1] In addition to expressing of various forms of
nationalism, Black Power era poetry was also very much a literary expression
of Third World solidarity and revolutionary internationalism.

With the historical narrative of the Black Power movement being male-centered and placing an immense value on traditional sources of knowledge, privileging biographies, autobiographies, and archival materials, those on the margins of this history—women, queer- identifying people, disabled people, nonblack people of color, and others—face historical erasure. The voices of women have gone unrecognized and undocumented within the mainstream Black Power historical narrative. Elaine Brown, Kathleen Cleaver, and a handful of other women who were able to ascend to power or notoriety have written their own works, but the voices of everyday women, those comprising the rank and file of the Black Power movement, including nonblack women of color, have largely gone unrecognized and even unmentioned.[2] This chapter is an effort to recover those voices and insert them into this history. By placing poetry at the center of this discourse we can reframe our understanding and lend new perspectives and voices to the historical narrative of the Black Power era.

Sanchez asks who will do the work—the work of dismantling racism, capitalism, ableism, classism, cis- and heteronormativity, sexism, et cetera, all of which heavily impact women of color. Beyond displacing women from the historical narrative of the Black Power movement, so much of the material produced on the period neglects to reinforce the importance of collective activism and solidarity between blacks and other people of color. Laura Pulido's *Black, Brown, Yellow, and Left: Radical Activism in Los Angeles* and Jeffery Ogbar's "Rainbow Radicalism: The Rise of Radical Ethnic Nationalism" speak to this history, but there is a visible gap in the literature when discussing black and Asian solidarity. More focused contributions to the documentation of Afro-Asian activism have been made by Daryl Maeda, Nico Slate, Dianne Fujino and a few others. (I will use the term "Afro-Asian" throughout this work to denote collective activism between the two groups within a U.S. context.) A great deal remains left uncovered, though, especially perspectives from women. In addition to centering poetry, this work centers the voices of black and Asian American women poets immersed in activism primarily in the Bay Area, as this region quickly radicalized after World War II, producing and serving as home to countless poets, activists, and organizations during the 1960s and 1970s. Moreover, the U.S. West, but the Bay Area in particular, became a place where blacks and Asians migrated to the region simultaneously and lived in close proximity, dealing with many of the same oppressions: limited access to housing and education, increased unemployment, poor compensation and working conditions, and racial discrimination generally.

Asian American protesters in front of Oakland courthouse, l969. *Courtesy Roz Payne.*

The increased migration of blacks and Asians to California has run parallel since the discovery of gold in the state in 1848. The pre-Civil War racial climate and legalized enslavement prevented many blacks from venturing to California freely. Blacks were often brought with their 49er enslavers, but some Blacks from the North—including Canada—came autonomously, and some had luck striking gold and settling in the state. Across the Pacific, China was recovering from the first opium war. With word of the discovery of gold in California, coupled with the need for a labor force to complete the transcontinental railroad, the state would soon witness the immigration of "strangers from a different shore."[3] The Chinese were among the first Asian immigrants to settle in California. During the early years of the gold rush, just a few hundred Chinese settled in the state, but by 1870 there were nearly 63,000 Chinese in the United States, 77 percent of whom were in California.[4] A vast majority of those settled in San Francisco, as the nearby Angel Island was a principal immigration station. As "strangers" and "outsiders," the Chinese population presented the state with a challenge as they disrupted the strictly enforced racial binary.

By the 1870s, the two groups were identified by the state as the clearly inferior races, as schools were segregated, housing marginalized, Chinese immigration halted (with the Chinese Exclusion Act of 1902), and jobs, once plentiful, became scarce and paid less. The Chinese in San Francisco created an immigrant community and enclave that came to be known as Chinatown. Many Chinese immigrants also chose to reside across the bay in Oakland, creating another but smaller Chinatown. Following the 1906 San Francisco earthquake, residents of that city's Chinatown sought refuge in Oakland, as much had been destroyed. At the turn of the century, Japanese immigration to California skyrocketed, as many came to fill cheap labor positions.[5] During World War II, while the Japanese were forced into internment camps, the Bay Area presented some of the greatest opportunities for African Americans in what was heralded as the "largest shipbuilding center in the world," and decent-paying jobs were plentiful.[6] Between 1940 and 1945, Oakland and the nearby city of Richmond, witnessed a combined 5,341.1 percent increase in African American population, as many moving west in search of opportunity and to escape the Jim Crow South.[7] Many African American Bay Area migrants came from Louisiana, Texas, Arkansas, Mississippi, Alabama, Georgia, and Oklahoma, and most of these people were no more than two generations removed from slavery.

What this abbreviated history illustrates is that blacks and Asians have always been in close proximity with each other in the Bay Area and fared with similar conditions with regard to race relations, housing, and access to resources. Moreover, the exploited labor of these two groups, as well as labor by Mexicans, other Latin Americans, and Native Americans, helped California generate its wealth. After World War II, conditions went downhill for blacks in California, with deindustrialization and reduced employment opportunity. By 1966, black frustration and anger was coming to a head, and many grew disillusioned with the civil rights movement and tired of living in what many felt was a police state. A younger generation helped usher in the Black Power movement, forming organizations including the Black Panther Party, US Organization, the Revolutionary Action Movement (RAM), the Third World Liberation Front (TWLF), and a host of other campus and community-based groups. Moreover, the movement also inspired artists countrywide who wanted to lend their support and engage in the struggle.

BAM! The Explosion of the Black Arts Movement
and Ethnic Artistic Expression

While the Black Power and Asian American movements comprised an on-the-ground fight against various systems of oppression, their activism and spirit was manifested in literature, scholarship, and art. Within the civil rights movement, the Freedom Singers, Fannie Lou Hamer and others often expressed their activism through song, and "We Shall Overcome" became the unofficial anthem of the movement. By the 1960s, with the emergence of writers like Amiri Baraka, Sonia Sanchez, Nikki Giovanni, and others, poetry moved to the forefront. Black poets often supported and amplified the views and goals of Black Power organizations and the movement at large.

While the Black Arts Movement and Black Power were interconnected and both grounded themselves in cultural nationalism, there were tensions between the two, the most obvious being with the Black Panther Party. BPP founders Huey Newton and Bobby Seale fought for the rights to the Black Panther name with a rival organization, the Black Panther Party of Northern California, that had known links to the US Organization.[8] US founder Maulana Karenga's Kawaida philosophy can perhaps best be described as a neo-African counterculture.[9] Newton, Seale, and other early members of the BPP found the US Organization's fixation on culture to be unproductive, as it didn't fully address the problems being confronted by the masses. Poets Amiri Baraka (who had ties to US), Sonia Sanchez, and Askia Touré were all called out to the Bay Area between 1966 and 1968 and had their contributions to black freedom discounted as cultural nationalism by many members within the local Black Panther chapters. While these poets were brought to California to radicalize and help the Black Arts Movement grow, they too were shaped and molded by circumstances there, including the student movement at San Francisco State. The formation of the TWLF—a coalition of students from the college's BSU, Filipino American Students Organization, Latin American Students Organization, American Indian Students Organization, BPP members, and others—helped shift the political mind-set of Sanchez and Baraka from cultural nationalism to radical internationalism and Marxism as they witnessed expressions of solidarity on campus and recognized that the students' struggle was global and inextricably linked to class struggle.[10]

But art has a direct role in this struggle, Maulana Karenga argued: "Black art must be for the people, by the people and from the people . . . that is to say that it must be functional, collective and committing."[11] Moreover, black art must make a statement. These sentiments echoed Mao Zedong:

> In the world today all culture, all literature and art belong to definite classes and are geared to definite political lines. There is in fact no such thing as art for art's sake, art that stands above classes, art that is detached from or independent of politics. Proletarian literature and art are part of the whole proletarian revolutionary cause. . . . Revolutionary culture is a powerful weapon for the broad masses of people. It prepares the ground ideologically before the revolution comes and is an important, indeed essential, fighting front in the general revolutionary front during the revolution.[12]

Thus, according to Mao and Karenga, black and Asian artists have a responsibility to voice the concerns of the masses, and they are integral to the revolution and struggle. During the Black Power era, the United States was simultaneously involved in the Vietnam War, occupation of Okinawa, and other international disputes that took black men and other men of color out of the country. But these servicemen were kept informed of the movement back home. Thanks not only to media by and about the Black Panthers and the US Organization but also to BAM-inspired poetry, many would returned home and joined Black Power organizations and contribute to the Black Arts Movement.[13] Political art can keep people informed who may not be immersed in a movement and, conveyed via media, can link the masses no matter where they are—and thus help the movement grow.

Black women were key poets during the era. Cheryl Clarke's book *"After Mecca": Women Poets and the Black Arts Movement* investigates the role black women's contributions to documenting, challenging, and engaging in struggle. They were writing and performing what they witnessed in their communities, asserting a political stance, and challenging white supremacy, oppressive notions of blackness, and especially sexism and hyper-masculinity. The current historical narratives of all three movements (Black Power, Black Arts, and Asian American) continue to rely on traditional discourses, and the poetry that has been integrated into these narratives tends to speak to the male experience (e.g., that of Larry Neal, Amiri Baraka, Sterling Plumpp) or feature voices from a small pool of women whose works have been most popular—Sanchez, Gwendolyn Brooks, Nikki Giovanni, and a few others.

Why is it that so few black women poets' voices have been heard from this period? Knowledge is typically constructed monolithically as a means to control and limit its complexities and maintain exclusivity. Furthermore, this control continues today to oppress women, people of color, queer-identifying people, and others straddling the margins, as their voices, views, and knowledge are suppressed and subsequently undervalued and devalued.[14] Patricia Hill Collins argues that the Western conception of epistemology is maintained to protect the interests of powerful white men.[15] Digging into archives and the likes of Aristotle, Thomas Jefferson, and Michel Foucault is viewed as real research, and anything different from this is often called into question and considered inauthentic. Western scholarship and archival research is integral, but it provides little room for oppressed people to insert themselves into history on their own terms. We must move beyond this western framework in order to begin democratizing knowledge and provide new perspectives.

During the early postcolonial period—the 1960s and 1970s in the Global South, black and cultural nationalists, black feminists and others, made strides to reclaim cultural elements that were lost and systematically erased during colonialism. But the dominant culture maintains authority and continues to erase, whitewash, and depoliticize. In "Notes on Deconstructing 'the Popular'," cultural theorist Stuart Hall additionally argues that the internalization of such erasure and suppression of one's culture acts in the favor of the dominant group.[16] Reading this in tandem with Frantz Fanon's articulation of mental enslavement, as argued in *The Wretched of the Earth*, can crystallize our understanding of how it is in the interest of those in power to suppress the voices, culture, and knowledge of a people, as we are forced to see and experience life as "other."[17] However, with resistance and rejection of "other" status—as witnessed in the Black Power and Black Arts movements—come increased exploration and understanding of cultural identity. This is why culture is as integral to liberation as political views sharpened by the likes of Marxism and socialism.

Black women navigate a world of intersecting oppressions. Their thoughts, ideas, voices, and work have been suppressed under institutions and structures entrenched in both white supremacy and patriarchy. They are often coerced into subscribing to the dominant discourse, and their work is undervalued, something that is evident with women's poetry in the Black Arts Movement as well as within the academy in general. Barbara Ransby, Tracye Matthews, and Angela Davis have worked to disrupt and combat internal oppression and push for the inclusion of women's work and voices within the field of Black Power studies. During the Black Power era, women fought tirelessly for their voices to be heard, and poetry provided a seemingly autonomous space that was free from the in-your-face sexism and misogyny they experienced in the movement.[18] The BPP and US have both been critiqued for their poor gender politics and gross mistreatment of women comrades.

Ntozake Shange, Jayne Cortez, Wanda Coleman, Mari Evans, and Gwendolyn Brooks achieved some level of fame because of their canny ability to express struggle through poetry. At first just members of an informal collective of writers, they would eventually attain canonic status. Femi Funmi Ifetayo (Regina Micou) published her first book of poetry in 1970 when she was still a high school student in Detroit. While Ifetayo was very young at the time, her work expressed many of the themes and styles and much of the complexity of poetry from the movement. She opens *We the BLACK WOMAN* by stating that "these poems express the role of the black woman in America, in the search of manhood for black men. They also express the 'tom' ways of some black people."[19] Ifetayo makes it evident that she will be grappling with black nationalism, and throughout her work other themes emerge, including black capitalism and the commodification of the Black Power aesthetic, a tension within her own gender politics, the calling out of apathetic members of the community, and the challenging of sexism in the movement.

> To be black
> is not only the
> color of your skin
> the thickness of your natural
> the way you come on strong
> your beard
> or the dashikis, gowns, and tikis you wear
> a brother could be—
> natural back
> Afro-down
> With a beard and looking good
> but . . .
> Check him out
> To be black
> Is togetherness of your mind
> Your awareness
> Of what's going down
> Around you

And also the love, trust, and
Respect for your people
Especially for your women[20]

By listing characteristics of the Black Power aesthetic, Ifetayo is questioning authenticity, loyalty, and dedication to the movement. She challenges the consciousness of the black community by asking it to move beyond what has previously been written about of blackness and radicalism. While this poem and the entirety of Ifetayo's work are very much aligned with early 1960s black nationalism, she confronts this political orientation when she places her womanhood in the forefront. Her emphasis on women speaks to the call for inclusion and recognition of women's labor within the movement. This creates tension since historically women have often been oppressed and their labor unrecognized in black nationalist spaces, and shows how the thinking and politics of Black Power youth were evolving.

Similarly to the case of black women, Asian American women navigate a society with intersecting oppressions. In the groundbreaking anthology *Making Waves*, the editors state, "Asian American women grow stronger with the support of their communities and other activist movements. In the end, though, no one else can speak for them. They, like all of us, must speak for themselves. We can expect no one else to fight our battles; we must fight them ourselves. We must make our own waves."[21]

Historically, Asian American women's voices have been suppressed. *Making Waves* was one of the first books that sought to recover and create a space for these voices—in movement building and in history. It reflects the various modes in which Asian American women speak out, poetry being one of them—there are many poems featured in the anthology—and also shows how Asian American women have been greatly influenced by other people of color. Yuri Kochiyama and Richard Aoki, two prominent Afro-Asian activists, discuss how central and inspirational the Black Power movement was in their own radicalization and formation of the Asian American movement. Activists like Bea Dong, Vicki Wong, and other Asian American women activists were fighting for equality within student and community organizations like the Asian American Political Alliance (AAPA) and the Red Guard Party, both greatly modeled after the BPP. Others were inspired by Sanchez and the growing BAM scene in the Bay Area between 1967 and the early 1970s, which produced poets Tomi Tanaka, Janice Mirikitani, Nellie Wong, and others.

For many Asian Americans, poetry was a fluid space of expression, creativity, and literary nationalism where their work didn't have to ascribe to rigid Western grammatical restrictions. (For some, English was their second language.) Beyond activism, Asian American women's poetry discussed language, family, politics, migration stories, memories, and spirituality.[22] As the second-wave feminist movement, Asian American movement, and Black Power movement evolved, many poems by Asian American women developed feminist undertones and became critical of patriarchy and the gender politics in the Asian American movement. Tomi Tanaka's poem "from a lotus blossom cunt" describes the complications of gender in the Asian American movement and the trials of living within a patriarchal culture.

> I'm still with you, brothers
> Always
> But I'm so damned tired
> Of being body first, head last
> Wanting to love you when all
> You want is a solution to the glandular discomfort . . .
> Try to use us,
> And you'll lose us
> Join us[23]

Tanaka's poem was published in 1971 and was groundbreaking. Her Third World feminist critique stands with the works of Audre Lorde, Ntozake Shange (another poet based in the Bay Area during part of the Black Power movement), and bell hooks, as she refuses to have a "race first" outlook but is posing an intersectional fight. In "La Güera," Cherríe Moraga recalls her experience of seeing Ntozake Shange perform, saying that "she was speaking a language that I knew—in the deepest parts of me—existed, and that I had ignored in my own feminist studies and even in my own writing. What [Shange] caught in me is the realization that in my development as a poet, I have, in many ways, denied the voice of my brown mother—the brown in me."[24] Beyond their activist contributions, Tanaka and Shange provided a language for other women to use to begin voicing their frustrations and struggles.

By 1969 the Black Arts Movement was so successful that it spawned several publishing houses, including Broadside Press (Detroit) and the Third World Press (Chicago) founded by Dudley Randall and Haki Madhubuti. In the Bay Area between 1966 and 1975 the movement helped produce several underground magazines, journals, and anthologies, including *Aion* (the first Asian American literary magazine, edited by Janice Mirikitani); and the *Journal of Black Poetry* (published in San Francisco), and *Aiiieeeee! An Anthology of Asian American Writers* (published by Howard University Press, a black press).

The BPP, which, as mentioned, was skeptical of cultural nationalism, even began including a "Black Revolutionary Poetry" section in its newspaper. This would become one of the most dependable spaces in which to find works written by and about Panther women. In the May 4, 1969, *Black Panther*, almost all of the work featured is by women, but Marsha's poem, "POW," stands out for its eerie description of black death.

> His brain splattered to the dotted floor
> my people's hearts and pains
> created the pattern of red upon that dotted base
> I could see my mother on her
> knees
> Whimpering
> my stomach growling
> my knees shaking from cold created the blood stained patterns
> on the floor
> Bunchy, John—the result of this
> pigs' madness
> that sadistic half-dicked mother fucking fool
> and don't forget those who stand in the way
> the unconcerned
> shall also make a bloody pattern
> on the pavement
> for the vanguard has a pact with the people
> to fight the death
> 'cause it's time for the madmen
> to unclench their fists, and stop
> standing on their toes
> waiting to move
> papa's coming home
> Huey's coming home,
> and the oppressor shall vanish.

Marsha's poem sheds light on the harsh reality and by-products of violence and death within the BPP and the movement at large. It is very easy to romanticize revolutions and neglect to realize that human beings are dying and families left to eternally grieve. Marsha's vivid description of spewed blood seems to come from her firsthand experience of the tragic shootout between the US Organization and the BPP at UCLA in January 1969 which resulted in the death of Alprentice "Bunchy" Carter and John Huggins. She curses the police as they aren't concerned and probably got some sort of pleasure in witnessing the death of party members—after all, the police were at war with the Panthers. Marsha remains steadfast in holding hope that the movement will push forward with the return of Huey P. Newton, who at this point was in prison for the shooting of Oakland police officer John Frey. Newton was later released in 1970. Arguably, Marsha's adoration of Huey is rooted in messianism, which is contradictory to the foundation of the Black Power movement. Black Power activists sought self-empowerment and grassroots organizing and criticized the civil rights movement for its overreliance on leaders like Martin Luther King Jr. In a later issue of *Black Panther*, Ericka Huggins, a prominent member of the party and wife of John Huggins, follows up on Marsha's telling of the UCLA incident. In Huggins's poem she laments that her infant daughter Mai will spend her early years parentless: not only has her father been murdered, but also her mother is being hunted by the state.

Other Panther women used poetry to voice their views. The April 6, 1970, issue of the *Black Panther* features five poems by women members, four of which are by Afeni Shakur, New York Black Panther Party member who would later be known as the mother of poet and rapper Tupac Shakur. Shakur's "The Lesson" presents her solution to messianism:

> Malcolm awoke and saw what appeared to be the mountain of
> liberation—he was murdered
> Martin started up that mountain and found there was a beauty
> and lasting peace—he was murdered
> Huey went all the way up and came down again to speak to the world
> of the solidarity there—he was shot & kidnapped
> Eldridge saw my desire to go up and showed me the rugged path—
> he was forced into exile
> Bobby took my hand to lead me there and I found the way rough and
> exhilarating and of course he was gagged, beaten, and chained
> Fred overheard their directions and took to the hills for a closer
> look—what he saw made him go back down to share
> his happiness

When he came back in the valley, all I could hear him say was—
    I am a Revolutionary
But, it made no sense and so I just sat and listened
The next day I heard him repeat this melody as he prepared the
    morning meal for my child
I heard the words—and still I was quiet; Fred didn't seem to mind—
    he just kept doing things and singing his song
And then one day—the melody of his song was taken up by the evil
Winds of human destruction
They heard its message and handed to him, the salary of a people's
    servant
KA BOOM—
The air that breathed his message to me was alive with urgency.
The mountains became a reality
The tools became friends
The curves became mere objects of jest!
I could sit still no longer
I began to hum his song
As I climbed, as I fell and
Got up and fell again—I
Sang the song of liberation
I AM A REVOLUTIONARY!
I AM A REVOLUTIONARY!

Instead of placing her aspirations for activism within the male figures the names, Shakur views them as martyrs who have inspired her as she proudly proclaims, "I AM A REVOLUTIONARY!"

The Mission District of San Francisco, which is currently being ravaged by gentrification, was once home to, and served as a stage for, many BAM poets, including Ntozake Shange, Jessica Hagedorn, Alfonso Texidor, and Victor Hernandez Cruz.[25] In the neighboring community known as the Tenderloin, Janice Mirikitani juggled working for Glide Memorial Church, editing multiple literary and poetry journals, and organizing with the AAPA. In 2000 she would be named the city's poet laureate, and while her political and humanitarian work have certainly left a mark on the city, her poetry speaks to a poetic space black and Asian women shared in solidarity, articulating their struggle. Her "Jungle Rot and Open Arms" is a reflection on the care Asian American women provided their brothers

returning from war and the near emptiness women experienced. Dedicated "For
a Vietnam Veteran brother, ex-prisoner," after two opening stanzas it continues:

> my anger
> for the enemy heads
> of states
> boiled to nothing
> nothing
> in the wake of his rage
> jungle rot
> had sucked his bones
> his fell
> like the monsoon
> his brain
> in a cast in Leavenworth
> In the midst
> of genocide
> he fell in love
> in Vietnam.
> "Her hair was
> long and dark—like yours"
> he said
> "her eyes held the
> sixth moon
> and when she smiled
> the sky opened
> and I fell through
> I would crawl in the tall grasses to her village
> and sleep the war
> away with her
> like a child on my thighs
> I did not know
> of the raid
> and woke
> with her arm
> still clasping mine
> I could not find

The rest of her
So I buried her arm
and marked my grave"
We sat in silence
That mocks fools
That lifts us to the final language
his breath sapped by B-52's
his eyes blinded by the blood of children
his hands bound to the bayonets
his soul buried in a shallow grave
I stood amidst
his wreckage
and wept for myself.
so where is my
political education? my
rhetoric answers to everything? my
theory in practice? My
intensification of life in art?
words
are
like
the stone
the gravemarker
over an arm
in Vietnam[26]

This poem details the trials Asian American men endured in Vietnam, including falling in love with women there. It possess a certain ambiguity as it is unclear if this "brother" is a family member or a lover, but in either case Mirikitani is left with emptiness, as he can longer love her. He is "jungle rot," yet she still finds words to embrace, care for, and love him. This nonreciprocal relationship leaves her lonely, depressed, and in search of her own identity. These feelings could have taken over and deprived her of any sort of life, but she recognizes that there is much more that she must do and instead symbolically buries her brother in Vietnam, and his death is a catalyst for her turning to activism.

The poets mentioned throughout this chapter provide a different optic for use in analyzing the late sixties and early seventies and Afro-Asian activism in the Bay Area. For Asian American and black women, poetry provided an escape from the gross sexism they encountered on the ground. It was an area in which they possessed control and agency of their thoughts and expression. Their words helped craft the political education, rhetoric, and now history of the movement. These women poets' radical, pioneering efforts and those of other Third World youth in the multicultural Bay Area helped expand a movement of black and cultural nationalism into one of intersectional awareness and international-ism. They responded loudly and clearly to Sanchez's rhetorical question as to who would create something more of black rhetoric. The answer: "We will!" The voices of these women not only addressed oppression and challenged the movement but also created a Third World feminist rupture, establishing that feminism was not owned by whites and that the Black Power movement was not owned by men, and humanized what it meant to struggle. Their sometimes blunt articulations, stripped of romanticism, remind us of the casualties of the movement from friendly fire.

These poems are especially valuable today and should serve as cautions in the Movement for Black Lives and related movements (#nativelivesmatter, #say-hername, #translivesmatter, and #asians4blacklives) against state-sanctioned violence, white supremacy, and systemic racism and capitalism.

Notes

Chapter epigraph: Sonia Sanchez, *We a BaddDDD People* (Detroit: Broadside Press, 1970), 15.

1. James Edward Smethurst, *The Black Arts Movement: Literary Nationalism in the 1960s and 1970s* (Chapel Hill: University of North Carolina Press, 2005).
2. See Trayce Matthews, "'No One Ever Asks What a Man's Role in the Revolution Is': Gender and Politics in the Politics of the Black Panther Party, 1966–1971," in *The Black Panther Party Reconsidered*, ed. Charles Jones (Baltimore: Black Classic Press, 1998).
3. Ronald Takaki, *A Different Mirror: A History of Multicultural America* (New York: Back Bay Books, 2008), 79.
4. Ibid.
5. Diane Fujino, *Samurai among Panthers: Richard Aoki on Race, Resistance, and a Paradoxical Life* (Minneapolis: University of Minnesota Press, 2012), 2–3.
6. Albert Broussard, "In Search of the Promised Land: African American Migration to San Francisco 1900–1945," in *Seeking El Dorado: African Americans in California*, ed. Lawrence DeGraaf, Kevin Mulroy, and Quintard Taylor (Seattle: University of Washington Press, 2001), 190.
7. Ibid.

8. Bobby Seale, *Seize the Time: The Story of the Black Panther Party and Huey P. Newton* (New York: Random House, 1970), 113, 115, 119, 124–25.

9. Smethurst, *Black Arts Movement*, Kindle location: 3967.

10. Ibid.

11. Maulana Karenga, *The Quotable Karenga* (Los Angeles: US, 1967), 22.

12. Mao Tse-Tung, *Quotations from Chairman Mao Tse-Tung* (Peking: Foreign Language Press, 1966), 299–300.

13. Smethurst, *Black Arts Movement*, 34. See also Yuichiro Onishi, *Transpacific Antiracism: Afro-Asian Solidarity in 20th-Century Black America, Japan, and Okinawa* (New York: New York University Press, 2013), 138–82.

14. Cheryl Clarke, *"After Mecca": Women Poets and the Black Arts Movement* (New Brunswick, N.J.: Rutgers University Press, 2005), 1.

15. Patricia Hill Collins, *Black Feminist Thought: Knowledge, Consciousness, and the Politics of Empowerment*, 2nd ed. (New York: Routledge, 2000), 253.

16. Stuart Hall, "Notes on Deconstructing 'the Popular,'" in *Cultural Theory and Popular Culture: A Reader*, ed. John Storey (New York: Routledge, 2008), 508–18.

17. See Frantz Fanon, *The Wretched of the Earth* (New York: Grove Press, 1963.

18. See Jeanelle Hope, "Black, Yellow, and Shades of Purple: Radical Afro-Asian Collective Activism in the San Francisco Bay Area From the Perspectives of Women in the Struggle, 1966–1972" (master's thesis, Syracuse University, 2014).

19. Femi Funmi Ifetayo, *We the BLACK WOMAN* (Chicago: Third World Press, 1970), 11.

20. Ibid.

21. Asian Women United of California, "Part Seven Introduction," in *Making Waves: An Anthology of Writings by and about Asian American Women* (Boston: Beacon Press, 1989), 348.

22. *Between the Lines: Asian American Women's Poetry*, directed by Yunah Hong (New York, NY: Women Make Movies, 2001), DVD.

23. Tomi Tanaka, "from a lotus blossom cunt," in *Roots: An Asian American Reader*, ed. Amy Tachiki, et al. (Los Angeles: University of California, Los Angeles, Asian American Studies Center, 1971), 109.

24. Cherríe Moraga, "La Güera," in *This Bridge Called My Back: Writings by Radical Women of Color*, ed. Gloria Anzaldua and Cherríe Moraga (Watertown, Mass: Persephone Press, 1981), 31.

25. James Edward Smethurst, *The Black Arts Movement: Literary Nationalism in the 1960s and 1970s* (Chapel Hill: University of North Carolina Press, 2005), Kindle ed., 3983.

26. Janice Mirikitani, *We, the Dangerous: New and Selected Poems* (Berkeley: Celestial Arts Press, 1995).

6 Apartheid in Arizona?

HB 2281 and Arizona's Denial of Human Rights to Peoples of Color

Julian Kunnie

It's just like the old South, and it's long past time that we prohibited it.

—Tom Horne, Arizona superintendent of public instruction, 2010

On the afternoon of May 11, 2010, Arizona governor Jan Brewer made international news that drew criticism from United Nations human rights experts when she signed Arizona's "Ethnic Studies" Law, HB 2281, coming at the tail end of a recent state senate bill, SB 1070, that authorized state police to detain any individual who does not provide documentation of evidence of US citizenship, particularly targeting Latina/o persons and other immigrants of color as part of an "immigration reform" initiative. This chapter interrogates the antecedents of HB 2281 and its implications for education and social justice.

The Background of HB 2281

In 2006, United Farm Workers leader and social justice activist Delores Huerta delivered a speech at Tucson Magnet High School in Tucson, Arizona, in which she criticized the Republican Party for its lack of support for Latina/o issues, specifically around the problems that Latin Americans have faced around US immigration policy. News of her remarks quickly reached the ears of the now former chief of Arizona schools, Republican Tom Horne, who won the position of attorney general with 52 percent of the vote in the 2010 state elections. Horne's

This chapter originally appeared in *Black Scholar* 40, no. 4 (Winter 2010): 16–26. Copyright by Taylor & Francis, Ltd. Reprinted with permission.

candidacy appealed to racist sentiments on immigration and crime and other social issues affecting Latin Americans in particular, since Latinas/os constitute the largest community of color and are a rapidly growing political force in the state and country. As superintendent of public instruction, Horne was quick to condemn Huerta's remarks, which he quoted out of context in reactionary fashion and seized on as an example of political attacks on the Republican Party at a public school. The principal of Tucson Magnet High School, Abel Morado, was summoned by Horne and asked to explain Huerta's comments. Further attention was then directed toward the "politicized" role that Raza–Mexican American studies played within the Tucson Unified School District (TUSD), particularly in subscribing to the Freireian dialogic approach in education deriving from Brazilian educator Paulo Freire's classic work *Pedagogy of the Oppressed*, which Horne disparaged and dismissed as "Marxist."[1] He castigated the TUSD Mexican American Studies program for promoting what he described as "ethnic chauvinism" and "racial resentment toward whites."[2]

In my capacity as director and professor of Africana Studies, I was involved in several programs in the late 1990s and over the past decade organized by the Mexican American Studies and African American Studies departments at TUSD, especially in discussing issues of Indigenous cultures, the experiences of enslavement of African people, and the manner in which blacks and Latinas/os had so much more in common than both communities realized. Ethnic studies at TUSD was the result of the Fisher-Mendoza court order (*Fisher v. Unified Tucson School District*) that required educational redress for the decades of discrimination against people of color within the Tucson school system.[3] In 2008 the court mandated order was lifted after a Tucson judge ruled that the desegregation requirement of the court order had been satisfied, a ruling that many working within ethnic studies in Tucson questioned seriously.

There is no question that the rapidly expanding Latin American community in the southwestern part of the U.S., particularly in California and Arizona, has generated a revanchist, racist backlash from the right-wing segment of the diminishing white population. Latinos and Latinas are about 35 percent of Arizona's population of seven million people, and the state's proximity to Mexico has added to the sense of insecurity among many white residents in central Arizona, in Maricopa County specifically, because of the looming presence of people of color in a traditionally European American state.

Arizona has had a much-checkered history when it comes to respecting the languages and cultures of people of color. This history of hostility dates back to the U.S. war against Pancho Villa in the nineteenth century. It includes the use of black cavalry members against Indigenous nations (cavalrymen who came to be known as Buffalo Soldiers); the history of rigid segregation of schools like the Lawrence Dunbar School for African Americans from the beginning of the twentieth century; the statewide resistance to the adoption of a state holiday honoring Martin Luther King, Jr. in line with the rest of the country in 1992, which provoked a national boycott of the state, including by the NBA; and in 2000 the passage of Proposition 203, which prohibited bilingual education in public schools and targeted the teaching of curricular materials in Spanish, constituting a major setback for Latin American immigrants in the state.[4] In the early twentieth century, Mexicans and Chinese immigrants were classified as "non-white" in Arizona, and whereas blacks could work in mines in the state because whites felt more comfortable with black people, Mexicans legally could not.[5] To demonstrate the absurdity of racial classifications in Arizona, the case of Mexican classification defied all human logic: Mexicans were classified as white in 1870, 1880, 1890, 1900, 1920, 1950 and 1960, but not in 1930, and in 1940 Mexicans were classified as white if they were not Native American or some race other than white.[6] As the educational chief in Arizona, Tom Horne ought to have been educated about the monstrous role that racism has played in Arizona's history and should have recognized that there is a set of facts that all students regardless of ethnic background are entitled as citizens to know regarding the history of oppression and humiliation of peoples of color in Arizona.

The signing of SB 1070 by Governor Brewer in April 2010, which legally protects the racist practice of profiling and interrogating individuals based on physical attributes, and the subsequent signing of the Ethnic Studies Law, HB 2281, continue the racist pattern of repression of the rights of people of color within the state of Arizona, sanctioned through state legislation. On July 29, 2010, the oppressive elements of SB 1070 were temporarily struck down by Federal District Judge Susan Bolton in response to the challenge to the law by the Barack Obama presidential administration on July 6. In her decision, Judge Bolton wrote that the law impinged on the role of the federal government in determining immigration policy and could further jeopardize the rights of citizens and legal immigrants because "there is a substantial likelihood that officers will wrongfully arrest legal resident aliens" and noted that "Arizona could not make it a state crime for non-citizens to be in the state without proper documents, nor could it allow the police to conduct arrests without warrants if officers believed the offense would result in their deportation."[7] It should come as no surprise that nine other states filed papers supporting Arizona's immigration law, underscoring the point that Arizona is certainly not alone in its advocacy of the attack on undocumented migrants and exhibiting of racist inclinations. The assertion that SB 1070 is "little more than a modern-day Chinese Exclusion Law" akin to the California exclusion law of 1858 that declared it a state crime, punishable by a serious fine or imprisonment, to transport any Chinese or "Mongolian" person to land at a California seaport, is thus not far-fetched. California's law was later nationalized with the adoption of the Chinese Exclusion Act of 1882 that legally prohibited people of Chinese descent from becoming naturalized as US citizens.[8] The assumption of a state government's right to criminalize migration is a continuation of the same train of racist exclusion and marginalization of people of color: first with Indigenous peoples in their own land during the European-Indigenous encounter, then with enslaved Africans, who were defined in the Constitution as three-fifths of a human being, followed by the criminalization of Chinese migration, and heralded now with the criminalization of Latina/o persons in particular. The kind of legal strictures in the United States against people of color are ironic in face of the fact that the European settlers in North America did not receive legal authorization from the First Nations of this hemisphere when they landed on these shores in the fifteenth century.

Consider the terms of the Arizona's 2010 educational law HB 2281. It forbids any courses or classes that include any of the following:

Promote the overthrow of the U.S. government.
Promote resentment toward a race or class of people.
Are designed primarily for pupils of a particular ethnic group.
Advocate ethnic solidarity instead of the treatment of pupils as individuals.

The roots of these laws derive from the colonial history of the United States, from colonization and close to near extermination of Indigenous nations and the subsequent enslavement of Africans in plantation slavery that provided the basis for profit accumulation and maximization through the emergence of industrial capitalism that defined the United States from the seventeenth century through the present.[9] Racism and colonialism have been intrinsic to the United States since its formation, and the ideology of European settler-colonialism that propagated the mythology of Columbus's "discovery," the "New World," the civilizing of the "western wilderness" (Manifest Destiny), and the eventual propounding of the "American Dream" came to dominate the economic, political, social, cultural, and educational landscape of the country.[10] After the Spanish-American War of 1898, Senator Albert J. Beveridge's utterances captured the imperialistic role of the

United States in religious and social Darwinist terms: "The American Republic is a part of the movement of a race—the most masterful race of history—and race movements are not to be stayed by the hand of man. They are mighty answers to Divine commands. . . . The inherent tendencies of a race are its highest law."[11] On yet another occasion, Beveridge melded themes of political imperialism, race, Darwinism, social gospel, manifest destiny, and territorial theft:

> God has not been preparing the English-speaking and Teutonic peoples for a thousand years for nothing but vain and idle self-contemplation and self-admiration. No, he has made us master organizers of the world to establish a system where chaos reigns. He has given us the spirit of progress to overwhelm the foes of reaction through the earth. He has made us adept in government that we may administer government among savage and senile peoples. Were it not for such forces as this the world would relapse into barbarism and night. And of all our race, he has marked the American people as his chosen.[12]

Religious legitimization was conjoined to this ideological construct, in which the United States became viewed as being the singular recipient of providential favor, not unlike the chosen people of Israel in the ancient Hebrew tradition, leading to the basis of the now routine closing line of presidential speeches, "God Bless America!"

The dominant white, masculine, Anglo-Saxon Protestant culture that exists in the United States permeates all segments of society, education being one of the most contentious, particularly in wake of the civil rights, Black Power, women's, and peace movements of students and communities around the country that demanded that the histories and cultures of peoples of color be included within all college curricula. The San Francisco Bay Area, San Francisco State University specifically, witnessed the gyration of protest and demand for educational and cultural diversity in higher education that propelled the formation of black studies, for example, and many other institutions, like the University of Chicago, Yale University, and Penn State University, followed suit.[13] Subsequently, during the Ronald Reagan presidential era that continued throughout the 1980s, many of the gains around cultural diversity and ethnic studies that issued from the previous two decades were dismantled or reversed, using supply-side economics and socially conservative ideology as the basis. As a strong pro-Republican state with defining legacies of right-wing Senator Barry Goldwater and then Judge William H. Rehnquist, who openly advocated denying people of color equal rights in voting yet went on to become a U.S. Supreme Court justice, the agenda of political narrowness and ethnic exclusiveness became firmly entrenched within the body politic of the state of Arizona in the 1990s and into the present.

As state educational superintendent, Horne seized the opportunity in the eruption of attacks on Mexican American Studies at TUSD to characterize its curriculum as unpatriotic, making reference to the Rudy Acuña book *Occupied America*, and he proceeded to denounce the program for its critical philosophical standpoint: "So I think this is mostly dysfunctional for the students that are in this Raza studies program being subject to a revolutionary curriculum, a curriculum that tells them that we took Arizona and other states from Mexico and it should go back to them, that tells them that the enemy is capitalism, that they're oppressed and they should be resentful."[14]

The ironic inference here is that the history of North America—which included theft and expropriation of Indigenous nations' lands all across the continent and the eventual annexation of five regions of Mexico that eventually were incorporated into the United States following the U.S.-Mexican War of 1848 (California, Texas, Colorado, New Mexico, and Arizona)—cannot be taught in Arizona schools because such facts would constitute a "revolutionary curriculum." The incredible point here is that the erstwhile educational chief of the schools in a state, Arizona, maintains in effect that teaching factual history is unacceptable. Thus forcing students to learn historical untruths rekindles the specter of ideological propaganda discussed in extensive detail in James Loewen's *Lies My Teacher Told Me: Everything Your US History Textbooks Got Wrong*.[15] This kind of dictatorial legislation parallels the statutes of the apartheid charter in South Africa that legally enshrined racism against black people as part of its national constitution. Now that apartheid has been formally abolished in South Africa since 1994, Arizona has seen fit to pass legislation that represses and violates the rights of all students to understand the actual history of the United States and by extension the Americas and the world.

The background of the Arizona Ethnic Studies Law resides in an unabashed racism that foists a dominant Eurocentric colonial ideology on the young people of the state, under the pretext of a "color-blind" society that invokes Martin Luther King Jr.'s admonition that persons should not be judged by the color of their skin but by the content of their character. A similar appeal was made by Ward Connerly, the University of California Regents member who led the campaign for the dismantling of affirmative action policies in California, even though he himself was African American and a self-admitted beneficiary of such programs. The insidious nature of racism and its repressive effects are evident in HB 2281, which clearly employs the convoluted logic that typically issues from ideological stalwarts of white supremacy.

The nature of white supremacy and its convoluted reasoning needs to be seriously interrogated with the promulgation of HB 2281. Even as ideologues like Arthur Schlesinger (*Disuniting America*), Thomas Sowell (*Dismantling America*), Abigail Thernstrom (*Voting Rights and Wrongs*), and Dinesh D'Souza (*What's So Great about America*) contend for a "melting-pot" United States, for the elimination of references to particular histories, cultures, and experiences of peoples, and for the mythic adoption of a "generalized American identity," it is abundantly palpable that the embracing of this kind of broad social projection implies the perpetuation of a hegemonic Eurocentric, ruling-class, WASP political and social culture.[16] Such ideological constructs reproduce Eurocentric colonial concepts of knowledge in the world that continue under the rubric of ostensibly "universal" disciplines like philosophy, psychology, literature, and so on, which in practice actually reflect Western cultural and historical biases. The Constitution enshrines the rights of individuals, not groups, and Arizona's Ethnic Studies Law seeks refuge in the constitutional provisions around individual rights, ignoring fundamentally that colonialism, racism, sexism, classism, religious intolerance, and sexual discrimination are based on singling out group identities. The use of racial profiling in police arrests in the United States is a case in point. African Americans are singled out not as individuals during police arrests of drug users but because they are perceived to be part of a group that already has stereotypes of criminality associated with such a grouping. The fact that 13 percent of drug users in the United States are black but constitute 35 percent of those arrested and 54 percent of those convicted lends basis to this criminalization of persons because they are perceived to be members of certain groups.[17]

Implications of HB 2281 for Education in Arizona and the U.S.

The United States continues to struggle with the colonial legacy of racist repression at the core of its social, economic, political, educational, and cultural operation as a society, a legacy summed up in the title of the book *The House that Race Built*.[18] What is evident is the very poor track record that the United States has as a society in redressing the issues of racism and white supremacy after over fifty years of desegregation and interethnic social "integration," in which students from diverse ethnic and cultural backgrounds study and learn together in classrooms across the country. The question of race continues to fester principally because

Chanting Mexican American studies supporters shut down a Tucson Unified School District Governing Board Meeting in opposition to TUSD's ethnic studies ban, 2012. *Courtesy Andrea Kelly on behalf of the Estate of Will Seberger.*

the rapidly diminishing white population in the country generally refuses to acknowledge the history of racism and cultural exclusion in the formation and development of U.S. schools. Colleges and universities in particular continue to dodge the subject of cultural and ethnic pluralism and divergence of social experience based on histories of racial, ethnic, and religious exclusion and marginalization in the United States. The operating philosophical assumption here is that the issue of institutionalized and social racism and even racial and ethnic conflict will disappear if the subject is buried or hidden from view and scrutiny.

Such persistent efforts toward obscuring this important subject obfuscate reality and perpetuate injustice against Indigenous peoples, African Americans, Latin Americans, Asian Americans, and all other peoples whose descent falls outside that of WASP culture. Sidestepping foundational white supremacy, class privilege, and gender injustice assures the social fragmentation and disintegration of U.S. society.[19] By overlooking social and cultural differences and languages, U.S. society robs people of color of their inalienable right to be who they were meant to be culturally as members of ethnic groups. A similar argument can be made regarding the tenacity of sexism and patriarchy in U.S. society and the world; silence or diffidence about the issue only serve to further the oppression and subjugation of women. In this sense, proscriptions against curricula that reflect and teach the experiences of peoples of color within the United States contribute to a self-negation of peoples of color and thus can ultimately lead to self-inflicted harm. Communities of color need to be able to understand and share their histories and cultures from their respective community points of view for such knowledge to be educationally authentic.[20]

The repressive character of HB 2281 violates the fundamental human, constitutional, and educational rights of freedom of expression and viewpoints, particularly in a society where such freedoms are enshrined in the UN Charter on Human Rights.[21] The educational process and experience is about freeing and opening up the mind to new and creative possibilities. HB 2281 has the consequence of stifling the thought process of all students at Arizona schools because it dictates what and how they are taught. In essence, the educational message being conveyed through this draconian legislation is that education is essentially a process of indoctrination and conformity to a status quo that may be inimical to the interests of people of color. Ethnic studies at the secondary school level is first and foremost designed to urge all students to think deeply about the diverse cultural and ethnic makeup of the world and to become sensitive to this diversity in social relations. It is also geared toward understanding the values that are culturally intrinsic to various ethnic groups. HB 2281 is a law that criminalizes group solidarity. It is racist because it outlaws studies that enhance the social cohesion of individual communities of color, when such cohesion is vital for the sustenance and well-being of the group. Education is about unearthing all of the facts about the world and being able to hear diverse, even divergent or conflicting perspectives on reality. It is through openness to diverse viewpoints and critical thinking that students become equipped at the high school level to prepare them for college, where cultivation of critical thinking and analytical skills is considered a hallmark of any decent educational experience. Freedom to think and digest complex and diverse educational materials is the index of a healthy educational journey for students at all levels of schooling.

Notes

Epigraph: Associated Press, May 12, 2010.

1. See Paulo Freire, *Pedagogy of the Oppressed* (New York: Continuum, 1970). Horne was cited in "Arizona Schools Chief Says Ethnic Studies Law Takes Focus off Race," *CNN,* http://www.cnn.com/.

2. Quoted in "Arizona Ethnic Studies Law Signed by Governor Brewer, Condemned by UN Human Rights Experts," *Huffington Post*, May 11, 2010, http://www.huffingtonpost.com/.

3. For instance, in 2001, I screened my second DVD production, *Black and Brown: An Afro-Latino Journey*, which documents the history of African peoples in Mexico from 1200 BCE, during the height of the Olmec civilization in Mesoamerica to the migration of Africans freed from enslavement in Cuba and the rest of the Caribbean, and most black and Latina/o students expressed disbelief about the significant number of black people in southern Mexico. The film draws upon the work of Ivan van Sertima, *They Came before Columbus: The Ancient African Presence in America* (New York: Random House, 1976).

4. A growing movement against Proposition 203 in which I was involved began in 1999, but the initiative passed, changing the law authorizing bilingual education to require that all classes be taught in English except for "English learners," whose mother tongue was a language other than English. See "List of Arizona Ballot Measures," Ballotpedia, http://www.ballotpedia.org/wiki/index.php/ List_of_Arizona_ballot_measures#tab=2000.

5. Linda Gordon, *The Great Arizona Orphan Abduction* (Cambridge, Mass.: Harvard University Press, 1999), 104.

6. Ibid., 356.

7. Randal C. Archibold, "Judge Blocks Arizona's Immigration Law," *New York Times*, July 29, 2010.

8. "Is SB 1070 a Modern 'Chinese Exclusion Law'?," *Reappropriate: Writings of an Asian American Feminist*, May 12, 2010, http://reappropriate.co/2010/05/is-sb-1070-a-modern-chinese-exclusion-law/.

9. See, for instance, Eric Williams, *Capitalism and Slavery* (Chapel Hill: University of North Carolina Press, 1994); Walter Rodney, *How Europe Underdeveloped Africa* (New York: Howard University Press, 1980); W. E. B. Du Bois, *The World and Africa* (New York: International Publishers, 1979); Joseph Inikori, *Africans and the Industrial Revolution in England: A Study in International Trade and Economic Development* (New York: Cambridge University Press, 2002); John Hope Franklin, *From Slavery to Freedom* (New York: Alfred Knopf, 2004); Manning Marable, *How Capitalism Underdeveloped Black America* (London: Pluto Press, 2000); Eugene Genovese and Elizabeth Fox-Genovese, *Fruits of Merchant Capital: Slavery and Bourgeois Property in the Rise and Expansion of Capitalism* (New York: Oxford University Press, 1983); Howard Zinn, *A People's History of the United States* (New York: HarperCollins, 2003); Angela Davis, *Women, Race and Class* (New York: Vintage, 1983); Colin A. Palmer, *Passageways*, vol. 1, *An Interpretive History of Black America* (New York: Thompson Learning, 2002).

10. See Vine Deloria, Jr., *Custer Died for Your Sins: An Indian Manifesto* (Norman: University of Oklahoma Press, 1988); James Wilson, *The Earth Shall Weep: A History of Native America* (New York: Grove Books, 2000); M. Annette Jaimes, ed., *The State of Native America* (Boston: South End Press, 1992); Luis Riviera, *A Violent Evangelism:*

The Political and Religious Conquest of the Americas (Louisville: Westminster/John Knox Press, 1992).

11. Introduction to Barry N. Schwartz and Robert Disch, *White Racism: Its History, Pathology and Practice* (New York: Dell, 1970), 37.

12. Ibid., 37–38.

13. See, for instance, Fabio Rojas, *From Black Power to Black Studies: How a Radical Movement Became an Academic Discipline* (Baltimore: Johns Hopkins University Press, 2007).

14. "In Defense of Arizona's Ethnic Studies Law," Fox News, May 14, 2010, http://www.foxnews.com/story/2010/05/14/in-defense-arizona-ethnic-studies-law.html.

15. James Loewen, *Lies My Teacher Told Me: Everything Your American History Book Got Wrong* (New York: Touchstone, 1995).

16. Examples of works that are core texts for white supremacist ideologues are Arthur Schlesinger's *Dis-uniting America: Reflections on a Multicultural Society* (New York: W. W. Norton, 1998); Abigail Thernstrom, *Voting Rights and Wrongs: The Elusive Quest for Racially Fair Elections* (Washington, D.C.: American Enterprise Institute Press, 2009); Thomas Sowell, *Dismantling America* (New York: Basic Books, 2010); Dinesh D'Souza, *What's So Great about America* (New York: Penguin, 2003).

17. See "Racial Disparities in Sentencing: Hearing on Reports of Racism in the Justice System of the United States," American Civil Liberties Union, October 27, 2014, https://www.aclu.org/sites/default/files/assets/141027_iachr_racial_disparities_aclu_submission_0.pdf. Also see Michelle Alexander, *The New Jim Crow: Mass Incarceration in the Age of Colorblindness* (New York: New Press, 2010), 178–220; E. Ann Carson, *Prisoners in 2014* (U.S. Department of Justice, Bureau of Justice Statistics, 2015), http://www.bjs.gov/content/pub/pdf/p14.pdf.

18. Wahneema Lubiano, ed., *The House that Race Built* (New York: Beacon, 2002).

19. A positive example of a core text on education against racism, still highly relevant for educational curricula today, is Peggy Macintosh, "White Privilege: Unpacking the Invisible Knapsack," Peace and Freedom Magazine, July–August 1989, 10–12, National SEED Project, https://nationalseedproject.org/white-privilege-unpacking-the-invisible-knapsack. Other cardinal texts are Schwartz and Disch, *White Racism*; Joe Feagin, Hernán Vera, and Pinar Batur, *White Racism: The Basics* (New York: Routledge, 2000); Joel Kovel, *White Racism: A Psychohistory* (New York: Columbia University Press, 1984); Tim Wise, *White Like Me: Reflections on Race from a Privileged Son* (Berkeley: Soft Skull Press, 2007); Tim Wise, *Between Barack and a Hard Place: Racism and White Denial in the Age of Obama* (San Francisco: City Lights, 2009); Paula Rothenberff, ed., *Race, Class, and Gender in the United States* (New York: Worth, 2007).

20. See Chinweizu, *The West and the Rest of Us: White Predators, Black Slavers, and the African Elite* (New York: Random House, 1974), 326.

21. "The Universal Declaration of Human Rights," United Nations, http://www.un.org/en/universal-declaration-human-rights.

░ Black Population of Fargo-Moorhead Has Nearly Tripled in Past Decade

As part of the conversation about twenty-first-century migration patterns, the following article explores the reason for the latest arrival of
blacks to booming metropolises like Fargo-Moorhead, North Dakota.
From 2006 to 2014 its black population nearly tripled from 2,937 black
residents to 8,654. In the passage below, the reader will also learn about
the diverse ethnicity of black newcomers.

Chandra Smith has watched Fargo-Moorhead's black population rise through the ledger
of her weave shop.

As co-owner of Fargo's Weaves of the World, Smith sells hair extensions primarily to black
women, and starting a year and a half ago, business began to boom. She estimates it was
up 20 percent for a time. Then came the competition.

Since September 2014, at least three new weave shops have opened in Fargo-Moorhead.

"With all the extra stores, we're down now by 20 percent," said Smith, 34, who moved
to Fargo four years ago.

The expanding weave market is a sign of change for Fargo-Moorhead, with its historically
low black population. Even today, the metro has a lower proportion of black residents than
most similarly sized metros, according to census data.

Experts say this dates to the so-called Great Migration from 1910 to 1970, when Fargo's
distance from the South and lack of industry failed to attract black workers moving north.

But Fargo-Moorhead is beginning to see a reversal of its history.

The percentage of black residents in the metro has more than doubled in recent years—
from 1.57 percent in 2006 to 3.79 percent in 2014, the most recent year of census data. Including
people who are black in combination with other races, that's a jump from 2,937 black residents
to 8,654—meaning the population almost tripled.

Source: Grace Lyden, "Black Population of Fargo-Moorhead Has Nearly Tripled in Past
Decade," *Forum of Fargo-Moorhead*, January 18, 2016.

Some of the newcomers are refugees and immigrants [primarily from West Africa], but many come from other areas of the United States. People of all races have been looking for jobs and hearing about opportunities in Fargo-Moorhead. As a result, the metro area is steadily becoming more diverse.

A New Migration

Fargo-Moorhead has something to offer migrants today that it didn't have during the Great Migration: jobs.

"Black people are going to move for the same reason white people do: opportunities," said Aaron Renn, a senior fellow at the Manhattan Institute for Policy Research who has studied demographics of the Midwest. "Fargo, in general, is just doing very well economically."

Renn has observed a recent movement of black (and white) workers away from the cities that attracted them during the Great Migration, such as Chicago, and back to the South or into the Great Plains, where economies are better.

"People are moving to places of opportunity, and quite often minorities are those who are leading the charge, particularly immigrants," said Mark Schill, vice president for research at Praxis Strategy Group, an economic development firm based in Grand Forks.

Foreign-born blacks who aren't multiracial comprised 48 percent of Fargo-Moorhead's black population in 2014.

At 3.1 immigrants per 1,000 residents, Fargo-Moorhead has a higher immigration rate than Chicago or St. Louis, according to an analysis by Schill, who ranked metros by their average immigration rates from 2011 to 2014. Out of 381 areas, Fargo-Moorhead ranked 77th.

Likewise, Fargo-Moorhead ranked 27th in Schill's analysis of domestic migration rates—a list that is "dominated by the nation's most dynamic economies and high-amenity regions."

Schill attributes these rankings to a shift in Fargo-Moorhead's economy, which used to be regional and primarily agricultural but is now global and flush with opportunities in science, technology, engineering and math.

Following the 2008 recession, F-M became known for its jobs.

"The story's out in the last five or 10 years," Schill said.

The Rev. Reuben Duncan, 48, of Christ International Assembly in Fargo, can testify to the appeal of a good economy. Originally from Monrovia, Liberia, he said that's why many immigrants come here.

The promises proved fruitful for Duncan, who is also co-owner of Manifold LLC (one of the new weave shops) and head of a nonprofit that helps the local Liberian community acclimate.

"I've been in this country 11 years, but I've never seen such prosperity and good people (as in Fargo)," he said.

Challenges Remain

The rising population hasn't gone unnoticed by local black residents.

"I've seen a lot of change," said Cedric Allbritton, a 33-year-old master barber at Skill Cutz in Fargo, who's been here close to nine years. Today, when he goes to the grocery store, "I see more faces, when before it was kind of like, 'Am I the only one here?'"

Eric Asa, an associate professor of construction management and engineering at North Dakota State University, echoed that.

If you go to Walmart or if you go to Kohl's and other places, you see lots of black kids working there, which is very encouraging," said Asa, originally of Mamfe, Ghana, who's been here since 2004. "It makes me also feel comfortable that I live life with other blacks here."

That doesn't mean it's easy to live in a place where blacks comprise 3.79 percent of the population, compared to 13.85 percent of the country, as of 2014.

Among 30 metropolitan statistical areas that are closest in size to Fargo-Moorhead, just nine places reported a lower percentage of black residents in 2014.

When Mario Williams moved to Moorhead from San Diego in 2013, he was stunned by the lack of people who look him.

"I'm used to seeing more minorities in the area," said the 20-year-old junior at Concordia College. "It was a big culture shock."

On campus, women sometimes tell Williams they've "never seen a black guy before," he said. And last year, while walking to a party off campus, he and his friends were attacked.

"As we were walking down the street, you know, a car drove by and said, 'Go back to Africa,' you know, called us all types of monkeys and then pelted us with eggs," he said.

Nothing like that happened to Williams in San Diego, and he doubts it would have happened here if there were a larger black population.

Allbritton, too, said he sometimes feels like people here act strangely around him because of his race. Shortly after he came to Fargo, he went to a job interview with a man who was clearly intimidated by him.

"It was obvious he was nervous and looking the other way," said Allbritton, who's from the Chicago area. "It was just weird. That was the first time I experienced anything like that."

Some, however, say they haven't experienced any negativity as a result of living here.

In 11 years here, Asa has never been pulled over by Fargo or West Fargo police, though he was pulled over regularly when he lived in Moscow, Idaho.

"Most people around here are educated, so it makes it easy to integrate," said Duncan, the Liberian pastor, who thinks the presence of so many colleges has made for an open-minded region. "I believe that almost everybody here understands about the real world."

Regardless of personal experiences, all of the black residents interviewed for this article said they hope the numbers continue to grow, enriching Fargo-Moorhead with culture and new ideas.

Smith, the co-owner of Fargo's Weaves of the World, wants her 4-year-old biracial son to grow up seeing diversity.

"It's good for him to know that people come in all different shapes, sizes and colors," she said. "There's not only one type of people."

The trend is likely to continue, as friends and family of current black residents hear the "good news" about Fargo-Moorhead, said Renn, the senior fellow at the Manhattan Institute.

"As people move and stay, then over time those networks become established," he said. "To the extent that your economy keeps doing well and people are made to feel welcome, I would expect the flow would continue."

PART 3

Political Expression

7 Multicultural Garveyism in the Far West

Holly Roose

Between 1916 and 1925 Marcus Garvey, a recent Jamaican immigrant, created in the United States what would later be recognized as the largest black mass movement in world history. His Universal Negro Improvement Association and African Communities League (UNIA) is estimated to have reached an official membership of more than a million members by the 1920s, with hundreds of thousands of Black Americans who followed and vicariously supported his organization even if they were not always dues-paying members. In the United States, the UNIA, which began with thirteen members in 1916, had by the early 1920s more than seven hundred chapters spread through thirty-eight states (most U.S. branches were in the southern states). Internationally there were hundreds of branches stretching across forty-one countries. The publications produced by Garvey, primarily through the official UNIA organ, the *Negro World*, were read and quoted around the world. Garvey's speeches had a wide audience, albeit a sometimes hostile one, that stretched to the halls of power in the national government and the imperial administrations of Europe. Typically the Garvey movement is examined as primarily a West Indian, Black-only movement that focused mostly on the eastern United States, where the movement began. This essay challenges that narrative by revealing the interracial collaborations of Garveyites with other nonwhite nationalists in the Far West.

Like all social movements, Garveyism did not exist in a vacuum. The individuals who worked closely within and alongside the Garvey movement were powerfully influenced by larger world events. Why Garveyites on the West Coast would need or want to work with other people of color or organizations cannot be understood without some knowledge of the circumstances of those other groups of color. The rise of Garveyism represented one element in the efforts of colored and colonized peoples throughout the world to liberate themselves from white domination during the World War I era and beyond. Representatives of these groups migrated to various American western destinations where they became significant components of the labor force. It was in cities like San Francisco, Los Angeles, Portland, and Seattle that these groups converged and found common ground. Yet their experiences in dealing with racism and with other racial groups of color in the United States were fluid and dynamic. At times they competed bitterly for employment in the lowest paying jobs to which workers of color were relegated. At other times, they worked together to protest policies like the Alien Land Laws, which barred Asian immigrants from owning property. At no time did all of these groups work harmoniously to support a common cause. This chapter will focus on those important moments of solidarity between the Black Garveyites and the other racial and ethnic groups, and on how the circumstances in the West made the Garvey movement in that region unique.

As Garveyism was rising in popularity on the East Coast, Indian and Japanese nationalism on the West Coast was also gaining prominence. In San Francisco, Indian nationalists founded the Ghadar movement in an effort to organize opposition to English colonialism in India. Concurrently, throughout California, Japanese Americans mobilized to fight restrictions on immigration. In addition, Mexican American immigrants fleeing political turmoil in Mexico became another potential ally of western Black nationalists. In response, the white population spawned racist organizations such as the Oriental Exclusion League and the Asiatic Exclusion League, and rushed to join preexisting racist organizations such as the Ku Klux Klan. As these organizations ramped up activities that targeted populations of color, and as the U.S. government simultaneously restricted immigration and put incoming Indian and Japanese immigrants under surveillance, the pressure on these groups to form mutually beneficial coalitions increased dramatically. Nowhere was this more apparent than on the West Coast.

Coalition building came as a result of the fact that Black populations on the West Coast were small. Figures from the 1920 census show 15,579 Blacks in Los Angeles, 5,489 in Oakland, 1,556 in Portland, 2,414 in San Francisco, and 2,894 in Seattle.[1] When Blacks did trickle into the Far West, it was primarily through the railroad industry that word of conditions and opportunities there were carried back to the South and East.

The Pullman Company had become the largest employer of Black workers in the early twentieth century.[2] The rise of small Black communities sprinkled across the West "can be explained by the use of black sleeping-car porters, railroad men, waiters, and cooks of the Southern Pacific Railroad."[3] It was through these Black rail workers, as well as to a lesser degree, Black shipyard and merchant marine workers, that word of the West spread to Black communities in the South and East. It was also in the first decades of the twentieth century, via rail and ships, that Garveyism and Garvey's *Negro World* spread to the Far West.[4]

Many of the discriminatory practices of southern Jim Crow also existed in the West. There was little that Blacks could do on their own to contest Jim Crow racism in the West because their numbers were so small. In places like Seattle, for instance, residential segregation enforced by restrictive covenants had become commonplace. In an effort to improve their circumstances, Blacks established local chapters of organizations such as the NAACP, the UNIA, the Urban League, and the National Negro Congress.[5] The color line in the West, however, was concerned with more than Black-white relations. Prevailing white oppression considered any nonwhite individual or group as eligible for special restrictions and discrimination. The immigrant populations from the Pacific Rim, like Chinese, Japanese, and other Asians (as well as residents from Mexico), found themselves facing in the West racial injustice and discrimination similar to what the Black population faced.[6]

Consequently the struggle for justice and equality for people of color in the West took a different form than in the southern, eastern, and northern parts of the country. More typically in the West the battle could assume multinational and multiracial forms, as it did, According to Quintard Taylor, "Black civil rights organizations formed temporary alliances with Asian groups such as the Filipino Community of Seattle. These alliances became the hallmark of a very different type of urban politics from that practiced in much of black urban America at the time."[7]

An event that demonstrates a need for multiracial cooperation was the growing presence of a large Klan movement in the West. As Garveyism expanded in the West in the early twentieth century, Black nationalists, relatively small in number in western cities, would come to rely on Mexican American and Asian collaborators in their efforts against the Klan. The Klan organized not only against Blacks but also against Jews, Catholics, and immigrants. In San Diego, "most Klan activities were clandestine, and aimed at keeping recently arrived Mexicans from participating in community politics."[8] The lynching of Mexicans as they attempted to cross the border was not uncommon.[9] From 1901 to 1928 there were at least 117 documented lynchings of Mexicans in the American West, though there were probably many more.[10] In Oregon, "Klansmen and their allies in the

United Negro Improvement Association meeting in Oakland, 1924. *Courtesy of African American Museum of Oakland.*

1923 legislature resurrected controversial racial and religious issues rejected in earlier years. A bill prohibiting the ownership of land by aliens, aimed primarily at Japanese immigrants, passed easily."[11]

The Klan existed in nearly every western state. In Oregon, Klan membership reached its height in the 1920s, and it was "routine to witness large Klan parades in full hooded regalia, with floats and bands included, down the main streets of Oregon towns and cities, including Portland." In Oregon, a popular pastime was to hold a "mock lynching" in which "the victim would be kidnapped by a group of hooded men, taken to a remote location, have a noose put around their neck, and be hoisted off the ground but lowered before death resulted and then ordered to leave the state."[12] In Washington, the Klan presence was heavy in Seattle and Bellingham. In 1925 the Klan made front-page news as approximately twenty-five thousand assembled in the town of Lynden, just north of Bellingham. The local paper reported: "The largest crowd that has ever assembled in the Lynden district gathered Saturday evening at the Northwest Washington Fair Grounds to witness the public demonstration of the Ku Klux Klan."[13] To the south, in California, by the 1920s the Klan had established itself in small cities like Bakersfield, where the police chief and the magistrate were both Klansmen. It also organized in big cities like San Francisco, where Klan members included deputy sheriffs, fire fighters, police, ministers, and public officials.[14] Likewise, it spread to Los Angeles, Sacramento, and other towns and counties throughout the state. Thus, Blacks in the West, facing oppressive racial circumstances similar to those found in other parts of the country, saw in the Garvey movement a potential pathway to progress.

The UNIA in Seattle was established in 1919 when Marcus Garvey presented his nationalist vision to a crowd of two hundred Seattleites at the Madison Street Theater.[15] The UNIA in San Diego also formed in 1919. The Los Angeles branch of the UNIA, the most profitable and the largest in the West, with approximately one thousand members, formed in 1920. The Black population of Los Angeles represented only 2.71 percent of the city's population (15,579 out of 576,673) in 1920.[16] But by the time the UNIA materialized there the city boasted a Black YMCA and YWCA, an NAACP, a branch of the National Negro Business League, and several Black newspapers, as well as Black hospitals, hotels, and restaurants.[17] Even with the existence of these established Black institutions, the Los Angeles UNIA chapter quickly emerged as an important force in local racial affairs.

One reason for its high profile was that the founding group included individuals from the elite strata of the city's Black leaders. These figures included John Wesley Coleman, a local Black businessman, and J. D. Gordon, a popular Black preacher and the future assistant president general to Marcus Garvey. Meetings in the Los Angeles UNIA division were held at Reverend Gordon's Tabernacle Baptist Church on Central Avenue, which boasted a large congregation. Other prominent Black leaders in the UNIA included Joseph and Charlotta Bass, the editors of the *California Eagle*, the most widely read Black newspaper in Los Angeles. Noah Thompson, the only Black journalist in Los Angeles who worked at the white newspaper, the *Los Angeles Evening Press*, became the local UNIA president.[18] Furthermore, Thompson was good friends with then governor Hiram Johnson, who proposed Thompson for the position of U.S. minister to Liberia.[19] The rhetoric of Noah Thompson in his speeches to the UNIA Los Angelenos was clear regarding the desire for unity of all people of color. In one such presentation, Thompson stated: "This movement means that every person not white is behind every other person not white, regardless of his standing intellectually, socially, or financially."[20]

The prominence and influential connections of this cadre of Black leaders in Los Angeles stood in contrast to the problematic relationship that Garvey himself had to East Coast elites, both white and Black. Over time, leaders of the NAACP and others saw him as an outsider and linked him to the lower Black masses, rather than to what Du Bois referred to as the "Talented Tenth." In Los Angeles, however, these organizations had a very different relationship. Charlotta Bass, who served as president of the UNIA Los Angeles women's chapter for a time, also worked in a leadership position for the NAACP. In Los Angeles, the UNIA and the NAACP held meetings in the same church.[21] Noah Thompson, in conjunction with his role as a leader in the UNIA Los Angeles division, was also the founding leader of the Los Angeles Urban League. On the East Coast Garvey and his UNIA were bitter enemies of the NAACP and the Urban League, and such interorganizational cooperation was unthinkable there.

Just as UNIA chapters in the East and West varied, West Coast UNIA chapters also differed from each other significantly. Economically, in some areas (e.g., Los Angeles) divisions between Garveyites and the Black middle class were practically nonexistent.[22] In Seattle, though, the UNIA chapter split along class lines. As mentioned, the first UNIA chapter was organized there in 1919, but "by 1924 Seattle had a second UNIA chapter, Division 97. Internal dissention and class differences probably prompted the formation of the second group, which consisted of two lawyers, a real estate agent, and the owner of the city's only black trucking firm, but virtually no working-class Garveyites."[23] The opposite was true in Oakland, California. There the movement was a reflection of the working-class concerns and circumstances. In Oakland, "Garveyites built on the labor organizing of Black dining car workers. Fewer than 10,000 African American men lived in the Bay Area in the 1920s, but one third of them were employed by the transcontinental railroads."[24]

San Francisco and Oakland were especially important multinational cities for Garveyism and other nationalist movements. Together they constituted a major international shipping port that connected the Pacific Coast to Asia, South America, Central America, the West Indies, and the Pacific Islands. "Interspersed with Chinese, Mexican, and Filipino communities, African American neighborhoods absorbed and supported the international struggles of many colonized groups."[25] In the West, Garveyism grew to maturity alongside other populations of color, all struggling against the same forces of imperialism that had characterized the nineteenth century both globally and in the United States. This close proximity and common enemies predictably worked to create opportunities for collaboration.[26] These interracial collaborations represent an important difference between Garveyism in the West and Garveyism in other parts of the country.

It would be a mistake, however, to assume that such alliances were automatic in spite of the common enemy, racism. There were numerous factors in western multiracial relations that created conflict between the various groups of color. A chief factor was the few economic opportunities available to people of color in a region historically dominated by white supremacist practices. Nonwhite groups of every kind found themselves, in essence, competing against each other for the economic leftovers of the dominant white population. Sizeable Asian populations in the West predated the arrival of a significant Black population. Mexican descendent populations had an even earlier and larger involvement in the West and Southwest than both Blacks and Asians. The potential for conflict between these groups of color was evident.

Seattle, in the late nineteenth and early twentieth centuries, witnessed such competition. The Asian presence there preceded the Black presence by two decades, the latter arriving in the city in the 1880s. Chinese laborers had come to Seattle as early as the 1860s to build railroads and work in nearby mines, forests, and canneries, among other forms of working-class labor. Later, large numbers of Japanese migrants came to Seattle to work in the fishing and agricultural industries. They also worked in the service industry, an industry generally relegated to blacks in other parts of the country. In the early twentieth century, Seattle held the second largest Japanese population in North America after Los Angeles.[27]

The large and established Asian communities could at times create conflict between groups of color in the labor force. This was particularly true for Black women workers, who had a difficult time in Seattle because "at a time when black women increasingly formed the majority of the servant class in the nation's largest cities, Seattle's black females faced competition from old rivals such as Japanese males and Swedish females, but also increasingly from Filipino men who began migrating to the city in the 1920s."[28] The intergroup cooperation that emerged in some western cities in the Garvey movement is all the more significant because of this economic context of competition for jobs.

Overall, in the early decades of the twentieth century there were significant global and local dynamics that worked toward an increase in cooperation among groups of color. For example, following World War I Blacks globally (such as in the Caribbean) and in the United States supported the Japanese and Japanese Americans. At the 1921 peace conference at Versailles, in which the Allied Powers imposed harsh restrictions on Germany, Japan attempted to add an amendment to the treaty, an amendment calling for the end of global racial discrimination. The article for racial equality "received eleven out of seventeen votes. China [who distrusted Japan in every other way] sided with Japan. Nevertheless, [President Woodrow] Wilson as chair, ruled the measure defeated on the grounds that the decision was not unanimous" even though other initiatives that passed were not approved unanimously.[29] The willingness of Japan to raise the issue highlighted the increasingly contentious role race would play in the global battles over colonialism in the post–World War I era.

On the national level, Marcus Garvey himself often collaborated with the Japanese from his base in Harlem. But there were major differences between Garvey's interactions with the Japanese in New York and those between Japanese residents and immigrants and West Coast Garveyites. The primary difference was that most of the Japanese men who met with Garvey were not residents of the United States. They were not personally subjected to the oppressive racial conditions that Japanese Americans experienced in the West.

In New York, Garvey's economic interest in the Japanese centered on the possibility that Japan might provide financial aid to the UNIA and its steamship corporation, the Black Star Line (BSL), and negotiate a trade agreement between Japan and the UNIA. A major ideological component of the Garvey movement was to establish trade with the colored world in an effort to end reliance on Europeans. In October 1920 it was reported that Garvey, at a meeting with two Japanese officials in New York, had had a lengthy discussion of opening trade networks between the UNIA and Japan through the BSL. According to government reports, the Japanese officials "had credentials from the premier of Japan" and had "promised to offer their merchandise at prices much lower than what the U.S. could sell, and to convince the Negroes that it would be far more advantageous to throw their lot in with Japan."[30] Japanese delegates were invited to speak at the 1921 UNIA convention in New York City to spur collaboration between the non-European races. Garvey wished to establish a connection with a bank in Japan in order to obtain financial backing for his second attempt at a shipping line. These East Coast interactions between Japanese officials and Garvey himself were for the most part economically motivated business negotiations. In the American West, the interactions between local Garveyites and the resident Japanese were more personal, intimate, and focused on a shared need for social justice.

In the West, Japanese residents, like other groups of color, were forced to live with racial policies that worked to keep them economically depressed. The Garveyites understood that with such small numbers in the West, the Black population would need to lend support to the Japanese residents in order for their own movement to gain momentum. For example, in California in 1913, when the Alien Land Act went into effect, Japanese citizens were prohibited from owning or leasing land. UNIA members in California worked together with Japanese Americans to protest this act. Garveyites in the West were very much aware of the efforts made by Japanese delegates at the Versailles peace conference, and they knew that it was the Japanese who had pushed for global racial equality, going so far as to walk away from the table when their amendment was not passed. At a UNIA meeting in Los Angeles, J. D. Gordon "advised his hearers not to countenance or assist the Anti-Alien Land Law and the Anti-Japanese Movement. He said the Japanese are our best friends because they injected into the peace conference the equality of the races, without regard to color."[31]

Furthermore, all along the West Coast, "large Japanese and Chinese communities may have helped make ethnic nationalism respectable."[32] UNIA divisions in San Francisco were funded by Japanese interests.[33] UNIA organizers as far west as Honolulu "received contributions from a number of Japanese and Chinese."[34] While these mutual support activities were not successful in reversing the anti-Japanese and anti-Chinese policies, they do stand as evidence of the multiracial and multinational vision of racial progress that flowed between West Coast Garveyites and Asian populations in the era.

An even clearer connection between the strategies of West Coast Garveyites and the growing anticolonial struggles of the early twentieth century is displayed in the relationships Garveyites forged to demand the end of English colonial domination in India. For Indians to work in conjunction with black nationalists was not unreasonable. The advent of World War I distracted England from its colonial domination of India, weakening the bonds of control necessary for efficient colonization. As a result, the Indian anticolonial movement had increased opportunities for resistance against English domination. Indian nationalist groups organized both within and outside of India, including in California. In the early twentieth century, Indian intellectuals and students traveled abroad to organize against colonialism.[35] In the American West, the primary city in which Indian nationalists organized was San Francisco.

The global Indian anticolonial movement was not limited to intellectual elites. During the nineteenth century, Indian workers were often turned to as an indentured labor force used to replace slave labor in other European colonies as systems of slavery were abolished. This created resident Indian-descended populations in those colonies and former colonies with a distinct blue-collar orientation. Indian migration to the American West in the early twentieth century reflected a similar working-class consciousness. For many Indians living in the U.S. West, there was no escaping the restrictions and discrimination directed at the colored population. Resistance to such repression was linked to Indian nationalism.[36]

One example of the kind of racism Indians faced is evident in the Asiatic Exclusion League, which was established in San Francisco in 1906 and then moved up the coast to the Pacific Northwest. The Asiatic Exclusion League was formed in reaction to the perceived large numbers of Japanese, Chinese, and other Asian immigrants. In the early twentieth century, the league added Indians to its list of those to be excluded.[37] It was not long until violence ensued in the form of a race riot targeting Indian immigrants. In Bellingham, Washington, in 1907 more than two hundred white workers attacked dozens of Indian laborers employed in the lumber industry. The whites were said to have been "determined to drive the 'Hindoos' out of the city, [and] the mob dragged Indian mill workers from their beds, threw their belongings into the streets, beat them and warned them to leave Bellingham at once."[38] The Indian laborers made their way to Vancouver, British Columbia, assuming perhaps that since India was a British colony, and Canada a British protectorate, they would have protection. On the contrary, responding to rumors that hundreds of Indians were about to descend upon Vancouver, whites there organized and began the largest race riot in that city's history.[39]

In reaction to the treatment they received in the United States, Indian laborers in the Pacific Northwest formed the Pacific Coast Hindi Association to address their mistreatment and to organize in the work camps. According to Seema Sohi, "What emerged out of these meetings between the spring of 1912 and the fall of 1913 was a revolutionary anticolonial politics that would coalesce into the Ghadar Party, the most revolutionary group of Indians to organize against the British Empire outside of India during the early twentieth century."[40] The Ghadar Party quickly swelled to include Indian students and intellectuals in conjunction with the laborers. Led by Sohan Singh Bhakna, the Ghadar Party organized unity meetings to discuss revolutionary tactics and give anticolonial speeches in Vancouver, Portland, and Seattle, as well as Oxnard, California, Astoria, Oregon, and other towns along the West Coast.[41]

There were numerous connections between this emerging Indian militancy and the elements of the black population that comprised an important constituency of the co-emergent Garvey movement.[42] The British West Indies for example, where Garvey was born, was also the location of a significant Indian population descended from earlier generations of indentured servants. The fact that India and the West Indies were both British colonial spaces gave these two groups a shared experience against a common oppressor. Both Indian and Black groups were targeted by discriminatory racist practices. Indians immigrating to the United States became disillusioned as they experienced the same racist attitudes, as can be seen in the *San Francisco Chronicle* determination that Indians should be excluded "because their minds and manners are different from ours. That applies to Hindus even more than to Chinese or Japanese."[43]

Furthermore, the emerging pan-African anticolonial movement in the early twentieth century was reflected in Garvey's demand to end European colonial control of that continent. The Indian anticolonial movement found much common ground with the West Coast Garveyites, who were fighting a similar enemy in the American racial color line and who saw in the pan-African anticolonial movement many parallels to Indian militant nationalism.

Much like the Garvey movement, the Ghadar Party also spread rapidly across continents, and it eventually included contingents in the Philippines, Africa, and Central America. Even before the Garvey movement and its *Negro World,* the Ghadar's primary method of ideological expansion lay in the publication of the *Ghadar,* a weekly that printed anticolonial rhetoric and promoted unity among England's colonial subjects. The *Ghadar* told its readers that "the paper had reached China, Japan, the Philippines, Hong Kong, Sumatra, Fiji, Java, Singapore, Egypt, Paris, British East Africa, South Africa, South America, Panama, and Trinidad."[44] The Ghadar Party promoted unification of all the colored races of the world and demanded they take a stand against their white oppressors. Garveyites were comfortable with this sentiment.

The Ghadarites developed a "by any means necessary" approach to their nationalist agenda, and their activities did not stop at proclamations. During World War I they organized an attack on English colonialists from the shores of San Francisco where "at least 1,000 Indians from British Columbia, Washington, Oregon, and California joined 7,000 Indians from Panama, the Philippines, Hong Kong, and Shanghai and boarded ships bound for India fired up with the goal of overthrowing British rule."[45] As the revolutionaries set sail, Indian intellectuals met in Germany with German officials in the hopes of securing arms and ammunitions.[46] The English were aware of the conspiracy, and thousands of Ghadarites, upon landing, were confined to homes and villages, imprisoned, or executed. The Ghadar movement reached its peak in the mid-1920s and did not formally disband until after World War II when the goal of freedom from English colonialism was finally achieved.

England reached out to both Canada and the United States to help crush the revolutionaries. Indian anticolonialists came under U.S. government surveillance, just as the UNIA had, because, as Sohi writes, these "expressions of unity between black Americans and Indian anticolonialists were alarming to US and British officials alike, who seized upon such racial solidarities to justify and expand their inter-imperial surveillance apparatus. By 1919, British officials were arguing that there were dangerous links between radicalism in their West Indian colonies, American black militancy, and international communism."[47]

In San Francisco, a government informant working for the Office of Naval Intelligence met regularly with a UNIA leader, whom he described as "a Hindu passing as a black man," named James Farr. Farr, a former bootblack, had put down his brush and polish and devoted his energies to his new position as the president captain of the Pacific Street UNIA chapter in San Francisco. Farr and another man from India, whose name is listed only as Chatterji, worked closely in an effort to organize across racial lines, incorporating Southeast Asians as well as Pacific Islanders into the Black nationalist agenda. According to the informant, who followed UNIA organizing on the West Coast closely, "Negro agitators [Farr and members of the UNIA] approached the Hawaiians in this city in order to persuade them to join their colored peoples union plan, which includes not only Negroes, but also all other races other than white. The Hawaiians, who are on the whole very loyal to the United States, are beginning to feel certain racial pride and, coupled with it, racial hatred."[48]

The informant also indicated that he had learned that "there are several Japanese, such as *Fujii* and *Yoneyama* of the Japanese Central Association who are very friendly toward the Negroes and the Hindus and the Mexicans and planning to organize what they call the 'Colored Peoples' Union,' which will include all the people on earth except whites." According to the investigator, Farr asserted, "[The UNIA] means to and will in time have something to do and something to say about all the colored races."[49] Through this interaction between the informant and Farr, it is clear that the UNIA on the West Coast incorporated other racial groups into its vision. Whether Farr was actually Indian or black or a mixture of the two remains unclear. However, the similarities between Black and Indian experiences in the West were significant.

In conjunction with Asian interactions, Garveyites in the West developed complex relationships with both Mexican Americans and the Mexican government itself in pursuit of their objectives. These relationships unfolded against a backdrop of social and political instability in Mexico. With its troubled transnational past and the reality of Mexico's shared border with the United States, it was inevitable that Mexico would be drawn into the changing racial dynamics of World War I and the postwar years with its northern neighbor.

While the Mexican social, economic, and political situation was chaotic in the early twentieth century, the country possessed considerable wealth in natural resources, potential markets, and other economic possibilities, including railroad infrastructure and industrial development. Mexican president Porfirio Díaz adopted policies favorable to opening the Mexican economy to U.S. corporate interests, which quickly rushed to take advantage of the opportunities. Given the exploitative history that already existed between the countries, Díaz's actions incensed many Mexicans and brought anti-American feelings to a boiling point. It also fueled a strong Mexican nationalist sentiment. When political opposition came to Díaz in the form of a political opponent, Francisco Madero, Mexico fell into a near constant state of revolution which lasted from 1910 to 1920. The turmoil often blurred the border as chaos ensued between the United States and Mexico.[50]

Pancho Villa, a revolutionary in these years whose base of operations was in the Mexican state of Chihuahua, which borders New Mexico, created a calamity that led to a major U.S. military event before the country entered World War I. In March 1916, in retaliation for U.S. support of his competitors in Mexico, Villa led an attack on the border town of Columbus, New Mexico. President Woodrow Wilson reacted quickly to the attack and "within a week a punitive expedition, initially composed of 5,800 men and later increased to 10,000 under the command of General John J. Pershing, invaded the Mexican state of Chihuahua."[51] The danger of a second Mexican American War was real.

Americans never captured or even saw Pancho Villa in the invasion of Mexico, but the intrusion of U.S. military forces stirred anti-American hatred and increased the fervor of Mexican nationalism on both sides of the border. Nevertheless, the incident did not create the strong anti-U.S. nationalism that prevailed in that era among Mexicans and Mexican Americans. Rather, Mexican nationalism had its foundation in the long national history of Mexican complaints against U.S. exploitation. An event in the small Texas-Mexico border town of San Diego in 1915 illustrates the depth of anti-U.S. sentiment in the Mexican American population that long preceded the Garvey movement. A group of Mexican Americans in San Diego, Texas, in that year drafted what they called the Plan de San Diego.[52] The plan was a radical nationalist proposal to retake the Southwest (including California) from the United States and put it back into Mexican hands. In a gesture of racial solidarity against white oppression, the plan included other nonwhite races as beneficiaries. The hope was that Blacks and other groups of color would join the plotters in the attempt to reclaim the American West, and the plan "further vowed to secure territory for other racial minorities victimized by Anglos: six more states for African Americans to establish an independent republic and the restoration of Native American ancestral lands."[53] The Plan de San Diego makes clear that Mexican nationalists were aware that Black nationalists were hoping to establish Black colonies within the United States and outside of it for the purposes of political and economic independence. However, "once Anglo-Texans believed that an organized rebellion against US rule was underway, they responded fiercely, killing Mexicans, most of whom were not connected [to the plot]."[54] The U.S. government took these antiwhite threats seriously. One report by a secret government agent declared that "some Mexican military men believed that in case of a German-American war, hundreds of thousands of German Americans in the United States would rise and that they might spearhead a revolt by blacks and Mexican Americans against the U.S. government."[55]

Conditions that existed for both Blacks and Mexican Americans in the United States at the time did little to discourage such thinking on the part of these two groups. Often both groups received the same treatment at the hand of the government, as seen after the Bureau of Investigation "began investigating alleged draft evasions by conducting 'slacker' raids, especially among California's African American and Latino populations."[56]

With Mexico's close proximity, immigration to the United States from Mexico was significant, with half a million Mexicans crossing the border with permanent visas in the 1920s.[57] Many came to work in the agricultural sectors, in mining, or in transportation, but there were also increasing Mexican American urban populations. Mexican Americans in the United States suffered from redlining and other discriminatory policies just as blacks and Asians did. As they moved into designated nonwhite neighborhoods, they brought with them their nationalist pride. According to Theodore Vincent, "Mexican-American communities in the early 1920s exhibited strong undercurrents of nationalist pride stemming from the Mexican Revolution."[58] Furthermore, in urban centers, Mexican American alliances in California with Garveyites may have been strengthened by the close proximity of Mexican American barrios to Black ghettos.[59]

Mexican Americans lived in the same neighborhoods as Blacks in cities like Los Angeles and San Diego. Furthermore, like the Garvey movement and the Ghadar movement, the Mexican nationalists also utilized the free press to get their agenda out to their constituency. Many of their editorials were in reaction to the Klan's perpetuation of mob violence and lynchings of Mexicans and Mexican Americans.[60]

In general, UNIA interactions with Mexico and Mexican Americans fell into two categories. In one category existed the interactions that Garveyites had with the Mexican government such as in Baja California, Mexico. In the second category was the relationship that western Garveyites had with local resident Mexican American populations. The best example of first category can be seen in the attempt by the UNIA to push for the creation of a Black colony in Baja, California, which was led by local western UNIA activists in California. In 1917, Hugh Macbeth Sr., a wealthy black lawyer in Los Angeles and supporter of the Garvey movement, was the driving force behind a colony he called Little Liberia, a clear reference to Liberia in Africa, which was also the destination for Garvey's "Back to Africa" movement. Although Macbeth had no intentions of actually living in the colony himself, he saw the potential for an agricultural center that could aid in the push toward black economic independence. He quickly came under investigation for his colony plan, when Bureau of Investigation agents suspected him of forming the community in order to encourage blacks to dodge the draft during World War I. But this did not deter his plans. In 1921 he sent a letter to UNIA official J. D. Gordon requesting funding for the project from the UNIA, and Gordon replied positively.[61] The Mexican government at least temporarily supported the possibility of trade and cooperation between Black Americans and Mexico. Furthermore, the governor of Baja California, Esteban Cantú Jiménez, hired "James N. Littlejohn, an African American highway and sewer contractor from Los Angeles, to begin road construction from Ensenada to Calexico in 1917."[62] The Mexican government also hired Macbeth as the Baja highway company's attorney.

In California, Black UNIA members and resident Mexican American populations worked less along lines of macro-economic interest. They formed associations around common issues of social oppression. In an effort to promote interracial cooperation, Charlotta Bass, in her editorials in the *California Eagle*, "regularly reported on events such as 'Mexican Cultural Nights,' organized by Latino activists."[63] Bass also regularly invited Mexican Americans to UNIA meetings.

Thus, in the shadow of World War I, black nationalists on the West Coast worked in conjunction with Asians, Mexicans, and other nonwhite groups in order to form a united front against their shared experiences of white oppression. This interracial cooperation did not mean that competition among or within these groups did not exist, nor does it suggest that all nationalist groups had identical goals. However, it does add complexity to previous descriptions of Black nationalism as a racially exclusive narrative. Black nationalists in the early twentieth century on the West Coast were few in number and needed the support of other groups to help meet their racial agenda. Similarly, Indian nationalists, Japanese nationalists, Mexican American nationalists, and other groups of color needed and worked with Garveyite Black nationalists in pursuit of their respective visions of justice and equity in the American West.

Notes

1. Quintard Taylor, *The Forging of a Black Community: Seattle's Central District from 1870 through the Civil Rights Era* (Seattle: University of Washington Press, 1994), 56.
2. Jervis Anderson, *A. Phillip Randolph: A Biographical Portrait* (Berkeley: University of California Press, 1986), 159.
3. Emory Tolbert, *The UNIA and Black Los Angeles* (Los Angeles: Center for Afro-American Studies, UCLA, 1980), 31.
4. Ibid.
5. Taylor, *Forging of a Black Community*, 85.
6. For a more detailed account of discrimination faced by nonblack racial groups in the American West, see Mae M. Ngai, *Impossible Subjects: Illegal Aliens and the Making of Modern America* (Princeton: Princeton University Press, 2004); Tomás Almaguer, *Racial Fault Lines: The Historical Origins of White Supremacy in California* (Berkeley: University of California Press, 1994).
7. Taylor, *Forging of a Black Community*, 88.
8. Carlos M. Larralde and Richard Griswold del Castillo, "San Diego's Ku Klux Klan, 1920–1980," *San Diego Historical Quarterly* 46, no. 2 (Spring/Summer 2000): 3.
9. Ibid.
10. William D Carrigan and Clive Webb, *The Forgotten Dead: Mob Violence against Mexicans in the United States: 1848–1928* (New York: Oxford University Press, 2013): 30.
11. Eckard Toy, "Ku Klux Klan," *The Oregon Encyclopedia*, Oregon Historical Society, https://oregonencyclopedia.org/articles/ku_klux_klan.
12. Darrell Millner, "Oregon," in *Black America: A State-by-State Historical Encyclopedia*, vol. 2, ed. Alton Hornsby Jr. (Santa Barbara, Calif.: ABC-CLIO, 2011), 692.
13. *Lynden (Wash.) Tribune*, October 1, 1925.
14. David M. Chalmers, *Hooded Americanism: The History of the Ku Klux Klan*, 3rd ed. (Durham, N.C.: Duke University Press, 1987), 119.
15. Taylor, *Forging of a Black Community*, 90.
16. Tolbert, *UNIA in Black Los Angeles*, 89.
17. Ibid., 40.
18. Ibid., 54.

19. Delilah Beasley, *Negro Trail Blazers of California* (Los Angeles: Times Mirror Printing, 1919), 255.

20. "Report by Bureau Agents A. A. Hopkins and E. J. Kosterlitzky" (February 19, 1921), *UNIA Papers* (Los Angeles: University of California Press, 1984), 3:224.

21. Theodore Vincent, *Black Power and the Garvey Movement* (San Francisco: Ramparts Press, 1970), 169.

22. Ibid.

23. Taylor, *Forging of a Black Community*, 91.

24. Robin Dearmon Jenkins, "Linking up the Golden Gate: Garveyism in the San Francisco Bay Area, 1919–1925," *Journal of Black Studies* 39, no. 2 (November 2008): 271. See also Shirley Ann Wilson Moore, *To Place Our Deeds: The African American Community in Richmond, California 1910 to 1963* (Berkeley: University of California Press, 1996).

25. Jenkins, "Linking up the Golden Gate," 271.

26. See Scott Kurashige, *The Shifting Grounds of Race: Black and Japanese Americans in the Making of Multiethnic Los Angeles* (Princeton: Princeton University Press, 2008).

27. Taylor, *Forging of a Black Community*, 109.

28. Ibid., 57.

29. Marc Gallicchio, *The African American Encounter with Japan and China: Black Internationalism in Asia, 1895–1945* (Chapel Hill: University of North Carolina Press, 2000), 24.

30. "Report by Special Agent P-138" (October 22, 1920), *UNIA Papers*, (Los Angeles, C.A.: University of California Press, 1984) 3:62.

31. "Report by Bureau Agent H. B. Pierce on Negro Activities," April 25, 1921 *UNIA Papers*, (Los Angeles, C.A.: University of California Press, 1984) 3:364.

32. Vincent, *Black Power and the Garvey Movement*, 171.

33. US Navy/Chief of Naval Operations/Office of Naval Intelligence, Entry 78: [Formerly] Confidential General Correspondences, Weekly Report Japanese Activities, Week Ending March 18, 1922, p. 10, box 31, record group 38, National Archives, Washington, D.C.

34. Vincent, *Black Power and the Garvey Movement*, 171.

35. Seema Sohi, *Echoes of Mutiny: Race, Surveillance, and Indian Colonialism in North America* (New York: Oxford University Press, 2014), 21.

36. See ibid.

37. Ibid., 25.

38. Ibid.

39. Ibid.

40. Ibid., 46.

41. Ibid., 56.

42. See Gerald Horne, *The End of Empires: African Americans and India* (Philadelphia: Temple University Press, 2008) for a more expansive account of Black interactions with Indians in the United States.

43. Quoted in Erika Lee and Judy Yung, *Angel Island: Immigrant Gateway to America* (New York: Oxford University Press, 2010), 149.

44. Sohi, *Echoes of Mutiny*, 61.

45. Ibid., 153.

46. Ibid.

47. Ibid., 202.

48. Week Ending February 4, 1922, p. 8, box 31, record group, 38, National Archives, Washington, D.C.

49. "J. J. Hannigan, Commandant, Twelfth Naval District, to the Director, Office of Naval Intelligence" (December 3, 1921), *UNIA Papers*, (Los Angeles, C.A.: University of California Press, 1985), 4:236.

50. For an extensive discussion of Mexican relations with the United States, see the excellent John Mason Hart, *Empire and Revolution: The Americans in Mexico since the Civil War* (Berkeley: University of California Press, 2002).

51. Friedrich Katz, *The Secret War in Mexico: Europe, the United States, and the Mexican Revolution* (Chicago: University of Chicago Press, 1981), 303.

52. See Benjamin Heber Johnson, *Revolution in Texas: How a Forgotten Rebellion and Its Bloody Suppression Turned Mexicans into Americans* (Chicago: R. R. Donnelly & Sons, 2003).

53. Carrigan and Webb, *Forgotten Dead*, 85.

54. Ibid., 23.

55. Katz, *Secret War in Mexico*, 514.

56. Lawrence B. de Graaf, Kevin Mulroy, and Quintard Taylor, eds., *Seeking El Dorado: African Americans in California* (Seattle: University of Washington Press, 2001), 159.

57. Nicolás Kanellos and Claudio Esteva-Fabregat, eds., *Handbook of Hispanic Culture in the United States: Anthropology* (Houston: Arte Público Press, 1993), 47.

58. Vincent, *Black Power and the Garvey Movement*, 170.

59. Ibid., 170–71.

60. See Carrigan and Webb, *Forgotten Dead*.

61. Although evidence of funding sent to aid the colony has not been found, for further information regarding this letter, see *UNIA Papers* (Los Angeles: University of California Press, 1984), 3:321–22.

62. De Graaf, Mulroy, and Taylor, *Seeking El Dorado*, 161.

63. Sarah Schrank, *Art and the City: Civic Imagination and Cultural Authority in Los Angeles* (Philadelphia: University of Pennsylvania Press, 2011), 73.

8 Brothers Taking Action

African American Soldier Activism
at Fort Hood, Texas, 1948–1972

Herbert G. Ruffin II

There are all these people who came here with individual
problems for the Congressman—but there's a Brother over
here with a problem, and there's another over there with
the same dam[n]ed problem. We ain't got no personal
problems—we're oppressed people! Blacks are just flunkies
around here. We can't solve our problems individually,
but as a group.
　　—People's Justice Committee member

An anonymous black soldier stationed at Fort Hood in Killeen, Texas, in 1971, spoke for the more than two hundred African American soldiers in attendance. "Blacks are just flunkies around here," he told an independent hearing led by Representative Louis Stokes (D-Ohio), a member of the Congressional Black Caucus. Stokes was at the base investigating racism in the U.S. Armed Forces to build a case for long-overdue institutional reforms. In this setting, black soldiers were fundamentally demanding an end to racism in the military justice system, promotion of military personnel, and duty assignments; an end to religious discrimination against Nation of Islam members; and more black officers. They were supported by one hundred additional soldiers from the mostly white Fort Hood United Front. This resulted in the formation of a black soldier organization, the People's Justice Committee (PJC).[1] Although the PJC was short-lived, the black GI movement that inspired it made notable contributions to the wider GI, peace, civil rights, and Black Power movements. It took the U.S. armed forces to task over their failure to live up to claims of color-blindness and forced radical reform on most matters concerning race.

This is a story that has been rarely told. Following the 1980s, the erasure from history of soldier activism went hand-in-hand with the popular reframing of the Vietnam War to U.S. citizens. Many Americans' attitudes and reflections on war were heavily influenced by the Rambo mythology of the redeemed abandoned soldier and redeemed superpower nation that had failed to achieve most of its strategic military goals. By the Gulf War in 1990, this restructured national consciousness resulted in the common perception that to be antiwar was to be "against the troops."[2]

Moreover, journalists and scholars have not focused on the black GI movement in Texas but rather seen it as an extension of the white-led GI movement. This movement centered on organizations such as the Fort Hood United Front and alternative institutions such as the Oleo Strut coffeehouse and the GI newspaper the *Fatigue Press*. Since historian William Leckie's *The Buffalo Soldiers: A Narrative of the Negro Cavalry in the West* (1967), most of the tales about black soldiers in Texas have been heroic, "beyond the call of duty" stories of Buffalo Soldiers and of black service in World War II, America's "good war," citing units like Fort Hood's 761st *"Black Panther" Tank Battalion*.[3]

In this chapter I argue that the emergence of the black GI movement uncovered a broken system in the military in urgent need of repair. This system clearly reflected the broken U.S. society of the late 1960s, built on and continuing to function on unequal race, class, and gender relations. In her book *The New Jim Crow*, Michelle Alexander argues that legal racial discrimination has been perpetuated despite the ostensible success of the civil rights movement, discrimination manifest in the War on Drugs, the prison industrial complex, and policing practices. Likewise I argue that while racial discrimination in the military was publicly ended with President Truman's Executive Order 9981 in 1948, that discrimination was subsequently restructured in terms of the draft, the dearth of black officers, and unequal application of nonjudicial punishment and dishonorable discharge.[4] Similar to being marked a felon, dishonorably discharge was, and still is, the mark of an outcast, someone who is ineligible for veterans' benefits, welfare, and living wage employment—a status often resulting in drug abuse, homelessness, poverty, and prison. The discussion in this chapter will be framed by Alexander's *The New Jim Crow*, Peniel E. Joseph's *Waiting 'Til the Midnight Hour*, Quintard Taylor's *In Search of a Racial Frontier*, and James Weiderheider's *The African American Experience in the Vietnam War*, which in an intersectional manner address de facto structural racism, the black freedom movement as a conduit for civil rights and human rights, and blacks in Texas as a place in the South and West, and infuse social history into military history.[5]

The U.S. Armed Forces and Race Reform

The need for racial reform has been long-standing in the U.S. armed forces and U.S. society in general. The two intersect and cannot be separated in popular discourse or in public policy (such a separation is continually attempted and continually fails). The health of race relations in civil society is reflected in race relations in the military. In Texas, African Americans' troubled legacy in the U.S. armed forces goes back to the Buffalo Soldiers, who from 1866 to the 1890s played a crucial role in opening the West to U.S. expansion.[6] Similar to the role black soldiers would be called upon to play during the Vietnam War, African Americans were used to fight other people of color, in this case Native Americans and Mexicans. These soldiers were agents of a government that made promises that it could not or would not keep. Black soldiers were a reflection of those they were fighting, while the military was characterized by white entitlement, white supremacy, and white privilege wherever it went. Even though the Buffalo Soldiers helped "civilize" the West, whites in the West would see the black soldiers as inferiors unfit for military service and first-class citizenship. Examples of this are evident in the Brownsville riot of 1906 and the Houston riot of 1917. In the latter, "police roughed up a black soldier and woman and arrested a black policeman . . . [which] stimulated a retaliatory raid of about one hundred fifty troops [from the black Twenty-Fourth Infantry, keenly aware of the long Texas history of lynching black people] in which seventeen persons were killed and sixteen wounded. "Twenty-nine of the soldiers involved received the death penalty and sixty-three" life imprisonment.[7] Twelve major U.S. riots between 1919 and 1923—two in Texas (Longview in 1919 and Waco in 1919) were sparked by "white fears of black migration to cities, labor competition, and demands for greater equality by returning [black] soldiers," Alwyn Barr writes in *Black Texans*.[8] This pattern of racial violence and property destruction would repeat in riots and urban uprisings in the 1940s and again in the mid- to late 1960s.

After World War II, institutional racism within the armed forces was finally addressed after the War Department and President Truman were pressured from several sources. A. Phillip Randolph's League for Non-Violent Civil Disobedience against Military Segregation threatened to organize a march on Washington if its demands were not met, there were concerns about rioting, and there was also the perceived need to live up to rhetoric about democracy and equality during the Cold War.[9] Thus the U.S. armed forces were the first federal bodies to be legally desegregated (at "all deliberate speed"), starting with the navy in 1946. Two years later, following Executive Order 9981, a similar process was theoretically undertaken in all military branches, including the army. Under the John F. Kennedy administration in 1962, racism in the military was further addressed, at least nominally, through the creation of an assistant secretary of Defense for Civil Rights, a move emboldened by the Civil Rights Act of 1964, which legally outlawed racial discrimination in the military, in civil service, and in institutions receiving federal funding.[10]

For black soldiers like George Brummell, this hypothetically reformed version of the U.S. armed forces provided African Americans a clear path to live upwardly mobile lives and escape inner city America and the Jim Crow South. Brummell was born in New Orleans and raised in Federalsburg, Maryland. He joined the army in 1962, several years before the Gulf of Tonkin Resolution authorized the escalation of U.S. troops and U.S. involvement in Vietnam. After briefly serving in Korea and Germany, Brummell was stationed at Fort Hood in Killeen, Texas, from the summer of 1962 to February 1964.[11] Like many black soldiers Brummell joined because he felt he had to prove himself. Like many soldiers, he also had a John Wayne complex: he entered the service with cowboys and combat on his mind, seeing the army as the ideal path to manhood, a step taken without fully assessing the possible consequences.

During the Vietnam War era (1965–75), black men driven to pursue a reckless, egotistical, and hypermasculine military career constructed an entirely different equation for the formulation of manhood than did their white counterparts. Unlike black soldiers, white soldiers were not the disproportionate victims of the draft, did not serve a disproportionate percentage of frontline duty, and were not systematically denied service promotion. White soldiers' limited personal interactions with African Americans meant that their understanding of blacks was limited at best, prone to stereotypes gained from mass media that often equated the civil rights movement to a communist invasion.[12] It the may have been the 1960s, but an early-twentieth-century white notion still held on some level: the urban "coon," the African American man whose goal "was leisure . . . spent strutting, styling, fighting, avoiding real work, eating watermelons, [either being dominated by their wives or being sexually aggressive without attachments], and making a fool of himself."[13] Tracing back to the American Revolution, GIs like Brummell and black Central Texans I interviewed from the Ball, Hall, and

Ruffin families were determined to prove to whites that black people were intelligent, courageous, and deserved full citizenship and equal opportunity.[14] This dynamic resulted in two wars being fought simultaneously: on the battlefield against the North Vietnamese and in the barracks, home bases, and after-hour clubs against racism.

The Tale of Two Cities

Even though Brummell enjoyed his military career, he and other black soldiers at Fort Hood dealt with "off-base hostility" and said that "Killeen" stood for "Kill each and every nigger."[15] Situated between Austin and Waco, Texas, Killeen at the time was changing from desolate, all-white cotton town to military boomtown. It served the needs of what had been called Camp Hood during World War II and then renamed Fort Hood in the postwar period.[16] Prior to Camp Hood's establishment in 1942, Killeen had been a two-block virtual sundown town with just two African American residents.[17] Its social order was maintained by racial segregation, and the Ku Klux Klan annually marched on Avenue D and famously warned blacks with a giant sign that read, "Nigger, don't let the sun set on you."[18] When blacks did come into Killeen as day laborers, they came in at the back of the train with the shades pulled down or rode into town at the back of the bus from segregated communities such as nearby Temple and East Austin. Once in Killeen, they were constantly reminded of their place, whether at the train station, which had "colored" and "uncolored" washrooms, or at restaurants that often refused to serve them.[19]

Jim Crow in Killeen began to fade in the 1940s with the emergence of Camp Hood and popular support to defeat fascism abroad. The army's need for tank battalions and foot soldiers created a demand for black GIs.[20] During the war, the most vocal protesters to this restructuring of Killeen's racial order were white business owners who tried to make the military bend to local customs. In one instance, local Winfred Bell saw them join "hands like a rope . . . stretched from one side of the street to the other and . . . down the street . . . where some [black] people had gone to a filling station to get some gas for a car. And they literally pushed these [black] people . . . and literally drove them out of town."[21]

What changed this behavior was Killeen's economic dependence on Camp Hood. This became evident after the base was recommissioned as Fort Hood in 1950 and became one of the largest bases in the Western Hemisphere in population and acreage.[22] This sparked the rapid infrastructural and population growth of Killeen, similar to growth of postwar military towns such as Seaside, California, and Colorado Springs, Colorado. Killeen's population grew from 1,410 in 1910 to 35,507 in 1970, with most of the population in 1970 working at Fort Hood, which had a soldier population as high as 95,000 during the peak period of the Vietnam War.[23] The federal presence resulted in Killeen becoming one of the first cities in Texas to undergo desegregation immediately following the *Brown v. Board of Education* verdict in 1954–1955. As a result, black children of enlisted men were able to attend Killeen High School and play on integrated sports teams almost ten years before the rest of the state went through this process in nearby school districts in Austin, La Vernia, New Berlin, and Seguin.[24] Still, before the 1970s, black soldiers did not find housing in Killeen but continued to live in segregated communities like Temple and on base. Many also did not feel comfortable socializing in Killeen's growing downtown, which had matured by 1968.

In the midst of this transformation, Killeen and cities across the country became powder kegs following President Johnson's 1965 resolution to escalate the U.S. presence in Vietnam. The Vietnam War became a point of contention that split the African American community along the lines of young and old, moderate and radical, and civil rights and Black Power. Early 1968, with the Tet Offensive and the assassination of Dr. Martin Luther King Jr., was a tipping point, however. More and more came to agree that the United States was fighting an ambiguous and never-ending war, with the potential loss of a generation of black men as casualties. The U.S. public also began to question the wisdom of making GIs serve in Vietnam not just as fighters but also as nation builders, diplomats, and pacifiers. But the main points of contention for black civilians were the draft and high casualty rates. For black soldiers there were the draft, preponderance of frontline deployments, high casualty rates, lack of representational officers, nonjudicial punishment (authorized by Article 15 of the Uniform Code of Military Justice), pretrial imprisonment, and dishonorable discharge.[25]

The Era of Individual Dissent, 1965–1967

Similar to the draft during the World War II and the Korean War, the Vietnam War draft, administered by the Selective Service Act of 1948, channeled African Americans mainly into the army and onto the front lines in a manner that appeared to be color-blind and impartial regardless of social class. But the reality was otherwise. Secretary of Defense Robert S. McNamara's controversial Project 100,000 (announced August 23, 1966) structured the Vietnam War into a white and rich man's war for U.S. superpower prowess, fought by black, brown, and poor people who, according to the Department of Defense (DOD), "lacked" the economic, educational, and intellectual aptitude to get deferments proportionate with their populations.[26] According to the DOD, by military would lower educational and mental fitness standards and thus provide the most disadvantaged people unprecedented opportunities to serve the United States while becoming productive members of society. There was no public mention of the project being a mechanism for conscripted manpower. As a result, just as middle- and upper-class white males were significantly overrepresented in deferments, eighteen-to-twenty-five-year-old African Africans were just as significantly overrepresented in Project 100,000, comprising 40 percent of its recruits.[27]

Young black men did not have to look far to know how authorities might punish them for draft evasion. All they had to do was review their own experiences and consider too how heavyweight boxing champion Muhammad Ali was treated by the Selective Service.[28] In 1967, Ali was stripped of his title and sentenced to five years for draft evasion for refusing to be conscripted, despite conscientious objection on the ground of his religious belief that members of the Nation of Islam "do not take part in wars that take human lives."[29] A Supreme Court decision in 1971 that refused to allow objection to a particular war triggered the defection from the United States of more than fifty thousand objectors who must have felt that they would receive similar treatment to that afforded Ali.[30] This post-1965 U.S. military was a fundamentally different than the once that Brummell had entered in 1962.

At Fort Hood, where Brummell was stationed, during the Vietnam War most soldiers were "veterans who had more than 90 days left to serve."[31] Their main tasks were riot control—a direct response to urban riots and rebellions were exploding throughout the United States—and training to fight a tank war against the Soviet Union in Europe.[32] While three out of four Americans continued to have a personal connection to the armed forces, stretching back to the advent of the draft in 1940, what had changed was that officers and career enlisted men more than ever before used force, intimidation, and harassment to maintain discipline.[33] Most draftees and recruits understood that soldiers had never been totally free. But arguably never before had enlisted men been treated so oppressively. Their First Amendment rights were systematically trumped by officers' excessive and unfair use of Article 15 and invocation of military necessity, conformity, and obedience, which had the backing of civilian and military courts.[34] Combined with the dramatic increase in black youth taken from urban plantations such as Birmingham, Alabama, and Watts, Los Angeles, to serve in the military, this reflected increased racial and class tensions in U.S. civilian society. It was no coincidence that black soldiers at Fort Hood were pioneers in a GI resistance movement at the same time as the rise of the Black Power and peace movements in 1966 and 1967.

Fort Hood's GI movement began on June 30, 1966, after Privates James Johnson (an African American), Dennis Mora (a Puerto Rican American), and David Samas (a Lithuanian and Italian American) openly opposed the war by publicly refusing deployment to Vietnam because they saw the war as "immoral, illegal, and unjust." They were the Fort Hood 3, and their protest took place eight months after the first Texas GI protest, at Fort Bliss in El Paso on November 6, 1965. (There in El Paso "a single GI" marched with thirteen other people to protest the war.)[35] The Fort Hood protest took place a month after Kwame Ture (Stokely Carmichael) and Mukasa Dada (Willie Ricks) called for Black Power in Greenwood, Mississippi. The Fort Hood 3 were arrested on July 7, 1966, on their way to speak at a rally in New York City held at Fort Dix, New Jersey, and released under immense pressure from the Fort Hood (Legal) Defense Committee and freedom rights groups such as SNCC, which organized mass demonstrations against their arrest and the Vietnam War. The trio became heroes to thousands of enlisted men who were increasingly malingering, deserting, substance abusing, and spontaneously rebelling in Vietnam and on stateside bases. Before long, in 1967, Martin Luther King Jr. and Muhammad Ali would speak out against the war and be arrested.[36]

The Era of Organized Dissent, 1968–1972

The GI movement at Fort Hood transitioned from spontaneous resistance to organized dissent in 1968, mirroring an organized antiwar and human rights struggle developing within the U.S. military. At the forefront of this development in Texas home were the most racialized, impoverished, and traumatized soldiers who had already witnessed mayhem abroad and were ordered to participate in more of the same as standbys for riot control in inner cities. Providing the space for them to organize against this were white-owned coffeehouses in towns adjacent to bases, such as the Oleo Strut in downtown Killeen.

The coffeehouse movement began in January 1968 near Fort Jackson in Columbia, South Carolina, at an establishment called UFO. It was founded by Vietnam reserve veteran Fred Gardner and Donna Mickleson.[37] In June 1968, Gardner's ambition to create a freedom rights and peace movement through coffeehouses resulted in the summer openings of the Oleo Strut in Killeen and Mad Anthony Wayne's in Waynesville, Missouri, near Fort Leonard Wood.[38] The Strut was named after a helicopter shock absorber, and the Strut's purpose, in part, was to

GIs outside the Oleo Strut in Killeen, Texas, circa 1970.

absorb the shock of soldiers stationed at Fort Hood.[39] At coffeehouses like this from 1968 to 1972, dislocated soldiers were able "to escape the authoritative grip of military command on stateside bases."[40] Here they were able to eat, hang out, listen to music, play games, read thought-provoking materials, and have political discussions with like-minded people. The voices of soldiers at Fort Hood were best heard in the GI newspaper the *Fatigue Press*, which was produced in the Strut and was one of an estimated three hundred GI newspapers from 1968–1974.[41]

The Strut's presence threatened Killeen's socioeconomic order, resulting in it being constantly attack by conservative locals, businessmen, and military officials who felt that it negatively impacted GI morale and military discipline.[42] This was especially true during the summer of 1968, with urban rebellions exploding in most major U.S. cities and the Tet Offensive forcing a beleaguered President Johnson to scale back bombings and ostensibly start negotiating a truce to end the war.[43] This turn of events produced a "severe breakdown in military morale and the appearance of a Peace [and Black Freedom] movement within the ranks."[44]

In this environment black enlisted men like Lionel Anderson increasingly began to read the *Fatigue Press* and the *Black Panther* newspaper. On August 22, 1968, black GIs also began meeting more formally at the Oleo Strut. On this night forty-three black soldiers met for the first time as a collective to do as Black Panther Party cofounder Bobby Seale suggested: seize the time to organize resistance to the wars in Vietnam and urban America.[45] A day later this group stopped trying to prove to white America that black people were worthy of first-class citizenship. They took a public stand despite perhaps foreseeing the response: military and law authorities quickly arrested them, and soon they were sentenced for refusing to follow orders. But as Seale had argued earlier, "Justice is gonna come when the masses rise up and see justice done."[46] With a similar mind-set the Fort Hood 43—as they were called—became known for defying orders to go to Chicago for riot control duty to reinforce the city's police at the Democratic National Convention. At that event, pro-segregationist governor George Wallace (D-Alabama) had hoped to win the presidential nomination. Outside the convention hall was a demonstration in which a large percentage of the demonstrators were African Americans. This prompted one Fort Hood 43 member to remark, "We came home from fighting Vietcong and now they want us to fight Americans."[47] Four years earlier Wallace had shut out the black Mississippi Democratic Freedom Party (MFDP) from fair representation within the Mississippi political structure despite the fact that blacks represented 80 percent of the county in which the MDFP was structured.[48]

At Fort Hood, the forty-three dissident ignored were systematically ignored in the *Armored Sentinel*, the base newspaper, which never mentioned the case. GI papers such as the *Fatigue Press* covered the case, of course, and this sparked a second generation of GI protest that was even more assertive and combined the politics of the black freedom and peace movements. More importantly, soldier-activists' demands began aligning with the demands of the American public. With Fort Hood on the verge of becoming a battlefield, the military courts gave most of the mutineers light sentences to avoid a base uprising.[49]

The on-base racial unity associated with support of the Fort Hood 43 did not last long. In 1969, white supremacy, black nationalism, and racial violence on the base increased. And while many black soldiers supported the Black Panther Party's dialectical struggle against oppression rooted in capitalism and racism, most did not view the country's principal problems as being centered on class struggle like the Panthers and their white ideological counterparts did.[50] Also, most black GIs were not hippies. While they appreciated the Oleo Strut, most were suspicious of it as a white-owned institution and its isolation in downtown Killeen. As a result, most black soldiers were intent on organizing their own movement. In February 1969, three hundred soldiers, black and white, met for a peace summit of sorts, but it was a failure. According to former Oleo Strut staffer and film director David Zeiger, what every white organizer discovered was that white soldiers did not have an identifiable antiwar and freedom rights organization, and whites had failed to consider that blacks had been socially isolated at Fort Hood, in Killeen, and in white America. Under these conditions, most African Americans had formed a strong collective mind-set that did not distinguish between white soldiers and white officers or "between individual racism and institutional racism." For most black soldiers too there could be no coalition with white soldiers as long as white soldiers were disorganized. Moreover, Strut staffers became aware of certain white supremacist tendencies "in trying to channel black organizing to fit the needs of the white [GIs]." During the remainder of the war, a few black soldiers used the Strut as a resource and hangout while staffers tried to cultivate an interracial antiwar culture by appealing to individual white soldiers who were not as inclined to organize in collective progressive politics, especially on an equal basis with black and brown soldiers.[51]

White soldiers' incentive to form an antiwar and freedom rights organization at Fort Hood picked up in 1970. At this time the Pentagon was trying to reform officer behavior, officers were fighting those reforms, and a culture of oppression had developed at bases like Fort Hood. Officers there increased efforts to discipline soldier-activists, determined to clamp down on minimal dissent and put an end to early releases and outside investigations of the base.[52] Under these conditions white GIs started to organize, starting with demands for the release of white antiwar and freedom rights activist Richard Chase, who had been given a dishonorable discharge and sentenced to two years at the U.S. penitentiary in Leavenworth, Kansas, for refusing riot control duty. His case was crucial to the military brass, who were trying to make an example of Chase so that others wouldn't do the same thing. In June 1969, six months after being granted "unofficial" conscientious objector status, Chase had begun organizing soldiers at Fort Hood and working at the *Fatigue Press*. On September 11, military brass had had enough of Chase's activism and ordered him to partake in riot control training. His refusal had led to his being sent to Leavenworth, but here Chase continued to organize soldiers. His case became a lightning rod for soldiers after December 18, when Chase's attorneys and GI newspapers learned that on four occasions he had been beaten by MPs while in solitary confinement.[53] "Free Richard Chase" became the rallying cry for enlisted men, who also used the occasion to successfully pressure the Pentagon to end the use of soldiers in riot and rebellion control. Simultaneously, white GIs developed common cause and organized the first public demonstration in Killeen since the Ku Klux Klan and World War II bond rallies in the 1920s and 1940s respectively.[54] On May 16, 1970, an Armed Forces Day demonstration—"Armed Farces Day"—took place at Killeen and in twenty-three other locales across the country.[55]

In Killeen, this demonstration had mixed results. Thirteen hundred to fifteen hundred enlisted men marched peacefully, but they failed to produce an antiwar and freedom rights GI organization.[56] That development was still months away and occurred after the Oleo Strut became a more relevant institution for soldiers, with the addition of a bookstore, counseling office, and star-studded fund-raising events. On December 20, 1970, its staffers and soldier-organizers used the "Free Kelvin Harvey and John Priest" cause to prod white GIs sitting on the fence to overcome their apathy and organize the Fort Hood United Front. Harvey and Priest had been placed in Fort Hood's stockade after participating in a minor incident at Fort Leavenworth that was later called a rebellion. They faced dishonorable discharge and imprisonment for up to sixty years if found guilty in a court-martial. Defending Harvey and Priest was the antiwar group American Servicemen Union, who took this opportunity to have a greater presence in the Fort Hood area. The formation of the United Front occurred during the peak of open dissent in all branches of the military. All charges against Harvey and Priest were dropped three days after a public gathering on their behalf on September 12, 1971.[57]

Most members of the United Front were white. In 1971, they organized antiwar demonstrations against Armed Forces Day and Veteran Day, the latter calling for an end to the war and freedom for all political prisoners.[58] On July 5 they organized a "Love-In" counterculture festival in Killeen's Condor Park that drew over two hundred people. Only a few African Americans attended the demonstrations, which to most seemed centered on outdated civil rights *movement* tactics.[59]

As 1971 moved into late autumn, the prospects for a strong interracial GI movement at Fort Hood seemed bleak, but looks were deceiving. Black congressman Ron Dellums (D-California)—who in April had chaired a congressional hearing on alleged U.S. war crimes—happened to take notice of Fort Hood's Veterans Day demonstration and contacted the Oleo Strut for assistance in publicizing a Congressional Black Caucus (CBC) hearing on racism at Fort Hood. The hearings were scheduled for November 15, to be led by Congressman Louis Stokes (D-Ohio).[60]

What organizers at Fort Hood and Killeen had to overcome was the wall of racial animosity between the soldiers and organizations such as a black separatist GI organization—the Five Percent—and the predominantly white United Front, not to mention the disproportionate disciplinary actions that white officers took against black and brown soldiers. For example, in August 1971 rumors of racial uprising impelled forty shotgun-carrying MPs to storm the barracks where the Forty-Second Signal Battalion was stationed, forcing to the ground eight black soldiers who were barely dressed, "drag[ging] people out of bed, and arrest[ing] them," according to a black MP.[61] Altogether nineteen blacks and one white were arrested.

During the CBC hearings the soldiers came to a temporary truce under the leadership of Wes Williams, a United Front member and widely respected black GI from Oakland. Williams brought together the aims of the United Front and black GIs within the broader frameworks of the black freedom movement and international socialism movements, intersecting race and class. Two hundred African American soldiers attended and demanded that there be one public hearing instead of being split into several groups as the army intended. One hundred members of the United Front supported this motion. With the intent of getting the most out of Congressmen Stokes's visit, after lunch African American soldiers met to form a black GI organization that would be aligned with the mainstream GI movement, while Stokes intentionally occupied the Army brass's attention with a prolonged tour of the base. The soldiers decided to go ahead with the plan but to address it at night and off base at the Oleo Strut, where they did not need authorization to meet. From that meeting emerged the People's Justice Committee (PJC), a revolutionary black GI organization. During its first three months it reflected the Black Panthers' views, espousing black socialism but allowing progressive whites to join, such as the Progressive Labor Party's John Pink.[62] This development resulted in the mass exodus of those who wanted the PJC to be a black movement for black soldiers. In the PJC's brief existence, from November 1971 though the summer of 1972, it tipped the domestic war at Fort Hood in favor of the GIs. Although its time was short, the PJC was part of a strong interracial GI movement occurring nationwide, one that put pressure on the Nixon administration to hasten the ending of the war and to support the troops by bringing them immediately home.[63]

Epilogue

At Fort Hood the racial unification of the U.S. antiwar movement came unhinged as soon as it became strong. In mid-November 1971, within the week that the PJC was formed, Fort Hood commanding general George P. Seneff requested that Wes Williams organize a "racial harmony team" that would regulate black militancy on the base. Williams refused and mentioned the hearings. The following day, MPs tailed him for intelligence and then informed Seneff about the PJC. That very night Williams was charged with possession of marijuana, with the possibility of being court-martialed and dishonorably discharged. This trumped-up charge united most soldiers at Fort Hood and at other bases, and one of the greatest political prisoner leaflet campaigns of the era led to Williams's acquittal on January 31, 1971, and honorable discharge three days later. During the campaign on behalf of Williams, the Fort Hood GI movement organized its greatest push to end the war and reform the U.S. military, which by 1973 included ending soldier deployments to South Vietnam, Cambodia, and Laos and reform of the draft, nonjudicial punishment, military justice, officer training, and promotional opportunities in stateside bases.[64] This was the peak of Fort Hood's GI movement during the Vietnam War.

Fort Hood's GI movement went into decline with the acquittal of Williams, who had a large group of soldiers testify on his behalf. Three days after his trail, he went back to another war zone as a civilian in Oakland. The loss of Williams led to a split in the base's GI movement. From November 1971 to April 1972, the PJC and United Front worked together, especially on campaigns to end the war, abolish Article 15 punishment and pretrial confinement, and improve the quality of living in the Killeen area. After Williams, white supremacy grew within the United Front, and black separatism grew within the PJC. This resulted in the PJC twice opting out of cosponsored events with the United Front that were planned when Williams was still an active soldier. The first was the "Free Billy Smith" national rally set for April. Smith was a black GI from Watts, charged (on circumstantial evidence) with fragging two officers in Vietnam. His rally occurred at the Oleo

Strut without the sponsorship of the PJC, who were interested in organizing their own rally without white GIs compromising their expression. The second event was the Armed Forces Day demonstration set for May 20, 1971. Three days before the march, the PJC told the United Front steering committee that it would not support the march and was planning its own demonstration because "they felt the march wouldn't do any good and most Black GIs wouldn't support it." What PJC members wanted was something more culturally relevant and institutionally transformative. As the PJC and Oleo Strut staffers predicted, the march was an uninspiring flop.[65] This was followed by a lessening of interracial unity and weakening of the GI struggle, hastened by a rash of early-out discharges. That said, this demise of Fort Hood's GI movement did not take away the tremendous contributions its soldier-activists had made to the peace and civil rights and Black Power movements.

After the heyday of the civil rights movement, the GI movement played a key role in democratizing the U.S. armed forces and opening up former sundown towns such as Killeen, Texas. At Fort Hood this was signified by the change in the name and focus of its newspaper, the *Armored Sentinel*, which became the *Fort Hood Sentinel* around 1973. To reflect the army's shift in focus it began addressing race relations, the valor and contributions of black soldiers dating back to Revolutionary War, military justice, and quality-of-life reforms.[66]

Waves of antiwar activity would take place at Fort Hood and in Killeen during the 1990–91 Gulf War and the subsequent War on Terror, addressing multiple deployments, untreated *post-traumatic stress disorder* and *traumatic brain injury*, overmedication, lack of personal support and quality mental health care, and stigmatization.[67] These are similar to what soldiers struggled with during the Vietnam War, with a fundamental difference: the military from 1973 on was voluntary, not conscripted, and wars today are fought more with machines and electronic technology and so forces are far smaller.[68] However, as in the past, black, brown, and poor people continue to fight wars on multiple fronts: against who they are ordered to fight and against institutional racism, classism, and sexism. Witness the Fort Hood shootings of 1991, 2009, 2014, a new GI movement organized at Killeen's Under the Hood Cafe and Outreach Center (2009–2014), and the underreported black freedom movement influence on international GI organizations such as March Forward! The latter represented a new form of erasure during the Barack Obama administration: self-censorship in the face of possibly embarrassing an African American president.

Notes

Epigraph: Quoted in James E. Weiderheider, *The African American Experience in the Vietnam War* (Lanham, Md.: Rowan & Littlefield, 2008), 144.

1. "Organized Protest: The Fort Hood United Front and the People's Justice Committee," in Weiderheider, *African American Experience in the Vietnam War*, 141–44; "Extensions of Remarks," *Congressional Record,* 92nd Cong., 2nd sess., October 14, 1972, 36582–85.

2. Mark Cronlund Anderson, "How to Win the Vietnam War: More Rambo," *West East Journal of Social Sciences* 2, no. 2 (August 2013): 11–22; John Hellmann, "Rambo's Vietnam and Kennedy' New Frontier," in *Inventing Vietnam: The War in Film and Television,* ed. Michael A. Anderegg, (Philadelphia: Temple University Press, 1991), 140–52.

3. See Alwyn Barr, *Black Texans: A History of African Americans in Texas, 1528–1995* (Norman: University of Oklahoma Press, 1996); Paul H. Carlson, *The Buffalo Soldier Tragedy of 1877* (College Station: Texas A&M University Press, 2003); Garna L. Christian, *Black Soldiers in Jim Crow Texas, 1899–1917* (College Station: Texas A&M University Press, 1995); Arlen L. Fowler, *Black Infantry in the West, 1869–1891* (Norman: University of Oklahoma Press, 1971); Bruce A. Glasrud, ed., *Brothers to the Buffalo Soldiers: Perspectives on African American Militia and Volunteers, 1865–1917* (Columbia: University of Missouri Press, 2011); Bruce A. Glasrud and Michael Searles, eds., *Buffalo Soldiers in the West: A Black Soldiers Anthology* (College Station: Texas A&M Press, 2007); William H. Leckie, *The Buffalo Soldiers: A Narrative of the Negro Cavalry in the West* (Norman: Oklahoma University Press, 1967); James N. Leiker, *Racial Borders: Black Soldiers along the Rio Grande* (College Station: Texas A&M University Press, 2002); Elizabeth D. Leonard, *Men of Color to Arms! Black Soldiers, Indian Wars, and the Quest for Equality* (New York: W. W. Norton, 2010); Fred L. McGhee, *Two Texas Race Riots* (New Delhi, India: Fidelitas, 2012); John H. Nankivell, *Buffalo Soldier Regiment: History of the Twenty-Fifth United States Infantry Regiment, 1869–1926* (Lincoln: University of Nebraska Press, 2001); Charles M. Robinson, *The Fall of a Black Officer: Racism and the Myth of Henry O. Flipper* (Norman: University of Oklahoma Press, 2008); Frank N. Shubert, *Voices of the Buffalo Soldier* (Albuquerque: University of Mexico Press, 2003); Quintard Taylor, *In Search of the Racial Frontier: African Americans in the West, 1528–1990* (New York: W. W. Norton, 1998); John D. Weaver, *The Brownsville Raid* (College Station: Texas A&M University Press, 1971); Kareem Abdul-Jabbar and Anthony Walton, *Brothers in Arms: The Epic Story of the 761st Tank Battalion, WWII's Forgotten Heroes* (New York: Broadway Books, 2005); Gina M. DiNicolo, *The Black Panthers: A Story of Race, War, and Courage—the 761st Tank Battalion in World War II* (Yardley, Pa.: Westholme, 2014); Charles W. Sasser, *Patton's Panthers: The African-American 761st Tank Battalion in World War II* (New York: Gallery Books, 2005); Joe Wilson Jr., *The 761st Black Panther Tank Battalion in World War II: An Illustrated History of the First African American Armored Unit to See Combat* (Jefferson, N.C.: McFarland, 2006).

4. Michelle Alexander, *The New Jim Crow: Mass Incarceration in the Age of Colorblindness* (New York: New Press, 2010), 1–19.

5. Alexander, *New Jim Crow;* Peniel E. Joseph, *Waiting 'Til the Midnight Hour: A Narrative History of Black Power in America* (New York: Holt, 2007); Taylor, *In Search of the Racial Frontier;* and Weiderheider, *African American Experience in the Vietnam War.*

6. Taylor, *In Search of the Racial Frontier,* 164–91; Glasrud, *Buffalo Soldiers in the West,* 153–216; Barr, *Black Texans,* 2–50, 86–88, 245.

7. Taylor, *In Search of the Racial Frontier,* 179–81.

8. Ibid., 138. Also see Darlene Clark Hine, William C. Hine, and Stanley Harrold, *Africans Americans: A Concise History* (Upper Saddle River, N.J.: Pearson, 2014), 359–63.

9. Herbert G. Ruffin, "A. Phillip Randolph," in *Icons of Black America,* vol. 3, ed. Matthew Whitaker (Westport, Ct.: Greenwood Press, 2011), 727–40.

10. Weiderheider, *African American Experience in the Vietnam War,* 124–25.

11. Gail Buckley, *American Patriots: The Story of Blacks in the Military from the Revolution to Desert Storm* (New York, Random House, 2001), 402–3.

12. Samuel Black, *Soul Soldiers: African Americans and the Vietnam War Era* (Pittsburgh: Senator John Heinz Pittsburgh Regional History Center and the Historical Society of Western Pennsylvania, 2006), 7; David Cortright, *Soldiers in Revolt: GI Resistance during the Vietnam War* (Chicago: Haymarket Books, 2005), 154; Weiderheider, *African American Experience in the Vietnam War,* 47; Jan Nederveen Pieterse, *White on Black: Images of Africa and Blacks in Western Popular Culture* (New Haven: Yale University Press, 1992), 30–101, 132–56, 224–35; Thomas Sugrue, *Sweet Land of Liberty: The Forgotten Struggle for Civil Rights in the North* (New York: Random House, 2008), 200–312.

13. David Pilgrim, "The Coon Caricature," Jim Crow Museum of Racist Memorabilia, http://www.ferris.edu/jimcrow/coon.

14. Persons in the Ball, Hall, and Ruffin families interviewed by the author in Luling, San Antonio, and Seguin, Texas in July 2009, July 2012, July 2015, who served in the military from the Vietnam War era to the present include James Alfred Ball, Shelby Ball, Ron Hall, Herbert Ruffin I, Honey Ruffin, and Jozette Ruffin.

15. Buckley, *American Patriots,* 403.

16. Gra'Delle Duncan, *Killeen: Tale of Two Cities, 1882–1982* (Killeen, Tex.: G. Duncan, 1984), 17–32.

17. *Killeen Historic Resources Survey: Killeen, Bell County, Texas* (City of Killeen, 2008), http://www.killeentexas.gov/, 23–24.

18. Quote from "John Cough," in "Killeen Pioneer Interviews," Spring 1977 (hereafter cited as KPI), 14, Killeen City Library Archives. Also see "Marion Denton," in KPI, 6; "Levy," in KPI, 4.

19. "Hellen Little" in KPI, 9.

20. "Ted Connell" in KPI, 4.

21. Quote from "Winifred Bell," in KPI, 17–18.

22. "Fort Hood History," Fort Hood, Texas, http://www.hood.army.mil/history.aspx.

23. Duncan, *Killeen,* 131–44; Carol Lynn McKibben *Racial Beachhead: Diversity and Democracy in a Military Town* (Stanford: Stanford University Press, 2012); U.S. Bureau

of the Census, *Thirteenth Census of the United States, 1910: Population by Counties and Minor Civil Divisions, 1910, 1900, 1890* (Washington D.C.: Government Printing Office, 1912), 510; U.S. Bureau of the Census, "Chapter A—Number of Inhabitants: Texas" (Washington D.C.: GPO, 1972), 45-15, http://www2.census.gov/prod2/decennial/documents/00496492v1p45s1cho2.pdf; "Fort Hood History."

24. See "Gerald Skidmore," in KPI, 6; "Hellen Little," in KPI, 14–15. Barr, *Black Texans*, 204–19; Anna Victoria Wilson and William E. Segall, *Oh, Do I Remember! Experiences of Teaching During the Desegregation of Austin's Schools, 1964–1971* (Albany: State University of New York Press, 2001); Herbert G. Ruffin II, "The Forging of an African American Community on the Outskirts of Alamo City: African American Suburbanization in San Antonio, 1980–2000," unpublished paper.

25. Weiderheider, *African American Experience in the Vietnam War*, 72–74, 141–44; "Tet Offensive," History.com, http://www.history.com/topics/vietnam-war/tet-offensive.

26. Black, *Soul Soldiers*, 141; Cortright, *Soldiers in Revolt*, 201–4; "Fact Sheet on GI Dissent," in *Library—Pamphlets, Supporting Materials for* Sir! No Sir!, http://www.sirnosir.com/archives_and_resources/library/pamphlets_publications/factsheet_on_gi_dissent/page1.html; Edward J. Drea, *McNamara, Clifford, and the Burdens of Vietnam, 1965–1969* (Washington, D.C.: Historical Office, Office of the Secretary of Defense, 2011); Janice H. Laurence, et al., "Effects of Military Experience on the Post-Service Lives of Low-Aptitude Recruits: Project 100,000 and the ASVAB Misnorming, Final Report 89–29," ERIC, 1989, http://eric.ed.gov/?id=ED366751; Ron Hall, J. A. Ball, and Honey Ruffin interviewed by the author, July 2012.

27. See Black, *Soul Soldiers*, 141; Weiderheider, *African American Experience in the Vietnam War*, 17–36.

28. David Zirin, *What's My Name Fool? Sports and Resistance in the United States* (Chicago: Haymarket Books, 2005), 53–72; Clayborne Carson, David J. Garrow, Gerald Gill, Vincent Harding, Darlene Clark Hine, eds., *The Eyes on the Prize Civil Rights Reader* (New York: Penguin, 1991), 439–59.

29. Quoted in Nisa Islam Muhammad, "Conscientious Objector Status 101," *Final Call*, July 21, 2004, http://www.finalcall.com/.

30. Ibid.

31. Quoted in Clay Coppedge, "Ode to the Oleo Strut," *TexasEscapes.com*, September 3, 2007, http://www.texasescapes.com/ClayCoppedge/Ode-to-the-Oleo-Strut.htm. Also see Jonathan Stein, "Sir, No Sir! An Interview with David Zeiger," in *Mother Jones*, September 1, 2005, http://www.motherjones.com/politics/2005/09/sir-no-sir-interview-david-zeiger.

32. First Cavalry and Fort Hood historian Richard Powell, interviewed by the author, Fort Hood, Texas, July 20, 2015.

33. See Jim Garamone, "Carter Asks Execs to Find New Ways to Work with Military," *Fort Hood Sentinel*, July 16, 2015.

34. Samuel Black, *Soul Soldiers*; Cortright, *Soldiers in Revolt*, 200–219; "Soldiers Suit against Army Heard in Federal Court," in *Library—Pamphlets, Supporting Materials for* Sir! No Sir!, http://www.sirnosir.com/archives_and_resources/library/

pamphlets_publications/Black_Panther/46.html; "Few Soldiers Think Art. 15s as 'Bennies,'" *Fort Hood Sentinel*, August 24, 1973; Stu Simms, "Article 15—the Most Frequent Military Discipline Action," *Armored Sentinel*, November 5, 1971; Wallace Terry, *Bloods—Black Americans on the Vietnam War: An Oral History* (New York: Presidio Press, 2006); Weiderheider, *African American Experience in the Vietnam War.*

35. "The GI Movement in Texas, 1965–1969," GI Press Project, http://gipressproject. blogspot.com/2011/04/gi-movement-in-texas-part-1-1965-1968.html; Howard Zinn, "Jun. 30, 1966: Fort Hood Three Release Public Statement on Vietnam Refusal," in *Zinn Education Project*, https://zinnedproject.org/2014/06/fort-hood-three.

36. "The Fort Hood Three: The Case of Three G.I.'s Who Said 'No' to Vietnam," in *Library—Pamphlets, Supporting Materials for* Sir! No Sir!, http://www.sirnosir.com/ archives_and_resources/library/pamphlets_publications/ft_hood_3/p6.html; Stokely Carmichael, and Ekwueme Michael Thelwell, *Ready for Revolution: The Life and Struggles of Stokely Carmichael* (New York: Scribner, 2003), 501–19; Martin Luther King Jr., "A Time to Break Silence," in Carson, Garrow, Gill, Harding, and Hine, *Eyes on the Prize Civil Rights Reader*, 387–93.

37. Cortright, *Soldiers in Revolt*, 53–54.

38. Barbara Dane, "The Oleo Strut," originally published in the *Guardian*, July 30, 1968, in *Library—Pamphlets, Supporting Materials for* Sir! No Sir!, http://www.sirnosir.com/ archives_and_resources/library/articles/guardian_01.html; Eric Ruder, "The Story of the GI Coffeehouses," *Socialistworker.org*, December 14, 2007, http://socialistworker. org/2007-2/656/656_10_Coffeehouses.shtml.

39. Dane, "The Oleo Strut"; Stein, "Sir, No Sir!"

40. Quoted in Ruder, "The Story of the GI Coffeehouses."

41. *Library—Pamphlets, Supporting Materials for* Sir! No Sir!, http://www.sirnosir.com/ site_sections/library.html.

42. "History of the Oleo Strut," 6, in *Library—Pamphlets, Supporting Materials for* Sir! No Sir!, http://www.sirnosir.com/archives_and_resources/library/pamphlets_publications/ history_of_the_oleo_strut/cover.html; Cortright, *Soldiers in Revolt*, 57.

43. "Tet Offensive."

44. Morelock, "Tet Offensive and the Media."

45. "History of the Oleo Strut"; Bobby Seale, *Seize the Time: The Story of the Black Panther Party and Huey P. Newton* (Baltimore: Black Classic Press, 1970).

46. "Letters from Disgruntled Black GIs in Vietnam," in Weiderheider, *African American Experience in the Vietnam War*, 139; "Organized Protest," 144.

47. Coppedge, "Ode to the Oleo Strut"; Cortright, *Soldiers in Revolt*, 56; "Organized Protest," 144; Ina Jaffe, "1968 Chicago Riot Left Mark on Political Protests," *NPR*, August 23, 2008, http://www.npr.org/.

48. Carson, Garrow, Gill, Harding, and Hine, *Eyes on the Prize Civil Rights Reader*, 166–69, 176–79, 186–89.

49. "Fact Sheet on GI Dissent."

50. Huey P. Newton, *War against the Panthers: A Study of Repression in America* (New York: Harlem River Press, 1996), 5–10.

51. "History of the Oleo Strut" 5.

52. Cortright, *Soldiers in Revolt*, 155; Weiderheider, *African American Experience in the Vietnam War*, 81–113.

53. *"Free All Political Prisoners," in Library—Pamphlets, Supporting Materials for* Sir! No Sir!, *http://www.sirnosir.com/archives_and_resources/library/articles/left_face_06.html*.

54. "Jim Lindley" in KPI.

55. Quoted in *"Other Scenes . . . Other Voices . . . Armed Farces Day, 1970," in Library— Pamphlets, Supporting Materials for* Sir! No Sir!, *http://www.sirnosir.com/archives_ and_resources/library/articles/gigline_08.html. Demonstrations* took place at Fort Ord, California; Grissom Air Force Base, Indiana; Fort Benning, Georgia; Fort Jackson, South Carolina; Fort Meade, Maryland; Fort Bragg, North Carolina; Grand Forks Air Force Base, North Dakota; Key West, Florida; Aberdeen Proving Grounds, Maryland; Fort Rucker, Alabama; Altus Air Force Base, Oklahoma; Sacramento, California; Goldsboro, North Carolina; Fort Polk, Louisiana; Quantico, Virginia; Andrews Air Base, Virginia; McDill Air Force Base, Florida; Phoenix City, Alabama; Great Lakes Naval Training Center, Illinois; Picatinny Army Base, New Jersey; U. S. Army Aviation Systems Center, St. Louis; U.S. Army Tank Center, Detroit; and Charleston Naval Base, South Carolina.

56. Ibid.; "History of the Oleo Strut," 8.

57. "History of the Oleo Strut," 16; David L. Parsons, *Dangerous Grounds: Antiwar Coffeehouses and Military Dissent during the Vietnam Era* (Chapel Hill: University of North Carolina Press, 2017), 57.

58. Gerald D. Skidmore, *Historic Killeen: An Illustrated History* (San Antonio: Historical Publishing Network, 2010), 104.

59. Cortright, *Soldiers in Revolt*, 56; "History of the Oleo Strut," 18; Carson, Garrow, Gill, Harding, and Hine, *The Eyes on the Prize Civil Rights Reader*, 333–586; Joseph, *Waiting 'Til the Midnight Hour*, 241–95; Sugrue, *Sweet Land of Liberty*, 286–531; Mark Edelman Boren, *Student Resistance: A History of the Unruly Subject* (New York: Routledge, 2001), 122–200.

60. Citizens Committee of Inquiry, ed., *The Dellums Committee Hearings on War Crimes in Vietnam* (New York: Vintage Books, 1972); "History of the Oleo Strut," 20.

61. "Organized Protest," 142–43.

62. William L. Van Deburg, *Modern Black Nationalism: From Marcus Garvey to Louis Farrakhan* (New York: New York University Press, 1997), 118; "History of the Oleo Strut," 20–21.

63. See "History of the Oleo Strut," 20–21; "Organized Protest," 141–44; "Extensions of Remarks."

64. "History of the Oleo Strut," 20; Cortright, *Soldiers in Revolt*, 160; Weiderheider, *African American Experience in the Vietnam War*, 105–13.

65. "History of the Oleo Strut," 20–21.

66. James Toms, "A Black Man Fell First," *Armored Sentinel*, June 5, 1970; "Black Soldiers Save Rough Riders," *Armored Sentinel*, November 24 1971; "Blacks Had to Beg for Equal Basis," *Armored Sentinel*, December 3, 1971; "Racial Slurs 'No Mocking Matter'

to Minorities," *Fort Hood Sentinel*, November 9, 1973; Linda Prellwitz, "From Family to Finance, Facing Problems Head-on," *Fort Hood Sentinel*, February 1, 1974; Stu Simms, "Article 15," *Armored Sentinel*, November 5, 1971; "Few Soldiers Think Art. 15 as 'Bennies'"; A. D. Pittman, "Blacks Included throughout American History," *Fort Hood Sentinel*, February 7, 1975.

67. Quoted from "Under the Hood Responds to This Week's Tragic Events at Fort Hood," Under the Hood Café and Outreach Center, April 4, 2014, http://underthehoodcafe .org/.

68. Edward Tick, *Warrior's Return: Restoring the Soul after War* (Boulder, Colo.: Sounds True: 2014); Cortright, *Soldiers in Revolt*, 160–61.

9 Black Women in Spokane: Emerging from the Shadows of Jim and Jane Crow

Dwayne A. Mack

Black women in Spokane, after their earliest migration to the Inland Northwest, made significant contributions to black communities on every level, yet they remained in the historical shadows of their male counterparts. However, during the summer of 2015, Rachel Dolezal—a white woman who appropriated black culture, had masqueraded for almost a decade as an African American, and had even been elected president of the Spokane chapter of the National Association for the Advancement of Colored People (NAACP)—brought controversial media attention to the city. Her egregious hoax of wearing the mask of black womanhood victimized Spokane's African American community and set the stage for spotlighting true African American women engaged in activism for at least a century. Yet social critics, activists, and the general public missed the opportunity to celebrate the pivotal role that African American women have played in the cultural, social, and political evolution of Spokane's black community.

Scholar activist Pauli Murray personally understood the Jim Crow challenges African Americans faced from the mid-twentieth century, but she also identified the debilitating sexist and racist challenges as "Jane Crow." Besides encountering white supremacy, black women experienced intra-racial and interracial sexism.[1] Nevertheless, African American women served as catalysts for the black freedom struggle in a city not known as a hotbed for such activity. Although the gender balance in Spokane's black community was somewhat even, historians have marginalized the accomplishments of black women. But their place in the shadows of

---

Parts of this chapter originally appeared in Dwayne A. Mack, *Black Spokane: The Civil Rights Struggle in the Inland Northwest* (Norman: University of Oklahoma Press, 2014).

historical scholarship fails to diminish their impact on all aspects of community life. They chose the black church as their initial platform and then spread their influence to other social and cultural venues.

Black Religious and Cultural Expression

The African American pioneers who migrated to Spokane in the late nineteenth century formed religious organizations like those elsewhere in the country. Calvary Baptist Church, Spokane's first black church, established in 1890, and Bethel African Methodist Episcopal Church, founded in 1901, served the spiritual needs of the black population. As historian Herb Ruffin II describes in his study on African Americans in Santa Clara, California, black women during the turn of the twentieth century guided the "daily operations" of the church, "broadening its public arm."[2] Such was also the case in Spokane. Through the black church, African American women formed the social cultural outlets that revealed their ability to promote spiritual, cultural, and social awareness and to cope with racism and discrimination. They organized picnics, dances, athletic events, and literary societies—group activities that formed the core of community life.[3]

Out of the Spokane limelight and excluded from white organizations, black women were thus forced to create their own outlets. As historian Quintard Taylor describes in his study on black Seattle, African Americans "were bound together by an intricate web of mutually reinforcing kin, fraternal, religious, and social relationships." Often people who did "not belong to the same . . . social club or fraternal order, met at other community functions" and organizations.[4] In Spokane too, secular black organizations—fraternal lodges, women's clubs, the Booker T. Washington Community Center, and other social service institutions—evolved from the local churches. These black organizations had "broad-based membership" in Spokane that included African American women from diverse social, economic, and religious circles.[5]

In 1903, black men in Spokane had established a sense of cultural solidarity through the Inland Empire Number Three Masonic Lodge.[6] Its auxiliary, the Eastern Star, established a chapter decades later in 1925 for black women. The latter promoted a strong code of Christian ethics, including honesty, financial assistance to the black community during times of need, support of black community development, service to the infirm, and college scholarships for black students. Moreover, the chapter supported the nationwide civil rights struggle through its membership in the NAACP.[7]

In the face of continued segregation by white clubs, black women formed their own cultural and social organizations. On August 9, 1917, Mrs. J. C. Mapps founded the Washington State Federation of Colored Women's Clubs (WFCWC), the umbrella organization for other clubs throughout the state. The leadership of other prominent black women, including Mamie Hagans, Ada Cunningham Jones, and Lucile Perkins Parker, brought African American women from all across Washington to meet in Spokane during the WFCWC's early years.[8] The new clubs shared cultural and social interests of black women. Between 1910 and 1914, they created the Afro-American Woman's Charity Club of Spokane (May 1910), the Wednesday Art Club of Spokane (July 1913), and the Lincoln Helping Hand Club (1914), as well as the Dunbar Literary Club, the Nannie Helen Burroughs Art Club, and the Rose Art Club of Spokane.[9]

The Wednesday Art Club was more than an ordinary art club. Club members promoted black art in the "social, educational, and civic life of the community." Black women were committed to uplifting the community and preserving black cultural expression that helped define black culture in Spokane. Each year the club showcased its artists' works in watercolor, crayon, oil, and other media. Mayme Lee, a popular local African American artist, chaired most of these exhibits. The organization's greatest contribution to the broader black art world was its 1936 showing of the Harmon Foundation Art Exhibit of New York (a collection of several prominent African American Harlem Renaissance artists) at the Campbell Memorial Museum in Spokane.[10]

Through the women's club movement, African American women in Spokane played an active role in improving social conditions for blacks and all citizens in other areas. Besides serving the black community, Wednesday Art Club members collaborated with local white organizations that attempted to help the black community. Some of the club's women held memberships in the Young Women's Christian Association (YWCA), the Council for Family Life Education, and the Council of Church Women. Beyond supporting African American art, the club promoted "racial pride" through black history.[11] Along with supporting cultural awareness, they also financially contributed to the local welfare agency, black churches, the Red Cross, the Spokane Art Center, the "Tiny Tim" fund of Deaconess Hospital, and impoverished families, and provided college scholarships to African American students.[12]

Unfortunately the Great Depression reduced the cultural influence of the black women's club movement in Spokane. The outmigration of African Americans in search of job opportunities in larger cities, such as Seattle, contributed to the shrinkage of Spokane's WFCWC membership. Historian Turkiya Lowe argues that the shift of the state's black population to other Washington cities created tension in the organization. Although black women in Spokane had started it, much of its club activity traveled west of the Cascades to Seattle and Tacoma by the 1930s.[13]

The Early Formations of Black Agency

Historically, Spokane's black women looked beyond their cultural and social activities to the burgeoning nationwide civil rights movement. Dating back to the racial turbulence of the Red Summer of 1919, in an effort to defend and protect their civil rights at home, black residents followed the lead of other cities and mobilized to challenge such violence.

Some black women in Spokane approached civil rights agency with the same intensity as activists elsewhere. On March 3, 1919, Bertha Cravens, a local African American activist, initiated the first phase of the premodern civil rights movement. She tirelessly recruited eighty-one African American residents and raised eighty-three dollars to include in a charter application for the NAACP. A couple of months later, the national NAACP headquarters in New York City approved the city's chapter for full membership. The national office praised Craven, now the first secretary of the Spokane chapter, and other local leaders for founding a branch and expressed confidence that it would develop into an "active and influential unit." The Spokane NAACP's primary agenda was to legally challenge national and local racial injustices. In addition to challenging lynching, mob violence, and discrimination and segregation in education, transportation, housing, and voting, they passionately advocated passage of civil rights legislation. The civil rights protection of African Americans on military bases in the region eventually would serve as the branch's greatest challenge.[14]

Blacks initially joined the Spokane NAACP because they believed that their racial oppression was not as severe as the oppression that blacks elsewhere in the nation experienced. As a result, during the early years, they focused on assisting all black Americans struggling against racial injustice nationwide. Since most African Americans could not afford an attorney, many—locally and nationally—relied on free legal assistance from the NAACP. Besides its legal and political goals, Craven's branch supported the social maturation of the black community. In an effort to raise money and cultural awareness among African Americans women, the chapter organized an annual baby contest for prizes and the top honor as the community's most beautiful baby.[15] On a much broader level, ticket sales gave the national NAACP financial support, and the event galvanized the community through socialization at one of the largest churches and allowed black women to display racial price while celebrating youth to defy the prevailing racist attitudes that denigrated the physical characteristics of African Americans.

The Great Depression

By 1930 Spokane's population had increased to 115,514, but job scarcity during the Great Depression held the black numbers to only 617, 0.5 percent of the total.[16] Most of Spokane's black residents did not regret living as part of a small racial cohort. Some migrants sought such an isolated environment. Flexan Pierce's family migrated from Durham, North Carolina, in the early 1900s because her father "wanted better conditions."[17] For Pierce and other black migrants from the South, Spokane was the final stop in their search for inroads to racial equality.

As the financial crisis continued to grip the nation in the 1930s, black migration into Spokane slowly persisted. Following the lead of earlier black pioneers, African Americans arrived in search of racial harmony and especially employment. These migrants trickled into the city individually or married. Historian Moya B. Hansen observed that on a national level the "depression took its toll on all workers, but black women found themselves at a serious disadvantage."[18] Benefits from New Deal programs eluded most black women arriving in Spokane, most of whom had to settle for such menial jobs as domestics and waitresses. However, some African Americans, including women, participated in President Franklin D. Roosevelt's economic and educational initiatives that attempted to bring the United States out of the economic crisis.[19]

In 1937, Rosa D. Malone, an African American graduate of Alabama's Tuskegee Institute, arrived in Spokane on a Works Progress Administration (WPA) appointment to serve the needs of black children.[20] This New Deal program pumped millions of dollars into child-care facilities nationwide to assist destitute families of all races. The WPA was more effective than President Roosevelt's other New Deal programs, which failed to improve the socioeconomic status of most African Americans. The WPA opened child-care centers in black communities and provided jobs for the thousands of African American teachers, nurses, food service personnel, custodians, and construction workers left unemployed by the Depression.[21]

On February 1, 1937, with the support of the WPA, Malone became the director of the Booker T. Washington Community Center, a child-care center for the black community. For a couple of months it operated in the basement of Calvary Baptist Church, and in the spring of the same year it moved to a two-story house at 959 East Hartson. The center also served as a gathering place for the black community for parties, dances, and classes in dressmaking, piano, and voice lessons. During these Depression years, the facility also provided employment for some African American women in the community. Malone's WPA staff (all black women) included C. V. Evans, the center's recreational coordinator and chorus director; Bailey Pierce, the janitor; and Alta Finley, the facility's secretary.[22] Although some black women found employment through the WPA in Spokane, most continued to hold labor-intensive jobs as domestics through World War II.

Racial Segregation during World War II

Spokane underwent demographic changes during World War II. With expanded military and civilian work opportunities, the city's black population nearly doubled from 644 in 1940 to an estimated 1,200 in 1945.[23] Although Spokane was not a site for major defense production, a small number of mostly black men found work at Alcoa Aluminum, one of the area's most productive defense industry plants. The war also brought in a couple of dozen black women in the Women's Army Corps (WACs). Along with the male soldiers, the female military personnel who came through Fort George Wright and Geiger Air Field added to the increase in the local African American population.[24]

Military officials made minimal efforts to accommodate the black soldiers coming through the city. On August 8, 1943, the George Washington Carver United Service Organizations (GWCUSO), located on First and Division in the heart of the city, opened as a recreational facility to serve African American soldiers, male and female. Since racial segregation was still the official policy of the U.S. military, the facility was reserved for blacks only. As in most cases, black women turned Jane Crow into an opportunity to build community. The former director of the Booker T. Washington Center, Rosa Malone, became the GWCUSO's director. The board of governors included African American leaders such as Reverend Emmett Reed from Calvary Baptist Church and Mayme Lee from the Wednesday Art Club. With assistance from one hundred recruited African American hostesses, Eastern Star, and other fraternal organizations, Malone administered the USO's daily operations with a paltry $5,000 annual operating budget. She and her staff accommodated hundreds of soldiers who visited the facility. The USO offered an area for dancing and a lounge. Soldiers daily socialized in the backyard and enjoyed meals prepared at the barbecue grill.[25]

Malone's programming boosted the morale of African American soldiers by allowing them to relax and participate in recreational and social activities such as pool, table tennis, chess, checkers, and card games, including poker and the popular

Rosa Malone (*on left in white hat*) greeting Women's Army Corps members as they arrive in Spokane in 1945. *Courtesy of Eastern Washington Historical Society and Jerelene Williamson.*

"koon can tops," a variation of rummy popularized by African Americans. As another way of raising self-esteem, local African American women hosted recreational activities and formed their own successful GWCUSO-sponsored women's softball team. The facility offered soldiers a library of materials reflecting black life and culture. The GWCUSO also helped newly arrived soldiers to find housing.[26]

The Second Great Migration led many African Americans to move west, but Spokane's location and its relative lack of employment opportunities brought only a modest increase in its black population. Notwithstanding, local African American residents focused on community building and created their own entrepreneurial opportunities that served not only African Americans but the white community as well. Racial turmoil that surfaced in the next decade would undermine some of this progress and the spirit behind it.

African Americans in Spokane and elsewhere began preparing to resist the racism they had expected. By 1950 179 of 470 (38 percent) legal-aged black women workers found employment in an overall female workforce of 22,920. In contrast,

22,527 white women—out of a total legal-working-age population of 107,269 (21 percent)—found work. Approximately sixty black women worked in private households as domestics; most of them (fifty-four) lived in their employers' homes. The largest group of black female workers (sixty-eight), however, consisted of cooks, beauticians and manicurists, porters, waitresses, bartenders, counter workers, and laundry and dry-cleaning employees.[27]

Although white women effortlessly found employment in the sales profession, black women were perhaps most underrepresented in the retail trade. As sales clerks, whites totaled 2,073, but only five black women worked in the same capacity. The difference in annual salaries also represented the disparity between white and African American female employees: blacks averaged $1,300 a year compared to $2,200 of employed whites.[28]

The inequality in hiring white women and black women and the type of jobs they secured reflected the pervasive racism of whites in Spokane. Some business owners considered hiring blacks but refused to challenge the perceived public sentiment that blacks were unsuitable for employment in most areas. One unidentified white employer defended his policy of refusing black applicants. "Even if I were inclined to hire a qualified Negro in our profession, I would have to consider the feelings of our other employees."[29] Another employer worried about public opinion. "We employ one Negro woman, but feel we could employ no greater number because of public prejudice."[30]

In higher-paying, blue-collar jobs, only a small number of black civilians gained employment. Spokane's naval depot, for example, employed a substantial number of whites at the site, which had a dozen warehouses. Sybil Stafford, a longtime resident, claimed that she was the only black employee during her tenure at a military depot in neighboring northern Idaho. As the only black worker, Stafford performed the same tasks as her white coworkers: loading and unloading freight. She, unlike most African Americans working in white-dominated environments, could not remember experiencing racial animosity from her supervisor or coworkers. Her presence did not threaten the mostly white infrastructure at the warehouse. In white-dominated situations such as these, white workers in Spokane engaged in less racial antagonism.[31]

Postwar Police Brutality

After World War II, despite the attempts of activists to challenge white supremacy in Spokane and throughout the nation, African Americans continued to face unfettered racism. White efforts to exclude blacks were relatively isolated, but they occurred frequently enough and were serious enough to draw attention of the local African American community and civil rights groups such as the Spokane NAACP. Just as in the South, blacks—older residents, newcomers, and visitors alike—experienced denial of service at most white-owned hotels, motels, restaurants, department stores, barbershops, beauty parlors, real estate offices, employment agencies, and nightclubs. They commonly encountered restaurant window signs that read: "We Reserve the Right to Serve and We Won't Serve Colored."[32]

Most isolated acts of racial discrimination failed to become part of the public transcript, as local media rarely reported these white transgressions. The city's retail stores routinely adhered to Jim Crow customs against African Americans. Salespeople gave white customers preferential service. Fearful of losing white customers, a significant number of clothing stores refused to allow black women to try on the clothes before making a purchase. For the same economic concern of whites in the South, shoe stores in Spokane did not permit blacks to try on shoes before buying them.[33]

Despite the barriers to access to most white-owned businesses, some blacks asserted their right to receive fair and equal treatment. Most new black arrivals opposed discrimination by using what historian Robin D. G. Kelley described as "infrapolitics." In isolated incidents, they challenged white racist authority and policies through subtle resistance. These exchanges rarely received legal or media attention but nevertheless represented at least personal moral victories.[34]

Lydia Sims, for example, sometimes protested informally by refusing to comply with the discriminatory policies of the city's department stores. During the 1940s, while shopping for a housecoat at the Crescent, one of Spokane's largest department stores, Sims experienced such mistreatment. She asked a salesperson if she could try on a house robe, because she "didn't want to purchase an article of clothing and it not fit." When the salesperson refused her request, Sims defiantly replied, "Oh, really." She then took the item off the rack and went into a changing room and tried it on anyway. Sims brought the robe back to the salesperson and told her that she did not want it "because it didn't fit." The befuddled clerk did not reply, and Sims walked out of the store. Before moving to Spokane from Newark, New Jersey, Sims had always tried on clothes before buying them. It made no sense for her to take apparel home if it might not fit simply to accommodate white bias.[35]

Similarly, longtime resident Mabel Coates openly challenged a white salesclerk who mistreated her. While shopping at a hat store on Riverside Avenue, in the city's downtown area, she dealt with salesclerks who denied her service. Two white clerks, upon seeing Coates walk in, suddenly deployed a common strategy used to avoid black customers. They disappeared to the back of the store to avoid serving her. Coates defiantly and patiently tried on several hats. Before leaving, she shouted brazenly that the store should hire black clerks.[36]

Nearly all white-owned lodging facilities, including the largest and most prestigious hotel, the Davenport, located downtown, refused blacks. During the first five decades of the twentieth century, hotels barred such popular jazz vocalists, musicians, and civil rights activists as Louis Armstrong, Duke Ellington, Marian Anderson, and Paul Robeson. Spokane's black residents provided temporary lodging in their homes for entertainers, black soldiers, and other African American visitors.[37]

Although the United States achieved victory overseas, black soldiers experienced discrimination in public accommodations in Spokane. Because hotels prevented them from renting rooms and because their base offered too few social outlets, black soldiers found lodging and often socialized in the city. On July 29, 1946, an incident involving black soldiers attracted the attention of the civil rights community. A black resident, Ralph Thomas, had rented rooms to Women's Army Corps members Marguerite Meyers and Estella Franklin, both stationed at Geiger, along with two African American male soldiers from Seven Mile Camp. After receiving a disturbance call at Thomas's residence, Spokane law enforcement arrested the soldiers and fined Thomas for "conducting a disorderly house."[38] The police then booked the four soldiers on charges of vagrancy after they allegedly refused to obey orders from Geiger military personnel to leave Thomas's house.[39]

The arrest of the WACs aroused serious concern among the local civil rights community because one of them had claimed police brutality. Helen McCannon, secretary of the Spokane NAACP Equal Rights Committee, stood at the forefront of investigating the soldier's allegations. She prepared a detailed report of the controversial arrest and detainment of the women. The victimized WAC vividly described her ordeal. The two WACs had earned a weekend pass to Spokane. They had tried to find lodging, but the white-owned hotels had denied them this, and finally they had boarded at Thomas's house, where they socialized with Smith and Allen. During the early morning hours, as the women soundly slept, Spokane police detective Robert B. Piper "suddenly awakened" them by throwing cold water on them. Piper ordered them to get dressed so that he could escort them to jail. When one of the women said that she would rather dress in the other room, instead of in front of him, Piper responded violently, knocking down the petite soldier. After the women dressed, city police placed both WACs in a squad car where the one woman's physical abuse reportedly continued while in transit to the jail.[40]

The WACs' ordeal continued for two weeks. The police denied them visitors, phone calls, mail, and legal counsel. After the WACs appealed several times, Judge Raymond F. Kelly granted visitation privileges. A white female military official who visited with the women encountered police hostility as well. Piper referred to two WACs as Geiger's "prostitutes" and asked that the female officer "keep her girls off the streets after 8 o'clock at night."[41] His comments reflected longstanding negative attitudes that some whites had toward black female sexuality. Police brutality incidents involving women in uniform were common.

For African American soldiers, the WACs' incarceration represented a gross injustice. McCannon and her NAACP colleagues formally criticized Geiger authorities for not protecting the civil rights of the soldiers and local law enforcement for their poor conduct. They accused army officials of purposely ignoring military policy by allowing civilian authorities to prosecute the WACs. Moreover, Geiger officials had ignored the safety of other African American personnel because they had not requested Piper's "removal" or reprimanded him for his "brutal treatment" of the WAC.[42] Unfortunately the Spokane incident failed to attract the national media and so the NAACP's outrage at the attack was not widely known.

Without fanfare, Meyers and Franklin gained their freedom on August 24. Instead of waiting for a directive from NAACP national headquarters, the Spokane branch investigators suggested methods for improving race relations on the base. They encouraged residents to support the military's development of additional recreational facilities for black soldiers, and they expected African Americans to express their displeasure over recent events by protesting police brutality, especially against female personnel. The branch pressed the black community to demand an explanation from Judge Kelly as to why he had "denied the women their constitutional right to counsel." In the spirit of the "double V" campaign, the investigators reminded residents that Americans, including African Americans, had recently fought a war against the "race superiority falsehoods of Hitler and the Ku Klux Klan. We must see that they did not die [or fight] in vain."[43]

Despite its efforts and expectations, the NAACP chapter's activism failed to receive an immediate response from military or local officials. In Spokane and other cities, courtship among black soldiers operated clandestinely because military officials and white society refused to provide social outlets. Public and private displays of black sexuality caused great concern in the white community. Social constraints and the military officials' refusal to create a better social environment in Spokane and throughout the country forced black WACs to be confined to their bases to socialize in isolation.[44]

A Post–World War II Jane Crow Casualty

Despite the agency of the local NAACP, divisions arose in the black community. African Americans who had settled in Spokane between the late nineteenth and early twentieth century believed that they had succeeded because of their social bond with whites, which they perceived was better than that of blacks in other cities. Some of the old settlers saw the incoming blacks, including women, as migrants who would destroy their fragile coexistence with whites.[45]

During the postwar period, a wave of more socially conscious black Spokane immigrants challenged the older group's "claims to leadership and of status in the black community simply because those individuals had been there longer." After experiencing the restrictions placed on blacks and other marginalized groups, many new residents argued that the pioneers had failed to secure their civil rights in the region.[46] The new residents wanted instead to participate in the emerging national civil rights struggle. For instance, when Lydia Sims arrived from Newark, New Jersey, with her husband, she brought a more militant attitude to challenge discrimination. In her opinion, the established residents were not aggressive enough in fighting for civil rights. "The attitude of these established blacks was frightening to us. Some of the people who were already here were very complacent," Sims remembered.[47] Many of the new migrants hailed from northeastern cities, where blacks had defiantly contested racism and discrimination through their local branches of the NAACP, the National Urban League, and the Congress of Racial Equality.

While investigating civil rights abuses in Spokane, African Americans also grappled with internal issues that threatened their social progress. In 1947 the community experienced a struggle between well-respected civic leaders that eventually became embroiled in a bitter civil court battle. The controversy stemmed from the refusal of the local NAACP and other groups to support the Booker T. Washington Community Center (BTWCC), which reopened on August 1. The NAACP claimed that the BTWCC was a segregated organization that catered exclusively to blacks.[48]

At the center of this intense dispute was Rosa Malone, still a relative new-comer, and Frank Stokes, a pioneer in Spokane's civil rights movement. Both individuals had faithfully served the African American community. Stokes's civil rights career began at the turn of the twentieth century. In 1919 he co-organized Spokane's NAACP branch, for which he had served in various executive positions. Stokes was also active in all NAACP-sponsored projects, but more importantly he was instrumental in the chapter's representation on the Spokane Health and Welfare Federation (also known as the Community Chest), a city agency that supported local nonprofit organizations.[49]

Similarly, Malone had an impressive history of serving the African American community as director of the African American USO during the war and, as of August 1, 1947, as director of the reopened BTWCC, which received partial funding from the city. Its continued funding hinged on the results of the city's upcoming inspection.[50]

The leadership of the BTWCC focused on interracial cooperation. Similar to the city's racially segregated YWCA and YMCA, the BTWCC offered classes in sewing, food preparation, social etiquette, singing, and musical instruments. Its most important role within the community, however, was providing recreational activities—such as swimming, softball, and basketball—for black youth. The BTWCC served dozens of children daily.[51]

Celebration of the BTWCC's reopening was short-lived. During the summer of 1947, a heated public debate between old-time residents and newcomers over the need for the center polarized the community. On August 8, the Community Chest's board of directors received a letter from Spokane NAACP branch offi-cials—President James F. Morton, Secretary Frank A. Stokes, and the chair of the executive committee, Joseph W. Strong—opposing the Community Chest's continued funding of the BTWCC. They asserted that the facility promoted segregation by serving only blacks.[52] In fact, the BTWCC was the only facility to welcome African American children.

Spokane's NAACP male leadership brazenly continued to malign Malone, mailing postcard petitions that asked members not to support the BTWCC. The petition partly read, "Racial tension is the result of segregation and all other forms of discrimination." The organization requested that "members join the branch in petitioning the Welfare Federation [Community Chest] to cancel appropriations for the Booker T. Washington Center after September 30, 1947." The NAACP also asked members to sign and support the brief statement: "I protest Community Chest appropriation for the Booker T. Washington Center as a waste of public funds and a detriment to the Negro people." The branch stated, "There is no question that" the BTWCC "contributes to segregation and racial tension, and that its facilities are woefully inadequate."[53]

In response to the public accusations from Stokes, Malone infuriated the civil rights leaders even more when she sent a telegram to Roy Wilkins, editor of the NAACP's *Crisis* magazine. She warned, "F. A. Stokes and other Communists are mailing out literature, letters and cards using the name of the NAACP." "It is imperative," she wrote, "that one of your key men visit this branch in the near future or you may regret it seriously." Malone said that her only staunch ally, Reverend Reed, past president of the Spokane NAACP, had tried to stop the assault on her organization but failed. Malone sent the telegram in hopes that it would derail the attack on her organization, but her strategy backfired.[54]

Wilkins immediately contacted his longtime civil rights colleague Stokes about Malone's shocking communist claims. "Of course, we do not take this thing seriously," Wilkins emphasized. He asked for an explanation of the situation.[55] Wilkins's letter implicitly suggested support for the Spokane NAACP's campaign to dismantle the BTWCC. Subsequently, Stokes forwarded to the Community Chest the results of a petition it had circulated throughout the community. Out of some 200 responses, 150 favored halting the BTWCC's funding.[56]

Despite the NAACP's strong opposition to the BTWCC, a handful of civic leaders and residents supported the facility and Malone's efforts within the community. For example, Reed publicly refuted the local NAACP branch's allegations and argued that the BTWCC did not foster racial discrimination. As a member of the BTWCC's board of directors, he claimed the board was a harmonious multiracial group that promoted racial diversity.[57]

The personal attacks from both parties evolved into a bitter civil lawsuit. On January 22, 1948, Stokes filed a suit against Malone at the Superior Court of the State of Washington in Spokane. He sought $10,000 in monetary damages for his "health and reputation." Stokes claimed in court documents that Malone had made publicly slanderous statements when she labeled him a communist and that Malone's telegram to the NAACP's national office was "false and untrue."[58] Malone filed a countersuit for the same amount. She claimed that Stokes had injured her reputation when he said that the BTWCC promoted "racial segregation and racial prejudice."[59]

The lawsuits, which were unfortunate but inevitable, pointed to close ties between the national NAACP and the local branch. At that time, a number of blacks who belonged to organizations such as the Congress of Racial Equality embraced public patriotism driven by the general paranoia of the Cold War. Local and national officials were fearful of communist subversion of individual branches, as had already happened in the San Francisco chapter after World War II. NAACP leaders correctly feared that if the public perceived their organization was a communist front, it would lose its credibility and its support from local and national political leaders.[60]

Not surprisingly, former friends and allies in the fight for racial justice parted company as NAACP leaders openly denounced prominent black figures such as entertainer and civil rights activist Paul Robeson and W. E. B. Du Bois, a scholar, activist, and NAACP cofounder who refused to repudiate the radical Left. During World War II, Robeson and Du Bois had expressed sympathy for the Soviet Union, but by 1946 the Cold War meant that the Soviet Union and its supporters were branded as enemies of the United States.[61] Fearing political backlash, Charles Stokes, a black Republican state representative from Seattle, publicly condemned Robeson in 1950 on the floor of the Washington state legislature.[62] These political attacks stifled the careers of Robeson and Du Bois. The federal government revoked Robeson's passport for eight years in 1950 and for Du Bois a year later. The government's effective anticommunist crusade forced some black leaders to conclude that if they appeared sympathetic toward communism or communist supporters, it could jeopardize their organizations.[63] The Cold War hysteria intimidated the NAACP's leadership, thus molding its sociopolitical agenda in the 1950s. Seeing how this hysteria affected African American leaders across the nation, it is not surprising that similar sentiments divided black Spokane during the Stokes-Malone trial.

Before the trial began, without surprise, the Community Chest withdrew its BTWCC funding. In response to that agency's decision, the *Spokane NAACP Bulletin* thanked branch members and supporters "who helped so valiantly and so courageously in its battle against segregation in Spokane."[64] The wave of support from the national office that followed reflected a closing of the ranks among men within the organization against threatening black female leadership. Looking back, the NAACP's support of Stokes served as a smokescreen for its patriarchal attitude toward a popular and progressive African American woman.

The trial began on November 19, but Stokes's personal attacks and the discontinued funding had already destroyed Malone's reputation and organization. Seven days later, the jury returned a verdict in favor of Stokes but ordered Malone to pay him only $5,000.[65] Following the jury's decision, Judge Charles W. Greenough made a final judgment on the compensation. First, he attempted to repair the image of the BTWCC and its former director. The judge ruled that the BTWCC did not contribute to segregation, since it catered to both "Negroes" and whites. "White people," according to Greenough, "were not excluded from any" of the facility's "activities and participated in many of them," and they "attended educational meetings along with colored children and participated in their activities." He praised Malone's years of valuable service to the black community, asserting that her direction of the USO and the BTWCC had provided the "only places in Spokane at which colored people felt that they were wholly welcome at any time and occasion."[66] Based on his conclusion that Stokes's reputation remained in good standing, the judge ruled the $5,000 award excessive and reduced it to $300, earning Stokes little more than a token victory.[67]

Unfortunately for Malone, the lawsuit ultimately neutralized her effectiveness as a community leader. The conflict clearly divided the African American community. "They [Malone and Stokes] could have settled the dispute without coming up with a suit, I think," Elmo Dalbert, a longtime black resident, told me in conversation in 2000. The situation had caused him anguish as two people he had admired fought publicly. "You had to make a decision on which one you were going to join," he recalled. His wife, Alta, had happily worked for Malone, but the Dalberts, as well as the Spokane community, respected Stokes, who served as Bethel A.M.E.'s Sunday school teacher. Thus it was difficult for anybody to take sides, Dalbert said.[68]

Another Spokane newcomer was stunned over the squabble between the two community leaders. Lydia Sims, a resident of only a few years at the time, bitterly recalled to me that Malone and Stokes "were poles apart." For her, the dispute was a pointless episode that reflected the disunity within the black community. It was an incident "where you just shrugged your shoulder and said 'what's this nonsense?'" There "were far larger battles" to be fought in the city.[69]

Sims's assessment was correct, because local black youth became the ultimate victims of the Malone-Stokes controversy. The conflict confused most of the BTWCC's enrollees. Jerrelene Williamson later observed that Malone "was a person who wanted to run things, and they [Stokes and the NAACP] did not like that fact."[70] Spokane residents missed a golden opportunity to mobilize behind the cause of victimized black soldiers and black youth. Instead Stokes's campaign to discredit Malone and Jane Crow attacks derailed the momentum of the black community's push for racial equality. Despite the efforts of some Spokane residents to expose their city's race problems during the 1940s, discrimination continued through the decade that followed.

A Challenge to Black Entrepreneurship

Employment discrimination emerged as the most serious grievance of Spokane blacks during the 1950s. Because blacks failed to find decent jobs, they were unable to buy better homes, use the best public accommodations, or press for other civil rights. Therefore employment became the key to racial progress and the NAACP leaders' priority.[71] Concerning black unemployment, local NAACP leaders argued that Spokane did not "compare favorably" with Seattle, Tacoma, and Bremerton because blacks had more employment opportunities in those port cities. As a result, most young and college-educated blacks born and raised in Spokane migrated to cities in western Washington or to California for employment. Furthermore, the NAACP charged that the state employment agency in Spokane refused to refer blacks to job assignments that were not "menial."[72] The outmigration of employable African Americans reflected their displeasure with the dismal employment opportunities.

NAACP leaders also revealed that throughout the decade African American men and women in Spokane continued working almost exclusively in service-oriented positions. According to branch officials, these jobs included maintenance and janitorial work in office buildings and department stores. An NAACP survey revealed that private and public sector employers refused to hire African Americans in such occupations as sales associates, administrative personnel, hotel and restaurant cooks, bank tellers, meter readers, and elevator and telephone operators.[73] For black women especially, meaningful employment opportunities failed to materialize. For example, shortly after graduating from high school, longtime resident Jerrelene Williamson applied for an operator position at the Bell Telephone Company in the early 1950s. However, as she was leaving the human resources department, she heard the receptionist tear up her completed application.[74]

Although some blacks were fortunate to hold jobs, a handful followed the lead of the city's earlier pioneers and became entrepreneurs. Some scholars have termed this "defensive entrepreneurship," because blacks founded businesses after being excluded from most places of employment.[75] In Spokane, for instance, some blacks owned and operated an auto body shop, a laundry, a construction company, a hotel, and restaurants, taverns, and apartment buildings to serve the needs of the black community (both as employees and customers). In actuality, from the World War II era on, these primarily black-male-owned businesses served the entire Spokane community, white and black.

During this period, the local NAACP's civil rights agency contributed to the increasing momentum of the local movement, but some white-owned establishments still refused service to blacks. For this reason, some African Americans continued to operate businesses that served the black community, but in the 1950s an African American woman opened the decade with a legal challenge to racial and gender barriers that decreased the ability of black entrepreneurs to earn a decent living.

Although African Americans had operated businesses in Spokane, the state prohibited black-owned establishments that sold liquor from serving the white public. This economic double standard enraged members of the civil rights community. In March 1951, Carl Maxey, the community's only black attorney, then serving as president and legal counsel for the Spokane NAACP, requested a hearing before the Washington State Liquor Control Board (WSLCB). According to Maxey, the lead investigator of the board's Spokane office, Guy Hill, had recommended a restrictive license to Shirley Allen and Fred Trexler, African American owners of the Keystone Tavern. NAACP leaders asked the WSLCB to clarify the intent of a license because Maxey considered a letter from WSLCB superintendent A. J. Cohn to the tavern owners racially offensive. The tavern's liquor license stated that beer and wine could be sold to "Negroes only." The regulation meant that the black-owned tavern was required to refuse service to whites.[76]

The NAACP argued that the liquor board had indicated that it would not permit "a Negro to operate a tavern where he can serve white and colored trade." The board's regulation, therefore, forced blacks to establish their businesses "under different laws from other people."[77] This form of economic apartheid limited profits, thus preventing Allen and her partner from competing with white-owned bars. Maxey maintained that a permit restricting the sale of any product to only African Americans "automatically deprives the Negro of his vested right to enter business on the terms enjoyed by other citizens."[78]

A representative from the WSLCB inspection department argued that the NAACP had "misinterpreted" the board's intention. The official claimed that the board had never meant to "deny the right of the owner to serve" whites but instead to "exclude unattended, unescorted white women."[79] The concern of city officials over "white women" reflected their desire to prohibit interracial relationships in bars, especially between those black soldiers entering the city during World War II. Regardless of the board's intentions, it denied Allen and her partner the opportunity to serve customers regardless of their race and, more importantly, earn revenue from them.[80] Maxey justified the NAACP's involvement, saying that "if this policy is continued, then it would be illegal, for example, for an Italian to serve a Greek."[81]

The NAACP's advisory role in the tavern licensing provided the impetus behind eventual legal action. In late March 1951, through their white attorneys Thomas Lynch and Henry Opendack, Allen and Trexler filed a civil lawsuit against the WSLCB and Guy Hill in the U.S. District Court, Eastern District of Washington. The plaintiffs sued for $3,500—the value of the property and the cost of the license to operate it.[82]

Rather than defend its position in a potentially lengthy and costly court battle, the board acquiesced to Allen and her partner's demands. On April 9, 1951, the WSLCB accepted the conditions and removed the licensing restriction regarding the race or color of the customer. At the same time, they attempted to clear the WSLCB of accusations that it practiced racism and discrimination.[83] On April 13 the plaintiffs, after careful deliberation, moved to dismiss the charges against the WSLCB. They accepted the board's promise to discontinue its policy of racial discrimination.[84]

The court's mediation marked the first major civil rights victory for African American women, and Spokane's NAACP had helped dismantle an economic barrier for a local black business co-owned by an African American woman in the post–World War II era. The NAACP's involvement had sent a strong message to municipalities practicing discrimination. More importantly, Allen and her partner's case had highlighted the growing importance of the nationwide effort to dismantle mechanisms of gender discrimination and racial discrimination in public accommodations.[85]

During the 1960s, black women in Spokane continued to tell a story of white intolerance and bigotry. Unlike the openly racist environment in the South, in Spokane discriminatory practices were camouflaged. The overt Jane and Jim Crow practices of prior decades were fading as the city's most popular diners in the Crescent Department Store and Newberry's now served African Americans and whites side by side. But some African Americans noted the inequality of service. An African American married couple, Emelda and Manuel Brown, who had moved to Spokane in 1960, recalled that white customers almost invariably enjoyed preferential treatment. According to Emelda Brown, "We may not have had any trouble in getting served, but if there were other people there waiting to be served and some came after we had gotten there, we were always the last to be asked." For her, racism in Spokane was more covert than in the South. "It may have been hidden, but it was here," she said.[86]

Spokane civil servant Lydia Sims and her husband, James Sims, circa 1970. *Courtesy of Spokesman Review.*

Dynamic NAACP Leadership Shift

On the heels of the civil rights movement and the struggle for gender equality, black women such as Shirley Chisholm and Barbara Jordan became political trailblazers. The 1970s began with hope and promise about employment opportunities for black Spokanites. Some black leaders in Spokane were able to ride the political wave started by their cohorts in other cities with larger African American communities, but the federal government's dismantling of antipoverty programs hindered progress for the masses.[87]

On the local level, the city government hired Lydia Sims in 1975 as its first affirmative action specialist. A year later she joined the city's newly established Affirmative Action Department. In her position, Sims closely monitored the city's efforts to adhere to affirmative action policies, and she assisted women, African Americans, and other people of color in finding job opportunities. Concurrent with her appointment, officials implemented the city's first six-year affirmative action hiring goal.[88] Sims's role in city government reflects the level of agency attained by some black migrants. She brought to her position a tempered militancy.[89]

Sims's civil service did not go unnoticed in the civil rights community. Her commitment to removing barriers at the workplace for African Americans fit the NAACP's continued black employment agenda. With little surprise, Sims won election to its presidency in December 1976, becoming the first African American female president of the small (113-member) branch.[90] She entered the position with an impressive record of civil service and advocacy. Like Bertha B. Cravens some fifty-eight years before her, Sims was poised to promote the directives of the organization.

Always at the forefront of the struggle to improve the economic situation of African Americans, Sims established an NAACP job fair in 1978 that would become an annual event. Under her leadership, the organization adopted the title Summer Jobs Awareness and Career Planning Program and invited area businesses to recruit potential employees. Sims opened the fair to all people of color but focused primarily on attracting black high school and college students. She was instrumental in recruiting juniors and seniors from Spokane high schools—Lewis and Clark, North Central, Rogers, Shadle Park—and Medical Lake High School in nearby Medical Lake.[91]

African American professionals were invited from other cities to participate in the program. James and Lydia Sims's son Ronald, a consumer specialist with the Federal Trade Commission in Seattle, conducted an employment workshop at the 1978 job fair. During that same event, Lydia Sims's efforts attracted some thirty businesses and an equal number of students. According to the NAACP's report on the job fair, fourteen of the students (40 percent) received job offers from places such as Crescent Department Store, Kaiser Aluminum, Central Pre-Mix Concrete Company, Fidelity Bank, and Seattle First Bank.[92] Sims's greatest success in encouraging companies to hire blacks came in the area of banking. By the end of the 1970s, 27 African Americans—mostly women—were hired as tellers compared to 833 white tellers in Spokane.[93]

Despite Lydia Sims's efforts, the general employment situation for blacks remained bleak in the public and private sectors. She became openly critical of continued employment discrimination in the city. As NAACP president, she constantly reprimanded businesses in the media for failing to comply with affirmative action hiring laws. Sims publicly revealed, "There are contractors in this city, with federal contracts, who are not adhering to directives from the government regarding affirmative action in hiring for jobs. The only pressures we can bring to bear on employers who discriminate in hiring are moral and legal. But it is apparent [that] change will not come from the goodness of people's hearts."[94]

During the decade, black Spokanites were unable to mount a serious challenge to the final vestiges of Jim Crow because of their small population, a problem since they first arrived in the area. Sims realized that the size of the black community prevented "effective boycotts, sit-ins and similar activities to bring public pressure on persons causing problems for them."[95] Her assessment of the black socioeconomic condition accurately reflected census data. During the 1970s, most blacks continued to find employment in only service-oriented professions. They worked in restaurants as food preparers and waiters. In fact, 282 African American men and women found employment in the service industry, while some 140 blacks carried on the work of their predecessors by serving as maids and butlers.[96]

Sims also approached city government agencies in noncompliance with affirmative action regulations. She constantly challenged police and fire department officials to hire African Americans. Sims organized public NAACP forums for the leadership of both the police and fire departments to address their failure to hire African Americans and to discuss their affirmative action plans.[97] Despite all her tireless advocacy, blacks failed to fill these positions. Census data at the end of the decade reveals that the police department did not hire a single black officer in a force of 560, while the fire department hired only two blacks compared to 319 whites.[98]

In the 1980s, African American leadership and progress in Spokane reached its pinnacle. Black women in Spokane no longer stood in the shadows of civil rights agency. In some ways the NAACP partly redeemed its sexist attitude toward black women like Rosa Malone by electing Lydia Sims to the presidency. Unfortunately, following the end of Sims's tenure in city hall and as NAACP president, African Americans failed to build upon her momentum and encourage significant inroads in black migration and employment. As the 1980s were winding down, so did the civic and political journey for some black women in Spokane. At the end of the decade, the black population had reached only 3,416 compared to an overwhelmingly white majority of 165,284.[99]

Over the next two decades the civil rights community in Spokane experienced ruptures in its leadership. By the 1990s, the voice of the leadership had all but faded out entirely. Age, retirement, and death contributed to muting the voices of these leaders active since the postwar period. Without their challenges to contemporary forms of white supremacy, the intensity of civil rights advocacy declined. A combination of outmigration of African Americans and a miniscule black population further created a dysfunctional and fragmented NAACP chapter in the twenty-first century. These factors opened the door for Rachel Dolezal to intentionally misidentify her race and wear the mask of black womanhood. Unfortunately, Spokane's black community and the national conversation failed to bring authentic black women in Spokane out of the shadows of history.

Notes

1. Sarah Azaransky, "Jane Crow: Pauli Murray's Intersections and Antidiscrimination Law," *Journal of Feminist Studies in Religion* 29, no. 1 (2013): 156.
2. Herbert G. Ruffin II, *Uninvited Neighbors: African Americans in Silicon Valley, 1769–1990* (Norman, University of Oklahoma Press: 2014), 66.
3. James Ralph Jones interview by Joseph Franklin, n.d., Inland Northwest Black History Collection, Eastern Washington University Archives and Special Collections, Cheney, Washington (hereafter cited as INBHC); Mabel and Earl Coates interview by Joseph Franklin n.d., INBHC.
4. Quintard Taylor, *The Forging of a Black Community: Seattle's Central District from 1870 through the Civil Rights Era* (Seattle: University of Washington Press, 1994), 136.
5. Ibid., 139. Taylor's explanation of the importance of social organizations in Seattle also applies to Spokane.
6. Samuel P. Debow and Edward A. Pitter, eds., *Who's Who in Religious, Fraternal, Social, Civic and Commercial Life on the Pacific Coast* (Seattle: Searchlight, 1927), 10.
7. Sylvester and Pauline Lake interview, January 5, 1979, INBHC; Joseph Franklin, *All through the Night: The History of Spokane Black Americans, 1860–1940* (Spokane: Ye Galleon Press, 1989), 88.
8. "A History of Spokane Clubs," typed manuscript (Spokane, 1952), Northwest Room, Downtown Branch, Spokane Public Library.
9. Turkiya L. Lowe, "The Washington State Federation of Colored Women's Clubs: Social Activism in Washington State's African American Women's Club Movement, 1917 to 1951" (PhD diss., University of Washington, 2010), 38; Franklin, *All through the Night*, 84–86.
10. "A History of Spokane Clubs."
11. Ibid.
12. Ibid.; Mabel and Earl Coates interview, INBHC; Sylvester and Pauline Lake interview. The Community Chest distributed funding locally to various organizations.
13. Lowe, "Washington State Federation of Colored Women's Clubs," 175–76.
14. National Association for the Advancement of Colored People, Branch Files, folder NAACP Spokane, Washington, 1915–1926, group I/box G, container 213, Manuscript Division, Library of Congress, Washington, D.C.; Franklin, *All through the Night*, 109–11.
15. Franklin, *All through the Night*, 75. Historian Susan Bragg also discusses the dynamics of such contests in "Marketing the 'Modern Negro': Race, Gender, and NAACP Activism, 1909–1945" (PhD diss., University of Washington, 2007).

16. U.S. Bureau of the Census, *Fifteenth Census of the United States, 1930*, vol. 3, *Population, pt. 2* (Washington, D.C.: Government Printing Office, 1933), 1222; Calvin F. Schmid, Charles E. Nobbe, and Arlene E. Mitchell, *Washington State Planning and Community Affairs Council Non-White Races: State of Washington* (Olympia, 1968), 29.

17. Flexan Pierce interview by Quintard Taylor, October 30, 1972, Black Oral History Interviews, 1972–1974, Manuscripts, Archives, and Special Collections, Washington State University Libraries, Pullman.

18. Moya B. Hansen, "Try Being a Black Woman! Jobs in Denver, 1900–1970," in *African American Women Confront the West, 1600–2000*, ed. Quintard Taylor and Shirley Ann Wilson Moore (Norman: University of Oklahoma Press, 2003), 212.

19. Dwayne Mack, *Black Spokane: The Civil Rights Struggle in the Inland Northwest* (Norman: University of Oklahoma Press, 2014).

20. Franklin, *All through the Night*, 117.

21. Harvard Sitkoff, *A New Deal for Blacks: The Emergence of Civil Rights as a National Issue; The Depression Decade* (New York: Oxford University Press, 2008), 69–72.

22. Franklin, *All through the Night*, 117.

23. U.S. Bureau of the Census, *Sixteenth Census of the United States, 1940*, vol. 2, *Population, pt. 7* (Washington, D.C.: Government Printing Office, 1942), 408.

24. Mack, *Black Spokane*, 27.

25. "Negroes to Have U.S.O. Clubhouse," *Spokesman-Review*, April 2, 1943; Coleman M. Campbell, "George Washington Carver U.S.O. Gay," *Spokesman-Review*, December 26, 1943. Clippings in the United Service Organizations George Washington Carver Vertical File, Northwest Room, Downtown Branch, Spokane Public Library.

26. "George Washington Carver U.S.O. Gay."

27. U.S. Bureau of the Census, *Seventeenth Census of the United States, 1950*, vol. 2, *Population, pt. 47* (Washington, D.C.: Government Printing Office, 1952–53), 115, 186, 188. The census indicated that approximately seventy-six black males worked in service-oriented positions.

28. Ibid.

29. Eugene Hamilton Breckenridge, "The Employment of Negroes in Spokane" (master's thesis, Whitworth College, 1949), 46–51. This quantitative and qualitative analysis accurately reflects the level of employment discrimination in the late 1940s.

30. Ibid., 51.

31. Sybil Stafford interview by Joseph Franklin, n.d., INBHC.

32. Carl Maxey interview by Joseph Franklin, n.d., INBHC; Sylvester and Pauline Lake interview by author, August 10, 2000; Sylvester and Pauline Lake interview, January 5, 1979, INBHC.

33. Tolbert H. Kennedy, *Survey of Racial Conditions in Spokane, Washington, 1945* (Pullman: State College of Washington, 1945), 100.

34. Robin D. G. Kelley, "We Are Not What We Seem: Rethinking Black Working-Class Opposition in the Jim Crow South," *Journal of American History* 80, no. 1 (June 1993): 77–78.

35. Lydia Sims interview by author, July 2, 2000.

36. Mabel and Earl Coates interview.

37. Maxey interview; Wallace Hagin interview by author, June 30, 2000.

38. "Negroes in Service Receive Sentences," *Spokane Daily Chronicle*, July 29, 1946.

39. Ibid.; Spokane County Jail Register, 1944–1947, 147, in Spokane County Sheriff, Fleet Services, Spokane, Washington.

40. National Association for the Advancement of Colored People, Branch Files, folder NAACP Spokane, Washington, 1940–1955, box II, C 213, Manuscript Division, Library of Congress, Washington, D.C. (hereafter cited as NAACPBFLOC-bII/C213).

41. Ibid.

42. Ibid.

43. Ibid. Each soldier paid a $2.50 fine and received a thirty-day sentence at the Spokane County Jail.

44. Mack, *Black Spokane*, 61.

45. Kennedy, *Survey of Racial Conditions in Spokane*, 155–57; Tolbert H. Kennedy, "Racial Tensions among Negroes in the Intermountain Northwest," *Phylon* 8 (1946): 359–60; Quintard Taylor, "Migration of Blacks and Resulting Discriminatory Practices in Washington State between 1940 and 1950," *Western Journal of Black Studies* 1 (1977): 69.

46. Taylor, "Migration of Blacks," 69.

47. Lydia Sims interview.

48. "Negro Center to Open August 1," *Spokesman-Review*, July 13, 1947; Civil Case #120950, Spokane County Clerk's Office, Archives Division.

49. NAACPBFLOC-bII/C213.

50. Ibid.; Mack, *Black Spokane*, 69.

51. "Negro Center to Open August 1."

52. NAACPBFLOC-bII/C213; "Group Objects to Chest Funds," *Spokane Daily Chronicle*, September 12, 1947; Civil Case #120950, Spokane County Clerk's Office, Archives Division.

53. Petition in NAACPBFLOC-bII/C213.

54. Malone telegram to Roy Wilkins, September 2, 1947, NAACPBFLOC-bII/C213.

55. Wilkins to Stokes, September 3, 1947, NAACPBFLOC-bII/C213.

56. NAACPBFLOC-bII/C213; "Group Objects to Chest Funds"; Civil Case #120950.

57. "Reverend Reed Raps View of Morton on Centers Funds," *Spokane Daily Chronicle*, August 14, 1947, NAACPBFLOC-bII/C213.

58. Civil Case #120950; "Mrs. Malone Named in Suit," *Spokane Daily Chronicle*, January 23, 1948.

59. "Recess Ordered in Damage Suits," *Spokesman-Review*, November 24, 1948, 9.

60. Manning Marable, *Race Reform and Rebellion: The Second Reconstruction in Black America, 1945–2006*, 3rd ed. (Jackson: University Press of Mississippi, 2007), 25–26.

61. Ibid., 21–22.

62. Taylor, *Forging of a Black Community*, 182–83.

63. Marable, *Race Reform and Rebellion*, 25–27; Carol Anderson, "Bleached Souls and Red Negroes: The NAACP and Black Communists in the Early Cold War, 1948–1952," in *Window on Freedom: Race, Civil Rights, and Foreign Affairs, 1945–1988*, ed. Brenda Gayle Plummer (Chapel Hill: University of North Carolina Press, 2003), 93–113.

64. *Spokane NAACP Bulletin*, Summer 1948, NAACPBFLOC-bII/C213.

65. "$5000 Damages Granted Stokes," *Spokesman-Review*, November 27, 1948; Civil Case #120950, 2–3.

66. Civil Case #120950 SCCO, 3.

67. Ibid.; "Judge Reduces Stokes' Reward," *Spokane Daily Chronicle*, January 22, 1949.

68. Elmo Dalbert interview by author, July 27, 2000.

69. Lydia Sims interview by author, July 2, 2000.

70. Jerrelene Williamson interview by author, July 2, 2000.

71. Mack, *Black Spokane*, 79.

72. "Discrimination Rating Denied by Negro Leader," *Spokane Daily Chronicle*, March 2, 1957. For detailed data on black employment and the labor-intensive jobs blacks had in Spokane, see U.S. Bureau of the Census, *Eighteenth Census of the U.S., 1960*, vol. 1, *Characteristics of the Population, pt. 49* (Washington, D.C.: Government Printing Office, 1963).

73. Ibid.

74. Jerrelene Williamson, e-mail to author, April 1, 2013.

75. Ivan Light and Judith Rosenstein, *Race, Ethnicity, and Entrepreneurship in Urban America* (Hawthorne, N.Y.: De Gruyter, 1995), 160–61.

76. "Negroes to Ask Ruling Change," *Spokane Daily Chronicle*, March 15, 1951.

77. "Meeting," Eleanor Barrow Chase Collection, Folder Chase Family Scrapbook—Music Items 1940–1951, box 6 of 7, Eastern Washington State Historical Society, Northwest Museum of Arts, Spokane, Washington.

78. "Negroes to Ask Ruling Change."

79. Ibid.

80. Mack, *Black Spokane*, 94–95.

81. "Group Attacks Liquor Policy," *Spokesman-Review*, March 31, 1951.

82. Liquor Control Board Files, Folder Shirley Allen and Fred Trexler v. State Liquor Board and Guy Hill, box 71, Washington State Archives, Olympia, Washington.

83. U.S. District Court, Eastern District of Washington, Northern Division, record group 21, box 83, Case 51CV939, Folder Spokane Civil Case Files, 1938–1962, National Archives, NW Pacific Region, Seattle, Washington.

84. "Tavern Racial Rule Is Killed," *Spokane Daily Chronicle*, April 13, 1951.

85. Mack, *Black Spokane*, 97.

86. Emelda Brown, interview by Rebecca Nappi; Scott Sines, "A Bumpy Ride to Freedom," *Spokesman-Review*, February 18, 2001. The Emelda Brown interview once appeared in the *Spokesman-Review* website under the title "Through Spokane's Eyes," a feature that celebrated Black History Month 2001. The interview is a part of a series held by Manuscript Archives and Special Collections, Washington State University Libraries,

Pullman. The recording can be found at "Emelda and Manuel Brown Discuss Racial Prejudice in Spokane in the 1960s," WSU Libraries Digital Collections, http://content .libraries.wsu.edu/cdm/ref/collection/cvoralhist/id/15.

87. Mack, *Black Spokane*, 131.

88. Edward Coker, "For Minorities Here: Jobs, Housing Difficult," *Spokesman-Review*, December 19, 1976; "Affirmative Action Director Appointed," *Spokane Daily Chronicle*, October 4, 1979.

89. Ken Sands, "County, City Hiring of Minority Stalls," *Spokesman-Review*, August 21, 1983.

90. Spokane NAACP Branch Files, SPC 979–0092, folder 1:2, Eastern Washington University Archives and Special Collections, Cheney, Washington; "NAACP Group Elects First Woman President," *Spokesman-Review*, December 14, 1976; "Affirmative Action Director Appointed," *Spokane Daily Chronicle*, October 3, 1979.

91. "Job Fair Report, 1978," in Spokane NAACP Branch Files, SPC 979–0092, folder 1:2, Eastern Washington University Archives and Special Collections, Cheney, Washington.

92. Ibid.

93. U.S. Bureau of the Census, *Twentieth Census of the United States: 1980* (Washington, D.C.: Government Printing Office), 1:328.

94. Edward Coker, "For Minorities Here: Jobs, Housing Difficult," *Spokesman-Review*, December 19, 1976.

95. Ibid.

96. U.S. Bureau of the Census, *Twentieth Census of the United States*, 1:329.

97. Spokane NAACP Branch Files, SPC 979–0092, folders 1:3 and 2:1, Eastern Washington University Archives and Special Collections, Cheney, Washington.

98. U.S. Bureau of the Census, *Twentieth Census of the United States*, 1:329.

99. U.S. Bureau of the Census, *Census of Population, 1990*, vol. 1, *Population, pt. 49* (Washington, D.C.: Government Printing Office), 314.

▦ Albina Residents Picket the
Portland Development Commission, 1973

In the spirit of carefully exploring the black response to Jim Crow and de facto racial discrimination in the West, this article focuses on the intense black grassroots challenge to urban renewal in the Rose City. African Americans in Portland mobilized to challenge their forced displacement from the once exclusively black Albina district.

Beginning in the 1960s, the City of Portland, with the cooperation of the Portland Development Commission (PDC) and Emanuel Hospital, began to lay the groundwork for redeveloping the Albina neighborhood by tearing down existing buildings to make room for a hospital expansion. The historically black neighborhood was labeled "blighted" and marked for urban redevelopment, which allowed the city to condemn hundreds of homes and businesses. Clearing land for the project displaced a significant number of Albina neighborhood residents, as hundreds of buildings were razed. The tear-down included the Black Panther's [*sic*] Fred Hampton Memorial People's Health Clinic on North Williams Avenue, prompting the group to organize a protest. Other residents who faced losing their homes and businesses joined the protest against the PDC in front of Emanuel.

Portland's black community had faced a long history of displacement in Portland. A significant number of African Americans had migrated to the area during World War II to take jobs in the shipyards, but housing was scarce. Most of the 20,000 to 25,000 African Americans who migrated during the war lived in Vanport, a federally funded city built specifically for war workers and their families that grew to become the second most-populated city in Oregon. The housing in Vanport was not meant to be permanent, but it became so for many African American families who stayed after the war was over. In 1948, the Columbia River flooded, and the dike protecting Vanport broke, leaving nearly 17,000 people homeless. Those who needed new housing were disproportionately African American.

Source: Tania Hyatt-Evenson, Sarah Griffith, and Amy E. Platt, "Albina Residents Picket the Portland Development Commission, 1973," in *Oregon History Project* (Oregon Historical Society, 2002; updated 2014), http://oregonhistoryproject.org/.

After the flood, many African Americans moved to northeast Portland to the area that is now known as the Rose Quarter. It was one of the few sections of the city open to black residents, who had been the victims of housing discrimination and redlining. In November 1965, as part of the development of Portland's downtown and the inner east side, the city decided to build a sports coliseum in the Rose Quarter. The city planning commission claimed that housing in the area was substandard, and the neighborhood—including much of the thriving Williams Avenue—was leveled.

Successive postwar construction projects in the Albina neighborhood—the Memorial Coliseum in the 1950s, Interstate 5 in the 1960s, and the Emanuel Hospital expansion plan in the 1970s—resulted in a steady migration northward by black Portlanders. When the federal funding for redevelopment of the Albina neighborhood fell through, the expansion was delayed and the once-populated neighborhood sat as empty lots for over forty years.

PART 4

Entertainment and Representation

10 The New Negro Frontier

Jean Toomer, Wallace Thurman, and
African American Modernism in the West

Emily Lutenski

In 1929, New Negro writer Wallace Thurman wrote a series of letters to a white
collaborator, journalist and playwright William Jourdan Rapp, with whom he
would most famously work on the show *Harlem: A Melodrama of Negro Life in
Harlem*, which was produced that year. He was stationed in Salt Lake City, Utah,
at the time, the western locale where he had largely grown up in the household
of his grandmother, Emma Jackson, whom he affectionately called "Ma Jack."
Thurman was often unwell; he had survived the influenza pandemic of 1918,
and he subsequently suffered from alcoholism and eventually tuberculosis. He
would die from this in 1934, at the age of thirty-two. In New York, caught up
in the heady atmosphere of Harlem and perhaps intuiting that he was not long
for this world, Thurman gained a reputation for hard living. At times, during
periods of sickness, he returned to Salt Lake City, where he sought respite from
the distractions that often exacerbated his health problems. In his letters to Rapp,
Thurman described a camping trip he took to the mountainous landscape outside
Salt Lake City during one of these flights. The trip, he reported, made him "feel
like a million bucks." He hiked. He fished. He wrote poetry. "Such is the result
of three days in a canyon with a copy of *Cane* by Jean Toomer," he told Rapp.[1]

This is a rather unexpected tale from the 1920s and 1930s flowering of African
American artistic, political, and intellectual work most often known as the Harlem
Renaissance. Even today, Salt Lake City is not known for having a large African
American community. One year after Thurman wrote this letter, the 1930 U.S.
Census recorded only 681 blacks as part of the total population of 140,267. Fur-
thermore, Thurman—perhaps even more than other New Negro writers—became
almost entirely associated with New York. Indeed, in 1932, drama critic Theophilus
Lewis was able to pen an article proclaiming Thurman a "model Harlemite."[2]

In Thurman's letter, it is not only his position in Salt Lake City that seems incongruous with his Harlem-centered notoriety. It is also his mention of Jean Toomer's 1923 publication *Cane*. *Cane* was a touchstone for many New Negro writers whose work followed in its wake. Harlem Renaissance intellectuals ranging from Langston Hughes in "The Negro Artist and the Racial Mountain" (1926) to William Stanley Braithwaite in "The Negro in American Literature" (1925) mention it as the harbinger of something new in black literature. As a result, while it is not surprising to learn that Thurman would be rereading the book in 1929, it seems mismatched to his getaway in a Utah canyon. While *Cane* is intensely place-based, like much of New Negro writing it vacillates between the rural South and the urban North, the more familiar trajectories of the black Great Migration. Reading *Cane* in a canyon is unlike, say, reading Willa Cather's *The Professor's House* (1925), the mesa setting of which seems more fitting to the environment Thurman sought to commune with during this camping trip spent, as he put it, "roughing it in general."[3]

By 1929, however, Toomer, like Thurman, could himself be found in the American West. He was first invited there in 1925 at the invitation of *salonnière* Mabel Dodge Luhan, who was interested in his work on behalf of his esoteric teacher George Gurdjieff. She offered to fund an "Institute for the Harmonious Development of Man" in Taos, New Mexico, which would resemble the one that Gurdjieff had earlier established in Fontainebleau, France. Up until 1947, which was long after his relationships with both Luhan and Gurdjieff eroded, Toomer continued to travel to New Mexico, where he would live in Taos or Santa Fe and write. There he came to believe, perhaps, that New Mexico could continue to offer him the spiritual, personal, and racial fulfillment and integrity that he had not experienced elsewhere. Although Toomer grew up in Washington, D.C., crafted *Cane* after trips to Georgia, and later moved to Chicago and New York (although he did not live in Harlem), he was able to write in a 1935 essay, "New Mexico after India," that it was New Mexico that "retains its hold upon my heart as home."[4]

Despite their differences in setting and in geographical trajectory, the western writings of Thurman and Toomer have commonalities. Firstly, like so many other figures of the Harlem Renaissance—including Arna Bontemps, Anita Scott Coleman, Louise Thompson, and even Langston Hughes—much of their writing about the West has been unpublished until recently or remains accessible only in their archives. But perhaps more surprising is that both Toomer and Thurman use western settings in order to rethink and reimagine the institution of marriage and its bearing on the construction of race in the United States.

Jean Toomer in Taos, New Mexico, 1935. *Courtesy of Jill Quasha on behalf of the Estate of Marjorie Content.*

By the time Jean Toomer arrived in New Mexico in 1925, its terrain had already witnessed centuries of black travel and settlement. As early as 1539, an enslaved Moor, Esteban, accompanied the Spanish conquest in the land that would one day be New Mexico. Although he was not the only enslaved black to end up there during this period, the African-descended population remained small throughout the Spanish colonial period. The nineteenth century saw the arrival of free black trappers and adventurers, as well as enslaved African Americans, although they were still few in number. After the Civil War, freed blacks arrived in New Mexico, which had become a territory of the United States in 1850 after the land was ceded from Mexico with the 1848 Treaty of Guadalupe Hidalgo. Like African Americans elsewhere, these settlers came in search of land, livelihood, and freedom. Buffalo Soldiers were stationed in New Mexico at Fort Bayard from its 1866 founding until 1899 when it became an army sanitarium where they were deployed, in the service of manifest destiny, against Geronimo and other Apaches. The second part of the nineteenth century saw New Mexico's black population grow due to a boom in mineral mining and then again subsequently due to the expansion of railroad networks. Black towns like Blackdom and Vado were incorporated in the early twentieth century. Overall, however, the African American population in New Mexico remained small. In 1920, before Toomer made his initial visit, there were but 5,733 African Americans counted as part of the total population of 360,350 New Mexicans. Furthermore, Taos County, where Toomer often stayed, had no African American residents in 1920, and Santa Fe, where he would also go, recorded only sixty-five.[5]

The sites where Toomer arrived were home not to black communities but to longstanding Native American and Mexican American communities—and the white modernist artists who flocked there, inspired by them. As historian Flannery Burke has documented, these artists and intellectuals were largely intrigued by their fantasies of New Mexico as a pristine landscape harboring Indigenous people who were similarly untouched by the modern world. When they failed to find the utopia they imagined there, figures like Luhan manufactured the image of it—and to lasting effect. For example, a view of New Mexico as "a world apart," Burke points out, continues to inform its image as a tourist destination. Dodge's invitation to Toomer to visit New Mexico was part of her effort to enact this fantasy. She understood through her acquaintance with white Harlem Renaissance promoter Carl Van Vechten, who had recently taken her Pueblo Indian husband, Tony Lujan, to Small's cabaret in Harlem, that African American culture was compelling for both black and white modernists. Seeing Harlem as somewhat of a draw from Taos, she sought to incorporate the New Negro movement into her southwestern utopian vision, making efforts to consider how Native American and African American cultures might relate to each other as sources of white primitivist allure, and then—to an extent—to assimilate African Americans into her vision of Taos. There were many reasons why Dodge's efforts to subsume Harlem with Taos were not successful. First, she failed to interest Van Vechten in Taos. While he had a nice visit there, it never became as exciting to him as Harlem. Furthermore, when she became attracted to Toomer as more than a Gurdjieffian teacher, her husband was understandably hurt by her infidelities. Additionally, her plan backfired when Toomer's spiritual guru squandered the $14,000 she gave him to develop a facility in Taos. She never saw that money again. And finally, by the time that Toomer arrived in Taos, he had already disclaimed identification with black culture.[6]

As early as *Cane*'s publication, although he conceived of the book as a "swan song" for African American folk life, Toomer balked at being represented as a "Negro" writer in promotion for the book. He wrote to his publisher, Horace Liveright, "My racial composition and my position in the world are realities which I alone may determine. . . . I do not expect to be told what I should consider myself to be." From there he went on to decry his inclusion in Alain Locke's 1925 anthology *The New Negro*, claiming his work was used without his permission. In 1930, he rejected James Weldon Johnson's effort to give him audience through the revised *Book of American Negro Poetry* (1931). He wrote to Johnson, "My view of this country sees it composed of people who primarily are Americans. . . . I do not see things in terms of Negro, Anglo-Saxon, Jewish, and so on. . . . I see myself as an American, simply an American." In accordance, he could not permit his work to be republished as "Negro poetry"—a move he grew to regret, as he regarded Johnson's work as "one of the best."[7]

In his autobiographical writing, Toomer describes his step away from African American identity as a "general countermovement," using a spatial metaphor to describe his process of dis-identification. Toomer's African American contemporaries, like Langston Hughes, tended to also see Toomer's casting off of blackness as spatially ordered. In his 1940 memoir *The Big Sea*, Hughes writes that Toomer chose "after Paris and Gurdjieff, to be merely American," and now he "is married to a lady of means—his second wife—of New York and Santa Fe, and is never seen on Lenox Avenue any more. Harlem is sorry he stopped writing." To leave Harlem and turn toward someplace like Santa Fe is—regrettably, in Hughes's estimation—to abandon African America. This is despite the fact that Hughes also engaged with the West—even New Mexico—in his writing. He once even depicted an interracial trio of "red, white, yellow skins" in his poem "A House in Taos" (1926)—which was rumored to be based on Toomer's affair with Luhan (an allegation Hughes denies elsewhere in *The Big Sea*). Nonetheless, his suggestions in *The Big Sea* are characteristic of the way Toomer's racial self-identification and departure from Harlem have long been received.[8]

Hughes's comment also reveals another story that has shaped assessments of Toomer's declaration of the American race: the story of his marriage. For not only does he slyly jab at Toomer for marrying a "lady of means," but he brings into the orbit of Toomer's "general countermovement" Toomer's first wife, Margery Latimer. After the publication of *Cane*, Hughes notes, "The next thing Harlem heard of Jean Toomer was that he had married Margery Latimer, a talented white novelist, and maintained to the newspaper that he was no more colored than white—as certainly his complexion indicated." Ever since Hughes made this declaration, scholars have returned to the suggestion that it was Toomer's marriage to a white woman that precipitated his racial abandonment—so much so that he has been accused of passing as white. Harlem Renaissance writer Arna Bontemps said Toomer "faded completely into white obscurity" after the publication of *Cane*, becoming the subject of "rumors he had crossed the color line," and being "on record as having denied later that he was a negro." More recently, Rudolph P. Byrd and Henry Louis Gates Jr. have followed suit: "It is our carefully considered judgment," they write, "based upon an analysis of archival evidence previously overlooked by other scholars, that Jean Toomer—for all of his pioneering theorizing about what today we might call a multi-cultural or mixed-race ancestry—was a Negro who decided to pass as white." One of the pieces of evidence they present to support this claim is Toomer's marriage certificate from his 1931 nuptials with Latimer.[9]

The Harlem Renaissance era was full of sensationalist reportage of marriages and divorces. The ostentatious wedding of poet Countee Cullen to Yolande Du Bois dominated the pages of the *Crisis* during the summer of 1928. Among African Americans, marriages such as this one could function as a symbol of respectability in the judgmental eyes of the white world. Uplift-conscious middle-class blacks, as historian Anastasia Curwood has shown, embraced marriage as one way to counter stereotypes about predatory black hypersexuality. When Cullen and Du Bois's union dissolved rapidly less than one year later, after the groom—accompanied by his longtime companion, Harold Jackman—left the bride for Paris, it undermined the image of respectability Yolande's father, W. E. B. Du Bois, had tried so hard to engineer and became the talk of the town. Interracial unions and divorces were also the subject of much attention in both black and white media outlets, such as the well-known Rhinelander divorce case of 1925 and Nella Larsen's difficult 1933 divorce from physicist Elmer Imes after he cheated on her with a white woman. Toomer's marriage to Latimer played into the same fears of miscegenation and debunked the same respectability politics that caused such melodrama around these other couples' stories.[10]

Toomer and Latimer were married in Latimer's hometown of Portage, Wisconsin, in October 1931 to little fanfare save a few local wedding announcements (e.g., "The marriage of Margery Latimer, youthful novelist and protégé of Zona Gale Breese, and Jean Toomer, Chicago psychologist and essayist, will take place at Portage Friday afternoon"). In such announcements, Latimer tends to get more attention than Toomer does as a writer. His authorship of *Cane* goes unnoticed. It wasn't until March 1932 that newspapers began to discover that Toomer might not be what many Americans considered white. Pursued by the press while honeymooning in Carmel, California, and asked to answer to the rumors that dogged the couple, Toomer issued his most famous statement about the American race:

> There is a new race in America. I am a member of this new race. It is neither white nor black nor in-between. It is the American race, differing as much from white and black as white and black differ from each other. It is possible that there are Negro and Indian bloods in my descent along with English, Spanish, Welsh, Scotch, French, Dutch, and German. This is common in America; and it is from all these strains that the American race is being born. But the old divisions into white, black, brown, red are outworn in this country. They have had their day. Now is the time of the birth of a new order, a new vision, a new ideal of man. I proclaim this new order. My marriage to Margery Latimer is the marriage of two Americans.[11]

The newspapers did not interpret Toomer's announcement charitably, and reportage about the couple became more lurid. Few failed to remark that Toomer and Latimer met as part of what they insinuated was a cultish "experiment" in human psychology. *Time* magazine poked fun at Toomer's suggestion that "America . . . is like a great stomach into which are thrown the elements which make up the life blood. From this source is coming a distinct race of people. They will achieve tremendous works of art, literature, and music. They will not be white, black or yellow—just Americans."[12]

In August 1932, ten months after she married Toomer as one of "two Americans," Latimer passed away after delivering their first child. Even reports of her death emphasized that Toomer was "part Negro" and, not insignificantly, that Latimer was a descendant of poet Anne Bradstreet and Puritan clergyman John Cotton. Her whiteness, these articles suggest, could not remain unsullied by Toomer's "one drop" of black blood. Sensationalist headlines screamed: "Woman Novelist Called by Death: Death Ends Romance of Two Races—White Wife of J. Toomer, Novelist of Negro Blood, Expires in Childbirth." The birth of the new American race, which Toomer announced when he spoke to the press about his marriage, was literalized in the birth of his child. Latimer's tragic death subsequently became an allegory for the perceived threat of miscegenation to white women.[13]

That interracial marriage and miscegenation would be concerning for, say, enthusiasts of Lothrop Stoddard's popular tract *The Rising Tide of Color against*

White World Supremacy (1920) probably goes without saying. But as literary critic Daylanne K. English has shown, New Negro thinkers also harnessed eugenic discourses when they thought about marriage. In the *Messenger* in 1927, for example, Alice Dunbar Nelson suggested that "Woman's Most Serious Problem" in African America was a low birth rate: "No race can be a growing race," she admonished, "whose birth rate is declining." W. E. B. Du Bois, English asserts, was one of the most forceful articulators of this outlook. His hope for his daughter's wedding was not just respectability but also the cementing of a racial future: a "utopian world 'remade' by the united intellectual, political, *and reproductive* efforts of first-rate men and women of color." For both whites and for blacks, then, Toomer's marriage to Latimer was roundly considered a failure.[14]

Toomer and Latimer visited Taos once together in 1931, shortly after their wedding. In the aftermath of Latimer's death, Toomer wed again, marrying photographer Marjorie Content in 1934. The service took place at the office of the Taos justice of the peace. They returned there in 1935, this time with Toomer's daughter with Latimer, Argie, and again in 1939, after a trip to India. They visited occasionally throughout the 1940s until their final trip in 1947. During these stays Toomer wrote an array of pieces across genres: notes, plays, memoirs, essays, short prose sketches, and poetry. These show that he saw in New Mexico the hope of a place where his concept of the American race might finally come to fruition.

For example, in a notebook Toomer kept on New Mexico, he uses the physical geography to describe racial identities. The mountains, the rivers, the horizon, and other landmarks are used to describe the emergence of the American race realized in the West: "Two mountain ranges face each other across the river, across the valley," he writes. "To the east is the Sangre de Cristo, to the west the Jémez. . . . If you are between two worlds, which way?" This description of two mountain ranges, their faces descending to meet in the valley below, suggests an image of two slopes that reappears in Toomer's "Sequences," a series of sketches also written about New Mexico. There, he muses, "Man, in the valley, has the choice of climbing one or the other" of "two slopes (symbolized by the Sangre and the Jémez ranges)." The epigraph for Toomer's play "A Drama of the Southwest" also mentions these slopes. He ties them to the multiethnic American race that emerges from the desert landscape: "Taos is the end-product. It is the end of the slope. It is an end-product of the Indians, an end-product of the Spaniards, an end-product of the Yankees and [P]uritans. It must be plowed under. Out of the fertility which death makes in the soil, a new people with a new form may grow." The language of fertility and fecundity in the arid desert soil mimics modernist tropes of regeneration. The "new people with a new form" that grow from this environment are Toomer's multiethnic American race.[15]

He continues to tie race to the New Mexican landscape elsewhere in "Sequences." He writes:

> Oh traveler, oh modern tourist rolling rubber, as you shuttle to and from auto court in Santa Fe to cabin camp in Taos, from auto motor court in Taos to motel in Santa Fe, stop your car just once where the highway passes the side of the Chama gap, get off the paved road and touch the earth and take into yourself the dust of your people. Those ancient people had red skins, and some dark skins, and a few white. What matter the skin color of them or yourself. They are your people. My people are the people of the earth. Today, yesterday, tomorrow.

At this point in the text, Toomer draws a triangle. Then he writes: "They touch at points, at angles only." When he scrawls this triangle, much like the three curves drawn at the beginning of *Cane*'s three sections, Toomer provides a geometric expression of his ideas about race. This triangle is a reminder of the northern New Mexico mountain ranges—the "slopes" of the Sangre de Cristo and Jémez, since the triangular form visually replicates the mountain peaks he describes in language. Furthermore, its three sides join together like the Indian, black, and white influences that mingle in Toomer's conception of the new American race—the "red skins, . . . dark skins, and a few white."[16]

In an essay titled "To This Land Where the Clouds Fall," Toomer expands on his role as progenitor of this new American race. Here he envisions a fecundity much like Latimer did when she wrote to a friend in October 1931 about her marriage: "You don't know how marvelously happy I am and my stomach seems leaping with golden children, millions of them," she wrote. In kind, Toomer asserts:

> I am one. Here I am I. In these grand spaces I feel grand, with largeness in me, and my body in the world. I tell myself that this geography must in the future as it has in the past produce a great race. I see this future, mountains beyond mountains, and the sun. I buy land, a large tract. I build a big house and smaller ones. I have fields and cattle. My children grow up. Their children grow up. With my friends and workers I inhabit it, building in New Mexico my world of man.

In this passage, Toomer imagines New Mexico as an ideal homeland for a mixed-race subject. Toomer, himself mixed-race, is at home in the New Mexican environment. "Here I am I," he writes, and his racially ambiguous body is peaceful "in the world" of the New Mexican West. He describes members of the new American race springing from the earth, almost as if they had been farmed there, like his "fields and cattle." His offspring and his offspring's offspring—the millions of golden children leaping from Latimer's womb—circumvent images of New Mexico's desert landscape as barren.[17]

The same year that Toomer initially arrived in Taos, Thurman first ventured into New York, where, as Lewis remarks in his sketch of Thurman as "model Harlemite," "he began to live on Labor Day 1925." So fully did he throw himself into the milieu of Harlem that Thurman's western upbringing seemed remarkable to his contemporaries. In a biographical essay about Thurman, Dorothy West suggests that the West was provincial and entirely incompatible with Thurman's cosmopolitan outlook: "after his failed attempt to revolutionize the West" by beginning a literary magazine, the *Outlet*, in Los Angeles, and thereby bringing the New Negro Renaissance there, she writes, "Thurman headed East," where eventually "the name of Wallace Thurman [became] more typical of [the New Negro movement] than the one or two more enduring names that survived the period." Even the eulogy delivered at Thurman's Harlem funeral in 1934 insisted that the West "wasn't ready yet" for his efforts to "establish the movement of the 'New Negro' there." The general sense in recollections of Thurman was that it was necessary for him to go to Harlem to find an environment open-minded enough to incorporate his artistic vision and bohemian attitudes.[18]

In his own writing, however, Thurman seems to express some exasperation that his western origins were such a source of bemusement to his colleagues. In 1926 he penned an essay about Utah titled "Quoth Brigham Young—This Is the Place," which was published in the *Messenger* as part of its series "These Colored United States," which ran from 1923 to 1926. This series was meant to serve as a counterpoint to a similar set of essays titled "These United States," which was published in the *Nation* between 1922 and 1925. "These United States," the *Messenger* pointed out, provided little in the way of black perspectives on place, and so set out to provide a corrective. While Thurman's piece certainly does not challenge some of the assumptions his peers had about Utah (he insists it provided him with little but "many dull hours" surrounded by "many dull people"), he also chafes a bit at how it "invariably furnishes me with material for conversation" among New Yorkers who cannot imagine he is actually from there.[19]

Despite the sparseness of Utah's African American population when Thurman was living there, it had a long history of African American travel and settlement.

More than twenty years before Utah Territory was established in 1850, formerly enslaved trapper James P. Beckwourth had explored its craggy mountain passes. In the 1840s, John C. Frémont's expeditions through the region had included Jacob Dodson, a free black who worked for Senator Thomas Hart Benton, Frémont's father-in-law. Blacks, however, largely did not settle in Utah until the Mormon migration that arrived there in 1847, when the place the Latter-day Saints named Deseret was still part of Mexico. Some of them were enslaved. The 1856 Republican Party platform denounced as "the twin relics of barbarism" both slavery and Mormon polygamy, which were seen as morally and sexually depraved. As part of the Compromise of 1850, slavery became legal in Utah, but its black codes were milder than many legislated elsewhere, and slavery never flourished due to the environment that made large-scale agriculture impossible. Mormon leaders Joseph Smith and Brigham Young both saw slavery as biblically permitted but suggested that enslaved people should be treated humanely. African Americans were baptized into the Mormon Church, but they were banned from the priesthood beginning in the 1850s—a ban that was not rescinded until 1978. It was not until the late nineteenth century that the black population of Utah became more visible and entrenched as African American railroad workers and soldiers took up residence. Eventually the 1890s saw black institutions take root. In Salt Lake City there were black literary societies, Masonic lodges, and social clubs, as well as several African American newspapers. The Trinity African Methodist Episcopal Church was established to serve black parishioners, as was the Calvary Missionary Baptist Church, of which Thurman's grandmother was a founding member.[20]

Ma Jack had been born in Missouri in 1862. She traveled west with her husband, Thomas Stewart, and settled in the mining community of Leadville, Colorado in the 1880s. There the couple had two children, the oldest of whom was Thurman's mother, Beulah. After Thomas's death, Ma Jack married a man named Wallace P. Jackson, and the family relocated to Salt Lake City in 1892. Ten years later, Thurman was born—as he described it, "within the protective shadows of the Mormon Temple and the Wasatch Mountains." Shortly after his birth, Thurman's biological father left Salt Lake City for Los Angeles. As Thurman grew up, he lived a somewhat transient life as his mother repeatedly remarried and moved to cities like Chicago, Omaha, Boise, and Pasadena. Later he would take classes at both the University of Utah and the University of Southern California, and he lived in Los Angeles for three years before his "hectic hegira to Harlem." Overall, his most stable upbringing occurred in Salt Lake City under the watchful eye of Ma Jack, and it is to her he would return when he visited home.[21]

Langston Hughes and Wallace Thurman in
California, 1934. *Courtesy of Elise Erickson on behalf
of the Langston Hughes Estate and Beinecke Rare Book
and Manuscript Library, Yale University.*

During his visits to Salt Lake City in 1929, as Thurman's letters to Rapp show,
he was in the midst of the breakup of his marriage to Louise Thompson. During
the divorce proceedings, Thurman accused Thompson of taking advantage of
a youthful indiscretion when he first came to New York, in order to strengthen
her claims for alimony. As he narrated to Rapp, "In 1925, a young colored lad
anxious to enter a literary career came to New York. He had a little stake which
was soon gone. He found no job. He owed room rent and was hungry. . . . At 135th
St., he got off the Subway, and . . . went into the toilet. There was a man loitering
in there. The man spoke. He did more than speak, making me know what his
game was. I laughed. He offered me two dollars. I accepted." For her part, in an
interview later in her life Thompson admitted, "I *never* understood Wallace. He
took nothing seriously. He laughed about everything. He would often threaten

to commit suicide but you knew he would never try it. And he would never admit that he was a homosexual. *Never, never,* not to me at any rate." While neither Thurman nor Thompson was part of the black elite, their divorce was tinged with rumors about Thurman's sexuality, similarly to the Cullen–Du Bois dissolution, which was happening concurrently. Like that other failed marriage, Thurman and Thompson's also flew in the face of the politics of respectability that undergirded so much of New Negro politics.[22]

Thurman was virtually a professional gadfly to politics of respectability, so his denial of gay identity seems somewhat out of character. Although Thurman may have denied being gay, he can certainly be understood as queer—as, in the words of theorist Lisa Duggan, "dissent[ing] from the dominant organization of sex and gender." Scholars who have situated him in kind have seen his queerness emerging from the "sexual topography" of "gay New York" as described by George Chauncey. But like Harlem, the West—and Salt Lake City, in particular—had a reputation for non-normative sexual postures. Richard Bruce Nugent, the only Harlem Renaissance figure to write transparently about same-sex desire, created a fictionalized version of Thurman in his novel *Gentleman Jigger* (written 1928–33, published 2008): Henry Raymond Pelman, known as Ray. Ray's western genealogy is explained as follows: His maternal great-grandmother abandoned her Mormon husband in protest of a black sister-wife. She married a half-mulatto, half-Jewish man and bore a dark-skinned daughter. This daughter would become Ray's grandmother, Emma—sharing a name with Thurman's real-life grandmother. Emma married a mixed-race man and bore a daughter, Hagar, who became Ray's mother after an affair with a dark-skinned man. Ray's origins, therefore, are written not only as interracial but also as polymorphously perverse. In Nugent's six-page description of Salt Lake City, he mentions polygamy, miscegenation, incest, same-sex and intergenerational desire, rape, impotence, pimping, and prostitution.[23]

Nugent's representation of Salt Lake City's sexual transgressions is clearly outsized, but Thurman also grappled with its history of non-normative configurations of marriage, family, and desire. Plural marriage was so unpalatable to the rest of the nation that it delayed Utah statehood for forty-six years. As historian Sarah Barringer Gordon points out, it was thought to be thoroughly un-American. African Americans were seen as both morally suspect and sexually unhinged, and they were thus thought to be particularly susceptible to Mormon conversion. In the face of such stereotypes, blacks in Salt Lake City may have felt a singular pressure to use respectability to bolster their claims for racial equality. In 1890, two years before Ma Jack settled in Salt Lake City, the Church of Jesus Christ of

Latter-day Saints proclaimed it would no longer expect its members to practice polygamy, officially backing away from its endorsement of "celestial marriage." Six years later, Utah became a state. To Thurman, however, this was a tragedy. In "Quoth Brigham Young," he writes, "Utah was finally forced to come into the Union, and for coming in she had to abolish polygamy, and lose her individuality, for from that day on Utah was just another state, peopled by a horde of typical American booboisie with their bourgeoisie overlords, and today Utah is a good example of what Americanization and its attendant spores can accomplish."[24]

In a 1928 letter to Hughes, Thurman challenges the conformist politics of respectability that he claims undergird African American society in Salt Lake City, particularly around the institution of marriage:

> The only things of interest in Salt Lake are an epidemic of influenza, and the attitude of the older folk here toward me who have snubbed me with a vengeance because of an article I wrote three years ago in *The Messenger* about my home town and state. It seems as if I said that most of Utah's early Negro settlers were whores, gamblers and washerwomen, which is true of any of these western states. Somehow they got the idea that I said all of Utah's Negroes from the beginning until now were whores and gamblers. They didn't object to washerwomen. The younger folk have all been enjoying shot gun weddings since I left with the result that those whom I used to push around in a baby carriage are now pushing baby carriages of their own.

Here he scoffs at members of Salt Lake City's black community for their pretense of respectability, insinuating that it is a denial of historical fact and a denial of the present. The community, he observes, is still engaging in illicit sexual behavior—but it is quickly covered up via the institution of marriage. To Thurman, the conformist politics of respectability—with heteronormative marriage as figurehead—come at the cost of personal integrity.[25]

His letters from Utah reveal, however, that he was also using the site as a way to seek alternatives. He was completing research for a play based on the life of Joseph Smith and, in particular, Smith's "vision authorizing polygamy." In a letter to Hughes, he explained:

> I have began [*sic*] work on a perfectly intriguing play, again in collaboration with Wm. Jourdan Rapp. It is my idea. *Sultan Smith* is the title, it being woven around the experiences of Joseph F. Smith, founder of the Mormon religion. The scene of the action is Nauvoo, Ill., where for one brief moment

the Mormons lingered before being driven out and forced to migrate to Salt Lake. It was at Nauvoo that Smith received his vision authorizing polygamy. That is the kernel of the play.

There is no evidence that this manuscript has survived. Thurman's discussions of it, however, indicate that he did not find Utah's history as unexciting as he claimed in "Quoth Brigham Young." Indeed, he buried himself in research during his 1929 trip to Salt Lake City, writing to Rapp, "Since I am now enthroned in the citadel of Mormonism, where all available records can be found there seems no better time than now [to work on "Sultan Smith"]. I shall hie myself to the library and the Mormon library and read all I can find on the subject." In another letter he reports, "My room is crowded with books on Joseph Smith and the early Mormons. I even have a Book of Mormon, confessions of one of Brigham's wives and much other juicy material, both scandalous and serious. Some emancipated Mormons I know here have aided me in gathering material, and I have gone directly to the Church library for the rest."[26]

During the time Thurman was researching "Sultan Smith" and undergoing his breakup with Thompson, he was using Salt Lake City's polygamous past to envision new possibilities for marriage in the present. As early as his marriage to Thompson the previous year, he had expressed interest in new ways of thinking about the institution. In a letter to Claude McKay, he reported:

> I got married, which action I, who never and still do not believe in marriage for an artist of any type, will not try to explain. It's just one of those unexplainable things that happens to the best of us. My only point of extenuation is that I happen to have married a very intelligent woman who has her own career and who also does not believe in marriage and who is as anxious as I am to avoid the conventional pitfalls into which most marriages throw one. I assure you ours is a most modern experiment, a reflection of our own rather curious personalities.

While his efforts failed, Thurman's letter seems engaged with the idea of the companionate marriage promoted by another westerner, Colorado judge Ben B. Lindsey, who coauthored with Wainwright Evans *The Companionate Marriage* (1927). The book described the necessary conditions for couples to enter into equal partnerships, including birth control and easy access to divorce.[27]

Although Thompson traveled to Reno, Nevada—the divorce capital of the United States—to initiate the proceedings only a few months after her marriage to Thurman, their divorce was never finalized. In 1934, the year of his death, Thurman sent Hughes a telegram from Los Angeles. It announced: "FAY AND I MARRIED TODAY." It was followed up by a second: "DONT YOU REALIZE THE DIFFERENCE BETWEEN GIN AND MARRIAGE." The joke is threefold. Firstly, the telegram undermines the respectable institution of marriage by poking fun at it from the cynical position of a jilted spouse (Fay M. Jackson, the friend to whom Thurman refers to here, also had a messy divorce from her husband in 1930). Secondly, it questions homonormativity, given the rumors surrounding Thurman's sexuality. Thirdly, it hints at polygamy, since Thurman's divorce from Thompson had never actually happened. This multifaceted critique of marriage as a site of black respectability politics becomes possible because of Thurman's engagement with Salt Lake City and the West.[28]

In *Marriage, Violence, and the Nation in the American Literary West*, William R. Handley suggests that although the West is often thought of as a place where a hearty, masculine, individualism can flourish, it is actually marriage that provides "the literary West's recurring preoccupation." Marriage, he contends, following in the footsteps of historian Nancy F. Cott, has long been a microcosm that helps Americans understand themselves, and the West, which was populated by "marital nonconformists, such as Indians and Mormons," became a place of contention as "the nation constructed its identity"—particularly its racial identity—"out West." Given the marginalized position of African Americans during the Jim Crow years, it is unsurprising that Harlem Renaissance writers also turned to the West in order to understand their relationship to the nation. While many blacks—like those involved in what Thurman refers to as the "polite colored circles" of Salt Lake City—tried to insert themselves into the mold of mono-racial, heternormative marriage, Toomer and Thurman both found in the West space to challenge this notion through a range of equally western possibilities, such as interracial marriage and miscegenation, companionate marriage, queer sexuality, and divorce. In doing so, they do more than make claims for incorporation into a nation already envisioned; they make critiques to shape a nation still in the making.[29]

Notes

Portions of this essay have been published in Emily Lutenski, *West of Harlem: African American Writers and the Borderlands* (Lawrence: University Press of Kansas, 2015).

    1. Wallace Thurman, "Letter to William Jourdan Rapp [c. July 1929]," in *The Collected Writings of Wallace Thurman: A Harlem Renaissance Reader*, ed. Amritjit Singh and Daniel M. Scott III (New Brunswick, N.J.: Rutgers University Press, 2003), 153–54.

The sole biography of Thurman is Eleonore van Notten, *Wallace Thurman's Harlem Renaissance* (Amsterdam: Rodopi, 1994).

2. U.S. Bureau of the Census, *State and County QuickFacts: Utah*, http://www.census. gov/; Wallace Thurman, "Harlem: A Melodrama of Negro Life in Harlem," in Singh and Scott, *Collected Writings of Wallace Thurman*, 305–69; J. Martin Favor, "George Schuyler and Wallace Thurman: Two Satirists of the Harlem Renaissance," in *A Cambridge Companion to the Harlem Renaissance*, ed. George Hutchinson (New York: Cambridge University Press, 2007), 198–212; "Wallace Thurman Is Model Harlemite, Lewis Announces," *Atlanta Daily World*, March 13, 1932 (an earlier clipping of this article, with Lewis's byline, is contained in Wallace Thurman, "Clippings re: Wallace Thurman," box 3, folder 60, Wallace Thurman Collection, James Weldon Johnson Collection, Beinecke Rare Book and Manuscript Library, Yale University).

3. Langston Hughes, "The Negro Artist and the Racial Mountain," in *Double-Take: A Revisionist Harlem Renaissance Anthology*, ed. Venetria K. Patton and Maureen Honey (New Brunswick: Rutgers University Press, 2001), 40–44; William Stanley Braithwaite, "The Negro in American Literature," in ibid., 10–16; Willa Cather, *The Professor's House* (New York: Vintage, 1990); Wallace Thurman, "Letter to William Jourdan Rapp [c. July 1929]," in Singh and Scott, *Collected Writings of Wallace Thurman*, 153–54.

4. Jean Toomer, "New Mexico after India," in *A Jean Toomer Reader: Selected Unpublished Writings*, ed. Frederik L. Rusch (New York: Oxford University Press, 1993), 253.

5. Bruce A. Glasrud, ed., *African American History in New Mexico: Portraits from Five Hundred Years* (Albuquerque: University of New Mexico Press, 2013); William A. Doback and Thomas D. Phillips, *The Black Regulars, 1866–1898* (Norman: University of Oklahoma Press, 2001); Rodman Wilson Paul, *Mining Frontiers of the Far West, 1848–1880* (Albuquerque: University of New Mexico Press, 2001); U.S. Bureau of the Census, *Fourteenth Census of the United States Taken in the Year 1920*, vol. 3, *Population* (Washington, D.C.: Government Printing Office, 1922).

6. Flannery Burke, *From Greenwich Village to Taos: Primitivism and Place at Mabel Dodge Luhan's* (Lawrence: University Press of Kansas, 2008), 1–12, 89–111.

7. Jean Toomer, "On Being an American," in *The Wayward and the Seeking*, ed. Darwin T. Turner (Washington, D.C.: Howard University Press, 1982), 123; Jean Toomer, "Letter to Horace Liveright [September 5, 1923]," in Jean Toomer, *Cane*, 2nd ed., ed. Rudolph P. Byrd and Henry Louis Gates Jr. (New York: W. W. Norton, 2011), 170; Jean Toomer, "Fighting the Vice," in Rusch, *A Jean Toomer Reader*, 102–3; Jean Toomer, "Letter to James Weldon Johnson [July 11, 1930]," in ibid., 105–6; Toomer, "Fighting the Vice," 103.

8. Toomer, "Fighting the Vice," 103; Langston Hughes, *The Big Sea* (New York: Hill and Wang, 1993), 242–43; Langston Hughes, "A House in Taos," in *The Collected Poems of Langston Hughes*, ed. Arnold Rampersad and David Roessel (New York: Vintage Books, 1995), 81; Hughes, *The Big Sea*, 262.

9. Hughes, *The Big Sea*, 242; Arna Bontemps, "Commentary on Jean Toomer and *Cane*," in Jean Toomer, *Cane*, ed. Darwin T. Turner (New York: W. W. Norton, 1988), 186–92; Rudolph P. Byrd and Henry Louis Gates Jr., "Introduction: 'Song of the Son': The Emergence and Passing of Jean Toomer," in Toomer, *Cane*, ed. Byrd and Gates, xix–lxx.

10. Daylanne K. English, *Unnatural Selections: Eugenics in American Modernism and the Harlem Renaissance* (Chapel Hill: University of North Carolina Press, 2004), 35–64; Anastasia Curwood, *Stormy Weather: Middle-Class African American Marriages between the Two World Wars* (Chapel Hill: University of North Carolina Press, 2010); Earl Lewis and Heidi Ardizzone, *Love on Trial: An American Scandal in Black and White* (New York: W.W. Norton, 2002); George Hutchinson, *In Search of Nella Larsen: A Biography of the Color Line* (Cambridge, Mass.: Harvard University Press, 2006).

11. Jean Toomer, "A New Race in America," in Rusch, *A Jean Toomer Reader*, 105.

12. "Margery Latimer, Novelist, U. Grad, to Wed Chicagoan," *Capital Times* (Madison, Wis.), October 25, 1931; "Just Americans," *Time*, March 28, 1932.

13. "Margery Toomer, Novelist, Dies in West: Wife of Psychologist Was Descendant of Prominent New England Pioneers," *New York Times*, August 18, 1932; "Woman Novelist Called by Death: Death Ends Romance of Two Races—White Wife of J. Toomer, Novelist of Negro Blood, Expires in Childbirth," *Los Angeles Times*, August 18, 1932.

14. Lothrop Stoddard, *The Rising Tide of Color against White World Supremacy* (New York: Charles Scribner's Sons, 1920); Alice Dunbar Nelson, "Woman's Most Serious Problem," in Patton and Honey, *Double-Take*, 115; English, *Unnatural Selections*, 59 [emphasis in original].

15. Jean Toomer, "Notebook: Contains Notes about New Mexico," Jean Toomer Papers, James Weldon Johnson Collection, Beinecke Rare Book and Manuscript Library, Yale University; Jean Toomer, "Sequences: Notes and Drafts," ibid.; Jean Toomer, "A Drama of the Southwest: Notes," ibid.

16. Toomer, "Sequences."

17. Latimer quoted in Cynthia Earl Kerman and Richard Eldridge, *The Lives of Jean Toomer: A Hunger for Wholeness* (Baton Rouge: Louisiana State University Press, 1987), 199; Jean Toomer, "Unidentified: Typescript [To This Land Where the Clouds Fall]," Jean Toomer Papers, James Weldon Johnson Collection, Beinecke Rare Book and Manuscript Library, Yale University.

18. "Wallace Thurman Is Model Harlemite"; Dorothy West, "Elephant's Dance," in *The Richer, the Poorer* (New York: Anchor Books, 1995), 215–16; "Personal Papers—Biographical Sketches by Harold Jackman and Hughes Allison," Wallace Thurman Collection, James Weldon Johnson Collection, Beinecke Rare Book and Manuscript Library, Yale University. Notes indicate this eulogy was written by playwright Hughes Allison and delivered by the Reverend William Lloyd Imes.

19. Wallace Thurman, "Quoth Brigham Young—This is the Place," in *These "Colored" United States: African American Essays from the 1920s*, ed. Tom Lutz and Susanna Ashton (New Brunswick, N.J.: Rutgers University Press, 1996), 263.

20. Ronald G. Coleman, "A History of Blacks in Utah, 1825–1910" (PhD diss., University of Utah, 1980); Notten, *Wallace Thurman's Harlem Renaissance*, 60.

21. Notten, *Wallace Thurman's Harlem Renaissance*, 59; Wallace Thurman, "Autobiographical Statement," in Singh and Scott, *Collected Writings of Wallace Thurman*, 91–92.

22. Wallace Thurman, "Letter to William Jourdan Rapp [Tuesday, May 7, 1929]," in Singh and Scott, *Collected Writings of Wallace Thurman*, 138–39; Thompson quoted in Arnold Rampersad, *The Life of Langston Hughes*, vol. 1., *1902–1941: I, Too, Sing America* (New York: Oxford University Press, 2002), 172.

23. Lisa Duggan, "Making it Perfectly Queer," in *Theorizing Feminism: Parallel Trends in the Humanities and Social Sciences*, ed. Anne C. Herrmann and Abigail Stewart (Boulder, Colo.: Westview Press, 2000), 223; George Chauncey, *Gay New York: Gender, Urban Culture, and the Making of the Gay Male World, 1890–1940* (New York: Basic Books, 1994), 23; Richard Bruce Nugent, *Gentleman Jigger: A Novel of the Harlem Renaissance* (Philadelphia: Da Capo, 2008), 13–18.

24. Sarah Barringer Gordon, *The Mormon Question: Polygamy and Constitutional Conflict in Nineteenth-Century America* (Chapel Hill: University of North Carolina Press, 2001); Thurman, "Quoth Brigham Young," 264.

25. Wallace Thurman, "Letter to Langston Hughes [Tuesday, December 5, 1928]," in Singh and Scott, *Collected Writings of Wallace Thurman*, 117.

26. Wallace Thurman, "Letter to Langston Hughes [Wednesday, n.d.]," in Singh and Scott, *Collected Writings of Wallace Thurman*, 126; Wallace Thurman, "Letter to William Jourdan Rapp [c. July 1929]," in ibid., 153; Wallace Thurman, "Letter to William Jourdan Rapp [Saturday, n.d.]," in ibid., 156.

27. Wallace Thurman, "Letter to Claude McKay [October 4, 1928]," in Singh and Scott, *Collected Writings of Wallace Thurman*, 164–65; Rebecca L. Davis, "Not Marriage at All, but Simple Harlotry: The Companionate Marriage Controversy," *Journal of American History* 94, no. 4 (2008), 1137–63.

28. Jani Scandura, *Down in the Dumps: Place, Modernity, American Depression* (Durham, N.C.: Duke University Press, 2008); Wallace Thurman, "Telegram to Langston Hughes [April 24, 1934]" and "Telegram to Langston Hughes [April 29, 1934]," in Singh and Scott, *Collected Writings of Wallace Thurman*, 129; Lael L. Hughes-Watkins, "Fay M. Jackson: The Sociopolitical Narrative of a Pioneering African American Female Journalist" (master's thesis, Youngstown State University, 2008).

29. William R. Handley, *Marriage, Violence, and Nation in the American Literary West* (New York: Cambridge University Press, 2002), 2–4; Nancy F. Cott, *Public Vows: A History of Marriage and the Nation* (Cambridge, Mass.: Harvard University Press, 2000); Wallace Thurman, "Letter to William Jourdan Rapp [August 1929]," in Singh and Scott, *Collected Writings of Wallace Thurman*, 159.

11 Containing "Perversion"

African Americans and Same-Sex Desire in Cold War Los Angeles

Kevin Allen Leonard

According to reports in two weekly African American newspapers in Los Angeles, on May 19, 1948, Ruth Foster, a twenty-year-old African American, repeatedly stabbed her lover, Louise Ford, a forty-three-year-old African American, in the home they shared on South Avalon Boulevard in Los Angeles. Foster killed the woman to whom she had been a "wife," because Ford intended to end their five-year relationship. Ford had found another woman who had more money than Foster did. After Ford taunted her, Foster said: "A strange frenzy came over me, and I grabbed a steak knife and began stabbing her." One of the two newspapers, the *California Eagle*, referred to the relationship between Foster and Ford as "strange" and "unnatural."[1] In a front-page article, the *Los Angeles Tribune* suggested that Foster should have been ashamed of her relationship with Ford. The newspaper reported that Foster's "truthfulness and lack of guile or shame" in discussing her relationship with Ford "startled a squad of sophisticated policemen." The *Tribune* also noted that Foster's attorney, Walter L. Gordon Jr., would argue that she was "not guilty by reason of insanity." Gordon told reporters that Foster's "alleged insanity grew out of 'illicit love'" and that she was "obviously mentally deficient."[2]

Two months later, Foster was sentenced to one to ten years in prison for manslaughter. The sentence prompted a third African American newspaper, the *Los Angeles Sentinel*, to observe that "life is extremely cheap when Negroes murder Negroes." In a front-page editorial, *Sentinel* editor and publisher Leon H. Washington Jr. criticized the sentence (which the editorial described as lenient),

---

This chapter originally appeared in the *Journal of the History of Sexuality* 20, no. 3 (September 2011): 545–67. Copyright by the University of Texas Press. Reprinted with permission.

Gordon's defense of Foster, and the African American community's tolerance of same-sex relationships. The newspaper declared that the light sentence "creates the impression among others who might indulge and those who do indulge in this activity that they may commit whatever crime they see fit, even to the extent of taking a life, hire a smart lawyer, plead insanity, spend a few short years in the 'pen' and then come back into the community and practice their immorality." The editorial implied that Gordon's insanity defense was disingenuous, since Foster and Ford "both knew that they were committing a crime against society." Washington stated that "it is common knowledge this type of illicit so-called 'love' has flourished in this community. There have been many cases of homes being broken up. Many are brazen. Their activities are well known and are flaunted about in cocktail lounges, bars and our most 'decent society.'" The newspaperman insisted that "it is the duty of the district attorney of this county to uphold the law and to protect society from these indecencies."[3]

The articles in the *Eagle* and the *Tribune* and the editorial in the *Sentinel* reveal that some African Americans in Los Angeles engaged in same-sex relationships in the years following World War II. They also show that some community leaders, including the editors and publishers of the newspapers, viewed these relationships with disgust, contempt, and alarm. The existence of these relationships and the discourse surrounding same-sex desire within the African American community, however, have largely escaped the attention of historians of sexuality.

In the past thirty years, a number of scholars have explained the emergence of lesbian and gay communities, the formation of government policies dealing with those communities, and the rise of a gay civil rights movement. In his groundbreaking 1983 study, *Sexual Politics, Sexual Communities*, John D'Emilio argues that social changes brought about by U.S. participation in World War II created the spaces in which a gay subculture could emerge. Exclusively gay bars and organizations such as the Veterans Benevolent Association in New York emerged during or immediately following the war.[4] Allan Bérubé provides additional information about the ways in which military service allowed some men and women to come to terms with their same-sex desires.[5] In his sweeping reinterpretation of the emergence of gay identity, community, and politics, *Bohemian Los Angeles*, Daniel Hurewitz notes that wartime social changes expanded the network of gay bars and cruising areas throughout the Southern California metropolis.[6]

Most of these historians agree that official tolerance of same-sex behavior ended soon after the war. D'Emilio notes the efforts of U.S. federal, military, and state and local officials to remove all homosexuals from government employment and military service, and he provides evidence to show that local police forces harassed lesbians and gay men in many cities.[7] As David K. Johnson points out in *The Lavender Scare*, the U.S. Park Police launched a "Pervert Elimination Campaign" in October 1947, and Congress passed a sexual psychopath law for the District of Columbia in 1948.[8] Hurewitz argues that persecution of "homosexually active men and women" increased dramatically in the mid-1930s. This persecution abated somewhat during the war years, but after the war "the systematic persecution of such men and women expanded exponentially." Arrests for sex crimes rose dramatically in the late 1940s, and in the 1950s the California legislature doubled the sentence—from ten to twenty years in prison—for sodomy. The state also established facilities for housing and treating "sexual psychopaths."[9] In a recent article, Whitney Strub argues that efforts to classify homoerotic literature and film as obscene were also part of this effort to suppress the expression of same-sex desire.[10]

Early historians generally sought to make visible the experiences of homosexuals, whose very existence had been rendered invisible before the Stonewall riots. These riots, which occurred in New York at the end of June 1969, are generally regarded as the beginning of the modern gay liberation movement in the United States. These historians relied heavily on interviews conducted in the 1970s and 1980s. More recent historians have expressed both theoretical and methodological concerns about this early research. This new generation of scholars has recognized that many of the people who acted upon same-sex desires before 1969 did not identify themselves as homosexual or see themselves as part of a community of people defined by sexual orientation. Instead, older forms of same-sex interaction persisted even as new identities and communities emerged. Accordingly, such historians have been cautious about using labels such as "homosexual" or "gay" to describe all people who expressed and acted upon same-sex desires. These scholars have also recognized that the memories of individuals are often dramatically transformed by events that have occurred during a person's life. Some have focused more attention on sources produced in the pre-Stonewall era in order to understand the world that shaped emerging identities and communities. This study follows in the footsteps of these more recent scholars, analyzing newspaper articles in an effort to illuminate the ways in which people could articulate same-sex desire in a period characterized both by the emergence of new identities and communities and by persistent efforts to prevent the expression of sexual desires deemed undesirable by religious and political leaders.

Scholars have also devoted relatively little attention to the relationship between racial ideologies and emerging gay identities and communities. D'Emilio mentions the Knights of the Clock, an organization of "interracially involved homosexuals" that emerged in Los Angeles in the late 1940s.[11] Bérubé notes that "public drag balls, despite their decline in many cities, stayed alive during the war in Harlem and other black urban neighborhoods," and he acknowledges the existence of gay African American soldiers.[12] Hurewitz connects the rise of the Mattachine Society to broader civil rights activism in Los Angeles, but he does not present much information relating to perceptions of same-sex desire expressed by African Americans, Mexican Americans, or Asian Americans.[13] Strub argues that police harassment of "queers" paralleled police treatment of people of color: "Just like Mexicans, queers were inherently criminal (by virtue of sodomy laws and conduct ordinances), and just as people of color needed to be contained, kept out of respectable neighborhoods, so too did deviant queers."[14] Nonetheless, Strub does not discuss either the presence of same-sex desire or opinions about such desire among people of color.[15]

In a recent provocative examination of the relationship between sexuality and the African American struggle for civil rights, Thaddeus Russell observes that working-class African Americans were more accepting of homosexuality and other "nonheteronormative behavior" than were middle-class African Americans in the years before the growth of the civil rights movement in the mid-1950s. Drag balls and cabarets in African American neighborhoods attracted hundreds of participants, and national U.S. magazines such as *Ebony* and *Jet* as well as African American newspapers in cities such as New York, Chicago, and Detroit publicized these events. African Americans also embraced preachers whose appearance and behavior flaunted the norms of heterosexual masculinity. Charles Manuel "Sweet Daddy" Grace, whose United House of Prayer for All People had churches along the East Coast, for example, had shoulder-length hair and five-inch-long fingernails and wore gold and purple coats. Detroit's James Francis "Prophet" Jones wore a white mink coat and boasted, "I have never had sexual intercourse with a woman." Russell argues that these drag shows and flamboyant religious leaders "were most popular during the greatest crusade against sexual deviancy in U.S. history." In the late 1940s and early 1950s, federal, state, and local officials forced homosexuals from public jobs, police departments launched raids on gay bars and cruising areas, and newspapers published the names of the people who were arrested. "At no other time," Russell insists, "were the sexual cultures of black and white America drawn in starker contrast."[16]

By the early 1950s, however, the middle-class leaders of the emerging civil rights movement had initiated what Russell calls an ultimately effective "campaign to replace the freedom and entitlement of black working-class culture with obligation, discipline, and rejection of the self." In the ideology of middle-class civil rights leaders, he adds, "black homosexuals came to represent all the elements of African American working-class culture that civil rights leaders identified as obstacles to the attainment of citizenship." At the same time as the African American middle class attempted to eradicate working-class tolerance of homosexuality, Russell maintains, European American elites embraced a new ideology that "made explicit that the price of admission to American society for African Americans would be a surrender to heterosexual norms." Civil rights leaders criticized the sexual content of much African American music, and a growing number of recording artists turned to recording songs that extolled the values of marriage and monogamy. By the middle of the 1950s, newspapers and magazines stopped publicizing drag shows.[17]

Although Russell's evidence, drawn mostly from articles in *Ebony*, *Jet*, and newspapers in Detroit and New York, supports his interpretation, Russell generalizes too broadly about nationwide events. Evidence from Los Angeles indicates that middle-class African Americans' hostility toward homosexuality predated the rise of the mass movement for civil rights and reflected widespread beliefs about normality, morality, and criminality as well as class divisions within the community. The African American newspapers in Los Angeles did not publish positive articles about drag balls in the 1940s. Instead these newspapers characterized drag ball participants and other African Americans who tolerated same-sex desire as abnormal and immoral. Articles in these newspapers did not distinguish between various kinds of "sex crimes" but implied that adults who engaged in consensual same-sex relations were not fundamentally different from sex criminals who kidnapped, molested, mutilated, and murdered women and young children. They depicted same-sex desire as a mental disorder that frequently led to jealous rage and murder. At the same time, these hostile depictions of same-sex desire and of the people who felt such desire reflected divisions within the African American community. Class standing and conformity to certain community standards protected some individuals accused of acting upon same-sex desires. The poorest and least powerful members of the community, in contrast, most frequently bore the criticism of middle-class editors and publishers.

"A Sterile and Destructive Vice"

The African American community in Los Angeles grew dramatically in the 1940s and 1950s. Tens of thousands of African Americans moved to Los Angeles, mostly from southern and midwestern cities, during and after World War II. In 1940 about 75,000 African Americans lived in Los Angeles County. By 1950 the county's total African American population was nearly 218,000. The African American population continued to grow dramatically during the 1950s; accordingly, the 1960 census counted nearly 465,000 African Americans in the Los Angeles–Long Beach metropolitan area.[18]

Three major weekly newspapers served the growing African American population of Los Angeles between 1941 and 1960: the venerable *California Eagle*, which could trace its roots to the nineteenth century; the *Los Angeles Sentinel*, established in 1933; and the *Los Angeles Tribune*, established in 1941.[19] It is impossible to say exactly how many people read each of these newspapers, who these readers were, or how they read them. However, circulation figures suggest that a significant percentage of the city's African American residents read the newspapers. The publishers of the newspapers reported that in 1949 the *Eagle* printed 6,000 copies each week; the *Tribune*, 7,100; and the *Sentinel*, 13,872. In 1954 publishers reported that the circulation of the *Tribune* was 12,500; the *Eagle*, 18,750; and the *Sentinel*, 21,349.[20]

Both the cost and the contents of the newspapers suggest that middle-class African Americans were more likely than working-class people to read the *Eagle* or the *Sentinel*. Through most of this period a yearlong subscription to the *Eagle* or the *Sentinel* cost four dollars, and single issues cost ten cents, twice as much as any of the metropolitan daily newspapers. The *Tribune* was more affordable than its competitors. A yearlong subscription to the *Tribune* cost two dollars until 1952, when the rate rose to three dollars. By September 1952 a single issue of the *Tribune*, which had previously cost only five cents, cost ten cents.[21] Each issue of the *Sentinel* contained several pages of "social news" that would have been of interest primarily to wealthy members of the community—engagement, wedding, and birth announcements as well as reports on the activities of clubs, fraternities, and sororities. Two sociologists who conducted a content analysis of all three newspapers in the 1950s noted that the *Sentinel* "appears to define its readers as Negroes who have achieved some status in the racial community and who wish to disassociate themselves from issues which emphasize race *per se,* particularly when Communist or left-wing groups are involved." These sociologists also noted that the *Sentinel* described itself "as Democratic in its politics," although "it consistently supports Republican candidates. The net impression is one of middle-class conservatism."[22] Although the *Eagle* was far to the left of the *Sentinel* politically, like its more conservative rival it devoted a good deal of space to news of the social activities of Los Angeles's African

American elite. The *Tribune* attempted to appeal more to working-class readers than its competitors did. The newspaper was outspoken in its opposition
to communism, but it tended to support labor unions and liberal Democrats.
The *Tribune* devoted more space to long articles about sensational crimes than
to social news. All three newspapers published articles about sexual behavior
within the African American community, but the *Sentinel* and the *Tribune*
published such articles much more frequently than did the *Eagle*. Although all
three newspapers survived the 1950s, two ceased publication in the 1960s. The
Tribune went out of business in 1960, and the *Eagle* ceased in 1964. The *Sentinel*
continues to publish.[23]

Historians of sexuality have for decades argued that large cities created the
anonymous spaces that allowed people to experiment with same-sex behavior
and to accept homosexual identities.[24] It seems likely that the growth of the
African American population in Los Angeles led to an increase in the number and
kinds of spaces in which people might feel free to experiment with and express
same-sex desire. However, it is very difficult to draw definitive conclusions about
same-sex desire and gay identity in the African American community, since very
few sources of evidence allow historians to probe African Americans' attitudes
in the years before World War II. Some scholars have attached great importance
to drag balls. Russell, for example, argues that African American newspapers
and magazines published numerous articles about and photographs of these
events. A few articles from the 1930s indicate that Los Angeles, like other large
U.S. cities, was the site of large drag balls that attracted hundreds of participants
and thousands of spectators. In its December 20, 1934, edition, for example, the
Los Angeles Sentinel reported that more than five hundred female impersonators
had promised to attend such a ball at the Elks Temple.[25] The producer of that ball
later claimed that four thousand people had attended.[26] However, it is impossible
to determine if these balls continued. No advertisements for or articles about such
a drag ball appeared in the *Sentinel* between 1935 and 1946.[27] The Club Alabam,
a legendary Central Avenue jazz club that did not ordinarily encourage gay or
lesbian patronage, advertised a Halloween Fashion Show and Drag Ball in the
October 25, 1945, issue of the *Eagle*, but the club's advertisements in other years
did not mention a drag ball.[28]

Although the *Eagle* and the *Sentinel* published a few advertisements for drag
balls in the late 1940s, they rarely published articles about the balls, and they
never published photographs of these events. Only a handful of the articles
that were published about the balls could be described as neutral or positive.

Drag ball at the legendary Central Avenue jazz club, Club Alabam, Los Angeles, 1945.
Courtesy Los Angeles Public Library.

On October 31, 1946, the *Sentinel* published an article that reported that the managers of the Club Alabam expected "a record breaking attendance tonight at the club's annual Drag Ball." One of the club's managers noted that "this year's performance will represent the largest assortment of talent ever presented at this affair." The article also indicated that drag performers from as far away as San Francisco, Portland, and Seattle would participate.[29] An entertainment column in the October 30, 1947, *Sentinel* encouraged readers to hear Johnny Otis and his band at the Club Alabam, adding, "You'll be there at the Drag Ball on Hallowe'en night anyhow."[30] A similar column in the October 30, 1952, issue of the *Sentinel* simply noted that "the Elks Auditorium will be packed with thrills Halloween night when the drags, witches, and vampires settle there for their annual dance festivities."[31] These scattered advertisements and columns about drag balls suggest that such events were not generally encouraged by middle-class African Americans in Los Angeles.

Beginning in November 1947, the African American newspapers usually mentioned the drag balls in order to criticize the promoters of and participants in these events. Columns in the *Sentinel* described some of what occurred at these balls as indecent and immoral. In the November 6, 1947, issue of the *Sentinel*, for example, the column that one week before had suggested that readers would be at the drag ball denounced the participants in and promoters of the drag balls. The column expressed reluctance "to question or be intolerant of anyone's conception of a 'good time.'" Nonetheless, "there are some few things in this world that violate all canons of decency or morality. We frankly can't understand how anyone who witnessed or assisted in the promotion of the various 'Drag balls' last Hallowe'en evening can possibly look at themselves in the mirror for several days to come."[32] In the spring of 1948, Leon H. Washington Jr., the publisher of the *Sentinel*, described the people who participated in drag balls as "a group of degenerates and sexual perverts." He also characterized their behavior at these events as "immoral," stating that they "dress in women's clothes and parade their immorality before audiences."[33]

The approach of Halloween 1948 offered *Tribune* editor Almena Davis the occasion to publish the most expansive condemnation of participants in the balls. Davis's column, subtitled "Davis' Own Kinsey Report," began with an explanation for why she had refused an advertisement for a "so-called 'drag ball,'" which she explained was "the annual Hallowe'en exhibition of the local society of homosexuals." Unlike Washington, who had emphasized the immorality of drag ball participants, Davis dwelled on the illegality of female impersonation, and she described the appearance of men in women's clothing as "grotesque." Davis's column did not simply disparage female impersonation. It also decried African Americans for their tolerance of homosexuals, whom she depicted as "deformed" and "defective."[34]

Davis explained that the *Tribune* had refused to accept an advertisement for the ball because "the biggest part of the night's activities will be agin' the law." Expressing an unquestioning acceptance of the reasonableness of these laws, Davis noted that both the wearing of masks and female impersonation were illegal. Davis also explained that she did not reject the advertisement simply because illegal activities would occur there. Her primary objection to the drag ball, she insisted, was aesthetic. God had made women and men different, she asserted, although she acknowledged that it was not God who had commanded women and men to wear different styles of clothing. She declared that "there is nothing more grotesque than the sight of what God intended to be men cavorting about in what convention has decreed as women's dress." Davis's column perpetuated stereotypes of gay men as fashionable dressers (in men's clothing) and tasteful interior decorators. She stated that she had "never been able to reconcile the good taste of most homos of my acquaintance in art, interior decorating, clothing, etc., with their lack of it in their conduct."[35]

Davis wrote of homosexuality as a deformity and a defect. She stated that the drag ball was "the one occasion of the year in which these people have the opportunity to satisfy their inordinate desire for acclaim of themselves in their peculiarly deformed state." Davis also advanced the claim that homosexuals were "defective human beings," because they were not capable of "performing their normal sexual function and their normal human function, which is the reproduction of their kind." Davis further described homosexuals as exhibitionists. "All the homosexuals of my acquaintance seem to have the very greatest proclivity for self exhibition," she wrote. Davis denounced African Americans for their tolerance of homosexuality, which she called a "sterile and destructive vice." She observed that African Americans accorded more importance to drag balls than other groups of people did. She noted that "the newspapers headline their theatrical pages with news of it" and "pictures of homosexuals in female dress are published," even though there is no evidence that the *Eagle*, the *Sentinel*, or the *Tribune* had "headlined their theatrical pages with news of" drag balls or published photographs of drag performers. Davis admonished members of her community for their tolerance. "You don't take a machine which is bad, in that it won't do the work it is intended for, and say, 'There's nothing wrong with it; it's just different.'" However, she insisted, "that's what we seem to have done with the homosexuals."[36]

Drag balls in Los Angeles never received the kind of publicity in local newspapers that similar events received in newspapers in New York or in national magazines. Instead, from 1947 on, African American newspapers described the balls as indecent, immoral, illegal, and grotesque, and they used similar terms to describe the "defective" homosexuals who participated in the balls. Moreover, it is difficult to find evidence in the Los Angeles newspapers that might support the contention that the attacks on homosexuals and people who tolerated them were related to the emergent civil rights movement. Washington's and Davis's criticism of the drag balls seems to reflect the tendency, explored in greater depth in what follows, to connect homosexuality and other varieties of sexual expression with heinous crimes.

"A Dangerous Murderer, Robber, or Sex Pervert
May Be Hiding Out in Your Neighborhood"

In its January 30, 1947, issue, the *Sentinel* published a letter from an unnamed reader who endorsed the district attorney's suggestion that "all sex degenerates and proverts [*sic*] be fingerprinted and listed." The author of this letter connected "the recent 'Black Dahlia' murder, which according to detectives is an act of a sex fiend," with same-sex desire. The letter endorsed "a clean-up of the Central avenue district of both male and female sex-fiends." The author insisted that "these perpetrators of sexual crimes are bold and open with their lust and fiendish desire. Their acts are what they term 'the modern way.'" These "sex-fiends" were "not only found in joints and dives but many are well known and associate in clubs, social and religious circles." The author stated that "both men and women degenerates" had broken up many homes and observed that "school children are confronted and propositioned by both male and female degenerates." The letter mentioned the Halloween drag ball, at which "the Club Alabam gave the sexual dearranged [*sic*] a chance to parade in splendor and glory." It also stated that "there are many exclusive women parties in which sexually deranged women play upon other innocent women. The boldness of some of these is unbelievable. They make no secrecy of their filthy abnormal desires and the list of these would be shocking to the public and common decency."[37] As this letter indicates, some African Americans in Los Angeles saw a clear connection between expressions of same-sex desire and heinous crimes such as the "Black Dahlia" murder of Elizabeth Short in 1947, which also drew considerable media attention.[38] The author of this letter was not alone in seeing a connection between same-sex desire and violent crime. Newspaper editors, other community leaders, and countless elected and appointed officials outside the African American community agreed with the position expressed in this letter.

A number of scholars have identified the late 1940s and the 1950s as an era of "sex crime panic." Legislators in many states passed laws allowing for the incarceration and treatment of a new category of criminal: the "sexual psychopath."[39] In some places, officials included all homosexuals in their definitions of "sexual psychopaths," and even individuals who had not been accused of a violent crime or a sexual act involving a child were sent to mental hospitals for psychiatric treatment.[40] The historians who have investigated the sex crime panic have noted that lawmakers, law enforcement officers, many of the psychologists and psychiatrists who advised them, and the public often failed to distinguish between different kinds of criminalized behaviors. George Chauncey, for example, points out that newspaper articles "usually blurred the lines between different forms of sexual nonconformity." Chauncey observes that newspapers used "a single term, sex deviate, to refer to *anyone* whose sexual behavior was different from the norm." Chauncey notes that this term "made any variation from the supposed norm sound ominous and threatening, and it served to conflate the most benign and the most dangerous forms of sexual nonconformity." As Chauncey points out, this single term could be and was used to describe people engaged in very different behavior, such as "an adult engaging in consensual homosexual relations with another adult, an adult involved in consensual sadomasochistic relations—or a sadistic murderer of children."[41]

There is evidence for "sex crime panics" across the United States in the late 1940s and 1950s, and many legislators, including those in Congress, passed new or stronger sexual psychopath laws. Evidence from Los Angeles, however, raises questions about whether or not there was a similar panic in Southern California. Hurewitz observes that Los Angeles police began cracking down on female impersonators in 1932 and that the number of men arrested for "sex perversion" increased "steadily and dramatically" from 1940 to 1948.[42] Heinous crimes of a sexual nature occurred several times in Southern California in the 1930s and 1940s. Newspaper articles that described these crimes typically referred to the suspects as "degenerates." For example, on June 28, 1937, the *Los Angeles Times* reported that three girls, aged seven, eight, and nine, had disappeared from Inglewood's Centinela Park. The suburban community's police chief was "convinced that the children are in the hands of a degenerate."[43] The following day, when the bodies of the three girls were found in a ravine in the Baldwin Hills, three different articles in the *Times* described the suspect as a "degenerate."[44] When the *Times* reported that crossing guard Albert Dyer had confessed to the murders, it noted that he had "been found by alienists called by the prosecution to be a sadistic degenerate."[45]

Although the term "degenerate" was most frequently used in the 1930s and 1940s to refer to men who committed sexual crimes against adult women or girls, it also was used to describe people who engaged in same-sex acts. In 1940, when the Los Angeles Police Commission moved to restrict the impersonation of "a person of the opposite sex," the report in the *Los Angeles Times* made clear that the target of these actions was "degenerates," who would not be "entitled to an impersonation permit."[46] In a January 31, 1945, article about the growing presence of "vice" in Hollywood, the *Los Angeles Times* noted that speakers from a variety of organizations told the Police Commission of servicemen "who mixed in some 'spots' with degenerates." In both articles it is clear that the "degenerates" to whom the speakers referred were homosexuals.[47]

In the postwar years, the use of the term "degenerate" to describe people who engaged in a wide range of sexual behaviors declined. Instead, in the second half of the 1940s, articles more often referred to "perverts." As was the case with "degenerate" in the 1930s and early 1940s, "pervert" in the later 1940s and 1950s was used to refer to people who engaged in a wide variety of acts. At times it was used to refer to pedophiles and murderers; in other cases it was used to describe adults who engaged in consensual relations with other adults of the same sex. A January 15, 1948, article about immorality in Hollywood bars and clubs, for example, stated that witnesses before a committee of the California legislature, the Assembly Interim Committee on Public Morals, had testified that some clubs and taverns were "hangouts for perverts."[48] The November 17, 1949, issue of the *Los Angeles Times* declared that the city council had "adopted a resolution asking for more stringent State laws controlling sex perverts." This resolution was prompted by the murder of six-year-old Linda Glucoft.[49] By the end of the 1940s, as Chauncey notes, articles in the *Los Angeles Times* began to use the term "sex deviate" in much the same way that they had previously used the terms "degenerate" and "pervert."

The authors of articles, editorials, and letters to the editor in the African American newspapers in Los Angeles used terms such as "degenerate" and "pervert" in the same broad way that these terms were used in the *Los Angeles Times*. The *Sentinel* used the term "degenerate" only a handful of times before World War II. In its January 4, 1940, issue, it reported that a woman had been attacked by a "mad, sex degenerate."[50] A few months later, in its April 25, 1940, issue, the newspaper referred to the person who killed nine-year-old Dorothy Gordon as a "degenerate."[51] After the war, however, the *Sentinel* frequently referred to both "degenerates" and "perverts," often using the terms interchangeably. The *Sentinel* most often used these terms to describe men who attacked women or female children. For example, in its April 30, 1950, issue, the *Sentinel* reported that a woman had been held captive and raped by three "perverts."[52] A June 28, 1951, article reported that a "pervert" would soon face trial on charges of molesting a seven-year old girl.[53] The newspaper also used the terms "degenerate" and "pervert," however, to describe men who forced other men to engage in same-sex acts. An article in the June 5, 1952, *Sentinel*, for example, revealed that a man had been forced at knifepoint to have sex with a third man. The *Sentinel* referred to the suspects in this case as "two bold sex degenerates," and the headline referred to them as "sex perverts."[54]

Articles in the *Sentinel* and the *Tribune* used the term "perverted" to describe consensual same-sex activity, and they used the term "degenerate" to describe people who engaged in consensual same-sex acts. For example, on August 27, 1949, the *Tribune* reported that the police had arrested Edward Deason, a twenty-six-year-old hairdresser, for engaging in a consensual same-sex act. According to the article, Deason had "indulged in a perverted act in a public rest room" with a twenty-two-year-old white man.[55] An April 6, 1950, column in the *Sentinel* referred to eighty-eight people who had been fired by the State Department "for being Degenerates."[56] On June 3, 1950, the *Tribune* reported that a sixteen-year-old boy had admitted to soliciting a "perverted" sexual act with a forty-four-year-old man. The article makes clear that neither was forced into the activity.[57] As these articles indicate, the newspapers did not suggest that crimes involving coercion or violence were different from or worse than consensual homosexual relations. Instead they implied that people who sought consensual same-sex relations were comparable to rapists and child molesters.

Articles such as these, which reported on people arrested for consensual same-sex activity, did not simply connect same-sex desire to violent crime. They also were part of an effort to contain "perversion." These articles usually included the names and addresses of the men who were arrested. The publication of such details had dire consequences for these people, who might have then lost their jobs or faced social ostracism as well as police persecution. In 1950 the *Sentinel* encouraged its readers to contribute to its effort to contain "perversion." In its October 5, 1950, issue, the newspaper announced that it would publish photographs and descriptions of "dangerous and wanted criminals who are being sought by our police department." The *Sentinel* urged readers to notify "the nearest police officer if you should happen to see any one of the wanted criminals who will appear in this column." In underscoring the importance of community involvement in this effort, the *Sentinel* reiterated the connection it had previously asserted between any kind of "sex perversion" and violent crime. The newspaper warned that "a dangerous murderer, robber, or sex pervert may be hiding out in your neighborhood in [the] guise of a respected citizen."[58]

Some articles and editorials in the *Sentinel* and the *Tribune* provide deeper insight into these newspapers' tendency to conflate violent crimes with consensual sexual relations. These articles referred to any sexual desires other than "normal" desires as "inconsistencies" or a "degeneracy" that needed to be eliminated. For example, an editorial in the June 7, 1951, edition of the *Sentinel* noted that "apart from an ineffective law requiring the registration of known sex offenders nothing has really been done to curb or wipe out sexual inconsistencies." Even though the killing of ten-year-old Patty Jean Hull had prompted the editorial, it did not focus simply on people who abused and murdered children. The editorial endorsed "special emotional treatment and orientation" for "all known and convicted sex offenders" so that they would be "reasonably normalized before release to society."[59]

Two articles published in the *Tribune* also contrasted "normality" with a wide range of "degenerate" behaviors. According to the September 18, 1953, issue of the *Tribune*, Dora Barbour claimed that her husband's "unspeakable degeneracy and corruption" had driven her to kill him. The article noted that the "paper-backed sex books" that Roscoe Barbour owned "substantiated, in part, Mrs. Barbour's claims that her husband was a degenerate." It also reported that Dora Barbour stated that her husband had "attempted to force her into intimacies with other men, usually whites, and that he and another man had once forced her from their home because they wanted to make love to each other."[60] The following week, the *Tribune* published a full-page article based largely on an interview with Dora Barbour. This article portrayed Dora Barbour as a "normal" person who was the victim of her husband's abnormality. "The root of their trouble was that Dora wanted a normal life. She was just a normal, maybe anemic, girl who wanted to live an ordinary life, loving her guy, if he'd let her." In contrast, Roscoe Barbour engaged in numerous "abnormal" behaviors: he "drank, smoked marihuana, sniffed 'coke' or heroin, and enjoyed both men and women sexually."[61]

A series of articles in the African American newspapers offered evidence that same-sex desire was connected to violent criminality. These articles depicted any persons who acted upon same-sex desires as unstable, prone to jealous rages, and violent. Of the approximately eighty articles that dealt with same-sex activity published in the *Eagle*, *Sentinel*, and *Tribune* between 1948 and 1957, one-third related to cases in which a person was accused of assaulting or killing a lover or partner. Many of these articles, like those about Ruth Foster's killing of Louise Ford, discussed above, emphasized the relationship between same-sex desire and jealousy. The June 18, 1949, issue of the *Tribune* included an article about Claude A. Rhone's killing of Rufus Smith. According to the article, the thirty-year-old Rhone had been in a "love affair" with the forty-one-year-old Smith. The *Tribune* noted that the police reported that Rhone had killed Smith "because Smith had threatened to leave him for infidelity."[62] On November 6, 1953, the *Tribune* reported that a "Westside laborer" who acknowledged his "sex deviation" had confessed that "he stabbed an East 6th St. man who had 'taken' his 'boyfriend.'"[63]

Even in cases in which "sex perversion" was only one possible motive for a crime, the newspapers stressed the connection between "sex perversion" and violent crime. In its May 6, 1950, issue, for example, the *Tribune* reported that a Los Angeles man suspected of killing a man with whom he had traveled from Arkansas to Arizona three months earlier may have been motivated by "sex perversion." Although law enforcement officers in Gila County, Arizona, where the body of twenty-four-year-old Thomas Stafford was found, also thought that robbery and jealousy may have been motives for the crime, the *Tribune* highlighted the "possible sex perversion motive."[64]

The articles in the African American newspapers that connected "abnormal" sexual desires and practices with violent crime suggest that hostility toward homosexuality did not primarily reflect a concern with civil rights. Instead these articles suggest that the antigay positions expressed in the newspapers reflected both a tendency within the larger society to view all types of "perversion" as related and widespread concerns about crime within the African American community.

"Why Disturb the Public Mind, the Community Decorum, with Publication of It?"

Depictions of same-sex desire and the people who acted upon that desire in the African American newspapers did not simply reflect a broader societal tendency to link together all "sexual inconsistencies" or African American concerns about crime. These depictions also reflected political divisions within the African American community. Two cases reveal how these political differences shaped the depiction of same-sex desire and behavior. In the first case, from 1953, the *Tribune* challenged powerful community leaders to become more fully committed to the identification and elimination of "perversion" in African American churches. Four years later, the newspapers gingerly reported on the case of a professional football player who was accused of molesting teenage boys. These articles imply that the man's position in the community and his performance of a masculine gender role prevented him from being labeled a "pervert."

In August 1953 police arrested the choir director of the Victory Baptist Church, at Forty-Eighth Street and McKinley Avenue in the Central Avenue district of Los Angeles, after a thirteen-year-old boy accused him of sodomy. The article about the arrest in the *Tribune* stated that juvenile authorities believed that the child "was at the 'crossroads' in his sexual development" and therefore "was prey to anyone he happened to admire." The article also noted that the child "is afraid that he is now pregnant."[65] Two weeks later, the *Tribune* reported that the district attorney had dropped the charges against the choir director after determining that there was insufficient evidence to support them. The district attorney also acknowledged that the child's "fantastic stories" about menstruation and the possibility that he might be pregnant made his charges suspect. The *Tribune* rejected the district attorney's explanation. Its articles instead offered the possibility that the child's stories "were the outcome of 'trauma' or shock, resulting from the alleged act of sodomy," and that the district attorney had dropped the charges because the minister of the church had exerted "heavy pressure" on him.[66]

The dismissal of the charges prompted *Tribune* editor Almena Lomax—the former Almena Davis noted above, whose surname was changed after marriage in 1949—to criticize not only Reverend Arthur Atlas Peters, the minister of the Victory Baptist Church, but also other ministers who had expressed support for Peters and the accused choir director.[67] Lomax ridiculed Reverend John L. Branham of St. Paul Baptist Church for offering prayers during his radio broadcast for Peters but not for the young accuser.[68] Yet another article about the case in the August 28, 1953, issue implied that Peters was more concerned with the accumulation of wealth through donations to his church than with the investigation and elimination of immorality. The *Tribune* reported that a group of women had asked Peters to remove the choir director from television broadcasts until the charges against him had been settled. The *Tribune* stated that Peters had defended the choir director and told the women that "we don't draw any lines against anyone in our church. . . . The church is for the sick. Freaks and all . . . if they want to come here and get a healing." The newspaper also noted that Peters told the women that the previous Sunday's collection had brought in more money than ever before—two thousand dollars.[69]

The *Tribune* also directly attacked Loren Miller, the attorney and publisher of the *California Eagle*, for missing "his cue as a crusader and defender of the underdog." In a long editorial, the *Tribune* accused Miller and the community's other newspaper, the *Sentinel*, of attempting to suppress the news of the accusations against the choir director. The *Tribune* further argued that Miller believed that an African American newspaper should only print articles that depict "the Negro in conflict with the white oppressor." The *Tribune* blamed Miller for treating certain incidents within the community exactly as white people did. When an African American laid a charge of wrongdoing against another African American,

"Mr. Miller takes the same attitude that the white official takes—it is trivial, of no consequence . . . so why disturb the public mind, the community decorum, with publication of it?" The *Tribune* editorial defended the editor's decision to publish articles about the accusations. The *Tribune* insisted that it would have published the story if it had involved "some less prominently connected individual, . . . and there was no reason to exempt this one."[70] As these articles and editorials in the *Tribune* make clear, Almena Lomax and her staff questioned whether the most powerful members of the African American community were as committed as the *Tribune* was to the crusade against sexual crimes.

Another article in the *Tribune* about this case, however, also suggested that for the first time the newspapers had begun to separate same-sex desire that was expressed in consensual activity involving adults from other forms of "sexual deviation." Whereas previous articles and editorials had not drawn a clear distinction between consensual same-sex activity and any other criminalized sex act, this one suggested that homosexuals were not a threat to children. The article, published on August 28, 1953, included an "interesting observation by a psychologist, who asked to remain anonymous." The psychologist expressed the opinion that "a crime such as is alleged here would stamp the person committing it as not so much a homosexual as a 'psychopath' . . . the most dangerous type of sexual deviate." The psychologist further explained what made someone a "psychopath": "Anyone in any sex act . . . who ignores all normal considerations and heeds only the satisfaction of his lust, as in rape, is beyond mere sexual deviation, and is psychopathic, hence dangerous."[71] In these statements, the psychologist clearly implied that homosexuals were not simply motivated by "the satisfaction of their lust" and that homosexuality itself was not psychopathic, and the *Tribune* in reprinting this opinion did not disagree.

Politics within the African American community in Los Angeles also clearly influenced the newspaper coverage of the 1957 arrest and trial of Rommie Loudd, a former all-American football star at UCLA. Loudd was one of three men who ended up standing trial on charges of molesting three boys. The boys, ages twelve, thirteen, and fifteen, were wearing wigs and women's clothing when they were picked up on the street by a man who took them to the apartment where they encountered Loudd and four other men. Loudd's attorney was Loren Miller, the publisher of the *Eagle*. Articles in the *Eagle* depicted Loudd as a "normal" man who was not guilty of child molestation. The initial report of Loudd's arrest in the *Eagle*, for example, reported on the charges but also included several paragraphs of a statement in which Loudd denied his guilt by explaining what had happened in the apartment. According to the *Eagle*, Loudd decided to teach the boys a lesson by forcing all of the men and boys in the apartment to remove their clothing. "We all undressed down to our shorts and just to teach them a real lesson, I made them undress, too, all the way," Loudd said. "After this I lectured them and told them to get dressed. After that I told the kids to go on home." In addition to offering Loudd the opportunity to defend himself, the *Eagle* also emphasized Loudd's normality by observing that he was married and that his wife was expecting a baby. The newspaper's front page included a photograph of Mrs. Loudd.[72]

The depiction of Loudd as "normal" contrasted dramatically with the newspaper's depiction of the boys who had accused Loudd and Kelly of molesting them. The *Eagle* noted that the "obviously effeminate boys" "told conflicting stories of what happened" in the apartment where they encountered Loudd and Kelly. The newspaper never explicitly described the sexual contact between the men and the boys, and it pointed out that "all agreed that Loudd gave them a stern lecture on masquerading as girls and told them that they would wind up in serious trouble if they continued that course of conduct."[73] Articles in the *Sentinel* did not conclude that Loudd was innocent or discredit the boys, but they did suggest that Loudd was "normal." One article, for example, noted that a psychiatric examination "failed to show that" Loudd "was a sex psychopath." The same article was accompanied by a photograph of Loudd with his wife, Carrie.[74]

In contrast, the *Tribune* placed greater emphasis on the statements of the young victims than on Loudd's denial and thereby raised questions about his "normality." The *Tribune* portrayed the charges against Loudd and the other defendants as "practically unprintable accusations of brutality and lust." The *Tribune* characterized what allegedly occurred in the apartment as an "orgy" and as "acts of sodomy and other perversion." The newspaper also reported that all of the people present in the apartment identified Loudd as the "'ringleader' in the asserted crimes against the boys." In the final paragraph of the article about the charges, the *Tribune* noted that Loudd was married but added that he "had sent his wife off to the movies."[75] Although the *Tribune* did not label Loudd a pervert, it did not join the *Sentinel* and the *Eagle* in their efforts to depict Loudd as "normal" and innocent of the charges.

Loudd was eventually found guilty on two charges of child molestation. The *Sentinel* implied that Loudd's crimes were not serious by emphasizing the lightness of the sentence. Loudd was sentenced to six months in jail and five years of probation.[76] The treatment of the Loudd case in the *Sentinel* and the

Eagle suggests that a person's standing in the community and his conformity to community standards of masculine gender expression could shield him from the kinds of attacks leveled at others accused of the same actions. Because Loudd was unquestionably masculine—a football star—and had a wife, he was not labeled a "pervert," even though he was found guilty of acts that the newspapers had previously described as "perverted" or "degenerate." Also, the difference between the *Tribune*'s coverage of the charges against the choir director in 1953 and its coverage of the charges against Loudd in 1957 suggests that a change had begun to occur. The *Tribune* did not criticize Loren Miller in 1957, nor did it depict Loudd's actions as symptomatic of a larger social problem. Some of this difference undoubtedly was due to Loudd's standing in the community. However, it might also signal that the concern about sex crimes had begun to abate by the late 1950s.

"The Growing Influence of Abnormal Sex Practices"

In his study of the relationship between the civil rights movement and black sexuality, Thaddeus Russell argues that the campaign against working-class tolerance of a wide range of sexual behaviors began in 1951, when *Ebony* published an article by Adam Clayton Powell, Jr., the U.S. representative who was also the pastor of the Abyssinian Baptist Church in New York City's Harlem neighborhood, attacking "the growing influence of abnormal sex practices" among young African Americans.[77] Evidence from Los Angeles, however, indicates that the editors and publishers of Los Angeles's African American newspapers never tolerated the expressions of same-sex desire that their counterparts in some other cities did. Moreover, editors of popular newspapers in Los Angeles had condemned both the public displays of same-sex desire and African Americans' tolerance of homosexuality since 1947, four years before Powell's article appeared in *Ebony*. Some articles in the African American newspapers depicted homosexuals as "defective" people who were incapable of stable, "normal" relationships, and many articles linked any expression of same-sex desire, even that involving consenting adults, with rape, child molestation, and murder. However, class and political divisions in the community protected some prominent African Americans when they were accused of engaging in acts of "perversion."

Even in the 1950s, as homophile organizations emerged and began to question the prevailing medical and legal opinions about same-sex desire, the African American newspapers in Los Angeles resolutely defended these older opinions. Reporters and editors of the metropolitan daily newspapers continued to characterize homosexuality as an illness, although they also duly reported on changes in medical and legal thought. For example, several columns published in the *Los Angeles Times* in the 1950s assured readers that transvestites and homosexuals were not a threat to "normal" boys. Dr. Walter C. Alvarez, a physician-consultant at the Mayo Clinic, described laws governing cross-dressing and same-sex behavior as "stupid and cruel and unjust." Alvarez doubted "if transvestites ever bother boys" and "if homosexuals often bother normal boys." Instead, the doctor wrote, "homosexuals, when they do want to have experience with a boy, choose one whom they recognize as either definitely one of them or inclined that way."[78] A 1958 article in the *Times* also mentioned the Wolfenden Report in the United Kingdom, which had recommended the decriminalization of same-sex acts involving consenting adults.[79] Only one article in the African American newspapers—a column by a physician published in the *Tribune* in 1953—challenged stereotypes about homosexuality.[80] The remaining seventy-nine articles that dealt with same-sex desire or behavior depicted homosexuality as abnormal and undesirable, and they criticized or ridiculed homosexuals.

It is impossible to know exactly how African Americans responded to the negative depictions of same-sex desire in these weekly newspapers. The messages that these newspapers sent about same-sex desire, however, were unambiguous and clearly told their readers, especially middle-class African Americans and those who aspired to middle-class status, that same-sex desire could not be tolerated. The newspapers also informed their readers that even people who associated with "known homosexuals" could and should be punished. In a September 19, 1952, report of a raid on a "homo hang-out," for example, the *Tribune* noted that the police had arrested twenty-six men, including a seventeen-year-old student, and one woman "for associating with known perverts and homos," public drunkenness, and the illegal sale of alcoholic beverages. As at other times, the *Tribune* published the names and, for some, their addresses and occupations.[81] The newspapers' continued negative depictions of same-sex desire had profound effects on the African American community, leading many LGBT people to hide their feelings and actions and allowing heterosexuals to ignore important changes in the larger society.

Notes

1. "Strange Affair Ends in Murder," *California Eagle*, May 27, 1948.
2. "Ruth Foster 'Mentally Deficient,' Says Attorney; to Plead Her 'Not Guilty,'" *Los Angeles Tribune*, May 29, 1948.
3. "Score Light Penalty for 'Odd Love' Killer," *Los Angeles Sentinel*, July 15, 1948.
4. Gay men who had served in the military formed the Veterans Benevolent Association in 1945. The organization sponsored parties and dances, some of which attracted

hundreds of gay men. See John D'Emilio, *Sexual Politics, Sexual Communities: The Making of a Homosexual Minority in the United States, 1940–1970*, 2nd ed. (Chicago: University of Chicago Press, 1998), 24–32.

5. Allan Bérubé, *Coming Out under Fire: The History of Gay Men and Women in World War Two* (New York: Free Press, 1990), 109–23. For a brief discussion of the impact of World War II on homosexuality in Washington, D.C., see David K. Johnson, *The Lavender Scare: The Cold War Persecution of Gays and Lesbians in the Federal Government* (Chicago: University of Chicago Press, 2004), 51–53.

6. Daniel Hurewitz, *Bohemian Los Angeles and the Making of Modern Politics* (Berkeley: University of California Press, 2007), 233–34.

7. D'Emilio, *Sexual Politics, Sexual Communities*, 40–53.

8. Johnson, *Lavender Scare*, 56–63.

9. Hurewitz, *Bohemian Los Angeles*, 117, 232, 235–36. See also Lillian Faderman and Stuart Timmons, *Gay L.A.: A History of Sexual Outlaws, Power Politics, and Lipstick Lesbians* (New York: Basic Books, 2006), 71–103. For additional information about the "sexual psychopath" laws, see Estelle B. Freedman, "'Uncontrolled Desires': The Response to the Sexual Psychopath, 1920–1960," *Journal of American History* 74, no. 1 (1987): 83–106; Stephen Robertson, "Separating the Men from the Boys: Masculinity, Psychosexual Development, and Sex Crime in the United States, 1930s–1960s," *Journal of the History of Medicine and Allied Sciences* 56, no. 1 (2001): 3–35; Neil Miller, *Sex-Crime Panic: A Journey to the Paranoid Heart of the 1950s* (Los Angeles: Alyson, 2002), 76–89.

10. Whitney Strub, "The Clearly Obscene and the Queerly Obscene: Heteronormativity and Obscenity in Cold War Los Angeles," *American Quarterly* 60, no. 2 (2008): 373–98.

11. D'Emilio, *Sexual Politics, Sexual Communities*, 32.

12. Bérubé, *Coming Out under Fire*, 116.

13. See Hurewitz, *Bohemian Los Angeles*, 217–28.

14. Strub, "Clearly Obscene," 377.

15. A small number of historians have examined African American sexuality, but most have focused on the period before World War II, and most have focused on reproductive sexuality. See, for example, Mary Frances Berry, "Judging Morality: Sexual Behavior and Legal Consequences in the Late Nineteenth-Century South," *Journal of American History* 78, no. 3 (1991): 835–56; Christina Simmons, "African Americans and Sexual Victorianism in the Social Hygiene Movement, 1910–1940," *Journal of the History of Sexuality* 4, no. 1 (1993): 51–75; Kevin J. Mumford, *Interzones: Black/White Sex Districts in Chicago and New York in the Early Twentieth Century* (New York: Columbia University Press, 1997); Martha Hodes, *White Women, Black Men: Illicit Sex in the Nineteenth-Century South* (New Haven: Yale University Press, 1999); Christina Simmons, "Modern Marriage for African Americans, 1920–1940," *Canadian Review of American Studies* 30, no. 3 (2000): 273–300.

16. Thaddeus Russell, "The Color of Discipline: Civil Rights and Black Sexuality," *American Quarterly* 60, no. 1 (2008): 103, 105–7, 111, 112. See also Tim Retzloff, "Seer

or Queer? Postwar Fascination with Detroit's Prophet Jones," *GLQ: A Journal of Lesbian and Gay Studies* 8, no. 3 (2002): 271–96.

17. Russell, "Color of Discipline," 103, 113, 121–22, 114.

18. Population figures are taken from tables available from the U.S. Bureau of the Census. See, for example, table 21, "Characteristics of the Population, for Standard Metropolitan Statistical Areas, Urbanized Areas, and Urban Places of 10,000 or More: 1960," in *Census of Population: 1960 California—Volume I Part 6*, http://www2.census.gov/prod2/decennial/documents/12533879v1p6ch03.pdf. See also Josh Sides, *L.A. City Limits: African American Los Angeles from the Great Depression to the Present* (Berkeley: University of California Press, 2003), 36–56.

19. For a discussion of the history of the *California Eagle*, see Douglas Flamming, *Bound for Freedom: Black Los Angeles in Jim Crow America* (Berkeley: University of California Press, 2005), esp. 26–34.

20. Circulation figures come from *N. W. Ayer and Son's Directory: Newspapers and Periodicals* (Philadelphia: N. W. Ayer, 1949), 90, 94–95; *N. W. Ayer and Son's Directory: Newspapers and Periodicals* (Philadelphia: N. W. Ayer, 1954), 91, 96–97. Scholars have for many years accepted that the actual number of readers was significantly higher than the circulation of most African Americans newspapers, since multiple readers perused each copy of the paper. See Patrick S. Washburn, *The African American Newspaper: Voice of Freedom* (Evanston, Ill.: Northwestern University Press, 2006), 6.

21. *Ayer and Son's Directory* (1949), 90, 94–95; *Ayer and Son's Directory* (1954), 91, 96–97. For the six-month subscription rate for the *Sentinel*, see the newspaper's masthead, *Los Angeles Sentinel*, January 30, 1947. The ten-cent single-issue price is printed on the front page of the newspaper. The *Eagle*'s six-month subscription rate in 1947 was $2.25. See the newspaper's masthead, *California Eagle*, March 20, 1947, 2. For subscription rates for the *Tribune*, see *Los Angeles Tribune*, December 22, 1951, and March 7, 1952.

22. Leonard Broom and Shirley Reece, "Political and Racial Interest: A Study in Content Analysis," *Public Opinion Quarterly* 19, no. 1 (1955): 11.

23. For a discussion of the demise of African American newspapers, see Washburn, *African American Newspaper*, 179–96.

24. See, for example, D'Emilio, *Sexual Politics, Sexual Communities*, 10–13, 23–33; George Chauncey, *Gay New York: Gender, Urban Culture, and the Making of the Gay Male World* (New York: Basic Books, 1994), 131–36. For a critique of this interpretation, see John Howard, *Men like That: A Southern Queer History* (Chicago: University of Chicago Press, 1999), esp. 11–15.

25. "Collins to Stage Fashion Parade at Elks Temple," *Los Angeles Sentinel*, December 20, 1934.

26. "Manager Announces Drag Ball Will Be Held at Club Araby on Friday Night," *Los Angeles Sentinel*, July 11, 1935.

27. Copies of the *Sentinel* from 1941 to 1945 have not survived.

28. Advertisement for Club Alabam, *California Eagle*, October 25, 1945.

29. "'Drag' Ball at Alabam Tonight," *Los Angeles Sentinel*, October 31, 1946.

30. "Hitting the Nite Spots," *Los Angeles Sentinel*, October 30, 1947.

31. Hazel L. Lamarre, "All the World's a Stage," *Los Angeles Sentinel*, October 30, 1952.

32. "Hitting the Nite Spots," *Los Angeles Sentinel*, November 6, 1947.

33. Leon Washington Jr., "Wash's Wash," *Los Angeles Sentinel*, April 15, 1948.

34. Almena Davis, "How 'bout This . . . ?" *Los Angeles Tribune*, October 23, 1948.

35. Ibid.

36. Ibid.

37. Letter to the editor, *Los Angeles Sentinel*, January 30, 1947.

38. Short's body had been mutilated and sawed in half before it was dumped in a vacant lot. For a scholarly discussion of the "Black Dahlia" case, see Theodore Hamm, "Fragments of Postwar Los Angeles: The Black Dahlia in Fact and Fiction," *Antipode* 28, no. 1 (1996): 24–41.

39. Freedman, "Uncontrolled Desires," 84; Miller, *Sex-Crime Panic*, 76–89; Johnson, *Lavender Scare*, 55–63.

40. See Miller, *Sex-Crime Panic*, 93–138.

41. George Chauncey Jr., "The Postwar Sex Crime Panic," in *True Stories from the American Past*, ed. William Graebner (New York: McGraw-Hill, 1993), 170.

42. Hurewitz, *Bohemian Los Angeles*, 117, 121, 140.

43. "Three Children Feared Kidnapped; Hundreds of Police Join Hunt," *Los Angeles Times*, June 28, 1937.

44. "Three Girls Found Slain in Hills; Felon Hunted in Fiendish Crime," *Los Angeles Times*, June 29, 1937; "Grim Search Climax Told," *Los Angeles Times*, June 29, 1937; "Davis Returns to Assist Great Man Hunt for Killer," *Los Angeles Times*, June 29, 1937. Later articles that referred to the slayer as a "degenerate" include "Aid Authorities Hunt for Slayer of Girls," *Los Angeles Times*, June 30, 1937; "Inglewood P.T.A. Demands Protection in Centinela Park," *Los Angeles Times*, June 30, 1937; "Girl Relates Slayer's Visits," *Los Angeles Times*, July 1, 1937.

45. "Dyer, Cringing in Fear, May Deny Confession," *Los Angeles Times*, July 10, 1937.

46. "Police Commission Hears about New 'B-Girl' Racket," *Los Angeles Times*, January 10, 1940. For a discussion of the impact of this restriction on Julian Eltinge, a celebrated female impersonator living in Los Angeles, see Hurewitz, *Bohemian Los Angeles*, 146–49.

47. "Hollywood Vice Charged," *Los Angeles Times*, January 31, 1945.

48. "Some Hollywood Night Spots Draw Fire at Morals Hearing," *Los Angeles Times*, January 15, 1948.

49. "Council Urges Stricter Laws on Sex Offenders," *Los Angeles Times*, November 17, 1949.

50. "Women Victims of Sex Fiend," *Los Angeles Sentinel*, January 4, 1940.

51. Editorial, *Los Angeles Sentinel*, April 25, 1940.

52. "Woman Held Captive in Two-Day Sex Orgy," *Los Angeles Sentinel*, April 13, 1950.

53. "Trial Set for Charged Pervert," *Los Angeles Sentinel*, June 28, 1951.

54. "Westside Cops Search for 2 Sex Perverts," *Los Angeles Sentinel*, June 5, 1952.

55. "Hairdresser Eadward Starts 'em Talking about More than Hair Styles This Time," *Los Angeles Tribune*, August 27, 1949.

56. J. T. Gipson, *Los Angeles Sentinel*, April 6, 1950.

57. "Boy Admits Soliciting Perverted Act," *Los Angeles Tribune*, June 3, 1950.

58. "Wanted," *Los Angeles Sentinel*, October 5, 1950.

59. "Sex Criminals Need Treatment," *Los Angeles Sentinel*, June 7, 1951.

60. "Wife Says Brutality, Sexual Exhibition of Mate Cost Her Self-Respect," *Los Angeles Tribune*, September 18, 1953.

61. Almena Lomax, "Mate Took His Pleasures Where He Found Them, Says Barbour Killer in Story of Life with Husband, Described as 'Degenerate,'" *Los Angeles Tribune*, September 25, 1953.

62. "Rhone Trial to Bare Eastside Men's Love Life," *Los Angeles Tribune*, June 18, 1949.

63. "Sex Deviate Admits Cutting over Man," *Los Angeles Tribune*, November 6, 1953.

64. "Possible Sex Perversion Motive in Desert Slaying," *Los Angeles Tribune*, May 6, 1950.

65. "Choir Leader Took Advantage of Boy's Admiration to Seduce Him, Says Mother," *Los Angeles Tribune*, August 21, 1953. See also "Charges of Boy, 13, Jail Church Choir-master," *Los Angeles Tribune*, August 21, 1953.

66. "No 'Corroborative' Evidence of Child's Charges, Says D.A.," *Los Angeles Tribune*, August 28, 1953. See also "Frazier Freed! D.A. Refuses to Issue Complaint," *Los Angeles Tribune*, August 28, 1953.

67. See "Tribune Readers Rationed This Week; Here's Why," *Los Angeles Tribune*, July 10, 1948.

68. Almena Lomax, "Ministers Pray for Each Other, but None for Lonely Accuser, Observing Birthday in Juvenile Hall," *Los Angeles Tribune*, August 28, 1953.

69. "Rev. Peters Denies Appeal by Women to Remove Frazier from Television," *Los Angeles Tribune*, August 28, 1953.

70. "Loren Miller Misses Cue as Defender of Underdog," *Los Angeles Tribune*, September 4, 1953.

71. "'Queens' along 'Street of Dreams' Have Indignation Meeting," *Los Angeles Tribune*, August 28, 1953.

72. "Loudd Denies Sex Charge," *California Eagle*, April 4, 1957; "Ex-UCLA Grid Star in Sex Raid," *Los Angeles Sentinel*, April 4, 1957.

73. "Sex Trial Set for Grid Stars," *California Eagle*, April 18, 1957.

74. "Rommie Lee Loudd Found Guilty," *Los Angeles Sentinel*, July 4, 1957.

75. "UCLA All-American Jailed with Four for Child Molesting," *Los Angeles Tribune*, April 3, 1957. Two other articles in the *Tribune* largely echoed what was reported in the April 3 article. See "Loudd, Two Others Face Trial on Boy Charges," *Los Angeles Tribune*, April 10, 1957; "Loudd Case Testimony 'Rank'; Athlete Held," *Los Angeles Tribune*, April 24, 1957.

76. "Loudd Draws Six-Month Jail Term," *Los Angeles Sentinel*, August 29, 1957. Also see "Rommie Loudd, 64, Pro Football Coach," *New York Times*, May 18, 1998; "Jury Convicts Rommie Loudd," *Los Angeles Times*, November 22, 1975; "Loudd Paroled after Serving 3 Years in Florida Drug Case," *Los Angeles Times*, September 23, 1978.

77. Russell, "Color of Discipline," 112. Powell may have appeared to Leon Washington Jr. and Almena Lomax to be a latecomer to a campaign that they had been waging for several years. Nonetheless, Washington and Lomax publicized Powell's article. The *Tribune* published what appears to be a press release about the article in its October 13, 1951, issue. The *Sentinel* published exactly the same release in its October 25, 1951 issue. See "Powell Blasts Sex Degenerates in Negro Church in Ebony Article," *Los Angeles Tribune*, October 13, 1951; "Powell Blasts Sex Degenerates in Church in Magazine Article," *Los Angeles Sentinel*, October 25, 1951. See also "Sex in the Church," *Ebony*, November 1951, 27–34; Retzloff, "Seer or Queer?"

78. Walter C. Alvarez, "Dr. Alvarez Says: Nature Sometimes Mixes Up Sex at Birth," *Los Angeles Times*, March 21, 1955. See also Walter C. Alvarez, "Dr. Alvarez Says: Transvestites Cause of Parents' Distress," *Los Angeles Times*, July 4, 1956; Walter C. Alvarez, "Dr. Alvarez Says: Transvestites Called Harmless to Society," *Los Angeles Times*, January 30, 1957.

79. Howard Whitman, "Crisis in Morals: Spotlight Hits Dark Areas of Sex," *Los Angeles Times*, May 30, 1958.

80. Milton E. Stein, "Stein Says Homosexuality Much Discussed, Little Understood," *Los Angeles Tribune*, August 21, 1953.

81. "Police Bag 26 in Raid on Homosexual Hangout," *Los Angeles Tribune*, September 19, 1952. Probably addresses and occupations were published whenever known.

12 "Something 2 Dance 2"

Electro-hop in 1980s Los Angeles and Its Afrofuturist Link

Gabriela Jiménez

DJs, rappers, music producers, engineers, dancers, visual artists, radio personalities, listeners, music promoters, and entrepreneurs formed the Los Angeles hip-hop scene in the early 1980s.[1] Marked by a city's dynamism and diversity, Los Angeles–based hip-hop is one of many black expressive cultural practices that have been and continue to be fundamental to the metropolis's musical production.[2] Like jazz of the Golden Era (1920–29), the gospel innovations of the 1960s, and the soul explorations of the 1960s and early 1970s, electro-hop substantiates the ways in which musical innovation in black Los Angeles not only contributes to but also constitutes American culture. Electro-hop, or techno-hop, was an electronic music and dance practice produced almost exclusively in Los Angeles during the 1980s. Given the relatively short popular existence of electro-hop, roughly from 1983 to 1988, its practitioners assembled a formative scene that included an impressive list of artists, recordings, independent record labels, and widely attended events hosted at high schools, nightclubs, skating rinks, sports arenas, and coliseums. Furthermore, electro-hop's notoriety played a formidable role in the restructuring of radio station KDAY-1580 AM in Los Angeles.

As with hip-hop on the East Coast, electro-hop was produced, performed, and enjoyed primarily by young people of color who were also marginalized— though, in both cases, young black, Latino, and Afro-Latino males figured most prominently. Unlike East Coast hip-hop, which experienced much national attention through the 1980s, electro-hop remained largely a regional musical practice—even when groups like the L.A. Dream Team recorded and released studio albums with major record companies such as MCA. Whereas East Coast hip-hop producers sampled initially and primarily disco, funk, and soul, electro-hop practitioners focused mostly on producing their own beats with minimal use of sampling. And, just as hip-hop took the shape of a multifaceted scene in mid-1970s New York—composed of four elements: DJing, MCing/rapping, break dancing, and graffiti writing—electro-hop too involved derivations of similar expressive cultural practices.

As gangsta rap's direct precursor, electro-hop lacks visibility and audibility in formal academic literature and popular music histories at large. Celebrated accounts on hip-hop, for example, mention electro-hop in passing, if at all, when discussing gangsta rap.[3] The Los Angeles electro-hop scene demands consideration.

Most accessible information on electro-hop comes from producers and participants themselves as well as from dedicated fans. Some influential electro-hoppers like Egyptian Lover and Arabian Prince continue to produce, DJ, and/ or perform electronic dance music, thereby expanding upon the music they produced in the 1980s. Electro-hop practitioners take advantage of the Internet and use social media—formerly MySpace and now Facebook, SoundCloud, and YouTube—to share music, videos, memories, and other information. Electro-hop fans too, in both the United States and Europe, dedicate time and resources to the dissemination and collection of information by way of the Internet. Loyal fans have especially turned to Web forums and self-made websites to remember and memorialize electro-hop.

Electro-hop fans include Europeans, most often Germans. It is two Europeans—Sandro De Gaetani and Stefan Schütze—who were responsible for one of the most comprehensive and detailed sources on electro-hop, the website West Coast Pioneers.[4] This highly informative website includes many primary and secondary sources (interviews, information on recordings and independent record labels, photographs, biographies, and links to useful articles, videos, and other websites). What is more, West Coast Pioneers demonstrates just how American popular culture, vis-à-vis hip-hoppers' early fascination with German electronic group Kraftwerk, the U.S. military presence in post–World War II Europe, and what Moritz Ege has called Afro-Americanophilia in Germany, informs and is informed by local, national, global, and virtual processes.[5]

As a versatile scene grounded in expressive cultural practices, electro-hop is a product of the physical and discursive spaces of 1980s black, and to a lesser extent Latino, Los Angeles. From high school gyms to skating rinks to nightclubs, electro-hop was produced, performed, and practiced around South Central Los Angeles, the West Side (Venice and Santa Monica), and parts of the San Fernando Valley. Electro-hop, as I demonstrate, was a dynamic scene integral to Los Angeles musical history. Moreover, electro-hoppers used music, dance, and visuals to engage socially, collectively, and publicly with black L.A.'s pasts, presents, and futures. Electro-hop, in other words, was an Afrofuturist musical scene wherein Afro-diasporic lived experiences and mass representations underwent epistemological alterations vis-à-vis tropes rooted in and routed by technology, water, and outer and cyber space: "Afrofuturism . . . is concerned with the possibilities for intervention within the dimension of the predictive, the projected, the proleptic, the envisioned, the virtual, the anticipatory and the future conditional."[6] Furthermore and according to Alondra Nelson quoting Mark Dery, "Afrofuturism can be broadly defined as 'African American voices' with 'other stories to tell about culture, technology and things to come.'"[7]

An Electro-hop Overview

Electro-hop as a musical sound began in Los Angeles roughly in 1983–84, and as the decade materialized, young adults fostered a multidimensional scene involving dance, visual arts, fashion, and a range of performance venues. Producers, DJs, and rappers recorded and released music via newly founded independent record labels whose local popularity in large part influenced KDAY's transformation into the first all–hip-hop radio station, and whose leverage on the streets of Los Angeles attracted major record companies (e.g., MCA and Epic) toward the end of the 1980s. Pinpointing the exact moment something commences is problematic; nevertheless, the production, recording, pressing, release, and popularity of Uncle Jamm's Army's song "Dial-a-Freak" is a reliable, if incomplete, starting point in electro-hop history.

A collective of mobile DJs, Uncle Jamm's Army released "Dial-a-Freak" in 1984. This is not necessarily the first electro-hop song or the first recording of hip-hop music on the West Coast—most hip-hop historians point to 1981's "The Gigolo Groove" by Captain Crunch & the Funky Bunch and Disco Daddy and Captain Rapp's "Gigolo Rapp" as the first hip-hop songs on the West Coast—but its musical characteristics and popularity contextualize electro-hop in early-1980s Los Angeles. Released on Uncle Jamm's Army's imprint, Freak Beat Records, "Dial-a-Freak" exemplifies electro-hop's musical aesthetics.[8] The track demonstrates electro-hop's reliance on electrophones, which points to how the influence

Uncle Jamm's Army, circa 1982. *Top row*: Razor Sharp, Mr. Prinze (Rodger Clayton), Lester, Troy, Muffla, Mr. No Good, Egyptian Lover. *Bottom row*: Tomcat, Gid Martin, Bobcat. *Courtesy Egyptian Lover.*

of the German group Kraftwerk and other electro funk musicians (namely Afrika Bambaataa and the Soul Sonic Force, Cybotron, Twilight 22, Jonzen Crew, Man Parrish, and Newcleus) galvanized the scene.[9] Music producers used drum machines like the Roland TR-808, Oberheim DMX, E-mu SP-1200, Linn LM-1, and Akai MPC 60C in combination with synthesizers like Roland Jupiter-8 and Moog, turntables, and vocoders to manipulate the voice.[10] In "Dial-a-Freak" we hear drum machines, synthesizers, and vocoder. The song's fast tempo, prominence of the bass, and emphasis on repetitive motifs indicate electro-hop's role as dance music first and foremost.[11]

Lyrical content and delivery allude to the primacy of dance beats over vocal dexterity. Various recordings pronounce more interest in musical sounds, inclusive of vocal manipulation, than in lyrics. Raps in electro-hop tend to showcase minimal preference for complex rhyming patterns and, for the most part, make small use of literary devices (metaphors, alliteration, similes, etc.): "Here I am mind so blue / Freaks on my mind don't know what to do" or "Here we are under the stars at Venice Beach / You be the student in the class and I will teach." Prevalent in "Dial-A-Freak" are also electro-hop's major lyrical themes: technology ("I got an eight-way phone so I can call my freaks"), virility ("Should I sit here? / Or should I call up a freak to drive me up the wall"), dance ("Just ain't nobody like me / I'll make you break freaking ET"), eccentricity ("I'm so sexy, I'm so unique"), and Afrocentricity ("In pyramids, on the Nile / I ride my camels in the sand with style").[12]

Other representative songs include Unknown DJ's "808 Beats," an ode to his dexterity on the Roland TR-808 ("The music is devastating, it was easy to create / cause I am the master of the 808"); Arabian Prince's "Strange Life," which promotes uniqueness ("The end is not near so don't scream and shout / live a strange life until your time runs out); Egyptian Lover's "Egypt, Egypt," an example of Afrocentricity ("Egypt is the place to be"); the World Class Wreckin' Cru's "Cabbage Patch," which deals with dancing ("Here's a new dance that can't be matched / so just step to the floor and do the cabbage patch"); and "Freak-a-Holic" by Egyptian Lover (1987), which foregrounds virility ("All of my life I've been a freak / doing what I want seven days a week").[13] These topics appear throughout most electro-hop recordings.

Electro-hop artists were part of mobile DJ crews modeled on those of the 1970s, as discussed below, or solo artists or both. DJ crews like Uncle Jamm's Army began producing, recording, and selling their own music. They combined their knowledge of what people preferred to dance to and added rapping to it. Taking additional cues from the burgeoning East Coast hip-hop scenes and markets, DJ collectives and affiliated practitioners created their own musical practice: electro-hop. As such, Los Angeles–based hip-hop is a product of the 1970s mobile disco scene. It was in these DJ collectives where some of electro-hop's most influential figures got their start. For example, Uncle Jamm's Army enlisted Egyptian Lover, Arabian Prince, Kid Frost, Silky D, DJ Bobcat, and Chris "The Glove" Taylor, among others. Other collectives recording their own music and consisting of prominent electro-hop practitioners, some of whom also released solo projects, included the World Class Wreckin' Cru, the L.A. Dream Team, the Knights of the Turntables, Electrobeat Crew, Dark Star, and Bobby Jimmy and Critters.

Women also contributed to electro-hop. The exception rather than the rule, Silky D and Mona Lisa Young were respected DJs. In 1987, JJ Fad released their song "Supersonic" on Dream Team Records. The song served as the first single for their eponymous debut album in 1988. Approximately nineteen years later, the famous hip-hop producer and rapper will.i.am sampled the song for Fergie's

"Fergilicious" (2006), bringing electro-hop to the mind of contemporary hip-hop fans. The Mistress and DJ Madame E produced two singles, "I Got Your Wild Thang" (1989) and "Mic Jack" (1989), and one album, *Leather and Lace* (1989), on Techno Kut Records.[14]

Part of the 1970s mobile disco scene, electro-hop's audiences were those who attended DJ crews' events at house parties, high schools, skating rinks, clubs, sports arenas, and coliseums. They were young people of color from the city's socioeconomically segregated areas—South Central, Watts, parts of the West Side, and the San Fernando Valley. These thirteen- to twenty-one-year-olds attended skating rinks and clubs where electro-hop could be heard and danced to through the 1980s.[15] While gang members frequented electro-hop events, gang culture—as celebrated and imagined accounts of Los Angeles-based hip-hop project—was a peripheral rather than exclusive force in the scene's formation.[16] In the 1983 TV documentary *Breaking and Entering*, for example, electro-hopper Ice T states that those who did not wish to participate in gangs were often electro-hop's primary participants—DJs, producers, rappers, dancers, and audiences.[17]

As *Breaking and Entering* and photographs of the time and practitioners also reveal, fashion was central to the electro-hop scene. Tracksuits dominated for practical reasons; it is easier to dance in them. Equally prevalent was the by-then classic teenager outfit of jeans and T-shirts. Some electro-hop practitioners took more eccentric routes by wearing, for example, doctor costumes or dressing in Egyptian gear, or what they imagined that looked like.[18] Photographs reveal Prince's influence on electro-hop style as a means to comment on and alter extant notions of black, heteronormative masculinity.

Facilitating the production and circulation of electro-hop was the creation of independent label imprints established by DJs, producers, rappers, and other entrepreneurs. West Coast Pioneers has a detailed list of independent labels that released electro-hop music exclusively or as part of a wider catalog. Dream Team Records, Egyptian Empire Records, Electrobeat Records, Freak Beat Records, JDC Records, K.M.A. Records, Kru-Cut Records, On the Spot Records, Players Only Records, Rappers Rapp Disco Co., Rapsur Records, Saturn Records, Street Talk Records, Techno Hop Records, Techno Kut Records, and Macola Records are some of the most noteworthy labels.[19]

Founded in 1984 by Don McMillan and located then at 6209 Santa Monica Boulevard in Hollywood, Macola pressed records for anyone willing to pay the rate of $1,000 for five hundred copies, akin to Disc Makers.[20] This enabled electro-hop practitioners to sell their recorded products for profit at swap meets and similar venues.[21] Macola got rid of its open-door policy when people at the company realized it was more profitable to sign artists than to merely provide duplication services.[22] Although vinyl pressings may not indicate it on the label, a large majority of electro-hop recordings were pressed at Macola. The record and pressing company served as one channel for the circulation of electro-hop; it was KDAY that popularized the music via radio airwaves.

KDAY-AM 1580 played hip-hop music from the East Coast as well as music produced by local electro-hop artists; thus, the radio station contributed to hip-hop's visibility and audibility across Los Angeles. By 1983, when electro-hop experienced an upsurge in production, KDAY was an established urban contemporary radio station playing black popular music, meaning rhythm and blues, soul, and funk.[23] KDAY changed formats in 1984 when it became "the first radio station to have an all-rap format," and it remained the only all-rap station until it went off the air March 11, 1991.[24] Greg Mack, who was offered a job as an on-air personality at KDAY in 1983 while working at a radio station in Houston, Texas, was pivotal to KDAY's programming shift. After his relocation, he lived in South Central Los Angeles, where he became interested in the music that was popular among local youth. His conscious attempts (and business acumen) to play what resonated locally and KDAY's willingness to give local musicians airtime accorded electro-hop another medium for its circulation. KDAY's relationship with electro-hop practitioners also led to Mack's creation of the Mix Masters. These were DJs, at first Dr. Dre and DJ Yella, who recorded live mixes in Alonzo "Lonzo" Williams's garage that were played during Mack's radio show. Also involved with KDAY was Egyptian Lover, who according to Mack "created the sound [electro-hop]."[25] Russ Parr, "the morning guy" at KDAY, turned to electro-hop for his creative endeavors as well. He created a personality he called Bobby Jimmy and, with the Critters (one of whom was Arabian Prince), produced parodies of hit songs—"Roaches" (1986), a reinterpretation of Timex Social Club's "Rumours" (1986) being one example. Like other electro-hoppers, he formed his own label, Rapsur (Russ Parr spelled backwards after dropping an "s" and an "r").[26]

KDAY's commitment to electro-hop as well as the station's grasp of Los Angeles musical tastes meant that the station played records that other stations would not, such as Ice T's "6 'n the Mornin'" (1986) and Eazy E's "Boyz-n-the-Hood" (1987)—electro-hoppers' initial forays into what would subsequently be termed gangsta rap.[27] As the late 1980s manifested themselves, up-tempo dance songs gave way to more narrative-based, slower tempo songs. Gangsta rap rose in popularity beginning around 1988 as electro-hoppers turned their attention to more explicit social commentary. N.W.A.'s *Straight Outta Compton* (1988), especially the last track on the album, "Something 2 Dance 2," would serve in many ways as a remnant of change and of Los Angeles–based hip-hop's Afrofuturist links—an engagement with black Los Angeles pasts, presents, and futures.[28]

Local and National Cultural Influences:
Funk, Street Dances, and Mobile DJ Collectives

Local and national popular musical practices of the 1970s and early 1980s—funk, disco, and hip-hop—were fundamental to electro-hop. Funk, especially, was foundational to electro-hop, whereas disco was more influential to the East Coast sound.[29] The Godfather of Soul and founding figure of funk James Brown and his band the J.B.s were instrumental to a musical practice that other musical groups, like Sly and the Family Stone and George Clinton and Parliament/Funkadelic, expanded upon. This first wave of funk musicians shaped future funk practices such as electro-hop. Asked what they would play as DJs before the advent of electro-hop, Arabian Prince answered, "Back then it was Top 40. There was not much rap yet, so you played everything from Run-DMC to Cyndi Lauper to Grace Jones to Prince to Parliament. It was everything, and everyone partied to it all night long."[30] Egyptian Lover elaborated by adding, "Back in the day, I would play a lot [of] Prince, Roger and Zapp, Bar-Kays, Rick James, and funk/soul jams like that."[31] Arabian Prince discloses an eclecticism that affirms the musical and social diversity of black Los Angeles.[32] Moreover, Egyptian Lover's response announces how derivations of funk foregrounded electro-hop. Funk provided the soundtrack for dancing practices central to 1970s Los Angeles, later incorporated into electro-hop.

Dance crazes that arose in California beginning in the 1960s had, by the late 1970s and early 1980s, become popular in Los Angeles; here they coalesced as facets of the electro-hop scene. Locking and popping, despite common knowledge, developed independently of each other, although funk was preferred as the music for both. Dancers and dance researchers trace locking to late-1960s Los Angeles and popping to 1970s Fresno, California.[33] Locking and popping, and their East Coast counterpart, break dancing, became integral aspects of the Los Angeles mobile DJ scene from which electro-hop materialized. The 1983 TV documentary *Breaking and Entering,* starring electro-hopper–turned–gangsta rapper Ice T, provides a glimpse into the scene as it illustrates the multifaceted quality of electro-hop, which involved DJing, rapping, dancing, fashion, and graffiti.[34]

Throughout Los Angeles, local DJ collectives hosted popular events, and filling convention arenas was not unheard of; it was at these social gatherings where one could hear, see, feel, and dance to electro-hop's beginnings. Starting sometime in the early 1970s and inspired by Chicano dance parties such as "Chicano Woodstocks," individuals like Roger Clayton and Lonzo Williams formed mobile DJ groups: Uncle Jamm's Army in 1973 (originally Unique Dreams Entertainment) and Disco Constructions in 1975, respectively.[35] The success of these early crews led to the formation of other DJ collectives that performed throughout Los Angeles County—the Westside, South Central, Downtown, and Long Beach—and parts of Northern California, like Oakland.[36] These DJ collectives hosted events at high schools, skating rinks, sports arenas, and coliseums.[37]

DJs also performed at nightclubs. Three clubs are mentioned most frequently in interviews, fliers, and other primary and secondary sources: Radio, Eve After Dark, and Playpen. Radio, located near McArthur Park, initially opened in 1982 and later relocated to Downtown Los Angeles—1317 Palmetto Street, according to a flier.[38] Uncle Jamm's Army frequently performed at Radio as did popular hip-hop groups such as Run-DMC and pop star Madonna.[39] Lonzo Williams founded Eve After Dark. His first DJ collective, Disco Constructions, and his later group, the World Class Wreckin' Cru, performed there. The club, situated near Compton, catered to those who were unable to make the trek to Downtown Los Angeles.[40] Playpen was yet another venue where Uncle Jamm's Army hosted events.[41] These three clubs were some of the venues where young Angelenos formed the city's electro-hop scene, a scene shaping and shaped by the social and economic climate of 1980s black (and Latina/o) Los Angeles.

Post-1965 Black Los Angeles

Electro-hop has much to tell us about black L.A.'s post-1965 environment. In many ways, electro-hop serves to contextualize the cultural, social, economic, and political processes that would culminate with and in gangsta rap's assumed sounds of fury. After the Watts uprisings of 1965, there was an upsurge in local expressive cultural practices whose politics aligned with black nationalism. Musically, new locales for artistic expressions opened. Places such as the Watts Happening Coffee House and the Watts Writers Workshop established vibrant venues that were pivotal to groups like Watts Prophets.[42] This interest in poetry was accompanied by a musical scene dominated, in part, by jazz musicians such as John Coltrane, Archie Shepp, Ornette Coleman, Horace Tapscott, and Eric Dolphy.[43]

In post-1965 Los Angeles, political organizations such as the Black Panther Party and the US Organization formed. These groups were pivotal for collective material and symbolic survival, which the U.S. government realized and ultimately undermined. Infiltrating both factions, the FBI helped thwart their influence and catalyzed years of stalwart gang activity in Los Angeles. What is more, the apparent animosity between the groups served to justify the U.S. government's now-infamous COINTELPRO (Counterintelligence Program).

Gang activity and violence escalated from the 1970s through the 1980s. Black street gangs were not a novelty in Los Angeles; in fact, their origins can be tied to mass migrations of African Americans to the West Coast during the 1940s and subsequent changes in social and public life.[44] However, in the context of post-1965 Los Angeles the situation became markedly dire when the Bloods coalesced in response to the Crips, which had formed as a Black Panther splinter group.[45] Law enforcement implemented a program that harassed and criminalized young black men, called "Operation HAMMER." Mike Davis describes how, in 1988 alone, police officers narrowed down focus on "ten square miles of south central Los Angeles between Exposition Park and North Long Beach, arresting more Black youth than at any time since the Watts Rebellion of 1965."[46] Electro-hop participants, who mostly were not gang members, used expressive cultural practices to enact their own version of 1980s black Los Angeles.

Deindustrialization, Reaganomics, and Crack Cocaine

In early 1980s Los Angeles, deindustrialization, Reaganomics, and the growing presence of crack cocaine helped galvanize an environment that electro-hop practitioners sought to "code, adopt, adapt, translate, misread, rework, and revision."[47] As manufacturing industries closed, many young people of color faced bleak job prospects. Los Angeles, in general, witnessed an expansion of specialized industries; yet, as Robin D. G. Kelley describes, areas with a high percentage of people of color were inflicted by years of ghettoization: "The generation who came of age in the 1980s during the Reagan-Bush era were products of devastating structural changes in the urban economy that date back at least to the late 1960s. While the city as a whole experienced unprecedented growth, the communities of Watts and Compton faced increased economic displacement, factory closures, and an unprecedented deepening of poverty."[48] High levels of unemployment, "at least 50 percent for youths" in 1983–84, shaped and were shaped by the appearance of crack cocaine in 1983.[49] Gangs began pushing the drug, fueling their and its proliferation. Thus, a complex web of interrelated factors coalesced as electro-hop was being actualized. It was by 1983–84 that electro-hoppers had established the beginnings of a musical scene.

Electro-hop was another take on 1980s black Los Angeles. With electro-hop, young people of color forged a scene with music at its epicenter. This was "hip hop [as] black urban renewal."[50] Electro-hop practitioners turned to music production and performance to enact a Los Angeles, their Los Angeles. By the mid- to late 1980s, however, electro-hop's popularity began to decrease as gangsta rap gained not just local but also national notoriety. Ice T's "6 'n the Mornin'" (1987) and N.W.A.'s *Straight Outta Compton* (1988) would become markers of gangsta rap, Los Angeles hip-hop, and Los Angeles writ large.[51] Nevertheless, N.W.A.'s now infamous album *Straight Outta Compton* comes to an end with the song "Something 2 Dance 2." A dance tune, the song gestures toward electro-hop and commemorates, in sound, a musical scene that in some ways set the stage for, and complicates predominant understandings of, gangsta rap and its affective modalities against state-sanctioned violence, as songs like "Fuck tha Police" express. Moreover, "Something 2 Dance 2" would be the only track on the album to prominently feature Arabian Prince. Like him, the song was one of electro-hop's last explicit appearances in one of Los Angeles hip-hop's most celebrated and renowned albums; and like him, "Something 2 Dance 2" solidifies electro-hop's engagement with Afrofuturism.

Afrofuturism and Electro-hop

Electro-hop is an expression of Afrofuturism. Electro-hop practitioners' musical productions, performances, and practices were Afrofuturist. Afrofuturism appears dynamically across Afro-diasporic artistic media and is a component of Afro-diasporic expressive cultural practices. From literature (i.e., Octavia Butler's *Kindred* [1979]) to visual art (i.e., the work of Fatimah Tuggar), Afrofuturism is an epistemology from which to consider, engage with, create, and alter notions of blackness across African diasporas.[52] Tropes related to technology, water, and outer and cyber space dominate as concerns over alienation and otherness are encountered in complex and oftentimes satirical and exaggerated means, which are ultimately employed and deployed to create and affirm black-centered histories and alternate worldviews, and provide social prognoses of everyday life.

In the area of music, we hear Afrofuturism in Sun Ra and Alice Coltrane's jazz, Lee "Scratch" Perry's dub versions, George Clinton and Parliament/Funkadelic's intergalactic funk, and Prince's funk-rock-jazz. Electro-hop practitioners formulated a scene along similar lines, which included music, dance, and visual art. Its musical sounds drew from previous Afrofuturists such as Parliament/Funkadelic, Prince, and Afrika Bambaataa.[53] Like them, electro-hoppers used electronic instruments, including voice manipulators to situate themselves Afro-futuristically. Or as Egyptian Lover has stated: "I also love that robot voice and that electronic music—using real electronic sounds from spaceships from outerspace. To me, it was the best way to escape from where I grew up."[54]

The lyrics to Parliament's 1975 single "Mothership Connection (Star Child)" demonstrate electro-hop's Afrofuturist link. In both musical practices, issues concerning virility, dance, technology, eccentricity, and Afrocentricity are central. The synthesizer-laden song is an extraterrestrial quest wherein which the African American spiritual "Swing Low, Sweet Chariot" takes its rightful place as one of Afrofuturism's anthems. In the process, Parliament highlights their eccentricity ("Swing low / Time to move on / Light years ahead of our time / Free your mind, and come fly / With me / It's hip / On the mothership"), dancing ("Gettin' down in 3-D / Light year groovin'"), technology ("Face it, even your memory banks have forgotten this funk"), virility ("Well all right, if you hear any noise, it ain't nobody but me and the boys / Gettin' down / Hit it, fellas!"), and Afrocentricity ("We have returned to claim the pyramids").[55] They, like electro-hop practitioners in the 1980s, imagine, enact, and produce an outer, other space. For electro-hoppers this space was a black Los Angeles where they could collectively and publicly proclaim through an Afrofuturist vein, "Ain't nothing but a party, y'all." Yet electro-hop was, is, and will be much more than that.

Notes

1. See Will Straw, "Systems of Articulation, Logics of Change: Communities and Scenes in Popular Music," *Cultural Studies* 5, no. 3 (1991), 368–88. As noted above, a previous version of this chapter appeared in *Black Music Research Journal* 31, no. 1 (Spring 2011). The special issue, titled "Music of Black Los Angeles," was accompanied by a website, which still includes supplementary material (links, additional references, and a selected discography) and can be accessed at http://musicofblacklosangeles.blogspot.com/.

2. Jacqueline Cogdell DjeDje and Eddie S. Meadows, eds., *California Soul: Music of African Americans in the West* (Berkeley: University of California Press, 1998), 1.

3. Robin D. G. Kelley, "Kickin' Reality, Kickin' Ballistics: Gangsta Rap and Postindustrial Los Angeles," in *Droppin' Science: Critical Essays on Rap Music and Hip Hop Culture*, ed. William Eric Perkins (Philadelphia: Temple University Press, 1996), 117–58; Jeff Chang, *Can't Stop Won't Stop: A History of the Hip-Hop Generation* (New York: Picador, 2005).

4. West Coast Pioneers can be accessed via the Internet Archive (archive.org) by searching there for at http://westcoastpioneers.com.

5. Egyptian Lover and Arabian Prince, "Interview with Eddie Fleisher," *Wax Poetics* 32 (2008): 54–60; Eddie Fleisher, "Machine Funk," *Wax Poetics* 32 (2008): 54–60; Moritz Ege and Andrew Wright Hurley, "Introduction: Special Issue on Afro-Americanophilia in Germany," *Portal: Journal of Multidisciplinary International Studies* 12, no. 2 (2015), 1–14.

6. Kodwo Eshun, "Further Considerations on Afrofuturism," *CR: The New Centennial Review* 3, no. 2 (2003): 293.

7. Quoted in Alondra Nelson, "Introduction: Future Texts," *Social Text* 20, no. 2 (2002), 9. For more on subject, see Mark Dery, "Black to the Future: Interviews with Samuel R. Delany, Greg Tate, and Tricia Rose," in *Flame Wars: The Discourse of Cyberculture* (Durham: Duke University Press, 1994), 179–222; Alondra Nelson, "Afrofuturism: Past Future Visions," *ColorLines*, Spring 2000, 34–37.

8. Uncle Jamm's Army, "Dial-a-Freak" (12-inch single) (Los Angeles: Freak Beat Records, 1984); Sandro De Gaetani, and Stefan Schütze, "West Coast Pioneers: A Tribute to the Early West Coast Rap Scene," *West Coast Pioneers*, http://westcoastpioneers. com, last accessed July 5, 2016.

9. Egyptian Lover and Arabian Prince, "Interview with Eddie Fleisher," 56; Amin Eshaker, *Arabian Prince: Innovative life—The Anthology 1984–1989*, CD liner notes (Los Angeles: Stones Throw Records, 2008).

10. Brian Cross, *It's Not about a Salary . . . Rap, Race and Resistance in Los Angeles* (London: Verso, 1993), 22, 64; Egyptian Lover and Arabian Prince, "Interview with Eddie Fleisher," 59.

11. Uncle Jamm's Army, "Dial-a-Freak."

12. Ibid.

13. Unknown DJ, "808 Beats" (12-inch single) (Los Angeles: Techno Hop Records, 1984); Arabian Prince, "Strange Life" (12-inch single) (Hollywood, Calif.: Rapsur Records, 1984); Egyptian Lover, "Egypt, Egypt," in *On the Nile* (Los Angeles: Egyptian Empire, 1984); World Class Wreckin' Cru, "Cabbage Patch," in *The Best of the World Class Wreckin' Cru* (Los Angeles: Kru-Cut Records, 1987); Egyptian Lover, "Freak-a-holic," in *One Track Mind* (Los Angeles: Egyptian Empire, 1986).

14. See The Mistress and DJ Madame E, "I Got Your Wild Thang" (Los Angeles: Techno Hop Records, 1989); "Mic Jack" (Los Angeles: Techno Hop Records, 1989); *Leather and Lace* (Los Angeles: Techno Hop Records, 1989).

15. Don Snowden and Connie Johnson, "In Search of the Black Beat," *Los Angeles Times*, May 8, 1983.

16. Dwayne Simon, "Interview with Sandra De Gaetani," *West Coast Pioneers*, September 2006, http://web.archive.org/web/20070509014852/http://www.westcoastpioneers. com:80/interviews.html (hereafter Simon interview); Delphine Williams, "Interview with Stefan Schütze," *West Coast Pioneers*, July 2007, http://web.archive.org/web/20080705195758/http://www.westcoastpioneers.com/interviews.html.

17. Colin "Topper" Carew and Coleman A. Carew, *Breaking and Entering*, TV documentary (Los Angeles: Rainbow Television Workshop, 1983).

18. Egyptian Lover, "Open Your Books to Page Freak: Egyptian Lover; Interview with Dave Tompkins," *Stop Smiling*, April 9, 2007, http://www.stopsmilingonline.com/story_detail.php?id=786.

19. De Gaetani and Schütze, "West Coast Pioneers."

20. Ibid.; Eshaker, *Arabian Prince*, 10.

21. Alonzo Williams, "Interview with Stefan Schütze," *West Coast Pioneers*, May 2006, http://web.archive.org/web/20080705195758/http://www.westcoastpioneers.com/interviews.html.

22. Eshaker, *Arabian Prince*, 10.

23. James Brown, "'Knowledge Has No Color': A Perspective on Black Radio," *Los Angeles Times*, April 9, 1981.

24. Cheryl L. Keyes, *Rap Music and Street Consciousness* (Urbana: University of Illinois Press, 2002), 99.

25. Greg Mack, "Interview with Stefan Schütze" in *West Coast Pioneers*, October 2006, http://web.archive.org/web/20080705195758/http://www.westcoastpioneers.com/interviews.html.

26. Ibid.

27. Ibid.

28. N.W.A., *Straight Outta Compton* (Los Angeles: Ruthless Records, 1988).

29. De Gaetani, and Schütze, "West Coast Pioneers."

30. Egyptian Lover and Arabian Prince, "Interview with Eddie Fleisher," 56.

31. Ibid.

32. DjeDje and Meadows, eds., *California Soul*, 15.

33. Jorge Pabon, "Physical Graffiti: The History of Hip Hop Dance," in *Total Chaos: The Art and Aesthetics of Hip-Hop*, ed. Jeff Chang (New York: Basic Civitas Books, 2007), 22; Wendy Garofoli, "Urban Legend," *Dance Spirit*, April 1, 2008, 80.

34. Carew and Carew, *Breaking and Entering*.

35. Cross, *It's Not About a Salary*, 20; Raegan Kelly, "Hiphop Chicano: A Separate but Parallel Story," in Cross, *It's Not About a Salary*, 70; Eshaker, *Arabian Prince*, 6; Alonzo Williams, "Interview with Stefan Schütze"; Roger Clayton, "Interview with Stefan Schütze," *West Coast Pioneers*, September 2006, http://web.archive.org/web/20080705195758/http://www.westcoastpioneers.com/interviews.html.

36. Snowden and Johnson, "In Search of the Black Beat"; Cross, *It's Not About a Salary*, 20; Kelly, "Hiphop Chicano," 70; De Gaetani and Schütze, "West Coast Pioneers."

37. Snowden, and Johnson, "In Search of the Black Beat"; Cross, *It's Not About a Salary*, 20; Kelly, "Hiphop Chicano," 70; Chris Taylor, "Interview with Stefan Schütze," *West Coast Pioneers*, July 2004, http://web.archive.org/web/20080705195758/http://www.westcoastpioneers.com/interviews.html; Alonzo Williams, "Interview with Stefan Schütze"; Egyptian Lover and Arabian Prince, "Interview with Eddie Fleisher," 59; Eshaker, *Arabian Prince*, 6.

38. Cross, *It's Not About a Salary*, 20; De Gaetani, and Schütze, "West Coast Pioneers."

39. Cross, *It's Not About a Salary*, 20; Taylor, "Interview with Stefan Schütze."

40. De Gaetani, and Schütze, "West Coast Pioneers."

41. Taylor, "Interview with Stefan Schütze"; Egyptian Lover and Arabian Prince, "Interview with Eddie Fleisher," 59.

42. Cross, *It's Not About a Salary*, 10; Jeff Chang, *Can't Stop Won't Stop*, 310.

43. Cross, *It's Not About a Salary*, 11–12.

44. Mike Davis, *City of Quartz: Excavating the Future in Los Angeles* (New York: Vintage Books, 1992), 293.

45. Chang, *Can't Stop Won't Stop*, 313.

46. Davis, *City of Quartz*, 268.

47. Eshun, "Further Considerations on Afrofuturism," 301.

48. Quoted in Kelley, "Kickin' Reality, Kickin' Ballistics," 97. Also see Chang, *Can't Stop Won't Stop*, 314; DjeDje and Meadows, *California Soul*, 6.

49. Chang, *Can't Stop Won't Stop*, 315. For more on subject, see Davis, *City of Quartz*, 280.

50. Tricia Rose, *Black Noise: Rap Music and Black Culture in Contemporary America* (Middletown: Wesleyan University Press, 1994), 61.

51. Ice-T, *Rhyme Pays* (Hollywood, Calif.: Sire/Warner Bros., 1987); N.W.A., *Straight Outta Compton*.

52. Octavia Butler, *Kindred* (1979; repr., Boston: Beacon Press, 2003).

53. See Egyptian Lover and Arabian Prince, "Interview with Eddie Fleisher," 56.

54. Ibid.

55. Parliament, "Mothership Connection (Star Child)," in *Mothership Connection* (Wilmington, Del.: Casablanca, 1975).

▓ Ku Klux Klan's 1925 Attack on Malcolm X's Family Home in Omaha Heralded the Fight to Come

Most biographers of Malcolm X have focused little on his presence in the western landscape of his birthplace and first home in Omaha, Nebraska. His social activism in Harlem and other cities take center stage. Scholars also fail to connect his black nationalist legacy to his birthplace. During the 1970s, Omaha community activists Rowena Moore's campaigned to preserve Malcolm's home site in the cultural memory of the Great Plains. This history includes the rootedness of and violent nature of the Ku Klux Klan in young Malcolm Little's Omaha community. Along with the Garveyite beliefs of his father and the white racial hostility Malcolm's family experienced, it is clear how his childhood experiences shaped his contempt for white supremacy. In recent years, through the Malcolm X Foundation in Omaha, Malcolm's legacy, black agency, and white supremacy in the city and region are being resurrected.

As the place of his birth, Omaha seems like a brief footnote in the short life of Malcolm X.

Yet the frightening experience his family had here just before he was born undoubtedly shaped Malcolm's racial consciousness and played a role in his evolution as a civil rights firebrand.

Biography

Malcolm X leads his autobiography with the night the Ku Klux Klan rode up to his parents' house in north Omaha: "The Klansmen shouted threats and warnings at her that we better get out of town because 'the good Christian white people' were not going to stand for my father's 'spreading trouble' among the 'good' Negroes of Omaha."

Source: Erin Grace, "Ku Klux Klan's 1925 Attack on Malcolm X's Family Home in Omaha Heralded the Fight to Come," *Omaha World-Herald*, February 21, 2015.

Malcolm Little's parents, Earl and Louise, had come to Omaha to spread the back-to-Africa gospel of Jamaican orator and political leader Marcus Garvey in 1921. They settled in a house at 3448 Pinkney St. at a time when the Klan was exploding across America and digging in roots in Nebraska, according to late scholar and biographer Manning Marable.

Marable's 2011 book, *Malcolm X: A Life of Reinvention*, tells how the Klan had grown to 45,000 members in Nebraska by 1923, added a women's branch in 1925 and had Tri-K clubs for children. It held a state convention in Lincoln, and had 1,500 participants in a parade.

The night in 1925 that Klansmen visited the Little home, Earl was gone. Louise, pregnant with Malcolm, came to the door and told the men she was home with three small children. "Then the Klansmen took the butts of their rifles and knocked out all the windows," Malcolm X's autobiography reads.

The Making of Malcolm X

Malcolm Little was born at University Hospital in May 1925. The family moved in 1926 to Milwaukee and then to Lansing, Michigan, where their home was torched in 1929.

Earl Little died when Malcolm was 6. Louise suffered a breakdown and was institutionalized when Malcolm was 13. Malcolm bounced around foster homes, dropped out of school and, following a burglary, was in prison at age 21.

In prison, he became self-educated, joined the Nation of Islam and dropped his surname for "X," to symbolize the family name lost to slavery. He became a devout Muslim and, once out of prison, a rising star in the Nation, led by Elijah Muhammad.

Malcolm X was a powerful orator and a controversial figure who, like Muhammad, called whites the devil and advocated for black self-determination. He once said that if the government wasn't going to defend black people, blacks should use "any means necessary" to defend themselves.

A later pilgrimage to Mecca tempered his views on whites. He broke with the Nation of Islam and repudiated the group, causing a huge rift. He started a new group, the Organization of Afro-American Unity.

Malcolm started to talk about tolerance and global human rights, but because of the rift with the Nation and FBI and government surveillance, supporters feared for his life. In 1965, his home was firebombed. A week later, on Feb. 21, he was shot and died.

Memory

The old Little house at 3448 Pinkney was torn down but in 1970, an Omaha activist named Rowena Moore launched a decades-long effort to memorialize the slain activist.

Moore bought the lot where the Little house stood and eventually amassed a number of neighboring lots. The state erected a historical marker [on March 1, 1984]. The city named a street for Malcolm X. And a Malcolm X Foundation locally kept alive the dream for creating a Malcolm X educational center.

In 2010, the foundation opened a Malcolm X center inside an old Kingdom Hall at 34th and Evans Streets, which sits near the former Little home. The foundation runs a number of educational programs, including an African-themed event today to honor Malcolm's life.

⚅ The Black 14: Race, Politics, Religion, and Wyoming Football

In the wake of recent deadly shootings that go back to the murder of Trayvon Martin in 2012, NBA superstars Carmelo Anthony, Chris Paul, Dwyane Wade, and LeBron James started the 2016 ESPY Awards with an urgent call to action. Their stand was in honor of the late and great humanitarian Muhammad Ali, while simultaneously asking fellow athletes to "do the right thing." In this essay, Phil White connects the protests in 1969 of fourteen black University of Wyoming football players—the "Black 14"—to the growth of similar movements nationally that created pathways for traditionally white universities to become more racially diverse. But the Black 14's struggle was complex, as it also involved religion and freedom of speech: The players wanted to spotlight the policy of the Church of Jesus Christ of Latter-day Saints—the Mormons—that excluded blacks from the priesthood. For wearing black armbands to a meeting with their coach the day before a game against Brigham Young University—a meeting when they only wanted to talk about forms the protest might take—the coach immediately kicked them off the team. Events deteriorated from there. BYU's controversial stand did not subside until after the 1978 Revelation on the Priesthood.

During the second period of the season-opening football game against Arizona on Sept. 20, 1969, a packed house at the University of Wyoming's War Memorial Stadium watched as Cowboys' split end Ron Hill, a sophomore from Denver, caught a pass and took it 24 yards into the end zone. It was Wyoming's first touchdown in the 100th anniversary year of college football. . . .

But . . . football triumphs faded quickly from public memory when a controversy that fall linking sports, race, religion, and protest politics swung the nation's news spotlights to

Source: Phil White, "The Black 14: Race, Politics, Religion and Wyoming Football," *WyoHistory .org*, Wyoming State Historical Society.

Laramie, Wyoming at a time when Americans were already deeply divided over civil rights and the Vietnam War. Controversy erupted over the expulsion of 14 African-American football players from the Cowboys' varsity. They came to be known as the Black 14.

A Winning Team

The Cowboys ... were ranked 12th in the nation in the United Press International coaches poll [after four season-opening wins in 1969] as the players prepared for their next game against Brigham Young University. The UW team lead the nation in rushing defense.

Under Head Coach Lloyd Eaton, Wyoming had won three consecutive Western Athletic Conference championships ... had won 31 of the previous 36 games; defeated Florida State in the Sun Bowl and very nearly upset Louisiana State University in the Sugar Bowl on Jan. 1, 1968, after going undefeated during the 1967 regular season.

The 51-year-old Eaton, a native of Belle Fourche, S.D. was at the peak of his career. . . .

But on Friday morning, Oct. 17, 1969, the day before the BYU game, Eaton summarily dismissed [fourteen] African American players on the UW team when they appeared at his office as a group wearing black armbands on their civilian clothes. BYU is owned and operated by the Church of Jesus Christ of Latter-day Saints, better known as the Mormons. By wearing the armbands, the players were protesting the LDS policy then in force, which barred black men from the priesthood.

The coach's action deeply affected the players' lives, and soon caused the demise of his own coaching career. The university, too, was profoundly affected.

A Turbulent Time

The controversy came at the end of the turbulent 1960s. The decade profoundly changed the nation but had apparently had less of an effect, so far, on conservative Wyoming.

In October [1968] U.S. sprinters Tommie Smith and John Carlos indelibly linked sports to racial politics when, standing on the medalists' platform at the Summer Olympics in Mexico City, they raised black-gloved fists as the Star-Spangled Banner played over the loudspeakers.

In the western United States, some college athletes learned of the Mormon Church's policy of barring black men from the church's lay priesthood and thus from leadership in the church. The students felt they could bring attention to what they saw as an injustice by protesting when their teams played Brigham Young University. BYU, located in Provo, Utah, is wholly owned and operated by the Mormon Church.

In November 1968, at San Jose State in California, black football players boycotted a home game against BYU. . . . In April, 1969, black track athletes at the University of Texas at El Paso were ejected from the team when they refused to participate in a meet at Provo. . . .

Protest Comes to Laramie

About a week before the UW-BYU game, slated to be played on UW home turf in Laramie, Willie Black, a 32-year-old math doctoral student with a wife and four children living in student housing, had learned of the Mormon policy. Black was chancellor of UW's Black Students Alliance [BSA]. On the Monday before the game, he informed alliance members, including the black football players, of what he had discovered. On Wednesday, he delivered a statement entitled "Why We Must Protest" to the UW president and athletic director. The document announced plans for a demonstration at the stadium before the BYU game. . . .

Also on Wednesday, Laramie townspeople and students took part in the Vietnam Moratorium, a nationally coordinated series of demonstrations and teach-ins. . . .

After practice on Thursday afternoon, Oct. 16, Coach Eaton warned Wyoming's tri-captain Joe Williams about the coach's rule prohibiting participation by athletes in demonstrations. Williams conveyed this information to his fellow black players that night, and they decided to meet with Eaton to discuss the issue.

On Friday [morning], the 14 black players gathered at Washakie Center in the dormitory complex. They donned black armbands and walked to Memorial Fieldhouse where Eaton had his office, hoping to persuade the coach to allow them to show some solidarity with the BSA call for a protest.

Seeing them together, wearing armbands, Eaton . . . immediately told them that they were all off the team. After that . . . the coach insulted the players in an angry manner, which further polarized the situation.

On Saturday, the Cowboys, suddenly an all-white team, defeated all-white BYU 40–7 while the 14 dismissed black players watched from the student section of the stands. Fans on both sides of the stadium chanted, "We love Eaton." After the game, Eaton said, "The victory was the most satisfying one I've ever had in coaching."

The National Spotlight

The dismissal of the 14 brought camera crews from the three big TV networks to Laramie, and articles appeared in newspapers and magazines throughout the nation. The Nov. 3, 1969, issue of *Sports Illustrated* carried an article whose photographs included one showing 10 of the dismissed players sitting on the south steps of the Wyoming Union. . . .

Aftermath

In response to the dismissals, the UW Student Senate, with [ASUW President Hoke MacMillan] fully involved, adopted a resolution by a 15–3 vote alleging that "coach Eaton refused to grant a rational forum for discussion, choosing instead to degrade and arbitrarily dismiss each player." The resolution said the ASUW Senate "expresses its shock at the callous, insensitive treatment afforded 14 Black athletes. . . . [T]he actions of coach Eaton and the Board of Trustees were not only uncompromising, but unjust and totally wrong." . . .

Sorting It Out in Federal Court

he week after the athletes' dismissal, the National Association for the Advancement of Colored People sent a Detroit attorney, William Waterman, to Wyoming to file the federal lawsuit seeking an injunction ordering the reinstatement of the players and asking for damages for violation of their civil rights [which got hung up in court, with a judge supporting the coach]. . . .

Reversal of Fortunes

The events had a devastating effect on Wyoming football. After six games, UW was still unbeaten and still rated among the top 15 in the national polls. Many fans were convinced the Cowboys could continue their winning ways without any African-American players. But protests against Eaton's actions followed the Cowboys on the road, and they lost the last four games of the 1969 season by lopsided scores. The 1970 team . . . finish[ed] with one win and nine losses—the worst record since . . . 1939. It was the Cowboys' first losing season since 1948. And future prospects looked dim . . . [On] Dec. 6, 1970, Lloyd Eaton's coaching career came to an abrupt end. . . .

The negative publicity affected Wyoming's football program for years. . . . They had only one winning season during the 1970s.

Epilogue

A *Salt Lake Tribune* article published Nov. 6, 2009, relates that the Black 14 incident quickly provoked changes at BYU, according to Tom Hudspeth, BYU head coach in 1969. Hudspeth was quoted as saying that he "cannot remember the exact date or how he was 'made aware' that LDS Church leadership wanted him to add African-Americans to his team, and fast. The following year, BYU's team included Ronnie Knight, a black defensive back from Sand Springs, Okla." [Nine years later,] on June 9, 1978, the First Presidency of the Mormon Church, composed of President and Prophet Spencer Kimball and Counselors N. Eldon Tanner and Marion G. Romney, announced that a divine revelation had been received to open the Mormon priesthood to African-Americans, ending the longstanding tenet. . . .

Since the turn of the 21st century the University of Wyoming football team has had upwards of 25 African-Americans on its roster nearly every season. The 2016 roster include[d] about 40 African-Americans.

⌘ Part 5

Reconsiderations

13 African Americans in Albuquerque, 1880–1930

A Demographic Analysis

Randolph Stakeman

This study explores how the Albuquerque African American community sustained itself and developed the sociopolitical foundation crucial to New Mexico's civil rights struggle. The community was far from a passive one, and we can see its struggles to nurture and maintain itself even though it lacked the large numbers of other black communities. The small community size before World War II allows us to examine community life better. We can see the development in microcosm of the organizations and structures needed to sustain a community; the mobilization of people and resources; and the achievements of individuals against great odds. Although the bulk of the story belongs to what is known as the Second Great Migration of African Americans, which occurred during and after World War II, the roots of the story start in the period examined here.

This focus is a departure from the scant historical work that has been done about African Americans in Albuquerque, New Mexico. From Barbara Richardson's *Black Directory of New Mexico* (1976) to Maisha Baton's oral histories *Do Remember Me* (2004), most publications about New Mexico's black past were produced by people within the state's African American community. In 2013 *African American History in New Mexico: Portraits from Five Hundred Years*, edited by Bruce Glasrud, extended black New Mexico's coverage into the domain of western scholars. All of these are valuable, but they share limitations. Some try to cover so much ground both geographically and chronologically that each subject receives scant attention. Many are attempts by dedicated people who have little historical training and therefore approach the information uncritically. Their major concern was documenting this information before the elders who had experienced it slipped away. I am grateful that they did. Building on this scholarship this article uses quantitative and qualitative social science approaches to examine the barely researched Albuquerque African American community in the early twentieth century.[1]

Prior to Statehood

Albuquerque remained a small and isolated community throughout the nineteenth century until the advent of the Atchison, Topeka, and Santa Fe Railway, which linked New Mexico to the rest of the country.[2] A few prominent Albuquerque citizens, including Franz Huning, William C. Hazeldine, and Elias S. Stover, anxious to have the railroad, turned land speculators and bought up the land around the proposed route. They agreed to deed the land to the Santa Fe railroad for one dollar an acre in exchange for 50 percent of the price when the railroad company would later sell it at a greatly inflated price to commercial developers once the railroad came through. On April 22, 1880, the train reached what would first be known as New Albuquerque with a great celebration to mark its arrival.[3]

There were only sixteen African Americans listed in the first census of New Albuquerque later that summer.[4] Most of these were listed as cooks and domestics. Only one black family was listed among them. The census listings rarely tell the whole story of black ambitions and accomplishments. One man listed as a "cook" in the 1880 census was the proprietor of a business, the New Mexico Novelty Store, by 1883. The business lasted until 1896. A retired miller listed in the 1880 census was the proprietor of a rooming house in 1883. There were three black children in the Albuquerque schools in 1884, and that number peaked at thirty-four before the end of the century.[5] By 1885 an African American community had begun to emerge in Albuquerque patterned on African American institutions and local social life elsewhere. On this urban frontier African Americans developed their own institutions. An African American Methodist mission was organized in 1882. The church at first rented space in other buildings for its weekly service, because its first facility was not able to accommodate all of the church's congregation. A year later it was reorganized as the Colored Methodist Mission, and the township of Albuquerque donated land for it. Money to sustain the mission was raised primarily by its black women, who held socials. They were successful, and eventually a new brick building opened in 1892 at Coal Avenue and Third Street in Albuquerque.[6] By the end of the nineteenth century, therefore, African Americans had moved into Albuquerque in large enough numbers to form embryonic social institutions, some of which continue today.

In addition to the church organizations, several other self-help organizations were founded. In 1914 eight women became the charter members of the Home

Circle Club, which at first was part of the national Colored Women's Clubs but later struck out on its own. It was not only a women's social club: it also provided training in home economics, college scholarships for black youth, and encouragement of black family life. In 1919 the Little Forum was formed with seven child charter members, to "[create an] interest in attending high school, to attain and maintain a high standard in our manners and decorum . . . [and to promote] our social and intellectual advancement," in the words of its founder. A. L. Mitchell, a former teacher who was prevented from teaching when he moved to Albuquerque because the Albuquerque school system would not hire black teachers, was put in charge of the club.[7]

Both the AME church and a black Masonic lodge were in operation by the turn of the century. Judging from the names of the deacons and the officers of the lodge, the same people were instrumental in both. There was great turnover among these civic leaders of the black community. No more than a third of the church officers, stewards, and stewardess listed in the city directories were still in Albuquerque in the next census in 1910. Additional institutions formed, such as a branch of the fledgling National Association for the Advancement of Colored People (organized in 1913 but chartered in 1915) and an additional African American church, the Mount Olive Baptist Church, organized in 1909 although its members had been meeting since 1898.[8] A third black church, God's House Church, was founded in 1916 but would not get its own building until 1924.

Over time many of the institutions the community created, like the African Methodist Episcopal church, remained and were continued by succeeding black immigrants. The few black families that remained in Albuquerque therefore took on a crucial role in the continuity of the community and its institutions as the population continued to turn over.[9]

Since 1900 Albuquerque has had the largest black population in New Mexico. This city's demographics reveal the contours of African American urban life in New Mexico. Demographic statistics can be helpful as long as we remember that they only give a snapshot and an approximate look at the community. Their numbers give a false impression of precision and accuracy. As long as one remembers we are dealing with people rather than numbers and that the numbers themselves represent fickle data collection at best, demographics can be helpful.

In 1900, New Mexico was a predominantly rural place. Only 14 percent of the state's population lived in urban areas, while 86 percent of lived in rural areas as defined by the U.S. Census Bureau. New Mexican African Americans were a much more urban group than average, with 35 percent living in urban areas. Of the New Mexican black urban dwellers, 40 percent lived in Albuquerque. As we shall see when we look at their occupations, they filled a service niche in New Mexico's slowly changing economy that was more prevalent in urban areas. They lived in a community quite different from other New Mexico African American communities, particularly those engaged in farming, ranching, or mining.[10]

For example, the gender balance was quite different. In New Mexico as a whole, African American men outnumbered African American women 1,023 to 587. In the territory single black males outnumbered married ones by a wide margin. Even in urban areas there were 105 African American men for each 100 African American women. In 1900 Albuquerque there were equal numbers of black men and black women in total but among black adults the ratio was 110 black males for every 100 black females. Black women who lived in Albuquerque were much more likely to be married (55 percent of black women) than black women in the territory as a whole (43 percent of black women).[11]

The stories of the Collins and the Boyer families illustrate this. John Collins was born in Virginia and eventually joined the U.S. Army's Twenty-Fourth Infantry Regiment, part of what came to be known as the Buffalo Soldiers. He married before his regiment was sent to the Territory of New Mexico in 1879. When they started to have children he retired from the army, and they settled in Albuquerque. Collins was an entrepreneur and started a transport company in 1896. He eventually started a scavenger company in 1907, which collected and recycled junk. John and Melissa Collins thus came to Albuquerque as a couple, and they started a family and businesses that would flourish in an urban environment.[12]

The story of Frank Boyer is different. Boyer was a married schoolteacher in Georgia whose father had traveled to the West. His father regaled him with tales about the possibilities for African Americans in the West. Boyer and a male friend set out to walk all the way from Georgia to New Mexico in hopes of getting land and becoming independent. They stopped along the way to do odd jobs to survive and eventually reached New Mexico Territory after a year's travel. They settled in rural New Mexico and worked on a ranch until they had enough money to obtain land themselves. It was not until two years later that Boyer's wife joined him. This pattern of single black men in farming or ranching not bringing women along at first contributed to the gender imbalance.[13]

At the turn of the twentieth century Albuquerque's black community had all the attributes of recent settlement. Over a third of black males lived as lodgers in other people's households. The median age of the black community was high;

overall it was twenty-eight but among black males it was even higher, thirty-one. To put it into context, in 1900 the overall median age of the United States was nineteen, of all African Americans in the United States it was 19, but of all New Mexicans it was twenty-one.

In 1900 Albuquerque's African American community differed from the rest of New Mexico. The median age of Albuquerque African Americans was higher than the age of all blacks in New Mexico, which was high to start with at twenty-seven. As the national census figures show us, the states with a median age far above the average for blacks are those in which a large part of the African Americans are immigrants from other states.[14] The percentage of the population who were children was much less for the Albuquerque black population than for the New Mexico population as a whole. Adults both young and mature made up a greater percentage of the Albuquerque African American population than the New Mexico total population, and elders comprised less. All of these are demographic signs that the Albuquerque African American population was a community in flux.

The low percentage of children and the high percentage of adults suggest that the community's growth was being sustained by migration rather than natural increase. This was particularly true of the Albuquerque black male population, in which these trends were heightened.[15] The migration statistics bear out that this was a community formed by migration. Some 79 percent of African Americans living in New Mexico were born outside the territory, compared to only 22 percent of the white population being immigrants. Only 21 percent of the territory's African Americans were born in New Mexico, while the highest contributing states (all contributing less than 21 percent) were Virginia, Texas, and Missouri, in that order. In Albuquerque about the same proportion of the population was born in New Mexico (22 percent), while states contributing the most immigrants (all contributing less than 21 percent) were Texas, Missouri, and Kentucky. This wasn't the same for men and women. A greater proportion of the men had migrated into New Mexico. Eighty-three percent of the black men and only 75 percent of the women were born outside the territory. This trend continued through 1920 as a decreasing proportion of Albuquerque African Americans were born in New Mexico.[16] For example, Edward and Lottie Carson migrated from Arizona to New Mexico just before the turn of the twentieth century. He had worked building the railroad and making barbed wire fences. In Albuquerque he worked as a teamster and drove the first horse-drawn hack in town. Andrew James Clayton and Anna Williams Clayton were born in Texas

and Louisiana respectively and moved to Albuquerque about 1910 when James
started a barbershop in downtown Albuquerque. Dr. James Dennis migrated
from Maryland about 1912 and became the first black doctor in Albuquerque.
He was also one of the organizers of the Albuquerque NAACP branch. All of
them came not just for jobs but for opportunity.[17]

The early Albuquerque African American community also was a community
in transit. Of the 224 people found in the 1900 manuscript census, less than 10
percent were found in the 1910 manuscript census. This is at best only a rough
approximation of how many people stayed in Albuquerque. Women who stayed
may have changed their names through marriage; people may have stayed but
moved beyond the city limits. I have tried to correct for this by including the
areas just outside Albuquerque in the manuscript census and trying to discern
female holdovers through similar names, birthplaces, and parents' birthplaces.
One can conclude even from these rough estimates that the great preponderance
of the community had moved elsewhere by 1910.[18]

Another way to note the slow evolution to a more settled and less transitory
community is to look at home ownership. The manuscript census lists whether
the heads of household own or rent their residences. If we examine the figures
for the African American heads of households, we see some clear trends. The
first thing to note is that the number of household heads remains about the same
between 1900 and 1920. The major change is in the number of household heads
who own rather than rent their residences. Although the percentage of renters
remains significantly above 50 percent, the number and percentage of home
owners more than doubles. The movement toward more ownership also translates
to a movement of location. Using the Geographic Information System, we can
track where African Americans lived in Albuquerque through each manuscript
census from 1900 to 1940. We can use the addresses given in the census to map
where African American rentals or houses owned would have been located in
contemporary Albuquerque. A map of the 1900 census shows them in rentals
in the central city area.

As home ownership increased, however, we see them moving out of the central
city to the outer reaches of the city and beyond. The shaded area is the central city
(see map 3). On the map the O's represent houses owned by African Americans,
and the R's are rentals by African Americans. Note the area along the current
highway toward the south, at the bottom center of the map, because that South
Broadway area is where the black residences would cluster in decades to come.
It is important to note that these areas were not exclusively African American.

TABLE 13.1 **African American home ownership in Albuquerque, 1900–1920**

	1900	%	1910	%	1920	%
Heads of Household	66	—	70	—	66	—
Owned	10	15.2	10	14.3	26	39.4
Rented	52	78.8	60	85.7	38	57.6
Unknown	4	6.0	0	0	2	3.0

Sources: U.S. Bureau of the Census, Negroes in the United States, Bulletin 8 (Washington, D.C.: Government Printing Office, 1904), table 27, 188; Zellmer R. Pettet and Charles E. Hall, Negroes in the United States, 1920–32 (New York: Greenwood Press, 1969), 267 (table 28).

They were mixed-race areas where whites lived alongside people of other races. There was no predominantly black area as would develop after World War II. As we have already seen, the census-listed occupations of African Americans are not always reflective of their lives. Nevertheless, they are important in understanding the community. The occupations of Albuquerque African Americans differed a bit from African Americans in other parts of New Mexico as we can see in table 13.2. In all columns there the total number of people in each category is listed in parentheses. The first column lists the most prevalent occupations of New Mexico African American males in 1900. We can compare it to the next column, which lists the most common occupations of Albuquerque African American males in the same year. The third and fourth columns are the most common occupations for black females in New Mexico and Albuquerque respectively.

The first thing to note is that there were no black military men or miners in Albuquerque as there were in other parts of New Mexico. Nor were there many primary goods producers like herders, farmers, or agricultural laborers. African American men in Albuquerque were confined to service occupations like porter, teamster, janitor, waiter, cook, or unspecified laborer. This is not totally unexpected in an urban environment, which should concentrate service jobs. For example, one quarter of the black barbers and half of the black janitors in New Mexico were in Albuquerque. For the women, what is striking is how few black Albuquerque women worked outside the home at this time. Only fifteen listed occupations and only a few of them were working in other people's homes.

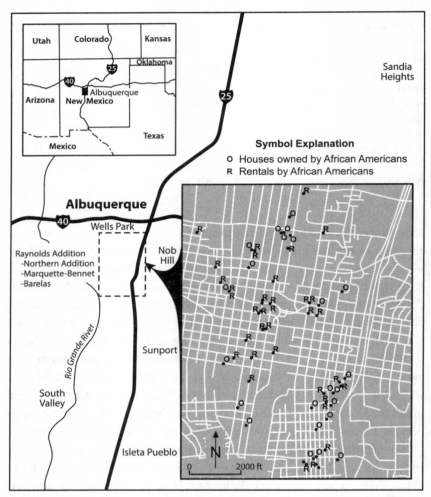

African American home ownership and rentals in Albuquerque, 1900. *Cartography by Joe Stoll. Copyright © 2018 by The University of Oklahoma Press.*

TABLE 13.2 African American occupations in Albuquerque, 1900

Males		Females	
New Mexico	Albuquerque	New Mexico	Albuquerque
Military (216)	Porters (15)	Servants (62)	Laundresses (7)
Miners (200)	Day laborers (12)	Laundresses (35)	Cooks (3)
Servants (102)	Teamsters (6)	Lodging house keepers (8)	Housekeepers (3)
Laborers (94)	Barbers (6)	Housekeepers (8)	Nurse (1)
Porters (30)	Janitors (6)	Laborers (5)	Lodging house keeper (1)
Barbers (22)	Laborers (6)	Nurses/midwives (5)	
Herders (20)	Waiters (5)		
Teamsters (19)	Cooks (4)		
Agriculture workers, farmers, janitors (12 each)	Teamsters, hod carriers, editors, housecleaners, herders, retired soldiers (2 each)		

Source: U.S. Bureau of the Census, Negroes in the United States, Bulletin 8, (Washington, D.C.: Government Printing Office, 1904), 182–86 (table 26).

When they had a choice, black women did not enter the work world at this time. Albuquerque was making the transition from rural hub to commercial and not industrial city, therefore there were no industrial jobs for African Americans, only service ones.[19]

After Statehood

In 1912 the Territory of New Mexico became a state, and the 1920 census is the first to reflect that change. The 1920 manuscript census shows that while the size of the Albuquerque African American community did not increase much, most of the community members were newcomers. These newcomers contained a group of highly educated African Americans who settled in the town from

1909 to 1915 and became the community leaders of the 1920s. They included S. W. Henry, a teacher who began to edit an African American newspaper, the *Southwest Review*, in 1924; James Dennis, a medical doctor; T. M. Brinson, a violinist and graduate of the Chicago Conservatory of Music; and A. L. Mitchell, a graduate of Wiley College in Texas. Several of the newcomers were retired army veterans who had served in the African American Ninth and Tenth Cavalries or the Twenty-Fourth or Twenty-Fifth Infantries, colloquially called the Buffalo Soldiers.[20] Although a few families did remain from 1910, an abnormal number of those who did stay had been widowed during the intervening ten years. Life was apparently precarious for black men at this time.[21]

A branch of the National Association for the Advancement of Colored People was chartered in 1915, just six years after the national NAACP was formed. By 1917 the local NAACP branch tried to get a civil rights bill introduced through the Albuquerque state representative to the New Mexico legislature. The bill would have made it illegal for owners of hotels, restaurants, and saloons to discriminate on the basis of race or nationality. The bill made it through the house judiciary committee, with a majority report recommending its adoption by the full house and a minority report recommending its rejection. The objections were based on the idea that it was a "social equality" bill that would cause "endless strife and trouble." The Mexican Americans on the committee and some in the full house supported the measure because they cited discrimination that they and Native Americans had received. Anglo Americans on the committee argued against it by saying that they had not witnessed any such discrimination. With the two conflicting reports, the bill was sent back to the committee to be reported back the next day. The next day the committee asked to be relieved of its responsibility to report back on the bill. A new bill was introduced with the same wording except that it only mentioned discrimination against Spanish Americans. This new bill was referred to a different committee, where it died.[22] Despite the support and solidarity between three nonwhite communities, the bill never made it out of the Committee on the Judiciary, to which it had been referred. Although the white majority easily broke apart the nascent coalition of Mexican Americans, Native Americans and African Americans, such a coalition presaged the future of a civil rights movement in New Mexico decades later.[23]

The Albuquerque NAACP grew because of discrimination faced in Albuquerque High School and elsewhere in Albuquerque public facilities. In 1907 the first African American girls ever scheduled to graduate from Albuquerque High School were Yolande Black, Frances Ellsworth, and Anedia Jasper. They had to graduate from the high school section of the University of New Mexico instead, when community members objected to their presence at the graduation ceremony. It was not until 1914 that the first African American, Birdie Hardin, graduated with her class from Albuquerque High School.[24]

Such slights did not stop African American parents from sending their children to school. In 1900 almost two-thirds of Albuquerque African Americans age five to twenty went to school. This was a higher percentage than New Mexican African Americans as a whole (43 percent in school) and New Mexican U.S.-born whites (42 percent in school). In 1910 the rate sank to 54 percent, lower than that of New Mexican blacks as a whole (58 percent) and New Mexican whites (61 percent), but it recovered in 1920 to a whopping 83 percent, surpassing New Mexican whites in school (66 percent) and even other urban blacks (70 percent). The manuscript census shows that it was those children aged five or six and those over sixteen who were most likely not to be in school. In other words, Albuquerque African Americans tended to start school a little later in life and leave a little earlier, perhaps because they had to enter the workforce earlier.[25]

We have already seen that from the beginning of black settlement in Albuquerque, African Americans were not just content to accept the roles that the white economy gave them: for example, porters and janitors for the men, domestic service as cooks or maids for the women. Black New Mexicans used those roles as stepping-stones to their own entrepreneurial projects as early as the 1880s.

Those black businesses that could serve the entire Albuquerque market are the ones that fared best. In the 1880s and 1890s there were black commercial farmers who could sell their produce to the New Albuquerque market. In 1907 William T. Thornton established a carpet and clothes-cleaning business that apparently had customers outside of Albuquerque as well. African Americans owned barbershops, tailoring establishments, shoemaking and shoe repair shops, and billiards or pool parlors. They often opened businesses that relied on skills they had developed elsewhere, as did former cavalry scout George Hutchinson, who opened a blacksmith shop next to his home in 1909.[26]

Black businesses became important sources of employment in the black community. Several businesses established after 1912 "provided jobs, experience and patronage for the black community," much as other Albuquerque ethnic businesses, like Jewish and Italian businesses, did.[27] A prime example of this was the Bryant Messenger Service established by the Bryant brothers, General, Heard, and Willard. They emigrated from Texas in 1906 and at first worked as general labors and porters. They had bigger dreams than that and started to open

Bryant Messenger Service, circa 1912. *Courtesy of William Cobb Collection, University of New Mexico Library.*

their own businesses. General Bryant opened that first black-owned restaurant in 1908 and a grocery store soon after. To supplement his income, he worked as a porter in the Commercial Club, where white business leaders met, relaxed, and presumably made deals or exchanged information. His brother Heard became a partner in a shoemaking venture. In 1912 General and Heard Bryant opened the Bryant Messenger Service, which gave employment to blacks as drivers or bicycle and motorcycle messengers. The company picked up baggage at the train station, carried messages to places without telephone service, and delivered to the tuberculosis sanitaria.[28]

In contrast, those ventures that relied on a predominantly African American clientele did not do as well. The Albuquerque African American community was too small to form commercially viable enterprises that catered to the community and too small to have the mainstream economy take its needs into account.

Although the community foundation had been laid by 1920, things had not changed much. One thing that had changed was that the black population of Albuquerque was becoming a smaller part of the city. From 1900 to 1920 Albuquerque's total population had risen from about 6,200 to a little over 15,000, while the African American population had basically stayed the same or even dropped a little, to a bit over 200. The result was that, as a percentage of Albuquerque's population, African Americans had dropped from 4 percent to 1 percent.[29]

The occupations open to Albuquerque African Americans in the economy also had not changed much. Of the black males age fourteen or older, eighty (or about 78 percent of them) were employed, and a third worked for the railroad. Only twenty-eight (or about 30 percent) of black women age fourteen or older were employed. Twelve (about 43 percent) were employed in private homes.[30] Almost 63 percent of the males were employed as porters, laborers, janitors, and cooks. Among black females, almost 80 percent were domestic servants, cooks, and laundresses. Less than a quarter of the males were unemployed by the mainstream economy, but over two-thirds of the women were able to withhold their labor from the dominant economy yet get by.[31]

In spite of the community size stagnating and the economic parameters being set, the 1920s saw attempts by the African Americans in Albuquerque to move their community forward. In 1925 the Albuquerque African American community was shaken by the state legislature's passage of a law that allowed the segregation of African Americans, and only African Americans, in separate schools if local school boards so wanted. Although some segregation had been practiced in New Albuquerque since its origins in 1880, the African American population had been able to rebuff segregation in the local schools and thwart proposed segregation on streetcars. The local NAACP had been formed to lead these fights. By the 1920s, although some establishments still refused to serve African Americans and the theaters each had a separate balcony area for blacks, there was only limited segregation in public facilities in Albuquerque. The state legislature's allowance of segregated schools was received as quite a blow to the black community.[32]

The change allowing segregated schools came in an omnibus bill in the state legislature reforming the school code that had been passed in 1923. In 1925 a state legislature more concerned with establishing a new way to finance schools, regulate school boards, depoliticize school board elections, and change teacher compensation, passed Senate Bill 95, which also contained an amendment to allow local school boards to set up separate schools for African Americans. The new law said that if the county or municipal school board and the state board of education thought that "it is for the best advantage and interest of the school that separate room[s] be provided for the teaching of pupils [of] African descent and such rooms are so provided, such pupils may not be admitted to school rooms occupied and used by pupils of Caucasian or other descent."[33] The bill passed the state house of representatives with only one dissenting vote, and the measure passed the state senate overwhelmingly (42–3).[34]

The New Mexico state constitution guranteed the right of New Mexicans of Latin American descent not to be forced to attend schools different from whites. A state legislature dominated by Republicans and a Democratic governor allowed a "Jim Crow" change in the school code, thus ignoring the interests of New Mexico African Americans. New Mexican African Americans were politically impotent and could not affect their statewide fate when the forces of racism prevailed.

The news hit the Albuquerque black community like a thunderbolt. There had been little racial discrimination in Albuquerque, and the black community felt it had escaped the racist mores of the South with their discrimination and segregation. The near unanimous passage of this law pointed out the precariousness of their position. Almost every legislator, no matter the political party, was willing to sacrifice the interests of black schoolchildren in order to get a new school code that put school systems on a firmer financial and organizational footing. More to the point, southern states' racism was making inroads into New Mexico. New Mexico had never been totally free of race prejudice, but the black community of New Mexico had convinced itself that things were better there than other places.

In fact, only the school boards in the southern part of the state, like that in Las Cruces, and in the southeastern part of the state, colloquially called Little Texas because of its large population of Texas immigrants and its proximity to Texas, organized separate schools for blacks. It has been reported that an official of the Albuquerque school board offered the African Americans their own school in the late 1930s but was turned down.[35] Altogether nine separate elementary schools were set up in the southern and southeastern New Mexico locales.[36]

By the Great Depression the number of African Americans in New Mexico had grown to 2,850 according to the 1930 census, an increase of about 33 percent. Albuquerque's black population had increased to over 400, thus doubling after two decades of stagnation.[37] If we group people into the same four age groups as before, children (0–15), young adults (15–34), mature adults (35–64), and elders (65+), we can see how the Albuquerque black community had changed. In 1930 much more of the black population were children, and there was a greater share of mature adults. There was a smaller proportion of young adults and of elders in the 1930 population. It is significant that most of these children (58 percent) were born in New Mexico. Even if we restrict our analysis to children who were not in the 1920 census, 45 percent were born in New Mexico. Of the children born after the 1920 manuscript census, over 79 percent were born in New Mexico. Although only 12 percent of the people listed in the 1920 manuscript census were also listed in the 1930 manuscript census, the increase in population is made up not only of new immigrants but of an increasing number of children within the stable core of Albuquerque's black population.[38] Thus the black population of Albuquerque was becoming less transient and more settled.

We can see from the numbers, therefore, that after the 1920s there was beginning to be a growing group of African Americans who would consider Albuquerque the place to put down roots, to start and to rear a family. This group augmented the small group of African Americans who had been settled in Albuquerque during the 1900 to 1920 period. By 1930 this core was enough to produce a growing maturity of African American social institutions and groups. The political, social, and economic institutions created by these African Americans would become crucial to the New Mexico's civil rights struggle in the decades ahead. The phenomenal growth of the black community during the 1950s because of the federal government's expansion in New Mexico and the civil rights movement, changed the community completely, but its roots were in this earlier period. The path that growth took was greatly influenced by what had gone before.

Notes

1. All charts, tables, maps, and statistics are based on the U.S. Census for Albuquerque for the relevant dates. The endnotes will indicate the source of all demographic information.

2. Maisha Baton, *Do Remember Me 2: Black Seniors of Albuquerque and Western New Mexico* (Albuquerque: privately printed, 2004), 4–5.

3. Marc Simmons, *Albuquerque: A Narrative History* (Albuquerque: University of New Mexico Press, 1982) 212–21.

4. "United States Federal Census Collection, 1880–1930: African Americans in Albuquerque," Ancestry.com; John Joseph Ellis, "Albuquerque's Black Entrepreneurs, 1880–1933" (bachelor's degree paper, University of New Mexico, 1976), 2.

5. "United States Federal Census Collection, 1880–1930," for 1880 and 1900, Ancestry.com; *Albuquerque Business Directory for 1883* (Albuquerque: Armijo & Borradaile, Daily Journal Steam Printing House,) 62, 74; Ellis, "Albuquerque's Black Entrepreneurs, 1880–1933," 2.

6. Bernice Ann Rebord, "A Social History of Albuquerque, 1880–1885" (master's thesis, University of New Mexico, 1947), 5–66; Marianne Hanson, "Grant Chapel AME Church, Albuquerque, New Mexico (1883–)," BlackPast.org, http://www.blackpast.org/aaw/grant-chapel-ame-church-albuquerque-new-mexico-1883.

7. Barbara Richardson, *Black Directory of New Mexico* (Rio Rancho, N.M.: Panorama Press, 1976), 40–41, 48–49.

8. Ibid., 26.

9. Hughes and McCreight, *Albuquerque City Directory and Business Guide for 1901* (Albuqueque: Albuquerque Daily Citizen, 1901), 19, 34.

10. U.S. Bureau of the Census, *Negroes in the United States*, Bulletin 8 (Washington, D.C.: Government Printing Office, 1904), 38.

11. Ibid.,112.

12. Richardson, *Black Directory of New Mexico*, 41–42.

13. Cindy Gaillard, *Colores: Blackdom* (Albuquerque: New Mexico PBS, KNME TV, 1996). This documentary can be viewed at http://www.pbs.org/video/1482083459.

14. U.S. Bureau of the Census, *Negroes in the United States*, 38.

15. U.S. Bureau of the Census, *1900 Census of Population*, vol. 3, *New Mexico* (Washington D.C.: Government Printing Office, 1904), 120–21.

16. U.S. Bureau of the Census, *1910 Census of Population*, vol, 4, *New Mexico* (Washington D.C.: Government Printing Office, 1911), 493ff.

17. Richardson, *Black Directory of New Mexico*, 38, 40, 48.

18. "United States Federal Census Collection, 1880–1930," for 1900 and 1910, Ancestry.com.

19. U.S. Bureau of the Census, *Negroes in the United States*, 182–86, table 26.

20. Richardson, *Black Directory of New Mexico*, 26.

21. "United States Federal Census Collection, 1880–1930," for 1920, Ancestry.com.

22. New Mexico Secretary of State, "Negroes back of Social Equality Bill Presented in Legislature," *Albuquerque Morning Journal*, March 3, 1917.

23. James Lewis, "Albuquerque NAACP Letter to National NAACP Executive Secretary, John Shillady, and New Mexico House of Representatives (February 28, 1919)" in National Association for the Advancement of Colored People Collection, group 1, box C128, Library of Congress, Washington D.C.

24. Richardson, *Black Directory of New Mexico*, 26, 46.

25. U.S. Bureau of the Census, *1900 Census of Population*, vol. 2, pt. 2, 156–57.

26. Ellis, "Albuquerque's Black Entrepreneurs, 1880–1933," 14.

27. Ibid., 26. See also Nicholas Ciotola, *Italians in Albuquerque* (Mt. Pleasant, S.C.: Arcadia, 2002); Naomi Sandweiss, *Jewish Albuquerque: 1860–1960* (Mt. Pleasant, S.C.: Arcadia, 2011).

28. Ellis, "Albuquerque's Black Entrepreneurs, 1880–1933," 23–24.

29. U.S. Bureau of the Census, *1900 Census*, vol. 1, 667; U.S. Bureau of the Census, *1920 Composition and Characteristics of the Population by States*, vol. 3 (Washington, D.C.: Government Printing Office, 1921), 19ff.

30. U.S. Bureau of the Census, *1920 Composition and Characteristics of the Population by States*, vol. 4, table 18, 449.

31. Compiled and calculated for Albuquerque from "United States Federal Census Collection, 1880–1930," for 1920, Ancestry.com.

32. "Legislature Passes Jim Crow Amendment to the School Code," *Southwest Review* (Albuquerque), March 14, 1925.

33. Senate Bill 95 (March 1925), New Mexico State Senate, New Mexico Records and Archives, Santa Fe.

34. "Secretary of State Journal (March 1925)," New Mexico Secretary of State, New Mexico Records and Archives, Santa Fe.

35. Roger W. Banks, "Between the Tracks and the Freeway: African Americans in Albuquerque," in *African American History in New Mexico: Portraits from Five Hundred Years*, ed. Bruce A. Glasrud (Albuquerque: University of New Mexico Press, 2013), 170–85.

36. Catherine Watkins Duncan, "A Survey of the Separate Elementary Schools for Negroes in the State of New Mexico" (master's thesis, University of New Mexico, 1938), 4.

37. Zellmer R. Pettet and Charles E. Hall, *Negroes in the United States, 1920–32* (New York: Greenwood Press, 1969), 9.

38. See "United States Federal Census Collection, 1880–1930," 1930, Ancestry.com.

14 Obscured Collaboration

African American Presence in
the Myth of the White West

Tracey Owens Patton

Oh, give me a home where the Buffalo roam,
Where the Deer and the Antelope play,
Where seldom is heard a discouraging word
And the sky is not clouded all day. . . .
How often at night, when the heavens are bright,
With the lights of the glittering stars,
Have I stood here amazed, and asked as I gazed
If their glory exceeds this of ours.
      —Brewster Higley, "Home on the Range" (1872)

The rousing campfire song "Home on the Range" encapsulates what many believe it means to be a cowboy on the western frontier before the onset of the industrial revolution. Where there was freedom of space, freedom from the overcrowded East Coast, and freedom of movement for white bodies, particularly white male bodies. According to John Lomax in introducing his 1911 collection *Cowboy Songs, and other Frontier Ballads*, "Out in the wild in far-away places, of the big and still unpeopled west . . . survives the Anglo-Saxon ballad spirit that was active in secluded districts in England and Scotland even after the coming of Tennyson and Browning. This spirit is manifested both in the preservation of the English ballad and the creation of local songs."[1] "Home on the Range" was supposedly one of these English- or Scottish-inspired ballads, but, although the song is credited to nineteenth-century otolaryngologist Brewster Higley, its source may actually have been an African American chuck wagon cook. African American contributions to the West are often overlooked—or erased—in favor of maintaining the myth of an "all-white West." The West and the expansion westward are considered to be almost synonymous with ideologically dominant Euro-American culture, but the West has rich multicultural traditions. By the time Frederic Remington created his iconic paintings and Owen Wister penned his novel *The Virginian*, the romantic West, where life was said to be simple, had disappeared. The great cattle drives were long gone, and railroad tracks spanned the country. Wister's imaginary West ended with the 1892 Johnson County War.[2] It can be argued that white people in the West before and after Wister erased the contributions of black people. Black men were often the cooks on cattle drives and an active part of cowboy culture, and historian Robert Cantwell asserted that "Lomax collected his most famous song, 'Home on the Range,' not from a golden-haired prairie Galahad but from a black cook, who once worked a chuck wagon on a Texas cattle trail, in a 'low drinking dive' of San Antonio . . . [Lomax] consistently obscured black collaboration."[3]

This chapter focuses on African American men in the West after 1965. From "Home on the Range" to the present, African Americans and other people of color have been co-collaborators in the construction of the West. While going from the nineteenth century to the years after 1965 may seem like quite a jump, this span is characterized throughout by the common themes of erasure, invisibility, and racism. These three concepts bound the experience of black people in the West. While we often reflect on progress, little has changed in how African Americans have been represented and re-represented in the West. The historical documentation of African American women is all but erased in favor of men's achievements, and these male achievements come gift-wrapped, sanitized, and sold as white history.

African American discoveries, experiences, and narratives are commonly found in the margins if they are not altogether erased in the historical re-creation of the West. The purpose of this essay is to examine African American representation in the West and in the cowboy cultural arenas post-1965, with a focus on men. Dominant themes of erasure, invisibility, racism, and power experienced by African American men will be explored. While scholars have written about literary and other representations of African Americans in the West, few have analyzed African Americans as cowboys from the sixties to the present. In addition to art, dime novels, and posters, television and film are particularly effective tools with which to disseminate dominate tropes of the West and rhetorically and visually perpetuate the myth of the white West. Examining cowboy culture and rodeos can challenge the stereotypes, and we can then place people of color in the center of the narratives of the West. African American women also ventured to the western frontier, but their voices and experiences are the most erased, and, therefore, the least seen in photographs, television, film, and writing.[4] Until recently, western television programs and films rarely had African American women as central characters. If anything, black women appeared as cooks or prostitutes, and this has maintained a white patriarchal West. Therefore, I focus on black men in western television, film, and cowboy culture, while keeping in mind erasure, invisibility, and racism, and I arrive ultimately at a depiction of the lone African American in the West.

The West as White Enthymeme

An enthymeme is a rhetorical deductive argument used in Greek antiquity that can be taken as the common sense or something implied. The use of an effective enthymeme requires one to have intimate knowledge with a culture, because an enthymeme can stand in for the unspoken or unsaid. The fact that rodeos and cowboys have been construed as automatically white (the enthymeme) is problematic, given that rodeo culture has part of its heritage in Africa, but this fact has long been forgotten or buried. Historians Joe Frantz and Julian Choate Jr. note, however, that the iconic longhorns of Texas trace back to "the plains of northern Africa and Andalucía" where the Moors raised them and tended to them for a thousand years.[5] Christopher Columbus took to Spain this African knowledge, which eventually made its way to Hispaniola and up through the Americas.[6] Eventually the sport of rodeo and the concept of cowboy culture exploded, with popular Wild West shows spotlighting feats of skill and bravery accomplished by women and men in the arena. While the numbers of ethnic minorities in rodeo in the United States have dwindled since the days of the open frontier and the major cattle drives, these drives employed over forty thousand cowboys before the twentieth century and, of that number, between 25 percent and 30 percent were African American, American Indian, or Latino.[7] To narrow this down, it is estimated that there were between five thousand and six thousand African American cowboys participating in cattle drives.[8] This leads one to ask, how did all these cowboys of color disappear from history?

The myth of the West, which not only lives in the minds of Americans but has also long extended across the Atlantic, began with the idea of Manifest Destiny, westward expansion, and the settling of a so-called uninhabited locale (as Lomax's "still unpeopled west"). Manifest Destiny (1812–1860) was a concept used to rationalize population expansion over North America to the Pacific

Ocean and to acquire California, Oregon, the Southwest—one justification for the U.S.-Mexican War. Ideas behind westward expansion were popularized in paintings and books, despite erasure, genocide, and the dire loss of land for African American and American Indian peoples. Frederic Remington (painter), Theodore Roosevelt (U.S. president), Frederick Jackson Turner (historian), and Owen Wister (author of *The Virginian*), promoted westward expansion as crucial to the progressive development of the young United States. Ideas promoted by Turner and others, including cultural values of courage, hard work, and individualism, were used to justify the displacement of Native peoples. Eventually dime novels popularizing the exploits of Daniel Boone and Davy Crockett, coupled with the notion of a romantic past and a simpler time, made the West all that much more attractive. The fact that the "simpler time" had disappeared with such developments as railroad tracks, barbed wire fencing, and law enforcement was of little consequence. Likewise the eventual extinction of western cattle drives and closing of wide-open spaces were invisible to the easterners to whom these stories were largely marketed. Tall tales spun by Wister and others kept in motion an American West that no longer existed.

Cultural narratives regarding expansionism were so wildly popular "that over 50,000 Americans in the early 1840s took to the Oregon Trail and migrated west."[9] In her research Joan Burbick, an English and American studies scholar, found westward expansion "promoted the cult of Anglo-Saxon masculinity by romancing the cowboy.... [T]he winning of the American West ... had become a permanent part of American culture."[10] Wister, in keeping his white audience in mind, conveniently erased the racial diversity that existed in the West. "In Wister's revisionist telling of the 'wild West' he recounts and admires only the hard, industrious work of white men."[11] Wister's *The Virginian* ignores the widely known and respected group of Buffalo Soldiers who were a prominent feature of the West. African American cavalry units and infantry regiments served in Arizona, the Dakota Territory, Kansas, Montana, New Mexico, Nebraska, Oklahoma, Texas, Utah, Wyoming, and as far south as Mexico following the Civil War and before the Spanish-American War. The Buffalo Soldiers helped make the cattle expansion possible and a career as a cowboy a reality.[12] Given this racially and ethnically diverse past, what are the repercussions for this white supremacist revisionist history of the construction of the West in post-1965 U.S. African American society?

Dime novel tales and narratives and paintings glorifying white male accomplishments and erasing people of color fit well with U.S. policy of that time. For example, Jim Crow laws were eventually established after the 1896 ruling in the U.S. Supreme Court case *Plessy v. Ferguson*. This ushered in an era of "separate but equal" policy that not only segregated black Americans physically but also curtailed their civil rights, ability to vote, and social and economic mobility. Violation of these laws could lead to imprisonment or even death. Jim Crow, C. Vann Woodward writes, "constituted the most elaborate and formal expression of sovereign white opinion upon the subject."[13] These laws remained in place through 1964, and it was not until 1965 that African Americans could freely exercise their right to vote with the Voting Rights Act. I argue that Jim Crow laws had one of the largest effects on African Americans in the West.

The White West and Rodeo after 1965

Through images, narratives, and the law, the identity of who *was* the West and who *built* the West was fully imagined. The white western male was the stereotype of what could be achieved through hard work, a six-shooter, and traditional gender roles. After 1965, African Americans were supposed to finally be the recipients of equality and the promises found in the Constitution, due to the passage of the 1964 Civil Rights Act and the 1965 Voting Rights Act. These were followed by the decade of the Black Power movement when people, in part, worked to "intervene in and alter those racist stereotypes that had always insisted black was ugly, monstrous, undesirable," as bell hooks puts it.[14] Black people now were encouraged to directly confront the overt and covert forms of racism and oppression they faced on a daily basis. The days of Jim Crow were thought to be relegated to history, which is what makes the continuance of the myth of the white West so problematic. If the West, for white people, was supposed to be the place to begin anew without the shackles of oppression, then where could African Americans begin anew after 1965?

In 1946 African American western pioneer Era Bell Thompson noted in her autobiographical *American Daughter* an initial belief that black people were welcome in the West. However, Thompson and her family learn that the West is no paradise. As Michael K. Johnson writes in *Hoo-Doo Cowboys and Bronze Buckaroos*, they and other black pioneers in the West have

> left behind black communities to become part of a strange white frontier world, which offers greater opportunity for landownership, less (but not a complete lack of) racism, a degree of safety from the antiblack violence erupting throughout much of early twentieth-century America, and escape

from the corrupt Jim Crow culture of segregation and second-class citizenship. That escape, however, comes at the cost of separation from African American culture and community. Is it preferable to remain isolated from "our people" in the relative safety of the frontier or to risk the dangers of antiblack violence in the civilized metropolis?"[15]

This question that Johnson posits about violence, safety, and racism would become the key concern in the West for African Americans after 1965. Generations earlier, some territories and states had opened doors for African American migration westward, as with the Exodusters in Kansas in the late 1870s. As black pioneer and autobiographer Mifflin Wistar Gibbs wrote, "With thrift and a wise circumspection financially, their opportunities were good; from every other point of view they were ostracized, assaulted without redress, disenfranchised and denied their oath in a court of justice."[16] After Jim Crow, what spaces and places were available for African Americans to attain the American Dream in the United States generally and in the West in particular? Since the West was crafted as a white space, African Americans are a smaller percentage of the population in the region than they are in the South and in the metropolitan North. After 1965 the myth began to be challenged that only the South was racist. Vivid documentaries like the PBS *Eyes on the Prize* series debunked this as they showed, for example, whites in supposedly progressive Boston fighting against bussing for school integration. Oregon banned black people from moving to and living in the state altogether until the law was repealed in 1927.[17] Wyoming, known as the "Equality State," had a lynch rate thirty times higher than states in the deep South and out-lynched all of the other western states.[18] According to NAACP records, from 1889 to 1918 Wyoming lynched thirty-four people. The state's closest western competitors were California, with twenty-six lynchings, and Kansas and Montana, each with twenty-two lynchings."[19] In the Equality State, it is said, 14.7 percent of those lynched "were considered colored. This large percentage is disturbing because blacks did not make up fourteen percent of Wyoming's population"; they made up 1 percent. In fact, between 1910 and 1920 the lynch rate in Wyoming was "369 per 100,000 [or] sixty-two times higher than the national lynch rate." Per 100,000 people during this same decade, "Alabama's lynch rate was five, Georgia's was twelve, Louisiana's was eight, [and] Mississippi's was three."[20] Lynching was used as a tool to expel black people or prevent them from moving to the state, and Wyoming's black population continues to hover at 1.5 percent.[21] So despite "rising black populations after the Civil War, with . . .

numbers increasing 'thirteen fold' in Idaho, Wyoming, Colorado, New Mexico, Arizona, Utah, and Nevada between 1870 and 1920," these population increases were not sustained because the West did not guarantee equality for African Americans.[22] This is particularly problematic given that from "the earliest incursions into the Americas by Spanish explorers to the California Gold Rush and the Oklahoma land rush, African Americans have been present at every frontier and have been active participants in transforming those frontier settlements into thriving communities."[23]

In the sports arena, "because Jim Crow laws regulated African Americans to second-class citizenry, few blacks were permitted to participate in black-promoted rodeos," Demetrius Pearson writes.[24] As George B. Kirsch, Othello Harris, and Claire E. Nolte have noted, the Professional Rodeo Cowboys Association (formerly the Rodeo Cowboys Association) never formally excluded blacks, but "prior to the 1960s racism and the lack of the blacks among the professionals . . . effectively kept them out of the white competitions."[25] Frequently those in cowboy culture encountered signs that read "no dogs, no Negroes, no Mexicans."[26] This despite the fact that African American cowboys changed the sport of rodeo, in the same way that African Americans changed the face of the West.

Historically, rodeo parallels American mass culture because it was participated in and influenced by minority athletes whose legacy has been marginalized and overlooked. An example of this omission is the story of Bill Pickett, an African American from Taylor, Texas, who is credited for having invented "bulldogging," a popular rodeo event commonly known as steer wrestling. Until he became a celebrity for his trademark bulldogging technique, Pickett was forced to masquerade as a Mexican toreador because rodeos did not admit black contestants.[27]

In addition to Bill Picket in the early 1900s, Jessie Stahl, an African American cowboy, became famous for his saddle bronc riding abilities, and in 1920 a newspaper reporter crowned Stahl the "best wild horse rider in the west."[28] Yet he too was faced with institutionalized and structuralized forms of racism within rodeo. Eventually segregation in rodeo led to the creation of the All Indian Rodeo Cowboys Association and the Southwestern Colored Cowboys Association, which afforded these cowboys (and cowgirls) of color opportunities to compete. However, the forced racial segregation perpetuated the myth that western spaces like rodeo were all-white, thus reinscribing the belief that the entire West was too. Further, segregation continues in rodeo today, not in rules excluding blacks from competing but in perpetuation of white spaces that people of color may not feel comfortable occupying.

African American cowboys were and are forced to endure racism that the Professional Rodeo Cowboys Association (PRCA) passively and actively supported in the 1950s, 1960s, and beyond. Because of this racism and segregation, black PRCA competitors today are small in number. The PRCA does not retain official statistics on race, but in 2005 African American bull rider Abe Morris estimated that the association comprised about 97 percent white cowboys.[29] Media depictions of white cowboys reinscribe and perpetuate the racism. Cowboys of color were forced to create their own segregated rodeo communities, such as the Bill Pickett Invitational Rodeo Circuit, Indian National Finals Rodeo, Canadian Indian Finals Rodeo, and the Soul Circuits. As Demetrious Pearson notes, Soul Circuits began in the 1940s in southern rural communities and were "unsanctioned weekend competitions close to home. None of these rodeos on the Soul Circuit was sanctioned by the PRCA, the largest national and international governing body of professional rodeo. Although these rodeos are viable professional competitions, the payouts are nominal and exposure is minimal; therefore, they rarely enhance the marketability of the rodeo athlete."[30] Rodeo scholar Sally Schedlock and I believe that Soul Circuits were transformed into the Southwestern Colored Cowboys Association, for which famed cowboy Myrtis Dightman rode.[31] Dightman, who has been called the Jackie Robinson of rodeo, was the first African American bull rider to qualify for the PRCA National Finals Rodeo, in 1967, and the first serious contender for the world title.[32] In the 1960s, when he asked what it would take for him to win the world title, he was told to keep riding a bull like he had been—and to turn white.[33] In his research Demetrious Pearson found, after 1965, that "on several occasions, African American cowboys recalled incidents in which they were not welcomed at some of the mainstream rodeos. Several recounted incidents in which they were required to ride before the fans had entered the arena, while others competed after they had left. Incidents of unfair judging and the refusal to pay individuals for winning or placing were also mentioned. These and other incidents were among the reasons given for the formation of ethnic rodeos, riding clubs, and associations."[34]

After 1965, but particularly from the 1990s forward, African Americans can attest to a society obsessed with the appearance of equality but not honoring this in practice. Images of the cowboy world showed no racial strife because they were entirely deracinated. In Hollywood westerns, it pays to depict a "simpler time," one void or nearly void of African American bodies and where the few African Americans can simply transcend race if they try. In reality, during the black freedom movements and beyond, there was social unrest and upheaval, and in the West there was racism. By the 1990s it may have no longer be accept-able to deny an African American cowboy his ride on an animal, but it is okay to compare him to one. The caption under an image of world champion calf roper Fred Whitfield in 1999's *Western Horseman's Rodeo Legends* reads, "Like a lion poised to pounce, Whitfield sets up for a winning run at La Fiesta de los Vaqueros Rodeo in Tucson." Likewise for the only other ethnic minority athlete featured, world champion team roper Leo Camarillo: his caption read, "Loop at the ready, The Lion poised to pounce."[35] None of the eighteen white contestants were compared to beasts. As Schedlock and I write in *Gender, Whiteness, and Power in Rodeo*, "The use of an animal moniker places the African American cowboy in the animal position of rodeo and so if the 'animal' wins, then the competition is lost."[36]

Charles Sampson began his rodeo career at the age of twelve, after meeting Myrtis Dightman, and in 1982, he became the first African American PRCA rodeo world champion bull rider.[37] Born in 1967, Fred Whitfield began his rodeo career at the age of seven, calf roping, and he eventually became a PRCA member in 1990. Well into his forties he still competes in team roping and calf tying and has won over eight world titles at the PRCA Finals in Las Vegas, Nevada. In 1999 he won not only calf roping but also the coveted all-around cowboy title, the first for an African American.[38]

James Pickens Jr., known to many as Dr. Richard Webber on *Grey's Anatomy*, is a steer roper and participates in team penning.[39] He has participated in the United States Team Roping Championships and regularly participates in the nation's only touring African American rodeo, the Bill Pickett Invitational Rodeo. How did he come by his love of cowboy culture? "I'm a child of the '50s," Pickens says, "and my father was a big fan of TV westerns. Back then each network had at least 10 or 11 westerns, and my brother and I would try to watch all of them. The horse has always been my favorite animal. It's so beautiful and powerful. There's something about them that epitomizes freedom."[40]

Sampson, Dightman, and Pickens are the exception, not the rule. Rodeo is still the embodiment and performance of conquering the West, and western films still turn the real lived experience of cowboy culture, which includes cowboys or color, into white western myth. In re-creating a false narrative of something ostensibly all-white and all-male, western historiography and rodeo have not evolved but rather continue to reflect and replicate racial and racist angst. But not only is mediated erasure and misrepresentation of people of color commonplace, so too is the erasure of racism. As feminist scholar Mary Thompson writes, "The

Myrtis Dightman is thrown from No. 434 Tex M (Inman) at the 1970 National Finals Rodeo in Oklahoma City. *Courtesy Dickinson Research Center, National Cowboy and Western Heritage Museum, Oklahoma City.*

invisibility of whiteness and white privilege intensifies with the belief that race no longer matters and that achievement is equally obtainable to all who seek it. Success, in such a worldview blind to structural inequalities and hidden privileges, is a matter of making good choices."[41] If an African American is not successful, particularly in the West, where the Horatio Alger myth lives on, this is seen as a personal problem and certainly not due to the white supremacist structural and institutionalized forms of racism that undergird the United States.

New Myth: African American Men and the West in Television and Film

Rodeos are empirical practices in western television and film. In keeping with the myth of the West that was constructed, Hollywood western film and television capitalized on two types of representation concerning African American men: the sidekick and the lone man on the trail. Referencing R. Philip Loy's research on sidekicks, Michael K. Johnson notes that "while white sidekicks went wherever the hero went in the Hollywood western and were considered 'buddies and social equals,' that was not the case when (as in *Haunted Gold*) the sidekick was African American, as the black character 'did not eat or sleep (unless it was outdoors around a campfire) with the hero.'"[42]

Moving from film representations of African Americans in 1932, when *Haunted Gold* was released, to such film representations after 1965, we see changes. For one thing, blacks were at least more visible in movies produced during the Black Power era (1966–ca. 1980). Quintard Taylor aptly notes a new trope: "the stereotype of the black westerner as a solitary figure loosened from moorings of family, home, and community."[43] Taylor refers to this as the new myth of the West. Here African American men are no longer absent from western history, but the solitary figure supports the stereotype that a black man in the West can transcend race in part, as Johnson writes, "by separating himself from the black (eastern) community to become a member of a black (western) society."[44] Only through segregating oneself from a larger African American community can one be successful in the West—on white terms. Put another way, stripping oneself of a community that has the ability to challenge structural and institutional racism in the United States is the only way for a solitary African American to be acceptable in the white supremacist construction of the West. This lone figure harks to the fear that rap group Public Enemy referenced in *Fear of a Black Planet*. Are African Americans such a threat to the myth of the West that they must be limited to a single representative in an otherwise all-white western town? Is an African American man in the West only tolerated if he comes sans family and community? This, I argue, is the ultimate form of African American erasure after 1965, particularly in the twenty-first century. African Americans, you are welcome, so long as you come alone. This trope of black man minus community and family is particularly problematic given the legacy of enslavement that African and African American people had to endure, with the intentional separation of families. This solitary figure is further problematic because of what it suggests about the future. One African American cannot alter or challenge the myth of the white West or the continuation of that myth through mediated rhetoric. The lone African American male figure emblematizes all of the people of color who made up and make up the population of the West while keeping whiteness centered.

Media, as cultural studies scholars Stuart Hall and Herman Gray have asserted, are the most popular way we come to understand the dynamic state of the world, and race falls under this rubric. As I wrote in an article with coauthor Julie Snyder-Yuly, "Media create a racial Xanadu or paradise where there are no hegemonic hierarchies and all things are possible if one works hard enough to overcome personal failings not related to race, gender, or institutional and structural forms of discrimination and racism."[45] In the mediated representation of the Horatio Alger myth, all that is missing is the singing of the national anthem. Famous African American cowboy Nat Love (also known as Deadwood Dick), in his 1907 book, *The Life and Adventures of Nat Love*, catalogs his life of "wild west adventures"—from slave plantation to Kansas to life with American Indian people—as one of individual achievement. Void of the entanglements of family and community, Love is able to carry out mythic adventures and be the kind of African American whites desired in the West: one without other black people. He becomes the stereotype of exceptionalism. The words of another African American cowboy—Jim Perry, a roper and cook who worked on the XIT ranch in Texas for twenty years in the late 1800s—certainly puts Love's stereotype in context. "If it weren't for my damned old black face," Perry is quoted as having said, "I'd have been boss of one of these divisions long ago."[46] Perry was up against a white supremacist affirmative action and could not get beyond the "whites only" mandate that relegated him to cowboy, roper, and cook. He would never be a foreman despite twenty years of experience.

Hollywood replicated this stereotype on the big screen. Johnson writes, "In westerns of the [early] era, black actors sometimes appear as entertainers . . . but more commonly these characters are associated with domestic spaces or duties, appearing as cooks, maids, servants, and/or as messengers, and they most often function in comic roles."[47] For example, there are *Cimarron* (1930), which won the Oscar for best picture in 1930 and had an African American cast as a servant, and the 1936 film *Red River Valley* (later retitled *Man of the Frontier*, in which the African American cast had to dance for whites in a saloon. While there were early films that challenged white depictions of African Americans in the West, these did not have the power to trump the tropes. These include, for example, *The Homesteader* (1919), *The Exile* (1931), *Haunted Gold* (1933), *Riders of the Black Hills* (1938), *Harlem on the Prairie* (1937), *Two-Gun Man from Harlem* (1938), *Harlem Rides the Range* (1939), and *The Man Who Shot Liberty Valance* (1962). One of the most popular movie and television characters was the Lone Ranger, believed to have been based on Bass Reeves, a famous and feared African American U.S. marshal in Indian Territory.[48] Yet, loath to challenge the trope of whiteness, Hollywood westerns still valorize whiteness, thus the 2013 *Lone*

Ranger film features white actor Armie Hammer in the title role (and white actor Johnny Depp as his sidekick Tonto).

Popular television shows *The Rifleman* (1958–63) and *Rawhide* (1959–65) had African American performers. Sammy Davis Jr. and Woody Strode made frequent guest appearances, yet race was never a topic of conversation, even while civil rights, race, racism, and voting rights featured prominently in news at the time. Even decades later the popular television miniseries *Lonesome Dove* (1989) could not get beyond the stereotype of the solitary black westerner, Johnson notes, "and in so doing increases the weight of the burden of representation on the sole African American character." *Lonesome Dove,* like so many other film and television westerns, "desire to include African Americans in the western's ongoing narrative of national belonging . . . [but] without generating controversy or causing offense," Johnson writes.[49] Hence the Lone Ranger (Bass Reeves) continues to be depicted as white.

It should be noted that there is a long history of African Americans making their own films and depicting their lives as they have seen them. As Johnson notes of these, "We must be conscious that the films both draw from the mainstream western and revise the genre to appeal to a specifically African American audience."[50] These films use story lines that challenge the traditional tropes and use African Americans as more than props for white actors. During the 1960s and 1970s westerns were actually made that focused on civil rights issues. Johnson writes, "The westerns of [this] era suggest contradictory positions on the possible outcomes of the civil rights movement, sometimes telling stories that suggest the relatively easy incorporation of African Americans into the western genre and the American nation and at other times spinning out narratives that reveal the intransigence of prejudice and difficulty of fully incorporating black Americans into either the nation or the genre."[51] In civil rights westerns such as the *Rawhide* episode titled "The Incident of the Buffalo Soldier" there were cautious approaches to social concerns, keeping a multiracial audience in mind. Western films such as *Buck the Preacher* (1972) and *Blazing Saddles* (1974) used humor and caustic satire to challenge racism and stereotypes while centering African American actors in the western genre. There were more explicit overtures to the trauma of racism and racist violence in a 1971 *Bonanza* episode, "The Desperado." In this episode, directly referencing to white racism, African Americans are on the top and whites are on the bottom. This sort of direct confrontation with racism was also seen in *Boss Nigger* (1975). More recently the television shows *Deadwood* (2004–2006) and *Hell on Wheels* (2011–2016) portrayed a multiracial and multiethnic settlement of the West beyond the black-white binary. Finally, sci-fi westerns have appeared: the television show *Firefly* (2002–2003) and movies *The Book of Eli* (2010) and *Django Unchained* (2012). In *Firefly* an African American woman appeared on the frontier—something rarely seen. Black women have been nearly erased from popular depictions of the western frontier. As journalist Danielle Belton notes, however, shows like *Firefly* "feature substantial black characters who are in a position of power but largely function as a helpmate to their white counterparts."[52] Still, in the sci-fi western genre, one can find African Americans featured in a variety of roles, as well as multiracial and multiethnic characters transcending race and righting a wrong (in *Django Unchained*), as well as story lines that have African American experiences, history, and signifiers embedded in the plots (in *The Book of Eli*).

At times Hollywood is able to place African Americans back into the West and even to center them, thus challenging its own all-white West that it seems to have been so keen on recycling. The problem lies in the fact that many of these films are so over the top with satire and parody (*Blazing Saddles*) or not historically accurate or plausible (*Django Unchained*) that viewers are able to walk away from such temporary inversions of power having seen them as temporary carnivalesque moments, the likes of which Bakhtin describes in *Rabelais and his World*. Through the concept of the carnival, Bakhtin reconstructs a type of world that challenges the hegemonic hierarchy through humor, laughter, masks, masquerades, and performance. The performance in this case is film. In these mediated moments, hegemony can be temporarily displaced and upended, but at the conclusion, life reverts to back to the status quo hierarchy. Given that the white, patriarchal West continues to be depicted, it can be argued that the temporary power inversions have not effectively debunked the stereotype of the all-white West but rather allow a multiracial West to exist side by side with it. White racism is periodically unmasked, but as soon as the show is over, the status quo is returned and whiteness centered. If African Americans in the West appeared front and center, it would no longer surprise people to think that the Lone Ranger was based on a black man, and a lone African American male would not represent all racial and ethnic diversity in the West. The important, but marginal, mediated inversions are not powerful enough to displace the dominant trope of white supremacy in the West. White supremacy has been embedded for far too long and continues to undergird the history of the country. Only when the very foundations of white supremacy are challenged will revisionist history be centered and last longer than a temporary, carnivalesque moment.

⊞

Behind the mediated depictions of an imagined all-white West, or a West where there is a lone African American male to represent everyone else, is another world. Here are the lives of African American men and women who actually helped make up the fabric of the West. Regardless of how diversity is represented in the West, race is the ever-present enthymeme. The West has never been all-white but has had a multiplicity of players: African Americans, American Indians, Chinese Americans, and Latinas/os, to name just a few groups. There have been African American cowboys and cowgirls, and there exist films, poems, songs, and stories that all provide a counter-narrative to the white supremacy that has been so embraced and perpetuated into the twenty-first century. These stories and experiences surmount the narrative of erasure, invisibility, and racism that are temporarily forced upon the visual and rhetorical palette. But even in current sci-fi westerns where there is more racial and ethnic diversity represented, one is forced to put race aside in favor of a post-racial ideal (there is one African American and race no longer matters). The lived reality for African Americans after 1965 is that there is no paradise in the West for them. Erasure, invisibility, and racism continue. One has to be able to see behind the screen and dig into the margins of history—and the margins of the present—to access African American people in the West.

Notes

Epigraph: "Home on the Range," lyrics by Dr. Brewster Higley (1840, 1927 1960), https://www.kshs.org/kansapedia/home-on-the-range/17165.

1. John Avery Lomax, *Cowboy Songs, and Other Frontier Ballads* (New York: Sturgis & Walton, 1911), xvii.

2. For an interpretation that challenges the myth of the white West, see Tracey Owens Patton and Sally M. Schedlock, *Gender, Whiteness, and Power in Rodeo: Breaking away from the Ties of Sexism and Racism* (Lanham, Md.: Lexington Books, 2012), 5. The Johnson County War, also referred to as the War on Power River, occurred in Wyoming in April 1892. This war stemmed from the proliferation of small ranches (run by cowboys who were forced to homestead) and their clash with the larger ranches run by cattlemen upset by the number of new ranches that had sprung up. A gunfight ensued and a two-day standoff between ranchers, hired guns, and law enforcement. Eventually the U.S. Cavalry, Wyoming senators, an acting Wyoming governor, and President Benjamin Harrison were dispatched to stop the fighting.

3. Robert Cantwell, *When We Were Good: The Folk Revival* (Cambridge: Harvard University Press, 1996), 72.

4. See Michael K. Johnson, *Hoo-Doo Cowboys and Bronze Buckaroos: Conceptions of the African American West* (Jackson: University Press of Mississippi, 2014); Tracey

Owens Patton, and Julie Snyder-Yuly, "The 'Tyra Tyrade': Reinforcing the Sapphire through Online Parody," in *Black Women's Portrayals on Reality Television: The New Sapphire*, Donnetrice C. Allison (Lanham, Md.: Lexington Books, 2016), 127–48.

5. Joe B. Frantz and Julian Ernest Choate Jr., *The American Cowboy: The Myth and the Reality* (Norman: University of Oklahoma Press, 1955), 20.

6. Richard W. Slatta, *Cowboys of the Americas* (New Haven: Yale University Press, 1990), 9.

7. Bob Jordan, *Rodeo History and Legends* (Montrose, Co.: Rodeo Stuff, 1993).

8. Dwayne Mack, "The Black West," in *Making of the American West: People and Perspectives*, ed. Benjamin H. Johnson, Perspectives in American Social History (Santa Barbara, Calif.: ABC-CLIO, 2007), 135–60.

9. Patton and Schedlock, *Gender, Whiteness, and Power in Rodeo*, 4.

10. Joan Burbick, *Rodeo Queens: On the Circuit with America's Cowgirls* (New York: Public Affairs, 2002), 21.

11. Patton and Schedlock, *Gender, Whiteness, and Power in Rodeo*, 5–6.

12. Ibid., 158.

13. C. Vann Woodward, *The Strange Career of Jim Crow* (New York: Oxford University Press, 2002), 23, 7.

14. bell hooks, *Killing Rage* (New York: H. Holt, 1995), 120.

15. Johnson, *Hoo-Doo Cowboys and Bronze Buckaroos*, 83.

16. Mifflin Wistar Gibbs, *Shadow and Light: An Autobiography* (1902), excerpts, National Humanities Center Resource Toolbox, ehttp://nationalhumanitiescenter.org/pds/ maai/identity/text4/gibbs.pdf.

17. Elizabeth McLagan and the Oregon Black History Project, *A Peculiar Paradise: A History of Blacks in Oregon, 1788–1940* (Portland, Ore.: Georgian Press, 1980), 25–30, 61, 157–71.

18. Todd Guenther, "The List of Good Negroes: African American Lynchings in the Equality State," *Annals of Wyoming: The Wyoming History Journal*, Spring 2009, 2–3.

19. Regan Joy Kaufman, "Discrimination in the 'Equality State': Black-White Relations in Wyoming history," *Annals of Wyoming: The Wyoming History Journal*, Winter 2005, 22–23.

20. Guenther, "List of Good Negroes," 23.

21. U.S. Census Bureau, "State and County Quick Facts," 2013, http:// www.census.gov/ quickfacts/.

22. Johnson, *Hoo-Doo Cowboys and Bronze Buckaroos*, 4.

23. Ibid.

24. Demetrious W. Pearson, "Shadow Riders of the Subterranean Circuit: A Descriptive Account of Black Rodeo in the Texas Gulf Coast Region," *Journal of American Culture* 27, no. 2 (June 2004): 192.

25. Quoted in Patton and Schedlock, *Gender, Whiteness, and Power in Rodeo*, 390. Also see Michael Allen, *Rodeo Cowboys in the North American Imagination* (Reno: University of Nevada Press, 1998), 243.

26. Patton and Schedlock, *Gender, Whiteness, and Power in Rodeo*, 164; Paul Wachter, "Fred Whitfield and the Black Cowboys of Rodeo: The Champion Calf Roper is

a Legend and an Outlier," *The Undefeated*, https://theundefeated.com/features/fred-whitfield-and-the-black-cowboys-of-rodeo.

27. Pearson, "Shadow Riders of the Subterranean Circuit," 192.

28. Philip Durham, and Everett L. Jones, *The Adventures of the Negro Cowboys* (New York: Bantam, 1969), 107.

29. Abe Morris, *My Cowboy Hat Still Fits: My Life as a Rodeo Star* (Greybull, Wyo.: Pronghorn Press, 2005), 339.

30. Pearson, "Shadow Riders of the Subterranean Circuit," 196.

31. See Patton and Schedlock, *Gender, Whiteness, and Power in Rodeo*.

32. George B. Kirsch, Othello Harris, and Claire E. Nolte, *Encyclopedia of Ethnicity and Sports in the United States* (Westport, Ct.: Greenwood Press, 2000), 390.

33. Andy Smith, "Bull Rider Paved Way for Blacks in Rodeo Arena," in *Conroe (Tex.) Courier*, November 11, 1997.

34. Pearson, "Shadow Riders of the Subterranean Circuit," 197.

35. Gavin Ehringer, *Western Horseman Rodeo Legends: 20 Extraordinary Athletes of America's Sport* (Colorado Springs, Colo.: Western Horseman, 1999), 205.

36. Patton and Schedlock, *Gender, Whiteness, and Power in Rodeo*, 173–74.

37. "2003 Hall of Fame Inductee, Charles Sampson," National Multicultural Western Heritage Museum and Hall of Fame, http://www.cowboysofcolor.org/profile.php?ID=3; Professional Rodeo Cowboys Association, http://www.prorodeo.com/.

38. "Biography," Fred Whitfield: The Official Website, http://www.fredwhitfield.com/ .

39. "About the Sports of Team Penning and Ranch Sorting," United States Team Penning Association, http://www.ustpa.com/index.php?cat=what.

40. Latoya M. Smith, "Backtalk with James Pickins, Jr.," *Black Enterprise*, July 2009, 96.

41. Mary Thompson, "Learn Something from This: The Problem of Optional Ethnicity on America's Next Top Model," *Feminist Media Studies* 10, no. 3 (2010): 335–52.

42. Johnson, *Hoo-Doo Cowboys and Bronze Buckaroos*, 115.

43. Taylor, *In Search of the Racial Frontier*, 22.

44. Johnson, *Hoo-Doo Cowboys and Bronze Buckaroos*, 11.

45. Patton and Snyder-Yuly, "The 'Tyra Tyrade,'" 130.

46. Richard W. Slatta, *Cowboy: The Illustrated History* (New York: Sterling, 2006), 75.

47. Johnson, *Hoo-Doo Cowboys and Bronze Buckaroos*, 103–4.

48. See Art Burton, *Black Gun, Silver Star: The Life and Legend of Frontier Marshal Bass Reeves* (Lincoln: University of Nebraska Press, 2006).

49. Johnson, *Hoo-Doo Cowboys and Bronze Buckaroos*, 164.

50. Ibid., 103.

51. Ibid., 158.

52. Danielle Belton, "Blacks in Space," *American Prospect* 20, no. 5 (2009), http://prospect.org/article/blacks-space, paragraph 14.

15 Kama'āinas and African Americans in Hawaii

Making Sense of the Black Hawaiian Experience
with Dr. Kathryn Waddell Takara

Herbert G. Ruffin II and Kathryn Waddell Takara

The following oral history encompasses black Hawaiian history and culture based on the testimony of black Hawaiian scholar Kathryn Waddell Takara. Herb Ruffin conducted this interview by phone on September 4, 2015. This unique history begins with Takara's youth in Jim Crow Tuskegee, Alabama. In 1959, as one of the few black students to attend the Quaker-run George School near Philadelphia, Pennsylvania, she began acquiring the ability to function as a dignified black person in white-majority spaces. Here she met future Black Panther Party leader Kathleen Cleaver and followed in the footsteps of another freedom rights movement activist, Julian Bond. In 1962, during the height of the civil rights movement, Takara attended Tufts University, and in the following year she met her husband during a civil rights movement North-South student exchange at the Tuskegee Institute. Her passion for justice deepened after 1966, starting with the death of her cousin, civil rights leader Samuel "Sammy" Leamon Younge Jr. While she was a UC Berkeley graduate student, her relationship with Cleaver deepened, and she and her husband allowed the Panthers to use their Oakland home as a safe house. With the urban crisis close at hand, the Takaras envisioned their freedom dreams being fulfilled abroad, and in a sense they made it halfway there: obtaining living-wage employment led to their decision to move to Hawaii in 1968.

In Hawaii, Takara immediately discovered that disempowerment of black people as a group and erasure of their collective present and past were typical of Hawaii's history and culture. Instead she found blackness in the Hawaiian Consciousness Movement of the late 1960s and the 1970s, a Hawaiian independence and cultural renaissance movement patterned in part on the Black Panther movement. She also found blackness addressed by people like local

African American journalist and labor activist Frank Marshall Davis, and Barack ("Barry") Obama's white grandfather, Stan, who understood that in order for Barry to remain principled on the mainland, he would have to be prepared for that experience in Oahu by understanding what it meant to be a stereotypical black man in America.

In 1971, Takara started producing knowledge on black Hawaiians as a University of Hawaii professor, scholar, and public historian. She has been responsible for uncovering the histories of many black Hawaiian, including Betsey Stockton, Wendell F. Crockett, and Alice Augusta Ball, who has a state holiday named after her. For Takara, in order for Hawaiian and U.S. West scholarship to evolve, scholars must begin intersecting new fields and ignored experiences, such as Africana studies and histories beyond the mainland United States—in Melanesia and Polynesia, for example. For persons of African descent this includes a rich black past that dates back to the reign of the first Hawaiian king, Kamehameha I (1782–1819), if not before.

Interview with Kathryn Waddell Takara

Herbert G. Ruffin II (HR): Who is Kathryn Waddell Takara?

Kathryn Waddell Takara (KT): I am from a long line of Tuskegee, Alabama, folk. Also, the other side of the family is kind of a Louisiana, Texas, Ohio line. I was born and raised in 1943 in Tuskegee, educated at Chambliss Children's House, the lab school to Tuskegee Institute, up to through my first year of public high school, when we had secondhand books passed over from the white schools and lagging enrollment of students due to planting and harvest seasons when many students had to work with their sharecropping families and missed a lot of school. My parents decided at that time to send me away to prep school in 1959 to acquire a first-rate education, which they both felt was necessary to my success as a black child. It was just when school integration was trying to happen but hadn't yet in Alabama. So I went to a Quaker boarding school in Pennsylvania. Before that I think I was fairly well prepared by going to the lab school at Tuskegee. My parents were both educators. My mother taught French [and] German and my father was a cofounder of the veterinary school and was a veterinarian. So I grew up with this intellectual setting all around and poor rural setting close by in Macon County, which was about 80 percent black in those days. When I went to the George School—where Julian Bond had attended a few years before me—I found myself in a sea of whiteness that I hadn't had contact with before. At that time, my feeling and view of whiteness was scary:

southern white power and violence. So here I was in this school with a lot of elite people's kids, and I had to make this adjustment from an all-black community to an all-white community.

Fortunately I had an English teacher at George School who encouraged me to write. I must add that I had begun journal writing during my earliest of years, when my mother would give me a diary each year for my birthday, and every day she encouraged me to write. Then I was encouraged by this teacher of English, Ken Keskenin, who told me, "You must write your stories." Because I was so homesick—I had seen so much already in the Deep South, and did yet not have my voice—I began to write stories, which was the foundation for my being a writer today. Meanwhile, I should mention that by the time I was four or five years old, not only did I know I was black and different from other people not in our community, but I had internalized other things about us as a group, such as that black people were ignorant, ugly, irresponsible, and inferior, which informed my being, despite my parents' and community's teachings to the contrary. Jim Crow was a powerful influence in our lives, minds, and sometimes our bodies.

The Quaker boarding school that I attended in my teens was in Pennsylvania in Bucks County. That was a good segregated train ride away, overnight. Social acceptance throughout my educational experiences was always an issue. Academic success and holding school offices, being in clubs, and on committees were not a problem, and I could excel, but because I was the only visible black, except for the kitchen help, when it came to anything like dating or visiting students' homes on long weekends and holidays, I was lonely. I did not get asked out on dates, and from high school through most of college that was always a big issue, especially when invitations were made and rescinded by parents of students. I completed my high school education at George School. During that time, the school's admission policy seemed to be that they would have one black student at a time or two, and there were some very distinguished people, including Julian Bond, Kathleen Neal Cleaver, and the son of the Chief Anderson who trained the Tuskegee airmen. That was its own kind of influence.

On to college at Tufts University, where I thought I wanted to study to be a doctor but not a veterinarian like my dad. Nor did I want to be a French and German professor like my mom. After my first year at Tufts, I went to France for a summer study program, lived with a French family in southern France, and felt free from prejudice, segregation, and discrimination for the first time in my life. I decided then that I would become a French major. I changed my major from pre-med to French because essentially I did not want to live in the

United States. When I returned to Tufts in 1962, the civil rights movement was heating up and getting really active.

In 1963, during spring break, I met my future husband, a white student at Wesleyan, who was at Tuskegee for a civil rights, North-South student exchange along with some other Wesleyan students. When I returned to Tufts and when he returned to Wesleyan, he called me, and we dated. We fell in love and got married after a year or a year and a half. I think I wanted to get out of the dormitory and the feeling of being an outsider. We were idealists, but also marriage took me away from the campus, the campus activities and feeling alienated. And I could develop my identity more on my own without always waiting to be accepted, welcomed, or invited someplace. I valued the courses that I was taking and the knowledge they provided.

In 1965 I was awarded a Fulbright fellowship, and we went to Bordeaux, France, where I translated West African and Caribbean poetry from French to English for one year and learned of the diaspora and themes of racism, colonialism, and struggles on an international stage. While in France, on January 3, 1966, my first cousin, Sammy Younge, a brother to me since I was an only child, and Student Nonviolent Coordinating Committee and Tuskegee Institute Advancement League activist, was shot in the head and killed in Tuskegee while trying to use a white bathroom. I was heartbroken and angry. Then my husband and I both got accepted to UC Berkeley, and so we went there for graduate school in 1966.

However, let me just interject that my husband's father . . . disowned him for marrying me but finally accepted him and me back into the family once we had a child. But he was full of hate. We had to keep him from the wedding because he threatened to come and kill us. We had to have some guards.

[The era of] 1966–68 at Berkeley was a very exciting time! Intellectually it was the Free Speech Movement. It was the creation of black studies, ethnic studies, the Weathermen, SDS, the United Farm Workers, antiwar protests, teargas. Everything was happening there, so it was a very exciting and mesmerizing time. I re-hooked up with Kathleen Neal Cleaver, whom I knew from Tuskegee. The Black Panther connection—its issues, community programs, and the police, in spite of my white husband—became a real force in our lives.

Inside Berkeley we received no static. We lived in Oakland. I wasn't on campus except for classes and student rallies. I got pregnant my second year, while I was teaching French as a teaching assistant, and had my first child.

HR: Did you live in the hills or did you live in the flatlands?

KT: We lived in the flatlands on Sixty-Second Street below Telegraph. We also lived in another community. The second year we lived on Delaware Street a half-block from San Pablo.

Black Migration and Settlement

HR: Can you briefly connect your story into this description of the black migration and settlement to Hawaii with emphasis on that post-1966 time period?

KT: Yes. With all the demonstrations, antiwar, as well as the Black Panther Party getting attacked by police officials—I mean the shoot-outs and all of that—security felt very precarious. Actually our house was kind of a safe house twice when people were on the run, which was interesting and very much on the edge. As I mentioned, I got pregnant. It was going to be a biracial child. We decided that we wanted to live out of the country again. So applications were made to Africa and various international agencies and Hawaii. Hawaii was the first job acceptance that came through. In 1968, when we arrived in Hawaii, my husband had a teaching job at Iolani School, which was primarily an Asian American prep school, although its diversity has greatly expanded since then. It was next to the Punahou School in terms of its elite reputation. We moved into the Honolulu community and had a bit of trouble finding housing, I think due to discrimination against blacks. We had our social activities through Iolani School. I quickly concluded I didn't like it here at all. I didn't like it because there was no visible black community except in the military, and our numbers in the Islands were about 2 to 3 percent. There also seemed to be a limited awareness of some of the race, ethnic, and class issues that I been involved with in Berkeley.

I found a group of progressive lawyers, ministers, and other types of activists. But the issue was more the Hawaiian Consciousness Movement and a cultural renaissance. What surprised me was that the Hawaiian activists, who were protesting when I arrived here in the late 1960s and early '70s, wore the black berets, the black leather jackets (even though it's hot here), and the black outfits modeled after the Black Panthers. They were also aware of their concerns and issues like the feeding project, the home project, the free stores and poverty, colonialism, imperialism, demonstrations, revolutionary rhetoric, and things like that. They were aware and outspoken. They were trying to stop land development over the local way of farming, the loss of Hawaiian lands, the loss of local power to mainland developers, corporations, and all of that. I hooked up with that movement and the antiwar movement because there wasn't really a black movement. When I got on it, I created some cultural and educational events to educate the larger community as to who black people are.

One of the events that I created was . . . titled "Blacks in Chinatown." It wasn't based on history. I organized and produced it at the Chinese Cultural Plaza in downtown Honolulu. And that was a month of activities that included our local black artists and intellectuals, as well as our social clubs who sponsored various events like a fashion show, hair braiding, talent, et cetera. That was a huge undertaking for me. I would say that was one of my bigger organizational projects, and when I became employed at the University of Hawaii at Manoa (UH) that experience served me well. I was able to organize and produce several national conferences and events at the university with outstanding African American intellectuals.

HR: When were you hired by the UH?

KT: I was hired part time at the University of Hawaii in 1971, full time in 1989, and stayed until I retired early in 2007. I spent my early years part time as a lecturer and as an instructor in French and ethnic studies. At that time, the university did not have a full-time tenure track position in ethnic studies for black studies. It took fighting by me and people in the community, as well as some administrators, to get that set up in 1989. I was a very popular teacher but also very outspoken. At UH, I never got tenure. I transferred to [the] Interdisciplinary Studies [Program], where I continued to create more courses on black and African studies, a total of six different courses.

This invisibility and political control is very typical of Hawaii's black history. Another example: There was a black man named English Bradshaw who was living here in the late 1960s. He got together with a Japanese professor named Dennis Ogawa, and they were the founders of the Ethnic Studies Program (now a department) in 1969 or 1970. Bradshaw approached me and asked me if I would be interested in teaching a course or two in black studies. I was eager and still hurt and angry after the death of my cousin Sam. I knew black history, made a solid proposal, and I got hired in '71 as an instructor of black studies. I had many students, sometimes seventy in a class in those early days, and great student evaluations up until the time of my retirement. My point is that Bradshaw was/ is never credited for his role in establishing [the] Ethnic Studies [Program] at the university with Dennis Ogawa.

HR: How many persons of African descent were on the faculty?

KT: At that time, in the 1970s to '90s, there might have been two or three professors in the College of Arts and Science at the main campus and a very few in the specialty schools. To this day, according to professor friends on campus, there probably are no more than eight black professors in arts and sciences, and not all are tenured.

HR: Is this institutional?

KT: Yes. I say it's that they don't recruit blacks, and that committees hire people that they know or friends of people that apply and are recommended. You know, it's an island. Those professors who went to Yale, they'll hire someone from Yale. I was never let in on the search teams, although I requested it. They had a program for exchanges with different colleges on the continental U.S. or the mainland, and I said that was a great place to recruit, because there were a few HBCUs [historically black colleges and universities] on the list who were available to participate in that program. I suggested that we could do active recruitment and add some other HBCUs to the list, or look at colleges and universities that had high black enrollment. But my ideas never went through.

When I arrived in 1968, . . . I found an active antiwar movement and a spreading Black Power (power to the people) movement. These attitudes were playing out in the military [in] black soldiers who had been to Vietnam and who felt they were still not being treated equally. Shortly thereafter, there was a small uprising at the Kaneohe Bay Marine Corps Air Station. I got involved with the black soldiers who were disproportionately incarcerated in the brig for often-minor infractions. A group of concerned civilians organized a group called CORPAS to deal with some of these issues and met with the admirals and commanders et cetera to help get some of these young men out of the brig. I worked with another black woman, named Cass Burnett, and some local residents. As a result of that involvement, Cass Burnett, I, and members of CORPAS started a small black cultural center, the first of its kind to my knowledge. It was located in Waikiki. We could only have access to the donated space on Sunday afternoons as it was used for a clinic the rest of the week. We provided a space for black military and others, and there was always a small crowd, from ten to twenty people, mainly military who would come together to discuss issues of the day and socialize. We had a small portable library. We cooked and offered free soul food. Sometimes there would be a speaker. We had music. It was a place where soldiers could see and meet with other community black folks in town and off base. That was the first black cultural center here in the islands.

Once I started teaching black studies, a woman in my very first class mentioned that Frank Marshall Davis lived in the islands and asked if I would like to meet him. Frank Marshall Davis was a writer who was included in an anthology that

I was teaching at the time. I learned soon thereafter that he had not only been a poet but an outstanding journalist and labor activist concerned with issues of race and class. I began my weekly visits with Frank Marshall Davis in 1972, which continued until his death in 1987. I eventually did my PhD research and dissertation on Davis, another sad story of an illustrious black man in Hawaii who has been overlooked and forgotten—that is, until President Obama was elected.

I'll just slip this in here: . . . I never met President Barack Obama, but I did meet his grandfather, Stan. His grandparents were helping to raise him while he attended Punahou, and his grandfather was best friends with Frank Marshall Davis. Davis was unique and lived in Waikiki at the time. His door was always open. He had jazz, books, and always had the news on. He was a great conversationalist and an intellectual. Stan recognized that Davis was a black intellectual devoted to social change and black culture, and I think he wanted to expose Barry [Barack Obama] to such a strong, influential, principled black man. There were surely a few other black intellectuals around, but they were tucked away in the military, or maybe Stan just did not have access to them.

Early Publications, Stories, and Race Relations

KT: I am going to put a pause in my talking about myself in Hawaii and move back to 1975, when I was asked to contribute a piece to a book called *Montage: An Ethnic History of Women in Hawai'i*. I was asked to contribute to the black component. I wrote a piece, "Who Is the Black Woman in Hawai'i?" It was published in 1977.

Before the publication of *Montage* by the University of Hawaii in 1971, I was interviewed for an article that was published in *Honolulu Magazine*. It was called "To Be Black in Paradise: The Myth of Racial Harmony in Hawai'i." A lot of the information that I shared in that article, I would say is still very correct. *Honolulu Magazine* is one of the most sophisticated, picturesque, and classy magazines here in the islands, not counting the literary journals. After publication of the interview, in the letters to the editor, people would say things like, "Well, why doesn't she go back to where she came from?" and "We don't have prejudice here."

The one thing that people who live in Hawaii should know is that it is offensive to many Hawaiians by blood and culture to call the local residents and immigrants Hawaiians. So we refer to each immigrant ethnic group by their place of origin or as local, particularly due to the large amount of interracial marriages. I wanted to make that distinction from Native Hawaiians, even when you said "black Hawaiians" for blacks who were born and raised in the Islands. Better to say "Hawaii blacks" unless one of the parents is of Hawaiian blood. It's a very sensitive and respectful way of talking and writing about the diverse people who live here. If they are people who have come here and lived here a long time like me, we are called "*Kamaʻāina.*" If people are born here and mixed-race with Hawaiians, then they are black Hawaiians or just Hawaiian. Otherwise, it's "blacks in Hawaii" or "African Americans in Hawaii" or "black residents of Hawaii" or "black families." The term "Hawaiian" is currently usually reserved for blood quantum, and it's a very touchy subject now since there is all this sovereignty movement, voting, protests, occupations, and all.

HR: Just to briefly break the train of thought, as you talk about sovereignty you mentioned leaving the mainland and said you and your husband were looking for a new place out of the country and mentioned Hawaii. What did you mean? Did you see Hawaii as a place out of the country, or were you talking about it in juxtaposition to leaving the mainland, continental U.S.?

KT: I think I was talking about mainland, but also that whole issue of having a nonwhite majority was attractive to both of us, although I knew very little about Hawaii except my hurried research at the last minute. It was the first job that came through, and we had just graduated. It was just over from California, so we made the decision to come here. The whole movement toward self-determination, nationhood, and all of that has become only much more active since I've been here. To the point now where they're protesting the observatories on Mauna Kea and Haleakala, the military occupation, and outside developments and destruction of agricultural lands. . . .

Returning to the issue of black history in Hawaii, I was asked to do this article for *Montage,* and what I found out was that I couldn't find anything about black women in Hawaii. We were totally invisible in history. I finally went to two main sources. One was the State Archives and the other one was the Mission House, where the writings of sea captains, sailors, missionaries, and settlers from the earliest of days of contact and relations may be found.[1] That is where I discovered nineteenth-century black history in Hawaii. The first woman that I found was Betsey Stockton, who was a freed slave from the president of Princeton University, Reverend Ashbel Green, who had recognized her brilliance and opened his library for her. She was caught up in the missionary fervor that many blacks at the period of time held and wanted to go to Liberia.

However, Stockton ended up coming to Hawaii in 1823 with the Reverend Charles Samuel Stewart family and friends of Reverend Green. After a brief sojourn in Honolulu, they proceeded on to Maui, which at that time was kind of a real economic center of the islands, what with the whaling and shipping industry and expansionism of the United States. She quickly recognized that there were no schools for commoners on Maui. So she established a small school and had students composed mainly of just regular folk, whether they were missionary kids or local Hawaiian kids. She was very knowledgeable in English, math, Latin, and all of the basic subjects. She also introduced the notion of industrial education, homemaking, and manual arts and crafts. Truth be told, she only stayed in the islands for about three years, with this family. Then Mrs. Stewart got very ill, and the decision was made to return home. Stockton decided to return to New Jersey and help her. It should be made clear that the Stewards announced at her arrival that Stockton was neither a slave nor a servant, because many of the missionaries immediately wanted her to come and help them. But no, she was a teacher, she taught, and she was a Christian.

Stockton also met and became friends with an earlier black settler who had arrived as a whaler and stayed. There were lots of black whalers at that time. In fact, I would say that up until the 1840s, blacks who jumped ship in Hawaii and stayed became entrepreneurs, musicians, married locally and felt good living in the islands. However, after the 1840s, when a lot of whites, and many of them southern planters and plantation owners familiar with slavery, began to come, then blacks stopped coming in any significant numbers, a pattern that remained essentially until the turn of the twentieth century, when they arrived once more in the military. . . .

The next person that I researched was Anthony Allen, an ex-slave, who greeted the early missionaries as an advisor to Hawaii's first king, Kamehameha I (1782–1819). With this role he was given land, wives, and started a boardinghouse, farm, grog shop, and small hospital for black seamen, among other accomplishments. Can you imagine? We don't hear about this stuff. . . . Do not let me get fired up.

By the 1880s, as more whites arrived and became planters and advisors to the monarchy, they considered several groups, including blacks, to import for cheap labor, because the Hawaiians were not suitable and/or willing. It was decided on the Chinese, Japanese, Portuguese, and the Filipinos in that order. The Asians were perceived as more passive, manageable, and thus more suitable for the job, whereas the lighter, more-European-looking Portuguese were used as "lunas" (or overseers) along with some native-born whites. I think that was because their skin color was white.

I would like to just make a small interjection, and that is: in Hawaii it seems like the politics of color still is very significant. I don't care whether you are dark-skinned Hawaiian or a dark-skinned African American or dark-skinned Polynesian: I think that there is something associated with the stereotypes of dark skin and blackness that preceded us.

HR: Has it changed? Do you see any shifts taking place in the post–World War II era?

KT: Yes. There are shifts, but I would say with African Americans the stereotypes still surge subtly forward. If they don't surge forward, they continue latently in many people's subconscious. There is more suspicion and reluctance to openly give "aloha" (i.e., affections, greeting and love) to African Americans. Especially, I think, due to the great majority of whites, some of whom (especially the older retirees) have definite attitudes about blacks and who have been settling here, perhaps to escape the racial tensions on the mainland. Part of it also might have to do with the fact that we have been so invisible in the history here. The numbers—we are around 3 percent; but with the re-categorization of the census—and the census has been a problem from the beginning—some early blacks were often categorized as Portuguese or "Other." More recently, those of mixed race do not own their African ancestry as much as their other ancestries. I'm certainly not talking everybody, but it seems to be a pattern associated with skin color that has continued after the Overthrow.

HR: What was the Overthrow?

KT: "The Overthrow" refers to the 1898 overthrow of reigning Queen Lili'uokalani and the Kingdom of Hawai'i by the U.S. government. At that time Hawaii became a territory. It was no longer a sovereign nation, and then it became a state in 1959. The longer that it was a territory, the more the stereotypes came. The stereotypes began with the planters. Then more were brought along with the Second World War in the 1940s by the soldiers because the military always has to protect its interests, and Americans had all these businesses over here, with the sugar plantation and the pineapple industry followed by tourism. The military has a huge presence in the islands, and although now there are black admirals, generals, officers, and even civilian employees, they are rarely featured or shown by the local media.

HR: How does what you are describing lead to the invisibility of black Hawaiians on the island from 1970 to the present?

KT: I will be very clear when I say "black Hawaiians"; I am meaning blacks who have been born here of Hawaiian ancestry. Likely the father might have been black in the military, whereas the Hawaiian mother, as nurturer and culture-bearer, most likely raised them. That in itself is a problem because the general population does not know black history, does not know our successes and our contributions. So the children who are born of these marriages, I would get a few of them as students at UH. They mostly had no sense of their African American identity, history, or culture. They knew they were different. They knew that people would call them "big lips" or "dark skin" or "nigger." Or their friends would say, "You should be a reggae singer" or "You need to smoke weed because you belong with us." I'm talking black Hawaiian. The students that I had were ever so grateful, and I'm still in touch with them because they discovered another sense of identity through knowledge gained in my classes. Some became my teaching assistants.

When we're talking about the immigrants, I'll talk contemporary. Since 2007, [in] my connection to university students and with African American social groups—that includes the NAACP and the Links—. . . the women that bring their family stories do not differ so much from thirty years ago when it's still sometimes difficult to find a living-wage job. Part of this is surely due to not being local. If you live in the local community you're accepted, but too often this is somehow an exception to the larger African American group, because negative or limiting stereotypes are often hiding beneath the surface. Unfortunately the local media has been no help and perpetuated these stereotypes and exclusion. It's been very apparent in terms of excluding blacks [from] almost any kind of local ads or featuring our accomplishments here in the islands. We're not visible. In national ads, we're visible. In local programming and in local news stories, we are portrayed mostly in an unfavorable light, that is as criminals committing a crime, the homeless, or as athletes on the university teams.

We have many outstanding people, including black generals, black doctors, black inventors, CEOs, et cetera. However, I have only seen them rarely on the news, maybe once or twice. There are many black celebrities or blacks who are outstanding in other illustrious ways and who have Hawaii connections, such as basketball legend Kareem Abdul Jabbar and media mogul Oprah Winfrey, who both have a house here in the islands. But you almost never see our local broadcasters featuring them. They instead do stories on black entertainers who pass through. Whereas, if it's local talented or outstanding persons, meaning Hawaiian, Japanese, Chinese, or especially white Americans, you see them often on TV. Locals and visitors seldom see us. When I'm on the plane coming to Hawaii . . . if I sit next to some tourist who's coming to the islands for vacation, they usually might ask, "How long will you be there?" There is never the assumption that black people live in Hawaii.

HR: So that they just come and visit —

KT: The assumption is that we come and visit, and that blacks do not live in Hawaii and certainly have no history here, except maybe in the military. In recent years, black tourism has grown, but it's still negligible. Black visibility has also grown since my arrival almost fifty years ago. I've seen a black policeman or two. I don't think I've seen a fireman. I've seen certainly a few in the federal jobs, in the city and county jobs . . . and the state jobs, most often if they relate to social services. We're still pigeonholed. If we're going to do something it's in social services, social work. African American professionals? You don't see them on television, hear them on the radio, or being interviewed in their role as a professional, except in Black History Month. That time was when people would always want to interview me.

We did recently have a black man and woman sportscaster. But both have moved on. Aside from those two, I can't recall black people being visible in the daily media except in negative roles. Finally, my Links sister is the city editor for Hawaii's main newspaper, the *Honolulu Star Advertiser*. But again, you rarely see feature stories on local African Americans in Hawaii, except during Black History Month.

HR: So it sounds like coalition politics with a small percentage is very important?

KT: It is.

HR: In terms of institutions themselves and those people who are in power, I understand that there's a large Asian descendant population inside Hawaii. However, are they in decision-making capacities, or is there a disproportionate amount of whites who are in those positions?

KT: Definitely at the university, it's whites with some exceptions, although in tourism many hotels are Japanese-owned. The Department of Education [DOE] has been traditionally controlled by local Japanese, and there have been discrimination suits by blacks against the DOE. When I first started teaching at the University of Hawaii, there were very few Asian professors and administrators, and almost no Hawaiians. Now there are more Asian American and local educators included at all levels, with still not too many Hawaiian and South Pacific Islanders represented, except in the Center for Hawaiian Studies, which was created since my arrival. African Americans are barely visible at all levels. We have had two black chancellors of the community colleges. . . . But it's like our roles as professors and administrators are the exception, and the few black people who are selected and rise to prominence sometimes don't have very "Negro" features and do not talk about race or rock the boat of the status quo and power elite.

HR: When you say "Negro," you're putting that in scare quotes, I'm assuming?

KT: Yes. I would like to add that there is another black man, Leon Richards, who was a dean at one of our community colleges. He has a PhD in political science, and he has been outstanding in building international programs. He was at one of the community colleges in a high position, but again there's usually that glass ceiling.

HR: I see.

KT: On one-to-one relationships African Americans do very well.

HR: One-to-one relationships?

KT: Yes. When just meeting people in the community, you often see a warm smile, you feel welcome and optimistic, but on a larger scale, the extended "aloha" so many people speak about and embrace, I think, has been absent or less open and visible for blacks. We don't have a mean police force, but we do have a disproportionate amount of blacks and Hawaiians in the jails and in the prisons. Even though African Americans in Hawaii have a higher degree of education proportionately than several other groups, we are more likely to be underemployed and even homeless.

Hawaii as a Racial Frontier

HR: What impact did Hawaii, and living in a place where people of color were the majority, have on . . . President Barack Obama's life? Is how he was raised a common experience for persons of African descent in Hawaii?

KT: The majority of our population here, which in 2010 was forty thousand, is connected to the military.[2] Of that population, I would estimate that 70 percent are military and their families. A few retire here, and many move on. There's a great turnover, which makes for a lack of continuity, status, and visibility. The transience of the black community is a hindrance, both politically and economically. What blacks bring to the islands culturally and historically, and how they raise their families, I would say is quite different than local people who have had their children here or even are born and raised here themselves. Black families who are long-time Hawaii residents or who have multiracial children have different sensibilities than their counterparts on the mainland. Barack

Obama's experience in Hawaii, and the kama'āina experience would be quite similar and typical. Their vision of the world would be more open, inclusive, multicultural, and probably even more economically diverse. Friendly, trusting, and giving are more the norms. It would be very different from the experience of an African American born and raised on the mainland, even in 2015. The environment of Hawaii creates a different kind of sensibility and a broader, more tolerant way of looking at the world.

I definitely think that President Obama's experience, both as multiracial and as a Hawaiian-born resident who attended school here in his formative years, was significantly different than what would be experienced on the mainland. I think he is more open to change, more open to diversity, warmer . . . more personal with people naturally, and less suspicious, with less armor around him than if he had been born and raised elsewhere.

HR: You're saying, I guess in an implicit way, that Hawaiians of African descent . . . are not living socially isolated lives?

KT: I think I'm saying that people of African descent in the islands may be less political and filled less with anxiety and despair. I think that all of them are aware of being black and what that means, that it's different and that they are unique in some ways. But unless the parents make a real effort to give them black history—and I think Stan, Obama's white grandfather, did this with Obama, cultivated him culturally through Davis's writing, through his politics, through his jazz, through his culture—I think that you have to make a special effort to ground African American children in their culture and history for them not to be indifferent to the value of culture and history in the formation of identity. It is an injustice to all to not expose children and students to political trends, the historical mistreatment of blacks, and racial injustice until they go to the mainland, and then, *Bam!*, they unexpectedly find themselves in situations for which they are ill-prepared, for Black Power and poverty and the rewards and consequences of all.

HR: It seems like a multiple consciousness has been occurring for most black Hawaiians?

KT: Yes.

HR: Can you talk about how with this background that you have just stated, how do black Hawaiians get to a point of not necessarily feeling socially isolated?

KT: We haven't had a Jack and Jill organization here in the past, but I understand one is being formed. But we do have the Greek fraternities, and we do have the Links, the Masons, the Eastern Stars, and of course the NAACP, which was organized here in the 1940s due to discrimination and segregation on the military bases. All of these groups have activities that include children. All of these groups meet regularly, and several celebrate Juneteenth and Kwanzaa, so that the children who live in diverse neighborhoods can get a sense of black community at these celebrations. Residentially there are very few neighborhoods that have a lot of blacks in them here. The ones that you find where blacks live in the same town are probably located close to a military base. For example, in my little town here, an hour from Honolulu, there might be two other black families. I don't even know if they're families with children. I've seen a couple of other blacks at the local post office. In Honolulu you see quite a few black faces these days, but most of the time . . . they are military or tourists.

Kama'āinas

HR: Can you give us an idea about Hawaii's geography? How easy or how hard is it to go between the islands as you talk about these black people coming together?

KT: It's expensive. It ranges from $163 to $250 to fly from Honolulu, Oahu, to Kahului, Maui, round-trip. Maui has its own African American Association, and [they] do events. Actually, they just had a monument installed to honor black history in the islands. It's in a multicultural garden where all of the other ethnic groups, except whites, are present—although whites have become the dominant group both numerically and economically. We do have a monument in a national park area with names of outstanding blacks listed on it, like Nolle Smith, the Crocketts, Betsey Stockton, Alice Ball, McCants Stewart—names of black historical figures. That's a very good start. So geography, demographics, and transportation back and forth between the islands . . . I would say that most of the 1.4 million people who live in the islands, especially black people, live on Oahu, which in 2010 had a population of 953,000.[3] Not including blacks who choose to not identify as African Americans on the census, as of 2013 in Honolulu County, Oahu, persons of African descent account for 2.3 percent of the county's population, which seems to be declining from earlier. Oahu has by far the greatest general and black populations out of the eight Hawaiian islands at 964,678 general and 22,246 black permanent residents.[4]

Every day I really rejoice when I see a black person working, for example, at a bank. I almost never see a black teller or manager at a bank because it's an island and they have these ways of inclusion and exclusion: "Who did you go to high school with?" "Who can you call?" It's that way. Even though there are blacks that are born and raised here, very often they either become entrepreneurs, state or city workers, get sucked away to the mainland for work and more affordable lifestyles, or some get sucked into the alternative economy.

HR: Which is?

KT: Which could be illegal or non-tax-paying activities: drugs, prostitution, and other forms of trafficking, fraud, fugitives, et cetera. In terms of African Americans connecting with other blacks in between the islands, I've made efforts in that area, because I write about African Americans in Hawaii, give lectures and poetry performances, and I write about some of the outstanding blacks on other islands.

I did want to quickly mention Nolle Smith, who migrated here in 1915. He was from a Wyoming ranching family and had gone to college at the University of Nebraska to study engineering, math, and to play football, basketball, and track. From this experience he had met famous swimmer, surfer, and former statesman Duke Kahanamoku, who had said, "Nolle, you need to come over to Hawaii."

He came over here to work as an engineer with the Honolulu Department of Public Works. The following year he became superintendent of docks for Matson Navigation Company at Kawaihae Harbor.[5] Then he went back to San Francisco and married his love, Eva Beatrice Jones, and brought her over here. He was quite the entrepreneurial type. He was the first one to organize the whole civil service system here in the islands from 1942 to 1946. He was also a statesman. He served in the territorial legislature. He had a big family. His daughters and son were all prominent. The girls stayed here on this island. The son became a cowboy, we call that a "paniolo," on the big island of Hawaii, and all of the children were successful. The grandchildren are still here. It's a very old island family. Nolle Smith. He was ambassador to Haiti. He was just outstanding and very strong.

Just about that same time there was a family, the Ball family. They were from Washington State. The father was a nationally renowned daguerreotypist who moved his family to Hawaii for health reasons. His daughter Alice Augusta Ball was interesting because she went to high school in Hawaii, then she went back to the state of Washington for college, and then she returned to Hawaii in 1914 for graduate school. The following year, she became the first woman to graduate with a Master of Science degree in chemistry from the University of Hawaii, which then, a land-grant college, was called Hawaii College. Alice Ball's research was on the awa plant and later the chaulmoogra tree and its possible cures for leprosy [Hansen's

College of Hawaii, class of 1915, including the first African American and woman
to receive a master's degree from the college, Alice Augusta Ball. The other two
graduates are Yakichi Kutsunai (*center*) and Tomoso Imai, both receiving bachelor's
degrees. *Courtesy University Archives Collections, Mānoa Library, University of Hawai'i.*

disease]. She was hired to teach some courses in chemistry and work on this cure
for leprosy, which was a big problem here in Hawaii in those earlier years. She was
hired by the chairman of the Chemistry Department, Arthur L. Dean. He was
her professor and her mentor. Ball invented a cure—I won't say it's a total cure,
but before the 1940s many people say the "Ball method" was a cure for leprosy.[6]

Then, shortly after her invention, she died. She was working both at Leahi
Hospital and on her research at the University of Washington in Seattle when
she prematurely died in 1916 of mysterious causes at the age of twenty-four. My
speculation is she caught the dreaded Hansen's disease. She got the pneumonia,
which was a symptom of Hansen's disease. Her professor, Arthur Dean, took her
work and continued to develop her research but never gave her credit, renaming
the treatment the "Dean method." It was not until 2000 that she was fully recognized for her contributions. This, seven-plus decades after U.S. public health officer

Dr. Harry Hollmann publicly exposed the fallacy in Dean's claims, and fifty-plus years after a Japanese reporter published Ball's exploits for a Japanese newspaper and called her a black Hawaiian in the header. . . . But she wasn't Hawaiian. She was an African American. In the late 1990s, I was asked by UH's Stan Ali to do further research on her. With his help, the University of Hawaii, myself, and other people who became interested in her story, we commissioned a painting of Ball, created a ceremony, invited residents from Kalaupapa (the old "leper colony" on Molokai), and planted a tree, the chaulmoogra tree, next to Bachman Hall, the administration building at UH. The painting of Ball now hangs in Hamilton Library. And the Hawaiian community began honoring Alice Augusta Ball after the governor declared February 29 to be Alice Ball Day in the state.

KT: The last black Hawaiians I will mention are an old island family called the Crocketts. The head of the family was Wendell F. Crockett. He was born in Virginia in 1859. He arrived in the islands as an attorney in 1901 with the first camp of black plantation workers, encouraged by the recommendation of Booker T. Washington. There were two separate groups of black plantation workers. The group that he was with went to Maui to a place called Spreckelsville Plantation.

HR: What type of agriculture was taking place on these plantations?

KT: Spreckelsville was a sugar plantation. Crockett came as a lawyer for the workers and later served Maui as county prosecutor. He had a wife who was very strong and very active. Her name was Annie V. Ryder Crockett. They came from Michigan, although they had spent some time in the South. They had several children, including Wendell Francis (Frank), who, after graduating from University of Michigan Law School, returned to Maui and became a renowned county prosecutor (1919–49), territorial senator (ca. 1950–54), circuit court judge (1959–61), and county supervisor (1963–65).[7] Annie Crockett became a principal. She was one of the first people to invent hybrid hibiscus. She was very well respected. In fact, most of the older, black kama'āina families, such as the Crocketts, who have stayed here either became politically active or they were in law or in education—like Helene Hale, who was nominal mayor of the Big Island in the 1940s and later a representative to the state legislature.

Politically, before African American political party realignment from the Republicans to the Democrats began during the New Deal in the 1930s, most early black Hawaiian families were aligned with the Republican Party, still then resonating with faint echoes . . . of President Lincoln's freedom party.

Today black Hawaiians are 95 percent Democrat.

Miseducation (and Oral History as a Tool for Historical Recovery)

HR: In terms of oral history, what can oral history accomplish in uncovering the lives of black Hawaiians that previous methods could not?

KT: For as long as I have been in the islands and before my arrival here, there has been a strong and constant need for the Department of Education to include black history in their curriculum. Unfortunately, apart from a Martin Luther King Day or a Black History Month event or assignment, there is little information given by public school teachers, and little learning in the classroom about African Americans. I feel it is especially important to not just talk about black history on the mainland, but to talk about the vital history of blacks in Hawaii. So, bit by bit, more and more articles are becoming available on this subject. If blacks saw a long and distinguished history here by some of these illustrious people, there might be more of a sense of curiosity to come over here and get to be a part of the mix, because I think that all of these people, including myself, have found Hawaii a very good place to live, whether it is nature, climate, multiculturalism, diversity. What is missing is African Americans in visible roles in Hawaii [or a role] that has history connected to it that can help to dignify and celebrate our contributions.

HR: Do you think the cost of living in Hawaii is a prohibitive factor?

KT: Well, we do have a large homeless population over here, very disproportionate, that come from the mainland because of the weather. I think that people can live wherever. That might make it easier to decide not to come, but I think people can survive, and, if they are willing, to work and get that job, be it in whatever area, at the city, state, or the federal [level] or just become entrepreneurs, work in the professions, and as enterprising entertainers, such as Maya Angelou, who was a torch singer here for a while. This tradition goes back to the reign of Kamehameha the Great, who had blacks in his band. Those early blacks probably came to the islands on whaling or trading ships. Later, the Royal Hawaiian Band as it is now called, with black musicians at the time, went from 1836 all the way up until the 1850s, when it was decided by the white settlers and advisors to the king that the monarchy, with its palace and all the trappings of Victorian-style international rule, needed to have a "proper" bandleader from Germany to formalize the Royal Hawaiian Band. After the arrival of the new bandleader, you didn't see a lot of blacks in the band. Similar to most of black Hawaiian history, although persons of African heritage were the foundation and beginning of the Royal Hawaiian Band, there is no public acknowledgment or celebration of this contribution.

Conclusion

HR: Closing out this wonderful conversation, what needs to change for future scholars and audiences to begin addressing the U.S. West beyond the mainland and to places such as Alaska and Hawaii?

KT: I think that the connection with the African diaspora, the modeling of Hawaii as a place where many cultures live together, play together, and work together, is important. I think Hawaii's connection to Asia is super-important. The challenges of our time and the twenty-first century are to see the connections and correspondences. Right now, Hawaiians are on a voyage of discovery and reconnecting with ancestors across the Pacific, the Indian Ocean, and down to Madagascar and on to South Africa, where they openly claim that they have ancestors. Truly a different paradigm to explore.

This concept of globalism can be a door opener as well as another way for dominance and colonialism to prevail. It is our responsibility to see what traces we can find of the African presence not only through India and through Malaysia but also all the way through the Pacific. Specifically, what about Melanesia? In Melanesia the people are very black. What about Fiji? People are very black. Interested scholars can contribute to a new paradigm that includes blacks in the West and beyond. I think that there is an urgent need for inclusion of blacks in American West history that becomes a global East. Connecting with the history and the oral histories of blacks in those under-explored sites of black history is a wide-open field.

Regarding future scholars, I think there is so much work to be done, and I think that Hawaii should have a center here for research of African connections to Asia and the Pacific. I made a proposal for that but just never got it done. I strongly believe that these links need to form. More research needs to happen so that scholars who are interested in a new paradigm of black inclusion and new ways of visiting world history can come from the mainland and Africa or other places of the African diaspora and beyond to study and research with a base in Hawaii. There are continuities and themes in art, cultural patterns, language structure, and spiritual practices that should no longer be ignored. And of course with DNA tests, the connections will become ever more apparent. Hawaii is the perfect base from which to launch new explorations and research, because it is an open field that has yet to be fully explored and developed. Imua!

Notes

1. Hawaiian Mission Houses Historic Cite and Archives, http://missionhouses.org.
2. U.S. Census Bureau, Population Division, "Annual Estimates of the Resident Population by Sex, Age, Race Alone or in Combination, and Hispanic Origin for the United States and States: April 1, 2010 to July 1, 2014," 1, http://files.hawaii.gov/dbedt/census/popestimate/2014-state-characteristics/PEP_2014_PEPASR5H_all.pdf.
3. Department of Transportation Services, City and County of Honolulu, "City and County of Honolulu: Department of Transportation Services, Public Transit Division, Title VI Program Report," http://www.honolulu.gov/rep/site/dts/dts_docs/Part_I_and_II_-_Title_VI_Progam.pdf.
4. U.S. Census Bureau, "2009–2013 5-Year American Community Survey," http://factfinder.census.gov/faces/tableservices/jsf/pages/productview.xhtml?pid=ACS_13_5YR_B02001&prodType=table
5. For more on Nolle Smith, see Miles M. Jackson, "Smith, Nolle (1888–1982)," *Blackpast.org*, http://www.blackpast.org/aaw/smith-nolle-1888-1982.
6. For more on Alice Augusta Ball, see Miles M. Jackson, "Ball, Alice Augusta (1892–1916)," *Blackpast.org*, http://www.blackpast.org/aaw/ball-alice-augusta-1892-1916.
7. Lynda Mair, *Wendell Francis Crockett* (Honolulu: Watumull Foundation Oral History Project, 1979), https://evols.library.manoa.hawaii.edu/bitstream/10524/48598/1/ocr_watumullohp_Crockett.pdf; John William Siddall, ed., "Crockett, William F.," in *Men of Hawaii: Being a Biographical Reference Library, Complete and Authentic, of the Men of Note and Substantial Achievement in the Hawaiian Islands*, vol. 1 (Hawaii: Honolulu Star-Bulletin, 1921), https://archive.org/stream/menofhawaiibeing02sidd/menofhawaiibeing02sidd_djvu.txt, 116.

⌘ Blanche Louise Preston McSmith: An Alaska Civil Rights Icon

Part 5 of this book, "Reconsiderations," reexamines the U.S. West in understudied sites. One site is African American history in Alaska. In this essay, black West pioneer Albert Broussard examines the state's early civil rights movement and the important role that Blanche Louise Preston McSmith had in the movement and in Alaska's public life.

The black presence in Alaska has been severely under recorded. This is particularly the case for the role of African American women. One of the most remarkable black leaders was Blanche Louise Preston McSmith, a native of Marshall, Texas, who, like the majority of African Americans residents, migrated to Alaska to seek greater economic opportunity.

Born May 5, 1920, Blanche Louise Preston graduated from Wiley College in 1941 and eventually earned a master's degree in social work from the University of Southern California in 1944. Preston married Los Angeles businessman William McSmith and the pair owned a local electronics business and real estate firm. In 1949, Blanche and William McSmith moved to Kodiak, Alaska Territory and the following year, settled in Anchorage, the Territory's largest city.

Blanche McSmith played a major role in organizing the Anchorage branch of the National Association for the Advancement of Colored People (NAACP) in 1951. Under her leadership as branch president, the Anchorage NAACP in 1959 pushed for a comprehensive civil rights bill when Alaska was admitted to the Union as the 49th state. The new Alaska State Legislature, however, failed to support the bill.

In that same year, Governor William A. Egan appointed McSmith to fill a vacancy for the 10th District, Alaska House of Representatives when Representative John Radar was appointed Attorney General. Her service in the Alaska legislature gave her the distinction of being the first African American to serve in that body.

McSmith worked tirelessly both in and outside the legislature to end housing and employment discrimination in Alaska. Her efforts culminated in the adoption of a fair housing ordinance by the Anchorage city council in 1967.

Source: *Albert Broussard,* "McSmith, Blanche (1920–2006)," *Blackpast.org.*

Employment discrimination proved equally troublesome for black Alaskans, and McSmith worked through the local NAACP to obtain employment opportunities for African Americans in both the public and private sectors.

In 1972, McSmith moved to Juneau, where she became the Director in the Office of the Governor for the Public Employment Program, a position she held until she retired in the early 1980s. Blanche Preston McSmith passed away on July 28, 2006, in Anchorage after waging a long and courageous struggle for economic and social justice in Alaska.

⌗ African American History Month Enacted in Alaska, 2015

On January 29, 2015, the governor of Alaska officially signed a proclamation recognizing African American history month. This occurred
thirty-nine years after the United States officially recognized Black History
Month in 1976 as part of the U.S. bicentennial. Black History Month dates
back to 1926, when Carter G. Woodson created Negro History Week. In
the West, one of the first adoptions of Negro History Week occurred in
San Jose in 1947, after the Santa Clara County NAACP pressured legislators
such as San Jose mayor Clark L. Bradley to enact it. In Alaska, activists
and concerned groups like George T. Harper's Blacks in Alaska History
Project have been on the front lines for decades in attempting to have
Black History Month officially recognized by the state. Although this
proclamation does not have the force of law behind it, the gesture is a
move in the right direction for better race relations in Alaska. This includes
rediscovering a rich black past that includes blacks in the Alaskan Gold
Rush, the African American U.S. Army Engineers who constructed the
Alaska Highway during World War II, U.S. Revenue Cutter Service captain
Michael A. Healy, and civil rights activist Blanche Louise Preston McSmith.[1]

WHEREAS, since 1976, February is recognized as African American History Month as a reminder
to Americans of the struggle for freedom and equal opportunity for African Americans; and

WHEREAS, African Americans have had a strong and positive impact on Alaska since before
Statehood. During Alaska territorial days, African American men migrated to Alaska to work
in whaling and fur trading and later to work in gold mining; and

WHEREAS, during the gold rush in 1899, members of the U.S. Army Company L, 24th Infantry, an
entirely African American unit, were stationed at Dyea and Skagway. Despite having to endure
racial tensions, these soldiers played an important role in maintaining law and order; and

Source: Bill Walker, "African American History Month," State of Alaska, Office of the
Governor, http://gov.alaska.gov/.

WHEREAS, African American Engineer General Service Regiments of the Army Corp of Engineers played a key part in building the Alaska/Canadian Highway (ALCAN) during World War II to safeguard Alaska from Japanese invasion. Alaska still owes these engineers a debt of gratitude for this important piece of infrastructure that endures to this day; and

WHEREAS, African American battalions were assigned to the Aleutian Islands during the World War II Aleutian campaign, and many African Americans have served in Alaska in the military or Coast Guard; and

WHEREAS, we honor Blanche Louise Preston McSmith, the first African American to serve in the Alaska State House of Representatives during the First Alaska Legislature in 1960; and

WHEREAS, African Americans have made and continue to make great contributions to our communities in Alaska in every field from science and the arts to business, politics, and government.

NOW, THEREFORE, I Bill Walker, Governor of the State of Alaska, do hereby proclaim February 2015 as: African American History Month in Alaska, to encourage all Alaskans to recognize African Americans' contributions to our state and to remember that no matter a person's color, ethnicity, or background, all Alaskans can make a difference in their communities.

Notes

1. APU/UAA Consortium Library, "Guide to the Blacks in Alaska History Project records, 1953–2004," https://consortiumlibrary.org/archives/FindingAids/hmc-0681.html.

Bibliographic Essay

The Twentieth- and Twenty-First-Century West

Herbert G. Ruffin II

Since the 1970s, the history of the African American West has evolved into an exciting branch of scholarship. In this period, the largest and most dynamic area of study has focused on the black urban experience in the twentieth and twenty-first centuries. The first regional synthesis to conceptualize how the African American western frontier connected to twentieth-century industrial-urban America was Quintard Taylor, *In Search of a Racial Frontier* (New York: W.W. Norton, 1998). This book was written in a manner that was mindful of the new western history and regional syntheses that preceded it or were published in the same year, such as Kenneth Wiggins Porter, *The Negro on the American Frontier* (North Stratford, N.H.: Ayer, 1971); Lawrence B. de Graaf, "Recognition, Racism, and Reflections on the Writing of Western Black History" (*Pacific Historical Review* 44, no. 1 [February 1975], 22–51); W. Sherman Savage, *Blacks in the West* (Westport, Ct.: Greenwood Press, 1976); William Loren Katz, *The Black West: A Pictorial History* (New York: Touchstone, 1987); Lillian Schissel, *Black Frontiers: A History of African American Heroes in the Old West* (New York: Aladdin, 1995); John W. Ravage, *Black Pioneers: Images of the Black Experience on the North American Frontier* (Salt Lake City: University of Utah Press, 1997); and Monroe Lee Billington and Roger D. Hardaway, eds., *African Americans on the Western Frontier* (Boulder: University Press of Colorado, 1998). What resulted was the fresh telling of history centered on the significance of the African American West, which fluidly intersected race, class, gender, multiculturalism, community formation, and political expression west of the Ninety-Eighth Meridian. With the exception of De Graaf's "Recognition," most regional surveys published before *In Search of a Racial Frontier* did not directly address the systematic erasure of twentieth-century black western history. They also took on the unnecessary burden of trying to make this history fit into the traditional West canon, a history that usually ended in 1890 and intentionally ignored the region's complex race relations, which included not just those of African American and European American but also those of Asian Americans, Latin Americans, and Native Americans on the "racial frontier."

Since *In Search, of a Racial Frontier*, several regional surveys have been published that have used the racial frontier framework, which has produced an invaluable expansion of western history. These surveys include Quintard Taylor and Shirley Ann Wilson Moore, eds., *African American Women Confront the West, 1600–2000* (Norman: University of Oklahoma Press, 2003), Douglas Flamming, African Americans in the West (Santa Barbara: ABC-CLIO, 2009), and Albert S. Broussard, *Expectations of Equality: A History of Black Westerners* (Wheeling, Ill.: Harlan Davidson, 2012).

In the 1980s, state-focused studies began to address the African American West beyond the nineteenth century and into the twentieth century as an urban, industrial region. In this historiographic period, black West surveys varied immensely in quality, usually addressing the subject via a "we were there" narrative or examining the significance of the African American western experience and race relations in a particular state. Early surveys that fit this description include Delilah L. Beasley, *The Negro Trail Blazers of California* (Los Angeles: *Times Mirror Printing and Binding House*, 1919); Melvin J. Banks, *The Pursuit of Equality: The Movement for First Class Citizenship among Negroes in Texas, 1920–1950* (PhD diss., Syracuse University, 1962); Charles Wollenberg, ed., *Neither Separate nor Equal: Race and Racism in California* (Berkeley: University of California Press, 1971); Roger Daniels and Spencer Olin Jr., *Racism in California: A Reader in the History of Oppression* (London: Macmillan, 1972); Alwyn Barr, *Black Texans: A History of Negroes in Texas, 1528–1971* (Norman: University of Oklahoma Press, 1973); Arthur L. Tolson, *The Black Oklahomans: A History, 1541–1972* (New Orleans: Edwards Print, 1974); Jimmie Lewis Franklin, *The Blacks in Oklahoma* (Norman: University of Oklahoma Press, 1980); Elizabeth McLagan, *A Peculiar Paradise: A History of Blacks in Oregon, 1788–1940* (Portland, Ore.: Georgian Press, 1980); Richard E. Harris, *The First 100 Years: A History of Arizona Blacks* (Apache Junction, Ariz.: Relmo, 1983); Franklin J. James, Betty L. McCummings, and Eileen A Tynan, *Minorities in the Sunbelt* (New Brunswick, N.J.: Center for Urban Policy Research, 1984); Michael R. Heintze, *Private Black Colleges in Texas, 1865–1954* (College Station: Texas A&M University Press, 1985); Charlotte K. Mock, *Bridges: New Mexican Black Women, 1900–1950* (Albuquerque: New Mexico Commission on the Status of Women, 1985); Marguerite Mitchell Marshall, Patricia Weisenburger, and Susan Barton, *An Account of Afro-Americans in Southeast Kansas, 1884–1984* (Manhattan, Kans.: Wheatland Books, 1986); Rudolph M. Lapp, *Afro-Americans in California* (San Francisco: Boyd & Fraser, 1979); Everett Louis Overstreet, *Black on a Background of White: A Chronicle of Afro-Americans' Involvement in America's Last Frontier, Alaska* (Fairbanks: Alaska Black Caucus, 1988); Alwyn Barr and Robert Carver, eds., *Black Leaders: Texans for Their Times* (Austin: Texas State Historical Association, 1990); Laurie Mercier and Carole Simon-Smolinski, *Idaho's Ethnic Heritage: Historical Overviews* (Boise: Idaho Ethnic Heritage Project, 1990); and Mamie O. Oliver, *Idaho Ebony: The Afro-American Presence in Idaho State History* (Boise: M. O. Oliver, 1990).

Since 1990, black urban history and civil rights history have been incorporated into

African American western history. Such state-focused surveys have been carried out by Beth Bailey and David Farber, *The First Strange Place: Race and Sex in World War II Hawaii* (New York: Free Press, 1992); Gretchen M. Bataille and Albert L McHenry, *Living the Dream in Arizona: The Legacy of Martin Luther King, Jr.* (Tempe: Arizona State University, 1992); J. M. Gaskin, *Black Baptists in Oklahoma* (Oklahoma City: Messenger Press, 1992); Sharon Bramlett, *Profile and Status of African American Women in Arizona: Background Report to the 1994 Arizona Black Town Hall* (Tempe: Arizona State University, 1994); Ruthe Winegarten, *Black Texas Women: 150 Years of Trial and Triumph* (Austin: University of Texas Press, 1995); France Davis, *Light in the Midst of Zion: A History of Black Baptists in Utah, 1892–1996* (Salt Lake City: University Pub., 1997); Bertha Calloway and Alonzo N. Smith, *Visions of Freedom on the Great Plains: An Illustrated History of African Americans in Nebraska* (Virginia Beach, Va. : Donning, 1998); Bruce A. Glasrud and Laurie Champion, eds., *Exploring the Afro-Texas Experience: A Bibliography of Secondary Sources about Black Texans* (Alpine, Tex.: Sul Ross State University, 2000); Lawrence B. De Graaf, Kevin Mulroy, and Quintard Taylor, eds., *Seeking El Dorado: African Americans in California* (Seattle: University of Washington Press, 2001); Bruce A. Glasrud and Paul H. Carlson, *Slavery to Integration: Black Americans in West Texas* (Abilene, Tex.: State House Press, 2007); Bruce A. Glasrud and James M. Smallwood, eds., *The African American Experience in Texas: An Anthology* (Lubbock: Texas Tech University Press, 2007); Debra A. Reid, *Reaping a Greater Harvest: African Americans, the Extension Service, and Rural Reform in Jim Crow Texas* (College Station: Texas A&M University Press, 2007); Bruce A. Glasrud and Archie P. McDonald, eds., *Blacks in East Texas History: Selections from the East Texas Historical Journal* (College Station: Texas A&M University Press, 2008); Bruce A. Glasrud and Merline Pitre, eds., *Black Women in Texas History* (College Station: Texas A&M University Press, 2008); Betti Van Epps-Taylor, *Forgotten Lives: African Americans in South Dakota* (Pierre: South Dakota State Historical Society Press, 2008); Bruce A. Glasrud and Charles A. Braithwaite, eds., *African Americans on the Great Plains: An Anthology* (Lincoln: University of Nebraska Press 2009); Daphne Barbee-Wooten, *African American Attorneys in Hawaii* (Kaʻaʻawa, HI: Pacific Raven Press, 2010); Bruce A. Glasrud, ed., *African Americans in South Texas History* (College Station: Texas A&M University Press, 2011); D. Molentia Guttman and Ernest Golden, *African Americans in Hawaii* (Charleston, S.C.: Arcadia, 2011); Gerald Horne, *Fighting in Paradise: Labor Unions, Racism, and Communists in the Making of Modern Hawaii* (Honolulu: University of Hawaii Press, 2011); Ingrid Banks, Gaye Johnson, George Lipsitz, Ula Taylor, Daniel Widener, and Clyde Woods, eds., *Black California Dreamin': The Crises of California's African-American Communities* (Santa Barbara: University of California, Santa Barbara, Center for Black Studies Research, 2012).

Prior to 1970, community studies of the black urban West appeared in novels, sociological monographs, and autobiographies. Some of the earliest novels on the black urban West include Lillian B. Jones, *Five Generations Hence* (College Station: Texas A&M University

Press, 1916); Langston Hughes, *Not Without Laughter* (New York: Scribner, 1930); Chester Himes, *If He Hollers, Let Him Go* (1945; repr., New York: Thunder's Mouth Press, 2002) and *Lonely Crusade* (1947; repr., New York: Thunder's Mouth Press, 1992), and John Alfred Williams, *The Angry Ones* (New York: Norton, 1960). Pioneering sociological monographs on the African American urban West include Ira De A. Reid, *The Negro Population of Denver, Colorado: A Survey of its Economic and Social Status* (Denver: Lincoln Press, 1929); T. Earl Sullenger and J. Harvey Kerns, *The Negro in Omaha: A Social Study of Negro Development* (Omaha: University of Omaha / Omaha Urban League, 1931); Charles S. Johnson, *The Negro War Worker in San Francisco: A Local Self-Survey* (San Francisco: Charles S. Johnson, 1944); Bennett M. Berger, *Working-Class Suburb: A Study of Auto Workers in Suburbia* (Berkeley: University of California Press, 1960); Warren M. Banner and Theodora M. Dyer, *Economic and Cultural Progress of the Negro in Phoenix, Arizona* (New York: National Urban League, 1965); Patricia Alder, *Paradise West: A Study of Negro Attitudes toward the City of Los Angeles* (Los Angeles: P. Adler, 1969). Important autobiographies that recorded aspects of the black urban West before 1970 include Alexander J. Somerville, *Man of Color: An Autobiography* (Los Angeles: L. L. Morrison, 1949); Charlotta A. Bass, *Forty Years: Memoirs from the Pages of a Newspaper* (Los Angeles: C. A. Bass, 1960); Horace R. Cayton, *Long Old Road: An Autobiography* (New York: Trident Press, 1963); Bobby Seale, *Seize the Time* (New York: Random House, 1968); Paul Bullock, ed., *Watts, The Aftermath: An Inside View of the Ghetto, by the People of Watts* (New York: Grove Press, 1969), and Jesse Kimbrough, *Defender of the Angels: A Black Policeman in Old Los Angeles* (New York: Macmillan, 1969).

From 1970 to 1990, the foundations of black urban West history developed mostly as social histories empirically addressing black agency and the African American impact on the metropolitan West in the late nineteenth and early twentieth centuries. These histories include J. McFarline Ervin, *The Participation of the Negro in the Community Life of Los Angeles* (San Francisco: R and E Research Associates, 1973); Francis M. Lortie, *San Francisco's Black Community, 1870–1890* (San Francisco: R and E Research Associates, 1973); Arthur E. Hippler, *Hunter's Point: A Black Ghetto* (New York: Basic Books, 1974); Keith E. Collins, *Black Los Angeles: The Maturing of the Ghetto, 1940–1950* (Saratoga, Calif.: Century Twenty One, 1975); Mike Garcia, *Adaptation Strategies in the Los Angeles Black Community, 1883–1919* (PhD diss., University of California, Irvine, 1985); Homer Broome Jr., *LAPD's Black History, 1886–1976* (Broome, 1978); Alonzo Smith, *Black Employment in the Los Angeles Area, 1938–1948* (PhD diss., University of California, Los Angeles, 1978); Zella J. Black Patterson, *Langston University: A History* (Norman: University of Oklahoma Press, 1979); Douglas Henry Daniels, *Pioneer Urbanites: A Social and Cultural History of Black San Francisco* (Berkeley: University of California Press 1980); Esther Hall Mumford, *Seattle's Black Victorians, 1852–1901* (Seattle: Ananse Press, 1980); Thomas C. Cox, *Blacks in Topeka, Kansas, 1865–1915* (Baton Rouge: Louisiana State University Press, 1982); Scott Ellsworth, *Death in a Promised Land: The Tulsa Race Riot of 1921* (Baton Rouge: Louisiana State University Press, 1982); Susan G. Greenbaum, *The Afro-American Community in Kansas City, Kansas: A History* (Kansas City, Kans.: The City, 1982); Mary Ellen Bell Ray, *The City of Watts, California, 1907 to 1926* (Los Angeles: Rising Pub., 1985); Esther Hall Mumford, *Seven Stars and Orion: Reflections of the Past* (Seattle: Ananse Press, 1986); Robert D. Bullard, *Invisible Houston: The Black Experience in Boom and Bust* (College Station: Texas A&M University Press, 1987); Donald E. Hausler, *Blacks in Oakland: 1852–1987* (Oakland: Donald E. Hausler, 1987); Lonnie G. Bunch, *Black Angelenos: The Afro-American in Los Angeles, 1850–1950* (Los Angeles: California Afro-American Museum, 1988); Lawrence P. Crouchett, Lonnie G. Bunch, and Martha Kendall Winnacker, *Visions toward Tomorrow: The History of the East Bay Afro-American Community, 1852–1977* (Oakland: Northern California Center for Afro-American History and Life, 1989); and Joseph Franklin, *All through the Night: The History of Spokane Black Americans, 1860–1940* (Fairfield, Wash.: Ye Galleon Press, 1989).

Black urban West histories have emerged since 1990 and fit nicely within the new western history as these local surveys emphasize the significance of race in the region through their examination of the Great Migration, World War II, and the civil rights movement. These contributions include DeCharlene Williams, *A History of Seattle's Central Area* (Seattle: Central Area Chamber of Commerce, 1990); Roy H. Williams and Kevin J. Shay, *Time Change: An Alternative View of the History of Dallas* (Dallas: To Be Publishing, 1991); Howard Beeth and Cary D. Wintz, eds., *Black Dixie: Afro-Texan History and Culture in Houston* (College Station, TX: Texas A&M University Press, 1992); Gary Reese Fuller, *Who We Are: An Informal History of Tacoma's Black Community* (Tacoma: Tacoma Public Library, 1992); Harriett Arnold, *Antioch, a Place of Christians: Chronicles of An African-American Church 1893–1993* (San Mateo, Calif.: Western Book Journal Press, 1993); Albert S. Broussard, *Black San Francisco: The Struggle for Racial Equality in the West, 1900–1954* (Lawrence: University Press of Kansas, 1993); Kimberly Moreland, *The History of Portland's African American Community, 1805 to the Present* (Portland, Ore.: Portland Bureau of Planning, 1993); Mark Baldassare, ed., *The Los Angeles Riots: Lessons for the Urban Future* (Boulder, Colo.: Westview Press, 1994); Anna Deavere Smith, *Twilight: Los Angeles, 1992* (New York: Anchor Books, 1994); Quintard Taylor, *The Forging of a Black Community: Seattle's Central District from 1870 through the Civil Rights Era* (Seattle: University of Washington Press, 1994); Gretchen Lemke-Santangelo, *Abiding Courage: African American Migrant Women and the East Bay Community* (Chapel Hill: University of North Carolina Press, 1996); Eddie Faye Gates, *They Came Searching: How Blacks Sought the Promised Land in Tulsa* (Austin, Tex.: Eakin Press, 1997); Mary T. Henry, *Tribute: A Guide to Seattle's Public Parks and Buildings Named for Black People: With Brief Biographical Sketches* (Seattle: Statice Press, 1997); Alan B. Govenar and Jay F. Brakefield, *Deep Ellum and Central Track: Where the Black and White Worlds of Dallas Converged* (Denton: University of North Texas Press, 1998); Hannibal B. Johnson, *Black Wall Street: From Riot to Renaissance in Tulsa's Historic Greenwood District* (Austin,

Tex.: Eakin Press, 1998); Kenneth Mason, *Paternal Community: African Americans and Race Relations in San Antonio, Texas, 1867–1937* (New York: Garland, 1998); and William H. Wilson, *Hamilton Park: A Planned Community in Dallas* (Baltimore: Johns Hopkins University Press, 1998).

From 2000 to 2015, community surveys became the largest and most dynamic genre of writing within African American West history. A few of these texts include Lawrence Bobo, *Prismatic Metropolis: Inequality in Los Angeles* (New York: Russell Sage Foundation, 2000); Maceo C. Dailey Jr. and Kristine Navarro, eds., *Wheresoever My People Chance to Dwell: Oral Interviews with African American Women of El Paso* (Baltimore: Imprint Edition, 2000); Larry Martin, *The Doctrines and Discipline of the Azusa Street Apostolic Faith Mission of Los Angeles* (Joplin, Mo.: Christian Life Books, 2000); Shirley Ann Wilson Moore, *To Place Our Deeds: The African American Community in Richmond, California, 1910–1963* (Berkeley: University of California Press, 2000); Calvin H. Bowers, *Realizing the California Dream: The Story of the Black Churches of Christ in Los Angeles* (Las Vegas: DocMo Enterprises, 2001); Dennis Domer and Barbara Watkins Domer, *Embattled Lawrence: Conflict & Community* (Lawrence: University of Kansas Continuing Education, 2001); Tim Madigan, *The Burning: Massacre, Destruction, and the Tulsa Race Riot of 1921* (New York: St. Martin's Press, 2001); Alfred L. Brophy, *Reconstructing the Dreamland: The Tulsa Riot of 1921* (New York: Oxford University Press, 2002); James S. Hirsch, *Riot and Remembrance: The Tulsa Race War and Its Legacy* (Boston: Houghton Mifflin, 2002); Sherry Lamb Schirmer, *A City Divided: The Racial Landscape of Kansas City, 1900–1960* (Columbia: University of Missouri Press, 2002); Robert O. Self, *American Babylon: Race and the Struggle for Postwar Oakland* (Princeton: Princeton University Press, 2003); Josh Sides, *L.A. City Limits: African American Los Angeles from the Great Depression to the Present* (Berkeley: University of California Press, 2003); Chris Rhomberg, *No There There: Race, Class, and Political Community* (Berkeley: University of California Press, 2004); Douglas Flamming, *Bound for Freedom: Black Los Angeles in Jim Crow America* (Berkeley: University of California Press, 2005); Charles E. Coulter, *Take up the Black Man's Burden: Kansas City's African American Communities, 1865–1939* (Columbia: University of Missouri Press, 2006); Kevin Leonard, *The Battle for Los Angeles: Racial Ideology and World War II* (Albuquerque: University of New Mexico Press, 2006); Martin Schiesl and Mark M. Dodge, eds., *City of Promise: Race and Historical Change in Los Angeles* (Claremont, Calif.: Regina Books, 2006); Jerelyne Castleberry Williams, *The Brackenridge Colored School: A Legacy of Empowerment through Agency and Cultural Capital inside an African American Community* (Bloomington, Ind.: AuthorHouse, 2006); Delia C. Gillis, *Kansas City (MO)* (Charleston, S.C.: Arcadia, 2007); Mary E. Abrums, *Moving the Rock: Poverty and Faith in a Black Storefront Church* (Lanham, Md.: AltaMira Press, 2009); Michelle M. Mears, *And Grace Will Lead Me Home: African American Freedmen Communities of Austin, Texas, 1865 to 1928* (Lubbock: Texas Tech University Press, 2009); Evelyn C. White, *Every Goodbye Ain't Gone* (Tuscaloosa: University of Alabama Press, 2009);

Darnell Hunt and Ana-Christina Ramon, eds., *Black Los Angeles: American Dreams and Racial Realities* (New York: New York University Press, 2010); Carol Lynn McKibben, *Racial Beachhead: Diversity and Democracy in a Military Town* (Stanford: Stanford University Press, 2011); Jason J. McDonald, *Racial Dynamics in Early Twentieth-Century Austin, Texas* (Lanham, Md.: Lexington Books, 2012); Bernadette Pruitt, *The Other Great Migration: The Movement of Rural African Americans to Houston, 1900–1941* (College Station: Texas A&M University Press, 2013); Kevin Fox Gotham, *Race, Real Estate, and Uneven Development: The Kansas City Experience, 1900–2010*, 2nd ed. (Albany: State University of New York Press, 2014); Herbert G. Ruffin II, *Uninvited Neighbors: African Americans in Silicon Valley, 1769–1990* (Norman: University of Oklahoma Press, 2014); G. S. Griffin, *Racism in Kansas City: A Short History* (Traverse City, Mich.: Chandler Lake Books, 2015; Marne L. Campbell, *Making Black Los Angeles: Class, Gender, and Community, 1850–1917* (Chapel Hill: University of North Carolina Press, 2016).

One of the faster growing subfields within black West historiography is focuses on the black freedom movement. This topic permeates most texts on the African American West, whether the focus is on rural, urban, or suburban space. The first studies on this subject included autobiographies such as Mifflin Wistar Gibbs, *Shadow and Light: An Autobiography* (Little Rock, Ark.: Gibbs, 1902), civil rights histories such as J. Alston Atkins, *The Texas Negro and His Political Rights: A History of the Fight of the Negro to Enter the Democratic Primaries of Texas* (Houston: Webster, 1932), nonfiction narratives written by journalist and activists such as Jerry Cohen and William S. Murphy, *Burn, Baby, Burn: The Los Angeles Race Riot, August, 1965* (New York: Dutton, 1966) and Bobby Seale, *Seize the Time* (New York: Random House, 1968). They became models for subsequent histories on the black freedom movement, including George Ruble Woolfolk, *Prairie View: A Study in Public Conscience, 1878–1946* (New York: Pageant Press, 1962); John Caughey and Laree Caughey, *School Segregation on Our Doorstep: The Los Angeles Story* (Los Angeles: Quail Books, 1966); Robert Conot, *Rivers of Blood, Years of Darkness* (New York: Bantam Books, 1967); Richard M. Elman, *Ill-at-Ease in Compton* (New York: Pantheon Books, 1967); John Crow, *Discrimination, Poverty and the Negro: Arizona in the National Context* (Tucson: University of Arizona Press, 1968), and Associated Students, University of Oregon, *Which Side Are You On? The Black Panthers in Eugene* (Eugene, Ore.: ASUO/Eugene Black Panther Party, 1969).

In the 1970s and '80s, civil rights movement and Black Power histories in the West continued in autobiographical accounts and ones focusing on school desegregation. They also began chronicling the social history of black public servants, black leadership, collective activism, and black empowerment, as in William Barlow and Peter Shapiro, *An End to Silence: The San Francisco State College Student Movement in the 1960s* (New York: Pegasus, 1971); Bobette Gugliotta, *Nolle Smith: Cowboy, Engineer, Statesman* (New York: Dodd, Mead, 1971); Dikran Karagueuzian, *Blow It Up! The Black Student Revolt at San Francisco State and the Emergence of Dr. Hayakawa* (Boston: Gambit, 1971); Ira Bryant,

Texas Southern University: Its Antecedents, Political Origin and Future (Houston: Bryant, 1972); Huey P. Newton, *Revolutionary Suicide* (New York: Harcourt Brace Jovanovich, 1973); Conrey Bryson, *Dr. Lawrence A. Nixon and the White Primary* (El Paso: Texas Western Press, 1974); Bobby Seale, *A Lonely Rage* (New York: Times Books, 1977); Ron Karenga, *Ron Karenga: Victim of Watergating* (Los Angeles: Pacifica Tape Library, 1978); Clara Luper, *Behold the Walls* (Oklahoma City: Jim Wire, 1979); E. Frederick Anderson, *The Development of Leadership and Organization Building in the Black Community of Los Angeles from 1900 through World War II* (Saratoga, Calif.: Century Twenty One, 1980); Emory J. Tolbert, *The UNIA and Black Los Angeles: Ideology and Community in the American Garvey Movement* (Los Angeles: Center for Afro-American Studies, University of California, 1980); Frank Hanawalt and Robert L. Williams, *The History of Desegregation in Seattle Public Schools, 1954–1981* (Seattle: Seattle Public Schools, 1981); Anne LaGrelius Siqueland, *Without a Court Order: The Desegregation of Seattle Schools* (Seattle: Madrona, 1981); Jacob Fontaine III and Gene Burd, *Jacob Fontaine: From Slavery to the Greatness of the Pulpit, the Press and Public Service* (Austin, Tex.: Eakin Press, 1983), Lawrence P. Crouchett, *William Byron Rumford: A Biography, The Life and Public Services of a California Legislator* (El Cerrito, Calif.: Downey Place, 1984); Doris Fine, *When Leadership Fails: Desegregation and Demoralization in the San Francisco Schools* (New Brunswick, N.J.: Transaction Books, 1986); Jim Schutze, *The Accommodation: The Politics of Race in an American City* (Secaucus, N.J.: Citadel Press, 1986); Marvin Dulavey, *Black Presence in Dallas: A History of Black Political Activism in Dallas from 1936–1986* (Dallas: Museum of African-American Life and Culture, 1987); Jamie Coughtry and R. T. King, eds., *Civil Rights Efforts in Las Vegas: 1940s–1980s* (University of Nevada Las Vegas, 1988); Angela Y. Davis, *Angela Davis: An Autobiography* (New York: Random House, 1988); Robert L. Allen, *The Port Chicago Mutiny: The Story of the Largest Mass Mutiny Trial in U.S. Naval History* (Berkeley: Heyday Books, 1989); and Paul Karlstrom, *The Spirit in the Stone: The Visionary Art of James W. Washington, Jr.* (Seattle: University of Washington Press, 1989).

Since 1990, the black struggle for civil rights and African American empowerment has been a central focus in the extension of African American West history as it developed beyond "we were there" narratives to address the historic significance of this experience. This has resulted in the black freedom movement becoming its own subfield that can be read about in Bettina Aptheker, *The Morning Breaks: The Trial of Angela Davis* (Ithaca: Cornell University Press, 1990); Ward Churchill and Jim Vander Wall, *Agents of Repression: The FBI's Secret Wars against the Black Panther Party and the American Indian Movement* (Boston: South End Press, 1990); Jamie Coughtry, ed., *Woodrow Wilson: Race, Community, and Politics in Las Vegas, 1940s–1980s* (Reno: University of Nevada Oral History Program, 1990); Jonathan D. Greenberg, *Staking a Claim: Jake Simmons, Jr., and the Making of An African American Oil Dynasty* (New York: Atheneum, 1990); Jamie Coughtry and Helen M. Blue, eds., *Clarence Ray: Black Politics and Gaming in Las Vegas, 1920s–1980s*

(Reno: University of Nevada Oral History Program, 1991); Raphael J. Sonenshein, *Politics in Black and White: Race and Power in Los Angeles* (Princeton: Princeton University Press, 1992); David Hilliard and Lewis Cole, *This Side of Glory: The Autobiography of David Hilliard and the Story of the Black Panther Party* (Boston: Little Brown, 1993); Eric Cummins, *The Rise and Fall of California's Radical Prison Movement* (Palo Alto: Stanford University Press, 1994); George Jackson, *Soledad Brother: The Prison Letters of George Jackson* (Chicago: Lawrence Hill Books, 1994); Philip S. Foner, *The Black Panthers Speak* (Philadelphia: Lippincott, 1995); Gerald Horne, *The Fire This Time: The Watts Uprising and the 1960s* (Charlottesville: University Press of Virginia, 1995); Christopher Darden and Jess Walter, *In Contempt* (New York: ReganBooks, 1996); George Jackson, *Blood in My Eye* (New York: Random House, 1996); Robyn Duff Ladino, *Desegregating Texas Schools: Eisenhower, Shivers, and the Crisis at Mansfield High* (Austin: University of Texas Press, 1996); James Richardson, *Willie Brown: A Biography* (Berkeley: University of California Press, 1996); Thomas R. Cole, *No Color Is My Kind: The Life of Eldrewey Stearns and the Integration of Houston* (Austin: University of Texas Press, 1997); Charles E. Jones, ed., *The Black Panther Party: Reconsidered* (Baltimore: Black Classic Press, 1998); Olen Cole Jr., *The African-American Experience in the Civilian Conservation Corps* (Gainesville: University Press of Florida, 1999); William Henry Kellar, *Make Haste Slowly: Moderates, Conservatives and School Desegregation in Houston* (College Station: Texas A&M University Press, 1999); Merline Pitre, *In Struggle against Jim Crow: Lulu B. White and the NAACP, 1900–1957* (College Station: Texas A&M University Press, 1999); and Wilson Edward Reed, *The Politics of Community Policing: The Case of Seattle* (New York: Garland Publishing, 1999).

Some black freedom movement histories published in the new millennium include Huey P. Newton, *War against the Panthers: A Study of Repression in America* (New York: Harlem River Press, 2000); Gretchen Cassel Eick, *Dissent in Wichita: The Civil Rights Movement in the Midwest, 1954–72* (Urbana: University of Illinois Press, 2001); Anna Victoria Wilson and William E. Segall, *Oh, Do I Remember! Experiences of Teachers during the Desegregation of Austin's Schools, 1964–1971* (Albany: State University of New York Press, 2001); Rusty L. Monhollon, *This Is America? The Sixties in Lawrence, Kansas* (New York: Palgrave, 2002); Scot Brown, *Fighting for US: Maulana Karenga, the US Organization and Black Cultural Nationalism* (New York: New York University Press, 2003); Ed Diaz, ed., *Horace Roscoe Cayton: Selected Writings* (Seattle: Bridgewater-Collins, 2003); Stephanie Stokes Oliver, *Song for My Father: Memoir of an All-American Family* (New York: Atria Books, 2004); Amilcar Shabazz, *Advancing Democracy: African Americans and the Struggle for Access and Equity in Higher Education in Texas* (Chapel Hill: University of North Carolina Press, 2004); Turkiya L. Lowe, *The History of the Greater Seattle Chapter of the Links Incorporated, 1955–2005* (Redmond, Wash.: Greater Seattle Chapter of the Links, 2005); Jeffrey O. G. Ogbar, *Black Power: Radical Politics and African American Identity* (Baltimore: Johns Hopkins University Press, 2005); Annelise Orleck, *Storming Caesars Palace: How Black Mothers Fought Their Own War on Poverty* (Boston: Beacon

Press, 2005); Matthew Whitaker, *Race Work: The Rise of the Civil Rights Movement in the Urban West* (Lincoln: University of Nebraska Press, 2005); David Hilliard, ed., *The Black Panther: Intercommunal News Service, 1967–1980* (New York: Atria, 2007); Robert Bauman, *Race and the War on Poverty: From Watts to East L.A.* (Norman: University of Oklahoma Press, 2008), Dr. Huey P. Newton Foundation and David Hilliard, eds., *The Black Panther Party: Service to the People Programs* (Albuquerque: University of New Mexico Press, 2008); Earnest N. Bracey, *The Moulin Rouge and Black Rights in Las Vegas: A History of the First Racially Integrated Hotel-Casino* (Jefferson, N.C.: McFarland, 2009); David Colvin, *Black Politics after the Civil Rights Movement: Activity and Beliefs in Sacramento, 1970–2000* (Jefferson, N.C.: McFarland, 2009); Jim Kershner, *Carl Maxey: A Fighting Life* (Seattle: University of Washington Press, 2009); George Henderson, *Race and the University: A Memoir* (Norman: University of Oklahoma Press, 2010); Samuel E. Kelly and Quintard Taylor, *Dr. Sam, Soldier, Educator, Advocate, Friend: An Autobiography* (Seattle: University of Washington Press, 2010); Gary M. Lavergne, *Before Brown: Heman Marion Sweatt, Thurgood Marshall, and the Long Road to Justice* (Austin, Tex: University of Texas Press, 2010); Kimberley Mangun, *A Force for Change: Beatrice Morrow Cannady and the Struggle for Civil Rights in Oregon* (Corvallis: Oregon State University Press, 2010); Paul T. Miller, *The Postwar Struggle for Civil Rights: African Americans in San Francisco, 1945–1975* (New York: Routledge, 2010); Donna Jean Murch, *Living for the City: Migration, Education, and the Rise of the Black Panther Party in Oakland, California* (Chapel Hill: University of North Carolina Press, 2010); Gregg Andrews, *Thyra J. Edwards: Black Activist in the Global Freedom Struggle* (Columbia: University of Missouri Press, 2011); Brian D. Behnken, *Fighting Their Own Battles: Mexican Americans, African Americans and the Struggle for Civil Rights in Texas* (Chapel Hill: University of North Carolina Press, 2011); Shana Bernstein, *Bridges of Reform: Interracial Civil Rights Activism in Twentieth-Century Los Angeles* (New York: Oxford University Press, 2011); Avel Louise Gordly, *Remembering the Power of Words: The Life on an Oregon Activist, Legislator, and Community* (Corvallis: Oregon State University Press, 2011); Joan Singler, Jean Durning, Bettylou Valentine, and Maid Adams, eds., *Seattle in Black and White: The Congress of Racial Equality and the Fight for Equal Opportunity* (Seattle: University of Washington Press, 2011); Aaron Dixon, *My People Are Rising: Memoir of a Black Panther Party Captain* (Chicago: Haymarket Books, 2012); Tekla Ali Johnson, *Free Radical: Ernest Chambers, Black Power, and the Politics of Race* (Lubbock: Texas Tech University Press, 2012); Joshua Bloom and Waldo E. Martin Jr., *Black against Empire: The History and Politics of the Black Panther Party* (Berkeley: University of California Press, 2013); Tobie Levingston, Keith Zimmerman, and Kent Zimmerman, *Soul on Bikes: The East Bay Dragons MC and the Black Biker Set* (St. Paul: Motorbooks, 2013); Alondra Nelson, *Body and Soul: The Black Panther Party and the Fight against Medical Discrimination* (Minneapolis: University of Minnesota Press, 2013); Dwayne Mack, *Black Spokane: The Civil Rights Struggle in the Inland Northwest* (Norman: University of Oklahoma Press, 2014), and Cheryl Elizabeth

Brown Wattley, *A Step toward* Brown v. Board of Education: *Ada Lois Sipuel Fisher and Her Fight to End Segregation* (Norman: University of Oklahoma Press, 2014).

Another rapidly growing subsection of urban African American West historiography comprises histories that examine multiculturalism. Most early work on this subject examined African American relations with Native Americans and Mexicans and Mexican Americans on the U.S. frontier via autobiographies and biographies of adventurers, black cowboys, and Buffalo Soldiers, and histories of enslavement. These works include James P. Beckwourth, *The Life and Adventures of James P. Beckwourth, as Told to Thomas D. Bonner* (New York: Harper and Brothers, 1856); Robert Elliott Flickinger, *The Choctaw Freedmen and the Story of Oak Hill Industrial Academy* (Pittsburgh, Pa.: Presbyterian Board of Missions for Freedmen, 1914); Annie Heloise Abel, *The Slaveholding Indians* (Cleveland: A. H. Clark, 1915); Nolie Mumey, *James Pierson Beckwourth, 1856–1866, An Enigmatic Figure of the West: A History of the Later Years of His Life* (Denver: Fred A. Rosenstock, 1957); William H. Leckie, *The Buffalo Soldiers: A Narrative of the Negro Cavalry in the West* (Norman: University of Oklahoma Press, 1967); John Upton Terrell, *Estevanico, the Black* (Los Angeles: Westernlore Press, 1968); Jesse Kimbrough, *Defender of the Angels: A Black Policeman in Old Los Angeles* (New York: Macmillan, 1969); John M. Corroll, ed., *The Black Military Experience in the American West* (New York: Liveright, 1971); and Arlen L. Fowler, *Black Infantry in the West, 1869–1891* (Westport, Ct.: Greenwood Press, 1971).

Since 1970, the subject of African American–Native American relations has become its own subfield. Most works in this genre examine the period from black enslavement to the early twentieth century, such as Daniel F. Littlefield, Jr., *Africans and Seminoles: From Removal to Emancipation* (Westport, Ct.: Greenwood Press, 1977); *The Cherokee Freedmen: From Emancipation to American Citizenship* (Westport, Ct.: Greenwood Press, 1978); *The Chickasaw Freedmen: A People without a Country* (Westport, Ct.: Greenwood Press, 1980); William Loren Katz, *Black Indians: A Hidden Heritage* (New York: Atheneum, 1986); Arthur T. Burton, *Black, Red and Deadly: Black and Indian Gunfighters of the Indian Territory, 1870–1907* (Austin, Tex.: Eakin Press, 1991); Kevin Mulroy, *Freedom on the Border: The Seminole Maroons in Florida, the Indian Territory, Coahuila, and Texas* (Lubbock: Texas Tech University Press, 1993); Katja May, *African Americans and Native Americans in the Cherokee and Creek Nations, 1830s–1920s: Collision and Collusion* (New York: Garland, 1996); Murray R. Wicket, *Contested Territory: Whites, Native Americans and African Americans in Oklahoma, 1865–1907* (Baton Rouge: Louisiana State University Press, 2000), Circe Dawn Sturm, *Blood Politics: Race, Culture, and Identity in the Cherokee Nation of Oklahoma* (Berkeley: University of California Press, 2002); Jeff Guinn, *Our Land before We Die: The Proud Story of the Seminole Negro* (New York: J. P. Tarcher/Putnam, 2002); Claudio Saunt, *Black, White, and Indian: Race and the Unmaking of the American Family* (New York: Oxford University Press, 2005); Tiya Miles and Sharon P. Holland, eds., *Crossing Waters, Crossing Worlds: The African Diaspora in Indian Country* (Durham: Duke University Press, 2006); Laura Pulido, *Black, Brown, Yellow, and Left: Radical*

Activism in Los Angeles (Berkeley: University of California Press, 2006); Kevin Mulroy, *The Seminole Freedmen: A History* (Norman: University of Oklahoma Press, 2007); Jun Xing and Erlinda Gonazles-Berry, *Seeing Color: Indigenous Peoples and Racialized Ethnic Minorities in Oregon* (Lanham, Md.: University Press of America, 2007); Celia Naylor, *African Cherokees in Indian Territory: From Chattel to Citizens* (Chapel Hill: University of North Carolina Press, 2008); David A. Chang, *The Color of Land: Race, Nation, and the Politics of Landownership in Oklahoma, 1832–1929* (Chapel Hill: University of North Carolina Press, 2010); Shirley Boteler Mock, *Dreaming the Ancestors: Black Seminole Women in Texas and Mexico* (Norman: University of Oklahoma Press, 2010); Kim Cary Warren, *The Quest for Citizenship: African American and Native American Education in Kansas, 1880–1935* (Chapel Hill: University of North Carolina Press, 2010); Josh Kun and Laura Pulido, eds., *Black and Brown in Los Angeles: Beyond Conflict and Coalition* (Berkeley: University of California Press, 2013).

Emergent literature that has extended the black West multiracial framework beyond African American–Native American relations in the nineteenth and early twentieth centuries includes Rufus P. Browning, Dale Rogers Marshall, and David H. Tabb, *Protest Is Not Enough: The Struggle of Blacks and Hispanics for Equality in Urban Politics* (Berkeley: University of California Press, 1984); Franklin J. James, Betty L. McCummings, and Eileen A. Tynan, *Minorities in the Sunbelt* (New Brunswick, N.J.: Center for Urban Policy Research, 1984); Sucheng Chan, Douglas Henry Daniels, T. Garcia, and Terry Wilson, eds., *Peoples of Color in the American West* (Lexington, Mass.: D. C. Heath, 1993), Edward T. Chang and Russell C. Leong, eds., *Los Angeles—Struggles toward Multiethnic Community: Asian American, African American and Latino Perspectives* (Seattle: University of Washington Press, 1993); H. J. Belton Hamilton, *Christmas and 33 Years inside an Interracial Family* (West Linn, Ore.: H. J. Belton Hamilton, 1994); Bradford Luckingham, *Minorities in Phoenix: A Profile of Mexican American, Chinese American, and African American Communities, 1860–1992* (Tucson: University of Arizona Press, 1994); Eui-Young Yu, ed., *Black-Korean Encounter: Toward Understanding and Alliance: Dialogue between Black and Korean Americans in the Aftermath of the 1992 Los Angeles Riots* (Claremont, Calif.: Regina Books, 1994); Neil Foley, *The White Scourge: Mexicans, Blacks and Poor Whites in Texas Cotton Culture* (Berkeley: University of California Press, 1997); Geta LeSeur, *Not All Okies Are White: The Lives of Black Cotton Pickers in Arizona* (Columbia: University of Missouri Press, 2000); Dan Moos, *Outside America: Race, Ethnicity, and the Role of the American West in National Belonging* (Hanover, N.H.: Dartmouth College Press, 2005); Mark Wild, *Street Meeting: Multiethnic Neighborhoods in Early Twentieth-Century Los Angeles* (Berkeley: University of California Press, 2005); Scott Kurashige, *The Shifting Grounds of Race: Black and Japanese Americans in the Making of Multiethnic Los Angeles* (Princeton: Princeton University Press, 2008); Neil Foley, *Quest for Equality: The Failed Promise of Black-Brown Solidarity* (Cambridge, Mass.: Harvard University Press, 2010); Brian Behnken, *The Struggle in Black and Brown:*

African American and Mexican American Relations during the Civil Rights Era (Lincoln: University of Nebraska Press, 2011); Mark Brilliant, *The Color of America Has Changed: How Racial Diversity Shaped Civil Rights Reform in California, 1941–1978* (New York: Oxford University Press, 2012); Robert Lee Johnson, *Compton* (Charleston, S.C.: Arcadia, 2012);Lauren Araiza, *To March for Others: The Black Freedom Struggle and the United Farm Workers* (Philadelphia: University of Pennsylvania Press, 2013); and Stacey L. Smith, *Freedom's Frontier: California and the Struggle over Unfree Labor, Emancipation, and Reconstruction* (Durham, N.C.: Duke University Press, 2013).

With the rise of black, cultural, ethnic, and media studies after 1970, the arts, entertainment, identity and representation have become increasingly important focal points in examining the urban black West. Literature that has examined the twentieth-century struggle for cultural democracy includes Newell Bringhurst, *Saints, Slaves, and Blacks: The Changing Place of Black People within Mormonism* (Westport, Ct: Greenwood Press, 1981); Bruce M. Tyler, *From Harlem to Hollywood: The Struggle for Racial and Cultural Democracy* (New York: Garland, 1992); Jessie L. Embry, *Black Saints in a White Church: Contemporary African American Mormons* (Salt Lake City: Signature Books, 1994); Larry Martin, *The Life and Ministry of William J. Seymour and a History of the Azusa Street Revival* (Pensacola, Fla.: Christian Life Books, 1999); Michael K. Johnson, *Black Masculinity and the Frontier Myth in American Literature* (Norman: University of Oklahoma Press, 2002); Bernice Love Wiggins, *Tuneful Tales* (Lubbock: Texas Tech University Press, 2002); Newell G. Bringhurst, and Darron T. Smith, eds., *Black and Mormon* (Urbana: University of Illinois Press, 2004); Blake Allmendinger, *Imagining the African American West* (Lincoln: University of Nebraska Press, 2005); Elizabeth Pepin and Lewis Watts, *The Harlem of the West: The San Francisco Fillmore Jazz Era* (San Francisco: Chronicle Books, 2006); Emory Douglas, *Black Panther: The Revolutionary Art of Emory Douglas* (New York: Rizzoli, 2007); Jane Rhodes, *Framing the Black Panthers: The Spectacular Rise of a Black Power Icon* (New York: New Press, 2007); R. J. Smith, *The Great Black Way: L.A. in the 1940s and the Lost African American Renaissance* (New York: PublicAffairs, 2007); Cynthia Davis and Verner D. Mitchell, eds., *Western Echoes of the Harlem Renaissance: The Life and Writings of Anita Scott Coleman* (Norman: University of Oklahoma Press, 2008); Laurie Champion and Bruce A. Glasrud, *Unfinished Masterpiece: The Harlem Renaissance Fiction of Anita Scott Coleman* (Lubbock: Texas Tech University Press, 2008); Keith A. Mayes, *Kwanzaa: Black Power and the Making of the African-American Holiday Tradition* (New York: Routledge, 2009); Daniel Widener, *Black Arts West: Culture and Struggle in Postwar Los Angeles* (Durham, N.C.: Duke University Press, 2010); Bruce A. Glasrud and Cary D. Wintz, eds., *Harlem Renaissance in the West: The New Negro's Western Experiences* (Boston: Pearson, 2012); Marta Effinger-Crichlow, *Staging Migrations toward an American West: From Ida B. Wells to Rhodessa Jones* (Boulder: University Press of Colorado, 2014); Matthew L. Harris and Newell G. Bringhurst, eds., *The Mormon Church and Blacks: A Documentary History* (Urbana: University of Illinois Press, 2015); Emily Lutenski, *West of Harlem: African American Writers and the Borderlands* (Lawrence: University Press of Kansas, 2015); and W. Paul Reeve, *Religion of a Different Color: Race and the Mormon Struggle for Whiteness* (New York: Oxford University Press, 2015).

Other areas where the examination of entertainment, identity, and representation has intersected with black western history include movies, music, and sport. Some books that examine the history of African Americans in Hollywood films and television include Donald Bogle, *Toms, Coons, Mulattoes, Mammies, and Bucks: An Interpretive History of Blacks in American Films* (New York: Viking Press, 1973); Daniel J. Leab, *From Sambo to Superspade: The Black Experience in Motion Pictures* (Boston: Houghton Mifflin, 1975); Thomas Cripps, *Slow Fade to Black: The Negro in American Film, 1900–1942* (New York: Oxford University Press, 1977); Gary Null, *Black Hollywood: The Negro in Motion Pictures* (Secaucus, N.J.: Citadel Press, 1977); Melvin Patrick Ely, *The Adventures of Amos 'n' Andy: A Social History of an American Phenomenon* (New York: Free Press, 1991); Thomas Cripps, *Making Movies Black: The Hollywood Message Movie from World War II to the Civil Rights Era* (New York: Oxford University Press, 1993); Manthia Diawara, ed., *Black American Cinema* (New York: Routledge, 1993); Ed Guerrero, *Framing Blackness: The African American Image in Film* (Philadelphia: Temple University Press, 1993); and Mark A. Reid, *Redefining Black Film* (Berkeley: University of California Press, 1993).

Since 1995, books examining black exploitation films and films of the post-1970s include Darius James, *That's Blaxploitation! Roots of the Baadasssss 'Tude* (New York: St. Martin's Griffin, 1995); Michael T. Martin, ed., *Cinemas of the Black Diaspora: Diversity, Dependence, and Oppositionality* (Detroit: Wayne State University Press, 1996); Lisa M. Anderson, *Mammies No More: The Changing Image of Black Women on Stage and Screen* (Lanham, Md.: Rowman & Littlefield, 1997); Valerie Smith, *Representing Blackness: Issues in Film and Video* (New Brunswick, N.J.: Rutgers University Press, 1997); Gerald Martinez and Denise Chavez, *What It Is . . . What It Was! The Black Film Explosion of the '70s in Words and Pictures* (New York: Hyperion, 1998); Susan Courtney, *Hollywood Fantasies of Miscegenation: Spectacular Narratives of Gender and Race* (Princeton: Princeton University Press, 2004); Krin Gabbard, *Black Magic: White Hollywood and African American Culture* (New Brunswick, N.J.: Rutgers University Press, 2004); Herman Gray, *Watching Race: Television and the Struggle for Blackness* (Minneapolis: University of Minnesota Press, 2004); Darnell M. Hunt, *Channeling Blackness: Studies on Television and Race in America* (New York: Oxford University Press, 2004); Christine Acham, *Revolution Televised: Prime Time and the Struggle for Black Power* (Minneapolis: University of Minnesota Press, 2005); Donald Bogle, *Bright Boulevards, Bold Dreams: The Story of Black Hollywood* (New York: One World Ballantine Books, 2006); Yvonne D. Sims, *Women of Blaxploitation: How the Black Action Film Heroine Changed American Popular Culture* (Jefferson, N.C.: McFarland, 2006), Donald Bogle, *Brown Sugar: Over 100 Years of America's Black Female Superstars* (London: Continuum, 2006); Stephane Dunn, *"Baad Bitches" and Sassy Supermamas: Black Power Action Films* (Urbana: University of Illinois Press, 2008), Josiah Howard, *Blaxploitation Cinema* (Godalming, England: FAB Press, 2008); David Walker and Andrew J. Rausch, *Reflections on Blaxploitation: Actors and Directors Speak* (Lanham, Md.: Scarecrow Press, 2009); Charlene B. Regester, *African American Actresses: The Struggle for Visibility, 1900–1960* (Bloomington: Indiana University Press, 2010); Mikel J. Koven, *Blaxploitation Films* (Harpenden, England: Kamera, 2010); Paul Mooney and Dave Chappelle, *Black Is the New White* (New York: Simon Spotlight Entertainment, 2010); Questlove, *Soul Train: The Music, Dance, and Style of a Generation* (New York: Harper Design, 2013); Mark J. Banville, *Theme '70: Tackling the Beast They Call Exploitation Cinema* (London: Headpress, 2014); Nelson George, *The Hippest Trip in America: Soul Train and the Evolution of Culture and Style* (New York: HarperCollins, 2014); Allyson Nadia Field, *Uplift Cinema: The Emergence of African American Film and the Possibility of Black Modernity* (Durham, N.C.: Duke University Press, 2015), and Roland Leander Williams Jr., *Black Male Frames: African Americans in a Century of Hollywood Cinema, 1903–2003* (Syracuse: Syracuse University Press, 2015).

Autobiographies and biographies of black Hollywood performers go back to Ethel Waters and Charles Samuels, *His Eye Is on the Sparrow: An Autobiography* (Garden City, N.Y.: Doubleday, 1951); Ethel Waters, *To Me It's Wonderful* (New York: Harper & Row, 1972); Diahann Carroll, *Diahann: An Autobiography* (Boston: Little, Brown, 1986); Carlton Jackson, *Hattie: The Life of Hattie McDaniel* (Lanham, Md.: Madison Books, 1990), and Richard Pryor and Tod Gold, *Pryor Convictions and Other Life Sentences* (New York: Pantheon Books, 1995). After 2000, this literature has become its own industry, and books include Bernie Mac, *I Ain't Scared of You: Bernie Mac on How Life Is* (New York: MTV Books/Pocket Books, 2001) and *Maybe You Never Cry Again* (New York: Regan Books, 2003); Rain Pryor, *Jokes My Father Never Taught Me: Life, Love, and Loss with Richard Pryor* (New York: Regan, 2006); Stephen Bourne, *Ethel Waters: Stormy Weather* (Lanham, Md.: Scarecrow Press, 2007); Sidney Poitier, *The Measure of a Man: A Spiritual Autobiography* (San Francisco: HarperCollins, 2007); Audrey Thomas McCluskey, ed., *Richard Pryor: The Life and Legacy of a "Crazy" Black Man* (Bloomington: Indiana University Press, 2008); Diahann Carroll, *The Legs Are the Last to Go: Aging, Acting, Marrying, and Other Things I Learned the Hard Way* (New York: Amistad, 2009); James Gavin, *Stormy Weather: The Life of Lena Horne* (New York: Atria Books, 2010); Pam Grier, *Foxy: My Life in Three Acts* (New York: Springboard Press, 2010); Aram Goudsouzian, *Sidney Poitier: Man, Actor, Icon* (Chapel Hill: University of North Carolina Press, 2011); Michael Seth Starr, *Black and Blue: The Redd Foxx Story* (Milwaukee: Applause Theatre & Cinema Books, 2011); Melvin Childs, *Never Would Have Made It: The Rise of Tyler Perry, the Most Powerful Entertainer in Black America* (Santa Cruz, Calif.: Touch 1 Media, 2012); Jimmie Walker, *Dynomite! Good Times, Bad Times, Our Times* (Boston: Da Capo Press, 2012); Kevin Cook, *Flip: The Inside Story of TV's First Black Superstar* (New York: Viking, 2013); David Henry and Joe Henry, *Furious Cool: Richard Pryor and the World That Made Him* (Chapel Hill, N.C.: Algonquin Books of Chapel Hill, 2013);

D. L. Hughley, *I Want You To Shut the F#ck Up: How the Audacity of Dopes Is Ruining America* (New York: Crown Archetype, 2013); Marty Gitlin, *Tyler Perry: A Biography of a Movie Mogul* (Berkeley Heights, N.J.: Enslow, 2014); Scott Saul, *Becoming Richard Pryor* (New York: HarperCollins, 2014); and Debbi Morgan, *The Monkey on My Back: A Memoir* (New York: Infinite Words, 2015).

Another popular focus of African American West scholarship is music, musicians, and the various music industries. Before 1990, the few existing studies included Ross Russell, *Jazz Style in Kansas City and the Southwest* (Berkeley: University of California Press, 1971); William W. Savage, *Singing Cowboys and All That Jazz: A Short History of Popular Music in Oklahoma* (Norman: University of Oklahoma Press, 1983); and Robert Gordon, *Jazz West Coast: The Los Angeles Jazz Scene of the 1950s* (New York: Quartet Books, 1986). After 1990, the field exploded, with studies of blues, jazz, and rhythm and blues music and musicians, and studies of the hip-hop revolution. For syntheses, see Ted Gioia, *West Coast Jazz: Modern Jazz in California, 1945–1960* (New York: Oxford University Press, 1992); Paul DeBarros, *Jackson Street after Hours: The Roots of Jazz in Seattle* (Seattle: Sasquatch Books, 1993); Jim Dawson, *Nervous Man Nervous: Big Jay McNeely and the Rise of the Honking Tenor Sax* (Milford, N.H.: Big Nickel Publications, 1994); Nathan W. Pearson, *Goin' to Kansas City* (Urbana: University of Illinois Press, 1994); Bette Yarbrough Cox, *Central Avenue—Its Rise and Fall, 1890–1955* (Los Angeles: BEEM Publications, 1995); Dave Oliphant, *Texan Jazz* (Austin: University of Texas Press, 1996); Clora Bryant, Buddy Collette, William Green, Steve Isoardi, and Marl Young, eds., *Central Avenue Sounds: Jazz in Los Angeles* (Berkeley: University of California Press, 1998); Jacqueline Cogdell DjeDje and Eddie S. Meadows, eds., *California Soul: Music of African Americans in the West* (Berkeley: University of California Press, 1998); Tom Stoddard, *Jazz on the Barbary Coast* (Berkeley: Heyday Books, 1998); Frank Driggs and Chuck Haddix, *Kansas City Jazz: From Ragtime to Bebop—A History* (New York: Oxford University Press, 2005); Steve Isoard, *The Dark Tree: Jazz and the Community Arts in Los Angeles* (Berkeley: Heyday Books, 2006); Robert Dietsche, *Jumptown: The Golden Years of Portland Jazz, 1942–1957* (Corvallis: Oregon State University Press, 2009); Anita G. Arnold, *Oklahoma City Music: Deep Deuce and Beyond* (Chicago: Arcadia, 2010); Roger Wood, *Down in Houston: Bayou City Blues* (Austin: University of Texas Press); Alan B. Govenar and Jay F. Brakefield, *Deep Ellum: The Other Side of Dallas* (College Station: Texas A&M University Press, 2013); David Keller, *The Blue Note: Seattle's Black Musicians' Union, a Pictorial History* (Seattle: Our House Publishing, 2013); Stephen C. Propes, *Old School 77 Years of Southern California R&B & Vocal Group Harmony Records, 1934–2011* (Seattle: CreateSpace Independent Publishing Platform, 2013); Stanley Crouch, *Kansas City Lightning: The Rise and Times of Charlie Parker* (New York: HarperCollins, 2014); Sean J. O'Connell, *Los Angeles's Central Avenue Jazz* (Charleston, S.C.: Arcadia, 2014); and Peter Vacher, *Swingin' on Central Avenue: African American Jazz in Los Angeles* (Lanham, Md.: Rowman & Littlefield, 2015).

Similar to black Hollywood books, autobiographies and biographies on West-based black musicians have become an industry. Some of these publications include Dave

Marsh, *For the Record 4: Sly & the Family Stone* (New York: Harper Perennial, 1998); Phil Pastras, *Dead Man Blues: Jelly Roll Morton Way Out West* (Berkeley: University of California Press, 2001); Horace Tapscott, *Songs of the Unsung: The Musical and Social Journey of Horace Tapscott* (Durham, N.C.: Duke University Press, 2001); Quincy Jones, *Q: The Autobiography of Quincy Jones* (New York: Doubleday, 2002); Sharon Lawrence, *Betrayed: The True Story of Jimi Hendrix* (London: Sidgwick & Jackson, 2004); Charles R. Cross, *Room Full of Mirrors: A Biography of Jimi Hendrix* (New York: Hyperion, 2006); Quincy Jones, *The Complete Quincy Jones: My Journey and Passions: Photos, Letters, Memories and More from Q's Personal Collection* (San Rafael, Calif.: Insight, 2008); Eddie Santiago, *Sly: The Lives of Sylvester Stewart and Sly Stone* (Raleigh, N.C.: Lulu.com, 2008); Jeff Kaliss and Sly & The Family Stone, *I Want to Take You Higher: The Life and Times of Sly & the Family Stone*, rev ed. (Milwaukee: Backbeat Books, 2009); Leon Hendrix and Adam Mitchell, *Jimi Hendrix: A Brother's Story* (New York: Thomas Dunne Books, 2012); Charles River Editors, *Legends of Music: The Life and Legacy of Jimi Hendrix* (Santa Barbara, Calif.: Praeger, 2013); Kathy Etchingham and Andrew Crofts, *Through Gypsy Eyes* (London: Gollancz, 2013); Jimi Hendrix, *Starting at Zero: His Own Story* (New York: Bloomsbury, 2013); and Dean Alger, *The Original Guitar Hero and the Power of Music: The Legendary Lonnie Johnson, Music, and Civil Rights* (Denton: University of North Texas Press, 2014).

The popularity of gangsta rap, Tupac Shakur, hip-hop's influence on nonblacks, and black resistance to the prison industrial complex and unfair policing practices has fueled the growth of surveys on the hip-hop or rap revolution in the West. For some of this scholarship, see Errol Henderson, "Black Nationalism and Rap Music," *Journal of Black Studies* 26, no. 3 (January 1996), 308–39), Michael Eric Dyson, *Between God and Gangsta Rap: Bearing Witness to Black Culture* (New York: Oxford University Press, 1998); Ronin Ro, *Have Gun Will Travel: The Spectacular Rise and Violent Fall of Death Row Records* (New York: Doubleday, 1999); Bakari Kitwana, *The Hip-Hop Generation: Young Blacks and the Crisis in African-American Culture* (New York: Basic Civitas Books, 2003); Randall Sullivan, *LAbyrinth: A Detective Investigates the Murders of Tupac Shakur and Notorious B.I.G., the Implication of Death Row Records' Suge Knight, and the Origins of the Los Angeles Police Scandal* (New York: Atlantic Monthly Press, 2003); Eithne Quinn, *Nuthin' but a "G" Thang: The Culture and Commerce of Gangsta Rap* (New York: Columbia University Press, 2004); Jeff Chang, *Can't Stop Won't Stop: A History of the Hip-Hop Generation* (New York: St. Martin's Press, 2005); Nelson George, *Hip Hop America* (New York: Viking, 2005); Michael Eric Dyson, *Holler If You Hear Me: Searching for Tupac Shakur* (New York: Basic Civitas Books, 2006); John Potash, *The FBI War on Tupac Shakur and Black Leaders: U.S. Intelligence's Murderous Targeting of Tupac, MLK, Malcolm, Panthers, Hendrix, Marley, Rappers and Linked Ethnic Leftists* (Baltimore: Progressive Left Press, 2008); Tricia Rose, *The Hip Hop Wars: What We Talk about When We Talk about Hip Hop—and Why It Matters* (New York: BasicCivitas, 2008); Alexis Wolfe, *Emerald City*

Hip Hop (Fresno, Calif.: Howl at the Moon Publishing, 2008); Sharma, Nitasha Tamar, *Hip Hop Desis: South Asian Americans, Blackness, and a Global Race Consciousness* (Durham, N.C.: Duke University Press, 2010); Frank Alexander and Heidi Siegmund-Cuda, *Got Your Back: The Life of a Bodyguard in the Hardcore World of Gangsta Rap* (New York: St. Martin's Press, 2011); Greg Kading, *Murder Rap: The Untold Story of the Biggie Smalls and Tupac Shakur: Murder Investigations by the Detective Who Solved Both Cases* (Las Vegas: One-Time Publishing, 2011); Maco L. Faniel, *Hip Hop in Houston: Origin and Legacy* (Mount Pleasant, S.C.: Arcadia, 2013); and Antonio T. Tiongson Jr., *Filipinos Represent: DJs, Racial Authenticity, and the Hip-hop Nation* (Minneapolis: University of Minnesota Press, 2013).

Since 1990, there has been a growing list of autobiographies, biographies, and oral histories about hip-hop performers and people who knew them. The list includes Ice-T, *The Ice Opinion* (New York: St. Martin's Press, 1994); James Earl Hardy, *The Day Eazy-E Died* (Los Angeles: Alyson Books, 2002); Cathy Scott, *The Killing of Tupac Shakur* (Las Vegas: Huntington Press, 2002); Jerry Heller, *Ruthless: A Memoir* (New York: Simon Spotlight Entertainment, 2006); Jacob Hoye and Karolyn Ali, eds., *Tupac* (New York: Atria Books, 2006); Ronin Ro, *Dr. Dre: The Biography* (New York: Thunder's Mouth Press, 2007); Verna Griffin, *Long Road Outta Compton: Dr. Dre's Mom on Family, Fame and Terrible Tragedy* (Cambridge, Mass.: Da Capo Press, 2008); Tupac Shakur, *The Rose that Grew from Concrete* (New York: Pocket Books, 2009); Tayannah Lee McQuillar and Fred L. Johnson, *Tupac Shakur: The Life and Times of an American Icon* (Cambridge, Mass.: Da Capo Press, 2010); Jake Brown, *Suge Knight: The Rise, Fall and Rise of Death Row Records* (Phoenix: Colossus Books, 2011); Joel McIver, *Ice Cube: Attitude* (London: Sanctuary, 2012); Ice-T and Douglas Century, *Ice: A Memoir of Gangster Life and Redemption—from South Central to Hollywood* (New York: One World Ballantine Books, 2012); Darrin Keith Bastfield, *Back in the Day: My Life and Times with Tupac Shakur* (New York: Ballantine Books, 2013); Stormey Ramdhan, *My Life with the Knight* (Savage, Md.: La' Femme Fatale' Productions, 2014); Simone Green, *Time Served: My Days and Nights on Death Row Records* (Boston: Golden Girls Publishing, 2015); Brad "Scarface" Jordan and Benjamin Meadows Ingram, *Diary of a Madman: The Geto Boys, Life, Death, and the Roots of Southern Rap* (New York: HarperCollins, 2015); Harris Rosen, *N.W.A—The Aftermath: Exclusive Interviews with Dr. Dre, Ice Cube, Jerry Heller, Yella and Westside Connection* (Toronto: Peace! Carving, 2015); S. Leigh Savidge, *Welcome to Death Row: The Uncensored History of the Rise & Fall of Death Row Records in the Words of Those Who Were There* (Los Angeles: Xenon Press, 2015); Felicia St. Jean and Jewell Caples, *My Blood My Sweat My Tears* (Detroit: Felicia St. Jean and Jewell Caples, 2015).

The first book to feature the African American athlete in the West was William McSweeny's biography of NBA legend Bill Russell, *Go up for Glory: Bill Russell* (New York Coward-McCann, 1966). From 1970 to 2000, books that critically examine the black athlete in the West have been dominated by autobiographies and biographies, such as Jackie Robinson and Alfred Duckett, *I Never Had It Made: An Autobiography of Jackie Robinson* (New York: Putnam, 1972); Wilt Chamberlain and David Shaw, *Wilt: Just Like Any Other 7-Foot Black Millionaire Who Lives Next Door: An Autobiography* (New York: Macmillan, 1973); Larry Fox, *The O. J. Simpson Story: Born to Run* (New York: Dodd, Mead, 1974); Betty Lou Phillips, *Earl Campbell: Houston Oiler Superstar* (New York: D. McKay, 1979); Sam Blair, *Earl Campbell: The Driving Force* (Waco, Tex.: Word Books, 1980); Harry Edwards, *The Struggle That Must Be: An Autobiography* (New York: Macmillan, 1980); Bill Russell, *Second Wind: The Memoirs of an Opinionated Man* (New York: Random House, 1980); Kareem Abdul-Jabbar and Peter Knobler, *Giant Steps: The Autobiography of Kareem Abdul-Jabbar* (New York: Bantam Books, 1983); Jules Tygiel, *Baseball's Great Experiment: Jackie Robinson and His Legacy* (New York: Oxford University Press, 1983); Reggie Jackson, *Reggie: The Autobiography* (New York: Villard Books, 1984); Randy Roberts, *Papa Jack: Jack Johnson and the Era of White Hopes* (New York: Free Press, 1985); Harvey Martin, *Texas Thunder: My Eleven Years with the Dallas Cowboys* (New York: Rawson Associates, 1985; Thomas Hollywood Henderson and Peter Knobler, *Out of Control: Confessions of an NFL Casualty* (New York: Putnam, 1987); Willie Mays and Lou Sahadi, *Say Hey: The Autobiography of Willie Mays* (New York: Simon and Schuster, 1988); Tony Dorsett and Harvey Frommer, *Running Tough: Memoirs of a Football Maverick* (New York: Doubleday, 1989); Barry Denenberg, *Stealing Home: The Story of Jackie Robinson* (New York: Scholastic, 1990); Bob Hayes and Robert Pack, *Run, Bullet, Run: The Rise, Fall, and Recovery of Bob Hayes* (New York: Harper & Row, 1990); Bo Jackson, *Bo Knows Bo* (New York: Doubleday, 1990); Woody Strode and Sam Young, *Goal Dust: An Autobiography* (Lanham, Md.: Madison Books, 1990); Wilt Chamberlain, *A View from Above* (New York: Villard Books, 1991); Ronnie Lott, *Total Impact* (New York: Doubleday, 1991); Rickey Henderson and John Shea, *Off Base: Confessions of a Thief* (New York: HarperCollins, 1992); Arthur Ashe and Frank Deford, *Arthur Ashe: Portrait in Motion* (Boston: Houghton Mifflin, 1993); Arthur Ashe and Arnold Rampersad, *Days of Grace: A Memoir* (New York: Alfred A. Knopf, 1993); Charles Barkley, *Outrageous! The Fine Life and Flagrant Good Times of Basketball's Irresistible Force* (New York: Simon and Schuster, 1993); Earvin Magic Johnson and William Novak, *My Life* (New York: Random House, 1993); Joe Morgan and David Falkner, *Joe Morgan: A Life in Baseball* (New York: W. W. Norton, 1993); Leroy Satchel Paige and David Lipman, *Maybe I'll Pitch Forever* (Garden City, N.Y.: Doubleday, 1993); Bob Gibson and Lonnie Wheeler, *Stranger to the Game: The Autobiography of Bob Gibson* (New York: Viking, 1994); Emmitt Smith and Steve Delsohn, *The Emmitt Zone* (New York: Crown Publishers, 1994); Roy Campanella and Jules Tygiel, *It's Good to Be Alive* (Boston: Little, Brown, 1995); George Foreman, *By George: The Autobiography of George Foreman* (New York: Villard Books, 1995); Hakeem Olajuwon and Peter Knobler, *Living the Dream: My Life and Basketball* (New York: Villard Books, 1995); John Klawitter, *Headslap: The Life and Times of Deacon Jones* (Amherst, N.Y.: Prometheus Books, 1996); Jerry Rice and Michael Silver, *Rice*

(New York: St. Martin's Press, 1996); Marcus Allen and Carlton Stowers, *Marcus* (New York: St. Martin's Press, 1997); Dennis Greenberger, Gene McGivern, Dennis Green, and Nicholas Copper-Lewter, *Dennis Green: No Room for Crybabies* (Champaign, Ill.: Sports Publishing, 1997); Ken Griffey and Mark Vancil, *Junior: Griffey on Griffey* (New York: CollinsPublishers, 1997); Ed McCoyd, *To Live and Dream: The Incredible Story of George Foreman* (New York: New Street Publishing, 1997); Paddy Joe Miller, *The Tyler Rose: The Earl Campbell Story* (Spring, Tex.: Schuromil Productions, 1997); Buck O'Neil and David Conrads, *I Was Right on Time* (New York: Simon & Schuster, 1997); Earl Woods and Tiger Woods, *Training a Tiger: A Father's Guide to Raising a Winner in Both Golf and Life* (New York: HarperCollins, 1997); Bill Gutman, *Ken Griffey Jr: A Biography* (New York: Pocket Books, 1998); Arnold Rampersad, *Jackie Robinson: A Biography* (New York: Knopf, 1998); John Strege, *Tiger: A Biography of Tiger Woods* (New York: Broadway Books, 1998); Earl Woods, *Playing Through: Straight Talk on Hard Work, Big Dreams, and Adventures with Tiger* (New York: HarperCollins, 1998); Earl Campbell and John Ruane, *The Earl Campbell Story: A Football Great's Battle with Panic Disorder* (Toronto: ECW Press, 1999); Deion Sanders, *Power, Money and Sex* (Nashville: Word Publishing, 1999).

After 2000, some of these texts include Charles Barkley, *I May Be Wrong but I Doubt It* (New York: Random House, 2003); Steven Travers, *Barry Bonds: Baseball's Superman* (Champaign, Ill.: Sports Publishing, 2003); John Bloom, *Barry Bonds: A Biography* (Westport, Ct.: Greenwood Press, 2004); Robert Cherry, *Wilt: Larger Than Life* (Chicago: Triumph Books, 2004); Clyde Drexler and Kerry Eggers, *Clyde Drexler: Clyde the Glide* (Champaign, Ill.: Sports Publishing, 2004); Thomas Henderson and Frank Luksa, *In Control: The Rebirth of an NFL Legend* (Thomas Henderson, 2004); Terrell Owens and Stephen Singular, *Catch This! Going Deep with the NFL's Sharpest Weapon* (New York: Simon & Schuster, 2004); Jacqueline Edmondson, *Venus and Serena Williams: A Biography* (Westport, Ct.: Greenwood Press, 2005); Murry R. Nelson, *Bill Russell: A Biography* (Westport, Ct: Greenwood Press, 2005); Richard Steins, *Arthur Ashe: A Biography* (Westport, Ct.: Greenwood Press, 2005); Terrell Owens and Jason Rosenhaus, *T. O.* (New York: Simon & Schuster, 2006); Geoffrey C. Ward, *Unforgivable Blackness: The Rise and Fall of Jack Johnson* (New York: A. A. Knopf, 2006); Wayne Stewart, *Alex Rodriguez: A Biography* (Westport, Ct.: Greenwood Press, 2007); Tommie Smith and David Steele, *Silent Gesture: The Autobiography of Tommie Smith* (Philadelphia: Temple University Press, 2007); Brad Snyder, *A Well-Paid Slave: Curt Flood's Fight for Free Agency in Professional Sports* (New York: Viking, 2007); Robert M. Goldman, *One Man Out: Curt Flood versus Baseball* (Lawrence: University Press of Kansas, 2008); Joe Posnanski, *The Soul of Baseball: A Road Trip through Buck O'Neil's America* (New York: W. Morrow, 2008); Jerry Rice and Brian Curtis, *Go Long! My Journey beyond the Game and the Fame* (New York: Ballantine Books, 2008), James S Hirsch, *Willie Mays: The Life, the Legend* (New York: Scribner, 2009); Jack Johnson, *My Life and Battles* (Westport, Ct.: Praeger, 2009); Lisa Leslie and Larry Burnett, *Don't Let the Lipstick Fool You* (New York: Kensington, 2009); Warren

Moon and Don Yeager, *Never Give up on Your Dream: My Journey* (Cambridge, Mass.: Da Capo Press, 2009); Jeff Pearlman, *Love Me, Hate Me: Barry Bonds and the Making of an Antihero* (New York: HarperCollins, 2009); Everson Walls, Kevin B. Blackistone, and Frank Deford, *A Gift for Ron: Friendship and Sacrifice on and off the Gridiron* (Guilford, Ct.: Lyons Press, 2009); John R. M. Wilson, *Jackie Robinson and the American Dilemma* (New York: Longman, 2009); Tom Callahan, *His Father's Son: Earl and Tiger Woods* (New York: Gotham Books, 2010); Larry Tye, *Satchel: The Life and Times of an American Legend* (New York: Random House, 2010); Aram Goudsouzian, *King of the Court: Bill Russell and the Basketball Revolution* (Berkeley: University of California Press, 2011); Neil Lanctot, *Campy: The Two Lives of Roy Campanella* (New York: Simon & Schuster, 2011); Shaquille O'Neal, *Shaq Uncut: My Story* (New York: Grand Central, 2011); Dayn Perry, *Reggie Jackson: The Life and Thunderous Career of Baseball's Mr. October* (New York: William Morrow, 2011); Gregory Jordan, *Willie Mays Aikens: Safe at Home* (Chicago: Triumph Books, 2012); Steve Richardson, *Ricky Williams: Dreadlocks to Ditka* (Champaign, Ill.: Sports Publishing, 2012); Grace Williams, *Williams Sisters: A Biography of Venus and Serena Williams* (San Francisco: Hyperink, 2012); Hank Haney, *The Big Miss: My Years Coaching Tiger Woods* (New York: Crown Archetype, 2012); Allen Barra, *Mickey and Willie: Mantle and Mays, the Parallel Lives of Baseball's Golden Age* (New York: Crown Archetype, 2013); Calvin Barry, *Barry Bonds: Life and Career*, Kindle ed. (Calvin Barry, 2012); Theresa Runstedtler, *Jack Johnson, Rebel Sojourner: Boxing in the Shadow of the Global Color Line* (Berkeley: University of California Press, 2013); Dave Sheinin, *RG3: The Promise* (New York: Blue Rider Press, 2013); Dave Zirin and John Wesley Carlos, *The John Carlos Story: The Sports Moment That Changed the World* (Chicago: Haymarket Books, 2013); Linda Pennington Black, *A Legend among Us: The Story of William "Youngblood" McCrary of the Negro Baseball League Kansas City Monarchs* (Linda Pennington Black, 2014); Sal Fradella, *Jack Johnson: They Didn't Know It Could Be Done*, Kindle ed. (Wellesley, Mass.: Branden Books, 2014); Reggie Jackson, *Becoming Mr. October* (New York: Doubleday, 2014); Hugh MacDonald, *The Williams Sisters: From the Ghetto to Glory* (Edinburgh, Scotland: Argyll Publishing, 2014); Richard Williams, *Black and White: The Way I See It* (New York: Atria Books, 2014); Rich Wolfe, *Tony Gwynn: He Left His Heart in San Diego* (Indianapolis, Ind.: Lone Wolfe Press, 2014); Bijan C. Bayne, *Elgin Baylor: The Man Who Changed Basketball* (Lanham, Md.: Rowman & Littlefield, 2015); Caron Butler and Steve Springer, *Tuff Juice: My Journey from the Streets to the NBA* (Guilford, Ct.: Lyons Press, 2015); and Brittney Griner and Sue Hovey, *In My Skin: My Life on and off the Basketball Court* (New York: It Books, 2015).

In the late-1960s, the black athletic movement in amateur and professional sports led to the development of the sociology of sport, and from this sprang books that analyze the intersections of sport with race, class, gender, and sexuality. Along with books in this category we have more recent ones (largely post-2000) that examine the collective experience of black westerners in sport. See Harry Edwards, *The Revolt of the Black*

Athlete (New York: Free Press, 1970); Donald Spivey, ed., *Sport in America: New Historical Perspectives* (Westport, Ct.: Greenwood Press, 1985); Janet Bruce, *The Kansas City Monarchs: Champions of Black Baseball* (Lawrence: University Press of Kansas, 1986); Robert Peterson, *Only the Ball Was White: A History of Legendary Black Players and All-Black Professional Teams* (Englewood Cliffs, N.J.: Prentice-Hall, 1970); Lyle Kenai Wilson, *Sunday Afternoons at Garfield Park: Seattle's Black Baseball Teams, 1911–1951* (Everett, Wash.: Lowell Printing & Pub., 1997); H. G. Bissinger, *Friday Night Lights: A Town, a Team, and a Dream* (Reading, Mass.: Addison-Wesley, 2000); Frank Fitzpatrick, *And the Walls Came Tumbling Down: The Basketball Game That Changed American Sports* (New York: Simon & Schuster, 2000); John B. Holway, Lloyd Johnson, and Rachel Borst, *Complete Book of Baseball's Negro Leagues* (Fern Park, Fla.: Hastings House, 2001); David K. Wiggins and Patrick B. Miller, eds., *The Unlevel Playing Field: A Documentary History of the African American Experience in Sport* (Urbana: University of Illinois Press, 2003); Amy Bass, *Not the Triumph but the Struggle: 1968 Olympics and the Making of the Black Athlete* (Minneapolis: University of Minnesota Press, 2004); Douglas Hartmann, *Race, Culture, and the Revolt of the Black Athlete: The 1968 Olympic Protests and Their Aftermath* (Chicago: University of Chicago Press, 2004); Don Haskins and Daniel Wetzel, *Glory Road: My Story of the 1966 NCAA Basketball Championship and How One Team Triumphed against the Odds and Changed America Forever* (New York: Hyperion, 2005); Ray Sanchez, *Basketball's Biggest Upset: Texas Western Changed the Sport with a Win Over Kentucky in 1966* (New York: Authors Choice Press, 2005); Dave Zirin, *What's My Name, Fool? Sports and Resistance in the United States* (Chicago: Haymarket Books, 2005); Lawrence D. Hogan and Jules Tygiel, *Shades of Glory: The Negro Leagues and the Story of African-American Baseball* (Washington, D.C.: National Geographic, 2006); Leslie A. Heaphy, ed., *Satchel Paige and Company: Essays on the Kansas City Monarchs, Their Greatest Star and the Negro Leagues* (Jefferson, N.C.: McFarland, 2007); Charles B. Kastner, *Bunion Derby: The 1928 Footrace across America* (Albuquerque: University of New Mexico Press, 2007); Mark Fainaru-Wada and Lance Williams, *Game of Shadows: Barry Bonds, Balco, and the Steroids Scandal That Rocked Professional Sports* (New York: Gotham Books, 2007); Michael E. Lomax, *Sports and the Racial Divide: African American and Latino Sport Experience in the Era of Change* (Jackson: University Press of Mississippi, 2008); Neil Lanctot, *Negro League Baseball: The Rise and Ruin of a Black Institution* (Philadelphia: University of Pennsylvania Press, 2008); Matthew C. Whitaker, ed., *African American Icons of Sport: Triumph, Courage, and Excellence* (Westport, Ct.: Greenwood Press, 2008); Don Yaeger, Sam Cunningham, and John Papadakis, *Turning of the Tide: How One Game Changed the South* (New York: Center Street, 2008); Tracy Callis, *Boxing in the Los Angeles Area: 1880–2005* (Bloomington, Ind.: Trafford, 2009); Larry Bird, Earvin Johnson Jr., and Jackie MacMullan, *When the Game Was Ours* (Boston: Houghton Mifflin Harcourt, 2010); Doug Merlino, *The Hustle: One Team and Ten Lives in Black and White* (New York: Bloomsbury USA, 2010); Phil S. Dixon, *Wilber "Bullet"*

Rogan and the Kansas City Monarchs (Jefferson, N.C.: McFarland, 2010); Rob Fink, *Playing in Shadows: Texas and Negro League Baseball* (Lubbock: Texas Tech University Press, 2010); John B. Holway, *Voices from the Great Black Baseball Leagues* (New York: Dover, 2012); Roger Craig, *Tales from the San Francisco 49ers Sideline: A Collection of the Greatest 49ers Stories Ever Told* (New York: Sports Publishing, 2012); David J. Leonard, *Commodified and Criminalized: New Racism and African Americans in Contemporary Sports* (Lanham, Md.: Rowman & Littlefield, 2012); Roger Kahn, *Rickey and Robinson: The True, Untold Story of the Integration of Baseball* (New York: Rodale, 2014); Charles B. Kastner, *The 1929 Bunion Derby: Johnny Salo and the Great Footrace across America* (Syracuse: Syracuse University Press, 2014); William C. Kashatus, *Jackie and Campy: The Untold Story of Their Rocky Relationship and the Breaking of Baseball's Color Line* (Lincoln: University of Nebraska Press, 2014); Larry Lester, *Baseball's First Colored World Series: The 1924 Meeting of the Hilldale Giants and Kansas City Monarchs* (Jefferson, N.C.: McFarland, 2014); Jeff Pearlman, *Showtime: Magic, Kareem, Riley, and the Los Angeles Lakers Dynasty of the 1980s* (New York: Gotham, 2014); John Rosengren, *The Fight of Their Lives: How Juan Marichal and John Roseboro Turned Baseball's Ugliest Brawl into a Story of Forgiveness and Redemption* (Guilford, Ct.: Lyons Press, 2014); Roberta J. Newman and Joel Nathan Rosen, *Black Baseball, Black Business: Race Enterprise and the Fate of the Segregated Dollar* (Jackson: University Press of Mississippi, 2015); and Darron T. Smith, *When Race, Religion, and Sport Collide: Black Athletes at BYU and Beyond* (Lanham, Md.: Rowman & Littlefield, 2015).

Contributors

Kendra Field is assistant professor of history and director of the Center for the Study of Race and Democracy at Tufts University. Field is the author of *Growing Up with the Country: Family, Race, and Nation after the Civil War* (Yale University Press, 2018). The book traces her ancestors' migratory lives between the Civil War and the Great Migration. Field served as assistant editor for David Levering Lewis's *W. E. B. Du Bois: A Biography* (Henry Holt, 2009) and has been awarded fellowships from the Ford Foundation, the Andrew W. Mellon Foundation, the Huntington Library, and Harvard University's Charles Warren Center for Studies in American History. Field has advised and appeared in historical documentaries, including Henry Louis Gates Jr.'s *The African Americans: Many Rivers to Cross* (2013) and *Roots: A History Revealed* (2016). Field received her PhD in American History from New York University. She also holds a master's degree in public policy from Harvard University's Kennedy School of Government and a BA from Williams College.

April L. Harris completed her PhD in the cultural foundations of education at Syracuse University in 2014. She has coauthored a number of articles on student success models and presented extensively on African American community, life, and history in the Greater North Bay Area of California, including exhibits such as at the Rosie the Riveter WWII Home Front National Historical Park in Richmond, California. Her research includes examinations of the Underground Railroad, the Harlem Renaissance, and the westward migrations of African Americans, particularly during the rise of black towns and settlements in the nineteenth century, and during World War II and the postwar period in her native Marin County, California. She is a consultant and licensed California real estate agent.

Jeanelle Hope is a PhD candidate in cultural studies at the University of California, Davis. Her current research looks at the ways in which Afro-Asian solidarity was manifest through grassroots organizing, art and culture, and digital activism. Her broader research interests include Afro-Asian studies, black radical feminism, transnational feminism, African American women's history, blacks in the West, Black Power studies, black queer theory, and grassroots oral history. Prior to UC Davis, Hope received her master's in Syracuse University's Pan African Studies graduate program, where she won the university's Outstanding Master's Thesis prize in 2015 for her research titled "Black, Yellow, and Shades of Purple: Radical Afro Asian Activism in the San Francisco Bay Area From the Perspectives of the Women in the Struggle, 1967–1972."

Gabriela Jiménez holds a PhD in ethnomusicology from the University of Toronto. Her research interests include popular music practices of and throughout the Americas, specifically in regard to gender, sexuality, urbanism, and technology. Working with a diverse group of musicians who explicitly use and work gender and sexuality to frame their musical performances, her current research considers musical performances as intersectional and multimedia encounters in contemporary Mexico City, Mexico. A transplant from California, Jiménez has also been published in *Black Music Research Journal*.

Julian Kunnie is professor of religious studies and classics at the University of Arizona. His teaching and research interests include Africana philosophy, history, political economy, geography, psychology, history of religions, racism and social change, and aesthetics of dance. He currently teaches courses in African and Indigenous religions, African American religion, and Malcolm X and Martin Luther King Jr. He is the author of four books, four education DVDs, and many articles. He is also the cofounder of the Nyakweri Ecological Restoration and Preservation Project, which is concerned with studying the impact of global warming and climate change on the Nyakweri Forest Preserve, Kenya. His most recent publication is *The Cost of Globalization: Dangers to the Earth and Its People* (McFarland, 2015).

Kevin Allen Leonard is professor of history and chair of the Department of History at Middle Tennessee State University. For twenty years he was a faculty member at Western Washington University. His research focuses on race relations in Los Angeles during and after World War II. He is the author of *The Battle for Los Angeles: Racial Ideology and World War II* (University of New Mexico Press, 2006).

Emily Lutenski is assistant professor of American Studies at Saint Louis University, St. Louis, Missouri. Her research interests include comparative ethnic studies, gender studies, modernism, place, and region. Her book *West of Harlem: African American Writers and the Borderlands* (University Press of Kansas, 2015) introduces African American writers best known as part of the Harlem Renaissance to the scope of the borderlands West. *West of Harlem* was a finalist for the 2015 Weber-Clements Prize for best nonfiction book on southwestern America, awarded by the Clements Center for Southwest Studies and the Western History Association.

Dwayne Mack is professor of history and Carter G. Woodson Chair of African American History at Berea College, where he teaches U.S. and African American history. His research interests include the black West, the civil rights movement, and educational development. He is the coeditor of *Violence against Black Bodies: An Intersectional Analysis of How Black Lives Continue to Matter* (Routledge, 2017) and of *Law Enforcement in the Age of Black Lives Matter: Policing Black and Brown Bodies* (Lexington Books, 2018). He is also the lead editor of *Mentoring Faculty of Color: Essays on Professional Advancement in Colleges and Universities* (McFarland, 2013) and author of *Black Spokane: The Civil Rights Struggle in the Inland Northwest* (University of Oklahoma Press, 2014).

Tracey Owens Patton is professor of communication in the Department of Communication and Journalism and adjunct professor in African American and Diaspora Studies in the School of Culture, Gender, and Social Justice at the University of Wyoming. She served as the director of the African American and Diaspora Studies Program from 2009 to 2017. Her area of specialization is critical cultural communication, rhetorical studies, and transnational studies. Her work is strongly influenced by critical theory, cultural studies, womanist theory, and rhetorical theory. She has authored a number of academic articles on topics involving the interdependence of race, gender, and power and how these issues interrelate culturally and rhetorically in education, media, and speeches. Patton recently published a coauthored book titled *Gender, Whiteness, and Power in Rodeo: Breaking away from the Ties of Sexism and Racism* (2012) and is at work on a book involving transnational and transracial studies in Germany.

Bernadette Pruitt is an associate professor of history at Sam Houston State University in Huntsville, Texas. Her teaching and research interests include black civil rights, internal migration, and community agency among Houston African Americans in the twentieth century. She has authored a number of articles and essays on the black experience in the United States, including *The Other Great Migration: The Movement of Rural African Americans to Houston, 1900–1941* (Texas A&M University Press, 2013) and "'For the Advancement of the Race': African-American Migration to Houston, Texas, 1914–1940" (*Journal of Urban History*, 2005). She was the recipient of the Huggins-Quarles Award from the Organization of American Historians, and the Mary M. Hughes and Fred White Jr. Research Fellowships in Texas history from the Texas State Historical Association. She is also the winner of the Ottis Lock Best Book Award from the East Texas Historical Association. Pruitt earned her PhD from the University of Houston in 2001.

Holly Roose received her PhD in history with an emphasis in black studies from UC Santa Barbara and her master's degree in African and African American studies from Columbia University. Holly is interested in transnational social movements and the global black experience. Her research focuses on black nationalism, specifically the Garvey movement and the ways in which Garveyites in the American West established multiracial partnerships in the early twentieth century. Her *Black Star Rising: Transnational Garveyism in* *the Far West* is under contract and scheduled to be published in 2017 by the University Press of Colorado. Her next book project will examine the rise of Garveyism in Africa.

Herbert G. Ruffin II is associate professor and chair of the Department of African American Studies at Syracuse University. His research and teaching interests includes African American history, Africana studies, digital history, public history, race and ethnic studies, sports history, urban history, U.S. social history, and U.S. West history. His research specifically examines the African American experiences in his native Silicon Valley, California, San Antonio, Texas, and the process of black urbanization and suburbanization in the American West from 1945–2015. He is the author of *Uninvited Neighbors: African Americans in Silicon Valley, 1769–1990* (University of Oklahoma Press, 2014) and *Illuminations on Chinua Achebe: The Art of Resistance*, coedited with Micere Githae Mugo (Africa World Press, 2017), and has a coedited book on the African American urban West forthcoming with Quintard Taylor. In addition, Ruffin has authored numerous articles, been featured in many education videos (such as C-SPAN's *Booknotes*), and is advising the production of several documentaries that focus on court watching in the Silicon Valley and on the Syracuse Nationals basketball team and the desegregation of the NBA.

The Shared History Program in the History Department at the University of Nevada, Reno, is a multifaceted program that incorporates public, oral, and digital history. Its purpose is to offer students valuable hands-on experience in acquiring and applying historical skills. The Oral History Archives, now incorporated into Shared History, are a legacy of the original Oral History Program. The interviews in the program's collections, which date from the mid-1960s to the present, contain firsthand recollections of topics including mining, ranching, casino gaming, university history, politics and government, Great Basin Indians, and the experiences of various ethnic groups in the settlement and development of the West. The collection also features numerous biographical volumes of individuals whose lives illuminate important themes in the history of the state and region.

Randolph Stakeman is Associate Professor Emeritus of African and African American history at Bowdoin College, Maine, where he was a driving force in the college's commitment to diversity as the chair of its Department of Africana Studies and as an executive administrator. His research interests include African Americans in New Mexico history, African Americans in Maine history, pan-Africanism, Latin American studies, women's studies, and gender studies. Stakeman has also made several documentary films, including *Heritage Day* (1994), and is currently using the digital humanities to document the African American experience in Albuquerque, New Mexico, and to document NAACP executive secretary Walter Francis White.

Kathryn Takara is Professor Emeritus of Ethnic Studies and Interdisciplinary Studies at the University of Hawaii at Manoa. She has authored eight books, published over three hundred poems in literary journals, and in 2012 was honored with the American Book Award, for her book *Pacific Raven: Hawaii Poems*. In retirement Takara works as a prolific writer and publisher with her company Pacific Raven Press. Together with *Love's Seasons* and *Zimbabwe Spin*, the book *Shadow Dancing* completes a trilogy of her recent poetry. Looking ahead, Takara plans to publish a collection of essays, titled *Black Orchids*, about racialized black women in Hawaii. Moroever, she is writing *Trembling Leaf: A Poet's Memoir* and a monograph titled *Colonialism and Erasure: Oral Histories of Black People in Hawai'i*. In recognition of her dedication to justice, peace, and the pursuit of truth, Takara was awarded the 2016 Lifetime Achievement Award by the Honolulu NAACP as an "agent of change."

Quintard Taylor is the Scott and Dorothy Bullitt Professor of American History at the University of Washington, Seattle, which is the oldest endowed chair at the university. He is the author of *The Forging of a Black Community: Seattle's Central District from 1870 through the Civil Rights Era* (University of Washington Press, 1994), *In Search of the Racial Frontier: African Americans in the America West, 1528–1990* (W. W. Norton, 1998), and *Dr. Sam: Soldier, Educator, Advocate, Friend—An Autobiography* (University of Washington Press, 2010), the latter coauthored with Samuel Kelly, and has a coedited book on the African American urban West forthcoming with Herbert G. Ruffin II. Taylor is also the author of over fifty articles that have appeared in *Western Historical Quarterly, Pacific Historical Review, Oregon Historical Quarterly, Journal of Negro History, Arizona and the West, Western Journal of Black Studies*, and *Journal of Ethnic Studies*. In 2011 Taylor served the Western History Association as its fiftieth president. He retired in 2015, but in retirement he continues to teach and to work as editor of the Race and Culture in the West Series for the University of Oklahoma Press and as a members of the board of directors of the largest reference center of the Africana experience, *BlackPast. org*, which he cofounded.

Index

African American West historiography, xiii–xiv, 3–4, 74n6, 363–85; African American–Native American relations, 373–74; autobiographies/ biographies, 365–66, 369, 373, 377–79; Billy Ray Flowers, 3; black popular culture, 375–84; black urban West, 363–68; cinema, 376–78; Civil Rights–Black Power/black freedom movement, 364–65, 369–73; community surveys, 365–66, 368–69; music, 378–80; Quintard Taylor, xiii–xv, 3–4, 330, 363; racial frontier, 321, 334, 363, 373–76; regional surveys, 363; sports, 380–84; state studies, 364. *See also* U.S. West, conceptual framework
African diaspora, 163–78. *See also* Migration
Allensworth, Calif., 7
Arizona, black communities in: Phoenix: 12, 13, 14, 15, 34n41; Tucson, 146–54
art and politics: Afeni Shakur, 140–41; Afrofuturism, 280, 288; Broadside Press, and the Third World Press, 138; Femi Funmi Ifetayo, 136–37; Ntozake Shange, 136, 138, 141. *See also* Black Arts movement; New Negro Movement

Asian Americans, 10, 18–19, 25, 26, 38n69, 102, 255, 346, 348–49, 355; Asian American/Asian immigrant women writers, 137–38; Asian American freedom rights movement, 129–30, 137–38, 141, 143–44; Asian American Political Alliance, 129, 137, 141; Asian Indian, 164, 171–74, 178; California Chinese exclusion law of 1858, 149; Chinese Americans/immigrants, 19, 38n69, 131–30, 169, 171–73, 334, 348–49; Chinese Exclusion Act of 1882, 132, 149; Filipino Americans, 19, 165, 168–69, 346; Ghadar movement, 164, 172–73, 176; Janice Mirikitani, 137, 141, 143; Japanese Americans/immigrants, 19, 38n69, 132, 164–66, 169–71, 173–74, 178, 342, 346, 348–49; Melanesia, 338, 357; Pacific Coast Hindi Association, 172; Red Guard Party, 129, 137; Tomi Tanaka, 137. *See also* Garvey, Marcus; Hawaiian identity; white supremacy
athlete activism: black, 14, 296–99; Black Students Alliance, 298; ESPY Awards (2016), 296; Muhammad Ali, 187, 296; San Jose State University Boycott, 297; Tommie Smith and John Carlos, 18, 297; University of Texas at El Paso

athlete activism *(continued)*
boycott, 297; University of Wyoming
Student Senate, 298; Willie Black, 298.
See also Black Power movement

Beckwourth, James P., 243
Black Arts movement, 18, 25, 128–29,
133–44, 286
black celebrations, 24: Juneteenth, 24,
352; Kwanzaa, 352
black church, 59, 65: Antioch Baptist
Church, 54; Bethel African Methodist
Episcopal Church, 203; Black
Baptist Convention, 54; Calvary
Baptist Church, 203, 206–7; Calvary
Missionary Baptist Church, 243;
Houston Baptist Academy, 54;
Huntsville Union Church, 47; Mount
Vernon Methodist Episcopal Church,
65; in New Mexico, 304–5; Our
Mother of Mercy Catholic Church,
62; Pilgrim Congregational Church
and Library Association, 63; St. John's
Baptist Church, 66; Trinity African
Methodist Episcopal Church, 243;
Trinity Methodist Episcopal Church,
54
black civil servants; judges, 15;
politicians, 14, 221–23. *See also*
electoral politics
black community, economy of, 6–7,
10–13, 17, 19–21, 24, 48, 58, 60–63,
108–12, 218–20, 287–88; black business
flight, 110–12; black middle class,
18–24, 108–9; GI Bill, 102; poverty,
101. *See also* black suburbanization;
deindustrialization; housing;
post–Cold War class formation; post–
World War II urban development;
Second Great Migration; Third Great
Migration
black community architects: A. L.
Mitchell, 305; Ball family, 6–7;

Edward McCabe, 119–20; Emmett J.
Scott, 54–57, 62–63, 69; Frank Boyer,
306; Hugh Macbeth Sr., 177; Jennie
Covington, 64–65; John Bell Brown,
54; John Collins, 306; Joshua Houston
and family, 47–54, 70–71; Kathleen
Evans Stewart, 66; Lullelia Harrison,
65; Mariah Sharkie, 54; Richard Allen,
54; Rowena Moore, 293–94; William
Eagleson, 119. *See also* Thompson,
Constance Houston, and Hortense
Houston Young
black community institutions and
celebrations, 24, 243; African
American Association (Maui, Haw.),
352; Ancient Order of Pilgrims,
63; black cultural center, Waikiki,
Haw., 343; Black Masons, 63–64,
203, 305, 352; Booker T. Washington
Community Center, 206, 213–15, 217;
Club Alabam, 258–59, 262; Colored
Carnegie Library, 63; Eastern Star,
203, 352; Emancipation Park, 54;
Grand Court Order of Calanthe, 64;
Home Circle Club, 304–5; Malcolm
X Foundation, 293–5; Young Men's
Christian Association, 167, 214; Young
Women's Christian Association,
64–65, 167, 204, 214. *See also* black
church
black cowboys, 6, 320–34: All Indian
Rodeo Cowboys Association, 326;
Bill Pickett, 326–28; Bill Pickett
Invitational Rodeo, 327–28; Charles
Sampson, 328; cowboy culture, 326;
James Pickens Jr., 328; Jim Perry, 331;
Myrtis Dightman, 327–29; Nat Love,
331; Professional Rodeo Cowboys
Association, 326; racism in rodeo
culture, 320–34; Soul Circuits/
Southwestern Colored Cowboys'
Association, 327; Southwestern
Colored Cowboys Association, 326–27

black GI movement: black nationalism and the GI movement, 181–82, 190–95; Fort Hood 43, 190–91; Free Billy Smith rally, 194–95; March Forward! 195; People's Justice Committee, 181–82, 193–95; Wes Williams, 193–94. *See also* Black Power movement; U.S. Armed Forces

Black History Month: Alaska, 361–62; Blacks in Alaska History Project, 361; Carter G. Woodson, 361; Hawaii, 349; San Jose, Calif., 361

Black Lives Matter, 25, 99, 144

black newspapers and magazines: *Black Panther*, 190; *California Eagle*, 167–68, 177, 252, 257–58, 261, 266, 268–71; *Chicago Defender*, 87; *The Crisis*, 238; *Ebony*, 256, 271; *Houston Defender*, 59, 63; *Houston Informer*, 59, 63; *Jet*, 256; *Las Vegas Voice*, 90–91; *Los Angeles Sentinel*, 259–62, 264–66, 270; *Los Angeles Tribune*, 257–58, 260–61, 265–72; *The Messenger*, 240, 242, 246; *Negro World*, 163, 165, 173; *The Outlet*, 242; *Sentinel Voice/The Missile*, 90–91

black newspapers and magazines, authors, editors, and publishers: Adam Clayton Powell Jr., 271, 277n77; Almena Davis/Lomax, 268–69; Charlotta Bass, 167–68, 177; Clifton Frederick Richardson Sr., 59; Ida B. Wells, 118–19; Leon H. Washington Jr., 253–54, 260–61; Loren Miller, 268–69, 271

Black Power movement, 17–19, 27, 128–30, 132–44, 181–82, 188–94, 287, 324, 330, 337–38, 340–41; Black Panther Party, 129, 132–34, 136–37, 139–40, 190–91, 287, 337, 340–41; Bobby Seale, 18, 133, 190; Colored Peoples' Union, 174; Huey P. Newton, 18, 133; Kathleen Neal Cleaver, 337, 340–41; Maulana Karenga, 133–34; Nation of Islam, 18, 181, 187, 294; Revolutionary

Action Movement, 132; Third World Liberation Front, 132; United Nations Charter on Human Rights, 154; U.S. Organization, 18, 132–34, 140, 287. *See also* athlete activism; Black Arts movement; black GI movement; civil rights movement; Garvey, Marcus; Malcolm X; Student Nonviolent Coordinating Committee (SNCC)

black suburbanization, 20–23, 101–4, 108–12

black towns: Little Liberia, Baja California, Mexico, 177; in Oklahoma, 7, 115–17, 119–24. *See also* Allensworth, Calif.; Dearfield, Colo.; Nicodemus, Kans.; western emigration

black women's movement: Blue Triangle YWCA, 63–65; feminist/womanist movement, 130–44; #LaughingWhileBlack, 99–100; National Council of Negro Women, 71; Washington State Federation of Colored Women's Clubs, 204–5; Wednesday Art Club, 204; women's rights, 50

Brownsville Riot of 1906, 183

Buffalo Soldiers, 8, 27, 183, 235–36, 306, 312, 323. *See also* Brownsville Riot of 1906; Houston Riot of 1917; U.S. Armed Forces

California, black communities: Anaheim, 11; Fresno, 285; Long Beach, 286; Los Angeles, 8–9, 11, 14, 17–19, 24–25, 164, 167–69, 171, 176–77, 278–88; Marin City, 99–104; Monterey, 11; Moreno Valley, 21; North Bay Area, 99–104; Oakland, 11, 13, 18, 25, 132, 140, 164, 168, 193–94, 286, 340–41; Orange County, 15, 19–20; Richmond, 11–12; Sacramento, 167; San Diego, 11, 165, 167, 175–76; San Fernando Valley, 280, 283; San Francisco, 11–12, 14, 25, 129,

California, black communities (continued)
141, 164, 167–68, 171–74; San Jose, 10,
21; Santa Ana, 20; South Central Los
Angeles, 280, 283, 286–88; Vallejo,
99–104. See also Allensworth, Calif.
civil rights legislation and court rulings,
57, 70, 324: affirmative action, 151,
221–23; Brown v. Board of Education
of Topeka, Kans., 14–15, 57, 186; Civil
Rights Act of 1964, 15–16, 324; Fair
Housing Act of 1968, 19–20, 101–2;
James v. Marinship, 12–13; McLaurin
v. Oklahoma State Regents, 15; Mendez
et al. v. Westminster School District,
15; Moulin Rouge Agreement, 26,
87, 89–98; public accommodations,
91–97, 98n3, 210–11; Public
Accommodations Act, Nevada,
98n3; Public Accommodations Act,
Utah, 16; Senate Bill 95, 315; Sipuel
v. Board of Regents of the University
of Oklahoma, 15; Smith v. Allwright,
13–14, 70; Sweatt v. Painter, 15; Voter
Rights Act of 1965, 324. See also civil
rights movement; education
civil rights movement: Carl Maxey,
219; Congress of Racial Equality
(CORE), 213; desegregation 11–17,
19–21, 24–25, 96–97; Greater Phoenix
Council for Civic Unity, 13–14;
Hawaiian consciousness movement,
337, 341; Joseph James, 101; Julian
Bond, 337–39; Lincoln and Eleanor
Ragsdale, 13; Links, 348–49, 352;
march on Las Vegas Strip, 92–97;
Mississippi Freedom Democratic
Party, 190; reperiodization of civil
rights movement concept, 72n4–5;
Samuel "Sammy" Leamon Younge
Jr., 340; sit-ins, 16–17; Spokane
Health and Welfare Federation, 214;
Texas Commission on Interracial
Cooperation, 50, 69–70; Tuskegee

Institute Advancement League, 340;
Urban League 88, 165, 168, 213. See
Black Power movement; civil rights
legislation and court rulings; Du
Bois, W. E. B.; education; King, Dr.
Martin Luther, Jr.; NAACP (National
Association for the Advancement of
Colored People); Student Nonviolent
Coordinating Committee (SNCC)
class: black middle class, 48, 51–57, 65,
255–59, 272; black working class, 51,
53, 74n6, 83n66; criticisms of black
middle-class editors and publishers,
256–72. See also black community
architects; black community,
economy of; employment; hip-hop
and rap; post–Cold War class
formation; post–World War II
urban development; politics of
respectability; Second Great
Migration; Third Great Migration
Cold War, 216
Colorado, black communities: Aurora,
110, 112; Denver, 110–12; Five Points,
Denver, 110–12. See also black towns;
Dearfield, Colo.

Dearfield, Colo., 7
deindustrialization, 13, 21, 24, 101–4,
287–88
demography, 4, 6, 9–11, 14, 20, 22–23, 46,
57, 108–9, 123, 157–59, 164, 207, 208–9,
223, 233, 236, 257, 304–11, 313, 315–17,
323, 325, 350, 352
Douglass, Frederick, 117
Du Bois, W. E. B., 216, 238, 240, 245

education, 48–52, 55, 57, 62, 64–68, 312–13,
315–16; Albuquerque High School,
312–13; Arizona public schools,
146–54; black student movement,
18, 128, 133; black studies, 340,
342–43; Booker T. Washington High,

70–71; Denver Public Schools, 112; Department of Education in Hawaii, 349; desegregation, 12–17, 19–21, 14–25, 185–86, 218–23, 315–16, 352–53; ethnic studies, 128, 146–54, 340, 342; George School, Bucks County, Pa., 337–39; historically black colleges and universities, 48, 52, 62, 337–38, 340, 343; Iolani School, 341; Killeen High School, 186; Mexican American studies, 147, 151, 153; Prairie View Normal and Industrial School/College, 48, 52; Proposition 203, 148, 155n4; San Francisco State University, 18, 128, 133, 150; Tucson Unified School District, 147, 151; UC Berkeley, 62, 337, 340; UCLA shootings of 1969, 140; Union school, 48; University of Hawai'i at Manoa, 342, 344, 349, 353–55; University of Nebraska, 353; University of New Mexico, 313; Wheatley High School, 62, 67. *See also* civil rights legislation and court rulings

electoral politics, 8–9, 12–14, 24, 221

employment, 48, 58–59, 88–89, 97, 101–2, 104, 158, 160, 164–65, 208–9, 218–23, 287–88, 306, 309, 311, 313–14, 349–50; Bryant Messenger Service, 313–14; fair employment movement, 359–60; hiring practices, 100–2, 104; National Negro Business League, 167; Pullman porters, 164–65; Ruby Duncan and Operation Life, 24; science, technology, engineering, and mathematics (STEM), 104. *See also* deindustrialization

Esteban (enslaved explorer), 4, 235

First Great Migration, 6–9, 46–47, 57–71, 163–77, 204–7, 234; Beatrice Morrow Cannady, 8–9; Great Flood of 1927, 62; McCants Stewart, 8–9. *See also* Second Great Migration, Third Great Migration

Garvey, Marcus: appeal to Hawaiians, 174; Black Star Line, 170; interracial collaborations, 164–65, 168, 170–78; Noah Thompson, 167–68; Universal Negro Improvement Association and African Communities League, 69, 163–78, 293–94. *See also* Black Power movement

Hawai'i, black communities; Honolulu, 11, 24, 171, 341–42, 345, 352; Maui, 355

Hawaiian identity, 345, 350–55; black identity, media and power relations, 338, 341, 347–51; Chinese, 342, 346, 348; Filipino, 346; Japanese, 346, 348; myth and stereotypes, 344, 347–48; native and immigrant relations, 337, 341, 344–45, 347–48, 350–55; Pacific Islander, 349; Polynesian, 338, 347

Hawaiians, 337–57; Alice Augusta Ball, 338, 353–55; Anthony Allen, 346; Betsey Stockton, 338, 345, 352; Cass Barnett, 343; early publications of black Hawaiians, 344–45, 355; Duke Kahanamoku, 353; Kamehameha I, 338, 346, 356; Kathryn Waddell Takara, 337–57; Leon Richards, 350; McCants Stewart, 352; Nolle Smith, 352–53; Royal Hawaiian Band, 356–57; Spreckelsville Plantation, 355; Wendell F. Crockett, 338, 352, 355. *See also* Obama, Barack

hip-hop and rap, 25, 278–89, 379–80; Afrika Bambaataa, 281, 289; Alonzo "Lonzo" Williams, 284, 286; Arabian Prince, 279, 282, 284–85, 288; *Breaking and Entering*, 283, 285; disco, 279, 282–83, 285; East Coast hip-hop, 279, 282, 285; Eazy E, 284; Egyptian Lover, 279, 282, 284–85, 289; electro funk, 281; electro hop, 278–86, 288–89; Eve After Dark, 286; four elements of hip-hop scene, 279; funk/soul, 278–79, 284–85; gangsta rap/street knowledge

hip-hop and rap *(continued)*
music, 279, 284–86, 288; George
Clinton and Parliament/Funkadelic,
285, 289; Greg Mack, 284; Ice-T, 284,
288; James Brown, 285; KDAY-1580
AM, 278, 280–85; L.A. Dream Team,
279, 282; Macola Records, 283–84;
Mix Masters, 284; N.W.A., 285, 288;
popping and locking, 285; Prince, 283,
285, 289; Public Enemy, 330; Roland
TR-808, 281–82; Run-DMC, 285–86;
Sly and the Family Stone, 285; Uncle
Jamm's Army, 280, 282, 286; West
Coast, 280–89; West Coast Pioneers,
279; women in, 282–83; World Class
Wreckin' Cru, 282, 286
housing: black homeownership, 108,
308–10; fair housing movement, 11–13,
18–24, 359; housing discrimination,
6–8, 11–13, 101–4, 165, 185–86, 229–30,
352; median housing income, 108–9;
Proposition 14, Rumford Act, Calif.,
12. *See also* black suburbanization;
post–World War II urban development
Houston Negro Hospital, 63, 69
Houston Riot of 1917, 8, 69, 85n77, 183

infrapolitics, 210

Johnson, Lubertha, 26, 87–97

Kansas, black communities: Kansas City,
8; Topeka, 12, 14–15; Wichita, 16–17.
See also Nicodemus, Kans.
King, Dr. Martin Luther, Jr., 148, 151, 186,
188

Latin Americans 146–49, 153, 278, 316;
Afro-Latin Americans, 155n4. *See also*
Mexican Americans/Mexicans

mainstream press: *The Age*, 90; Hank
Greenspun, 91–93, 95; *Las Vegas Sun*,
91; *Review-Journal*, 89–90

Malcolm X, 293–95; Nation of Islam, 294;
North Omaha, 293–95; Organization
of Afro-American Unity, 294. *See also*
Black Power movement
Mexican Americans/Mexicans, 7, 10,
14–16, 18–19, 25–27, 102, 174–78, 183,
236, 255, 312, 316, 326, 373–75; Brown
Berets, 129; Chicana/o culture, 286;
Delores Huerta, 146–47; Mexican
American/Chicana/o civil rights
movement, 18, 146–47; Mexican
immigrants and immigration,
146–49, 176–77; Mexican Revolution,
174–76; Pancho Villa, 175–76. *See also*
Latin Americans
Migration: African, 103, 108–9, 158–60;
Asian, 102, 149; black cultural
retention: 111–12; black flight, 102–4,
108–9; border city migration/"Other
Great Migration," 7–8, 11, 304–11;
British West Indies, 172–73; chain
migration networks, 8, 58–59;
intraregional migration, 52–53, 57–60,
108–12; Mexican, 102; migration and
class formation, 108–9, 111–12; reasons
to migrate, 52–53, 57–60, 108–12, 325; to
Vancouver, British Columbia, 172. *See
also* black towns, First Great Migration;
Second Great Migration; Third Great
Migration; western emigration
Murray, Pauli, 202
NAACP (National Association for the
Advancement of Colored People),
8–9, 12–17, 63, 65, 69, 167–68, 299,
308, 312, 315, 325; Albuquerque, 308,
312, 315; Blanche Louise Preston
McSmith, 28, 359–60; Hawaii, 348,
352; Las Vegas, 87, 90–97; Seattle, 165;
Spokane, 202–3, 205, 210–20, 222–23;
San Francisco, 12, 216; San Jose, 361
National Negro Congress, 165
Native Americans, 26, 38n69, 120–22,
183, 236, 312, 323, 331, 334, 373–74;

American Indian movement, 18, 128; Indian nations–freedmen controversy 120–21

Nevada: Las Vegas, 11, 23–24, 26, 87–97; Reno, 247–48; North Las Vegas, 96; West Las Vegas, 89–91

New Deal, 87, 206–7, 355; Great Depression, 12, 206–7; Works Progress Administration, 206–7. *See also* World War II

New Mexico: Albuquerque, 13–14, 19, 28, 303–17; New Mexico Territory, 304–11; Santa Fe, 235–37, 241; Taos, 234–37, 240–42

New Negro Movement, 47, 52, 57, 59, 63–71, 85–86n77, 233–48: *Book of American Negro Poetry,* 237; *Cane,* 237–39, 241; Emma "Ma Jack" Jackson, 233, 243, 245–46; Harlem Renaissance, 233–34, 236–38, 245, 248; Jean Toomer, 233–42, 248; Langston Hughes, 234, 237–38, 244, 246, 248; *The New Negro,* 237; "Quoth Brigham Young—This Is the Place," 242, 246–47; racial identity, 234, 237–42; William Jourdan Rapp, 233, 244, 246–47. *See also* black newspapers and magazines; Thurman, Wallace

Nicodemus, Kans., 7

Obama, Barack, 108, 148, 338, 344, 350–51: and Frank Marshall Davis, 338, 343–44; and Stanley Armour Dunham, 338, 344, 351

Oklahoma, black communities: Indian Territory/Oklahoma, 115–24; Langston City, 7; Oklahoma City, 10, 16–17; Tulsa, 8. *See also* black towns

Oregon, black communities: Albina, Portland, Oregon, 27, 229–30; Portland, 8–9, 11–13, 21, 27, 31n19, 229–30; Rose Quarter, 230; Vanport, Portland, Oregon, 229

Pan Africanism, 18, 69, 163–78. *See also* Black Power movement; Garvey, Marcus

politics of respectability, 245–46, 268. *See also* black women's movement; civil rights movement; New Negro Movement; sexuality

popular culture and myth, 320–34, 376–85: concept of carnival (Bakhtin), 333; historical erasure, 321–24, 329–32, 334; Lone Ranger/Bass Reeves, 331; television shows, 329–33

post–Cold War class formation, 103–4, 108–9

post–World War II urban development: central city underdevelopment, 11–25, 286–88; gentrification and displacement, 108–9, 229–30. *See also* black community, economy of; black suburbanization; civil rights movement; deindustrialization; demography; housing; Second Great Migration; Third Great Migration; War on Drugs

Reconstruction, 47–48, 117–18; Fourteenth Amendment, 8–9

Robeson, Paul, 211, 216

Robinson, Jackie, 11, 327

Sanchez, Sonia, 128–30, 133–34, 137, 144

Second Great Migration, 7–19, 88–89, 101–2, 132, 183–88, 207–21, 229–30, 257, 303, 359–60. *See* civil rights movement; deindustrialization; post–World War II

Second Great Migration *(continued)* urban development; World War II

761st "Black Panther" Tank Battalion, 11, 182

Sims, Lydia, 210, 221–23

slavery, 4, 6, 8, 45–48, 53, 55, 58, 70, 121, 235, 243

social media, 25, 279

sports, 296–99, 380–85. *See also* African American West historiography; athlete activism

Stonewall riots, 254

Student Nonviolent Coordinating Committee (SNCC), 340. *See also* Black Power movement; civil rights movement

Texas, black communities: Austin/East Austin, 4, 6, 8, 20, 185; Beaumont, 11, 13, 25; Dallas–Fort Worth, 7, 20–21; Dodge, 51; El Paso, 8; Houston, 7–8, 13, 24, 26, 46–71; Huntsville, 47–51, 59, 71; Independence Heights, Houston, 60–61, 63; Killeen/Fort Hood, 11, 181, 194–95; San Antonio, 6–7, 20, 197n14; Tarrant County, 20; Temple, 186; Third, Fourth, and Fifth Wards, Houston, 60–63; Walker County, 7, 47–51

Third Great Migration, 19–25, 109–12, 157–60, 341–45, 347–50; and Information Age metropolises, 21, 103–4; Rae Lowry, 20; T. J. Owens, 21. *See also* post–World War II urban development

Thompson, Constance Houston, and Hortense Houston Young, 48, 70–71

Thurman, Wallace, 233, 242–48

Urban uprisings and riots: Carrollton massacre of 1886, 117–18; Kaneohe Bay Marine Corps Air Station uprising, 343; Los Angeles uprising of 1992, 4, 25; Memphis lynching of 1892, 118–19; Red Summer of 1919, 205; Watts riot/uprising of 1965, 17–18, 286–87. *See also* Brownsville Riot of 1906; Houston Riot of 1917; post–World War II urban development; Stonewall riots

U.S. Armed Forces: Armed Forces Day, 195; Article 15, 186–87, 194; assistant secretary of defense for civil rights, 184; Base Realignment and Closures Commission, 103; Camp Hood, 185; Congressional Black Caucus hearings, 181, 193; Executive Order 9981, 184; *Fatigue Press*, 182, 190–91; George Brummell, 184, 187; Fort Hood 3, 188; Fort Hood shootings, 195; Fort Hood United Front, 181, 192–95; Free Kelvin Harvey and John Priest movements, 192; GI movement, 181, 186–95; Gulf War, 195; John Wayne complex, 186; Oleo Strut coffee house, 188–89, 192; Pentagon reforms (1970–73), 191, 194–95; post–draft era antiwar activism, 195; postwar military towns, 185–86, 343, 352; post–World War II base closures, 13; Project 100,000, 186–87; Rambo mythology, 182; Richard Chase, 191–92; riot control, 187, 190–92; Tet Offensive, 186, 190; U.S. Army of Engineers, 361; Vietnam War, 143, 182–88, 190, 194–95. *See also* 761st "Black Panther" Tank Battalion; black GI movement; Buffalo Soldiers

U.S. West, black communities: Anchorage, Ala., 359–60; Boise, Id., 7; Cheyenne, Wyo., 16, 325; Fargo-Moorhead, N.D./Minn., 157–60; Omaha, Nebr., 7–8, 13, 28, 293–95; Salt Lake City, Utah, 15–16, 243–48. *See also* black towns; *names of individual states*

U.S. West, conceptual framework, xiii–xv, 3–4, 47, 240, 248, 320–21, 323, 330, 334, 334n2. *See also* African American West historiography; popular culture and myth

War on Drugs, 24, 287–88

Washington, Booker T., 54–56, 63, 67–69, 77n32, 115–16, 121–22, 355

Washington State, black communities: Bellingham, 166, 172; Renton, 109; Seattle, 10, 13–14, 19, 21, 25–26, 108–10, 164–69, 172, 354; Spokane, 11, 14, 27, 202–24; Tacoma, 10

wellness and health, 68–69. *See also* Houston Negro Hospital

western emigration, 115–24, 323, 325

white supremacy: Asiatic Exclusion League, 164, 172; Black Codes, 120; Church of Jesus Christ of Latter-day Saints (Mormons), 15–16, 243, 246–48, 296–99, 375; COINTELPRO, 19; Compromise of 1850, 243; James/Jane Crow, 27, 87–97, 213–24, 183, 186–95; Jim Crow, 6, 8, 14, 27–28, 51, 57, 62, 88–89, 123–24, 165, 183–87, 312–13, 315–16, 323–26; Ku Klux Klan, 9, 28, 164–67, 177, 185, 212, 293–94; lynching, 51, 118–19, 165–66, 177, 325; Manifest Destiny, 149, 322–23; neoliberalism, 24; Oriental Exclusion League, 164; police brutality, 24, 209–13; post-racialism, 20, 329–34; Rachel Dolezal, 202, 224; U.S.-Mexican War and Treaty of Guadalupe-Hidalgo, 235, 322–23; westward expansion and U.S. conquest, 147–51, 322–23. *See also* War on Drugs

World War I. *See* First Great Migration

World War II, 100–101; Double V campaign, 212; Executive Order 8802, 9, 100; Fair Employment Practices Commission, 9, 100; George Washington Carver United Service Organizations, 207–8; Mare Island, Vallejo, Calif., 100, 103; Marinship, Sausalito, Calif., 100–101; Rosa D. Malone, 206–8, 214–17; Women's Army Corps, 207, 211–13. *See also* 761st "Black Panther" Tank Battalion; Second Great Migration